Medieval to modern suburban material culture and sequence at Grand Arcade, Cambridge

McDONALD INSTITUTE MONOGRAPHS

Medieval to modern suburban material culture and sequence at Grand Arcade, Cambridge

Archaeological investigations of an eleventh- to twentieth-century suburb and town ditch

By Craig Cessford and Alison Dickens

With contributions by
Martin Allen, Steve Allen, Tony Baggs†, Rachel Ballantyne, Steve Boreham, Richard Darrah†, Andrew Hall, David Hall, Jen Harland, Kevin Hayward, Vicki Herring, Lorrain Higbee, Rosemary Horrox, Philip Mills, Quita Mould, Richard Newman, Mark Samuel, David Smith, Simon Timberlake, Ian Tyers, Anne de Vareilles and Alan Vince†

With a foreword by Martin Biddle

Graphics by Vicki Herring with Andrew Hall

Principal photography by Craig Cessford and Dave Webb

Cambridge Archaeological Unit Urban Archaeology Series
The Archaeology of Cambridge Volume 1

Published by:

McDonald Institute for Archaeological Research
University of Cambridge
Downing Street
Cambridge, UK
CB2 3ER
(0)(1223) 333538
(0)(1223) 339336 (Production Office)
(0)(1223) 333536 (FAX)
eaj31@cam.ac.uk
www.mcdonald.cam.ac.uk

Distributed by Oxbow Books
United Kingdom: Oxbow Books, 10 Hythe Bridge Street, Oxford, OX1 2EW, UK.
Tel: (0)(1865) 241249; Fax: (0)(1865) 794449; www.oxbowbooks.com
USA: Casemate Academic, P.O. Box 511, Oakville, CT 06779, USA.
Tel: 860-945-9329; Fax: 860-945-9468

ISBN: 978-1-902937-78-6
ISSN: 1363-1349 (McDonald Institute)

Base maps in figures 1.2, 3.1, 3.2, 3.27, 4.55, 4.61, 4.69, 4.70, 5.69, 6.1, 6.6, 6.19 and 6.20 are reproduced by permission of Ordnance Survey on behalf of HMSO. © Crown copyright [and database rights] [2018] OS [100048686].

On the cover: *Aerial view of Grand Arcade, facing northwest, with outlines of areas of investigation and various features shown. Compare to fig. 1.11E (photograph courtesy of Bovis Lend Lease Ltd.).* On the back cover: *View of the excavation of the main area at Grand Arcade, facing west.*

Cover design by Dora Kemp, Andrew Hall and Ben Plumridge.
Typesetting and layout by Ben Plumridge.

Edited for the Institute by James Barrett (*Series Editor*).

Printed and bound by Short Run Press, Bittern Rd, Sowton Industrial Estate, Exeter, EX2 7LW, UK.

CONTENTS

Supplementary Material

Contributors

MARTIN ALLEN
Senior Assistant Keeper, Department of Coins and Medals, Fitzwilliam Museum, Trumpington Street, Cambridge CB2 1RB (coins and jettons)
Email: mra25@cam.ac.uk

STEVE ALLEN
Wood Technologist, Conservation Department, York Archaeological Trust, 47 Aldwark, York YO1 7BX (wood species)
Email: sallen@yorkat.co.uk

TONY BAGGS†
Freelance specialist (standing buildings)

RACHEL BALLANTYNE
Research Associate, McDonald Institute for Archaeological Research, Downing Street, Cambridge CB2 3ER (environmental remains)
Email: rmb51@cam.ac.uk

STEVE BOREHAM
Senior Technical Officer, Department of Geography, University of Cambridge, Downing Place, Cambridge CB2 3EN (pollen)
Email: sb139@cam.ac.uk

CRAIG CESSFORD
CAU (principal author, plus modern pottery, clay tobacco pipes, metalwork, stone objects, worked bone and miscellaneous items)
Email: cc250@cam.ac.uk

RICHARD DARRAH†
Freelance specialist (wood and timber)

ALISON DICKENS
Director Granta Heritage, formerly CAU (principal author and standing buildings)
Email: alison@grantaheritage.co.uk

ANDREW HALL
CAU (modern pottery, metalwork)
Email: afh21@cam.ac.uk

DAVID HALL
Freelance specialist, Pinfold, Hargrave, Northamptonshire NN9 6BW (Middle Saxon to Early Post-Medieval pottery and field systems)
Email: hargravefields@aol.com

JENNIFER HARLAND
Archaeology Institute, University of the Highland and Islands, East Road, Kirkwall, Orkney KW15 1LX (fish bone)
Email: jen.harland@uhi.ac.uk

KEVIN HAYWARD
Building Material Specialist, Pre-Construct Archaeology, Unit 54 Brockley Cross Business Centre, 96 Endwell Road, Brockley, London SE4 2PD
Email: KHayward@pre-construct.com

LORRAINE HIGBEE
Senior Zooarchaeologist, Wessex Archaeology, Portway House, Old Sarum Park, Salisbury SP4 6EB (animal and bird bone)
Email: l.higbee@wessexarch.co.uk

ROSEMARY HORROX
Fellow & Director of Studies in History, Fitzwilliam College, University of Cambridge, Storey's Way, Cambridge CB3 0DG (documentary sources)
Email: reh37@cam.ac.uk

VICKI HERRING
CAU (illustrator, modern glass)
Email: vh252@cam.ac.uk

PHILIP MILLS
Freelance specialist, Hon. Research Fellow, University of Leicester, 21, Dalby Road, Anstey, Leicester LE7 7DL (ceramic building material)
Email: tilemanandson@gmail.com

RICHARD NEWMAN
CAU (Christ's Lane excavations, East Fields)
Email: rn276@cam.ac.uk

QUITA MOULD
Barbican Research Associates, 51 Whin Common Road, Denver, Downham Market, Norfolk PE38 0DX (leather)
Email: quita@onetel.com

MARK SAMUEL
Architectural Historian, Architectural Archaeology, 15 Grove Road, Ramsgate CT11 9SH (stone mouldings)
Email: twoarches@aol.com

DAVID SMITH
Senior Lecturer in Environmental Archaeology, Department of Classics, Ancient History & Archaeology, Institute of Archaeology and Antiquity, University of Birmingham, Edgbaston, Birmingham B15 2TT (insects)
Email: d.n.smith@bham.ac.uk

SIMON TIMBERLAKE
Freelance specialist and Affiliate Scholar McDonald Institute, formerly CAU, 19 High Street, Fen Ditton, Cambridge CB5 8ST (worked stone objects and slag and metalworking remains)
Email: simon.timberlake@gmail.com

IAN TYERS
Freelance specialist, Dendrochronological Consultancy Ltd, Lowfield House, Smeath Lane, Clarborough, Retford DN22 9JN (dendrochronology)
Email: ian@dendro.co.uk

ANNE DE VAREILLES
Freelance specialist, formerly CAU (environmental remains)
Email: ak.vareilles@gmail.com

ALAN VINCE†
Freelance specialist (thin section and ICPAES analysis).

DAVE WEBB
CAU (photographer)
Email: dww25@cam.ac.uk

Figures

Tables

Dedication and acknowledgements

This work is dedicated to the memory of two distinguished archaeologists with long standing Cambridge connections who influenced it in very different ways. Tony (Anthony) Paget Baggs (1934–2006) had a long career in architectural recording at the Royal Commission on Historical Monuments for England and the Victoria County History. Following his retirement in 1997 he continued working in a freelance capacity and undertook many projects for the Cambridge Archaeological Unit, including the work at Grand Arcade which he unfortunately did not live to complete. Tony was always generous with his time and immense knowledge, his presence was one of the most enjoyable aspects of the fieldwork at Grand Arcade. This book owes much to him and is undoubtedly the poorer through his demise. John Amyas Alexander (1922–2010) conducted numerous excavations in Britain, Africa and elsewhere. The investigations of the King's Ditch that he directed in 1969–71 only rank amongst his more minor achievements, but it was a great pleasure to be able to show him around our subsequent excavations over three decades later (see Fig. 5.93B). We must also mention two other contributors to this volume who are sadly no longer with us, Richard Darrah and Alan Vince. Richard possessed an unparalleled understanding of woodworking that has greatly enhanced this volume and will be greatly missed. Similarly Alan Vince provided unique specialist knowledge.

First and foremost this work is based upon the dedication, skill and commitment of the Grand Arcade and Christ's Lane excavation teams, although they are too numerous to list particular appreciation goes to Richard Newman and Letty ten Harkel. Alison Dickens managed both projects for the CAU and finds processing was overseen by Norma Challands and later Gladwys Monteil. Both projects were monitored by Andy Thomas, Principal Archaeologist, Land Use Planning, of the County Archaeology Office. The work in the field also benefited greatly from the work of Rosemary Horrox on documentary sources and the prompt spot-dating of the pottery by David Hall. The main authorship of the volume broadly corresponds to the two principal author's responsibility, with Cessford dealing mainly with the below ground excavated remains and Dickens with the above ground standing buildings although a great deal of cross-over has occurred. The structure of the volume has benefited from input by Chris Evans and Sam Lucy, the latter of whom proof-read the volume, and we are also grateful for the comments of the two anonymous reviewers.

The graphics are primarily the work of Vicki Herring with oversight and input from Andrew Hall. Photographs are principally by Dave Webb, Craig Cessford and member of the excavation team. The timber drawings are largely based upon original drawings by Nigel Randall, with the exception of a number of illustrations supplied by Richard Darrah (Figs. 4.8C, 4.41C, 4.42C, 4.45D, 4.47D, 5.87D). Drawings of stone mouldings are based upon illustrations by Mark Samuel (Figs. 4.34A–H, 4.63C–G, 4.64, 5.11A–D, 5.11G, 5.26, 5.36, 6.15), whilst the leather drawings were informed by sketches by Quita Mould. Images from the digital model of the standing buildings owe much to the work of Marcus Abbott. A number of images are courtesy of the Cambridgeshire Collection, Cambridge Central Library (Figs. 1.10 lower image, 3.24, 5.59, 5.77C–D, 5.78A–B, 5.83, 6.3B, 6.14, 6.17D), and are reproduced thanks to the assistance of Chris Jakes. Aerial photographs of the Grand Arcade site (front cover and Fig. 1.4) are courtesy of Bovis Lend Lease Ltd. and the Cambridge University Collection of Aerial Photographs (Fig.1.14). The leather jug (Fig. 5.6B) is copyright MOLA, Faith Vardy. Some animal bone photographs are by Lorrain Higbee (Fig. 3.12C, 3.14A–D, 3.25D–E, 4.14E, 4.26B, 4.50B, 4.69) and the fish bone photo (Fig. 4.27B) is by Jen Harland. The portrait of Barnett Leach III on a box lid (Fig. 7.3) is courtesy of Ric Leach. The pottery from the Fitzwilliam Museum (Fig. 5.34A) although photographed by Craig Cessford is reproduced by permission of the Syndics of The Fitzwilliam Museum, Cambridge, and the pottery from his personal collection (Fig. 7.15) was photographed by Peter Stoivin. The images in Fig. 7.2 are courtesy of Charles French (A–D), Kevin Hayward (E–K) and Alan Vince (L–S). Emmanuel College bottles (Fig. 5.60A–B, 5.60E) are courtesy of Emmanuel College although drawn by Vicki Herring and access to College material was obtained with the assistance of Sarah Bendall, the curator of the Emmanuel College Douglas Finlay Museum of College Life. The 1629 survey of the King's Ditch is courtesy of the Cambridge Antiquarian Society publication, but we have unfortunately been unable to trace the current owner of the plan (Fig. 3.23). Plans from college archives are reproduced by kind permission of the Master and Fellows of Christ's College Cambridge (Fig. 6.17B), the Master and Fellows of Emmanuel College Cambridge (Figs. 5.58, 5.63B, 5.70C, 6.13A) and the Master and Fellows of Jesus College Cambridge (Figs. 5.19B–C, 5.79). The plan in Fig. 1.15 is based upon an original in the John Lewis Partnership Archive Collection and Fig. 5.84 (middle) and Fig. 5.88B derive from the same source.. The x-rays that are reproduced were undertaken by York Archaeological Trust particularly Ian Panter, Jo Dillon of the Fitzwilliam Museum and English Heritage. Graphs and charts are largely based upon versions supplied by the relevant specialists. For the eBook version of the monograph, figures that incorporate Ordnance Survey data have been altered so they only incorporate Ordnance Survey OpenData products that are permitted under the Open Government Licence. The affected illustrations are Figs. 1.2, 3.1, 3.2, 3.27, 4.55, 4.61, 4.69, 4.70, 5.69, 6.1, 6.6, 6.19 and 6.20.

A number of college archivists responded helpfully to queries concerning documents, maps and other material: Geoffrey T Martin (Christ's College), Amanda Goode (Emmanuel College), Madeleine Patston (Gonville & Caius College), Frances H. Willmoth (Jesus College), Malcolm Underwood (St John's College) and John Pollard (Trinity Hall). The radiocarbon dating was undertaken by the Waikato Radiocarbon Dating Laboratory with the assistance of Fiona Petchey and Alan Hogg. Access to documents and material was assisted by the staff of the Cambridge Records Office, the Cambridgeshire Collection and the Cambridge University Museum of Archaeology and Anthropology, particularly Anne Taylor, while Quinton Carrol arranged for access to archives and material held at the Cambridgeshire Archaeological Store and Julia Poole arranged for access to material held by the Fitzwilliam Museum. Mark Ashton kindly arranged access to St Andrew the Great. Additionally a number of individuals supplied helpful information and insight on a range of topics. These include Peter Addyman (the 1959 investigations), John Alexander (the 1969–71 investigations), Alasdair Brooks (Modern ceramics), Peter Carter (the Eel grig), Joanne Cooper of the Natural History Museum, Tring, (bird bone identification), Peter Kuniholm and Tomasz Wazny from the Malcolm and Carolyn Wiener Laboratory for Aegean and Near Eastern Dendrochronology, Cornell University (the Ottoman barrel), Gavin Lucas (Modern ceramics), Tim Murray (Modern material), Harvey Sheldon (the 1971 investigations). Peter Stovin (college ceramics), Chris Swaysland (the cattle burials), Robin Wood (the European Maple jug), Rachel Wroth (college servants). Conservation of various materials was undertaken by the Museum of London, English Heritage and the York Archaeological Trust.

The work at Grand Arcade would have been impossible without the generous support of John Chesters of Grosvenor Plc on behalf of the Grand Arcade Partnership and Doug Dawes from the principal contractor Bovis Lend Lease Ltd, who acted as archaeological liaison. The Grand Arcade excavations were funded by the Universities Superannuation Scheme and Grosvenor Developments Ltd. as joint funders under the auspices of the Grand Arcade Partnership. The Christ's Lane excavations were funded by Land Securities Properties Ltd. (now Landsec Securities Group), and undertaken with the assistance of their agents SDC Construction. This publication has been principally funded by the Grand Arcade Partnership, with Land Securities Properties Ltd. funding the Christ's Lane element.

Foreword

Martin Biddle

From 1956 to 1988 four hundred volunteers and a small band of professionals worked together to save evidence of the original nucleus of prehistoric and Romano-British Cambridge on Castle Hill before it was destroyed by modern development. This was a pioneering and remarkable effort, but with one single exception it was to be some time before any attempt was made to mount a similar programme on the main site of the medieval town on the opposite bank of the Cam.

The single exception was the work of Professor T. McKenny Hughes who between 1873 and 1915 recorded the remains of medieval Cambridge revealed by building operations. No attempt was made to follow his example in the hey-day of Victorian and Edwardian rebuilding or indeed down to the late 1950s, when it appeared that another period of reconstruction was about to begin and that 'the progress of modern development will destroy more and more of the archaeology of the town' Addyman & Biddle 1965, 76).

Some forty years later Peter Addyman and I did what we could mostly in term time 1958–61 on a few sites – Bradwell's Court, Corn Exchange Street, and Post Office Terrace, for example – and warned of coming problems (Addyman & Biddle 1965, especially p. 76):

> In a few years the redevelopment of the largest single site ever to be rebuilt in the town in modern times – the Lion Yard – will destroy the archaeology of a large area within the King's Ditch. Its prior excavation on an adequate scale is imperative. The progress of modern development in Cambridge will destroy more and more of the archaeology of the town. The constant observation and systematic recording of this work is necessary if any adequate

picture of the development and topography of early medieval Cambridge is to be achieved. In very few English towns has this need been met, but the recording of medieval Oxford provides an example which Cambridge should follow.

The archaeology of Lion Yard was almost entirely lost and little else was done for the next quarter of a century. Medieval Cambridge was far from the interests of academic archaeology in Cambridge then or for decades to come and it was only with the coming into force of Planning Policy Guidance 16 in 1990 that things began rapidly to change. Much of this welcome new work was, however, done in central Cambridge, within the line of the King's Ditch.

The singular and wholly exceptional achievement of the present volume is that it represents what is probably the largest area of *suburban* development ever investigated in an English or to my knowledge European city:

- throughout time, from the beginnings of settlement to the present day,
- covering every kind of documentary, artefactual and environmental evidence,
- without social bias, from the most simple to the most elevated,
- and closely related in visual and recording to the actual patterns created and, most important, to the elements that will now survive into the future.

The innovative element is the way the archaeological evidence (excavation and standing buildings) is presented together with the evidence of the written sources and with historic images of every kind. And this is not done in the 'traditional ' way of separate, usually sequential, sections devoted to each kind of evidence, but rather by the way in which the sources

Figure 0.1. *In the summer of 1959 the earliest feature excavated at Corn Exchange Street was a 13th-century 'ditch', the waterlogged fills of which contained wooden planks, posts, wicker-work, laths and two large circular blocks (Addyman and Biddle 1965, 77–8, 124). 46 years later in 2005 the feature was re-excavated, with the fill of 'clean blue clay' (Addyman and Biddle 1965, 77) and the trench excavated into it in 1959 clearly visible. While the larger exposure meant the feature could now be identified as a substantial pit, unfortunately the fills had almost entirely dried out and c. 2.0m of later sequence had been removed. For all the richness of the archaeology presented in this volume, an elegiac note for what was lost in the 'disastrous failure' of the Lion Yard development (Heighway 1972, 51) is ever present.*

are assembled so that the relevant parts of the evidence are woven together, phase by phase.

For the present writer, the whole approach of this remarkable volume is demonstrated by a single exciting photograph (Fig. 2.6). This looks across the excavation towards the standing buildings on Hadstock Way and shows how the line of an excavated early 12th-century boundary ditch coincides precisely with a property division still in use today.

Martin Biddle
5 December 2018

Summary

Large-scale excavations undertaken by the Cambridge Archaeological Unit in 2005–6 at the Grand Arcade and Christ's Lane sites in Cambridge allowed extensive and intensive investigation of both the town ditch and two street blocks of a suburb lying outside it. The town ditch, known as the King's Ditch, was created in the eleventh or twelfth centuries and was then recut on a number of occasions with a surviving sequence extending until the mid-sixteenth century including a timber bridge, plus some later features. In the suburb dispersed occupation began in the mid-eleventh century with a planned layout following in the early twelfth century. Significant proportions of the backyard areas of 14 plots founded at this time were investigated and their development traced up to the present day, including a detailed programme of standing building recording plus intensive documentary and cartographic analysis. Substantial assemblages of a wide range of artefact types were recovered, including large quantities leather and timber preserved in waterlogged conditions. Major assemblages of pottery, animal bone and stone mouldings were analysed. The material includes a large number of substantial mid-eighteenth to early twentieth-century assemblages of pottery, glass, clay tobacco pipe and other materials that have been analysed in detail. There was also extensive environmental sampling, including pollen and insect analysis. As well as the scale of the assemblages there were a range of individually significant items including leather and wooden jugs and an imported Ottoman barrel from Greece. A considerable number of distinctive college related ceramic and glass items were also found.

The main feature types were pits, wells, postholes, beamslots, gullies, animal burials, ovens and ditches. From the eighteenth century onwards there were increased levels of building activity, during the early nineteenth century in particular the area became much more heavily built up and became urban rather than suburban in character. The features of this phase were largely brick built and consisted of walls, floors, wells, cellars and soakaways. Of particular note is the fact that the depth of the development meant that the bases of all but the deepest features were investigated, uncovering the lower portions of features such as wells that are often left in situ by developer funded excavations.

Overall the work presents a detailed picture of the medieval town ditch on a scale that is previously unparalleled in Britain, one of the most comprehensive archaeological pictures of the development of the plots of a medieval and later suburb and treats eighteenth–twentieth-century material culture in a manner unparalleled in a British context.

Chapter 1

Introduction

Craig Cessford and Alison Dickens

'I still hold ... that the suburbs ought to be either glorified by romance and religion or else destroyed by fire from heaven, or even by fire-brands from the earth.'
The Coloured Lands (1938, 108)
by G.K. Chesterton (1874–1936)

At one level this is a book concerned with the excavation of a small portion of the boundary ditch of a particular medieval and later British town and part of a suburb that lay outside it. Whilst the sheer quantity and quality of archaeological remains presented are of inherent interest, this potentially relatively parochial and recent subject matter is of more global and current significance. Although this is in many respects a conventional publication, covering the largest archaeological investigations ever undertaken in Cambridge (Figs. 1.1–1.2), it can also be conceived of as not so much a study of what happened in the past *per se*, but how the present situation was reached. Although it represents the first major archaeological study of this urban centre, it is concerned principally with fringes, peripheries and boundaries and the University for which Cambridge is best known is an ever-present but off-stage entity. It is almost a cliché that just over half the world's current population live in urban areas (53 per cent in 2014), rising to 80 per cent for the United Kingdom. Humankind has in a sense become *Homo Urbanus* and this trend is likely to continue, with estimates that by 2050 70 per cent of the world's population will live in urban areas. This trope is, however, only true if a simplistic urban–rural binary division is adopted. The origins and early development of urbanism have long been a major concern of archaeologists and over the course of the twentieth century more recent urban centres have increasingly attracted significant archaeological attention. This book is concerned principally with a single excavation in a single urban centre, the town being Cambridge and the main time frame starting in the mid/late eleventh century. As Cambridge is a still thriving urban centre, being granted city status in 1951 for 'exceptional' reasons, as it possessed the only historic British university not located in a city or royal burgh, the archaeological evidence described has many more links with present day urbanism than with the river valleys of Mesopotamia, India, China, and Egypt around 3000 BC where urbanism began. The contribution of this book is therefore one firmly rooted in the present (albeit a present that is in some senses 2005–6 rather than the date of publication) which treats all periods from the site's inception to the 'contemporary past' as equally worthy of archaeological investigation.

This book is not, however concerned with the urban core of Cambridge, and indeed the fact that the city is still a thriving urban centre means that this area will probably only ever be subject to piecemeal and small-scale investigations, remaining in a sense an off-stage metaphorical 'heart of darkness'. This is, however, in some respects a strength, as the urban–rural dichotomy has never been absolute, as suburbs have been an integral part of most urban centres including ancient Mesopotamian cities (van de Mieroop 1997, 68–72) and Classical Rome (Mandich 2015). Suburbs have formed one of the major foci of Romano-British archaeology in recent decades (Fulford & Holbrook 2015) and the same is true for medieval and later periods. Over 40 per cent of the population of the United Kingdom may be defined as living in suburbs (ITC 2004) and a truer value is almost certainly over 50 per cent. We might therefore modify the idea of *Homo Urbanus* to *Homo Suburbanus*. The modern suburb where such a high proportion of the population live, particularly with its focus upon commuting and association with rail and road infrastructure, is largely a product of the nineteenth and twentieth centuries, albeit one with earlier antecedents. It is these relatively recent suburbs that have formed the principal focus of academic 'suburban studies', with earlier suburbs and

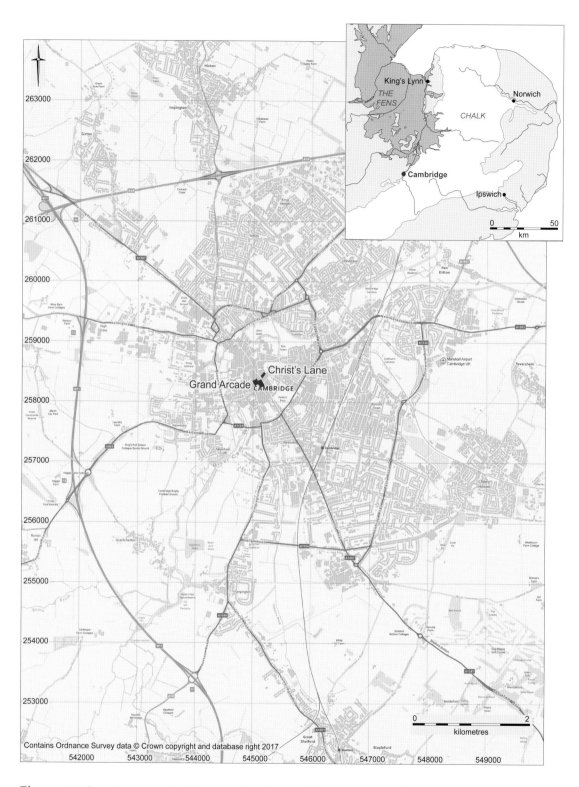

Figure. 1.1. *Location map, showing the principal sites discussed in this volume.*

archaeology at best playing a peripheral introductory role (Vaughan 2015; see also Kruse & Sugrue 2006). Ironically, although there have been studies of such nineteenth and twentieth century Cambridge suburbs (e.g. Bryan & Wise 2005), this book is only peripherally part of that particular narrative, as it was at precisely at this time that the area of Cambridge under consideration effectively ceased to be a suburb. It can therefore

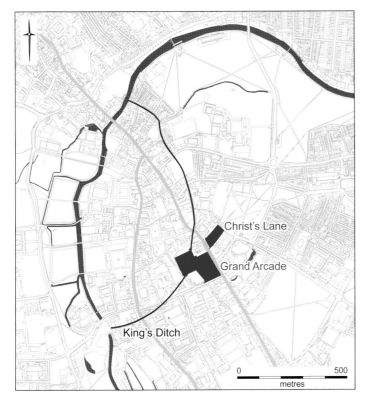

1. Fisher Square watching brief, CAU 2007
2. Corn Exchange Street watching brief, CAU 2007
3. St. Andrew's Street watching brief, CAU 2007
4. No. 21 St. Andrew's Street watching brief, CAU 2007
5. Lion Yard, Alexander 1969-70
6. Nos. 14–15 Corn Exchange Street, Addyman & Biddle 1959
7. Masonic Hall, Hughes 1914
8. Holiday Inn, Malim 1989
9. McDonald Institute, CAU 1992
10. Bird Bolt Hotel, Hughes 1905
11. Emmanuel College, CAU 1993
12. Bradwell's Court, Addyman & Biddle 1959 and Christ's Lane CAU 2006–7
13. Post Office Terrace, Addyman & Biddle 1959
14. St. Andrew the Great, CAU 1992
15. Lion Yard, Partridge 1973

A. Emmanuel College Kitchen, CAU 1992
B. Prudential buildings, Craster 1957
C. No. 62 St. Andrew's Street, Hughes 1880
D. No. 63–4 St. Andrew's Street, Hughes 1880
E. Christ's College Library extension, Hughes 1895
F. Downing Place, CAU 1998
G. Post Office, Hughes
H. Foster's Bank, Hughes 1891
I. Hunnybun's premises, Hughes
J. Bowling Green, Hughes
K. New Museums, Various
L. Cork and Child, Hughes
M. Falcon Yard, Hughes

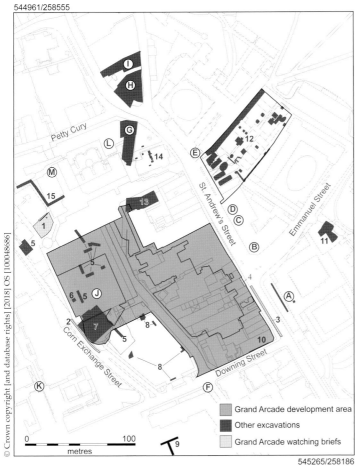

Figure 1.2. *Location of Grand Arcade and Christ's Lane within Cambridge, plus King's Ditch (upper), and all archaeological investigations undertaken within the Grand Arcade street block and its immediate vicinity (lower). Major investigations are numbered, whilst minor investigations are lettered.*

be conceived of as forming the medieval and later 'prehistory' of the Modern suburb.

Although concerned with one particular place – the Barnwell Gate suburb, one of five suburbs situated around the outskirts of medieval Cambridge – this book deals with a range of themes that are germane to the broader subject of suburbanism as a whole, as well as the medieval, post-medieval and modern archaeology of British towns. At the core of the work lie the results of a substantial open-area excavation that was undertaken by the Cambridge Archaeological Unit (CAU) in advance of the construction of the Grand Arcade shopping centre in 2005–6. Encompassing most of a street block in area, the size of this project permitted the detailed excavation of a large proportion of numerous contiguous suburban properties, as well as a considerable portion of the adjacent town boundary ditch. Important evidence pertaining to the suburb's long-term development, spanning its eleventh-century origins through to the early twenty-first century, was recovered.

Methodologically, the detailed treatment of all remains at the site, up to and including those of the twentieth century – allied with the excavation of the lowest portions of all but the very deepest features, the integration of the below-ground archaeology with extensive standing building recording (Fig. 1.3) and the widespread use of documentary and cartographic evidence – renders this a significant example of 'total archaeology'. Moreover, when combined with the results obtained from additional excavations undertaken within a second, nearby street block – the Christ's Lane development – as well as several other small-scale investigations situated in the immediate vicinity, the scale of this work is such that the Barnwell Gate suburb now represents one of the most intensively and extensively investigated suburbs of any British town. Similarly, the excavation of the town's boundary ditch also represents one of the largest and most detailed examples of its kind yet undertaken.

Lying on the southeastern outskirts of Cambridge, the Barnwell Gate suburb developed along one of the town's principal approach roads. In terms of both its size and composition it was relatively typical of contemporary suburbs located all across England. Unlike some examples, however, it did not serve a particular, specialized role and nor did it contain a significant industrial focus. Instead, its narrative is predominately one of stable, continuous and incrementally expanding domestic and commercial occupation. Although pronounced archaeological changes did occur, these primarily pertained to the dominant feature- and material-types in use altering, rather than anything more profound. Yet such a stable

pattern is in itself relatively atypical. The majority of English towns appear to have undergone much more pronounced cycles of growth and decline, which in certain instances – such as that of Stafford, for example – have been described as an 'extraordinary switchback ride of boom and bust' (Carver 2010, preface). Any broader understanding of the excavated sequence is thus inextricably bound up with that of the town itself.

Throughout the majority of the study-period, Cambridge was a relatively minor English county town. Initially established during Roman times as a small settlement located to the north of the River Cam (Alexander & Pullinger 1999), the town was subsequently to remain an 'economically viable backwater' until the mid-tenth century (Hines 1999, 136). Rapid expansion then followed, both physically and economically. Occupation soon extended to the south of the river, where, between the mid-tenth and early fourteenth centuries, a flourishing inland port developed. Numerous religious institutions were founded and the town quickly emerged as a dominant regional centre. In 1209, further stimulus was provided by the foundation of the University of Cambridge; an institution that was subsequently to become central to Cambridge's growing and changing economy. Topographically, the town gradually expanded until, at the beginning of the nineteenth century, the inclosure of the surrounding open fields facilitated a rapid escalation of its suburban growth.

Overall, the large-scale excavations that have been undertaken within the Barnwell Gate suburb, allied with the integrated methodological approach that was adopted and the extensive material assemblages that were recovered, present an opportunity to examine its growth and development in unparalleled detail. The results of this work are thus of local, national and international significance, and make an important contribution to the larger project of global historical archaeology.

Circumstances and background

A century ago the Reverend H.P. Stokes published a slim volume entitled *Outside the Barnwell Gate: another chapter in the intimate history of medieval Cambridge* (Stokes 1915). This work dealt with the medieval and post-medieval development of this suburb, based primarily on documentary and cartographic evidence but also incorporating the results of a small quantity of antiquarian fieldwork. In many respects, therefore, the present book can be regarded as an enlarged and updated reappraisal of Stokes' study. However, the excavations reported on here represent a quantum leap in terms of both the scale and intensity of archaeological investigation in Cambridge. This can be demonstrated by a simple statistic. The town's medieval core – as defined by its encircling boundary ditch – occupied *c.* 37.7 ha; the Grand Arcade development alone is equivalent to *c.* four per cent of this area, or *c.* three per cent of the overall medieval town when its five suburbs are also included.

In retrospect, Stokes' volume was published at the end of what can now be regarded as the heyday of antiquarian investigation in Cambridge. Beginning around the middle of the nineteenth century, a flourishing – and, in some respects, ground-breaking – tradition of observation and artefact recovery was established. A diverse range of individuals were involved, many of whom were associated with the University, and much of their work was conducted during the extensive range of building projects that were then being undertaken. Foremost amongst these figures was Cambridge's Woodwardian Professor of Geology, Thomas McKenny Hughes (1832–1917), who was actively locally from *c.* 1873 to 1915. Not only did Hughes undertake a large number of investigations but he also published his results in detail within the Cambridge Antiquarian Society journal. These papers continue to form an important resource, particularly in relation to areas where little subsequent development has occurred.

For much of the succeeding eight decades, Cambridge saw little in the way of sustained archaeological investigation. One notable exception was the work of Dr John Alexander (1922–2010) – lecturer in the Department of Archaeology – who was active locally from 1956 to 1988. Alexander undertook a number of important excavations in the town's Castle Hill area, although these were primarily focused on Roman remains (Alexander & Pullinger 1999). To the south of the river, however, within Cambridge's medieval core, very little work took place. In a few isolated instances, some College fellows undertook investigations while construction work was being conducted at their respective institutions. These individuals included Glyn Daniel (1939), James Graham-Campbell (1968) and Peter Salway (1996). However, the only sustained investigations to have been undertaken within the core of Cambridge during this period were those conducted by two undergraduates – Peter Addyman and Martin Biddle – between 1958 and 1961 (Addyman & Biddle 1965; Biddle 2008), both of whom went on to become major figures in British urban archaeology.

Despite recognition in the early 1970s that Cambridge's archaeological provision was inadequate (Browne 1974, foreword; Heighway 1972, 48), not uncommon at this time, the 'Rescue' boom of the 1970s and 1980s largely bypassed the city. This is perhaps ironic given the important roles that were played by Martin Biddle at Winchester (Biddle 2005; Biddle 2008; Collis 2011) and Peter Addyman at York (Addyman 1997; Addyman 2005). The dearth of fieldwork may have resulted in part from a lack of support by the Department of Archaeology, at least at a corporate level; it was certainly noted that the department had 'taken no official part in excavations' (Heighway 1972, 48). Yet there were also a number of additional factors. Firstly, the absence of significant Roman, Middle Saxon and Viking remains within the settlement to the south of the river limited potential interest, as these periods were then regarded as the most important for archaeological investigation. Secondly, the majority of attention was focused on larger towns at this time, partly because these were perceived of as more important (Dyer 2003) but also because, at a practical level, it was difficult to sustain the necessary volume of archaeological work in smaller urban centres.

By the early 1970s, around 30 per cent of Cambridge's medieval core had already been redeveloped or was in the process of being built on (Heighway 1972, 48, map 7). By the end of the 1980s this figure had probably exceeded 40 per cent, with perhaps a further 20 per cent rendered permanently inaccessible via the presence of numerous University and College-associated listed buildings. The situation altered somewhat in the 1990s, with the advent of PPG16 and the rise of developer-funded archaeology. Nevertheless, although these changes have led to a marked increase in the frequency of archaeological fieldwork, the majority of town-centre excavations in Cambridge have been limited to some extent by occurring within an urban environment that is still occupied and indeed thriving. Consequently, the majority of such investigations have been both small in scale and trench-based in nature. Despite this, however, a number of significant discoveries have been made and our knowledge of the town continues to increase.

Previous archaeological investigations
As the above account makes clear, the most recent phase of excavations did not occur within an archaeological vacuum and the Barnwell Gate suburb has been subject to investigation in one form or another since the mid-nineteenth century. The quantity of such work, and its scale in relation to the substantial size of the Grand Arcade development, is demonstrated graphically in Figure 1.2. Here, it is apparent that the site is surrounded by a scatter of earlier observations and additional, smaller-scale investigations.

Following on from a limited number of isolated antiquarian observations, made between *c.* 1840 and 1870, a much more sustained programme of

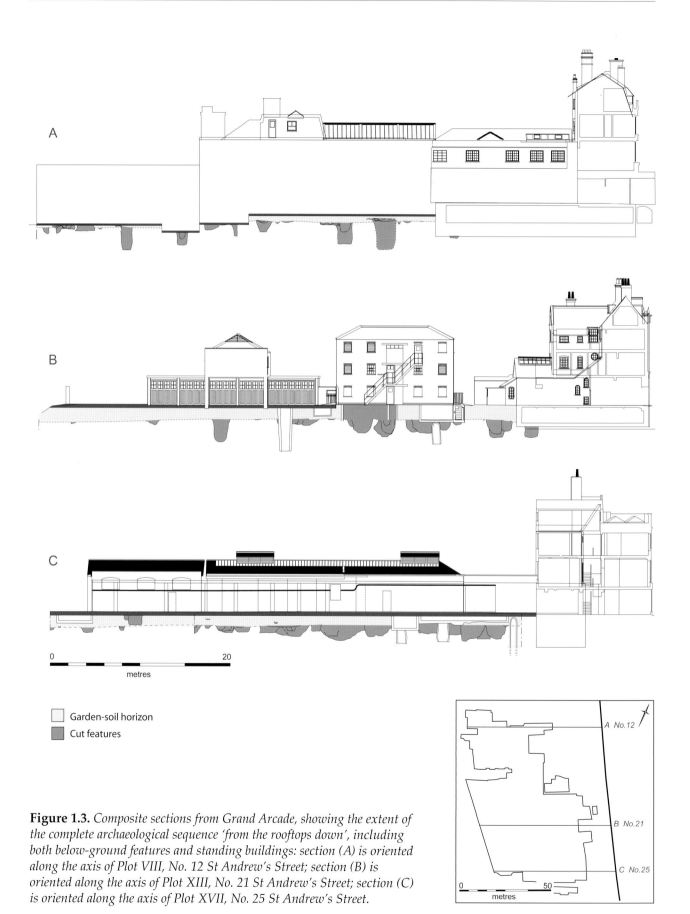

Figure 1.3. *Composite sections from Grand Arcade, showing the extent of the complete archaeological sequence 'from the rooftops down', including both below-ground features and standing buildings: section (A) is oriented along the axis of Plot VIII, No. 12 St Andrew's Street; section (B) is oriented along the axis of Plot XIII, No. 21 St Andrew's Street; section (C) is oriented along the axis of Plot XVII, No. 25 St Andrew's Street.*

investigation was undertaken by Thomas McKenny Hughes from *c.* 1873 to 1915. Replicating the wider pattern that predominated all across Cambridge, Hughes observed works undertaken at 11 different sites in the vicinity (Fig. 1.2). The most significant of these comprised his investigations at the Birdbolt Inn (Hughes 1907a; Fig. 1.2, no. 10) and Masonic Hall (Hughes 1915a; Fig. 1.2, no. 7). Following Hughes, however, a prolonged hiatus occurred until a series of small-scale investigations were undertaken by Peter Addyman and Martin Biddle in 1958–61. Significant sites that were investigated during this latter period included the courtyard of 14–15 Corn Exchange Street, the Bradwell's Court shopping centre – subsequently to form the focus of the Christ's Lane development – and Post Office Terrace (Addyman & Biddle 1965, 77–82, 85–8; Fig. 1.2, nos. 6, 12, 13).

The succeeding three decades, *c.* 1960–90, were characterized by a significant dearth of archaeological investigations. This absence is rendered particularly significant because, despite earlier warnings (Addyman & Biddle 1965, 76–7; Hurst 1956, 50), the extensive Lion Yard shopping centre development was undertaken during the 1970s immediately to the north of Grand Arcade. Scant archaeological provision was allocated (Alexander 1970; Alexander 1972; Hurst 1970, 180; Fig. 1.2, nos. 5 and 15) and this development – which resulted in the destruction of an entire medieval street block – was subsequently described as a 'disastrous failure' (Heighway 1972, 51). Throughout the 1970s–1980s, moreover, the situation continued to decline; a series of developments took place without any form of archaeological intervention whatsoever. By the late 1980s things had begun to improve slightly. A small number of extremely limited investigations took place in advance of ongoing development (e.g. Malim 1990, 2; Fig. 1.2, no. 8).

Following the implementation of PPG16 in 1990, the situation altered markedly. Since that time a number of archaeological investigations have been undertaken in the area, principally by the CAU. These initially consisted of small-scale evaluations such as those conducted at St Andrew the Great (Miller 1992; Fig. 1.2, no. 14) and the McDonald Institute (Gdaniec 1992; Fig. 1.2, no. 9). A watching brief was also undertaken at Emmanuel College kitchens in 1992 (Dickens 1992; Fig. 1.2, A), plus an evaluation and subsequent excavation in the Master's forecourt of Emmanuel College in 1993 (Dickens 1993; Dickens 1994; Fig. 1.2, no. 11). More informal recording of works not covered by PPG16 also took place (White & Mortimer 1998; Fig. 1.2, F). Yet with the exception of evidence of a major fourteenth-century building Emmanuel College (Dickens 1999a), none of these investigations produced particularly notable results. Cumulatively, however, a broader understanding of the archaeological deposits that were present in the area was constructed. Where pertinent, the results of these various investigations have been fully integrated into the following account.

Grand Arcade and related developments
The Grand Arcade development was initially proposed in 1997. A draft planning brief was issued in 1998 and subsequently approved by Cambridge City Council in 2000. From the outset, it was apparent that this 1.5 ha development area represented not only the largest site that had yet been made available for archaeological investigation in the town, but also – due to the difficulties inherent in securing a large contiguous area within a densely occupied, multi-tenanted urban landscape – the largest that was ever likely to occur. Moreover, the fact that the proposed site partially overlapped with the scene of the 'disastrous failure' of the Lion Yard development added to the sense that it represented a unique opportunity. The scale of the resultant excavation is well-demonstrated by an aerial photograph taken partway through (Fig. 1.4).

As part of the initial planning stage of the project a desk-based assessment was undertaken (Dickens 1997a), a brief covering archaeological excavations issued (Kaner 2000) and a statement of archaeological strategy produced (Dickens 2001b). Several phases of preliminary ground investigations were monitored at the site (Dickens 2001; White 1998), whilst two archaeology-specific test pit evaluations were undertaken (Dickens 1999c; Dickens & Cessford 2003). Practical considerations meant that the evaluation phase was restricted to the observation and/or excavation of 37 small holes, with a combined area of *c.* 27 sq. m. This represented a sample of the site of less than 0.2 per cent, much lower than the 2–5 per cent generally considered appropriate for an evaluation (Hey & Lacey 2001). Nonetheless, the test pits did confirm the survival of *in situ* archaeological deposits, although their nature and extent remained unclear. Following this phase the original desk-based assessment was revised and updated (Dickens 2003) and a written scheme of investigation produced (Dickens 2004).

The Grand Arcade development was jointly funded by the Universities Superannuation Scheme and Grosvenor Developments Ltd under the auspices of the Grand Arcade Partnership, which was formed in December 2002. The CAU was employed as a subcontractor by Grosvenor Developments Ltd in its role as Development and Project Manager. An archaeological presence was first established at the site in November 2004 and the excavations themselves were undertaken between 7 February 2005 and 11 July

Figure 1.4. *Aerial view of Grand Arcade, facing southwest, taken in May 2005 partway through the ongoing archaeological investigations. The red line indicates the extent of the development area (photograph courtesy of Bovis Lend Lease Ltd.).*

2006, with a short break between mid-December 2005 and early April 2006. The on-site team consisted of a director, two supervisors, a surveyor and up to 25 field archaeologists.

As is common on developer-funded urban excavations, the site was not made available for archaeological investigation as a single, cohesive entity. Instead, the initial scheme of investigation subdivided the site into five areas, which were in turn to be excavated in 10 relatively coherent blocks. In practice, however, the exigencies of the demolition, piling and construction processes meant that the excavation programme was subject to constant amendment and the site was actually partitioned into a much larger number of diminished and less coherent sub-blocks, numbering around 40 in total. For similar reasons, it was rarely possible to excavate the entirety of the below-ground

remains within a particular block in a single, unbroken sequence. Rather, the investigation of such an area typically involved between five and seven stages.

Prior to the commencement of any demolition works, all extant standing building remains were recorded. Depending on accessibility and survival, a second phase of building recording was sometimes required during the demolition process itself. Any archaeological features that were revealed by the buildings' removal were then subject to controlled excavation. Where present, the underlying garden-soil layer was also subject to test-pit investigation at this stage (Fig. 1.5). This latter material was then mechanically removed under close archaeological supervision, while any discrete remains that were encountered during this process were hand-excavated and recorded. The next stage comprised the excavation of those features

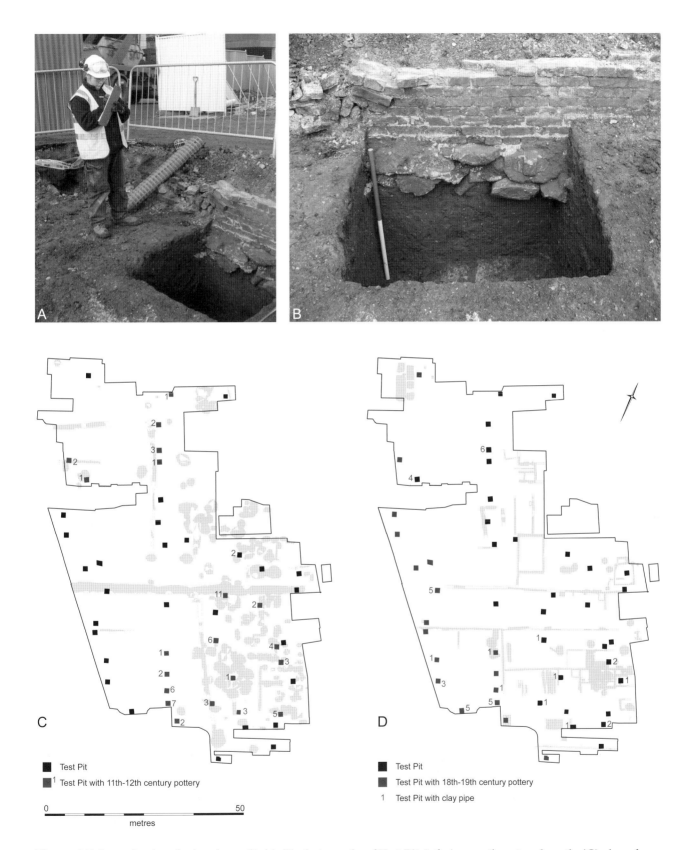

Figure 1.5. *Investigating the 'garden soil': (A–B) photographs of Test Pit 4, facing northwest and north; (C) plan of test pits showing distribution of eleventh- to twelfth-century pottery; (D) plan of test pits showing distribution of clay tobacco pipe fragments and eighteenth- to nineteenth-century pottery.*

that had been stratigraphically sealed beneath the garden-soil horizon. Finally, the lowest portions of deep features, such as wells, occasionally required an additional stage (or stages) of mechanical excavation in order to ensure continued safe access.

Overall, the Grand Arcade excavations were undertaken in a relatively standard manner and were recorded using a modified version of the Museum of London Archaeology Service single context system (Spence 1994). The principal innovation adopted during the recording process comprised the use of a – then relatively newly available – Leica TPS reflectorless theodolite to facilitate planning. This digital system allowed the numerous horizontal and vertical 'fault lines' that had been introduced by the multi-staged excavation process to be repaired during the post-excavation phase. The latter culminated in the production of grey reports covering both the excavations (Cessford 2007) and standing building recording (Baggs & Dickens 2005; Dickens & Baggs 2009). Finally, an updated project design was also produced (Dickens 2007). Much of the specialist analysis was completed during the period 2008–10 and although some updating has taken place this has not been universal.

Very similar methodologies were also adopted at the other sites that have been incorporated into this volume, most notably the Christ's Lane development (Newman 2007). These sites will be discussed in greater detail in Chapter 6, where information pertaining to their background circumstances will also be presented.

Structure and organization

As stated above, the principal focus of this book comprises the long-term development of the Barnwell Gate suburb, alongside that of the adjacent town boundary – known historically as the King's Ditch – which defined the perimeter of medieval and later Cambridge. To this end a variety of evidence is employed, a large proportion of which is archaeological in nature; first and foremost are the results from the excavations at Grand Arcade. A large number of archaeological features were encountered (Fig. 1.6), in addition to the extensive material assemblages and the wide variety of standing buildings (see Fig. 1.12). Consequently, a conventionally organized volume – with all results afforded equal weight and discussed at a consistently high level of detail – would be prohibitively lengthy and unwieldy.

To mitigate this issue, a bipartite approach has been adopted. The printed volume forms a self-contained, stand-alone work. Supplementing this, however, is a second digital-only volume archived in the University of Cambridge Repository (https://www.repository.cam.ac.uk/), and also available via the McDonald

Institute for Archaeological Research website. The latter includes – but is by no means restricted to – additional detailed feature-specific information, historical sources and artefactual and ecofactual data. It is intended that, whenever additional information is desired or a greater level of detail sought, the two mediums can be used in conjunction. To facilitate this, the same chapter-by-chapter organizational structure has been adopted in both instances. In order to restrict unwarranted repetition and maintain internal cohesion, direct cross-referencing between the two volumes has been kept to a minimum.

Whilst not necessarily ideal, it is felt that this arrangement preserves the integrity of a single volume account whilst also permitting a greater level of detail to be accessed as and when required. Moreover, by placing the additional material online, within the University of Cambridge's institutional repository, it is rendered both accessible and searchable.

One of the main underlying principles of this publication, which extends to both the print-based and digital-only material, is *integration*. Wherever practicable the available archaeological, artefactual, environmental, architectural, historical and cartographic information has been combined to provide a multi-faceted, diachronic account (Taylor 1974a; Taylor 1974b). In the main, this material has been organized into a broadly chronological narrative. Firstly, Chapters 2–5 present the results that were obtained from the large-scale open-area excavation undertaken at Grand Arcade, beginning with the earliest evidence of pre-suburban activity at the site (Chapter 2). Next, the entire King's Ditch sequence is explored, from its initial creation to its eventual infilling (Chapter 3). This feature is considered in isolation from the over-arching chronological framework due to its limited stratigraphic overlap with the adjacent suburb, allied with the desire to present a coherent, in-depth analysis of the ditch's formation, development and usage.

Following this brief temporal disjunction, the narrative returns to a predominately chronological examination of the patterns of medieval (Chapter 4), post-medieval and modern (Chapter 5) development within the Grand Arcade street block. Similarly, the extensive artefactual, economic and environmental remains that relate to these periods are also incorporated on a chapter-by-chapter basis. In Chapter 6, the perspective shifts outwards to an examination of the Barnwell Gate suburb's wider environs. Here, the results obtained from the nearby Christ's Lane development are presented, alongside those from the surrounding East Fields and other Cambridge suburbs. Once again, this material is considered out of its position in the temporal sequence, in order to highlight any potential differences between the various sites. Finally, the volume concludes

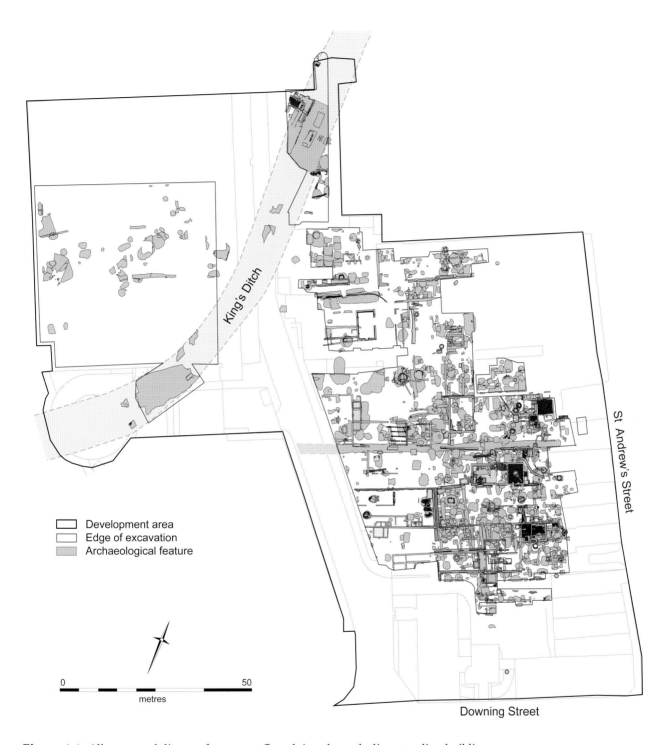

Figure 1.6. *All excavated discrete features at Grand Arcade, excluding standing buildings.*

with a series of thematic essays that address some of the wider issues raised within the foregoing text (Chapter 7).

The last chapter is particularly important. It is the inherent tendency of a chronological framework to fracture the narrative into a series of period-specific sub-sections, each of which is effectively discussed in isolation. This in turn serves to marginalize, and potentially even obfuscate, the impact of long-term processes of change and development as well as general themes (such as the nature of suburbanism) and particular issues (such as the impact of global trade). The thematic essays are thus intended to counteract this imbalance. Moreover, by engaging with issues of local, national and international scale, as well as addressing

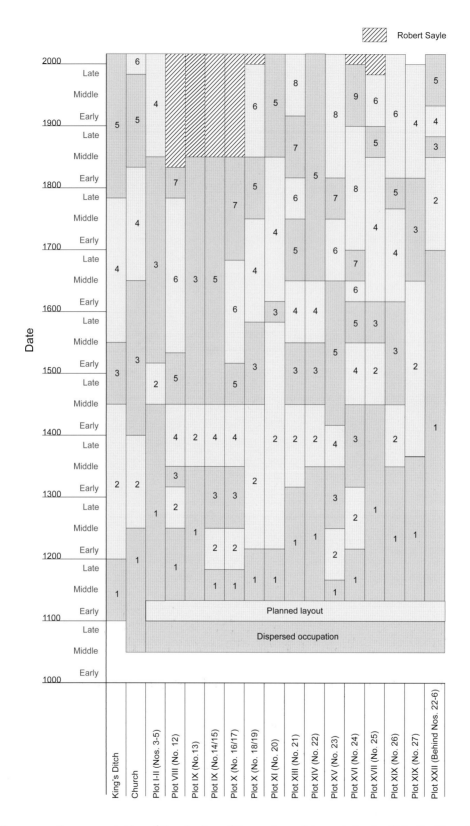

Figure 1.7. *Diagrammatic representation of the phasing of the various plots contained within the Grand Arcade street block. Note the diverse trajectories that were followed by the majority of plots, with little evidence of cohesive, site-wide phasing. Individual phase numbers (1, 2, 3, etc.) are entirely plot-specific; they are based upon the particular archaeological sequences that were encountered. For plot locations see Fig. 5.2.*

key topics such as the archaeology of modernity, they also serve to contextualize the volume's results in terms of a broader global historical standpoint.

Spatial dimensions are also of significance. Indeed, it would have been equally possible to organize this book according to a predominately spatial as opposed to temporal framework. There are several reasons why this approach has not been adopted. Firstly, up until the early seventeenth century the necessary quantity of documentary, cartographic and closely dated archaeological data is not available. Consequently, the segregation of the material into a series of discrete spatial elements would be an unwarranted imposition. After this date, however, such an approach is not only warranted but is – arguably, at least – desirable. Therefore, this spatial dimension, presented in the form of a series of discrete 'tenement narratives' (see Bowsher *et al.* 2007; Hall & Hunter-Mann 2002), an increasingly important facet of the discussion from that point onwards (Chapter 5). The second reason is that, throughout the majority of the suburb's existence, little or no evidence of classic site-wide phases or 'levels' can be identified.

This situation can be demonstrated graphically via a diagrammatic representation of each identified plot's individual developmental trajectory (Fig. 1.7). By presenting the data recovered from the Grand Arcade street block in this fashion, it becomes apparent that no significant changes occurred across all, or even the majority, of plots either at one single point in time or over a relatively discrete period. Nevertheless, a number of recognizable commonalities are apparent. These generally relate to 'thresholds', whereby particular feature- or material-types became increasingly common and thus effectively achieved the status of a site-wide choice. Such nebulous distinctions do not comprise a suitable basis for the organization of an entire volume, and have not therefore been adopted. Yet it is important that some form of mechanism be provided in order to allow the spatial aspects of the sequence to be adequately incorporated into the accounts presented below. To this end, a terminological distinction has been adopted between *plots*, which are primarily based upon documentary/cartographic evidence, and *properties*, which are primarily based upon archaeological evidence.

For ease of reference, the Grand Arcade street block has been subdivided into 23 plot-units (see Fig. 5.2, Plots I–XXIII; Table 1.1), each of which is based to some degree upon the surviving documentary evidence. Whilst some of these plots relate directly to discrete, self-contained entities, others pertain to larger property holdings owned by a single institution and a final category comprise less well-documented

Table 1.1. *Archaeologically investigated plots within the Grand Arcade street block (* = includes part of Plot XII, located to west).*

Plot	Equivalent street number (1870s onwards)	Area excavated (m²)	Overall percentage excavated
I–II	Nos 3–5 St Andrew's Street	125	4
III	No. 6 St Andrew's Street	-	-
IV	No. 7 St Andrew's Street	-	-
V	No. 8 St Andrew's Street	-	-
VI	No. 9 St Andrew's Street	-	-
VII	Nos 10–11 St Andrew's Street	75	15
VIII	No. 12 St Andrew's Street	420	49
IX*	Nos 13–15 St Andrew's Street	560	33
X*	Nos 16–19 St Andrew's Street	990	45
XI*	No. 20 St Andrew's Street	610	59
XIII	No. 21 St Andrew's Street	530	50
XIV	No. 22 St Andrew's Street	180	72
XV	No. 23 St Andrew's Street	165	66
XVI	No. 24 St Andrew's Street	210	74
XVII	No. 25 St Andrew's Street	155	65
XVIII	No. 26 St Andrew's Street	145	60
XIX	Nos 27–29 St Andrew's Street	135	15
XX	No. 30 St Andrew's Street	-	-
XXI	Nos 13–14 Downing St	-	-
XXII	Behind Nos 22–26 St Andrew's Street	360	22
XXIII	North of St Andrew's Hill	-	-

units of uncertain attribution. It is important to note that the static numbering system employed here – and maintained consistently throughout the volume – does not necessarily imply the absolute stability of these plots' boundaries, or an unbroken continuity to their sequence. A system which took account of all known and potential changes would be so complex and unwieldy, running to several hundred spatio-temporal entities, as to be rendered unusable for all intents and purposes. Given the much more restricted scale of the archaeological investigations undertaken within the Christ's Lane street block, a less complex spatial framework has been adopted in Chapter 6.

It should also be noted that the relationship between the various different sources employed in this volume is often rather problematic; not because one is more or less correct than another, but because each operates on different spatial and temporal scales. At a spatial level, for example, the archaeological remains principally comprise individual features, such as pits and wells, whilst the documentary evidence relates

Figure 1.8. *Photographs of the initial clearance of part of the main Grand Arcade area, facing southeast (upper) and excavations ongoing within part of the main Grand Arcade area, facing west (lower).*

mainly to larger, grouped entities such as plots. While the archaeological features certainly fell within properties, the precise relationship between the two is often unclear, especially during the earlier medieval period.

At a temporal level documentary sources can often be dated very precisely, to a particular year or even day, whilst archaeological evidence is rarely more precise than half a century (although there are some notable exceptions). Therefore, it is often impossible to correlate a particular feature to a documented property and even when this can be done, it may not be possible to link the feature to a specific, documentarily attested owner or lessee. This issue also has broader implications, since historians are increasingly examining short, nuanced periods of a few years in duration; periods that can very rarely be distinguished in the archaeological record.

Figure 1.9. *Photograph of excavations ongoing within part of the main Grand Arcade area, facing southeast.*

Some doorways and windows to the past

This inset is effectively a 'greatest hits' medley of one of the plots excavated at Grand Arcade. In urban archaeology sequence is all, although if life and history are just 'one damn thing after another' urban archaeology is frequently lots of things happening at the same time, or at least with overlapping temporalities. Although sequence is crucial, this need not constitute a simplistic linear narrative, or narratives. Indeed it is often the resonances – be they temporal, spatial, social, economic etc. – of the sequence that are most informative. Archaeology is often defined as the study of the material remains of the past, but it also deals with the contemporary and the future, especially if the 'archaeological present' in this context is defined as 2005–6 when the Grand Arcade excavations took place.

Some of the frontage buildings on St Andrew's Street have been retained, one of which is No. 21 (Plot XIII), which since it re-opened in 2009 has housed Chocolat Chocolat (Fig. 1.10). The website for the business notes states:

> Cambridge has one of the oldest universities in the world and is a city full of tradition, within a few short steps you can peak into the glorious spires of King's, the quadrangles of Christ's College, Trinity and many more each steeped in over 800 years of tradition. Voted Cambridge's favourite chocolate shop Chocolat Chocolat is found in [the] historic centre of the city opposite Emmanuel College and just around the corner from Downing College in a nineteenth century building. Since it opened in 2009 Chocolat Chocolat can't claim to have the same long history as the rest of the city, but the shop and its range of luxury chocolates are steeped in the traditions of the independent chocolatier.
> (http://www.chocolatchocolat.co.uk/about/ accessed 7 April 2016)

Although the Chocolat Chocolat website refers to the heritage and tradition of Cambridge, it is the grand narrative of the University rather than the particular story of the property that it occupies. Indeed the one particular fact it mentions, that the building is nineteenth-century, is incorrect. The evidence in this volume demonstrates that this property, like the others investigated, possesses a tradition that exceeds the 800 years of the University.

The current building was constructed c. 1912–13 and is in the Queen Anne revival style, which was popular c. 1875–1920 but harks back to the English Baroque architectural style of approximately the reign of Queen Anne (1702–14) (Fig. 1.10). Also prominently displayed is a stone sign that reads EMMANUEL/THE CHALICE, depicting the college coat of arms above a chalice (see Fig 5.77B). Emmanuel College acquired the property at the time of its foundation in 1584, and the property was the Chalice Inn by 1578 and until 1616/37. By the early twentieth century the plot had not been known as the Chalice for over 250 years. When the current building was constructed the history of the Barnwell Gate suburb was being assiduously researched by the Reverend H.P. Stokes (1915) and in 1910–12 one of the occupants was the Revered Fredrick George Walker (c. 1858–1936), secretary to the Cambridge Antiquarian Society. This suggests that the sign is a self-consciously antiquarian statement, which may have been inspired by Walker who excavated at Godmanchester and elsewhere in Cambridgeshire before becoming organizing secretary and editor of the Egypt Exploration Society in 1913. Whilst living at the premises Walker donated a post-medieval iron key with a cusped bow, piped stem and flat 'S'-shaped web 'found in yard, at the back of Flack and Judge, St Andrew's Street' to the Cambridge Museum of Archaeology in 1907.

When the property stopped being the Chalice in c. 1616/37 the property was occupied by a sequence of chandlers, grocers and wine merchants for c. 370–90 years until 2005, with a remarkable degree of retailing continuity spanning around a dozen generations of occupants and which effectively still continues today. While many of these occupants have left little discernible archaeological trace of their presence, the five sets of initials linked to the household of the grocer Edward Jay that mark Standing Building 70 constructed in 1845 communicate particularly eloquently of a moment in time (see Figs. 5.47–5.50). The best evidence relates to the Headley family of tallow chandlers and grocers, who resided there for around 90 years c. 1723–1815 and who can be linked to two assemblages that speak vividly of their domestic material culture (*Pit 57 c. 1760–80* and *Soakaway 2 c. 1813–23*; see Figs. 5.27 and 5.46). These contain many intriguing items, such as a soup bowl from Trinity College from *Soakaway 2* (see Fig. 5.46E) when there is no evidence for a connection to that college and at a time when soup had to be ordered as an extra. The Headley family were also probably responsible for the construction of *Well 45* in the 1720s. This had a baseplate of Norwegian Scots pine felled after 1714 and a lining of reused stone that included blocks from two domestic windows of *c.* 1570–1640 (see Figs. 5.24–5.26). In all likelihood these windows had previously graced the frontage building of the property, but one itself incorporated reused stone from a window of *c.* 1200–70. One potential origin for this stone is a window of the Dominican Friary founded *c.* 1221–38, which later became the site of Emmanuel College.

The period when the property was the Chalice Inn *c.* 1578–1616/37 is archaeologically attested most vividly by the construction and later backfilling of *Cesspit 16*, probably linked to the commencement and cessation of the property being an inn (see Figs. 4.37B, 4.43 and 5.5–5.6). The discarded material, which is likely to derive from the inn, includes some elements of timber-framing that were being removed from a building and some unused poor-quality small wooden pegs, intended to be used in a door or window. More personal items include an exceptional near-complete moulded leather drinking vessel (see Figs. 4.37B and 5.6B), wooden spoons (see Fig. 5.5G–H), a bone apple or cheese scoop, leather shoes (see Fig. 5.6A) and parts of some wooden boxes or drawers (see Fig. 5.5A–E), whilst amongst the waterlogged plant remains were seeds of cucumber and grains-of-paradise. The presence of the latter of these, a West African member of the ginger family used as a spice, provides indirect testimony to the rise of the Second Atlantic slave trade in the 1620s.

Prior to the mid-sixteenth century documentary evidence directly relating to this property is lacking and all that survive are a few passing references in leases of adjacent properties. We are therefore almost wholly reliant on the archaeological evidence, which suggests three phases of occupation spanning the mid-fifteenth–mid-sixteenth, early fourteenth–mid-fifteenth and mid-twelfth–early fourteenth centuries. Continuing our progression backwards though time, the defining feature of the mid-fifteenth–mid-sixteenth century phase is cask-lined *Well 39* (see Fig. 4.35), but perhaps the most striking elements are two large water filled features *WFF 14–15* both of which had upright ladders left in them when they were backfilled (see Figs. 4.46 and 4.48). Such abandonment of ladders is unparalleled in Cambridge and extremely rare nationally. The preceding mid-fourteenth–mid-fifteenth century is defined by wattle-lined *Well 29* and also has two large water filled features *WFF 6–7*, possibly used for soaking cattle horns or retting flax (see

Fig. 4.18). Probably associated with this phase, although it could be earlier, was *Pit 22*. This was just one of many such pits dug to extract gravel and is typical in its form and size. When it was backfilled 3400 bones – but very little other material – were dumped in it. This rapidly deposited animal bone represents *c.* 700kg of meat or *c.* 2,550 person days of consumption, suggesting some kind of major feasting event at a level much greater than a single household. The earliest mid-twelfth–early fourteenth-century main occupational phase also has a wattle-lined well (*Well 13*), plus *Cesspit 10* – which lay within a timber building – and *Cesspit 11*. The mixed composition of the wood used to construct the two wattle-lined wells, with both utilizing the dominant willow but with significant quantities of ash (*Well 13*) and hazel (*Well 29*), suggests that it was acquired non-commercially as 'cut-it-yourself' wood. This potentially relates to the fact that woodland was relatively easily accessible from a suburban locale.

Although the mid-twelfth century marks the beginning of the main suburban sequence, the northern boundary of this plot was defined by a slightly earlier *Ditch 1*. *Ditch 1* was the most significant element of the early twelfth-century planned layout and its location still marked a boundary until the early twenty-first century (see Fig. 2.6). Additionally from the mid/late eleventh century this area had been occupied with evidence for a well (*Well 1*), cesspit (*Cesspit 1*) and timber building (*Building 1*) (see Fig. 2.3). *Cesspit 1* in particular produced some semi-complete pottery vessels, plus timber boards probably from a building. These boards come from an oak tree felled in 1029, which began to grow in 802 taking us back to the Middle Saxon period before the conquest of the area by the Kingdom of Wessex (917) and the Danelaw (875–917), to a period when the area was on the boundary between the kingdoms of Mercia and East Anglia. In the early ninth century there is no evidence of an urban settlement at Cambridge, or even that it fulfilled any central place functions. What little we know of the period suggests scattered rural settlements, plus a ford across the river Cam and an abandoned Roman 'city' or 'camp' still visible because of its fourth-century stone walls. Finally, in archaeological terms, what would later be this plot was crossed by a Middle Iron Age (350–50 BC) gully (see Fig. 2.1). By this point any meaningful connection has of course been lost, as demonstrated by the radically different alignment of this feature.

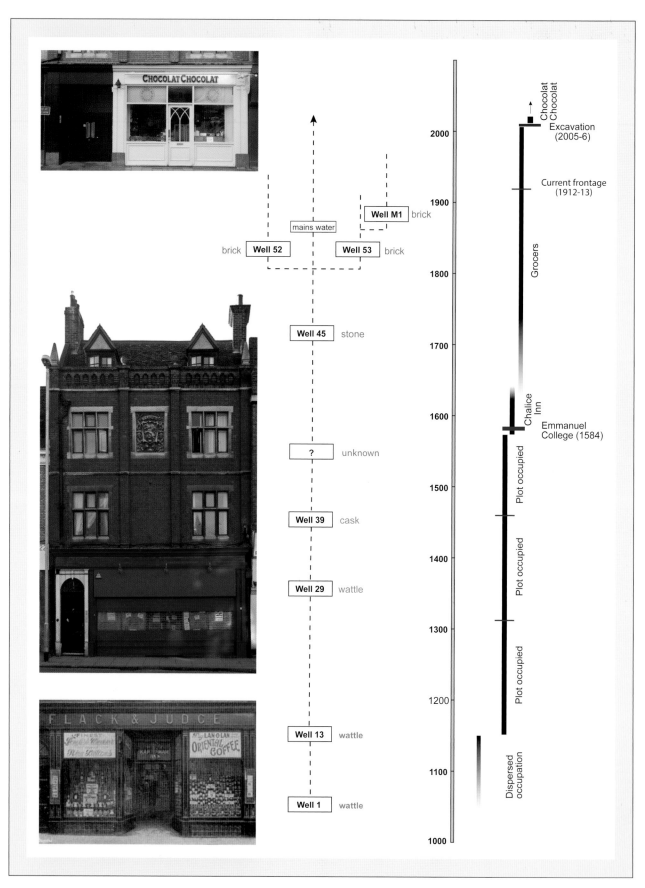

Ignoring the Middle Iron Age gully and the Middle Saxon oak tree, as preludes that relate to 'space' rather than meaningful 'place', the true beginning of the sequence dates to the mid/late eleventh century or the mid-twelfth century depending upon definition. This 850–950 year sequence probably represents 30–35 familial generations. Whilst many fundamental aspects of human existence have remained effectively unchanged during this period, a staggering amount of social, economic, political, technological and other change has taken place. Archaeologically this is expressed in many ways, two obvious examples due to their archaeological visibility being ceramics and water supply. In terms of ceramics, the backfilling of *Cesspit 1* in the early twelfth century contained four unglazed Thetford-type ware and St Neots type-ware jars and bowls, and it is possible that these represent a significant proportion of the pottery owned by one household (see Fig. 2.3A–D). In contrast when material was deposited in *Pit 57* in *c.* 1760–80 by the Headley family, the 18 items would only have represented a small proportion of ceramics that they owned (see Fig 5.27). Although many of the ceramics were manufactured in England there were vessels from Westerwald in Germany and China (see Figs. 5.27H–I). These vessels indicate the consumption of global products, including tea from China and coffee from Central or South America, whilst a clay pipe (see Fig. 5.27K) demonstrates the smoking of tobacco from North America. The Headley family probably sold all these products from their grocery shop – several of which were slave grown products and can therefore be linked albeit indirectly to that phenomenon as can the earlier grains-of-paradise. Whilst there is no direct evidence for the drinking of chocolate it is likely that they also sold this; other contemporary assemblages from Cambridge include chocolate cups (Cessford *et. al.* 2017, fig. 20), providing a link to the current occupants Chocolat Chocolat. Even the relatively utilitarian chamberpot from Westerwald provides

a counterpoint to the sanitary conditions associated with *Cesspit 1*, in which the early twelfth-century pottery was deposited. The exoticism of the global should not, however, obscure the local and some of the pottery deposited in *c.* 1760–80 was produced in Ely, which is closer to Cambridge than the likely sources for the twelfth-century Thetford-type and St Neots-type wares. Additionally the North American tobacco was smoked in a pipe produced by Samuel Wilkinson at 11 Sidney Street, less than five minutes' walk away.

Water is one of the most fundamental human necessities and wells are amongst the most visible archaeological features, creating a potent interpretative combination. The earliest occupants obtained water from a series of wattle-lined wells located in the middle of the plot for around 300 years (*Wells 1, 13, 29*; see Fig. 2.3G). In the mid-fifteenth century they switched to a cask-lined well (*Well 39*; see Fig. 4.35), which in the mid-sixteenth century was apparently replaced by a well of unknown type located at the rear of the property. In the 1720s a stone-lined well was constructed at the front of the property (*Well 45*; see Figs. 5.24–5.26). In 1845 this well was supplemented by two brick-lined wells; one was located in the middle of the property (*Well 52*; see Fig. 5.49), while the other was sealed under a warehouse (*Well 53*). Both supplied water to pumps via lead pipes rather than being directly accessed via buckets. Sometime between 1862 and 1880 the mid-sixteenth-century stone-lined well was backfilled; this probably corresponds with the property being connected to the mains water supply. Other wells continued in use, however, and there is even evidence that a further brick-lined well was constructed inside a building at the rear of the property in 1885 (*Well M1*). The brick-lined wells eventually went out of use, for example *Well 53* was backfilled *c.* 1908–26, but it was only in the 1970s that water was obtained solely via mains supply. Whilst the changes in well linings from wattle to stone to brick are undoubtedly significant material transitions, the inhabitants of the property still essentially obtained their water from a single well. It was really only in the 1840s, when the number of wells rose to three and water was obtained from pumps, and then in the 1860s or 1870s when mains water was provided that fundamental change occurred.

It is something of a cliché to view archaeology as a metaphorical doorway or window to the past,

Figure 1.10. *Past (early twentieth century), present (2005) and future (2016) frontages of Plot XIII (No. 21 St Andrew's Street), plus Harris matrix-style depiction of water supply and general timeline (lower image courtesy of the Cambridgeshire Collection, Cambridge Central Library).*

yet it is perhaps acceptable in the case of Grand Arcade, as buildings such as No. 21 still possess historic doorways and windows and copious evidence for older stone and timber doorways and windows was incorporated into the linings of various features. The property that ultimately became No. 21 has probably had dozens of doorways and windows that numerous generations of occupants have walked and looked through. A few still survive *in situ* and a few more have left distinctive archaeological traces, but most have disappeared without trace. In contrast some of the doorways and windows that were recovered through excavation never actually fulfilled their primary function at the site. Similarly this whistle-stop highlights tour of the past, present and future of one of the investigated properties at Grand Arcade has included a range of themes central to the whole book, which are based on a variety of partial types of evidence. These include the nature of suburban and property tail archaeology, change in a particular locale over a period approaching a millennium, modernity, the local and the global and connections to the Colleges of the University.

Finally, some mention should be made of the terminology that is employed within the following account. In general, the archaeological remains are discussed in terms of features as opposed to contexts. Although contexts were utilized as the primary units during the initial recording process, they often proved to be less meaningful interpretively; hence, such labels have only been retained where they have been thought particularly significant. Arbitrary feature numbers were assigned during the excavation and post-excavation phases. For publication purposes, these have largely been renumbered into individual sequences based instead on feature-type, using a number of abbreviations and acronyms (Table 1.2). As far as possible, the different numbering sequences have been organized chronologically by period and then spatially from north to south. Features that were previously identified during earlier investigations are denoted by a site-specific prefix (Table 1.2).

Table 1.2. *Table of concordance, detailing the abbreviations and acronyms used and the contexts in which they appear.*

Abbreviation	Meaning	Context
AB	Addyman & Biddle's 1959 excavations	All contexts
ADP	Animal Disposal Pit	Plans only
AL	Alexander's 1969–71 excavations	All contexts
B	Building	Plans only
C	Cesspit	Plans only
CAU	Cambridge Archaeological Unit	All contexts
Ce	Cellar	Plans only
D	Ditch	Plans only
E	Elite	Tables only
EC	Emmanuel College	Tables only
F	Flesh side of leather	Figures only
G	Grain side of leather	Figures only
M	Malim's 1989 excavations	All contexts
MNBU	Minimum Number of Butchery Units	All contexts
MNI	Minimum Number of Individuals or Items	All contexts
MSW	Mean Sherd Weight	All contexts
NISP	Number of specimens Identified to SPecies	All contexts

Abbreviation	Meaning	Context
NS	Not Studied	Table only
O	Oven	Plans only
PB	Planting Bed	All contexts
PF	Percolation Fill	Tables only
PH	Planting Hole	All contexts
POSAC	Parts Of Skeleton Always Counted	Tables only
R	Rural	Tables only
RF	Redundant Feature	Tables only
S	Surface	Plans only
SB	Standing Building	Plans only
So	Soakaway	Plans only
SP	Specialized Pit	All contexts
St.And.St	St Andrew's Street	Tables only
Su	Suburban	Tables only
U	Urban	Tables only
VSA	Vessels in Studied Assemblages	Text only
W	Well	Plans only
Wa	Wall	Plans only
WFF	Water-Filled Feature	All contexts

Site sequence

The predominately chronological framework that has been adopted to present the archaeological results in this volume conveys a number of significant strengths. Yet it also serves to fracture the overall sequence into a series of discrete, period-specific chapters. Whilst this has a relatively limited impact on the more minor sites that are discussed – as these were often fragmented in turn by the limited, piecemeal nature of their investigation – it is a particular drawback in relation to the large, open-area excavation that was conducted at Grand Arcade. Here, an intimate and nuanced view of a substantial proportion of a suburban street block has been obtained. Therefore, the opportunity will be taken to present a brief synopsis of the principal phases of activity at this site prior to their detailed, chapter-by-chapter analysis. The following account is centred on a series of simplified, schematic plans that outline the distribution of the most significant features related to each respective phase (Fig. 1.11).

In the first instance – following on from scattered evidence of occasional, non-domestic activity during the later prehistoric to early medieval periods (Fig. 11A) – an initial mid–late eleventh-century pattern of dispersed occupation was present (Fig. 1.11B; Chapter 2). This was succeeded during the early twelfth century by a planned initiative consisting of a large-scale imposed layout (Fig. 1.11C). At this time, a number of rectilinear plots were established, aligned perpendicular to the main Hadstock Way frontage, which comprised part of a newly emergent ribbon development situated on the outskirts of the town (Chapter 2). Shortly thereafter, the new layout was profoundly impacted by the early/mid-twelfth-century creation of the King's Ditch (Fig. 1.11D). A substantial and imposing boundary, the creation of this feature effectively created the suburb by formally demarcating the division between *within* and *without* the urban core (Chapter 3).

Subsequently, throughout the remainder of the twelfth century, the street block developed as part of a relatively thriving, densely occupied suburb (Fig. 1.11E). Numerous properties were established, within which large numbers of features and material assemblages were encountered (Chapter 4). The succeeding thirteenth–mid-fifteenth centuries then appear to represent a broadly consistent period of stability and continuity (Fig. 1.11F–G). Occupation continued, and may well have increased in intensity, while distinctions began to emerge between larger properties – which possessed extensive, spacious backlands – and smaller properties, wherein a comparable number of features were present in much denser profusion (Chapter 4). Throughout this period, the King's Ditch remained

a significant, well-maintained presence. This pattern of relative stability is consistent with the ranking of Cambridge as around the twentieth most important English town during this period (see Dyer 2000).

Between the mid-fifteenth and mid-sixteenth centuries, the overall level of archaeological activity appears to have declined (Fig. 1.11G) as does its intensity of occupation, based upon the lower number of wells that were now being created (Chapter 4). Whilst it does not appear that any of the properties were 'abandoned' in the strictest sense, some may have ceased to be used for domestic occupation. This was a gradual process, which in particular instances may later have been reversed. Similarly, at roughly the same time the King's Ditch was less well-maintained; although it was recut much more frequently, it was also increasingly utilized for refuse disposal. This pattern of apparent decline is somewhat counteracted by the evidence provided by contemporary material culture, which suggests that any diminution in the levels of occupation and activity at the site coincided with a rise in living standards and increased material prosperity.

Between the mid-sixteenth and early seventeenth centuries, a period of archaeological 'invisibility' predominated. This is perhaps best interpreted as evidence of a further period of relative stability. Subsequently, however, the mid-seventeenth–early eighteenth centuries witnessed a period of growth (Fig. 1.11H), as evinced by a considerable investment in certain properties at particular points in time (Chapter 5). Archaeologically, there is then evidence for a substantial increase in occupational and commercial activity during the eighteenth century (Fig. 1.11I); effectively marking the rise of the modern period and the commencement of many of the processes that were to continue throughout the succeeding centuries. A large number of frontage buildings were substantially rebuilt in brick, while the building coverage – the relative

Figure 1.11 *(following six pages). Simplified, schematic plans of the core investigation area at Grand Arcade over time, including: (A) Middle Iron Age gully; (B) mid/ late eleventh-century dispersed occupation, including the distribution of identifiably eleventh-century pottery; (C) early twelfth-century planned layout; (D) initial, mid-twelfth-century layout of the King's Ditch; (E) mid–late twelfth-century occupation; (F) thirteenth–fourteenth-century occupation; (G) fifteenth–sixteenth-century occupation; (H) seventeenth-century occupation; (I) eighteenth-century occupation; (J) nineteenth-century occupation; (K) twentieth-century occupation; (L) early twenty-first-century redevelopment as the Grand Arcade shopping centre.*

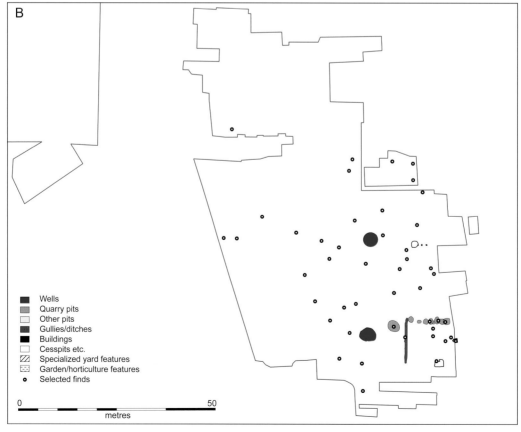

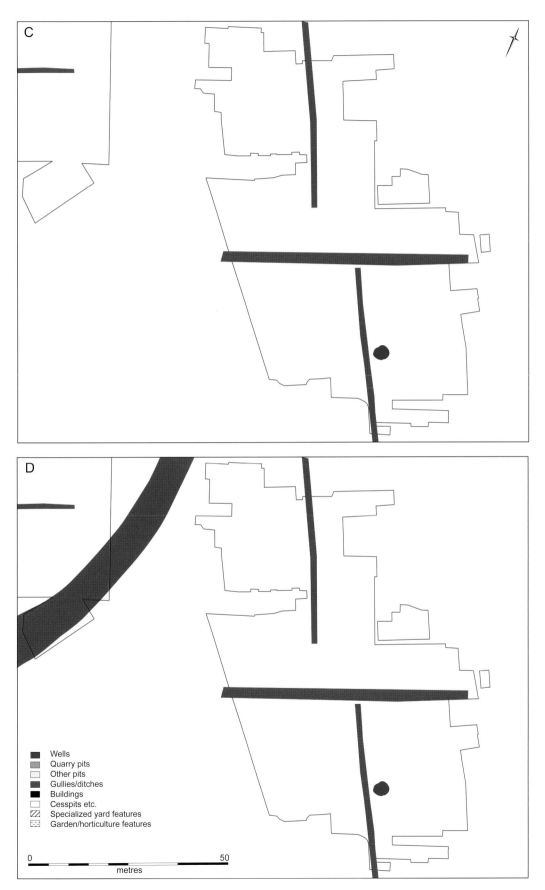

Wells
Quarry pits
Other pits
Gullies/ditches
Buildings
Cesspits etc.
Specialized yard features
Garden/horticulture features

0
50
metres

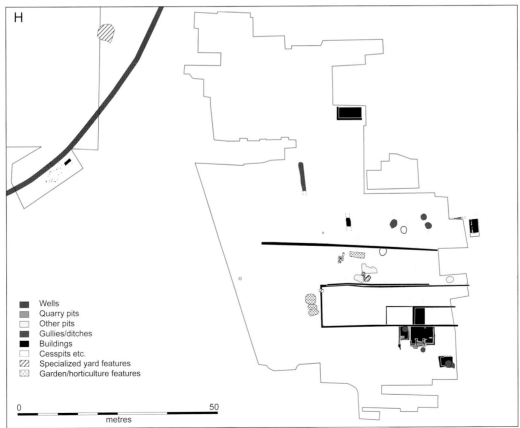

	Wells
	Quarry pits
	Other pits
	Gullies/ditches
	Buildings
	Cesspits etc.
	Specialized yard features
	Garden/horticulture features

0   50

metres

Wells
Quarry pits
Other pits
Gullies/ditches
Buildings
Cesspits etc.
Specialized yard features
Garden/horticulture features

0   50

metres

percentage of individual properties covered by buildings – increased, although a substantial proportion of the street block remained open space. Similarly, the material culture in use expanded markedly, in both range and quantity, from the mid-eighteenth century onwards (Chapter 5). Attitudes to such material also changed, as exemplified by the deposition of large 'feature group' assemblages on a hitherto unprecedented scale.

During the nineteenth century, the character of the street block changed significantly. The degree of building coverage escalated rapidly, doubling or quadrupling on most properties. For the first time, therefore, open space comprised a minor component of the site's topography (Fig. 1.11J). Several areas were developed into densely packed slum-like courts while, contrastingly, a substantial area was developed as a relatively unified entity by the Robert Sayle department store (Chapter 5). The range of material culture in use also continued to expand. Commercial activities now predominated, although a strong residential component was retained. This led to a frequent separation between the businessmen who utilized premises for commercial purposes and the householders who resided at the site, often leading to property fragmentation. Subsequently, during the twentieth century, the area effectively became a 'non-place' (see Augé 1995) that was almost entirely commercial in nature (Fig. 1.11K; Chapter 5). This in turn led to the early twenty-first-century shopping 'experience' of Grand Arcade – and, to a lesser extent, Christ's Lane – which, for good or ill, is emblematic of contemporary society.

The Grand Arcade development itself removed a significant proportion of the street block's former layout (Fig. 1.11L). In many respects, therefore, this most recent phase represents a form of 'year zero' for the area that is unparalleled since its early twelfth-century planned layout. One way in which this change can be articulated is via an examination of the fluctuating levels of population within the street block. During the late twelfth–fourteenth centuries, for example, the estimated population comprised *c.* 100–120 individuals. This fell to *c.* 80 during the sixteenth century before rising again to *c.* 120 in the late seventeenth century, climbing finally to 351 in 1881. The level then declined sharply over the course of the twentieth century, eventually falling to zero if the definition is restricted to permanent residents alone. At a more significant level, however, the Grand Arcade development can be seen as a direct continuation of broader trends in commoditization, retailing and capitalism that can be traced back to the eighteenth and more especially nineteenth centuries; particularly the rise of the Robert Sayle department store.

Starting at the end

Before proceeding to the chronological, chapter-by-chapter narrative it is worthwhile to 'begin at the end'. By so doing, several of the overarching themes that are to arise at points throughout this book can be introduced well before their nominal position in the sequence. Moreover, such a starting point also provides an opportunity to present a practical demonstration of the theoretical framework that is to underpin much of the following account. From the outset, the Grand Arcade project was conceived of as being, as far as was practicably feasible, a 'total' investigation. Below ground the proposed basements, extended car park and road alterations were to remove any and all surviving remains to a depth of 6–8m; for all intents and purposes, 100 per cent of the site's archaeological remains. Moreover, this level of destruction equally extended to most of the above-ground structures, which up to early 2005 filled the space now occupied by the Grand Arcade shopping centre. The necessity for the recording of these structures, unhindered by presumption of 'worth', was embodied in the conditions placed on planning, combined with the Listed Building Consent required for 22–25 St Andrew's Street (Plots XIV–XVII; for plot locations see Fig. 5.2).

In combination, these conditions required a record to be made of all structures erected both before and after 1939 (the extent of which are shown in Figs. 1.12–1.13). Much of this phase of work was carried out during the three to four months between the closure of the Robert Sayle department store and the commencement of the subsequent demolition phase, but continued for much longer within the buildings that were retained along the St Andrew's Street frontage. In practical terms, the standing building record consisted of three main elements: photography (in excess of 3000 film and digital images were taken); 'traditional' building recording in the form of notes, measured sketches *etc.*; and a full 3D model of the exterior, which was constructed using a Leica TKS 1200 reflectorless theodolite. The latter captured a particular point in time, November/December 2004, into virtual space within around three weeks.

Whilst this short preamble introduces the practical necessities of the building recording it is, perhaps, more important to reflect on the broader vision involved. Very early in the fieldwork phase of the project, the local press seized upon the throwaway comment that this project comprised 'archaeology from the rooftops down'. Whilst on the one hand a shorthand remark intended for the general public, this phrase does encapsulate the philosophy behind the approach. The buildings and the uppermost layers of stratigraphy are

Figure 1.12. *All surviving eighteenth–twentieth-century standing buildings at Grand Arcade, as they stood at the site in November 2004.*

not merely an impediment to be removed in order to reach the below-ground archaeology, but themselves comprise an inherent part of the narrative. In some recent publications, the built elements of archaeological sites – extant or otherwise – have been given due recognition; most notably, perhaps, in the London Guildhall volume with its detailed reconstructions and extensive study of documentary sources (Bowsher *et al.* 2007).

At Grand Arcade it was felt that the standing buildings component, although it should certainly be addressed at the appropriate point in the chronological

sequence (Chapter 5), does not form the inevitable 'conclusion' of that story: hence, starting at the end. Of course, inherent in this approach is the perennial problem of how to integrate the above-ground building recording with the below-ground archaeological record. Although conceived of as a seamless continuum, the buildings were recorded at a different time, and using a different methodology, to the archaeological remains. A further issue is embodied by the observation that, although a particular building may be constructed at one fixed point in time it could subsequently remain in use, with relatively few alterations,

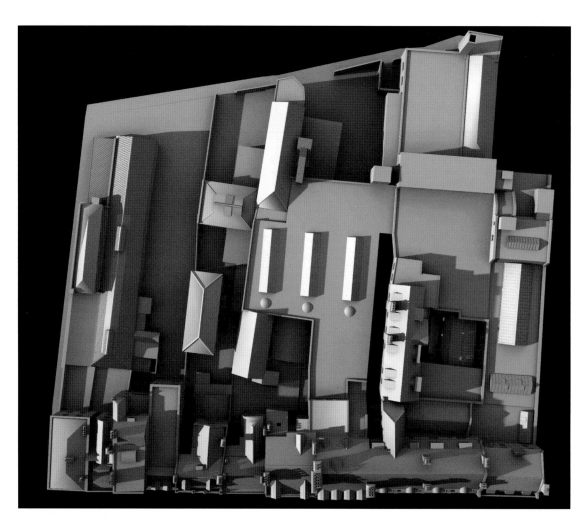

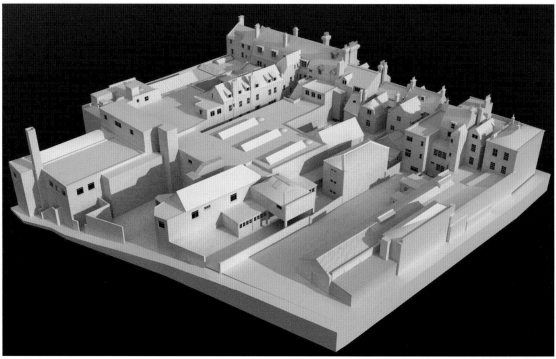

for decades if not centuries. Thus, any given building may represent a palimpsest and aggregation of numerous actions undertaken by the individuals and groups that were associated with it over time. The same is also true of long-lived below-ground features, such as wells, which sometimes remained in use for several centuries. Consequently, the long-term sequences of many such elements can potentially be fragmented by the volume's predominately chronological structure.

In the broadest terms, the standing frontage structures have their roots in the medieval origins of the suburb outside the town ditch. Based on the results of the archaeological investigations, the earliest evidence of occupation dates to the mid/late eleventh century, while the area became increasingly organized and densely occupied from the early twelfth century onwards. Within the buildings as they stood in November 2004, however, no fabric earlier than the early eighteenth century was evident. Figure 1.12 summarizes the pattern of the standing buildings' survival and indicates the general dates of their construction (see also Figs. 1.13–1.14). Elements of 20 and 22–25 St Andrew's Street (Plots XI and XIV–XVII) partially or substantially retained eighteenth-century fabric, with the most complete buildings on the site being *Standing Buildings 42/65*, which dated to the later eighteenth century.

Lengths of surviving eighteenth-century boundary or garden wall were also recorded, while others were incorporated into later *Standing Buildings 94* and *96*. Overall, this period represents about seven per cent of the standing structures, with 33 per cent being nineteenth-century and 60 per cent twentieth-century in origin. Figure 1.12 also demonstrates the proportion of land that was built on as opposed to being open. In some plots, noticeably behind Nos. 22–23 (Plots XIV–XV), the yard area was less covered-over than it had been in the aerial photograph of 1968, whereas behind Nos. 12–20 the only areas open to the sky comprised a short length of the former alleyway between Nos. 15–16 (Plots IX–X) and the service yard on Tibb's Row. Both areas are reflections of the changes that were brought about by the realignment of Tibb's Row during the early 1970s.

To the average Cambridge inhabitant, prior to 2004 the Robert Sayle department store *was* this street block (see Chapter 5). Although even the later story of this city block is not just that of a department store, indeed far from it, the development of this one store has had a significant impact on the area and the way in which parts of it developed and altered; the topic of most significance to this present discussion. Robert Sayle opened his shop at 12 St Andrew's Street (Victoria House, Plot VIII) in 1840. Over the next 164 years the store developed and expanded until by the time it was removed, temporarily, to Burleigh Street in September 2004, it occupied Nos. 12–17, 18/19, part of 24 and 25 St Andrew's Street (parts of Plots VIII, IX, X, XVI, XVII) as well as much of the ground and buildings between them and Tibb's Row. In some instances this had involved major structural alteration and rebuilding and in other places almost none at all.

The Robert Sayle department store retained the name of its founder for 167 years until the move back to St Andrew's Street in November 2007 when, in keeping with national policy, all John Lewis stores lost their local names and the store reopened as John

Lewis, Cambridge. In those intervening years the store had several owners. From 1840 until his death in 1883 Robert Sayle was the sole proprietor. Then, from early 1884, ownership was transferred to Robert Sayle & Co. with three individual partners. Subsequently, in August 1919, the business became a private company, Robert Sayle & Co Ltd., while in November 1934 it was sold to Selfridges' Provincial Stores who sold it on in turn to the John Lewis Partnership in February 1940 (Sieveking 2004, 123). Each of these different ownerships had an impact on the fabric of the store. Before 1979, non-Robert Sayle department store-related structures occupied 33 per cent of the ground between Nos. 12–25 St Andrew's Street (Plots VIII–XVII) and the re-aligned Tibb's Row, although by 1988 that had shrunk to only 17 per cent. The more important distinction; however, is between the structures of the main store to the rear of 12–17 St Andrew's Street (parts of Plots VIII–X; almost 59 per cent of the area), which were the focus of the realization of the Robert Sayle department store as a purpose-built retail entity.

By 1877, and probably a little earlier, the Robert Sayle department store occupied most of the No. 12 plot (Plot VIII) apart from its rearmost area, all of Nos. 13–17 and the areas to their rear, as well as the rear of Nos. 18–19 (Plots IX–X). A series of plans, part of the leasehold record for the properties held by Jesus College (see Fig. 5.79), show the development from individual house/shops to a purpose-built retail establishment, with its ancillary and support structures, over a period of about 40 years. Unfortunately, although No. 12 (Plot VIII) is just as much part of this story, it belonged to Emmanuel College, and so does not appear on the plans until the one drawn up by Selfridges' Provincial Stores in 1938 (Fig. 1.15). As time passed the space closer to Tibb's Row was gradually infilled, most noticeably in *c.* 1862–89. Sitting amongst these newer buildings, however, was *Standing Building 42*, which had been constructed during the late eighteenth century. It appears that this and the attached *Standing Building 65* were the only buildings on the 1862 leasehold plan that were still standing intact in 2004.

According to Lintonbon (2006) two main models of retailing emerged towards the end of the nineteenth century. One endeavoured to create an architecture integral to the development of sales; the other was more concerned with the concentration of retail identity within a branded business where the architecture of the shop building mattered less than its signage and fittings. The late nineteenth–early twentieth-century redevelopment of the Robert Sayle department store would seem to express the former rather than the latter. When Robert Sayle opened his first shop in 1840 the retail world was at a point of change. Rather than selling only the component materials for clothing, new manufacturing techniques and an awareness of fashion was paving the way for a readymade clothing market. This, coupled with the arrival of the railway and the telegraph, allowed goods to be ordered, dispatched and handled with much greater efficiency than ever before. Lintonbon, following other writers (*e.g.* Laermans 1993), identifies another trend, particularly observed in the drapery trades, which was to 'departmentalize' businesses. This allowed such businesses to benefit from economies in increased buying power and had the attraction for customers of finding many related goods conveniently within one shop. The Bon Marché shop in Paris, completed *c.* 1865, is sometimes considered to be the world's first department store, although this is disputed.

Departmentalization, however, had obvious spatial implications because of the need for additional display space and the requirements of handling and storing large quantities of goods. By adopting these newer sales methods, Robert Sayle in effect created the situation whereby the business had to change physically to cope with the increasing demands on an infrastructure that had ceased to be fit for purpose. This provides the context for the store's initial phase of redevelopment starting in 1876, during which the entire standing fabric of the store (excepting *Standing Buildings 42* and *65* and some minor structures since removed) was demolished and rebuilt. The demands of modern selling methods led to the use of

Figure 1.13 *(opposite). Views from the digital model constructed of the standing buildings: overhead view of roofscape (upper) and general view of area from the southwest (lower).*

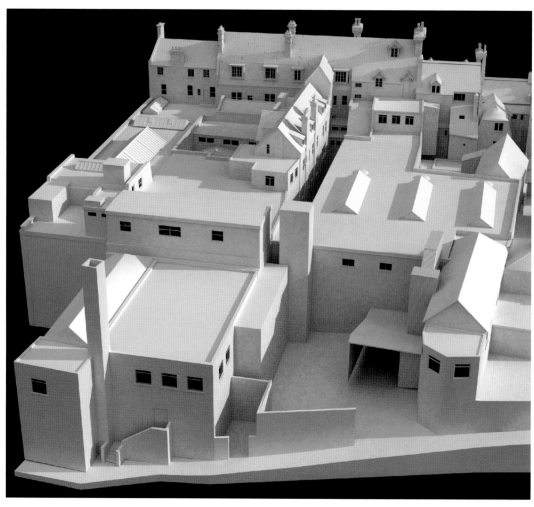

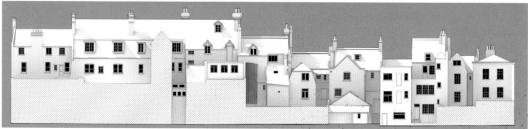

Figure 1.14. *Views from the digital model constructed of the standing buildings: the main Robert Sayle buildings from the southwest (upper) and rear view of Nos 12 to 25 St. Andrew's Street (lower).*

the most modern construction methods, iron and steel girder frames, to create the spaces in which to carry them out. In Cambridge this change was further boosted in 1882 when University academics were allowed to marry for the first time, creating a whole new potential customer base right on the Robert Sayle's department store doorstep.

This event roughly coincides with the second phase of the store's redevelopment, involving chiefly Nos. 16–17 (part of Plot X). This seems most likely to be the point at which the classical decorative scheme across the main shop floor areas was established, the main sweeping staircase installed and the intricate moulded plaster and wood embellishments added. A further six or so years later No. 12 (Plot VIII) was itself rebuilt in an entirely different style

externally, although inside the decorative scheme was extended, at least in part. In this instance, in the absence of evidence to the contrary, it seems likely that the wishes of the landlord – Emmanuel College – overrode any unifying desires of the lessee. Yet even this was something of a compromise, as no breakthrough between Nos. 12 and 13 (Plots VIII–IX) took place until Selfridges' ownership during the 1930s.

Even within its new, purpose-built shell, space was at a premium throughout the Robert Sayle department store's history. Storage space became shop floor, workshops became stores, bedrooms became stores and offices and the footprint occupied by buildings was increased, though only significantly in the later years

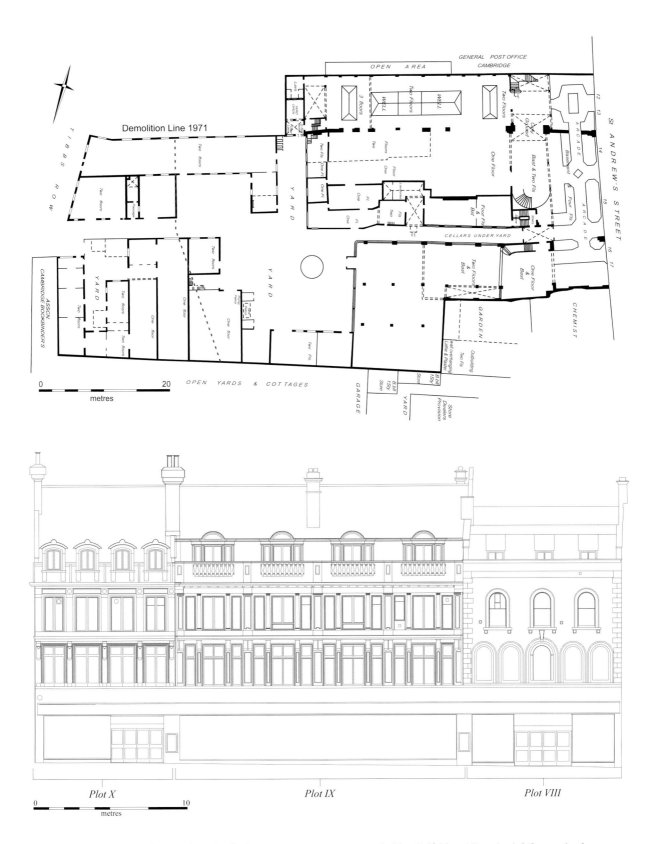

Figure 1.15. *1938 plan of the Robert Sayle department store, as recorded by Selfridges' Provincial Stores (redrawn from an original held in the John Lewis Partnership Archive Collection) (upper) and drawing of the Robert Sayle frontage as it existed in 2005 (lower).*

of the twentieth century. While the outer shell remained relatively intact, the interior was altered to suit changing needs and fashions. This is seen in part in the contrast between interior photographs of 1933–35 where the long dark wooden counters of the Victorian shop are replaced by the lighter, more open units of the twentieth century. The shop is also more open, following the breakthrough between Nos. 12 and 13 (Plots VIII–IX).

Selfridges only owned the department store from 1934–40, but the changes made at that time strongly influenced the shape of the next 65 years. The light and the more open aspect, however, did little to alleviate the need for more selling and storage space. Every available nook and cranny was in use, and most design decisions had the need for more space behind them. An arcaded front was created for more window space, but was removed in 1970 to expand the shop floor (*i.e.* the selling area). The area to the rear became more crowded, hugely exacerbated by the loss of about a fifth of the site under compulsory purchase when Tibb's Row was realigned as part of the Lion Yard development in 1971. Whilst this did allow for some expansion back towards Tibb's Row, the discussions in the early 1970s focused more on moving the store to a new location as opposed to expanding its own site (Gooch 2004, 135).

Although it was a true, purpose-built retail establishment, the Robert Sayle department store in Cambridge – however forward looking – was not conceived of on a sufficiently large scale to outlast changing times and the limitations of its own physical containment. The space given to the very first department store, Bon Marché, with its sky-lighted interior courts, or to other broadly contemporary English constructions such as the Walsh's store built in Sheffield in 1896 (five storeys high plus attic, with 3½ acres of floor space and frontages onto each thoroughfare of 200ft and 172ft), Lewis's in Liverpool and Manchester and Selfridges in Oxford Street, all dwarfed the Robert Sayle department store in terms of both scale and conception. Robert Sayle, both the man and the company, were nevertheless pioneers in their own area. The Cambridge store, begun in 1840 and remodelled on modern lines during the 1870s and 1880s, outlived all its local rivals; such as Laurie and McConnal in Fitzroy Street (1883–1977), Eaden Lilley on Market Street (1750–1999), Joshua Taylor in Sidney Street (1860–1991) and Mitcham's on Chesterton Road (1909–77).

Chapter 2

Preludes: prehistoric to early twelfth century

Craig Cessford

Space not place

Until it was given meaning by human beings, Cambridge was simply a 'space' rather than a 'place' (Relph 1976; Tuan 1977). Whilst the crossing point of the River Cam may have been a meaningful place in prehistory, in archaeological terms this 'placeness' is first recognisable in the first century AD with the foundation of a Romano-British settlement (Alexander & Pullinger 1999). As the Romano-British settlement was followed by a hiatus, although there were Early Anglo-Saxon settlements and cemeteries in the general vicinity (Dodwell *et al.* 2004), it can be argued that archaeologically an eighth century execution cemetery provides a more appropriate marker as it demonstrates a distinctive central place activity taking place (Cessford *et al.* 2007). These definitions are, however, effectively irrelevant in terms of the specific locale that is the concern of this book, as it is in the mid/late eleventh century that this becomes a place, albeit a relatively minor one. Whilst it would be tempting to ignore the earlier 'space', all 'places' have a prelude, which is outlined here.

Prior to the establishment of the long-lived and intensively occupied suburb that forms the principal focus of this volume, some limited evidence of earlier activity was encountered at the Grand Arcade site. In all, three phases of 'pre-suburban' activity have been identified (see Figs. 1.11A–C). As these predate the main period of study they will be discussed briefly here before the more substantive medieval and post-medieval material is presented. The earliest of the three phases, which was prehistoric to mid/late eleventh-century in date, pertained to the establishment and subsequent maintenance of a broad agricultural hinterland (Fig. 2.1). This period came to an end when the site was encroached on by a pattern of scattered, dispersed occupation (Figs. 2.2–2.4). Commencing no earlier than the mid-eleventh century, it appears that the area gradually became incorporated into the outermost periphery of Cambridge's expanding urban 'fringe'. Then, during the early twelfth century, a much more regular, grid-like layout was imposed on the site (Figs. 2.5–2.6). This phase appears to represent a marked intensification in the scale of occupation. Ultimately, however, the episode proved to be abortive. Around the mid-twelfth century a substantial ditch was created that truncated many of the pre-existing divisions and separated the site into two discrete portions. For the first time, this boundary – the King's Ditch (Chapter 3) – definitively segregated *within* from *without*: the Barnwell Gate suburb was born.

In addition to the following text, further detailed information – relating in particular to specialist analyses, feature descriptions and associated historical sources – can be found within the supplementary volume.

Prehistoric mid-eleventh century

Geologically, the Grand Arcade site is located upon well-drained *c.* 1–3m-thick Second Terrace Cam Gravels, which in turn overlie impermeable Gault clay. This rendered it a relatively attractive venue for occupation. Nevertheless, for the first few millennia of the site's history the overall level of activity appears to have remained low. Above the gravels, micromorphological analysis has revealed that well-developed argillic brown earths developed, indicating stable and well-drained wooded conditions that were cleared from the Neolithic period onwards (see Figs. 7.2A–D). The area was then incorporated into an extensive rural hinterland; residual flakes of struck flint were the only finds of Neolithic or Bronze Age date. Subsequently, however, during the Middle Iron Age – *c.* 350–50 BC – a gully was established (*Gully 1*; Fig. 2.1). Aligned northwest–southeast and extending over 100m in length, this feature measured *c.* 1.1m wide by over 0.3m deep. It contained six sherds of Middle Iron Age pottery, weighing 20g, and most probably functioned as a field boundary within an area of open pastoral farmland. A similar pattern also predominated during the succeeding Roman and Anglo-Saxon periods. Small quantities of residual pottery fragments of these dates were recovered that were most probably dispersed via manuring (e.g. Fig. 7.6 bottom), but no identifiable features or discrete areas of activity were encountered.

It thus appears that throughout this earliest phase of activity the site remained only a peripheral element within a broader agricultural landscape. Despite this, certain features within that

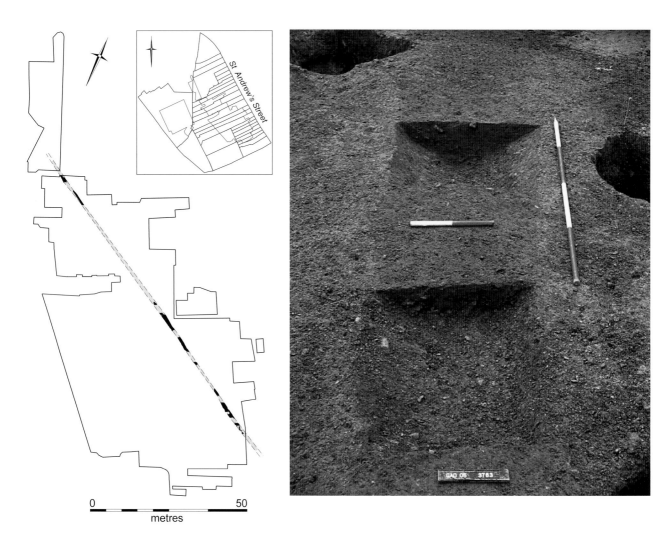

Figure 2.1. *Plan of Middle Iron Age Gully 1 plus photograph, facing southeast.*

landscape – albeit features that can only be archaeologically inferred as opposed to positively identified – are likely to have had a marked impact on the subsequent developments that occurred from the mid/late eleventh century onwards. The most significant was the former Roman road from Colchester to Godmanchester, which probably followed the same alignment as medieval Hadstock Way. Also likely to have been of influence were the Late Saxon field strips of *c.* 850 onwards that were associated with the East Fields of the nascent town (Hesse 2007). These presumably ran perpendicular to the Roman road. When occupation was first established at the site during the mid/late eleventh century, therefore, these topographic elements were already well-established. This implies that the extensive changes which occurred at this time were not a *tabula rasa*; indeed, certain long-lived elements were to persist for centuries.

Mid/late eleventh century

By the mid-eleventh century Cambridge was a well-established and economically thriving town and most archaeological investigations conducted within the urban core to the south of the river have produced evidence of eleventh-century occupation. The best evidence for the form of the settlement at this time is its churches, as these formed a central 'spine' running along Trumpington Street, the medieval High Street, indicating that this was then the most important

thoroughfare. In contrast, along the line of the former Roman road only three churches were present, implying that by the eleventh century this route had declined in significance. Occupation at the Grand Arcade site commenced around the mid/late eleventh century, although issues of dating and the degree of later truncation – which has potentially removed over 80 per cent of the relevant features – make certainty difficult. It is probable that the King's Ditch itself did not exist at this date, although it may perhaps have later followed the course of a pre-existing natural feature (Chapter 3). The major topographic influence on the area therefore remained the former Roman road, which by this date was known as Hadstock Way.

Within the Grand Arcade street block itself there is convincing evidence for at least two discrete areas of eleventh-century occupation (Fig. 2.2). Although many of the constituent features were heavily truncated, there is little to imply that this phase lasted more than around 50 years (from *c.* 1050–1100). Indeed, it may have been as short as 20 to 40 years; the average lifespan of a timber-built structure during this period (Bowsher *et al.* 2007, 317–18; Horsman *et al.* 1988). In the northern area (Area 1), the features were stratigraphically sealed beneath a ditch that was created in the early twelfth century. They consisted of timber *Building 1*, which comprised a row of three postholes that extended over 2.2m in length (Fig. 2.3E), *Cesspit 1* (Fig. 2.3F), which was located to the rear of the building, and wattle-lined *Well 1* (Fig. 2.3G). While there is no evidence that definitively proves that these features were contemporary, the most likely scenario is that they relate to a plot *c*. 36m in length that fronted onto Hadstock Way. Moreover, the combination of a building, a cesspit and well indicate a relatively high level of investment, consonant with permanent domestic occupation. The well and cesspit were deliberately backfilled around 1100. Their infilling contained a number of oak boards that derived from the demolition of a timber building – which had been constructed after 1049, on dendrochronological grounds – four jars and bowls (Fig. 2.3A–D) and a quantity of faunal remains.

Area 2, located a short distance to the south, lacked the direct stratigraphic dating associated with the occupation of Area 1. It can be identified because it contained a discrete concentration of stratigraphically early features containing pale, subsoil-rich fills alongside a significant proportion of eleventh-century material culture. The area of activity was 9.6m wide and around 38m long, covering *c*. 365 sq. m. Its northern perimeter was defined by a linear alignment of 12 intercutting gravel quarry pits (*Pit 1*). Pit rows such as this are frequently encountered on medieval urban sites (Schofield & Vince 2003, 80–1). The presence of such an alignment indicates that the area was already quite rigidly subdivided and

demarcated. Located 26m from the frontage was a 9.6m long gully (*Gully 2*), which probably demarcated the boundary of the plot's innerland and backland zones. Within the innerland were located the traces of a timber-built structure (*Building 2*) and two cesspits (*Cesspits 2–3*), whilst towards the rear of the property lay a wattle-lined well (*Well 2*) whose structure had been reinforced with reused mid-tenth-century cask staves. Also located in the backland zone were a number of gravel quarry pits. The backfilling of one of these – *Pit 2* (Fig. 2.4A) – contained portions of five pottery vessels (Fig. 2.4B), four worked bone objects (Fig. 2.4C) an iron knife (Fig. 2.4D) and hook, and almost 500 animal bones representing *c*. 42kg of meat. The latter included mutton, beef, pork and chicken, some of which indicate that the pit filled up over a period of several months.

It is possible that there were other, unrecognized areas of mid/late eleventh-century occupation at the site, as well as additional isolated eleventh-century features (principally gravel and clay quarry pits); although none can be identified with certainty. The distribution of tenth–eleventh-century pottery (Fig. 2.2) does however indicate that contemporary occupation was principally concentrated in Areas 1 and 2. Whilst the exact nature of this occupation is unclear, had the area been fully urban in character it is

Figure 2.2. *Plan of mid/late eleventh-century dispersed occupation showing distribution of identified features and typologically early St Neots-type ware, plus detail of the principal features associated with Areas 1 and 2.*

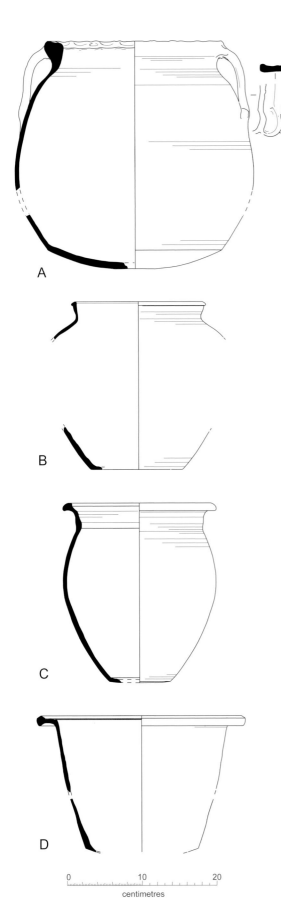

A

B

C

D

0   10   20

centimetres

Figure 2.3 *(opposite). Mid/late eleventh-century features in Area 1, plus associated material from early twelfth-century backfilling: (A) Thetford-type ware rounded wide jar with thumbed clubbed rim and two strap handles from Cesspit 1 ([35197]); (B) Thetford-type ware rounded jar with clubbed rim and fingernail decoration from Cesspit 1 ([35197]); (C) St Neots-type ware rounded narrow jar with clubbed rim from Cesspit 1 ([35197]); (D) St Neots-type ware rounded deep bowl with clubbed rim from Cesspit 1 ([35197]); (E) photograph of posthole from Building 1, facing north; (F) photograph of oak board(s) and overlying pottery in base of Cesspit 1, facing north; (G) photograph of wattle-lined Well 1, facing north.*

likely that more evidence would be identifiable. It therefore appears that some form of dispersed, and potentially intermittent, ribbon development existed at this time, stretching out along Hadstock Way. To the north, the church of St Andrew the Great had most probably been established (Fig. 2.2). There is unlikely to have been any formal boundary between the periphery of the settlement and the surrounding East Fields.

Early twelfth century
The early twelfth century was a time of pronounced change for Cambridge. In 1101 Henry I granted the fee farm to the town, meaning that in return for payment of a lump sum it was authorized to collect what had previously been payments to the crown. Then, in 1109, the town was transferred from the Diocese of Lincoln to the newly created Diocese of Ely. It was also around the turn of the twelfth century that the Grand Arcade street block was divided

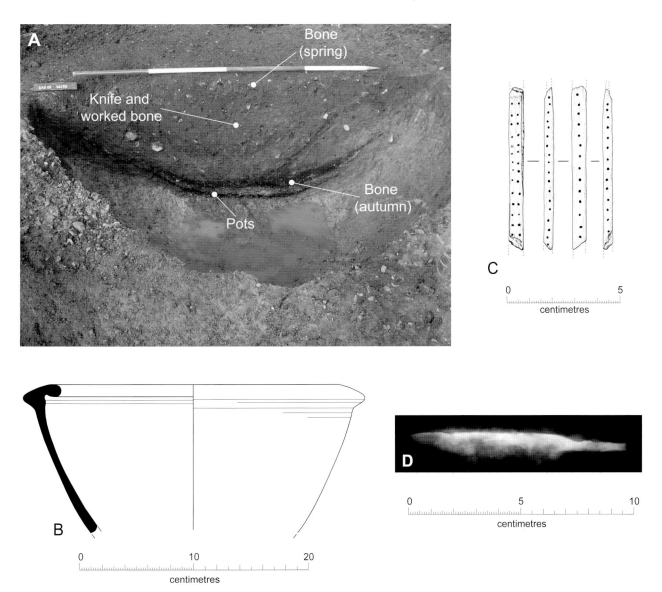

Figure 2.4. *Late eleventh–early twelfth century gravel quarry Pit 2: (A) photograph of pit, facing southeast; (B) St Neots-type ware rounded shallow bowl with flanged rim ([34261]): (C) square-sectioned object made from mammal long bone with dot decoration on all sides ([34258]); (D) iron whittle-tanged knife ([34258]).*

into four segments (Fig. 2.5). The principal boundary at this time was a substantial ditch that ran perpendicular to Hadstock Way – *Ditch 1* (Fig. 2.6) – parallel to which ran two shallower gullies (*Gullies 3–4*). *Ditch 1* would originally have measured *c*. 2.5m wide by 1.5m deep and there is evidence of a bank on its northern side. The gullies, which were probably dug immediately after *Ditch 1*, were only *c*. 0.3–0.4m deep by *c*. 0.3m wide. The primary function

of *Ditch 1* was presumably to demarcate a boundary, but it would also have provided effective drainage for the area. Whilst ditches are a common feature on broadly contemporary rural sites such as West Fen Road, Ely, (Mortimer *et al.* 2005, 116–20) and Cottenham (Mortimer 2000) they are rare in urban contexts. This is probably because space was at more of a premium. To the north of *Ditch 1*, lying *c*. 47–50m from Hadstock Way, was situated *Gully 3*. This

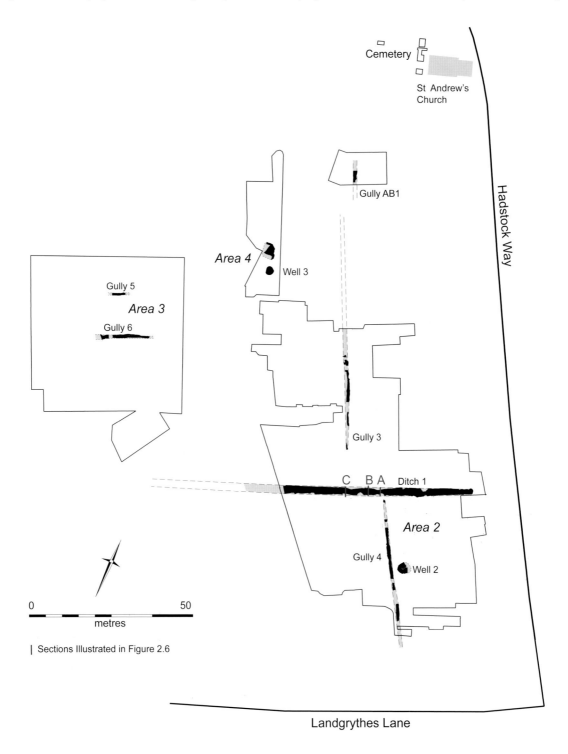

Figure 2.5. *Plan of features associated with the early twelfth-century planned layout.*

40

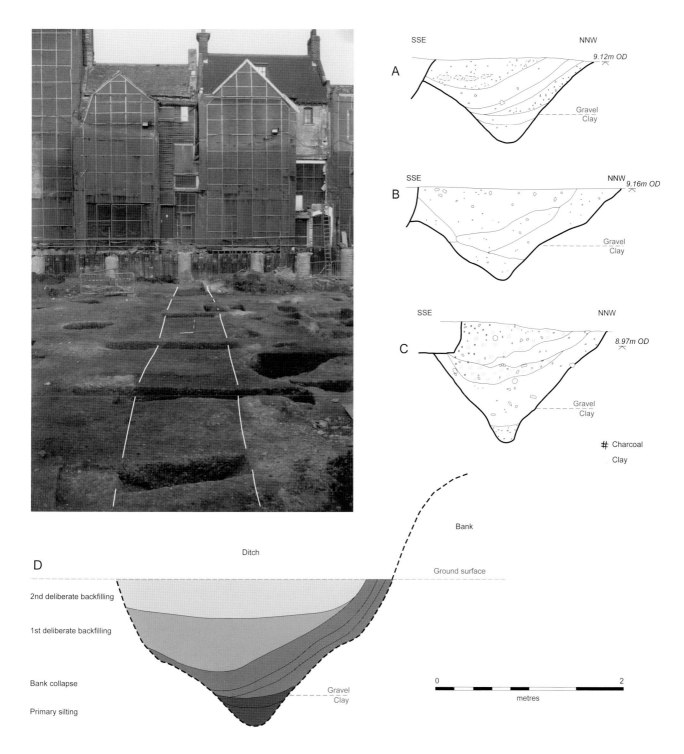

Figure 2.6. *Photograph of early twelfth-century Ditch 1 facing east-northeast with edges of feature highlighted; note how the ditch alignment matches the boundary between two twentieth-century standing buildings. Sections of ditch (A–C; locations shown in Fig. 2.5), reconstructed profile of original ditch and bank (D).*

feature measured a minimum of 28m in length and may represent a continuation of *Gully AB1* that was previously identified in 1959 (Addyman & Biddle 1965, 85, fig. 9). If this attribution is correct then it originally measured over 80m in length. *Gully 3* was relatively short-lived; it contained no evidence of recuts or material later than the twelfth century. To the south of *Ditch 1* lay *Gully 4*. This was located *c.* 40m from Hadstock Way and ran for over 40m in length. *Gully 4* had a more variable history than *Gully 3*, with some stretches rapidly going out of use during the twelfth century while others remained open until the fourteenth century.

Whilst some eleventh century features from Area 2, such as *Well 2*, appear to have continued in use into this period, Area 1 was effectively obliterated by the creation of *Ditch 1*. This latter feature, along with the associated gullies, effectively divided the area into four rectangular areas or quadrants (Fig. 2.5). Although it would be somewhat misleading to characterize this development as 'planned' rather than 'organic' in nature – an artificial and unhelpful dichotomy that often 'begins to dissolve on closer inspection' (Baker & Holt 2004, 376) – it represents the subdivision of a substantial area that was probably undertaken by the landowner rather than the individual occupants. Occurring during the mid/late eleventh century, the scale and layout of this development indicate that the King's Ditch did not yet exist (as this would have cut across the quadrants at an awkward, obtuse angle). Similarly, the obliteration of Area 1, allied with the 'clearance' of a relatively sizable quantity of domestic material in Areas 1 and 2, indicates that this development was directly imposed on the landscape by an outside agency. As such, it is likely to have been undertaken by a single landowner, although it is possible that the areas to the north and south of the ditch remained under separate control throughout.

It appears probable that the relatively large quadrants were intended to be further subdivided into smaller properties ready for domestic occupation. The surviving evidence suggests that this process did not occur immediately, but in a more gradual, piecemeal fashion, though it must be noted that delays of a few years or even decades are difficult to identify archaeologically. This situation is further complicated by the fact that the area was subsequently heavily affected by the creation of the King's Ditch. While it is likely that a considerable amount of activity predated this event, such a scenario cannot be proved (except in certain specific instances). More generally, within Cambridge's wider environs the development at Grand Arcade was by no means unique. Morphological evidence indicates that very similar, 'imposed' developments also occurred at a number of local villages during the late eleventh and/or early twelfth centuries. This situation has been identified archaeologically at Chesterton (Cessford with Dickens 2004; Newman 2015) and fits very well within the broader, national pattern of Norman expansion and control (Aston 1992, 71–81). The instigator of the early twelfth-century development is unknown, although a potential candidate might be the Benedictine monastery of Ely, founded in 970, which is known to have owned land in Cambridge (van Houts 1992, 64). If correct, the division might potentially have been linked to the foundation of the Ely diocese in 1109. A link with Ely is suggested by the fact that it was the patron of St Andrew the Great, although it is unclear how early this relationship began. It may be no earlier than 1225–8, although this may represent the restitution of an earlier relationship that existed in 1200 and at least one church in Cambridge belonged to Ely in 1086 (Otway-Ruthven 1938, 359).

There are three areas where a convincing argument can be made for early twelfth-century occupation at the Grand Arcade site. The first of these coincided with one of the earlier areas of occupation (Area 2), now located within the new southeastern quadrant, where *Well 2* continued in use. In the north-western quadrant (Area 3), two parallel west-southwest to east-northeast aligned gullies – *Gullies 5–6* – were identified, lying 12.3m apart (Fig. 2.5). As these features are aligned perpendicular to Hadstock Way, rather than with reference to any later alignment, it appears likely that they were associated with the occupation of this area prior to the establishment of the new town boundary. Located a short distance to the east, in Area 4, was a poorly preserved wattle-lined well (*Well 3*). This again must have predated the King's Ditch on stratigraphic grounds. Finally, close by *Well 3* was situated a cluster of intercutting pits. These features contained very little cultural material, and the uppermost pits in the sequence were also sealed by an early phase of the ditch. Additional features of early twelfth-century date may also have been present, although none could be conclusively identified.

Discussion

The open pastoral landscape that was created during the later prehistoric period persisted until at least the mid-tenth century. At this time Cambridge has been described as an 'economically viable backwater' (Hines 1999, 136) and it was around then that one of the reused cask staves in *Well 2* was felled (*c.* 930–70). Subsequently, the site was encroached on by mid/late eleventh-century dispersed occupation. This expansion coincided with the rapid economic development of the town, which by the late eleventh century had been transformed into a well-established county centre that contained a concentration of central-place functions. The pattern of scattered, piecemeal occupation which predominated at this time is consistent with that of the outlying urban fringe, indicating that the site probably lay on the periphery of the settled area. During the early twelfth century, however, a pattern of more regular planned urban development appears to have superseded the earlier, dispersed phase. A series of discrete topographic blocks was created and the overall level of activity seems to have increased.

Such a pattern is by no means unique to Cambridge. The eleventh–twelfth centuries were a period of major urban growth all across England. Large numbers of pre-existing settlements expanded and many new towns were established (Beresford 1988). Furthermore, a two-fold pattern wherein an initial phase of scattered occupation was succeeded by a more organized, imposed layout is also paralleled elsewhere, as at No. 1 Poultry, London, where these stages occurred during the later tenth and early eleventh centuries respectively (Burch *et al.* 2010). In the case of Cambridge, the degree of success that was enjoyed by the newly imposed development is somewhat unclear. The intention was probably to create a series of narrow rectangular plots aligned perpendicular to Hadstock Way, one of the town's two principal approach roads, in order to increase rental income and stimulate additional growth. Although both wider and longer than the majority of properties located within the urban core, such as those investigated at the Old Divinity School site (Cessford 2015a), these plots were nevertheless distinct from the large ditched enclosures that predominated in many rural contexts at this date.

What is less clear is the number of inhabitants who had taken up residence within the new development by the mid-twelfth century, when the landscape of the area was substantially altered (see Chapter 3). This uncertainty arises for two reasons. Firstly, the degree of later truncation obfuscated much of the earliest portion of the sequence, thereby making precise determination of the number of relevant features difficult. Secondly, the material culture that was in use during this period remained relatively unchanged for over a century, thus rendering fine-grained chronological distinctions difficult. Overall, it appears that this period was one of marked growth all across Cambridge, as indicated by the foundation of such religious institutions as the Augustinian Barnwell Priory (founded 1092, and transplanted to a new site *c.* 1112), the leprosarium of St Mary Magdalene (*c.* 1130) and the Benedictine nunnery of St Mary and St Radegund (1133). Nevertheless, the surviving evidence from Grand Arcade indicates that process of plot adoption on the urban fringe most probably remained relatively gradual and piecemeal as opposed to rapid and uniform in nature.

Chapter 3

The King's Ditch: from Anarchy to alleyway

Craig Cessford

Medieval town walls were impressive urban symbols when they were constructed and in use, a glamour that surviving examples still retain as heritage monuments. In comparison, town ditches have something of an image problem. Cambridge never possessed a town wall, but its ditch has both an actual and temporal scale that rendered its excavation a physical and intellectual challenge. This scale means that it is only extensive and intensive investigations that can do justice to the rich narratives that are embedded, both metaphorically and almost literally in some cases, in the muddy ditch fills. The large-scale investigations at the Grand Arcade, whilst still inconsequential in terms of the overall length of the ditch, were sufficient to achieve this in a way that has arguably never previously been possible in a British context.

At one level the narrative of the ditch is a relatively simple one: a large-scale construction project cutting a substantial line both through and around the town probably in a time of major national conflict (early/mid-twelfth century), followed by a period as a well-maintained element of the civic fabric (late twelfth–mid-fifteenth century). The ditch then became a much messier, less well-maintained increasingly and problematic townscape element (late fifteenth–late seventeenth century), before a relatively ignominious but prolonged afterlife (late eighteenth–early twenty-first century). Within this overall narrative there are many details and nuances, which deepen and enrich it so that this relatively bland summary is entirely inadequate.

Following on from the initial, somewhat piecemeal phase of eleventh- to mid-twelfth-century occupation at the site (Chapter 2), the topography was substantially altered when a large ditch bisected the western portion of the excavated area. Known historically as the *Fossatum Regis*, or King's Ditch, this feature formed part of an imposing boundary that enclosed the majority of medieval Cambridge lying to the south and east of the river Cam (Fig. 3.1).

At around 9.0m wide, at least 3.2m deep and *c.* 1340m long, the ditch formed a significant component of the local landscape. It was also very long-lived, surviving as a discrete entity until the late eighteenth century – albeit in a much reduced form – and remaining a local topographic presence into the early twenty-first century.

Due to the ditch's peripheral location relative to the main area of excavation – allied with the degree of later truncation it had sustained, which in many places had removed the uppermost two-thirds of its sequence – there was little if any surviving relationship between the ditch itself and the adjacent suburban plots. Moreover, the nature and complexity of the town boundary, which was recut and remodelled on numerous occasions, rendered it archaeologically distinct from the predominately domestic sequence encountered across the remainder of the site. Consequently, the following chapter addresses the entire King's Ditch sequence – from its creation to its infilling, as well as its subsequent 'afterlife' – in isolation from the largely chronological framework adopted throughout the majority of this volume.

The results of the recent excavations, which together constitute one of the largest and most detailed investigations of a medieval British town boundary ditch yet undertaken, are presented below in some detail. Where pertinent, the results obtained during earlier nearby investigations have also been incorporated. Because this material is discussed separately from the remainder of the Grand Arcade sequence, the relevant artefactual and ecofactual data has also been included, before turning to discussion of the wider issues surrounding the ditch's origin, form and function.

Previous investigations

Prior to the Grand Arcade excavations, the King's Ditch had been subject to relatively little archaeological investigation. Following initial *ad hoc* discoveries

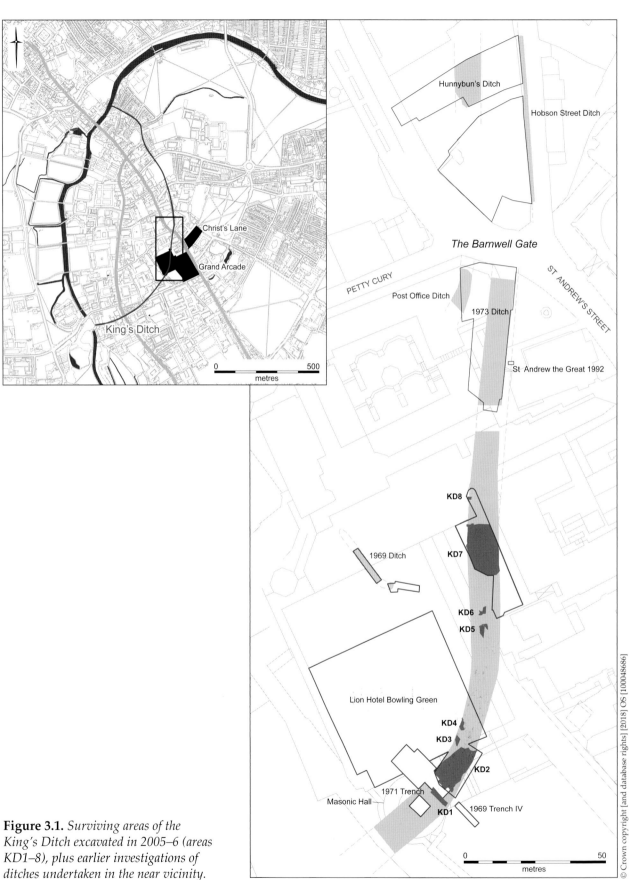

Figure 3.1. *Surviving areas of the King's Ditch excavated in 2005–6 (areas KD1–8), plus earlier investigations of ditches undertaken in the near vicinity.*

during building works in the mid-nineteenth century, a more systematic programme of investigation was undertaken by Professor Thomas McKenny Hughes between 1873 and 1914. During this period, Hughes observed building works undertaken along the line of the ditch at various sites across the town, several of which were situated in relatively close proximity to Grand Arcade. The ditch was readily identifiable during building works due to 'a bed of unmistakable black mud which appears to have been its most notable feature' (Atkinson 1907, 252). A little way to the north of the Grand Arcade site, Hughes observed construction works between Hobson Street and Sidney Street (Hunnybun's Ditch and the Hobson Street Ditch; Hughes 1894a, 37–40; Fig. 3.1) and at the Post Office site (the Post Office Ditch; Hughes 1894a, 40; Fig. 3.1). A little way to the south, he subsequently observed additional works undertaken during an extension of the Masonic Hall (Hughes 1915a, 19; Fig. 3.1) and also noted that the ditch 'passed across the corner of the bowling green of the Lion Hotel' (Hughes 1894b, 263; Fig. 3.1).

Unfortunately, each of these investigations was undertaken on a limited scale, that precluded detailed stratigraphic recording, and only small quantities of material culture were recovered. Moreover, it is probable that in each instance the ditch's basal deposits remained unexamined. Hughes nonetheless observed that there appeared to be:

> 'several ditches along the strip of land adjoining the King's Ditch... [and] it seemed that there were long periods of neglect during which the ditches got silted up, or choked with rubbish, and perhaps even purposefully filled and built over, and that then there occurred times of beating the boundaries, contesting encroachments, and cleaning out the ditches'
> (Hughes 1894b, 255).

The limited scope of the original exposures, allied with the relative paucity of Hughes' subsequent records, means that it is by no means clear whether his results pertained to a number of isolated, individual features or instead represented multiple recuts within a much larger, multi-phased entity.

Following Hughes' work a prolonged lacuna occurred until, between 1969 and 1971, a second campaign of investigation was conducted by John Alexander in advance of the construction of the Lion Yard shopping centre (Alexander unpubl.; Alexander 1972; Fig. 3.1). The most significant work undertaken during this phase took place in 1971, when a trench was inserted within the cellar of the former Masonic Hall. Here, the King's Ditch was identified and sectioned, although its sequence was not clearly elucidated, and an area to either side of it – totalling 45 sq. m within

and 12 sq. m without the boundary – was investigated. Despite the scale of this investigation, which was markedly more substantial than any previously undertaken, the site was 'excavated under considerable difficulties (natural and man-made) for area excavations were not possible' (Alexander 1972). Indeed, although 'several recuttings and clearings' were identified (Lobel 1975, 5) the results have since been described as 'rather unsatisfactory' (Taylor 1999, 77) and they were never published. In 1973, during construction of the Lion Yard shopping centre itself, a further c. 50m long stretch of the ditch was observed (Partridge 1973; Fig. 3.1), although this was not investigated archaeologically.

More recently, in July 1988, a portion of the King's Ditch was identified during a small excavation conducted at the Department of Metallurgy site on Pembroke Street. Here, it was found to be in excess of 2m deep and filled with 'black sticky soil [that] contained many animal bones, including horse, dog, sheep, cow and pig. One find was the complete skull of an elderly boar' (Taylor 1988). Taylor also noted that 'we are hoping to do more detailed work on the King's Ditch when the car park next to Lion Yard is developed'. This latter event took place in 1989, when the Crowne Plaza Hotel was constructed, but attempts to locate the ditch at this time failed (Malim 1990). Similarly, a further investigation conducted outside Christ's College at around the same time was also unsuccessful.

Subsequently, despite the introduction of Planning Policy Guidance 16 in November 1990, relatively few opportunities to investigate the ditch arose prior to the Grand Arcade development. Of the three small-scale commercial excavations that did take place along its route, all produced very limited results. Firstly, a little way to the north of Grand Arcade, two test pits were inserted in close proximity to the church of St Andrew the Great in 1992 (Miller 1992; Fig. 3.1). Here, a marked discrepancy in the depth of natural strata between the two pits suggests that the westernmost may have been situated on the periphery of the King's Ditch. A very similar result was also obtained from two small trenches that were excavated beside the ADC Theatre on Park Street in 2002 (Whittaker 2002). Once again, however, few details of the ditch itself could be determined. Finally, salvage recording conducted at the junction of Portugal Place and New Park Street in 1997 revealed evidence of a substantial, waterlogged feature (Regan 1998). This may have formed part of the King's Ditch, but could alternatively have been a large pit or tank.

As a result of the limited scope and extent of these various investigations, prior to the Grand Arcade excavations it was stated that:

'The origins and history of the King's Ditch still need some decisive archaeological work, single trenches through it being inevitably inconclusive as so much later scouring has destroyed its stratigraphy'
(Taylor 1999, 77).

Nevertheless, despite the limited data available, several theories have been put forward regarding the origin of the King's Ditch. These can be broadly sub-divided into two categories. The first, and much the most popular, has associated the ditch with the initial post-Roman occupation of the south bank of the Cam. In this model, first proposed at the end of the nineteenth century (Gray 1908; Maitland 1898, 99–100), the King's Ditch is regarded as a primary element in the creation of a tenth-century *burh* (which is in turn connected with the conquest of the area in 917 by the Kingdom of Wessex). In essence, this represents the importation of a previously identified pattern from other, larger and more intensively investigated Late Saxon towns, such as Oxford. With only occasional, minor amendments, this theory has since been widely accepted (*e.g.* Addyman & Biddle 1965, 90–103; Biddle 1976, 136–7; Cam 1934; Haslam 1984; Hines 1999, 136; Lobel 1975, 2–5; Taylor 1999, 44–50).

A second, less popular interpretation has been to regard the King's Ditch as a later imposition on a pre-established settlement (*e.g.* Stephenson 1933). Unlike the former model – which assigns the ditch a key role in the initial, planned layout of a Late Saxon town – this theory posits a more piecemeal developmental trajectory for the settlement to the south of the river. In this scenario, the King's Ditch was most probably created in direct response to a direct or perceived threat or crisis, such as the Norman Conquest (1066), the Anarchy period (1135–54) or the First Barons' War (1215).

Circumambulating the King's Ditch

Before embarking upon a detailed examination of the discrete portion of the King's Ditch lying in closest proximity to Grand Arcade, it is important to situate this study within the broader context of the town boundary as a whole. Comprising a broadly semi-circular enclosure of univallate – or single bank-and-ditch – form, each terminus of the King's Ditch was originally connected to the river Cam (Fig. 3.1). Consequently, the feature was at least partially water-filled, although it does not appear to have retained standing water perennially along its entire length. Furthermore, there is no evidence to indicate that a wall or similar fortification – of either timber or stone – was ever associated with the boundary. The sheer scale of the ditch itself, however, allied with the presence of an upstanding earthen bank or rampart, no doubt presented an imposing barrier; one both physical and psychological.

A medieval visitor nearing Cambridge from the south would initially have proceeded along one of the town's two principal approach roads: Trumpington Street and Preacher's Street. Both roads passed through extra-mural suburbs before culminating in a formal crossing over the King's Ditch where the town was physically entered, a distinct cultural practice that has attracted relatively little attention (Jütte 2014). Yet the precise form of these significant nodal points, the Trumpington and Barnwell Gates, remains unclear. No contemporary description or depiction of them has survived; indeed, little of their early history is known. The first documentary reference to a gate's existence – which pertained to the *Janua de Barnewell*, or 'Door of Barnwell' – occurred in 1235 (Reaney 1943, 42). By 1573, however, only one of the wooden uprights that constituted this structure remained extant (Caius 1568, 116). Moreover, in 1655 Thomas Fuller noted that the Trumpington Gate was 'now ruined' and the Barnwell Gate 'decayed' (Fuller 1840, 40–1). In fact, the latter appears to have been destroyed in a conflagration during the Late Medieval period (Stokes 1915, 3). From an early date, however, it is probable that a degree of official control had been maintained over access into the town's enclosed urban core. Physically, this may have taken the form of a drawbridge and/or portal (see Hughes 1894a, 35; Stokes 1915, 4), whilst the very act of entry for non-burgesses may itself have incurred a toll.

During the fourteenth century – when the King's Ditch comprised a long-established, but nevertheless still well-maintained, element of the urban townscape – a pedestrian attempting to circumambulate its circuit would have faced several obstacles. Amongst the most significant of these were the grounds of two substantial friaries, founded by the Franciscan and Augustinian Orders *c.* 1238 and 1290 respectively, which had expanded to straddle both sides of the ditch. In addition, numerous small-scale impediments would also have been encountered. Many of these are likely to have been associated with individual property plots that shared a direct physical relationship with the ditch (typical examples include fences, pits, industrial features and latrines that extended out over the channel itself). It is also notable that the northern terminus of the circuit lay within an area of low-lying marshland, which does not appear to have been reclaimed until the mid-to late fourteenth century (Newman 2008a) although there are indications that slightly further away from the river flooding episodes ceased in the twelfth century (Cessford 2017b). Despite these various obstacles, however, the route closely respected the underlying

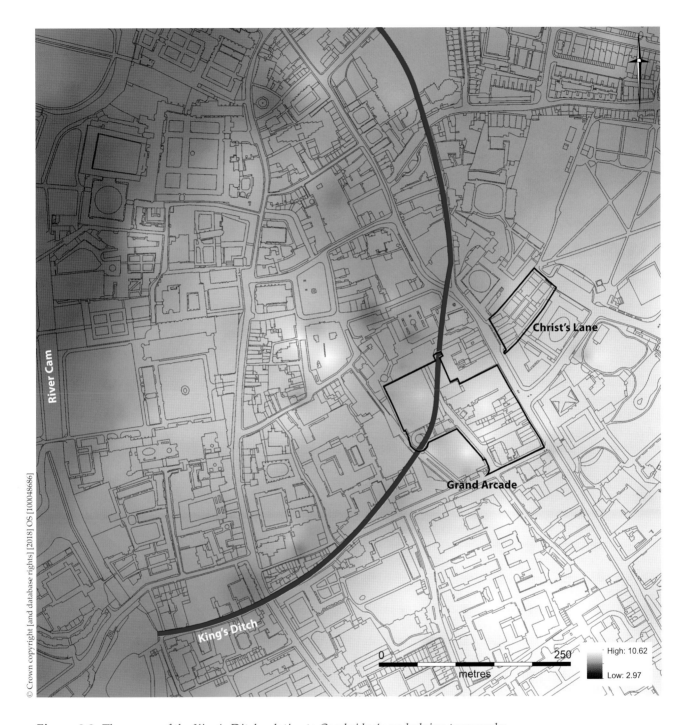

Figure 3.2. *The course of the King's Ditch relative to Cambridge's underlying topography.*

natural topography of the area (Fig. 3.2). Indeed, so marked was this association, it appears highly likely that topographic considerations played a significant role in determining the King's Ditch's course; this is because utilizing natural contours to form a 'line of least resistance' would have greatly facilitated the feature's construction. It is particularly notable, therefore, that the location of the Grand Arcade site upon a

localized outcrop of Gault clay was highly atypical of the remainder of its circuit.

A final point of interest concerns naming. During the medieval period, the term 'King's Ditch' – *Fossatum Regis* – was not solely applied to the ditch encircling the town. It was also used on an interchangeable basis to denote a canalized branch of the Cam at Garret Hostel Green as well as the various ditches surrounding the town commons (Willis & Clark 1886 vol. II, 405–6). Such a situation was by no means unusual, however; a similar pattern of nomenclature has been identified at many contemporary towns across England. The use of this particular term does not connote direct royal involvement, as has occasionally been assumed at Cambridge, but rather that the feature in question was owned/controlled communally as opposed to privately. Many major roadways were similarly termed *Via Regia*, or King's Highway, for example. As a result, the boundary's name provides an important insight into the way it would have been perceived by those who interacted with it on a daily basis.

The King's Ditch sequence

At the Grand Arcade site the King's Ditch was investigated in a series of eight discrete areas, denoted *KD1–8*, between February 2005 and May 2006 (Figs. 3.1 and 3.3–3.10). Six of these areas were relatively small in scale. In effect, they represented isolated 'islands' of stratigraphy, basal remnants of the ditch that had been extensively truncated by later development – principally during construction of the Lion Yard shopping centre in the 1970s. Topographically, the southernmost area, *KD1*, lay beneath the access ramp to the Crowne Plaza Hotel car park (Fig. 3.1); it was not excavated, but preserved *in situ*. To the north, areas *KD3* and *KD4* were situated within the basement of the Lion Yard multi-storey car park (see Fig. 3.10), while areas *KD5* and *KD6* were located beneath Tibb's Row. Finally, area *KD8* lay towards the northernmost limit of the site. In each instance, the archaeological sequence in these areas had been extensively denuded. Indeed, in places the tooth-marks of mechanical excavators were discernible, testament to the deliberate, wholesale removal of 'made-ground' deposits during the 1970s construction process.

Elsewhere, however, two much more substantial and well-preserved areas – *KD2* and *KD7* – were also excavated. The former was situated towards the southern limit of the investigated area, the latter towards the northern limit (Fig. 3.1). Area *KD2* measured 18.5m by 13.0m with deposits surviving up to 1.7m in depth, whilst area *KD7* measured 19.8m by 11.0m with deposits surviving up to 2.0m in depth. In both locations, complex archaeological sequences were encountered (Figs. 3.3–3.9). Multiple recuts were identified, for example, along with anaerobically preserved timbers and, from the mid-fifteenth century onwards, substantial dumps of material remains. Nevertheless, it is important to note that in excess of two-thirds of the twelfth–sixteenth-century deposits, along with the entirety of the seventeenth–nineteenth-century deposits, had been truncated in both areas. In order to partially redress this imbalance, the results of two earlier investigations – those conducted at the former Masonic Hall in 1914 (Hughes 1915a) and 1971 (Alexander 1972) – have also been amalgamated into the following account.

Based on this combination of evidence, the King's Ditch sequence can be divided into four broad phases:

1) The earliest surviving deposits (early/mid-twelfth century)
2) The well-maintained medieval ditch (late twelfth– mid-fifteenth century)
3) The shallow re-cutting and utilization of the ditch for refuse disposal (late fifteenth–late seventeenth century)
4) Afterlife as Tibb's Row (late eighteenth–early twenty-first century)

Despite the substantial size of the recent investigations, which rank amongst the largest of their type yet undertaken, as the King's Ditch measured around 1340m in length the excavated area constituted only *c.* 3.5 per cent of its overall extent. In effect, therefore, the investigated sample is more comparable in scale to an evaluation rather than a typical open-area excavation (Hey & Lacey 2001). Accordingly, the following results should not be regarded as uniformly indicative of the deposits present around the ditch's entire circuit; they pertain instead to the particular locale from which they were recovered. Elsewhere within the volume specialist data has been grouped into discrete sections. Here, however, because the King's Ditch is discussed in isolation from the remainder of the suburb, specialist analyses have been incorporated directly into the relevant phase sections.

Early/mid-twelfth century incorporating specialist information from Rachel Ballantyne, Steve Boreham, Quita Mould and Anne de Vareilles
The earliest evidence of activity to be recovered from the King's Ditch took the form of three distinct 'slots' in the feature's base (F.5075 in area *KD5*, plus F.5093 and F.5127 in area *KD7*; Fig. 3.8). These slots were rectangular in form and aligned longitudinally along the central axis of the ditch; each had straight sides, rounded corners, steep almost vertical sides and a relatively flat base. They measured 3.85–4.5m long by 1.8–2.15m wide and 0.4–0.55m deep. All of the slots had near-identical fill sequences, comprising an initial 0.1–0.15m thick deposit of grey clay that had washed in from the base of the ditch, followed by a mixed brownish grey slightly silty sand derived from erosion of the ditch sides. The only cultural material to be recovered was a single small fragment from a Niedermendig lava quern from one of the slot's upper fills. Overall, the form, fills, stratigraphy and lack of cultural materials in these slots combine to indicate that they were created either during the process of the feature's initial construction or, alternatively, a later episode of re-excavation that had removed all trace of any earlier deposits. As the slots were cut into the Gault Clay they would have rapidly filled with water, thereby keeping the rest of the ditch base relatively dry and forming convenient sumps to facilitate bailing. Once the

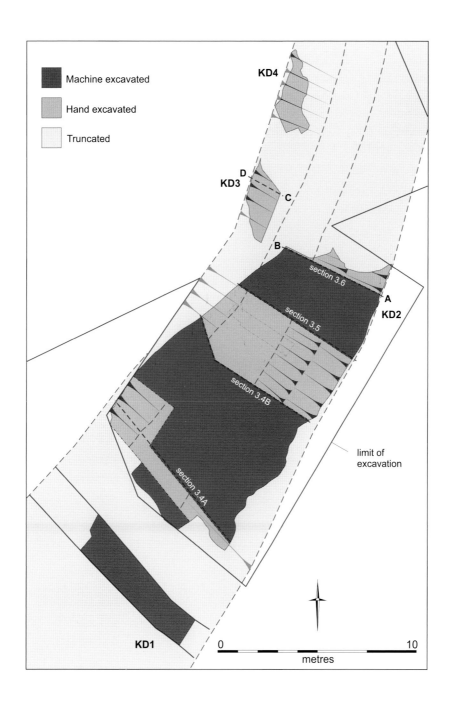

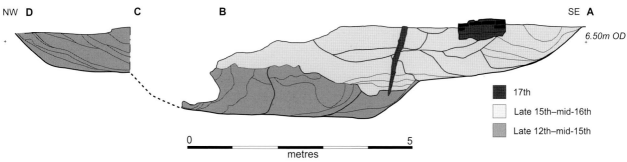

Figure 3.3. *Simplified plan of main southern area of excavation of the King's Ditch (KD2), plus phased section.*

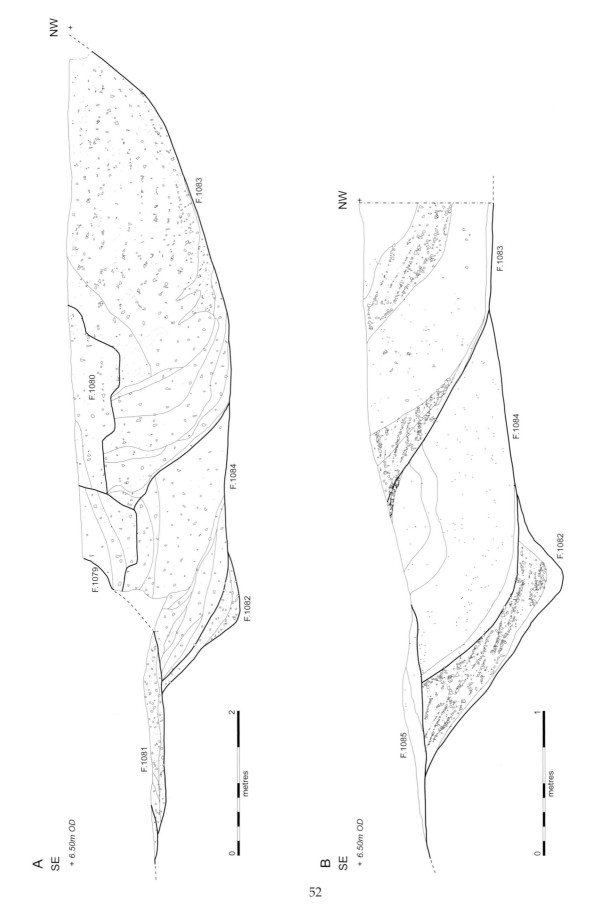

Figure 3.4. *Sections of the King's Ditch in area KD2, locations shown on Fig. 3.3.*

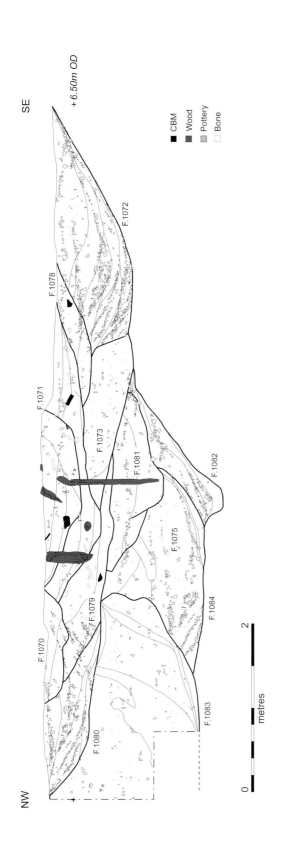

Figure 3.5. *Section and photograph of the King's Ditch in area KD2, locations shown on Fig. 3.3.*

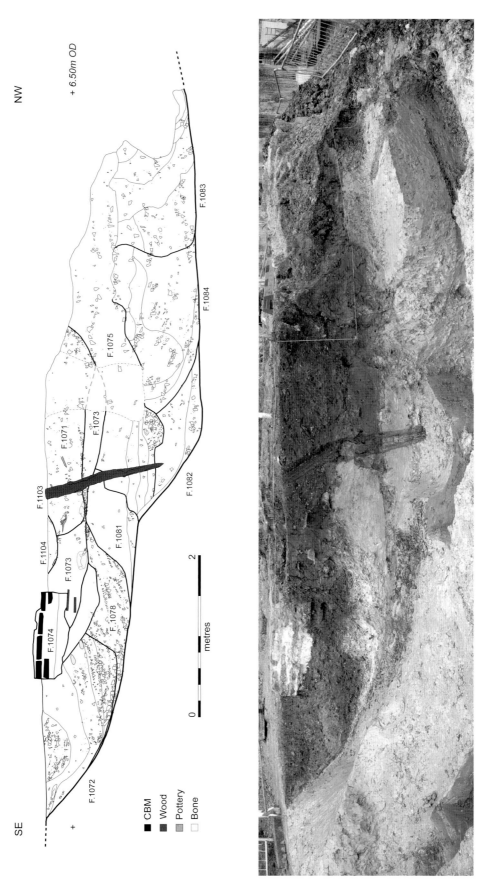

Figure 3.6. *Section and photograph of the King's Ditch in area KD2, locations shown on Fig. 3.3.*

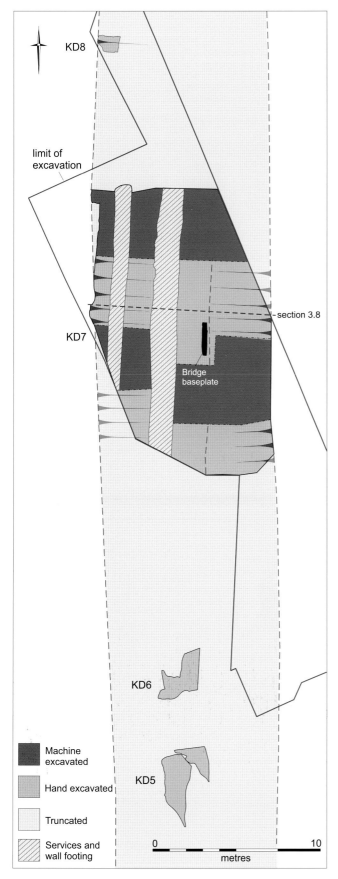

KD8

limit of
excavation

KD7

section 3.8

Bridge
baseplate

KD6

KD5

Machine
excavated

Hand excavated

Truncated

Services and
wall footing

0   10

metres

remainder of the work had been completed, the slots would have quickly silted up through natural processes.

A pollen sample recovered from slot F.5075 (Fig. 3.8) was entirely barren, indicating a highly weathered and oxidized environment. Similarly, the plant remains obtained from the same deposit revealed very little evidence for refuse or cess. The only charred plant remains consisted of one cereal grain and a low amount of charcoal. Waterlogged plants included one cabbage/mustard seed and some crumpled corncockle seeds, which could indicate low levels of human cess, and a great fen sedge leaf fragment. The majority of seeds were of ruderal plants and arable weeds that are likely to have colonized the land nearby. It is unclear if the arable weeds were feral from cereal by-products, or instead derived from nearby cultivated land. The lack of any waterlogged cereal chaff suggests the arable weeds do not directly represent crop cleanings. Although waterlogged remains (particularly numerous insect exoskeletons) show that this slot had been continuously wet from its formation until the present, there is good biological evidence that the early ditch was prone to drying episodes. The likely autochthonous plants were aquatics of shallow still water, such as celery-leaved buttercup (*Ranunculus sceleratus*) and duckweed (*Lemna* sp.) with other damp to wet land plants, such as pale persicaria (*Persicaria lapathifolium*) and golden dock (*Rumex maritimus*). The numerous unhatched winter-eggs of water fleas (*Daphnia* spp.) are significant as they only reproduce this way when under environmental stress, such as in shrinking water-bodies; fertilized winter-eggs can lie dormant until the return of more favourable conditions (Fitter & Manuel 1986).

Two radiocarbon determinations were undertaken on waterlogged plant remains recovered from slot F.5075 (Table 3.1; Fig. 3.11D). These indicate a date for the infilling of the slot between the mid-eleventh and early thirteenth centuries. Bayesian analysis (Buck *et al.* 1999; http://bcal.sheffield.ac.uk) suggests that this occurred in 1157–1223 (68 per cent probability) or 1066–1232 (95 per cent probability); the deposit may therefore be eleventh- (34.2 per cent probability), twelfth- (58.7 per cent probability) or thirteenth- (7.1 per cent probability) century in origin. Although there is some residual earlier material, the pottery from the ditch (Table 3.2) broadly favours a twelfth-century date for the earliest associated material culture.

Initially, it appeared that the three slots represented the only surviving elements from the earliest extant phase of the ditch; however, subsequent analysis indicated that a small island of stratigraphic material, not originally assigned to this phase during the excavation, also remained extant in area *KD7* (F.5199). The initial stimulus for this reappraisal came from the identification of a one-piece upper from a leather turnshoe dated stylistically to the early twelfth century (Fig. 3.8). The shoe came from a deposit of dark grey sandy clay that also contained St Neots-type ware (16 sherds, 64g) and environmental remains. The latter included frequent aquatics, as well as wasteland specimens such as stinging nettle, goosefoots, oraches and golden dock. Plants of known economic value included rocket (*Sisymbrium* sp.), water-cress (*Rorippa nasturtium-aquaticum*) and flax (*Linum usitatissimum*); however, these only occurred as one or two seeds. Pollen from this deposit (S.5016; Fig. 3.11C) was dominated by the goosefoot (55.2 per cent) and cabbage (23.1 per cent) families, plus grass, cereals, herbs, hazel and privet. The latter may indicate that hedges were present in the vicinity.

Although no direct stratigraphic relationship survived, this basal deposit from the main portion of the ditch almost certainly overlay the fills contained within the deeper slots. F.5199 was markedly different in character, for example, being much

Figure 3.7. *Simplified plan of main northern area of excavation of the King's Ditch (KD7).*

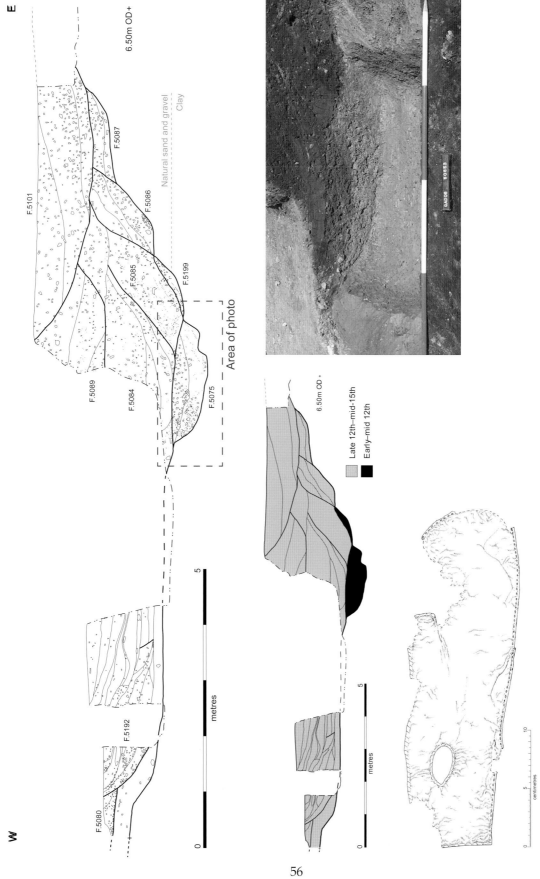

Figure 3.8. *Section of the King's Ditch in area KD2, photograph of earliest deposits relating to the initial construction of the King's Ditch, phased section and early twelfth-century leather turnshoe, left foot ([50394] F.5199), location of section shown on Fig. 3.7.*

Table 3.1. *Radiocarbon determinations from the King's Ditch.*

Laboratory no.	Context	Feature	Phase of ditch	Material dated	Radio-carbon age (BP)	δ¹³C (‰)	Calibrated date range (68.27% confidence)	Calibrated date range (95.45% confidence)
Wk-22895a	50384	5075	Initial construction	Charred cereal grain	911±33	-22.7±0.2	Cal AD 1044–1163	Cal AD 1032–1205
Wk-22895b	50384	5075	Initial construction	Charred cereal grain	869±30	-22.2±0.2	Cal AD 1154–1219	Cal AD 1046–1250
Wk-22895 combined	50384	5075	Initial construction	Charred cereal grain	888±22	-	Cal AD 1053–1205	Cal AD 1045–1216
Wk-22896	50405	5194	Later recut	Waterlogged wild plant seeds	791±30	-27.9±0.2	Cal AD 1222–1264	Cal AD 1190–1279
Wk-22892	10016	1000	Later recut	Charred cereal grain	797±33	-23.5±0.2	Cal AD 1219–1264	Cal AD 1183–1277
Wk-22893	50170	5191	Later recut	Charred cereal grain	661±32	-22.0±0.2	Cal AD 1284–1386	Cal AD 1276–1394
Wk-22894	50380	5192	Later recut	Charred cereal grain	596±30	-23.1±0.2	Cal AD 1310–1401	Cal AD 1298–1410

Table 3.2. *Pottery from the Grand Arcade (2005–6) and Masonic Hall (1914) excavations of the King's Ditch.*

Fabric	2005–6 No.	2005–6 Weight (g)	2005–6 MSW (g)	1914 No.	1914 Weight (g)	1914 MSW (g)	Fabric	2005–6 No.	2005–6 Weight (g)	2005–6 MSW (g)	1914 No.	1914 Weight (g)	1914 MSW (g)
Roman total	*8*	*113*	*14.1*	-	-	-	Misc. coarseware	130	2815	21.7	-	-	-
Maxey-type	1	36	36.0	-	-	-	*Medieval total*	*454*	*8666*	*19.1*	-	-	-
Ipswich	2	55	27.5	-	-	-	Babylon	66	470	7.1	54	3202	59.3
Middle Saxon total	*3*	*91*	*30.3*	-	-	-	Broad Street Gritty	9	1312	145.8	-	-	-
St Neot's-type	23	183	8.0	-	-	-	Broad Street Fineware	8	24	3.0	8	70	8.8
Thetford-type	44	1550	35.2	-	-	-	Broad Street Bichrome	-	-	-	2	75	37.5
Stamford	5	60	12.0	-	-	-	Dutch Glazed Red Earthenware	2	18	9.0	-	-	-
Early medieval Ely	3	50	16.7	-	-	-	Frechen	9	412	45.8	21	4022	191.5
Early grey coarseware	5	173	34.6	-	-	-	Glazed Red Earthenware	97	5387	55.5	80	9915	123.9
Saxo-Norman total	*80*	*2016*	*25.2*	-	-	-	Langerwehe	1	49	49.0	-	-	-
Boarstall/Brill	7	265	37.9	-	-	-	Midlands-type yellowware	-	-	-	5	134	26.8
Developed Stamford	2	20	10.0	-	-	-	Raeren	19	395	20.8	3	619	206.3
Medieval Ely	54	1174	21.7	-	-	-	Staffordshire type slipware	-	-	-	18	618	34.3
Ely-Grimston	41	791	19.3	-	-	-	Surrey Borders	-	-	-	1	12	12.0
Essex Greyware	23	390	17.0	-	-	-	Misc. coarseware	88	3413	38.8	27	3057	113.2
Essex Redware	99	1351	13.6	-	-	-	Misc. Fineware	-	-	-	2	35	17.5
Grimston	6	64	10.7	-	-	-	*Post-medieval total*	*299*	*11,480*	*38.4*	*221*	*21,759*	*98.5*
Lyveden/Stanion	29	457	15.8	-	-	-	**Overall total**	**844**	**22,366**	**26.5**	**221**	**21,759**	**98.5**
Cambridge-type Sgraffito	6	275	45.8	-	-	-							
Surrey Borders	57	1064	18.7	-	-	-							

darker; it also contained cultural material. The base of the slots lay at 4.97–5.12m OD, with the base of the main portion of the ditch at *c.* 5.5–5.8m OD. The contemporary ground surface lay at *c.* 8.5–9.0m OD, so the main ditch was *c.* 3.2m deep. There is a possibility that in the area of the ditch the contemporary ground surface was higher at *c.* 10m OD due to a localized ridge, in which case the ditch would

have been *c.* 4.2m deep, but this cannot be confirmed. The ditch is likely to have been *c.* 9.0m wide.

The summary of the 1971 investigations, located in area *KD1–2*, stated that 'there was no surviving evidence at this point of the medieval or earlier defences' and no evidence of any associated bank, palisade or wall (Alexander 1972). It seems likely that a bank did originally exist, as there is some evidence for bank material slumping into the ditch and also because the initial excavation of the feature would have produced considerable quantities of gravel and clay that would have required disposal. The bank is most likely to have been almost entirely removed by later activity, as is the case in most medieval towns. The evidence for slumping of the bank suggests that there was no significant platform or berm separating the bank from the ditch.

Late twelfth–mid-fifteenth century incorporating specialist information from Rachel Ballantyne, Steve Boreham, Richard Darrah, Andrew Hall, David Hall, Lorrain Higbee, Quita Mould, David Smith, Simon Timberlake and Anne de Vareilles

Throughout this phase, the King's Ditch remained well-maintained and its profile was regularly recut. Nevertheless, during the medieval period different sections of the ditch began to develop divergent sequences. This may have resulted in part from the feature's curvilinear form, which would have affected the flow of water through it, as well as the differing geological strata through which it cut. A further complicating factor was the varying pattern of adjacent occupation and activity along its route. Overall, the profile of the ditch remained relatively uniform; at around 9.0m wide and just over 3.0m deep, it had moderately sloping sides and a broad, flat base. There is no evidence to suggest that it ever had any form of revetment as there were no surviving timbers, or associated impressions, and the inner face was sloping rather than vertical, unlike town ditches elsewhere where revetments have been postulated (*e.g.* Isserlin & Connell 1997).

Based upon similarities in both form and deposit type, the investigated areas that contained Phase 2 deposits can be subdivided into two broad groups. The first was located in areas *KD1–4*, the second in areas *KD5–8*. Firstly, in area *KD2*, three recuts were identified (Figs. 3.3–3.6). The earliest (F.1082) had moderately angular sides sloping at *c*. 40–45° and a relatively narrow flat base, with a distinct step on its outer side that was 0.15m deeper; this most probably acted as a drainage slot. This recut was filled with remarkably sterile clay deposits that included lenses of gravel. Although it contained no dateable material culture, it was almost certainly thirteenth-century in date on stratigraphic grounds. A pollen sample recovered from the base of its sequence (S.1073.1; Fig. 3.11A) was dominated by the Goosefoot Family (Chenopodiaceae; 45.5 per cent), along with cereals (13.6 per cent), grass (Poaceae; 9.1 per cent) and a range of herbs including dock (*Rumex*), the Cabbage Family (Brassicaceae) and the Aster Family (Asteraceae). Trees were represented by hazel (*Corylus*) and birch (*Betula*), whilst fern spores reached 9.1 per cent. Some pollen from slightly later in the sequence of the recut (S.1073.2) had a low main sum, but nevertheless contained goosefoot, grass and hazel.

The second recut in this area (F.1084) shifted the location of the ditch inwards by *c*. 0.4m, although its base remained at roughly the same height. The ditch's overall profile remained largely unchanged, and the fills of this phase were similar to those of its predecessor. In material terms, they contained a small amount of animal bone and a square-shaped, smoothed and flattened chalk tablet that was crudely inscribed with a cross on its upper face; this was probably a Christian symbol (Fig. 3.12A). Composed of local Middle or Upper Chalk, the tablet measured 65mm by 60mm in extent and was 27mm thick; several knife marks were evident. The pollen sequence from this phase (S.1073.3) was similar to that of the preceding recut. The assemblage was dominated by grass (26.7 per cent), accompanied by members of the Goosefoot Family (23.3 per cent), cereals (6.7 per cent) and the Cabbage Family (6.7 per cent). The range of herbs was greater, however, with dock, plantain, aster, cow parsley, campion and deadnettle all present. The only trees were hazel and ash (*Fraxinus*).

Although nearby areas *KD3–4* were heavily truncated (Figs. 3.10 and 3.11B), the surviving deposits in this location (F.1000) correspond very closely to those in area *KD2*. Here, a small quantity of faunal remains and ceramic fragments dating from the Roman period to the fourteenth century were recovered. The most substantial piece was the upper portion of a buff coarseware jug with a strap handle and pulled-lip spout whose fabric has very little sand and some grits (Fig. 3.13A). A radiocarbon determination of 1181–1278 AD (95 per cent confidence) or 1219–63 (68 per cent confidence) (Wk-22892; 797±33) was derived from a context stratigraphically earlier than the jug (Table 3.1; Fig. 3.11D). Four pollen samples were also analysed. The earliest (S.1012.1) was dominated by grass and herbs including thistle, stinging nettle and the Cabbage Family. Meadowsweet, cereals and the Cow Parsley Family were also relatively abundant, while trees included alder, oak, hazel and privet. The second sample (S.1013.2) had a very low main sum, but was dominated by grass (36.4 per cent) along with the Cow Parsley Family, Bean Family, Goosefoot Family and privet. Fern spores reached 18.2 per cent and pollen of the emergent aquatic reedmace (expressed outside the main sum) reached 9.1 per cent. The third sample (S.1013.1) was dominated by grass (27.3 per cent) and the Goosefoot Family (22.7 per cent). Other herbs included aster, the Cabbage Family, cereals and the Cow Parsley Family. Trees included alder, hazel and privet, whilst the emergent aquatics reedmace and bur-reed together reached nine per cent. The final sample (S.1012.2) was dominated by grass (17.9 per cent) and the Cabbage Family (21.4 per cent), with fern spores, cereals, thistle and privet.

Attention now shifts to the second of the two identified area groups. In the southern part of this zone, within areas *KD5–6*, the archaeological sequence had been heavily disturbed and nothing could be determined of the ditch's form. Nevertheless, the fills in this area (F.5195, F.5196) consisted of soft black sandy clay that is closely akin to the material encountered in nearby area *KD7*. A small amount of fourteenth/fifteenth-century pottery (Fig. 3.13B) and animal bone was also present. The latter included the articulated vertebral column of a pig, the axis of which, along with five cervical and 12 thoracic vertebrae, had been chopped through the centrum (Fig. 3.12C). These marks result from the division of the carcass into sides (Sykes 2006, 69); although, in this instance, the butcher appears to have been relatively unskilled. Also recovered were a fourteenth/early fifteenth-century leather turnshoe sole and a fragment from its left upper (Fig. 3.12D).

A much more complete sequence was encountered in area *KD7*. Here, a minimum of six recuts were identified, several of which had associated timber structures. The fills in this area were also considerably darker and contained much more cultural material. Altogether, these deposits appear to have comprised a mixture of waterlain material plus various collapse and slumping events from the sides of the ditch, interleaved with relatively discrete dumps of refuse. The earliest phase (F.5087) had been heavily truncated and produced only a single sherd of fourteenth/fifteenth-century pottery. The subsequent recut (F.5086) was also heavily truncated, although it appears that the line of the ditch had shifted inwards somewhat at this time. Associated with this phase was a roughly square posthole (F.5061) that measured 0.30m by 0.36m in extent and over 0.33m deep. The post itself had been removed, but two associated willow stakes (both five year old and 40–45mm in diameter) remained.

In contrast to its predecessors, substantially more of the third recut (F.5085 plus F.5129) remained extant. By this time the ditch had shifted inwards a further *c*. 0.8m and had steep, angular sides sloping at *c*. 60° as well as a broad, relatively flat base. The small amount of pottery present spanned the twelfth–fourteenth centuries. In addition, 145 animal bones were recovered via controlled excavation, 87 of which were identified, whilst during later machining (F.5198) a further 664 bones were recovered. Of the former, 62 cattle horn cores, characteristic of waste from a horn-worker, accounted for 71 per cent of the total number of fragments (Fig. 3.14A); two sheep horn cores were also present. The cattle horn cores were derived from at least 32 animals (MNI), 16 from the left-hand side and 32 from the right. A large proportion (81 per cent) had been detached with part of the frontal bone and only eight had cut marks around the base from removal of the sheath. One core had been sawn in half, presumably because smaller sections of horn were required (Yeomans 2005, 71), and another had been sawn at the tip. Most were from adult animals (49 per cent), followed by sub-adults (32 per cent) and juveniles (19 per cent). Measurements on complete horn cores indicate that 81 per cent were derived from small horned cattle with the remainder from short horned cattle; it appears that both sexes are represented (Fig. 3.14E). Most of the remaining bones consisted of waste elements from primary butchery (*e.g.* mandibles and metapodia) or bones from non-food species (*e.g.* dog and frog); the final 30 per cent comprised beef and mutton joints (*c.* 17.6kg), plus goose (Table 3.3).

The assemblage from machining included 208 cattle horn cores (67 per cent NISP) representing at least 104 animals (MNI), plus four goat horn cores (Fig. 3.14D) from at least two animals (MNI). The cattle horns included 82 from both the left-hand and right-hand sides equally. A significant proportion (75 per cent) had been detached with part of the frontal bone and cut marks were observed around the base of 16 per cent. Three cores had been chopped through at the base to completely detach them from the skull, and four had been sawn in half. The majority (74 per cent) were from adult animals; these would have been the most useful to the horn-worker because of their larger size. There were also cores from sub-adults (22 per cent) and juveniles (4 per cent). In total 77 per cent of the complete cores were derived from small horned cattle, 21 per cent from short horned and the remaining two per cent from medium horned. Both sexes were represented, although there appear to have been significantly more females than males. The remaining 33 per cent consisted of bones from non-food species (37 per cent), domestic waste (20 per cent) and primary butchery (19 per cent). Non-food species included horses (MNI three, based upon right mandibles) and cats (MNI, two based upon right pelves). There were also disarticulated dogs (Fig. 3.14B; MNI three, based upon left mandibles) plus the semi-articulated remains of two partial adult dog skeletons. One dog had an estimated shoulder height of *c.* 0.36m and the other of *c.* 0.35m.

In addition to the meat provided by several joints of beef, mutton and pork (*c.* 37.1kg), there was also some rabbit, domestic poultry and a tibiotarsus and radius from a bittern, a high-status bird. Archaeological finds of bittern are extremely rare (Serjeantson 2006, 142), but include finds from medieval Lincoln (O'Connor 1982, 44), and post-medieval Ely (Cessford *et al.* 2006, 75, tab. 8). Bitterns were highly prized and peasants were frequently fined for catching them and stealing their eggs. Over a two year period in the early fourteenth century, 36 people from the manors of Sutton and Littleport were fined for taking bitterns and 'habitually' stealing their eggs (Stone 2006, 154), while early sixteenth-century court rolls for Waterbeach indicate that any bitterns and other prized birds taken within the commons were first to be offered to the lord of the manor to buy (Stone 2006, 159). Notably, the vast majority of this faunal assemblage appears to have been deposited from the suburban as opposed to urban side of the ditch.

Two pollen samples were analysed from this recut. The earliest (S.5017) was dominated by cereal pollen (17.6 per cent), grass (13.7 per cent) and the Goosefoot Family (11.8 per cent). Herbs included aster, the Cabbage Family and Cow Parsley Family. The proportion of fern spores reached 11.7 per cent and trees were represented by birch, pine, alder, hazel and privet. A slightly later sample (S.5018) was dominated by grass (25 per cent) and the Cabbage Family (20 per cent), with herbs including cereals, campion, meadowsweet and dock. Trees included oak, privet, pine (which is unusual and may represent deliberate planting in the vicinity) and lime (also probably from deliberate horticultural activity).

Table 3.3. *Minimum number of butchery units and meat weights from King's Ditch recut F.5085/F.5198.*

Methodology	Species	Joint	Total no. bones	MNBU	Estimated meat weight (kg)	Total estimated meat weight (kg) by meat type
Controlled excavation	Cattle	Thick flank	1	1	5.1	12.5
		Neck & clod	1	1	7.4	
	Sheep	Shoulder	2	1	2.9	5.1
		Leg	2	1	2.2	
	Goose		1	1		
Total			7	5	**17.6**	
Machining	Cattle	Thick flank	2	2	10.2	14.8
		Shin	2	2	4.6	
	Sheep	Shoulder	4	3	8.7	13.1
		Leg	2	2	4.4	
	Pig	Shoulder/hand	2	2	9.2	9.2
	Rabbit		2	1		
	Chicken		2	1		
	Goose		2	1		
	Duck		1	1		
	Bittern		2	1		
Total			21	16	**37.1**	

The fourth recut in area *KD7* (F.5084, F.5128) shifted the line of the ditch inwards an additional *c.* 1.5m. At this time, the feature had moderately sloping sides at *c.* 45° and a broad flat base. Its fills contained a repaired adult leather turnshoe vamp from a shoe fastening across the instep with a buckle and strap, a style popular in the late fourteenth/early fifteenth centuries (Fig. 3.12E). There was also a residual sherd of Middle Saxon Ipswich ware and a small amount of other pottery spanning the eleventh–fourteenth/fifteenth centuries. In addition, nine small, irregularly shaped hearth base fragments associated with secondary iron smithing were recovered. Three pollen samples were also taken, although one (S.5021) was entirely barren, indicating a highly weathered and oxidized environment. The others (S.5019 and S.5020) had similar pollen spectrums, dominated by the Goosefoot Family (*c.* 23–25 per cent) and grass (*c.* 21 per cent) along with cereals and a range of herbs.

During Phase 2 it appears that the townward side of the ditch was more thoroughly cleansed and maintained than the suburban side. Indeed, the earliest surviving deposits in the former area (F.5191–94) appear to equate to the fourth recut in the sequence. A radiocarbon determination from one of the earliest of these fills was dated to 1276–1394 (95 per cent confidence) or 1284–1385 (68 per cent confidence) (Wk-22893; 661±32; Table 3.1; Fig. 3.11D). Another determination of 1298–1410 (95 per cent confidence) or 1310–1401 (68 per cent confidence) (Wk-22894; 596±30; Table 3.1; Fig. 3.11D) derived from a slightly later fill is likely to have been 1–83 years (95 per cent probability) or 1–25 years (68 per cent probability) later. The pottery assemblage associated with these deposits contained

Figure 3.9. *Photographs of the King's Ditch during the 2005–6 excavations: investigation of deposits in area KD2 facing north, for the section that is being recorded see Figure 3.5 (upper left), initial cleaning in area KD2, facing northwest, with toothed bucket marks from 1970s truncation clearly visible (upper right); area KD7, facing northeast, for section see Figure 3.8 (lower).*

Figure 3.10. *Photograph of excavations inside the standing Lion Yard car park where areas KD3–4 were excavated.*

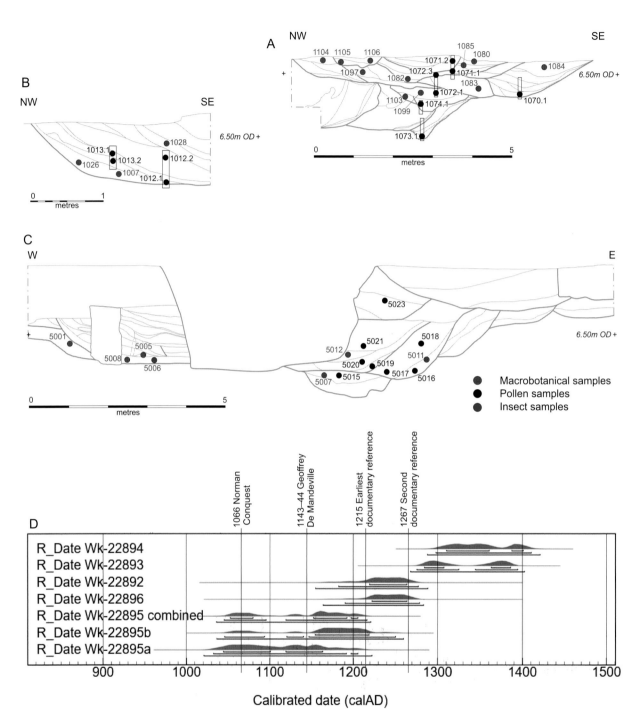

Figure 3.11 *(above). Analysed plant macrofossil, insect, pollen and radiocarbon samples from the King's Ditch; section (A) area KD2, corresponds to Figure 3.5; section (B) area KD4; section (C) area KD7, corresponds to Figure 3.8; (D) plot of radiocarbon determinations (OxCal v4.2.4; Bronk Ramsey & Lee 2013; r:5 IntCal 13 atmospheric curve; Reimer et al. 2013).*

Figure 3.12 *(opposite). Thirteenth–fourteenth-century artefacts recovered from the King's Ditch, including: (A) chalk tablet bearing a crudely inscribed cross ([10488] F.1084); (B) unidentified iron object ([50152] F.5192); (C) articulating pig vertebral column ([50945] F.5195); (D) turnshoe sole, adult left foot ([50930] F.5195); (E) turnshoe vamp, adult left foot ([50622] F.5084); (F) turnshoe sole, child's right foot ([50355] F.5192) (photograph C courtesy of Lorrian Higbee).*

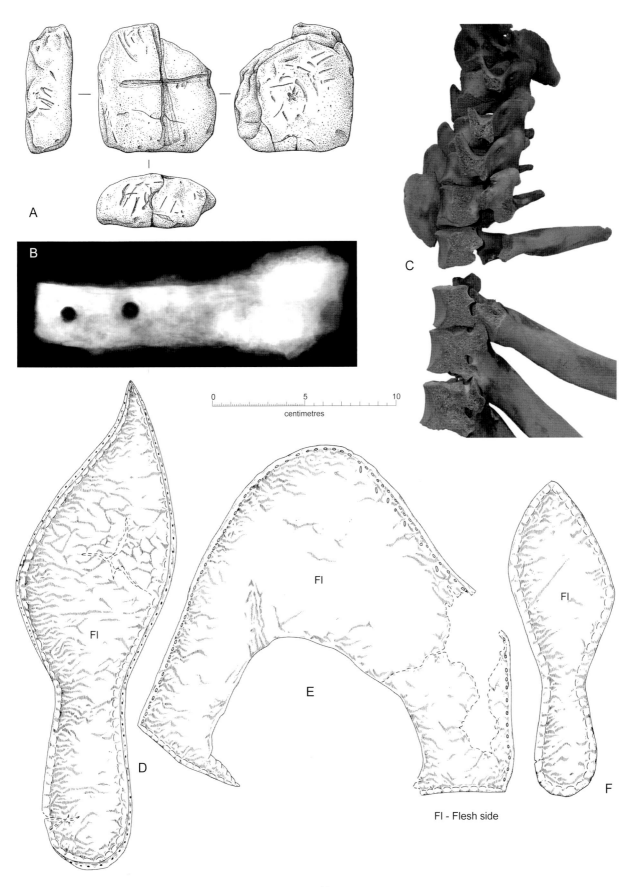

A

B

C

D

E

F

FI - Flesh side

0   5   10
centimetres

63

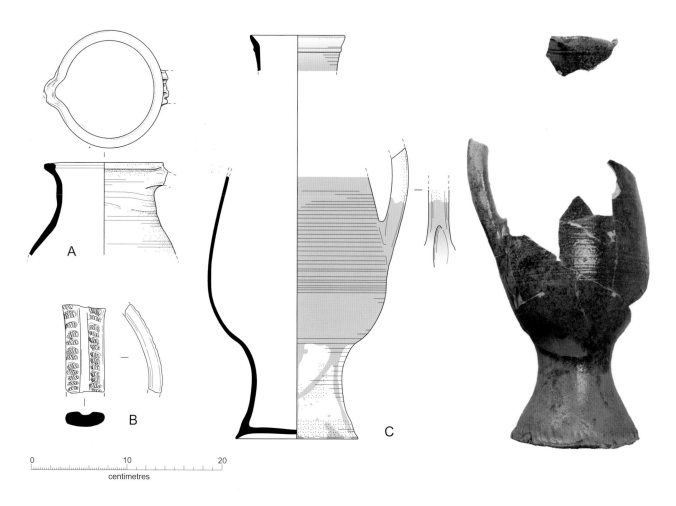

0   10   20
centimetres

Figure 3.13. *Fourteenth-century pottery recovered from the King's Ditch, including: (A) buff coarseware jug ([10030] F.1000); (B) grey coarseware strap handle with stamped decoration ([50757] F.5196); (C) Surrey Borders strap-handled baluster jug ([50355], [50338], [50361], [50357] F.5192).*

twelfth–fourteenth/fifteenth-century material, including a residual twelfth-century grey coarseware lamp (see Fig. 4.57L) and a group of Thetford-type ware (23 sherds, 433g). Also present was an almost complete thirteenth/fourteenth-century Surrey Borders baluster-shaped jug with rilled decoration, pinched spout and recessed base which had been inadvertently glazed (Fig. 3.13C); this was similar in form to fourteenth-century Kingston-type ware rilled baluster jugs (see Pearce 1992, 20–1). Nearby was a group of glass shards, probably from a fourteenth-century English potash goblet. There was also an unidentified heavily corroded iron object shaped broadly like an axe head, but with two perforations (Fig. 3.12B).

Additional finds from this area included a fragment of a little-used imported Scandinavian quartz schist whetstone, a piece of a shelly Oolitic limestone mortar and a small and very roughly shaped stone tablet made from Lower Greensand. One of the earliest deposits of this phase also contained a large dump of oyster shells (MNI *c.* 700) plus a few mussels (MNI one), whelks (MNI three) and cockles (MNI one), whilst a separate deposit contained a large number of leaves. Their presence suggests that deposition occurred during the autumn, although it is unclear whether they accumulated naturally or were deliberately dumped. Two leather turnshoes – one a fourteenth/early fifteenth-century child's sole (Fig. 3.12F), the other a left shoe that would have fitted an adolescent or small adult – were also recovered. Further discoveries included the partial,

semi-articulated skeleton of an adult dog with an estimated shoulder height of *c.* 0.59m, the remnants of at least two adult ravens (which were spread between four separate fills) and the relatively rare find of a swan tibiotarsus. All of this material had been deposited from the townward side of the ditch, where it was associated with a plot that was recorded from 1361 onwards. By the sixteenth century, this had become the Falcon Inn.

The insect remains recovered from this recut demonstrate clear evidence for the presence of slow moving or stagnant water.

Figure 3.14 *(opposite). Fourteenth-century animal bone recovered from F.5085/F.5198, including: (A) assemblage of cattle horn cores ([50742]); (B) dog skull with terrier-type morphology ([50394]); (C) sawn cattle horn cores ([50394], [50742]); (D) goat horn core ([50394]); (E–F) charts showing size variation of cattle horn cores derived from controlled excavation (E) and machined contexts (F) based upon their minimum (Wmin) and maximum (Wmax) basal diameter measurements. (photographs courtesy of Lorrain Higbee).*

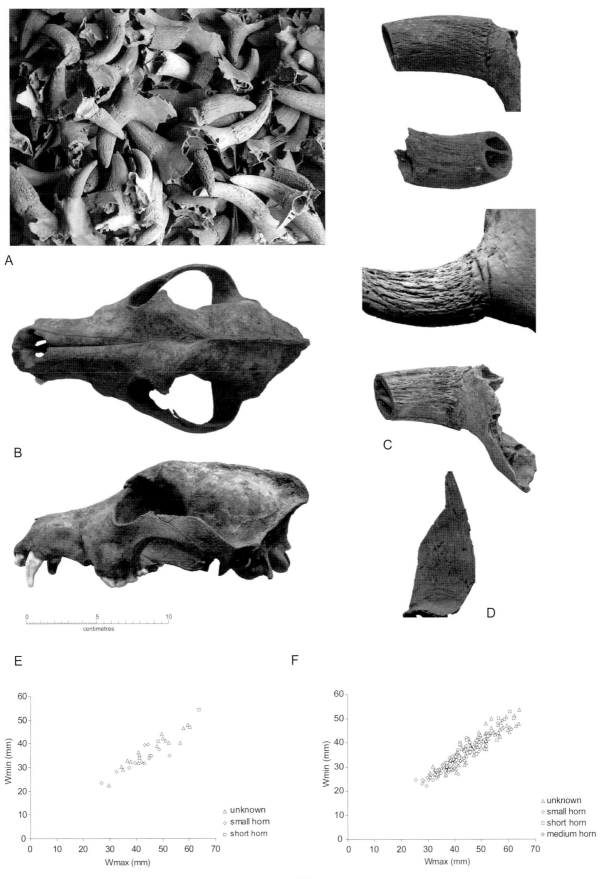

This is most clearly indicated by the species of hydrophiliid 'diving beetle' such as *Hygrotus inaequalis, H. palustris* and the *Agabus* species (Nilsson & Holmen 1995). This environment was also inhabited by a range of Hydreanidae and Hydrophilidae such as *Octhebuis minimus, Hydreana spp., Cercyon ustulatus, Laccobius* and *Chaetarthria seminulum* (Hansen 1986). There appears to have been little surface or marginal vegetation present in the ditch. Only single individuals of *Tanysphyrus lemnae,* which feeds on duckweed, and *Plateumaris braccata,* which feeds on *Phragmites* water reed, were recovered. This may suggest that the ditch was kept relatively clear of such vegetation. There are also indications from the presence of ground beetles and phytophage weevils present that a weedy and grassy area surrounded the ditch. There also appears to have been a large amount of settlement waste incorporated into the ditch throughout the period of its infilling. A large proportion of the fauna recovered consists of Kenward's 'house fauna' and a range of other synanthropic species. Equally, there is also some evidence from the fly pupae recovered (*Sepsis* flies and the 'rat tailed maggot' *Eristalis tenax*) for the presence of human cess (Smith 1989).

The fifth recut (F.5089, F.5124, F.5125) was noticeably shallower than in preceding phases, and consequently the base of the ditch now appears to have lain *c.* 1.0m higher. It remained in broadly the same location, however, and retained a near-identical profile. The fills of this recut were typical of those of its predecessors, consisting of mid to dark grey silts that contained variable amounts of sand and gravel and some thirteenth–fourteenth/fifteenth-century pottery. Also contemporary with this recut was an elm baseplate (F.5046) that formed part of a wooden footbridge (see inset: 'bridging the divide'). The sixth and final recut in area *KD7* (F.5101, F.5102, F.5197) had gently sloping concave sides and a broad rounded base. It contained a small quantity of residual twelfth–fourteenth/ fifteenth-century pottery, along with a small thin perforated slate whetstone. The pollen from this phase (S.5023) indicates a return to the tall herb community dominated by the Cabbage Family, whilst the relative paucity of aquatic pollen suggests an absence of perennial standing water.

Overall, the pollen evidence represents an admixture of material derived from the ditch itself as well as with the surrounding area. Waterlogged plant remains indicate that, in contrast to Phase 1, nettle-leaved goosefoot was now almost non-existent and oraches were less common. Instead, there was an increase in aquatics, particularly celery-leaved buttercup, and plants of damp soils. Differences between samples may reflect both local and temporal variations in hydrology. In general, however, all illustrate a vegetated wet ditch with well-established aquatics, which was surrounded by nettles, grasses and other annuals. Elder and willow remain the only tree species to have been identified. Crop weeds were also present and may have drifted into the ditch from nearby areas of crop-processing activities. Water-fleas, indicative of shallow stagnant water, were common, and altogether the insect remains indicate that the ditch was situated close to an area of pasture. Settlement rubbish and waste was also present in the vicinity, while one notable absence is any sign of extensive areas of waterside vegetation or reeds. The pollen evidence indicates that cereal cultivation was taking place close to the ditch and there were a few scattered trees in the vicinity, although much of the woody vegetation appears to be represented by hazel and privet scrub or hedgerow. It seems the ditch itself was treeless, although it is possible that occasional alders may have become established in wetter areas. The ditch was essentially dry for at least the summer months in some places, although at other times there is evidence for standing water. The vegetation of the ditch was in general a damp riparian meadow with tall herb communities, but particular plant communities developed at the base of the channel in response to specific local conditions at different times.

The plant macrofossils from area *KD7* show little change in flora to the preceding, twelfth-century phase, and the ditch environs – including the nature of nearby activities – appear to have remained relatively unchanged. There were still very few charred plant remains, mostly individual cereal grains (hulled barley, wheat/ rye) with no chaff or seeds, and low amounts of wood charcoal. A general trend from waterlogged seeds of annuals to perennials over time suggests the ground was disturbed less frequently or extensively; both goosefoots and chickweeds were now much less common, but the frequency of stinging nettles increased (all three taxa favour nutrient-enriched land). The fourth recut (F.5084) demonstrated evidence for much greater soil disturbance as nettles were absent, but numerous seeds of fumitories (*Fumaria* sp.) and fool's parsley (*Aethusa cynapium*) were present, annuals that thrive on open disturbed soils. The fifth recut had slightly greater evidence for watery conditions, in the form of rigid hornwort (*Ceratophyllum demersum*), plus numerous gypsywort seeds (*Lycopus europaeus*) and ostracod valves.

In terms of contemporary spatial variability, during the thirteenth–fourteenth centuries traces of human faeces were more widespread in the northern sub-group than the southern, as evidenced by various elements of the fourth recut in area *KD7*. One deposit (F.5191) included fig seeds (*Ficus carica*) in addition to cabbage/mustard and blackberries; fennel seed (*Foeniculum vulgare*) could also have been used as a condiment or have grown wild. Another deposit (F.5192) contained numerous seeds of black mustard (*Brassica nigra*) and cabbage/mustard, whilst a third (F.5084) included hops (*Humulus lupulus*) and fragments of wild or cultivated cherry stones (*Prunus avium*). Although the cultivation of hops in England did not begin on a significant scale until the early sixteenth century, these plants do occur naturally; nevertheless, hop seeds have also been found in eleventh-century cess deposits in Norwich, where they appear not to be of natural origin (Murphy in Ayers 1987, 121). Other deposits, however (such as F.5085 and F.5194), lacked any evidence of ingested seeds. These compositional irregularities suggest that faeces entered the ditch infrequently, and imply that some effort was made to maintain the cleanliness of the King's Ditch during this period.

Further to the south, areas *KD2–3* appear to have been slightly wetter than area *KD7* during the thirteenth–fourteenth centuries, as seeds of fool's-water-cress (*Apium nodiflorum*) occurred here consistently. The other major taxa were identical to those in area *KD7*, however, and included gypsywort, celery-leaved buttercup, pale persicaria, golden dock and duckweeds. One sample lacked nettles but included sun spurge (*Euphorbia helioscopia*), whilst both earlier and later samples had the inverse composition. These marked shifts in flora suggest extensive soil disturbance between the formation of the fills. The latest deposit appears to reflect overgrown rough ground due to the numerous seeds of wild parsnip (*Pastinaca sativa*), hemlock (*Conium maculatum*), thistles (*Carduus/Cirsium* sp.), and perennial sow-thistle (*Sonchus arvensis*) it contained. There were also low amounts of waterlogged ingested seeds, including figs, bramble, and blackthorn/cherry (*Prunus spinosa/avium*). Unlike area *KD7*, however, there were almost no arable weeds such as corncockle or stinking mayweeds. As charred remains were also completely absent, other than a great fen sedge leaf fragment, this area appears to have been completely disassociated from any cereal processing.

Historically, the earliest documentary references to the existence of the King's Ditch occurred during Phase 2. The first, dated 6 November 1215, was associated with the First Barons' War of 1215–17. At this time, King John (*b.* 1166, *r.* 1199–1216) commanded the Barons of the Exchequer to allow the bailiffs of Cambridge the costs they had incurred 'in enclosing the town and making pickaxes, spades and iron hooks; and for the carriage of arms, ladders, shields and cords' (Cooper 1842, 35). Given the radiocarbon dates derived from the basal fills of the ditch (Fig. 3.11D), this activity almost certainly pertained to a widespread episode of maintenance as opposed to its primary construction. John is known to have been at Cambridge on 9–10 March 1215 and it is possible that the work was ordered then; he returned to Cambridge on the 16–17 September

Bridging the divide incorporating specialist information from Richard Darrah, David Hall and Mark Samuel

The construction of the King's Ditch had a significant impact on the day-to-day lives of Cambridge's medieval occupants. In the short term, the physical process of its excavation doubtless caused significant localized disruption and destruction. But in the long term its primary legacy was the physical subdivision of numerous plots, institutions and parishes, thereby causing a considerable degree of inconvenience for their inhabitants. To mitigate this, from an early date a number of bridges were constructed across the divide. Whilst the formal crossing points into and out of the town were restricted to the Barnwell and Trumpington Gates, where a degree of regulation and control over access was almost certainly maintained, additional bridges were also erected at various points along the ditch's course. Some of these latter structures appear to have been both relatively substantial in scale and long-lived in duration, indicating that they may have received at least a degree of official sanction. Supplementing these, however, were a variety of less permanent bridges that seem to have been erected on a more informal basis, with most of them probably providing private access for individual householders to and from their property.

Historically, privately owned bridges across the King's Ditch were first recorded in the Hundred Roll of 1279 (Illingworth & Caley 1812–18, 352), although similar structures may have first been constructed relatively soon after the ditch itself. Due to the insubstantial and unregulated nature of many of these crossing points, their overall number is difficult to determine; nevertheless, despite a degree of temporal variability, the total almost certainly increased over time. As a result, their impact on the permeability of the town boundary is likely to have been high. Along with the physical structures themselves – predominately narrow timber footbridges which could have been easily slighted if required – each crossing point also incorporated a breach in the associated bank. A rare opportunity to examine a relatively typical informal crossing point was presented by the Grand Arcade site, where in area *KD7*, the remnants of a small fourteenth-century timber bridge were identified (Fig. 3.15).

Embedded into the base of the ditch was an elm baseplate (F.5046) made from the hewn rectangular baulk of a 30 year old trunk. This measured 1.94m (6ft 4in) long and had two 150mm (6in) long mortices on its upper surface that were situated 0.3m (12in) from either end, thereby leaving a 1.04m (3ft 6in) gap between the two uprights. A portion of one of these uprights had also survived. It was composed of fast grown roundwood oak and the presence of a redundant auger hole across the shoulder of the sawn tenon, which was situated too low to have attached a brace between the bridge's uprights, indicates that it had been reused. The pegs holding the tenons comprised fast grown cleft ash. The upper face of the baseplate into which the mortices were set had been carefully shaped, so that it was flat over the full width of the 280mm by 200mm (11in by 8in) plate, with the result that the face had been cut to within 50mm of the centre of the tree. The sides were roughly finished, creating a rectangle with wide waney edges, and the base was deliberately left rounded to make it easier to get into position. One end had been sawn straight across, while the evidence on the other end was missing through decay.

Both mortices measured 150mm by 65mm and 100mm deep and had rounded ends. There was no evidence that they had been drilled out as there were no auger marks at the bottom of the mortice, although these may have been removed by water action. On the inner face of the baseplate were five vertically set roundwood stakes (35–55mm diameter), which helped hold the baseplate in position during its installation. Overall, therefore, this baseplate comprised part of a minor bridge of Rigold's Type 2, with support from trestles rising from transverse soleplates without transverse bracing and with no shoring in the longitudinal direction (Rigold 1975, 56–7). The bridge trestle was almost certainly lowered into position prefabricated rather than built *in situ*.

Contemporary with the construction of the bridge a wattle-lined revetment was erected towards the townward side of the ditch, *c.* 3.3m from the baseplate. The lower part of this revetment (F.5190) consisted of a row of five multifaceted roundwood oak stakes (60–79mm diameter). Above these was situated a badly deformed wood revetment (F.5052) composed of 18 stakes made from smaller willow (12), oak (four) and ash (one) coppiced poles (33–60mm diameter), plus two pieces of reused oak board. Directly associated with one of the stakes was a fragment of a carved and decorated fine-grained sandstone tablet that may have been part of some half-open stone container or some simple stone tracery. This revetment represents a vertical step in the profile of the ditch, which would have had another baseplate for the bridge placed on top of it as it was not substantial enough to form an edge up to ground level. Deposits associated with this revetment (F.5140) contained twelfth–fourteenth/fifteenth-century pottery, including a group of refitting sherds from a fourteenth-century Medieval Ely ware jug copying Grimston ware.

Alongside the bridge's physical remains, additional documentary evidence can also be cited with regard to its probable function. Firstly, in topographic terms the crossing point was situated at the rear of one of the northernmost plots in the street block (Plot II; Fig. 3.15). In 1375, Agnes – widow of John Fulbourn, a skinner – released to Hugh Leche and Walter Bylneye all her rights by way of dower in the *messuage* and adjoining L-shaped garden that

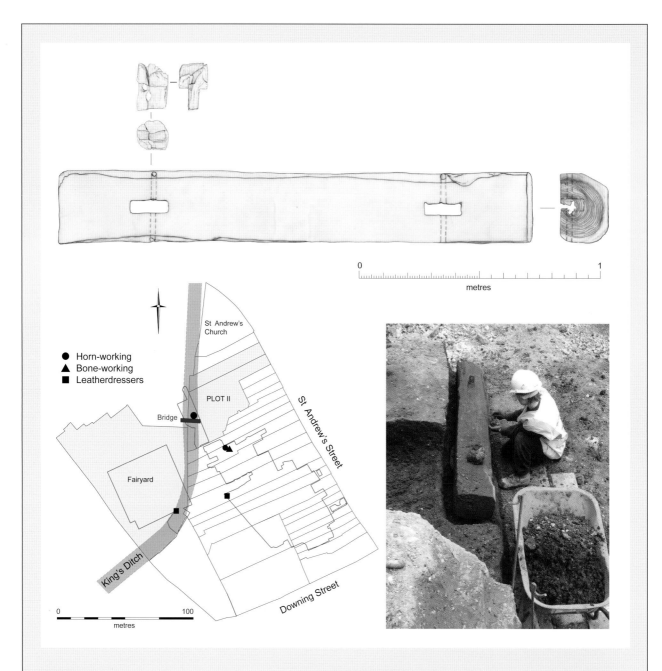

Figure 3.15. *Fourteenth-century Elm baseplate ([50275]), with oak upright ([50282]) above and south-facing photograph of the baseplate in situ. The location of the bridge is also shown in relation to contemporary deposits of horn-working, bone-working and leatherdressers' waste.*

together constituted this plot (Christ's, Cambridge A13). Further to the west during this period – on the opposing side of the ditch, to which the bridge connected – lay a large open area known as the Fair Yard that also functioned as a beast market. Significantly, in 1261 the same John de Fulbourn had witnessed a document relating to the lease of two empty pieces of

ground close by this area (CCCC09/10/15). Furthermore, in 1368 a certain John de Fulbourne, tanner, also issued a quitclaim to rights to a property in Petty Cury, which was again situated on the townward side of the ditch (CCCC09/10/16b). These documents therefore demonstrate a series of physical linkages that criss-crossed the King's Ditch at this point. Of at least equal importance, however, was the nature of John Fulbourn's occupation. As a skinner/tanner, access to the beast market would have been central to his trade. Moreover, archaeological evidence recovered from adjacent plots within the suburb demonstrates that both bone and horn working were widely undertaken during this period (see further Chapter 4). It thus appears quite probable that the fourteenth-century bridge formed part of a much larger 'co-operative supply network' associated with the use of animal by-products (see Yeomans 2005; Yeomans 2007).

1216, a month before his death. The second reference occurred in 1267, during the aftermath of the Second Barons' War of 1264–67. At this time, Henry III (b. 1207, r. 1216–72):

> 'On his arrival took measures for fortifying the town. He caused a ditch to be made on the south and east sides whereon he erected two gates, and he intended to have built a wall … the town should be cleansed from dirt and filth and kept clean, and that the watercourse should be opened and kept open as of old time it was used, so that filth might run off. That all obstacles that prevented the passage should be removed, and that the great ditch of the town should be cleansed, for doing whereof two of the more lawful burgesses in every street were to be sworn before the mayor and bailiffs'
> (Cooper 1842, 50–1).

As part of this process a 'walk' measuring 8ft (2.4m) wide was created inside the ditch, and compensation paid for houses that were pulled down to construct it. Then, in 1268, 'the King issued a writ … to the bailiffs at Cambridge of £27, which by the King's Command they had paid to divers men of the town for their homes lately pulled down near the King's Ditch' (Cooper 1842, 51). By 1279, the ditch was being encroached on in places (Cooper 1842, 59–60). It was also mentioned in various records of the first half of the thirteenth century as forming a plot boundary. Subsequently, in 1330 there were complaints about the ditch not being scoured (Cooper 1842, 85) and in 1348 there was a commission to decide 'what ought to be the breadth of the ditch, [and] who was bound of right to cleanse it' (Cooper 1842, 99–100).

Late fifteenth–late seventeenth century incorporating specialist information from Rachel Ballantyne, Steve Boreham, Richard Darrah, Andrew Hall, David Hall, Lorrain Higbee, Philip Mills, Quita Mould, Simon Timberlake and Anne de Vareilles

In the late fifteenth century, c. 1480–1500, the character of the King's Ditch changed markedly. It began to be recut much more frequently, at least once per decade; a total of eight recuts were identified in area KD2 within a 50 to 70 year period. These recuts were of a different character to their medieval precursors, being much shallower in form and consisting of numerous interconnected short lengths that were identified by the presence of distinct butt ends; on average, their surviving portions measured 5m+ in length by c. 2.5m+ in width and c. 0.5m+ in depth. Taken together, their size and form imply a segmented pattern of excavation, undertaken perhaps by individual plot holders rather than occurring under the aegis of a centralized authority. The fills were also considerably darker than in earlier periods and contained much more material culture, with substantial quantities of faunal remains, ceramics, leather and metalwork being recovered, plus occasional wooden objects and textiles (Figs. 3.16–3.21). The archaeological evidence is therefore consistent with contemporary historical accounts, such as one of

1502 that mentions the casting of 'dung and other filth and noxious matter and dead animals' into the ditch (Cooper 1842, 258).

Little of the sequence pertaining to Phase 3 had survived in area KD7, the only exception being two very heavily truncated recuts (F.5047, F.5136) with concave sides and rounded bases, which contained fifteenth–sixteenth-century pottery. In area KD2, however, a relatively well preserved stratigraphic sequence was encountered. Here, the earliest recut in the sequence consisted of two short sections (F.1075 and F.1080) with irregular, stepped profiles that were located in the centre of the ditch. These features contained no pottery, although an iron knife with a wooden handle was recovered (Fig. 3.16B). In addition, 48 animal bones were recovered, 34 of which were identified to species; 82 per cent were from sheep, the vast majority of which comprised metapodia from nine individuals (MNI), with 11 from the left-hand side and 14 from the right, all from animals over 1½–2 years of age. This group represents leatherdressers' waste, and is a by-product of treating sheep and goat hides with oil or alum to produce light coloured leather (Yeomans 2007, 99, 112, fig. 8.11). The pollen from this phase (S.1074.1) was dominated by the Cabbage Family (25.8 per cent), plus grass (19.4 per cent), the Cow Parsley Family (9.7 per cent), meadowsweet (*Filipendula*) (6.5 per cent) and cereals (6.5 per cent). Fern spores reached 12.9 per cent and the only trees were birch and privet (*Ligustrum*). Similarly, the pollen from a later fill in the same recut (S.1072.1) was again dominated by Cabbage Family (14.0 per cent) along with grass pollen (14.0 per cent) with cereals (12.3 per cent), cow parsley (Apiaceae) (10.5 per cent), and a range of herbs including thistle, aster, campion, deadnettle, plantain, buttercup and stinging nettle. Trees were dominated by privet with ash and hazel, whilst emergent aquatics reedmace (*Typha*) and bur-reed (*Sparganium*) were both present at low frequencies.

The second recut (F.1079) was heavily truncated but contained some fifteenth-century pottery, including Cambridge-type Sgraffito ware (Fig. 3.16A), and a leather turnshoe ankle boot fastened at the instep with a pair of buckles and straps of c. 1400–50 (Fig. 3.16D). The third recut (F.1081) was also heavily truncated, but had stepped sides and a wide flat base. It contained a small amount of fifteenth-century pottery, a leather sole repair and three pieces of secondary leather waste plus the partial remains of an articulated adult dog skeleton with an estimated shoulder height of c. 0.46m. The skull has a pronounced sagittal crest and is similar to the terrier-type morphology of small–medium-sized dogs from Castle Mall, Norwich (Albarella *et al.* 1997, 44). The main bones of the left pelvis had failed to fuse; this usually occurs at around six months (Silver 1969, 286, tab. a) and the cause of this aberration is uncertain. One possible explanation is that the animal suffered from congenital acetabular dysplasia (*i.e.* congenital dislocation of the hip joint). Also present were a swan humerus and femur. Although swans were amongst the most expensive birds to purchase (Wilson 1973, 118), they were one of the most common wild birds consumed by the medieval upper classes (Albarella & Thomas 2002, 34) and many estates established their own swanneries, such as one at Elm established by the Bishop of Ely in the early fifteenth century (Stone 2006, 157–8). The pollen sample from this phase (S.1072.2) had a low main sum and was dominated by alder (*Alnus*) pollen, with beech, buttercup and fern spores also present.

69

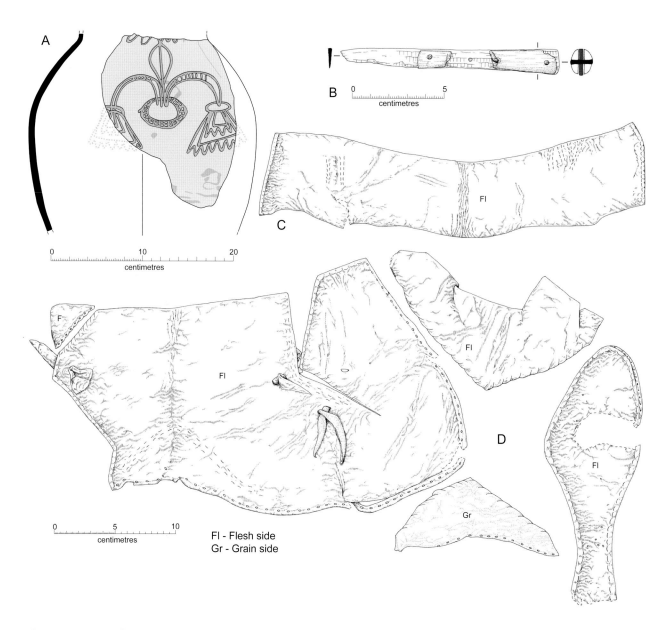

Figure 3.16. *Artefacts recovered from late fifteenth–early sixteenth-century recuts of the King's Ditch, including: (A) Cambridge-type Sgraffito ware jug in a red fabric with white grits and curving, possibly foliate, decoration ([10436] F.1079); (B) wooden handled scale-tanged iron knife ([10480] F.1075); (C) leg cut from a boot ([10491] F.1072); (D) turnshoe ankle boot with double buckle and strap fastening, left foot.*

The fourth recut, which was located on the suburban side of the ditch, consisted of two sections that butt ended against each other (F.1072, F.1077). It had a concave side on its suburban edge and a steeper, more angularly stepped edge on its townward side, with a wide flat base. There was little pottery, although one sherd appears to be sixteenth-century in date. In addition, part of a leather turnshoe and the upper part of a leg cut from a tall adult boot was also recovered (Fig. 3.16C). This dates from *c.* 1490–1550; presumably, the leather from the remainder of the boot leg was salvaged for reuse. Three pollen samples were analysed from this phase. The earliest (S.1070.1) was dominated by grass (46.2 per cent) and aster pollen (38.5 per cent), but its low main sum coupled with the presence of a few resistant taxa suggests that it has been

subjected to post-depositional oxidation and is not representative. The next sample (S.1070.2) was also dominated by grass (42.9 per cent), but contained fern spores (28.5 per cent), plus cereals, sedge, thistle and the Cabbage Family. Trees were represented by alder and hazel. Again, the low number of taxa and high proportion of fern spores suggests a degree of post-depositional modification. The final sample (S.1070.3) fared little better, having a very low main sum and being dominated by grass (30 per cent), with fern spores and the Cabbage Family; alder, beech, and aster were also present.

The fifth recut (F.1076) was heavily truncated, but had angular sides and a V-shaped profile. Similarly, the sixth recut (F.1078) was also heavily truncated, although in contrast to its predecessor it had gently sloping concave sides and a slightly rounded base. The

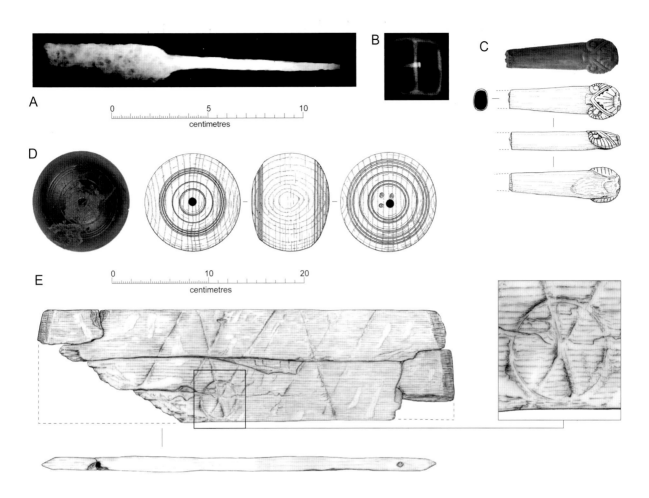

Figure 3.17. *Artefacts recovered from early/mid-sixteenth-century ditch recut F.1073, including: (A) whittle-tanged iron knife ([10435]); (B) square iron buckle with double looped frame and part of the pin still present ([10462]); (C) bone handle, probably from a knife, decorated with an intricate anthropomorphic design ([10438]); (D) wooden bowling ball ([10442]); (E) oak stave with race knife-carved owner's or maker's mark ([10575]).*

small pottery assemblage from this phase spanned the thirteenth–sixteenth centuries, while leather included a piece of secondary waste, a shoe rand and a piece of rolled welt from a welted shoe of no earlier than *c.* 1490–1550. The seventh recut, however (F.1073), was relatively well-preserved. It had partially concave sides on its suburban side and slightly steeper sides on its townward side, along with a relatively flat base that contained a steeper slot for drainage. The fills of this recut appeared to represent repeated episodes of deposition. These may indicate seasonal episodes of inundation and subsequent stagnation, combined with the partial removal of material in order to allow water to flow. A considerable amount of refuse was sporadically dumped over time, including over 6kg of pottery although some of this was residual Roman to medieval material. The stoneware was dominated by material from Raeren (Belgium) with a little from Frechen (Germany), indicating a date of *c.* 1500–50, while pottery from Ely is suggestive of a date of *c.* 1525–50; no clay tobacco pipe fragments were recovered.

Metalwork from this phase included a late fifteenth-century French copper alloy jetton, plus a Late Medieval square iron buckle with double looped frame and part of the pin still present (Fig. 3.17B), a knife blade (Fig. 3.17A), a 19mm-diameter unfired lead musket ball, a worked bone gaming piece or button and a bone handled whittle-tanged iron implement handle. The latter was made from a mammal long bone with a highly polished surface and intricate zoomorphic

decoration (Fig. 3.17C). In addition, a pair of ornately shaped bone scale handles with an all over decoration of parallel incised grooves were recovered. Rarer finds included a complete bowling ball or wood (100mm diameter by 81mm thick) with the standard incised pattern of lines and dots (Fig. 3.17D), a badly compressed woven round-based basket (Fig. 3.18) and a piece of textile.

Also present within the ditch during this phase were a number of timber fragments. These included several oak and ash boards, part of an oak cask head with an owner's mark carved on it with a race knife (Fig. 3.17E) and numerous pieces of ash, willow and hazel roundwood. Some of this material may have simply been discarded, although why it was not used as firewood is unclear, but at least some pieces appear to have been deliberately laid horizontally in order to provide a firm footing in treacherous conditions. One piece of fast grown roundwood was identified as blackthorn or sloe; this is the only identification of this species despite the fact that sloe stones are found throughout the site's occupation. Leather fragments from this phase included parts from at least six fifteenth-century turnshoes, including two ankle boots (Fig. 3.19A) and a shoe. The ankle boots fastened at the instep with either a single or a double buckle and strap, while the fastening straps on both ankle boots lacked looped strap 'keepers' to hold the strap ends in place, suggesting a date of *c.* 1400–50. There were at least four welted shoes (Fig. 3.19B–D). Two of these had broad

0   10   20
centimetres

Figure 3.18. *Early/mid-sixteenth-century woven basket ([10457] F.1073).*

round toes; one was for a young child, the other was a low-sided strap and buckle fastening shoe of adult size. Broad-toed shoe styles were worn *c.* 1490–1550 and one insole has a square toe, a shape most popular *c.* 1520–40 (Swann 1975, 22).

Also present were two latchets and a fastening strap (Fig. 3.19E) from a wooden-soled patten, worn to raise the feet from the mud of the streets. Altogether, these leather shoes span at least 50 years and probably closer to a century. None need postdate *c.* 1550, however, and distinctive styles of the later sixteenth century are absent from this and all the other investigated recuts of the ditch. Additional leather items included a piece cut from a decorated panel of calfskin (Fig. 3.20) and a length of plain strap. Leatherworking waste was also represented by a thick shaving or other unusable area of hide, which comprised primary waste, and a piece of secondary cattle hide waste produced when trimming a pattern piece to size.

Of the faunal assemblage of 909 bones from this recut, 277 were identified to species. Part of an articulated horse carcass was identified, consisting of the vertebrae, ribs, sacrum and pelvic girdle, plus disarticulated hind legs that had been placed across the rib cage. The horse was an adult with an estimated shoulder height of *c.* 13.1 hands that had pathological changes on its lower thoracic and lumbar vertebrae indicative of heavy labour. These changes included severe ankylosis (*i.e.* fusion) of some vertebrae; the changes were more severe on the right-hand side of the vertebrae centra, suggesting that the animal is likely to have been used as part of team (Jaques & Dobney 1996, 5). This animal had been processed for its hide and possibly also its flesh (see Yeomans 2007, 75). A small group of articulated dog bones was also present. The remainder of the faunal material comprised a mixture of industrial waste (34 per cent), domestic waste (27 per cent), butchery waste (21 per cent) and non-food species including dog, horse, cat and corvids (18

per cent). Sheep bones were the most common (36 per cent NISP) followed by cattle (27 per cent) and pig (8 per cent). Elements of industrial waste included a relatively large number of metapodia (63 per cent) and horn cores (37 per cent), mostly derived from sheep (MNI 13 and eight respectively) and accounting for 62 per cent of the sheep bone with 16 metacarpals, 23 metatarsals and 16 horn cores. A similar number of cattle horn cores were also present, although there were only nine metapodia, the majority of which had unfused distal epiphyses and are therefore from immature animals (MNI eight and four respectively). This material represents waste from the processing of sheep and calf hides, and possibly also horn-working; leatherdressers' waste is frequently associated with the partial remains of old horses.

Butchery waste included a significant number of cattle and sheep skull fragments, with several of the cattle skulls showing evidence of pole-axing or demonstrating cut marks on the occipital condyles where the head had been detached. One of the sheep skulls had also been split sagittally and the horn core removed. The domestic food refuse of *c.* 249.1kg (Table 3.4) included a significant quantity of beef joints, plus some mutton, pork, veal, hare/rabbit and domestic poultry. A complete tibiotarsus from an adult peafowl (or peacock) was the only bone of this species to be recovered.

Table 3.4. *Minimum number of butchery units and meat weights from early/mid-sixteenth-century King's Ditch recut F.1073.*

Species/meat	Joint	Total No. bones	MNBU	Estimated meat weight (kg)	Total Estimated meat weight (kg) by meat type
Cattle/beef	Leg	2	1	6.5	190.2
	Thick flank	1	1	9.3	
	Neck & clod	12	8	108	
	?Topside/silverside	1	1	11.5	
	Shin	1	1	4.1	
	Chuck & blade	6	2	39.4	
	Rump	6	1	11.4	
Cattle/veal	Chuck & blade	1	1	4	4
Sheep/mutton	Leg	7	4	13.2	32.3
	Shoulder	19	4	17.2	
	Scrag	4	2	0.6	
	?Chump/loin	1	1	1.3	
Pig (immature)/pork	Leg	6	3	13.8	22.6
	Shoulder/hand	5	2	5.8	
	?Chump/loin	1	1	3	
Hare/rabbit		3	2		
Chicken		8	2		
Goose		3	1		
Duck		5	1		
Pigeon		1	1		
Peafowl		1	1		
Total		**94**	**41**	**249.1**	

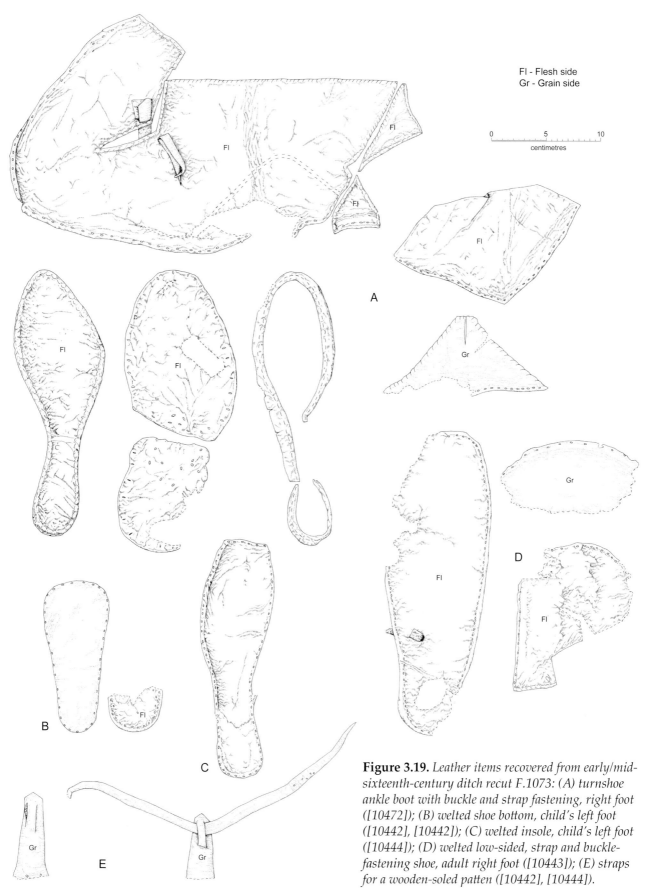

Fl - Flesh side
Gr - Grain side

0   5   10
centimetres

Figure 3.19. *Leather items recovered from early/mid-sixteenth-century ditch recut F.1073: (A) turnshoe ankle boot with buckle and strap fastening, right foot ([10472]); (B) welted shoe bottom, child's left foot ([10442], [10442]); (C) welted insole, child's left foot ([10444]); (D) welted low-sided, strap and buckle-fastening shoe, adult right foot ([10443]); (E) straps for a wooden-soled patten ([10442], [10444]).*

Peacocks were probably introduced into Britain by the Normans (Sykes 2007, 69) and are found on elite sites of this date, although it is only in later periods that they are found in towns (*e.g.* Bramwell 1986). Peacocks would have been kept in parks under controlled and closely managed conditions (Albarella & Thomas 2002, 34; Woolgar 1999, 14); they were expensive birds to purchase and were often elaborately displayed when served at feasts (Pluskowski 2007, 39).

Four environmental samples were analysed from this phase; three from F.1073 and one from F.1072. Celery-leaved buttercup, oraches, goosefoots and stinging nettle continued to occur in abundance. Plants from damp soils that had previously been common had declined, however, whilst others such as hemlock (*Conium maculatum*) had increased. Nevertheless, this does not automatically infer an ecological change as it may reflect a natural

distribution along the ditch's route. Fig and black mustard seeds now appeared more regularly, while strawberry (*Fragaria* sp.) was seen for the first time. Two pollen samples were also analysed (S.1072.3, S1071.1). These contained similar assemblages that were dominated by grass (*c.* 21 per cent), along with cereals, the Cabbage Family and a range of herbs including meadowsweet, aster, cow parsley and sedge. One contained a wide range of tree species with birch, alder, hazel, privet and sea buckthorn, whilst the other had only birch and privet. Insect remains were similar to those from earlier phases of the ditch, with evidence of slow moving or stagnant water, a weedy and grassy area surrounding the feature itself and the dumping of settlement waste including human cess.

The eighth and final recut in area *KD2* (F.1070, F.1071) was again heavily truncated. Its profile consisted of concave sides and

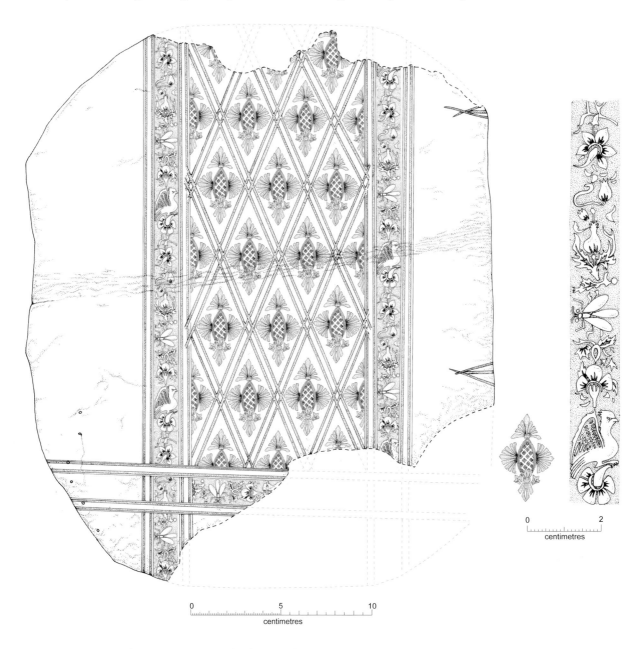

Figure 3.20. *Early/mid-sixteenth-century leather panel bearing elaborate stamped and tooled decoration ([10417] F.1073).*

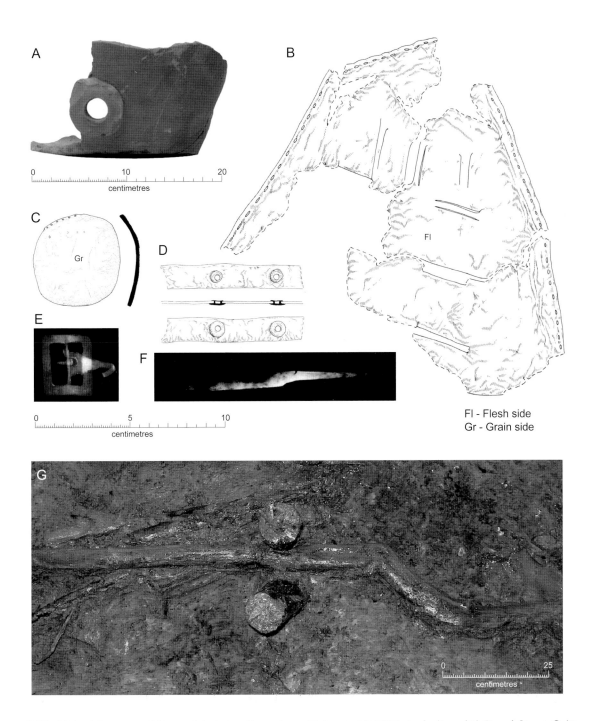

Figure 3.21. *Material recovered from mid-sixteenth-century ditch recut F.1071, including: (A) Broad Street Gritty Red Earthenware bunghole jar or cistern ([10452]); (B) welted vamp with slashed decoration, adult left foot ([10416]); (C) near-circular disc cut from a leather shoe sole ([10569]); (D) plain strap with lead alloy eyelets ([10451]); (E) typologically Late Medieval square iron buckle with double looped frame, pin still present ([10466]); (F) whittle-tanged iron knife ([10542]); (G) photograph of wattle revetment F.1107, facing north.*

a relatively narrow flat base. Associated with this phase was a poorly preserved, partially collapsed wattle fence line or revetment (F.1107; Fig. 3.21G). The upright stakes were composed of willow (2) and elm (1), while two horizontal rods were composed of elder. A small assemblage of fourteenth–sixteenth-century pottery (Fig. 3.21A) and tile was also recovered, while copper alloy finds included a thirteenth–fifteenth-century buckle with plain circular frame, a pierced disc, a lace-tag and a pin with a large spherical head. Iron items included a buckle (Fig. 3.21E), a knife (Fig. 3.21F) and a probable hinge pivot. One of the deposits contained some fallow deer bones and a single mute swan bone. The mute swan was formally assigned royal status in the Act of Swans of 1482, whereby owners of swans were required to mark them with a succession of nicks on the beak, although Fellows of St John's College are legally allowed to eat unmarked mute swans and there are swan traps built into the walls of the college alongside the river. King's College and Trinity College had swan-houses during the sixteenth–seventeenth centuries, and in the seventeenth–eighteenth centuries some colleges employed swanherds and kept swans on their rural estates (Willis & Clark 1886 vol. II, 594–6). Early seventeenth-century records for the London Company of Poulterers suggest that swans were still the most expensive birds to purchase at this time (Wilson 1973, 118).

Parts of several fragmentary welted shoes were also found. Two vamp fragments that were recovered from physically separate fills appear to derive from the same square-throated cattle hide shoe of c. 1490–1550. In addition, a calfskin vamp from a sixteenth-century welted shoe with slashed decoration (Fig. 3.21B), similar to examples from the Mary Rose (Evans & Mould 2005, 89–90), was also identified. It was composed of 2.01mm-thick calfskin, measuring c. 158mm long. There was also a plain strap with lead eyelets (Fig. 3.21D), whilst a neat circular disc that had been cut from a shoe sole was probably intended for use as a pump valve (Fig. 3.21C). A further leather find consisted of a torn sheet of thin bovine leather with a small area of linear tooled decoration, which had been heavily folded before being thrown away. The now delaminated leather may have originated from a purse or possibly a garment. A pollen sample from this final recut (S.1071.2) was dominated by grass (29.7 per cent) and cereals (17.6 per cent) plus a wide range of herb taxa including knapweed, aster and the Cabbage Family, while tree species were restricted to beech, hazel and privet.

Overall, the plant remains recovered from Phase 3 deposits included low amounts of charred material in addition to waterlogged remains. Charred barley and free-threshing wheat grains were identified, along with one unidentifiable chaff fragment, a few fragments of great fen sedge leaves and very infrequent wild seeds. The sporadic, low-density charred remains that occurred during this period are likely to have been greatly displaced in time and/or space from their original location. Within the three earliest, fifteenth-century samples, there were limited indicators of cess (including a small number of a fig, black mustard and corncockle seeds). By way of contrast, the range of wild plant seeds varied markedly during the fifteenth century. The earliest recut lacked any waterlogged remains at all. As the overlying fills remained waterlogged, this indicates that a dry spell occurred during the formation of the deposit. During the late fifteenth century, however, the plant remains were similar to those previously encountered during the thirteenth–fourteenth century, although annuals such as fat-hen (Chenopodium album) and chickweed were much more abundant, suggesting that nearby soils were being disturbed. Wet ground lying beside the ditch was also colonized temporarily by bur-marigolds (Bidens cernua and B. tripartita). At the close of the century, a broadly similar sequence was present, but with a much narrower range of water-associated plants. Pale persicaria and gypsywort disappeared, while golden dock, fool's water-cress and duckweed were also much less numerous. This trend appears to represent a genuine change in habitat, as opposed to differential preservation, because insect remains were still well-represented and a number of other taxa appeared, such as stinking mayweed, common mallow (Malva sylvestris) and shepherd's purse (Capsella bursa-pastoris).

The deposits contained with the various sixteenth-century recuts demonstrated good waterlogged preservation. They contained numerous ingested seeds, for example, suggesting that the King's Ditch was now being used regularly as a latrine. The most frequent food seeds were of fig, followed by black mustard and strawberries. Other probable food remains included blackberries, cabbage/mustard, domesticated plum and wild/cultivated cherry, with corncockle a frequent contaminant of flour. Although the preservation of numerous insect remains reveals that the base of the ditch still retained an element of standing water, aquatic and

semi-aquatic plants were almost entirely absent, with only celery-leaved buttercup abundant in the latest phases. Environmental conditions may have become unfavourable for many species following the increase in refuse disposal. The majority of wild seeds present within the sixteenth-century recuts represent plants of the type of damp, disturbed land that would be typical of ditch banks and closely adjacent areas. Although the results have been examined stratigraphically, there were no clear temporal trends. Stinging nettle, fat-hen, orache, chickweed, elder, hemlock thistles and perennial sow-thistle dominated most samples. The majority of the other, less well-represented plant species were also indicative of damp grassland or ruderal settings, and are consistent with the margins of human settlement. The final surviving recut was not waterlogged, potentially marking the limit of the permanent water-table.

The 2005–6 investigations encountered no in situ deposits that post-dated c. 1550; the upper portion of the sequence had been entirely removed by later truncation, primarily during extensive construction works conducted during the 1970s. Nevertheless, a small number of late sixteenth– seventeenth-century posts and footings that had been cut into the earlier sequence were identified in area KD2. These will be discussed further below. Firstly, however, it is worthwhile examining the results of two earlier investigations that had taken place at the Masonic Hall site. Situated in close proximity to area KD2 (Fig. 3.1), excavations were conducted here in 1914 and 1971. In both instances, these investigations took place prior to the extensive truncation of the area. Consequently, a minimum of 1m of additional overlying deposits were encountered, thereby extending the overall sequence onwards into the seventeenth century (Hughes 1915a, 23). As the 1971 investigation remains unpublished, it is Hughes' work in 1914 that necessarily forms the principal focus of attention.

The ceramics that were recovered in 1914 have been re-examined in order to render their identification consistent with that of the material recovered from Grand Arcade itself. The assemblage consisted primarily of sixteenth/seventeenth-century wares (Table 3.2). No material definitively earlier than c. 1550 was present, whilst the latest frequently occurring fabrics dated to the second half of the seventeenth century. Also present were seven clay tobacco pipe bowls of c. 1660–80 and a 'most curious piece … a fragment of a large vessel in grey coarse ware with a number of stems of tobacco pipes lying side by side in it obliquely to the rim, as if intended to hold it up while being fired' (Hughes 1915a, 24, fig. I). This is in fact a fragment of muffle from a clay tobacco pipe kiln (Cessford 2001b). Three generations of Cambridge pipemakers called Tobias Anthony lived in this area between the 1680s and 1730s (Cessford 2006), and it possible that this artefact was associated with them. An ornately decorated sixteenth-century leather book cover was also recovered (Hughes 1915a, 25, fig. II), which was probably discarded in the seventeenth century. This bore the mark of Garrett Godfrey, a bookseller and binder from the Netherlands who was active in Cambridge from 1502 until his death in 1539. He lived in Great St Mary's Parish and was one of three stationers or printers appointed in 1534 following the issuing of a charter to the University to print books.

Hughes also identified a 'large quantity' of leather, 'chiefly boots and shoes … there is a considerable difference in form and size. Some being small and pointed and others broad and rounded' (Hughes 1915a, 26). Relatively little of this material has survived, but what has been preserved is seventeenth/eighteenth-century in date. In addition, Hughes recorded the presence of a range of other material, including several 'old fashioned' seventeenth-century wine bottles, some 'thrown in' dog skeletons ('most of them of a powerful breed like a mastiff, and one or two of a small breed with a protuberant brow like a King Charles' spaniel only larger') and over 30 horses' heads, only one of which appeared to have been pole-axed (Hughes 1915a, 20–6). The finds from the 1971 excavations could not be located, but a contemporary photograph shows what appears to be small iron glazed cup or similar vessel with applied yellow coloured 'blobs' of decoration that form a flower. Parallels from Cambridge and elsewhere (*e.g.* Hall 1975) suggest that this can be dated to the mid/late seventeenth century.

A further important discovery made during the 1914 excavation comprised:

> 'The point of an oak pile [that] carries us back to the time when the ditch was being encroached upon, or perhaps to the still earlier period when a footbridge was thrown across the watercourse which became the ditch'
> (Hughes 1915a, 26).

A number of roundwood timber posts with multifaceted points were also recovered in 1971, whilst 58 posts of near identical form were present in area *KD2* (F.1103) (Fig. 3.22). The latter measured 50–90mm in diameter and each culminated in a multifaceted point; variations in the way these points had been created indicate that the posts were shaped by several different individuals. They were made from coppiced poles that could be up to 20ft (6m) high and a range of distinct growth patterns were identifiable, suggesting more than one source. The posts primarily consisted of elm (41; 71 per cent) plus willow (12), ash (two), oak (two) and alder (one). The predominance of elm indicates that the ditch and its environs remained a relatively wet environment at this time, as elm is more resistant to decay when permanently wet. Overall, these posts appear to represent several separate phases of activity, with perhaps three discrete rows aligned parallel with the ditch. Due to their size, they are unlikely to have functioned as piles for a structure; instead, they probably formed a sequence of fence lines. The surviving depth of some of the posts suggests that this fence was strongly constructed. Such measures may have been necessitated by the presence of large livestock such as cattle, which were either grazed locally or possibly kept in association with the beast market that was held in the area until 1842.

Also cut into the ditch in area *KD2* from a higher level during the seventeenth century was rectangular brick foundation F.1074 (Fig. 3.22). Aligned parallel to the course of the ditch, this foundation measured in excess of 1.8m long, 0.90m wide and over 0.35m deep; it had vertical sides and an irregular base. Initially, an off-white lime mortar had been poured into the base of the cut in order to create a level surface, on top of which the brick foundation was constructed from red handmade slop moulded bricks – measuring 230mm (9in) long, 110mm (4½in) wide and 75mm (3in) thick – which had been produced on the Isle of Ely. Overall, the foundation was in excess of 2m deep. It almost certainly functioned as a pier supporting a small bridge, making it a

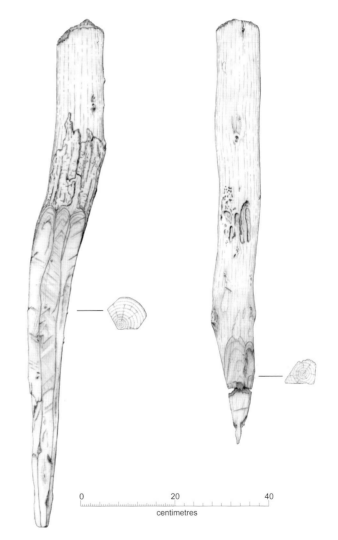

Figure 3.22. *Seventeenth-century brick-built foundation F.1074, facing southwest (top), and late sixteenth–seventeenth-century Elm and oak roundwood posts from area KD2 (bottom).*

77

successor to the previously identified fourteenth-century example (see inset, above). Indeed, by this date it appears that a multiplicity of bridges had been erected across the King's Ditch. Very similar footings have recently been identified *via* a geophysical survey conducted within the both the Master's and Fellow's Gardens at Sidney Sussex College, for example (Ferraby 2011a; Ferraby 2011b), whilst additional examples are known from other historical sources (Atkinson 1899; Atkinson 1907; see also Fig. 3.23).

Finally, located *c.* 3.1m to the northwest of the ditch was heavily truncated, plank-lined square or rectangular shaft SP7 (F.1031). This feature, which measured over 4.5m by 3.8m in extent, was constructed during the mid/late sixteenth century. Although only the bottom 0.65m of the shaft had survived later truncation, it would originally have been in excess of 2m deep. Its sides had been revetted with oak planks that were held in place by oak stakes (40–70mm diameter) with multi-faceted points. This timber lining appears to have formed a temporary 'box', which was then backfilled with stone and brick rubble. The infill included part of a glazed mullion that may have been derived from a fourteenth-century traceried window made of Barnack stone. This deep, rubble-filled shaft would have provided an extremely robust foundation, and its proximity to the King's Ditch implies that it may have comprised an additional pier relating to a further bridge.

Historically, a number of sources survive in relation to Phase 3 of the King's Ditch. In 1423, for example, the town treasurers paid 9s2d to the King's exchequer for a perambulation of its circuit (Cooper 1842, 170), while in 1494 John Keynshawn paid a 12d fine for erecting a footbridge over it (Cooper 1842, 243). During the fifteenth century it was referred to in contemporary documents as both the King's Ditch (*Fossatum Regis*) and the common ditch (*fossatum commune*). Subsequently, in 1502 there were references to sedges in the ditch, privies overhanging it, 'damaging' of the ditch and the casting of

'dung and other filth and noxious matter and dead animals' into it (Cooper 1842, 258). Then, in 1574 it was noted that the ditch:

> 'which in the first instance was set out with very deep and very wide excavations for the circumvallation and defence of the town, now provides fairly well for the cleansing of filth from the streets, and for washing dirt into the River Granta'
>
> (Cooper 1843, 323–4).

In the same year, in response to an outbreak of plague, it was argued that water could be diverted to the ditch 'for the perpetual scouring of the same, which would be a singulare benefit for the healthsomnes of the Universitie and of the Town' (Cooper 1843, 324). In 1610, there was a further agreement to cleanse the ditch (Cooper 1845, 37).

The earliest surviving cartographic sources for Cambridge, which date to the late sixteenth century, depicted the King's Ditch in the vicinity of Grand Arcade as a watercourse with open areas situated to either side of it (see Fig. 4.29). Subsequently, in 1629, a survey of the ditch recorded that in this locality it measured 36in (*c.* 0.9m) wide by 60in (*c.* 1.5m) deep (Atkinson 1907; Fig. 3.23). In addition, a small bridge was recorded at the rear of the Falcon Yard public house, in roughly the same location that the fourteenth-century timber bridge had occupied. Then, during the English Civil War of the 1640s, a rampart and ditch were erected for the defence of the town. The King's Ditch was not incorporated into this earthwork, however, as the newly constructed fortifications enclosed a much larger area (Osborne 1990, 23–4). In 1688, Loggan's map of Cambridge (see Fig. 5.1) depicted the ditch as an open watercourse, with only a few structures situated in its immediate vicinity. No eighteenth-century features or deposits associated with the King's Ditch have

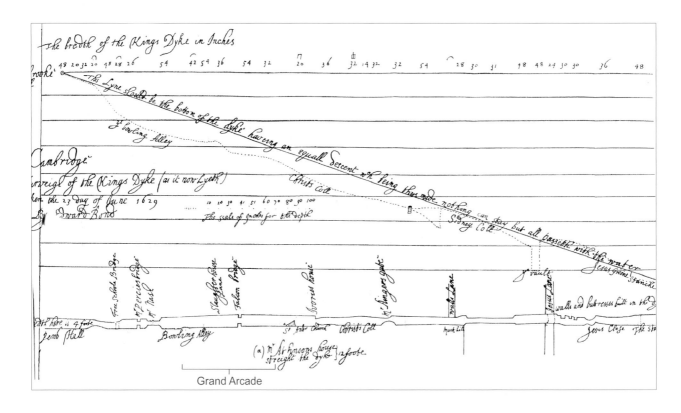

Figure 3.23. *1629 survey of the King's Ditch (reproduced from Atkinson 1907, plate XIV; courtesy of the Cambridge Antiquarian Society).*

been identified during any preceding investigation, although it is appears likely that it continued to exist as a shallow feature into which refuse was dumped. Indeed, despite its marked physical reduction, its alignment continued to be respected by surrounding developments until the late eighteenth century.

Late eighteenth–early twenty-first century
incorporating specialist information from Vicki Herring, Lorrain Higbee, Philip Mills, Quita Mould and Mark Samuel

Following the 1794 Cambridge Improvement Act (34 Geo. III), tenders were invited for 'filling up and bridging over the King's Ditch from Slaughterhouse Lane [Corn Exchange Street] to … Petty Cury'. By 1798 the line of the ditch was marked on William Custance's plan as *Tib Row* and it appears that the ditch was no longer open but had become a street with a number of buildings situated to either side of it (Fig. 3.24). Tibb's Row then gradually developed over the course of the late eighteenth and early nineteenth centuries as a secondary occupation road, or back lane. Along the eastern side of the street, in particular, there developed a series of tail-end plots that fronted on to the laneway (see Fig. 5.38). Within the area of excavation itself, these plots included 1–4 Tibb's Row, plus land to the rear of 20–21 St Andrew's Street along with the Falcon Yard and Vicar's Building. Discrete elements of the plots were discernible archaeologically via a series of shallow wall footings, cellars and drains (Fig. 3.24), although in general the level of preservation was poor. Complementing the archaeological data, however, are several nineteenth-century photographs of extant buildings in this area (Fig. 3.24).

The tail-end plots fulfilled a variety of largely commercial roles, although there was also a small amount of domestic occupation. In general, however, due to the location of the excavated areas only a small portion of each plot could be investigated, and within these portions few features survived to shed light on the nature of the activities that had been undertaken. The archaeological potential of this phase therefore appears rather limited. Nevertheless, a significant exception to this pattern occurred in relation to 4 Tibb's Row. Here, a larger percentage of the total plot was investigated and a number of relatively significant features were encountered. As a result, the historical and archaeological evidence pertaining to this plot will be presented in some detail. This focused case study-based approach has been selected in preference to a more generalized discussion of the poorly preserved and physically isolated features that constitute the remainder of this phases' remains.

During the nineteenth century 4 Tibb's Row, which lay at the rear of 12 St Andrew's Street (Fig. 3.24), was in the possession of Emmanuel College. It first emerged as a distinct entity in 1856 after Robert Sayle sublet the 'garden ground' in this area and then subsequently leased the 'ground in rear'. The plot measured 58ft (17.7m) wide at its frontage on Tibb's Row and was 68ft 7in (20.9m) long. By 1858 it had been occupied by Thomas Thoday and George Clayton, builders and undertakers. In 1860 the plot functioned as a timber yard; it included a number of structures situated along the frontage along with an open yard behind, although access was via 12 St Andrew's Street. Along Tibb's Row there was a warehouse, a house and stables with lofts over, as well as a counting house. Behind these were a number of less substantial lean-to buildings, including a dung pit, two gig houses, some open sheds and a stable yard. At the other end of the yard there was a nail shop. Only the central yard, the open sheds, the counting house and the nail shop were occupied by Thoday and Clayton; the other premises were split between three other tenants. In 1861 Thomas Thoday was living at No. 3 and the business employed 17 men and two boys. The firm undertook building work at Addenbrooke's Hospital in 1864 and were involved in a development at Bateman Street and Norwich Street with Robert Sayle in 1865.

By 1869–71 Clayton had left and the business passed to Francis Thoday and his manager, Thomas Reeve. In 1871 Thoday corresponded with the Vice Chancellor concerning building work, and by 1874 the plot had undergone significant changes. It was now entirely occupied by Thoday and the access from No. 12 had been sealed; entry was now gained via a gateway on Tibb's Row. The former buildings along this street had also been demolished and replaced by a single structure that was split into four parts and used as a stable, cement house, plumber's shop and office. Attached to the rear of this building was an open-sided wood shed and to one side of that there was a dung pit. Lying to the south of the open area was an open-sided timber shed containing a saw pit, while at the eastern end there was another open-sided timber shed with a workshop over. In 1877 Thoday was involved in the construction of King's College chorister's school and he leased a plot in Petty Cury from 1886 to 1890. At some point between 1874 and 1881, however, Thoday left 4 Tibb's Row and the builder's yard was converted into a public house. By 1881 the Carrier's Arms was occupied by brewer and publican Edward N. Marshall; his wife Emma took over in 1891–95.

Archaeologically, the most significant feature to be encountered within this plot comprised *Sawpit 1* (F.5177; Fig. 3.25A). This feature, which was constructed at some time after 1862 and depicted on a plan of 1874, was rectangular in form. Lined with bricks, the sawpit measured 8.7m long, 1.6m wide and over 0.5m deep. As it is unlikely to have originally been over 1m in depth it was most probably associated with the use of a circular saw. In 1874–81 this feature was partially converted into a sewer (Fig. 3.25B–C) before finally being backfilled. Its infill contained at least 76 'items', consisting mainly of pottery vessels (MNI 33) and glass vessels (MNI 30) plus three iron door hinges, a horseshoe, a ceramic door handle, a leather front-lacing adult man's boot of brass riveted construction, a spoon, part of a rubber belt or strap handle, a plastic comb, two pieces of marble, two clay tobacco pipes, occasional brick and tile and 56 bones including several clear examples of particular cuts (Fig. 3.25D–E).

Overall, the pottery assemblage consisted of 147 sherds weighing 5262g (MSW 35.8g) with an EVE of 4.41 (EVE per MNI 0.13). This group was highly fragmentary and pertained to a wide range of functions, with none dominant. There were three Willow pattern vessels and one of Asiatic Pheasant, plus two stoneware bottles stamped JOHN CLIFF & Cº/LAMBETH and …LAMBETH. John Cliff bought a works in Lambeth in 1858 which he occupied until 1869; he also undertook numerous improvements to the manufacturing process that became widely adopted (Blacker 1922, 204–5). The vessel glass assemblage (MNI 30) consisted of 23 utility bottles, three pharmaceutical bottles, three jars and one drinking glass. All of the material originated during the mid/late nineteenth century with the exception of a late eighteenth- or early nineteenth-century Georgian wine glass; this was presumably retained as a valuable item until eventually being broken. Three of the utility bottles, one of which was complete, comprised imported French or Belgian wine bottles of slender cylindrical form in green glass. 15 cylindrical bottles of typical English design, in green brown or 'black' glass, were also present, along with three Hamilton bottles and a Codd bottle. One of the Hamilton bottles was embossed …. ORNE/….[W]ATER/….ORY; this can be linked to J.H. Colborne who was working at 6 Newmarket Road, Cambridge, in 1875.

The clay tobacco pipe assemblage included a stem marked A·CLEEVER/CAMBRIDGE, which was manufactured by Anne Cleaver (active 1858, died 1864). A second stem marked C CROP/LONDON within a box was manufactured by Charles Crop of 36 Great James St, London (active 1856–70s, and under his sons until 1924; Oswald 1975, 133). Charles Crop and Sons were one of the largest late nineteenth-century pipe producers in London, eventually occupying a three-storey factory in the 1880s, and their pipes included high quality examples with ornate bowls

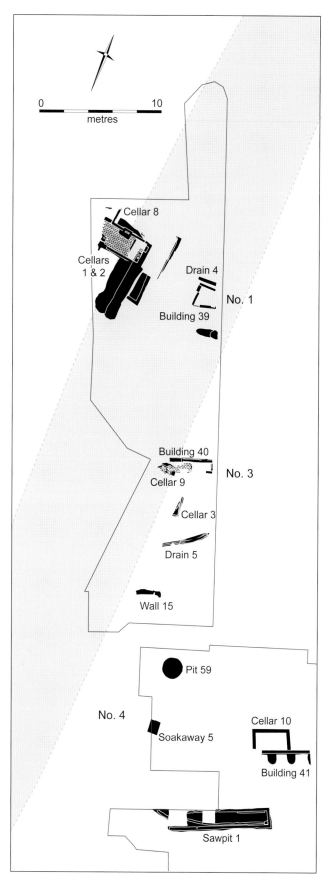

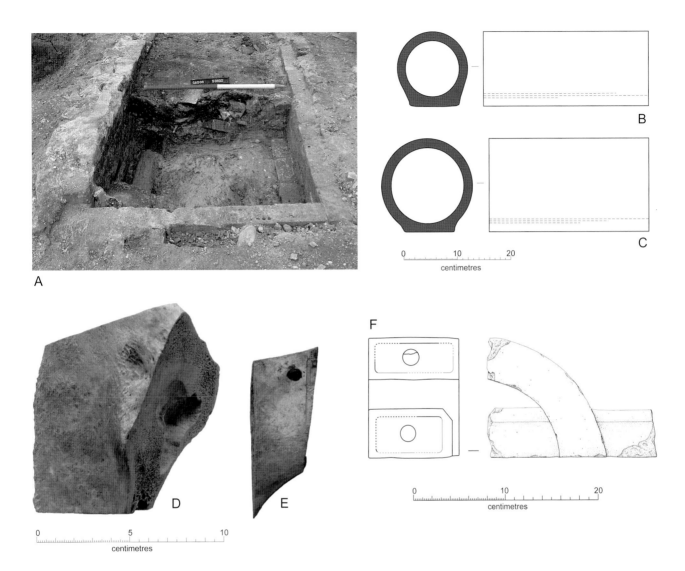

Figure 3.25 *(above). Sawpit 1, created 1858–74, along with material from its backfilling c. 1874–81: (A) photograph of the sawpit, facing west; (B–C) cylindrical ceramic pipes with flattened bases that were manufactured on or near the Isle of Ely ([50823]); (D) sawn cattle pelvis, silverside/topside meat cut ([50830]); (E) probable cattle bone, rump steak cut ([50824]); (F) fragment of architectural brick in a modern machine-made yellow fabric. The piece consists of a main trunk and an arching strut, both of which have circular holes in their ends to allow them to be attached to an adjoining brick. There is also a broken edge where a further strut has snapped off ([50831]) (photographs D–E courtesy of Lorrain Higbee).*

Figure 3.24 *(opposite). Plan of eighteenth–nineteenth-century archaeological features located within tail-end plots fronting onto Tibb's Row, plus photographs of houses on Tibb's Row c. 1880, facing south (upper right) and the Masonic Hall in 1968 just prior to its demolition, facing southeast (bottom right) (photographs courtesy of the Cambridgeshire Collection, Cambridge Central Library).*

(Hammond 2009, 246). The brick and tile assemblage included several interesting pieces, some of which may have been related to Thoday's business. There was a fragment of a white glazed wall tile marked in underglaze blue …N DEPT/[TRI]NITY COLLEGE, CAMBRIDGE, for example. A further fragment, which bore the legend [BR]OSELEY, had been manufactured in Shropshire, while a piece produced in an Isle of Ely fabric comprised a decorative architectural ceramic with a main trunk and an arching strut with hollowed ends (Fig. 3.25F). Also present were two piece of imported marble dated c. 1600–1840 that had been used as veneer.

Following the backfilling of the sawpit and the demolition of many of the structures formerly associated with Thoday's works, a series of buildings associated with the Carrier's Arms public house were constructed. The only archaeological remains that pertained to this phase were the footings of *Building 41* (F.5184), which was

81

identified as a stables, plus associated small brick-lined *Cellar 10* (F.5185); the latter measured 3.1m by 1.65m in extent and over 0.8m deep. Construction deposits associated with these two buildings contained part of a serving dish from Pembroke College. Two further features that may have been associated with either the builder's yard or the Carrier's Arms comprised brick-lined *Soakaway 5* (F.5169), whose backfill contained a George V penny that was minted in 1916, and *Pit 59* (F.5108), a vertically sided circular feature measuring 1.65m in diameter and over 1.6m deep that appears to represent a failed attempt to dig a well.

Part of the Carrier's Arms was taken over by Robert Sayle (Sieveking 2004, 67) and in 1927 it was let to Mr H. Waitling, who became the last proprietor as the public house ceased business in 1929–31. The buildings were then adapted for use by Robert Sayle,

with the result that *Cellar 10* was most probably backfilled *c.* 1929–31. These deposits contained at least 24 'items', including pottery (MNI eight), glass vessels (MNI eight), leather shoes (MNI eight), part of a knitted woollen garment such as a jumper, waistcoat or cardigan, a metal spoon, a long thin rod made from a mammal long bone and 14 additional bones. The pottery was highly fragmentary, but the leather and glass items were more complete. There were four adult leather shoes, for example (Fig. 3.26A–C), three of riveted construction, the other of welted construction. The best preserved was a woman's derby shoe of Adult size 4 (37) that laced up the instep through four pairs of lace holes with brass eyelets, and had a heavily worn, low stacked leather heel 1in (28mm) high. The fragmentary remains of a second front lacing shoe with five lace holes with brass eyelets may also have been derived from a shoe of similar style or possibly

Figure 3.26. *Leather items backfilled into Cellar 10, c. 1929–31 ([50009]): (A–C) shoes; (D) horse-grooming brush; (E) lengths of thick cattle hide strap, probably from a heavy harness.*

a Balmoral boot. One sole of riveted construction had a low, stacked leather heel, again *c.* 1in (30mm) high. The impression made by textile around the upper edge suggested that the shoe upper may have been of textile rather than leather. The only shoe bottom of welted construction was of large size – Adult 8/9 (42/43) – and was hobnailed, indicating it came from a heavy working shoe or boot.

Also present was a shoe with an organic sole and a textile upper, such as an espadrille or rope-soled deck shoe. There were also some leather items associated with horses including a grooming brush (Fig. 3.26D) comprising a pair of oval cattle hide panels 220mm by 113mm in extent, with brass wire that had held the bristles in place and the impression of a 56mm wide strap handle. In addition, three lengths of thick cattle hide strap were identified, one lined and two folded over at opposite ends secured together with a row of five iron nails to give a combined thickness of *c.* 34mm (Fig. 3.26E). These were probably derived from a heavy harness, possibly a trace. The straps measured 38mm (1½in) wide and 4mm thick. Two lengths of narrower, plain strap with buckle pin holes may also come from harnesses and a circular cattle hide washer 75mm in diameter and 4.5mm thick from a piece of machinery. Five of the glass vessels were complete, a bottle embossed DALE comes from the Dale and Co Ltd brewery on Gwydir Street, Cambridge. There was also a POND'S cream jar and a colourless inkwell.

Moving away from 4 Tibb's Row, a series of modern services had been inserted along the line of the King's Ditch itself during the twentieth century. These services, many of which were also encountered in 1971 (Alexander 1972), had severely impacted on the earlier deposits of the King's Ditch. Indeed, as part of the pattern of on-going development in the area, by the latter part of the twentieth century Tibb's Row itself had effectively ceased to exist. During the 1960s several buildings were demolished to make way for a telephone exchange, for example, while others were removed by the Lion Yard development in the early 1970s. As a result, although technically still extant, Tibb's Row now served solely as an access road for the Lion Yard shopping centre and telephone exchange and its route only followed the original line of the King's Ditch for a short stretch. Therefore, whilst it is still possible to follow much of the route of the King's Ditch through Cambridge along extant roads, the Grand Arcade street block represents one of several areas where even this topographic 'ghost' has been exorcized. The final death knell was sounded by the 2005–6 redevelopment itself, for although Tibb's Row still exists it no longer follows the line of the King's Ditch at all.

Discussion

The excavations of the King's Ditch detailed above represent one of the most comprehensive investigations of a British medieval town ditch yet undertaken (see Creighton & Higham 2005; Kenyon 1990, 197–9). This work has revealed that the earliest surviving archaeological evidence for the existence of a ditched boundary at Cambridge dates to around the mid-twelfth century. From then, up until the late fifteenth century, it appears that the ditch was well-maintained and kept relatively free from refuse. Following this date, however, its condition deteriorated rapidly; episodes of maintenance/repair became increasingly less frequent and less effective, whilst the degree of refuse disposal increased concomitantly. By the late eighteenth century, all trace of the ditch as a negative feature had disappeared. Despite this, its subsequent use as a laneway meant that it remained a discernible

topographic presence until the eventual construction of the Grand Arcade shopping centre in 2005–6. As a result, in one form or another, the King's Ditch comprised a significant component of the local landscape for over seven centuries.

In addition to its longevity, the recent investigations also revealed a pronounced pattern of variability between even closely adjacent sections of the ditch. This may in part be attributable to a gradual shift away from communal, town-wide episodes of maintenance during the medieval period towards more localized, individually instituted programmes in post-medieval times. But it also underlines the fact that the ditch shared a direct physical relationship with the rear portions of numerous properties in the town, within which a wide and varied array of activities were undertaken. Marked differences in its depositional sequence, along with the nature of any associated material remains, may thus have occurred over relatively short distances. These variations also serve to highlight the potentially misleading nature of the small sondages that were previously excavated through the King's Ditch; investigations conducted on such a limited scale are likely to have revealed little beyond the conditions prevalent within their immediate locale. This has potential implications for the other small-scale town boundary investigations that have previously been conducted elsewhere.

Due to the generally complex nature of medieval town boundary ditches – which, surviving as open features for several centuries, were frequently subject to repeated and intensive episodes of maintenance and modification – archaeological evidence alone is often insufficient to determine accurately the date of their construction. This is because the possibility that preceding iterations of the feature were entirely truncated prior to the deposition of the earliest extant material remains cannot be entirely precluded. Consequently, additional evidence is required in order to inform a broader, contextualized analysis of their origins. Both topographical and historical sources can be adduced in this regard. Cartographic evidence may also provide valuable information, although it must be borne in mind that for the majority of British towns, historic maps were only compiled from the sixteenth century onwards (the earliest surviving map to depict the King's Ditch, for example, was drawn in 1574).

In relation to the origin of the ditched boundary at Cambridge, topographic evidence is particularly informative. This can be demonstrated very clearly via a consideration of the following hypothesis. If, on the one hand, the King's Ditch comprised a primary element in the lower town's formation – as has been widely assumed – then it is probable that the majority of plot boundaries, both secular and ecclesiastical, were initially constrained *within* its bounds. Conversely, however, if the creation of the ditch post-dated the establishment of the settlement, then it is likely that its imposition instead *truncated* many pre-existing divisions. Accordingly, the relationship between the King's Ditch and the medieval urban parish boundaries – which comprise some of the longest-lived, and most closely dated, topographic elements in the town (Cam 1959, 123–32) – is of particular interest.

When their layouts are compared (Fig. 3.27), a marked discrepancy is immediately apparent. For the most part, the parish boundaries did not respect the line of the ditch. Indeed, of the parishes located within the ditch's circuit, five greatly exceeded its bounds. These included St Clement's (a saint who was widely venerated during the Viking period), St Botolph's (probably founded *c*. 970–1050, as the cult of St Botolph was promoted in East Anglia by Aethelwold, Bishop of Winchester 963–84), St Andrew the Great (pre-1200 on documentary grounds), Holy Trinity (pre-1174 on documentary grounds) and All Saints (1077–93 on documentary grounds). Based on both their physical extents and relative associations, it appears highly likely that in each instance the formation of these parishes predated the construction of the King's Ditch.

This impression is further reinforced by an examination of those areas where the route of the ditch and the limit of the remaining boundaries coincided (Fig. 3.27). Firstly, towards the northern end of its circuit, the town boundary concurrently comprised the western boundary of the Benedictine Priory of St Mary and St Radegund (founded 1133). Whilst this might, at first sight, imply that the ditch respected – and thus post-dated – the priory's establishment, the boundary was only transferred to this position in 1250 when the nuns enclosed a croft that lay between the monastery and the King's Ditch (Gray 1898, 22–3). Primarily, therefore, this conjunction demonstrates the substantial influence that the ditch was subsequently to exert on town's topography. As a wide, deep and relatively impermeable barrier, albeit one that was bridged in places (see inset), the King's Ditch represented a 'fixation line' that typically permitted expansion up to, but not beyond, its bounds (Conzen 1960, 58).

Further to the south, in the area of Grand Arcade itself, it appears likely that a similar pattern of expansion resulted in a second concordance of the parish and town boundaries (Fig. 3.27). This situation may in part have arisen from the awkward, irregular space that resulted from the boundary's marked curvature at this point (see further Chapter 4). A short distance away, however, along the route of present-day Pembroke Street/Downing Street, a different pattern appears to

have predominated. Here, geological evidence indicates that the route of the King's Ditch followed the course of an earlier, potentially natural topographic feature (Fig. 3.2). Indeed, this original association is preserved in the medieval name of this routeway, *Landgrytheslane*, which may mean 'long stream' (Reaney 1943, 47) and almost certainly relates to some form of boundary. As a significant local landmark, one that most probably predated the establishment of occupation in the area, this feature may already have been utilized as a boundary prior to the ditch's insertion.

Overall, therefore, the layout of Cambridge's medieval parish boundaries represents a complex mosaic of differing temporal relationships. In certain places, the reuse of pre-existing topographic features may have resulted in the coincidental alignment of earlier and later boundaries; conversely, at other points along its route the King's Ditch appears to have itself been adopted as a communal boundary due to its inhibition of later development. Predominately, however, the evidence cited above presents a compelling case for the majority of parish boundaries having *predated* the ditch's insertion. Thus, although by no means conclusive, the topographic data is nevertheless strongly suggestive that the King's Ditch originated after *c*. 1000 and probably after *c*. 1050.

What, then, of its historical context? As previously discussed above, the prevailing consensus has been that the King's Ditch originated during the first half of the tenth century as part of the planned layout of a large Late Saxon settlement. Yet the topographic evidence argues against this hypothesis. Moreover, whilst two excavations conducted within the historic core of Cambridge, to the south of the river Cam, have successfully identified settlement activity of early to mid-tenth-century date, this appears to have been limited in both scale and extent (Cessford 2015a, 54–6; Newman 2008c, 74–7); it is certainly not consonant with the establishment of a substantial *burh*. Instead, archaeological evidence indicates that occupation first became widely established in this area during the eleventh century. The resulting settlement appears to have developed in a largely organic, piecemeal fashion, with occupation extending first along the primary arterial routeways before gradually expanding into the riverside, waterfront zones. A key element in

Figure 3.27 *(opposite). The relationship between the King's Ditch and Cambridge's medieval parish boundaries (top), plus the location of the castle and the town's major religious institutions (bottom; also showing recent investigations undertaken in close proximity to the ditch).*

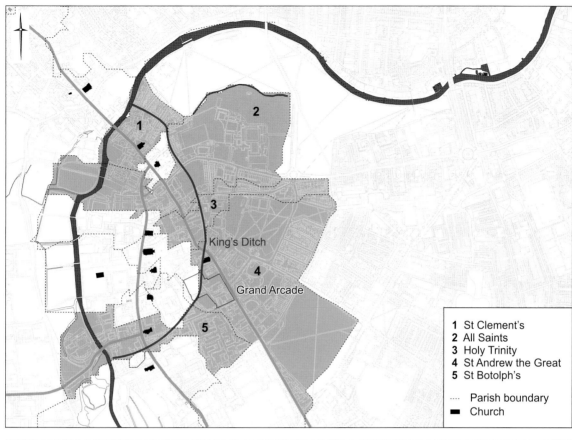

1 St Clement's
2 All Saints
3 Holy Trinity
4 St Andrew the Great
5 St Botolph's

···· Parish boundary
■ Church

King's Ditch

Grand Arcade

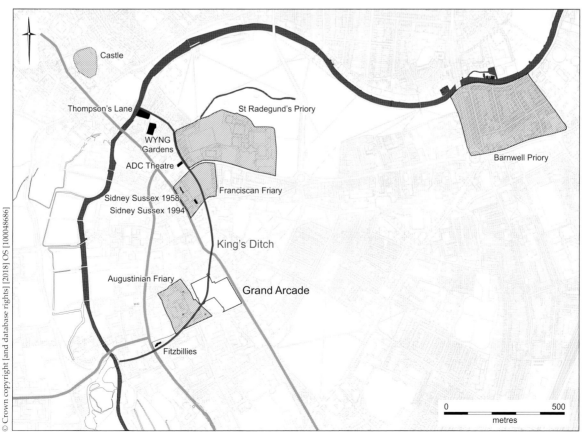

Castle

Thompson's Lane

St Radegund's Priory

WYNG Gardens

ADC Theatre

Franciscan Friary

Sidney Sussex 1958
Sidney Sussex 1994

King's Ditch

Augustinian Friary

Grand Arcade

Fitzbillies

Barnwell Priory

0   500
metres

this process comprised the construction of a series of churches along the medieval High Street, present-day Trumpington Street/King's Parade, during the first half of the eleventh century (Addyman & Biddle 1965, 99; Brooke 1985; Haslam 1984, 21).

Between *c.* 1050 (when the parish boundaries were becoming firmly established) and *c.* 1200 (when radiocarbon dates demonstrate that work upon the ditch had almost certainly been completed, Fig. 3.11D) there are a number of potential historical contexts for the construction of the King's Ditch's. It is important to note, however, that its insertion was not necessarily related to a single, documentarily attested event. Nevertheless, the scale of the undertaking – allied with the level of disruption and destruction it caused – implies that a level of centralized authority and/or widespread consensus was required for its implementation. Firstly, therefore, the ditch's construction may have been associated with the aftermath of the Norman Conquest in 1066. A motte-and-bailey castle is known to have been established at Cambridge in 1068, while the nearby Isle of Ely became the focus of sustained military activity in 1069–72 (Rex 2006). This latter action also affected Cambridge, as did the rebellion of Raulf de Gael, Earl of Norfolk, in 1074 (Cam 1959, 5).

Subsequently, in 1086, Domesday Book recorded that 27 houses were destroyed to make way for the enlargement of the castle (Cam 1959, 4). A comparable, if not greater, degree of destruction would undoubtedly have accompanied the creation of a substantial ditch enclosing the town. No such disruption was recorded in any surviving historical source, however, thereby indicating that the King's Ditch is unlikely to have been constructed during the period 1066–86. Two years later, in 1088, supporters of Robert, Duke of Normandy, destroyed Cambridge 'with fire and sword' (Cam 1959, 4); this provides a further potential context for increased militarization in the town. A rather different event then occurred in the 1120s, when a charter of Henry I (*r.* 1120–31) forbade 'that any boat shall ply at any hithe in Cambridgeshire, save at the hithe of my borough of Cambridge, nor shall any take toll elsewhere, but only there' (Maitland & Bateson 1901, 2–3). In order to be effective, a monopoly such as this would have required the strict definition of the boundaries of the town and may also have resulted in the formal demarcation of its perimeter.

Finally, perhaps the latest possible context for the construction of the King's Ditch is the Anarchy that prevailed during the reign of King Stephen (*r.* 1135–54). The inherent instability of this period provided circumstances in which an undertaking on such a scale might have occurred without being recorded documentarily. In particular, the years 1143–4 saw

significant military activity in and around the Cambridge area. In 1143, for example, the *Gesta Stephani* records that baron Geoffrey De Mandeville:

> 'took and pillaged the town of Cambridge, which was subject to the king, breaking into it when the inhabitants were off their guard, and smashed open the churches by burying axes in the doors, and after plundering their ornaments, and the wealth that the townsmen had laid up in them, set fire to them everywhere'
>
> (Potter 1976, 165).

In addition to sacking Cambridge, De Mandeville also seized the Isle of Ely and captured and fortified Ramsey Abbey. In response, King Stephen ordered the construction of an arc of castles north of Cambridge at Caxton, Swavesey, Rampton, Burwell and Lidgate, forming a chain 10–15km apart located at strategic points (Creighton 2005, 59). Shortly thereafter, however, military activity largely petered out following De Mandeville's death in September 1144.

All of the above events provide a potential context for the construction of a substantial ditch encircling the burgeoning transpontine settlement at Cambridge. With the exception of Henry I's charter, which may have provided an economic impetus for the ditch's insertion, the principal factor that unites each episode is essentially militaristic. Of these, perhaps the most significant, certainly at a wider regional level, was the latest. Unlike earlier episodes – which were primarily restricted either to the north of the Cam, in the case of those pertaining to the castle, or to events in which Cambridge played a relatively peripheral role, in the case of the Earl's Revolt – the threat posed by Geoffrey De Mandeville precipitated a concerted campaign of fortification along the fenland frontier. Moreover, the date of this episode, 1143–4, coincides very closely with the date of the earliest material to have been recovered archaeologically from the ditch's extant basal deposits. Overall, therefore, although certainty is impossible, it is this episode that comprises the most likely context for the King's Ditch's construction. (It is important to note, however, that this does not preclude the possibility that earlier events had prompted the establishment of a less substantial defensive perimeter; any pre-existing earthworks would have been superseded – and thus quite possibly entirely truncated – by the mid-twelfth-century works).

Until recently the Anarchy period has not received the same degree of detailed archaeological investigation to which other comparable historical episodes, such as the mid-seventeenth-century English Civil War, have been subjected (*e.g.* Harrington 2004) although this is changing (Creighton & Wright 2016). Indeed, the primary focus of its study has been restricted to castles, either in relation to the construction of new fortifications or else to siege works associated with pre-existing fortresses (*e.g.* Collard 1988; Everson 1988; Lewis 1989; Spurrell 1995). At a secondary level, the influence of the period has also been discerned in relation to coinage (Mack 1966), the deposition of hoards (Thompson 1956) and sculptural schemes (Hunt 2004). Historically, however, an important element of the Anarchy comprised the predominately urban context within which the majority of its military engagements took place (Matthew 2002, 170). This association coincided with a marked increase in both the overall number and relative size of towns throughout much of Britain, a pattern that escalated rapidly from the late eleventh century onwards. On the one hand, therefore, the assignation of the King's Ditch to this period provides an important addition to the known corpus of Anarchy-related archaeology. On the other, it serves to highlight the urban impact of this prolonged period of internecine conflict.

Two further questions remain with regard to the King's Ditch; they pertain to its form and function. As will be shown, these issues are closely related. At Grand Arcade, it was possible to reconstruct in some detail the changing profile of the town boundary over the course of its 650 year existence (Fig. 3.28). The ditch itself went through several iterations (which have been described in detail above). Up until the late fifteenth century, despite numerous episodes of maintenance and repair, its form remained relatively consistent. Following this date, however, it became gradually shallower and less clearly defined; eventually, it disappeared altogether. Due to the extent of later truncation, the upstanding portion of the circuit is less clearly understood. That an internal earthwork was present is demonstrated by the consistent slumpage of material into the ditch from its townward side. Similarly, the presence of such deposits indicates that little or no berm separated this bank from the ditch edge; a common pattern during the medieval period (Barley 1976b, 69).

In its initial mid-twelfth-century form, the upstanding earthwork appears most likely to have comprised a simple earthen rampart. Its external face was probably revetted, either with turf or timber, although due to the extent of later truncation no definite evidence of its construction technique could be determined. This was by far the most common form of town defence to have been constructed during the twelfth century (Kenyon 1990, 183). Somewhat unusually for a mid-sized prosperous town such as Cambridge, however, the rampart does not appear to have later been surmounted by a masonry wall. During the thirteenth and fourteenth centuries in particular, many earthen defences were upgraded in this manner

(Creighton & Higham 2005, 39–40; Kenyon 1990, 185). The reason for the absence of a wall at Cambridge is not clear. It is certainly notable that in 1267, during the aftermath of the Second Barons' War, one of the measures proposed by Henry III 'to fortify the town' was the construction of just such a wall (Cooper 1842, 51). Yet although various works are known to have been undertaken at this time, there is no evidence to indicate that work upon the wall itself ever commenced (Creighton & Higham 2005, 90; Lobel 1975, 12; RCHM(E) 1959, xliii).

Given what is known of the King's Ditch's shallow-sided, flat-bottomed form, it is unlikely that it would have comprised a particularly effective obstacle to a determined military force. This impression is further underlined by the absence of an associated wall, along with the timber as opposed to masonry construction of the town gates. When taken in combination, this evidence implies that the ditch was not primarily intended to act as a full-scale defensive boundary. Instead, it may well have functioned as a largely psychological deterrent. A significant factor that may have contributed to the limited scale of the town's fortification is its location. Initially, the small Roman settlement at Cambridge occupied a natural promontory situated to the north of the Cam (Alexander & Pullinger 1999; Evans & Ten Harkel 2010). This area comprised the primary focus of occupation until the mid–late tenth century, when the rapid economic growth of the town precipitated its expansion onto the opposing bank of the river.

Following this expansion, the original core of the town was quickly superseded in importance. The natural promontory nevertheless remained an important strategic location. In 1086, the Norman motte-and-bailey castle was established here; its subsequent development eventually resulted in the presence of a relatively substantial castle (Cam 1959, 116–18). The castle was jurisdictionally seperate, being within the royal manor of Chesterton, and although physically located within the town was divorced from the newly emergent urban townscape to the south where the majority of the population resided. This separation would have had a marked impact upon the defensibility of the transpontine portion of the town. Despite the limited military potential of the King's Ditch, however, it was regularly maintained by the town corporation – no doubt at significant cost and inconvenience – until the late fifteenth century. This implies that it may also have played an important secondary role.

In addition to defence, the physical demarcation of a town boundary also provided a significant economic benefit. It allowed control over the access of both goods and people and permitted the exaction of

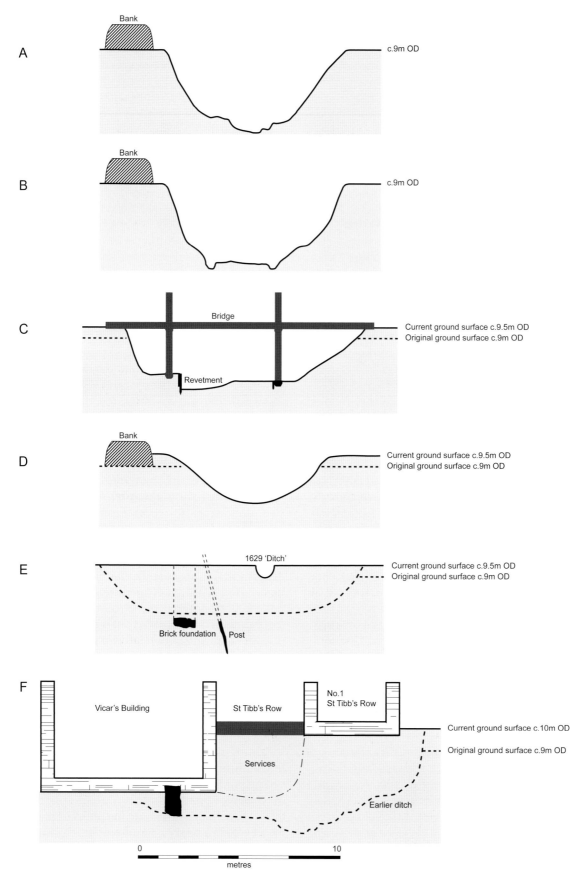

88

a toll. Indeed, instances are known of town gates being utilized almost exclusively for this purpose, without recourse to either a wall or a ditch; as at Banbury (Harvey 1969) and Glasgow (Kellet 1969). As the foremost borough in its county, through which a significant body of trade was conducted, Cambridge was well placed to take advantage of just such an opportunity (Lobel 1975, 5). Therefore, while it most probably originated in response to a particular military threat, it appears likely that the continued maintenance of the King's Ditch throughout the remainder of the medieval period owed more to its economic than its defensive potential.

As well as considering the King's Ditch in direct relation to the town that it enclosed, it is also important to situate this feature within its broader regional and national context. Locally, very few town boundaries have been investigated archaeologically, although a significant exception to this pattern occurred at St Neots, Cambridgeshire. Here, a substantial 8ft (*c.* 2.4m) wide by 7ft (*c.* 2.1m) deep ditch has been excavated (Rudd & Tebbutt 1973). This was V-shaped in form, with a rounded base that appears to have retained a shallow depth of standing water. Associated with the ditch was an internal earthen bank that demonstrated evidence of localized revetment. These defences appear to have originated during the Late Saxon period, when St Neots formed an important regional centre; the ditch eventually went out of use during the thirteenth century.

Moving away from an urban milieu, a further significant local comparator comprises artificial water channels. Several features of this type have recently been excavated in the surrounding area (*e.g.* Cessford *et al.* 2006; Sayer 2009; Spoerry 2007; Spoerry *et al.* 2008). At their most substantial, works in this category involved major alterations to extant river courses. Just such an endeavour was almost certainly undertaken at Cambridge itself, although the precise date and extent of the Cam's canalization requires further investigation. At a less substantial, but nevertheless significant, scale, a series of lodes were also constructed in the area. Dating predominantly to *c.* 800–1200, these man-made watercourses were primarily associated with extensive programmes of hydrological management; a secondary benefit of their construction was the facilitation of

water-borne transportation. In Cambridgeshire, these lodes varied between 3.6km to 5.3km in length and 6.7m to 12.2m in width (Oosthuizen 2000). Although, in many instances, their original depth remains unclear, it is likely to have been in excess of 2m. Consequently, their construction typically involved the extraction of between *c.* 48,000 cubic m and *c.* 130,000 cubic m of material. By way of contrast, the King's Ditch – at around 9m wide, at least 3.2m deep and *c.* 1340m long – constituted a much less substantial enterprise, involving the extraction of only *c.* 22,000 cubic m of material. Yet its construction nevertheless required significant financial investment along with the mobilization of a large labour force.

Nationally, relatively few town ditches have been the focus of concerted archaeological investigation. This dearth is the result of a combination of factors. Firstly, the intensive pattern of nineteenth-century suburbanization and redevelopment that occurred in the majority of British towns substantially altered and/or obscured their pre-existing layout; accordingly, 'town ditches are [now], in most places, inaccessible to the spade' (Barley 1976b, 69). Secondly, the substantial width and depth of many of these features has meant that, even when they have been encountered, it has rarely been possible to excavate a complete section across them. This severely reduces the value of the results that are obtained (see Kenyon 1990, 197–9). Thirdly, pressures of time and expense – allied with logistical and safety issues – have often resulted in the machine-excavation of a large percentage of the deposits, with a commensurate loss of fine-grained stratigraphic information. Finally, the majority of town ditch excavations, especially those conducted on a commercial basis over the past 20 years, remain unpublished. As a consequence of these various factors, the principal focus of study has been restricted to the upstanding portions of medieval town defences. In particular, ramparts and walls have been investigated (*e.g.* Creighton & Higham 2005) whilst their associated ditches have remained relatively neglected.

A summary of the form and dimensions of excavated medieval town ditches from across England and Wales, derived from the most pertinent published accounts, is presented in Table 3.5. In the majority of instances, these excavations resulted in the identification of a relatively simple archaeological sequence consisting of two or three distinct recuts. This contrasts markedly with the complex stratigraphic sequence that was identified within the King's Ditch itself. Whilst it is conceivable that an unusually intensive programme of maintenance and repair was instituted at Cambridge, thereby leading to a commensurate increase in the overall number of archaeological phases, this is very unlikely. Instead, it seems probable that the inherent limitations

Figure 3.28 *(opposite). The changing profile of the King's Ditch over time: (A) as originally constructed in the early/mid-twelfth century; (B) thirteenth–mid-fifteenth-century recuts; (C) fourteenth-century timber bridge (see also Fig. 3.15); (D) mid-fifteenth–mid-sixteenth-century recuts; (E) seventeenth–eighteenth century diminution; (F) nineteenth-century afterlife as St Tibb's Row (see also Fig. 3.24).*

Table 3.5. *Summary of the dimensions and form of published English and Welsh medieval town ditches.*

Site	Width (m)	Depth (m)	Profile	Reference
Abergavenny	6	2.8	V-shaped	Clarke & Bray 2003
Boteler's Castle	7	3		Jones *et al.* 1997, 86–8
Bristol	15.8	4.3+		Hebditch 1968
Bridgwater	4+	3+		Ellis 1985
Bridport	7.4	2.4	U-shaped	Bellamy 2006
Bungay	18	4		Martin *et al.* 1984, 327
Bury St Edmunds	4+	1.2+	Steep sided	West 1971a
Cambridge	9	3.2+	U-shaped profile, flat bottomed	This volume
Chesterfield	-	5	V-shaped	Schofield *et al.* 1981, 22
Chipping Ongar	14	5.5	U-shaped, flat bottomed	Priddy 1982, 136
Christchurch	-	2+	V-shaped	Davies 1983, 53–6
Coventry	10.5	2	Steep sided, flat bottomed	Gooder *et al.* 1964, 102
Devizes	9	5	V-shaped	Haslam 1978
Dunwich	12	4.5	Steep sided, flat bottomed	West 1971b
Farnham	8.3–10.0	2.5–3.0	V-shaped	Poulton 1998; Poulton & Riall 1998; Riall 1998
Flint	16	3	Flat bottomed	Miles 1998, 117–20
Hartlepool	5.2	4		Daniels 1986
Huntingdon, Bar Dyke	5	1	V-shaped, flat bottomed	Mortimer 2006
Leicester	4.9	1.5–3.1	Shallow sided, flat bottomed	Buckley *et al.* 1987, 22, 61
London, Aldersgate, all phases	17.5+	4.0	Shallow sided, flat bottomed	Butler 2001, 54
London, Aldersgate, 13th–14th century	11.24+	1.9+	Shallow sided, flat bottomed	Butler 2001, 54–5
London, Aldersgate, *c.* 1350–1400	8.30+	0.84+	Shallow sided, flat bottomed	Butler 2001, 55
London, Aldersgate, *c.* 1400–1500/50	10.46+	0.50+	Shallow sided, flat bottomed	Butler 2001, 55–7
London, Aldersgate, *c.* 1500	2.40+	0.89+	Steep sided with narrow flat base	Butler 2001, 57
London, Aldersgate, 16th century	10.90+	1.37+	Shallow sided, flat bottomed	Butler 2001, 57
London, Aldersgate, 17th century	5.25+	2.04+	V-shaped	Butler 2001, 57
London, Dukes Place	12–18	-		Maloney & Harding 1979
London, Houndsditch	18–22	1.35+		Maloney & Harding 1979
London, Cripplegate	15	-		Milne & Cohen 2002, 35
Maldon	4	3	Inner face near vertical	Isserlin & Connell 1997
Newark	5.2+	3.4		Barley 1961; Todd 1975
Northampton	4	2		Chapman 1998; Williams 1982
Nottingham	6.2+	3.5	Steep sided, rounded base	Carter, A. 1972
Oxford	18.3	3.35	Flat bottomed	Daniell & Leeds 1939
Pleshey	15	5		Eddy & Petchey 1983, 74–6
Rhuddlan	14	2.75		Quinnell & Blockley 1994, 88–90
Richard's Castle	5.9	3.7		Curnow & Thompson 1969, 117–19
Saffron Walden	3.65–6.2	1.5	U-shaped, flat bottomed	Bassett 1982, 67–70; Ennis 2007
St Neots	2.4	2.1	V-shaped, rounded base	Rudd & Tebbutt 1973
Swavesey	8	2	Shallow flat bottomed with steeply sloping sides	Haigh 1984
Tamworth	5.4	3.75		Rahtz & Meeson 1992
Taunton	10	4		Leach 1984, 72
Tonbridge	12.5	3.7	U-shaped	Streeten 1977
Warwick	6.7–7.6	3.7	U-shaped, steep sided with vertical inner face	Klingelhofer 1978, 89

of many of the other excavations resulted in the generic oversimplification of their respective sequences.

Despite the pronounced variability in size of the town ditches that have previously been investigated, their profiles were generally quite consistent; broad in form, with moderately to gently sloping sides leading to a flat or bowl-shaped base (Table 3.5; see also Barley 1976b, 69). The King's Ditch itself appears to have comprised a relatively typical mid-sized example of this type (Fig. 3.29). The relative significance of these marked variations in size is difficult to determine, however. It is possible that in certain instances the full dimensions of a ditch were not seen and/or recognized during its excavation, resulting in a partial skewing of the data. In addition, variations in the overall size of the town to which the ditch was associated, along with its relationship to any other associated defensive features (such as a rampart, wall or gate), may also have comprised important determinants.

One of the most comparable investigations to that conducted at Grand Arcade, although undertaken on a more limited scale, took place at Aldersgate in London (Butler 2001). Here, succeeding two earlier third–fourth-century and eleventh–twelfth-century ditches was a further boundary that had been established during the thirteenth century. This latter ditch was primarily broad and shallow-sided in form, with a flat base. Prior to its backfilling in the late sixteenth–early seventeenth century the feature was recut at least four times, with its various iterations measuring between 2.4m+ and 11.2m+ in width and 0.5m+ and 1.9m+ in depth (see Table 3.5). Subsequently, in the mid-seventeenth century, the ditch was briefly reinstated as part of London's defences during the English Civil War. Notably, both the stratigraphic sequence and the nature and constitution of the fills within the medieval Aldersgate ditch are closely comparable to the contemporary deposits in the King's Ditch.

There are also close parallels between the assemblages of refuse material that were dumped into both features. Significant groups of ceramic, leather and faunal remains were recovered from the Aldersgate ditch, for example, with the latter including both cats and dogs as well as packhorses (some of which had been disposed of as whole carcasses and some as dismembered joints). In addition, similar assemblages of pollen and bulk environmental remains were also recovered. These parallels are perhaps somewhat unsurprising, given that both ditches effectively contained 'generic' medieval urban assemblages derived from a wide variety of disparate sources. Nevertheless, their similarities are important as they demonstrate that the civic authorities in both Cambridge and London fought the same 'constant battle against … disposing of … rubbish in the ditch' (Butler 2001, 57). A further significant element of the Aldersgate sequence is that it can be directly contrasted with previous excavations of London's ditched boundary that were conducted on a much more hurried, 'rescue' basis (*e.g.* Maloney & Harding 1979). Unlike the detailed stratigraphic sequence that was elucidated at the former site, the results of these earlier investigations were characteristically lacking in nuance and complexity.

In common with the Aldersgate ditch, perhaps the most significant component of the later King's Ditch sequence comprised large assemblages of dumped material; these groups were predominately deposited during the late fifteenth–mid-sixteenth century (although occasional earlier dumps were also noted). Unfortunately, the interpretative potential of these assemblages is somewhat limited. This is because they represent decontextualized agglomerations of material,

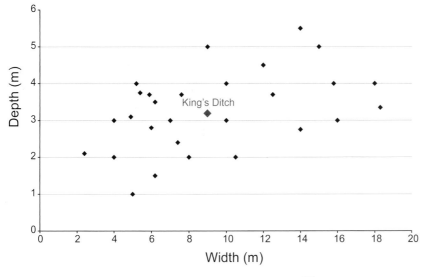

Figure 3.29. *Comparative widths and depths of excavated medieval English and Welsh town ditches (although it should be noted that inconsistencies in recording render these comparisons indicative rather then absolute).*

derived from a multiplicity of sources, which can no longer be linked to individual properties. A similar phenomenon has previously been noted in relation to waterfront sites, where a wide range of intermixed material was often utilized for land reclamation. Whilst such remains provide important dating evidence, and are generally indicative of the types of activities that were being undertaken in the wider vicinity, the material itself often lies within a secondary or even tertiary context, at some remove from its original location.

In conclusion, the recent investigations of the King's Ditch at Grand Arcade have made an important contribution to our understanding not only of Cambridge's town boundary itself, but also its impact upon the wider townscape of the period. Indeed, in this respect it has been suggested that:

> 'The elucidation of the defences of medieval towns, the walls, ditches and gates (with or without adjacent walls) is one of the most significant contributions archaeologists can make to the study of towns'
>
> (Schofield & Vince 2003, 52).

The King's Ditch undoubtedly comprised a major topographical and psychological constituent of the twelfth–eighteenth-century town, yet it was also a liminal zone – distinct from the urban core, but also segregated from the suburbs that lay outside its bounds. Aside from occasional episodes of maintenance, the ditch would rarely have been entered physically, yet its presence nevertheless had a marked impact on the day-to-day activities of many of Cambridge's inhabitants. As is often the case, the documentary sources that pertained to the ditch were primarily concerned with its detrimental impact; the cost of maintaining it, its misuse as a receptacle for refuse and its supposed role in spreading disease. For although town walls often became a source of civic pride – appearing proudly on many seals, for example – it was no doubt difficult to conceptualize a ditch in the same light. Dank and malodorous, such features were neither as imposing nor as appealing as their upstanding counterparts. Rarely, therefore, has the jargon of 'positive' and 'negative' archaeology appeared as apposite as it does in this context.

Chapter 4

The early suburb: mid-twelfth to sixteenth century

Craig Cessford

This chapter and the one that follows cover around 850 years of relatively rapid change in social and cultural history, from the mid-twelfth to early twenty-first century. Probably spanning slightly over 30 generations, it is likely that 10,000–20,000 individuals have lived in the street block for significant periods. Of these, relatively few are known by name from documentary sources and even a significant proportion of these are effectively anonymous, as we know nothing about them. With just over 2000 features, perhaps 200 of which might be deemed significant, many of these people are equally absent in the archaeological remains. Nonetheless a combination of archaeological and documentary evidence can place these individuals within the broad circumstances of their time. Additionally it is a particular strength of the urban archaeological record that aspects of many of these lives are often brought into sharper focus by archaeological traces of specific short lived events, be these the creation of a particularly distinctive archaeological feature or its backfilling with an assemblage of material.

From the mid-twelfth century onwards, following the establishment of the King's Ditch (Chapter 3), the Grand Arcade street block lay within a clearly defined suburb rather than on the urban fringe. In common with many other towns during this period, Cambridge's population continued to grow; concomitantly, over the course of the next 50 to 100 years the intensity of occupation at the site rapidly increased. Superseding the previous early twelfth-century layout of the area (Chapter 2) a series of long-lived properties were now established, many of which appear to have remained relatively unchanged throughout much of the remainder of the medieval period. Accordingly, this chapter presents evidence relating to the activities that occurred within the street block between *c.* 1150 and 1600. Although this period encompasses a number of notable changes, including transitions in the types of material culture that were in use as well as the types of feature that were created, there are a number of unifying factors which render it appropriate to consider the mid-twelfth–sixteenth-century material together, rather than as a series of isolated sub-phases.

Firstly, the degree of stratigraphic resolution that was possible during this period was very limited as little or no vertical strata remained extant. This situation, which is more commonly encountered during rural rather than urban excavations, is primarily attributable to the generation of substantial garden soil deposits across all investigated portions of the site. Similar in formation to 'dark earth', in that it represents an admixture of subsoil and later deposits/features that have been affected by biological and pedological processes (Macphail *et al.* 2003, 353; Verslype & Brulet 2004; see also Carter 2001), due to the homogenizing effect of this garden soil only two stratigraphic horizons were encountered; one that was effectively sealed *beneath* the deposit and a second which *succeeded* its formation. Significantly, all of the features that are discussed in this chapter lay beneath the garden soil. This circumstance had two major impacts on the degree of archaeological survival: first, the majority of stratigraphic relationships had been lost, meaning that artefactual dating and spatial interpretation become the primary tools of analytical analysis; second, ephemeral features – such as surfaces and structural remains, for example – are likely to be significantly under-represented within the surviving corpus.

A second factor that differentiates the archaeology of the mid-twelfth–sixteenth centuries from that of later periods is the variety of evidence that is available. From the seventeenth century onwards, the survival of extensive documentary and cartographic sources renders it possible to distinguish, and thus structure the discussion around, a series of discrete 'plots' whose boundaries can be adduced with a reasonable degree of certainty. Prior to this date, however, the more limited evidence pertaining to the medieval period – which is predominately, although not entirely, archaeological in nature – restricts interpretation to a series of putative 'properties', whose boundaries remain primarily inferential. Whilst it is probable that there is a high degree of correspondence between these medieval properties and the later post-medieval plots, this cannot be determined with certainty. Consequently, it is more appropriate to analyse the remains of the medieval period on a broader, site-wide basis, focusing upon events that occurred within individual properties only where sufficient evidence exists to warrant such analysis.

Despite these limitations, a substantial number of archaeological features and a large quantity of associated artefactual and environmental material pertaining to the medieval occupation of the Grand Arcade street block was encountered. Indeed, so extensive is this body of data that in presenting the material it is necessary to achieve a compromise between a distanced narrative overview – addressing the bigger 'questions that count' – and a more detailed and nuanced picture – focusing upon intimate 'stories that matter' – which can be obtained from certain well-dated individual features (see Hicks 2004). In order to strike a balance between these two equally valid perspectives, the following account includes both general discussions and more detailed, feature-specific case studies. The latter, in particular, represent an attempt to integrate the various categories of evidence and thus provide a level of 'thick description' (Geertz 1973) that complements the more general presentation of the majority of material.

Underpinning this approach is the observation that although archaeological features comprise discrete, bounded entities they also form a spatio-temporal locus, with connections that extend outwards in space as well as both backwards and forwards in time. This is related to the concept of cultural biography (Kopytoff 1986), which has been relatively widely utilized in archaeology although primarily in relation to artefacts (*e.g.* Joy 2009). Whilst artefact biographies can produce interesting results, it is features and assemblages that form the principal focus of investigation here. Although to some extent an inherently subjective choice, the features selected to serve as case studies generally represent typical examples of their type and period. In order to maintain a degree of consistency, a number of wells have been chosen, as this feature-type comprises one of the longest-lived at the site, occurring in all periods from the eleventh to the nineteenth centuries. The remaining case studies focus on the most apposite features that illustrate other facets of contemporary activity.

Structurally, this chapter has been divided into two sections. The first presents the mid-twelfth–sixteenth-century archaeological remains that were encountered, the second the contemporary artefactual and environmental assemblages that were recovered. In addition, the first section has been further sub-divided into three arbitrary chronological phases, each of which contains two case studies (Case Studies 1–6). Further detailed information, pertaining to both detailed feature descriptions and more extensive specialist analyses, can be found within the associated digital-only volume. To maintain coherency, direct cross-referencing between the two mediums has been avoided; nevertheless, it should be noted that the latter resource closely complements the following account and it is recommended that the two be used in conjunction.

This section is divided into three parts. Although essentially arbitrary, these sub-divisions – which comprise the mid–late twelfth century, the thirteenth–fourteenth centuries and the fifteenth–sixteenth centuries – allow the evidence to be presented on a period-by-period basis, thereby assisting in the elucidation of patterns of change over time.

Mid–late twelfth century

Archaeological remains

From the mid-twelfth century onwards, the Grand Arcade street block lay within the newly established Barnwell Gate suburb, close to that entry-point into the town (no record of its original medieval name has survived). Unfortunately, the degree of later truncation, combined with the lack of stratigraphic resolution and fine-grained phasing or dating, precludes a finely nuanced understanding of the mid–late twelfth-century development of the area. Nevertheless, numerous features belonging to this period were identified (Figs. 4.1–4.4) and relatively substantial artefactual and environmental assemblages were recovered. Consequently, several conclusions can be drawn.

Overall, the surviving evidence suggests that the density of occupation in the street block increased relatively rapidly over the course of the mid–late twelfth century, although the somewhat irregular distribution of many contemporary features and the apparent lack of standardized property widths suggest that the constituent properties were not all occupied immediately. Instead, occupation appears to have developed in a more *ad hoc* fashion than during the first half of the century (see Chapter 2), with new properties being incorporated into an increasingly densely inhabited palimpsest. Identifying the boundaries of individual twelfth-century properties is problematic. There are however several strands of evidence that can be employed in this regard (Table 4.1). These criteria can be used to identify 11 probable east-northeast to west-southwest-aligned mid–late twelfth-century boundaries lying to the east of the King's Ditch, all of which ran perpendicular to the Hadstock Way frontage (Fig. 4.2).

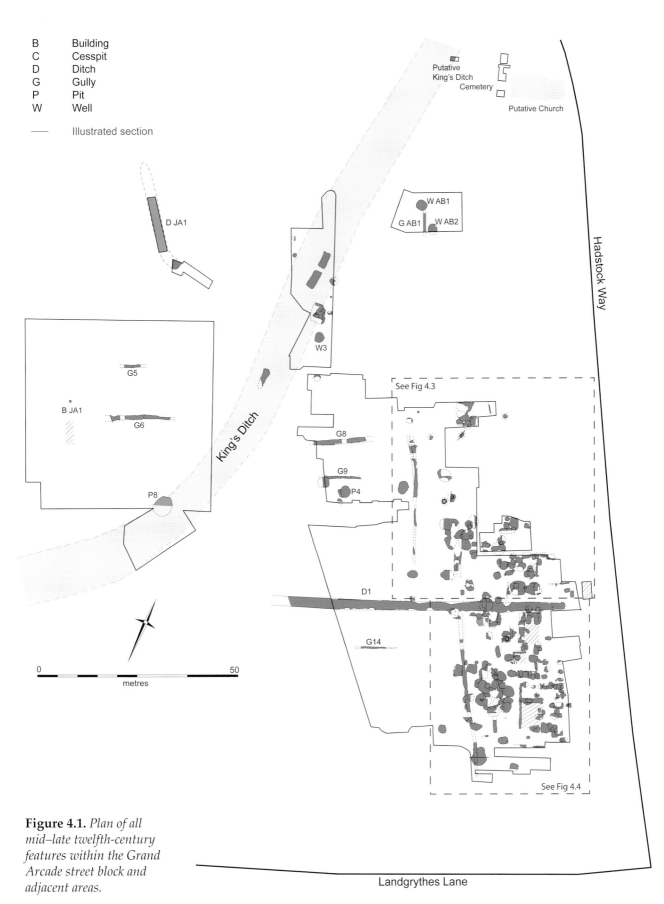

B   Building
C   Cesspit
D   Ditch
G   Gully
P   Pit
W   Well

———   Illustrated section

Putative
King's Ditch

Cemetery

Putative Church

Hadstock Way

D JA1

W AB1

G AB1   W AB2

W3

B JA1

G5

G6

See Fig 4.3

G8

G9

P4

P8

D1

G14

King's Ditch

0   50
          metres

See Fig 4.4

Landgrythes Lane

Figure 4.1. *Plan of all mid–late twelfth-century features within the Grand Arcade street block and adjacent areas.*

95

Figure 4.2. *The layout of putative mid/late twelfth-century property boundaries in relation to contemporary wells.*

A further south-southeast to north-northwest-aligned boundary – *Gully 4*, which like *Ditch 1* was originally established during the early twelfth-century imposed layout of the area – also appears to have remained in use during this period.

Despite the absence of surviving twelfth-century documentary evidence, additional support for this proposed layout can be found in the high degree of correspondence between these putative boundaries and the layout of many later, historically documented plots; of the 11 identified east-northeast to west-southwest aligned boundaries, for example, seven correspond to long-lived plot-divisions that subsequently remained in use for many centuries. Further circumstantial support

can also be found in the distribution of feature-types that were closely associated with the everyday, practical requirements of domestic settlement, such as wells and cesspits. It can be reasonably assumed that the majority of properties would have required both a source of fresh water and a latrine, and the disposition of such features can also be broadly correlated with the proposed plot divisions (Fig. 4.2).

It would thus appear that between 20 and 25 properties were present in the street block by the close of the twelfth century. Assuming a mean household size of 4.5, as was typical for the period (Holt 2000, 83), this implies a population of around 90–110 individuals. As the overall frontage of the street block was

Figure 4.3. *Plan of northeastern part of main excavation area at Grand Arcade in the mid/late twelfth century.*

Table 4.1. *Criteria for the archaeological identification of property boundaries.*

Criteria	Archaeological interpretation
Boundary features	Elements that directly constituted boundaries, such as gullies, ditches, postholes or hedge lines
Substantial features	Large features, such as specialized pits, whose location and alignment respected the boundaries of a putative property
Feature 'zones'	Discrete clusters of features, such as quarry pits, ovens or specialized features, which respected the boundaries of a putative property
Feature 'rows'	Discrete alignments of features, typically pits, which occurred alongside putative boundaries
Areas of absence	Blank 'strips', occurring laterally along a property, created by the avoidance of an upstanding boundary such as a fence or hedge that is not otherwise represented archaeologically

c. 170m long, this suggests a typical property width of *c.* 7m, although it appears that there was in fact a wide degree of variation, with no identifiably 'standard' width. Circumstantial evidence indicates that the area was initially divided into large primary units, perhaps around 10 perches wide (a perch being *c.* 5.8m), which were then divided into smaller properties that were two or three perches wide; these were then in turn divided into individual plots that were often around one perch in width (Rees Jones 2008, 73–4). Variations in the size of the smallest plot units at Grand Arcade appear to have occurred in ¼ perch increments, and there is evidence from elsewhere in Cambridge that 1½ perches (*c.* 8.5m) was a particularly favoured width.

It is known that in Winchester and London a free property market existed before the Norman Conquest, which was typified by the frequent buying, selling and renting of plots (Keene 1996, 95). A similar situation almost certainly prevailed in Cambridge by the twelfth

Figure 4.4. *Plan of southeastern part of main excavation area at Grand Arcade in the mid/late twelfth century.*

century, and – although contemporary documentary evidence has not survived – it seems likely that relatively soon after the large-scale layout of the area (Chapter 2), land ownership at Grand Arcade began to fragment into either small groups of adjacent plots or discrete individual properties. A very similar pattern of occupation occurred almost ubiquitously in urban and suburban contexts across England during the Middle Ages (Slater 1981). Predominately long and narrow, with a short frontage, the individual properties located in boroughs are known as *burgage plots*. Ownership of a burgage plot in a borough conveyed various legal, trading and financial privileges.

Following the Conzenian tradition (Whitehand 2001), burgage plots can be described with reference to a series of discrete spatial sub-units. In a typical plot, for example, 'the *plot head* at the front contains the *plot dominant* or main building, housing the essential part of the land use of the plot, together with its yard. The *plot tail*, generally the larger part in the case of burgages, is occupied by the 'garth' or garden and often accommodates subsidiary buildings or *plot accessories* (Conzen 1960, 31–2). This latter portion of the plot was itself frequently sub-divided into an *innerland* zone, within which a variety of domestic or craft-based activities may have been undertaken, and a *backland* zone that was often reserved primarily for horticultural use (Conzen 1968, 128). At Grand Arcade, due to the presence of retained and/or cellared buildings along the street frontage, the investigations were almost exclusively restricted to the plot tails.

Overall, utilizing a combination of evidence, it appears that around 20 to 25 burgage plots were present in the Grand Arcade street block by the end of the twelfth century. This number was to remain relatively consistent throughout the remainder of the medieval period. Defined primarily by gullies, most of the properties had their own individual well located in the property tail. Many also contained evidence for cesspits and timber buildings, although these feature-types have not survived as well and are almost certainly under-represented. Numerous pits were present, a significant proportion of which appear to have been utilized to quarry gravel. However, as there was an average of only 30–120 gravel quarry pits of eleventh–sixteenth-century date in each property, this equates to the creation of one pit every four to 15 years. Moreover, as it is likely that each feature was only open for a matter of days, or months at the most, they must therefore be regarded as a relatively uncommon phenomenon, despite their

archaeological prominence. Finally, a substantial garden soil deposit also began to accumulate, primarily as the by-product of horticultural activity.

Wells (incorporating specialist information from Richard Darrah)
In the twelfth century, the majority of wells were wattle-lined in form. These features were constructed by digging a relatively large oval or circular construction pit through the overlying deposits and gravel substrate (Fig. 4.5; see also Case Study 1). Such pits typically varied

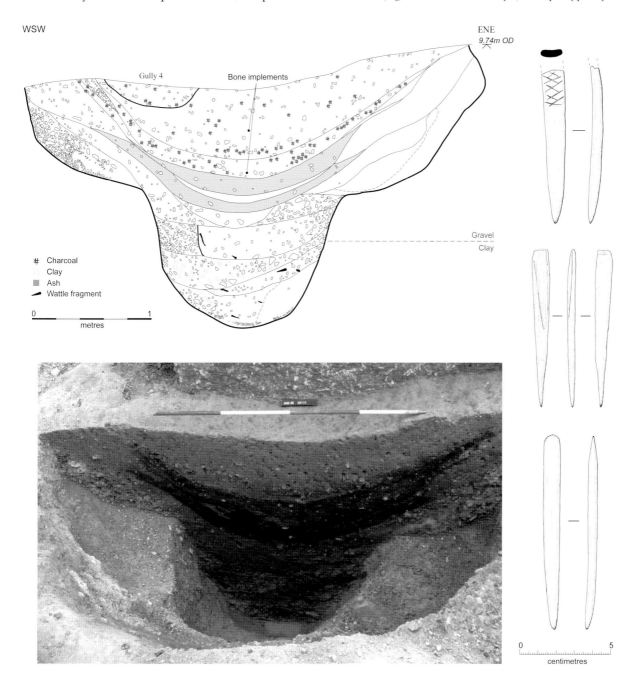

Figure 4.5. *Section and photograph, facing north, of twelfth-century wattle-lined Well 18 and twelfth–thirteenth-century recut of Gully 4; plus, right, three double-ended bone implements recovered from the construction deposits of Well 18 ([31983], [32001]), for location see Fig. 4.4.*

from 1.8–3.55m by 1.5–2.2m in extent and 1.5–2.0m in depth. A small circular shaft, averaging 0.7–1.35m in diameter and 0.5–1.0m in depth, was then dug at the base of the pit, penetrating the underlying clay. Into this shaft a pre-fabricated circular wattle lining was placed, and the outer portion of the upper construction pit backfilled. Willow was the most commonly used type of wood in this process (see Fig. 4.65A); it is still commonly employed in wattle constructions as it is flexible and physically well-suited to the role. Its principal drawback is that when structures are backfilled with soil the branches may take root and grow, although this is not an issue with wells. Ash was also quite commonly employed in wattle linings, whilst hazel – which pollen evidence indicates was growing locally during this period (Chapter 3) – oak and maple were occasionally used. The mixed composition of the wood employed in some of the wells at Grand Arcade (*e.g. Well 13*) suggests that it may have been obtained by theft or on a 'cut-it-yourself' basis, where small amounts of wood were obtained surreptitiously over time (Rackham 1980, 156).

Archaeologically, wells comprise one of the most readily identifiable feature-types at Grand Arcade because their distinctive linings usually survived below the level of the clay. In some instances, however, the dewatering effects of modern foundations or other factors had resulted in the decay of any organic lining. Nevertheless, such features could still be identified as wells on morphological grounds. Overall, wells comprise a particularly significant feature-type because they are unlikely to have been entirely removed by later truncation, often surviving under even the most adverse circumstances (*e.g.* Bruce-Mitford 1939). They also tend to be long-lived features, in many instances remaining in use for several centuries. Finally, they were relatively ubiquitous because they supplied a necessity of life. These factors render them ideal for inter-plot comparison. Several examples – such as *Wells 12, 13* and *15* – had some evidence of an associated timber superstructure, although it is not clear precisely what form this took. As a minimum, all of the wells probably possessed low curbs to prevent refuse entering and prohibit animals or people falling into them. Many are likely to have had more substantial superstructures to facilitate

the raising of buckets using either blocks and tackles or rollers with cranks (Skov 2009, 156–7).

Spatially, the wells were situated within a broadly north–south aligned zone that lay between 18m and 47m from the Hadstock Way frontage, with most located between 24m and 38m from the street (Fig. 4.2). Excluding *Wells 1* and *3*, both of which had gone out of use by the mid-twelfth century, 19 wells were in use during this period. Two of these – *Wells AB1* (F.14) and *AB2* (F.19) – were previously identified in 1959, while 17 – eleventh-century *Well 2*, which continued in use, plus *Wells 4–19* – were encountered during the 2005–6 excavations. It is likely that these features constitute approximately two-thirds of the number that were originally present across the entire street block, implying that there may have been around 30 wells in total. Two of the wells, which were situated in close proximity, were significantly different from the others. The first, *Well 7*, was much deeper than the majority, with a shaft cut *c.* 2.1m into the clay that would have held a significant quantity of water. The lining of the second, in contrast – *Well 6* (Fig. 4.6A–B) – utilized part of a reused cask. Imported wine casks from north-eastern France were widely reused as well-linings throughout north-western Europe at this time (Crone 2005); however, the cask in *Well 6* was probably a Mediterranean import that had been cut down for some other purpose before subsequently being reused in the well.

As wells filled with water that percolated through the surrounding gravels they would have functioned less effectively if placed in close proximity to one another. This suggests that not all the wells were in use contemporaneously and there is good evidence that some went out of use during the twelfth century and were replaced; *Well 7* appears to have been succeeded by *Well 6*, for example, *Well 9* by *Well 8* and *Well 15* by *Well 14*. In other instances there were wells that were situated further apart, but where replacement also seems to have occurred; such as *Well 9*, which is likely to have been replaced by *Well 10* located *c.* 7m away. This evidence suggests that around 20 to 25 wells may have been in existence at any one time in the street block. The most likely scenario is that each property had its own well. In some towns such 'private' wells would have

---

Case study 1: *Well 5* incorporating specialist information from Steve Allen, Richard Darrah and David Hall

Wattle-lined *Well 5*, which was constructed during the twelfth century, is relatively typical of the majority of the wells of the period (Fig. 4.6C–D). Unfortunately, the upper *c.* 1.2–1.5m of this feature had been destroyed in 1973–4 when the basements of the Robert Sayle department store were expanded westwards. Around 3000 sq. ft (*c.* 280 sq. m) of material – primarily consisting of archaeological deposits – was removed as part of this process (Gooch 2004, 149). As a result, only the lowest 0.8m of the well survived, although the feature must have been over 2.0m deep originally. This event also disassociated the well from its original context. It was one of only two features to have survived beneath the basement, in an area that had effectively been transformed into something akin to a plough-truncated rural site.

The construction cut of *Well 5* was sub-circular in form and measured 1.95m in diameter. Its central wattle shaft was 1.35m diameter and would have naturally filled with water to a depth of *c.* 1.8m, thereby holding *c.* 2.4 cubic m. The lining was composed of 16 groups of upright sails, each comprised of one to three pieces of wood; these were predominately ash (24), with some oak (four), hazel (two) and willow (one). The sails varied in diameter between 12–27mm, although most were 12–20mm. Their ages were fairly evenly distributed from three to 12 years, but there were fewer ash samples in the middle of the range when compared to the ends. In total 22 of the pieces were cut in autumn/winter, 15 in spring and nine in summer; there was no correlation between cutting season and wood species.

The rods were also predominately ash (24), plus some willow (11), hazel (four) and oak (one). They formed a cohesive group by both age and size, being 7–17mm diameter with one outlier at 22mm and though they ranged between two and 10 years only six were older than five years. A total of 26 were cut in autumn/winter, 13 in spring and one in summer. Overall, it appears the assemblage was formed from a group of ash rods, averaging 12–13mm in diameter and three to five years old, to which were added willow, hazel and oak rods with the aim of bulking out the quantity available. There was considerable overlap between the distributions of sails and rods, both in age and diameter, and they were probably derived from a single source. The smaller and younger pieces tended to be used for the rods, the larger and older for the sails. These patterns might be expected from a series of clear felled stools cut at slightly different times of the year, which have subsequently been amalgamated.

Well 5 was eventually abandoned in the mid-fourteenth century. Its basal fill, which represents the final silting up of the well during the last phase of its use, contained seven sherds of pottery weighing 582g. These refitted to form the near-complete upper portion of a distinctive fourteenth-century Hedingham ware rounded jug. Produced in Essex, the jug had a twisted rod handle and rows of cartwheel stamps and applied strip decoration (see Fig. 4.58K). No trace of the lower portion of the jug was found. This suggests that it was broken elsewhere and its upper portion thrown into the well in an *ad hoc* manner as it was being backfilled.

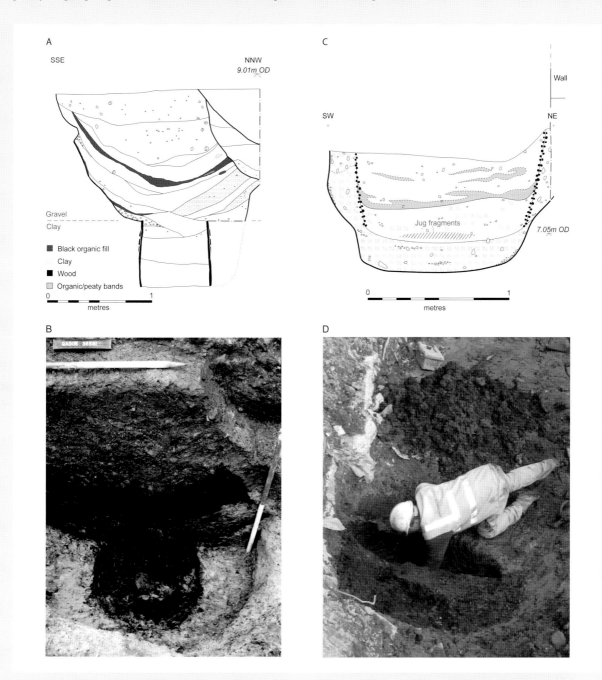

Figure 4.6. *West-facing photograph and section of twelfth-century cask-lined Well 6 (A–B), plus east-facing photograph and section of twelfth-century wattle-lined Well 5 (C–D).*

constituted a luxury and connoted a degree of wealth; however, in Cambridge, where underground water was easily accessed, they appear to have been ubiquitous. The lifespan of the wells at Grand Arcade varied considerably, but it is clear that a significant proportion remained in use for several centuries. This contrasts with broadly similar Bronze Age wells, which probably only had lifespans of a few decades (Masefield *et al.* 2003). This prolonged lifespan raises two specific issues. Firstly, it is likely that the wells would have silted up relatively rapidly and would thus have had to be cleaned out several times a century. Secondly, the condition of the wattlework was often remarkable, indicating that the features were very well-maintained (Masefield *et al.* 2003, 108–9).

Cesspits

Ten twelfth-century cesspits were identified within the Grand Arcade street block. While these were important features (Schofield & Vince 2003, 80, 82–3) it is unlikely that all the original cesspits have survived in a recognizable form, making them less significant than wells in determining contemporary patterns of occupation. In form, cesspits typically comprised carefully dug rectangular flat-bottomed features with vertical or near-vertical sides, averaging 1.35–2.7m long by 1.0–1.7m wide and *c.* 1.0–1.5m deep. They were usually revetted with either wood or wattle, in order to remain open for prolonged periods. Because of their relatively shallow depth, however, these linings have rarely survived, although the impressions that they left indicate that the majority were wattle-lined, with a much smaller number utilizing timber posts and boards. Most cesspits demonstrated evidence of distinctive cess-related green staining within their fills, which had occasionally leached into the surrounding deposits. A sequence consisting of several cess-related deposits was often present, capped by a clay sealing layer.

Some pits that were initially dug as gravel quarries or for other functions appear to have later been used as *de facto* cesspits (*e.g. Pit 13*); such pits have not been classified as cesspits unless there is clear evidence that the feature was specifically modified for this purpose, or that it was employed in this manner for a prolonged period. As with wells, cesspits were predominately situated within a discrete, broadly north–south aligned strip across the site, which in this case lay *c.* 11–35m from the Hadstock Way frontage. In some instances, one cesspit appears to have directly replaced another during the twelfth century, as with *Cesspit 9* succeeding *Cesspit 8*, for example. It is also likely that some, but not all, of the cesspits were originally located within timber privies or 'latrine buildings' (Spoerry *et al.* 2008, 182). The clearest examples of this practice comprised *Cesspit 10*, which lay within a *c.* 7.5m by 4.0m building, and *Cesspit 6*.

By *c.* 1160 some cesspits in London are known to have been shared by adjacent properties (Schofield & Vince, 2003, 82), although there is no evidence for this in Cambridge. The London Assize of Nuisance stipulated that the mouth of a cesspit should be at least 3½ft (*c.* 1.05m) from an adjacent property if it was 'walled in earth', which appears to cover all those without stone linings (Chew & Kellaway 1973). It is likely that similar rules applied in Cambridge.

Buildings

Evidence for a small number of twelfth-century timber buildings was identified. However, the principal buildings were presumably located in the plot heads along the Hadstock Way frontage and have either not survived or could not be investigated; the principal exception to this being *Building 3*, which was only excavated on a very limited scale. The remaining structures comprised secondary, plot accessory buildings situated in the property tails. They were timber-framed in construction and rectangular in form, with their long axes aligned perpendicular to the street. Although generally heavily truncated, making their original size and form difficult to reconstruct, most appear to have been 2.5–7.5m long by 2.0–3.0m wide. This group includes some structures that were directly associated with wells and cesspits; these have not been categorized as separate buildings.

Of the remainder, some of the 'buildings' appear to have been relatively small and flimsy and might more accurately be described as 'structures' but, because the degree of truncation renders such distinctions difficult to resolve, all identified structures have been classified as buildings. All of the buildings were situated within a relatively narrow zone that extended up to *c.* 27m from the frontage.

Archaeologically, the principal evidence for the existence of buildings consisted of linear vertically sided features with relatively flat bases that have been interpreted as beamslots. A number of postholes were also often found in close association with these beamslots. The earliest timber buildings appear to have been constructed from rows of simple earth-fast posts, post-in-trench slots and/or beamslots. Structures utilizing timber frames supported on earth-fast sill beams began to be constructed in the late twelfth century (Walker 1999), stimulated by the re-adoption of sawing as a technique *c.* 1180 which improved the squaring of timber and allowed better-built timber frames (Schofield & Vince 2003, 109). Timber-framed buildings are much shallower and therefore less visible archaeologically than those that utilized earth-fast techniques. Earlier construction methods such as earth-fast posts continued to be employed particularly for ancillary buildings (Meeson & Welch 1993). There were also a considerable number of single postholes, which could represent heavily truncated buildings but might equally well have belonged to fences or isolated posts. As in the eleventh century (Chapter 2), the twelfth-century buildings were relatively short-lived, with a typical lifespan of around 20 to 40 years. There are slight indications that some were rebuilt, although these are not conclusive.

Gullies

Gullies are linear features that can be distinguished from beamslots by their more rounded profiles and much greater length. Most were originally *c.* 0.3–0.4m deep and *c.* 0.3m wide, although typically only the bottom *c.* 0.1–0.2m survived (*e.g. Gully 4*, Fig. 4.5). Most of the gullies had been heavily truncated and therefore appeared discontinuous. It is likely that the majority functioned principally as boundaries between properties, although it is possible that some were also used for drainage. Many property boundaries were probably also delineated by stake and wattle fences (Hall & Hunter-Mann 2002, 807–10) and/or hedges (Bowsher *et al.* 2007, 23), features that have left no discernible traces apart possibly for some pollen evidence for privet (see below). To further complicate matters, how a particular boundary was defined may have varied along its length; boundaries may also have been discontinuous, with no physical demarcation for some stretches (Hall & Hunter-Mann 2002, 807–10). Broadly contemporary gully systems are known locally from a number of sites such as Chesterton (Cessford with Dickens 2004; Newman 2015); where, due to a lower degree of later truncation, they formed a more recognizably coherent system.

A number of the gullies corresponded quite closely to later, more securely identified boundaries. Some of the latter remained in use into the twentieth century, indicating a degree of long-term continuity and stability; examples of this include *Gully 8*, *Gully 9*, *Gully 11*, *Gully 14* and *Gully 17*. Overall, the distribution of gullies suggests that a range of property widths were present – the distance between *Gully 5* and *Gully 6* was 12.3m, for instance, between *Gully 8* and *Gully 9* 7.5m, *Gully 11* and *Ditch 1* 4.9m and *Ditch 1* and *Gully 14* 10.5m – thereby demonstrating a relatively irregular layout. At this time properties were laid out in multiples of perches, a measurement that varied nationally between 16.5ft and 20ft (5.0–6.1m; Crummy 1979). It is uncertain precisely what definition of perch was used in Cambridge, although circumstantial evidence suggests that it was *c.* 5.8m. Whilst some street blocks in central Cambridge appear to have been laid out in a 'top down' system with regular widths of 28ft (8.5m) and lengths of 65ft (19.8m), possibly prior to the Norman Conquest (Baggs in Hall & Brudenell 2003), the evidence from the Grand Arcade street block implies that a more 'bottom up' development took place and suggests that the properties may not all have been occupied immediately. Instead, they may have developed in a more *ad hoc* fashion with later properties being fitted into an increasingly densely occupied palimpsest.

Pits

Pits comprised the most common feature-type during this period. A significant proportion of twelfth-century pits at Grand Arcade were used for quarrying gravel but an even higher number are of unknown function. Gravel quarry pits are distinguished by the fact that they appear to have been open for only a short period, were cut either entirely or largely into undisturbed natural and showed no signs of any other function. They were generally relatively large, but their extent and depth varied considerably. The majority were sub-rectangular, with steep sides that were often vertical or even undercutting. Although pits comprised the most common type of feature they were relatively transient, standing open for no more than a few months before being either naturally or deliberately backfilled. While their presence indicates zones of activity they are in many respects less informative than other types of feature in determining patterns of occupation. A major issue with gravel quarry pits is that once they penetrated to the level of the natural gravel their original excavators appear to have deliberately avoided earlier features. This means that there is frequently no discernible stratigraphic relationship between adjacent features, or the relationship is so slight that it must be regarded as tenuous. Quarry pits were also frequently backfilled with garden soil, with the result that much of the material they contained was residual. These twin issues, of a lack of stratigraphic resolution and residuality, make dating the gravel quarry pits problematic.

During the eleventh–twelfth centuries gravel quarry pits had a relatively widespread distribution, although they were almost

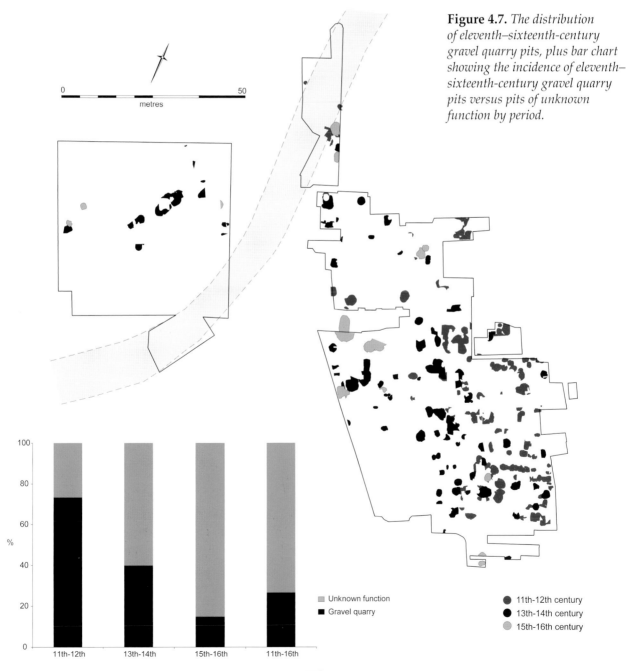

Figure 4.7. *The distribution of eleventh–sixteenth-century gravel quarry pits, plus bar chart showing the incidence of eleventh–sixteenth-century gravel quarry pits versus pits of unknown function by period.*

Case study 2: *Pit 5* incorporating specialist information from Steve Allen, Richard Darrah and David Smith

Gravel quarry *Pit 5* was a relatively typical example of the period. It was sub-circular in form and measured 2.7m by 2.9m in extent and over 1.7m in depth; it had straight, vertical sides and a flat circular base (Fig. 4.8A). The presence of Thetford-type ware, allied with additional stratigraphic evidence, indicates that it was twelfth-century in date. *Pit 5* would have passed largely without notice were it not for its distinctive fill, which contained large pieces of charred wood alongside numerous dark brown flattened oval lumps of fibrous plant material that measured roughly

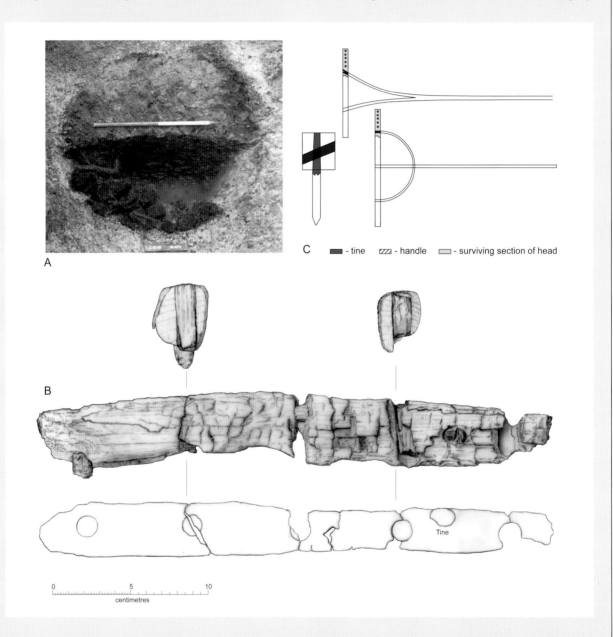

Figure 4.8. *Twelfth-century gravel quarry Pit 5: (A) a photograph of the pit, facing west; (B) the surviving rake head ([35870]); (C) possible reconstructions of the rake head (based upon an original drawing by Richard Darrah).*

0.05–0.08m in diameter and 0.1–0.2m thick. These lumps were initially interpreted as pieces of dried organic animal dung. Upon further examination, the carbonized wood proved to consist of three pieces of elder roundwood and part of the ash head of a hay rake with field maple tines (Fig. 4.8B–C), similar to medieval examples from York (Morris 2000, 2319–20, 2416).

The rake head was incomplete. The surviving remnant measured 300mm long and 40mm wide by 33mm thick; it had five tines whose centres were 65–70mm apart and a single angled hole for a handle. Other known rakes were made from ash and poplar or aspen (Morris 2000, 2319). The head was rectangular in cross section and the maple tines were all set into the 33mm-wide face in tapering round holes. The 13–14mm-diameter tine that was examined had six facets to fit this taper, although it is unclear whether the tapered round wood peg had caused the taper in the head when it was inserted or if the taper had been cut into the head and the peg then shaped to fit it. The handle hole was also 14mm in diameter; it was set in the 40mm-wide tined face at an angle of 120°. The section of the handle was wedged at its outer end. As only a single angled hole survived it was not clear whether this rake had a split handle that joined the head at two places or a handle with a brace where there would have been three holes to attach the handle and its brace to the head (Fig. 4.8C). This rake differs from the York examples as the tines were roundwood rather than being split and square where they were fitted to the head (Morris 2000, 2319). The complete rake cannot have been deposited in *Pit 5* whole, as its handle would not have fitted.

Hay rakes are known archaeologically from the second century onwards, although they were relatively small and split-handled rakes such as this example with a larger head around 0.6m long are only known from the eighth century onwards (Myrdal 1984). The rake from *Pit 5* would have been extremely similar to hay rakes made by traditional methods in Suffolk up to the 1980s (Bagshawe 1956; Tabor 1992), the only difference being the roundwood maple tines rather than round cleft ash tines, showing that the design of East Anglian rakes has remained remarkably unchanged for 700 years. In medieval Britain cutting grass with a scythe to make hay usually occurred in late June and July. The crop was then left to dry in the sun for some time before the rake was used to gather up the strewn hay, which was then thrown onto large piles known as haycocks using a fork. This would probably have been the most likely time of the year for a rake to break, transforming it from functional object to firewood.

Intriguingly, an iron scythe head was also found in nearby twelfth-century *Pit 6* (Fig. 4.9). Whilst this may be entirely coincidental, the close spatial and temporal proximity of two relatively rare and related objects raises the possibility that the deposition of these items was somehow linked. There is an increasing appreciation of 'special deposits' of material made at Anglo-Saxon settlements (Hamerow 2006) including agricultural tools (Thomas *et al.* 2016, 753–5). It is possible that this hay rake and scythe represent the continuity of such practices into the early Post-Conquest period. Hay rakes may have been invented and spread as part of an agricultural 'package' of more intensive stock breeding and rearing of which scythes were also part (Myrdal 1984), so the two items may well have been symbolically linked.

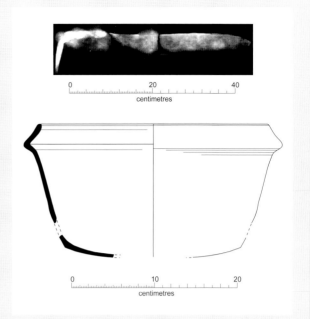

Figure 4.9. *Objects from twelfth-century Pit 6; x-ray of iron scythe head ([35886]) and St Neots-type ware rounded bowl with inturned rim ([35885]).*

The insect remains recovered from the oval lumps of fibrous plant material included a large proportion of 'house fauna' such as the usual range of cryptophagids and lathridiids, the 'spider beetles' *Ptinus fur* and *Ptinus unicolor* and a range of 'woodworms'. The latter include the 'furniture beetle' *Anobium puctatum*, the 'powder post beetle' *Lyctus linearis* and the 'fan bearing wood borer' *Ptilnus pectinicornis*. The wide range of staphylinid 'rove beetles', such as the *Omalium* and *Oxytelus* species, suggest the presence of rotting settlement waste, as does the Anthicidae *Anthicus floralis*. Human cess also appears to be present, since pupae of the *Sepsis* fly were recovered. Also identified were a small number of individuals of two species of 'granary pest' beetles. These are the 'saw-toothed grain beetle' *Oryzaephilus surinamensis* and 'the granary weevil' *Sitophilus granaries*, both associated with decayed grain. These species might indicate that small amounts of spoilt grain may have entered these pits either directly as waste or as part of human cess (*sensu* Osborne 1983).

Many of the insects present are not from settlement waste, but appear to derive instead from the environment surrounding the pit. This includes relatively large numbers of 'dung beetles' including *Onthophagus coenobita, Aphodius contaminatus, A. foetens* and *A, ater*, all associated with animal dung left out in the open (Jessop 1986). This is also the environment favoured by the Hydrophilidae *Sphaeridium lunatum* and the Staphylinidae *Platystethus arenarius* (Hansen 1986; Tottenham 1954). Similarly, many of the species of Carabidae 'ground beetles' recovered, such as *Harpalus aeneus, Pterostichus melanarius, Agonum dorsale,* and the *Calathus* and *Amara* species, are associated with open and grassy areas often in and around settlement (Lindroth 1974). The phytophages recovered from these two pits also indicate the existence of a similar environment. The presence of stinging nettle (*Urtica dioica*) is indicated by the Nitidulidae *Brachypterus urticae* and the weevils *Apion urticarium*, *Ceutorhynchus pollinarius* and *Cidnorhinus quadrimaculatus* (Koch 1992). Shepherd's purse (*Capsella bursa-pastoris*) is also a plant found in such weedy areas and is the food plant of the weevil *Cuetorhynchus erysimi*. Equally, *Apion craccae* and *A. pomonae* are associated with various species of vetches (*Vicia* spp.) and *Sitona flavescens* with clover (*Trifolium* spp.) (Koch 1992).

The 'soldier beetles' *Cantharus rufa* and *Malachius bipustulatus* are also common in rough grassland. Lastly, the 'leaf beetle' *Gastroidea viridula* is associated with dock (*Rumex* spp.). It is probable that most of these species are derived from the area within a few hundred metres of the pit and indicate the environment present. Another alternative is that they may have come into the deposit in hay and field grasses perhaps used as fodder (Kenward & Hall 1997). In addition, there are indications that the pit may have been periodically flooded. This is suggested by the numbers of water beetles recovered, including the 'diving beetle' *Hygrotus inaequalis*, the

hydraenids *Octhebius minimus*, *Hydraena* spp. and *Limnebius* spp. and the hydrophilids *Cercyon ustulatus* and *Coelostoma orbiculare*. All of these species are associated with very slow flowing or stagnant waters such as ditches and weedy ponds (Hansen 1986; Nilsson & Holmen 1995). Also recovered was an individual of the 'whirlygig' beetle *Gyrinus* spp. Flooding of these deposits is also probably indicated by the numbers of *Tanysphyrus lemnae* recovered, since this species feeds only on duck weeds (*Lemna* spp), and by the 'leaf beetle' *Macroplea*, which occurs on *Potamogeton* pondweeds and water milfoils (*Myriophyllum* spp.).

Gravel quarry *Pit 5* was probably only open for a few weeks at most and is distinguished from the hundreds of similar pits at the site only by the presence of what appear to be the partially burnt remnants of a small fire of animal dung and wood including a broken rake. The insects contained in this feature present a picture of the environment within a few hundred metres of the pit, providing a spatial link outwards, while the rake head acts as a temporal link forwards in time to local craft traditions that survived almost until the present day.

Table 4.2. *Gravel quarry pits and pits of unknown function by period.*

Century	Gravel quarry no.	Gravel quarry %	Unknown function no.	Unknown function %
11th–12th	163	46.4	59	11.4
13th–14th	113	32.2	169	32.8
15th–16th	28	8.0	159	20.8
Unphased 11th–16th	47	13.4	129	35.0
Total	351		516	

all located less than 40m from the street frontage (Fig. 4.7). At least six relatively distinct clusters of gravel quarry pits were present, consisting of around five to 15 pits apiece. This pattern indicates that each individual property may have had a favoured locale from which to obtain gravel. There was also a single distinct row of nine, *Pits 3*, which had numerous post and stake holes beside it, suggesting that there was a fenced property boundary with pitting to one side. It appears that the pits in this row were initially dug from east to west with gaps between them; these spaces were then quarried in turn from east to west by a second, succeeding row of features. As well as the pits themselves a number of thin 'blank' areas were present where pit digging does not appear to have occurred. These areas of absence may indicate the location of boundaries or other above ground features that were actively avoided (Schofield & Vince 2003, 80).

If the gravel quarry pits are considered in 200-year blocks then it is clear that they gradually declined over time (Table 4.2; Fig. 4.7). This pattern is further reinforced by the observation that the majority of the examples that could not be closely dated were probably early. Each pit would have produced approximately 2.0 cu. m of gravel. The temporal pattern for pits of unknown function is different to that of gravel quarry pits as they do not appear to have declined over time; in this instance, it is also less likely that the majority of the examples that could not be closely dated are early. One notable absence, with the single exception of *Pit 8*, is that no clay quarry pits were identified that predated the fourteenth century. Even after this date digging for clay remained a rare activity, suggesting that the main source of this material was the nearby fields.

Garden soil

During the twelfth century a rich homogenous dark brown to black sandy silt deposit – colloquially referred to as 'garden soil' – began to accumulate over the entire investigated area. This deposit became ubiquitous by the thirteenth century and the process of its formation continued until the late sixteenth/early seventeenth century. In places, it measured up to 1.1m thick. The garden soil has had two profound archaeological impacts. Firstly, it reduces the stratigraphic resolution by either removing or significantly decreasing the certainty of many stratigraphic relationships. Secondly, it effectively removes the contemporary ground level as a discrete surface, which is particularly important since people 'lived and undertook their daily tasks on surfaces, not down pits and postholes' (Drewett 1999, 98). These two effects mean that while 'sequence is all' in urban archaeology (Reece 1984) suburban sites dominated by garden soil are in some respects more akin to relatively dense rural sites, where artifactual dating and spatial logic are more significant analytically than the stratigraphic sequence. Despite this the garden soil does serve as an apposite reminder that until the nineteenth century over 90 per cent of the street block consisted of open areas used for horticultural cultivation, the keeping of animals, the storing of material such as wood and timber, middens and other activities that have left no trace as discrete features but whose presence can reasonably be inferred from artefactual and environmental evidence.

Thirteenth–fourteenth centuries

In general, the thirteenth–fourteenth centuries represent a continuation of the preceding mid–late twelfth-century pattern of occupation within the Grand Arcade street block. The two periods are considered separately, however, in order to provide a more finely nuanced chronological analysis of the archaeological sequence. This approach is greatly facilitated by the fact that the dominant ceramic fabrics in use at the site altered around the beginning of the thirteenth century, thereby allowing the later developments to be clearly distinguished. During this period the King's Ditch remained in use and was well maintained (Chapter

3); it thus comprises a significant 'off-stage presence' throughout the following discussion.

Across Cambridge more generally, the thirteenth–fourteenth centuries saw an increase in the number of religious institutions in the town. New foundations included the Hospital of St John the Evangelist (c. 1195) as well as monastic communities of Dominicans (c. 1221–38; see further Chapter 6), Franciscans (c. 1238), Friars of the Sack (1258), Augustinians (1277–89), Carmelites (1290) and Gilbertines (1291). Perhaps even more significantly, this period also encompassed the establishment – and early growth – of Cambridge's University. Although founded c. 1208–10 and with evidence of academic activities from the 1220s onwards (Zutshi 2012), the true rise of this institution began with the establishment of the first colleges – Peterhouse (1284) and King's Hall (1317) – and the granting to Cambridge the status of a *studium generale* by Pope John XXII in 1318 (Zutshi 2011). Following this, a number of additional colleges were founded in relatively rapid succession. These included Michaelhouse (1324), University Hall/Clare Hall (1326), Gonville Hall (1348), Pembroke (1347), Trinity Hall (1350) and Corpus Christi (1352).

The last of these establishments were effectively accompanied in 1348–9 by the Great Mortality, or Black Death, during which the town lost around a third of its population. Subsequently, in 1381, Cambridge was rocked by the Great Uprising, or Peasants' Revolt, which – although short-lived – united the richest burgesses and poorest commoners in a series of violent clashes between 'town' and 'gown' (Dunn 2004, 157–9). These events were then followed by a fire in 1385 and an outbreak of plague in 1389, the cumulative impact of which may well have caused many inhabitants to flee the town (Maitland & Bateson 1901, 35).

Although both documentary and archaeological evidence survives from this period, a number of difficulties are inherent in definitively reconciling these two sources. As a result, the street block is considered first as a series of documented *plots*, and then separately as a number of distinct archaeological *properties*. In each instance, additional detailed information can be found within the associated digital volume.

The documented plots Rosemary Horrox with Craig Cessford

From the thirteenth, and more particularly fourteenth, century onwards there are an increasing number of surviving documentary sources relating to individual plots at the site. These are preserved in the archives of the various 'perpetual institutions' (Keene 1996, 103) that were, or later became, part of the University of Cambridge. Nevertheless, the documentary

evidence presents only a partial view of the street block, with large areas of *terra incognito*; ironically, many of the best-documented plots are those that were the least investigated archaeologically. The earliest leases indicate that by the thirteenth century there was already a long-established system of land ownership in the suburb, which had gone through a significant number of modifications since its inception. In general, the plots were leased to, or owned by, relatively wealthy members of the burgess class, including several mayors. In many cases, however, these individuals sublet their plots and the actual occupants are therefore unknown.

Within the documents, the plots are most frequently described as *tenements*, from the Latin tenē(re) 'to hold'; this can simply mean land or real property which is held of another by any tenure, but most commonly refers to a dwelling house. The term *messuage*, from the Old French *mesnage* 'a domestic establishment or household', is also used; this denotes a dwelling house plus outbuildings and adjacent land assigned to its use. In addition, there are also occasional references to *gardens* and *land*, terms that denote areas without buildings (which, in the case of gardens, were enclosed). The only detailed description relates to the leasing of Plot IX to John Berlee in 1369 (see Case Study 4).

By the fourteenth century at least nine plots in the street block were in religious or collegiate ownership. Major absentee landowners included the Priory of St Mary and St Radegund (three plots) and Corpus Christi College (two plots); single plots were also owned by Barnwell Priory, the Hospital of St John the Evangelist, Clare Hall and the Premonstratensians. This accounts for between one-third and one-half of the total street block, with the bulk of the remaining area apparently residing in private ownership. Whilst the majority of the latter owners and lessees lived in Cambridge, plots were also in the possession of individuals from nearby villages such as Fulbourn, Horningsea, Hildersham and Toft, plus more distant locations such as Baldock and Barley in Hertfordshire, Walpole in Norfolk and Southwark near London (see Fig. 7.14A). Where recorded, the trades of the suburb's occupants – as distinct from those of the owners and lessees – included butcher, carter, draper, tailor and bladesmith.

Archaeological remains

In many respects, the archaeological evidence for thirteenth–fourteenth-century occupation in the street block is similar to that of the mid–late twelfth century; the number and distribution of features remained relatively consistent (Fig. 4.10). Over the course of the period the

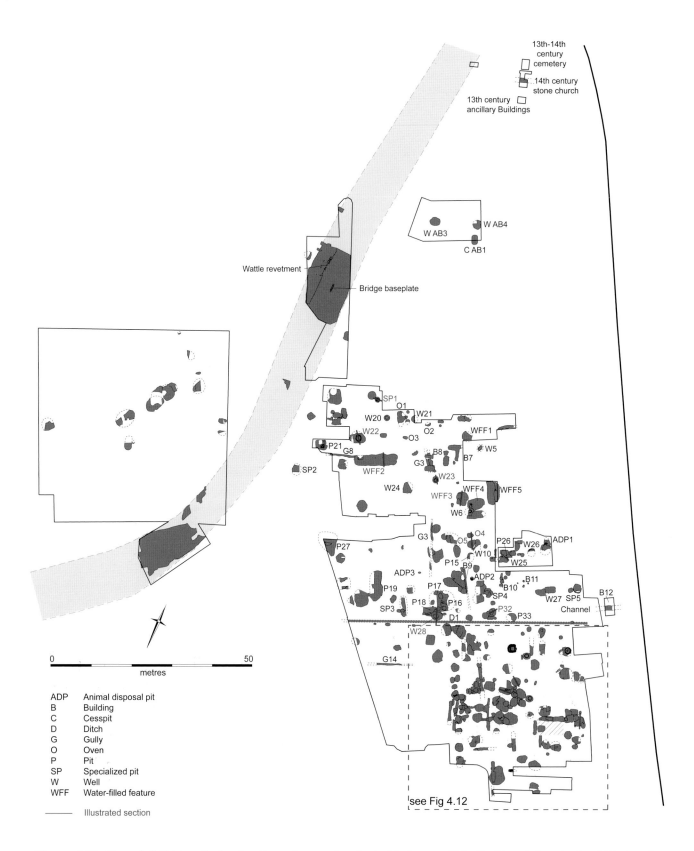

Figure 4.10. *Plan of all thirteenth–fourteenth-century archaeological features within the Grand Arcade street block and adjacent areas.*

108

Figure 4.11. *The layout of putative thirteenth–fourteenth-century property boundaries in relation to contemporary wells, plus the locations of documented plots and buildings from lease descriptions.*

number of properties also appears to have remained relatively stable. Indeed, in several instances the plots may have continued to expand, principally to the rear, albeit at a much slower rate than had occurred during the preceding period. Such a pattern is at odds with the general national trend, however, as the suburbs of many English towns are known to have contracted during the thirteenth century (Keene 1976, 78–9). Nevertheless, the presence of continued occupation at the site within a series of narrow, tenement-style properties fronting onto the Hadstock Way is clearly demonstrated by

the distribution of the thirteenth–fourteenth-century wells, which broadly correspond to the pattern of their mid–late twelfth-century predecessors. This indicates that each property continued to maintain its own individual well, located in the property tail, while the overall pattern of well replacement strongly suggests that the layout of these properties remained relatively stable over time (Fig. 4.11).

Despite this level of stability, however, a number of changes did occur during this period. Archaeologically, this is most clearly demonstrated by the appearance of

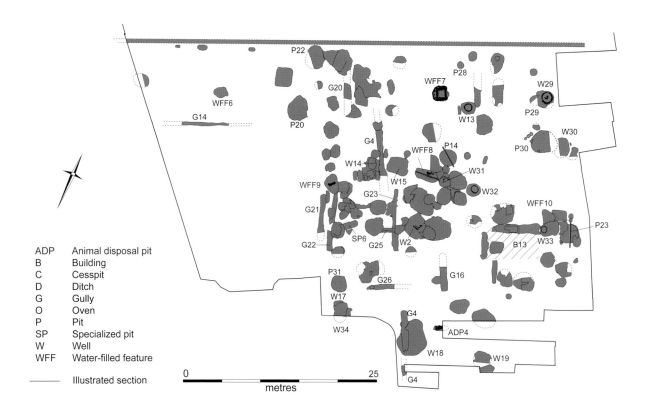

Figure 4.12. *Plan of southeastern area of main excavation area at Grand Arcade in the thirteenth–fourteenth century.*

a range of new feature-types, the most immediately visible of which were deep water-filled features. As with wells, the depths of these latter features are likely to have ensured that the majority of those that were originally created have survived to be identified. Given their relatively low overall number, therefore – especially when combined with their varied nature, scattered distribution and often quite prolonged lifespan – they do not appear to represent either a widespread pattern of land use or the residues of long-term intensive professional activity. Rather, they suggest that at various points over a period of centuries particular properties were occupied for a few decades by individuals who undertook certain specialized activities. The same is also true of the more general category of 'specialized pits', as well as the ovens that first appeared somewhat later during the fourteenth century.

In the case of both of these latter feature-types, however, the difficulties inherent in their interpretation are exacerbated by their greater susceptibility to later disturbance and truncation. One further category of feature also emerged during the fourteenth century. At this time, a number pits appear to have been dug specifically in order to receive the carcasses of horses and other animals. As it is unlikely that any such skeletons either went unrecognized, or else were entirely

removed by later activities, this practice appears to have been genuinely rare. Overall, it is unclear whether the emergence of new types of features such as these marks the adoption of a new set of activities by the inhabitants or simply the tailoring of individual features to specific tasks in contrast to the more opportunistic secondary or even tertiary reuse of generic feature-types that had occurred during the mid/late twelfth century.

Wells (incorporating specialist information from Richard Darrah and Mark Samuel)

Ten twelfth-century wells from the 2005–6 excavation area continued in use during this period and 15 new wells were constructed (Fig. 4.11). Although it is impossible to determine exactly how many wells were in use at one any point in time, the number appears to have been relatively stable and most new wells can plausibly be interpreted as direct replacements for features that had gone out of use. In most cases, the lining was still in good condition when the well was replaced and, while it is possible that the upper portions of the revetment above the water table had deteriorated, it appears that in most instances the act of replacement was part of a more general pattern of property reorganization rather than a structural necessity. The majority of the wells were situated within the same broadly north–south aligned strip, located between 18m and 47m back from the Hadstock Way frontage, as they had previously occupied during the mid–late twelfth century (Fig. 4.2).

Nevertheless, occasional outliers were present; most notably atypical stone-lined *Well 22* (Fig. 4.13), which was located 65m from the street. The majority of the thirteenth–fourteenth-century wells were wattle-lined (Figs. 4.14–4.17, plus Case Study 3) and were similar

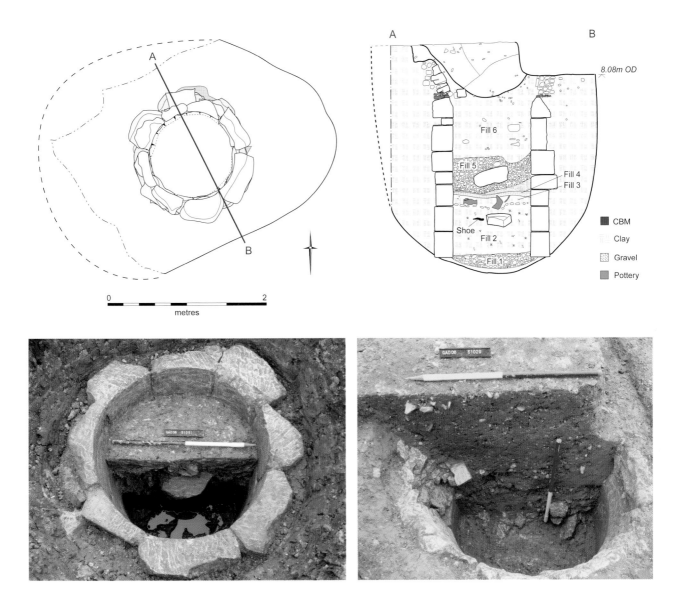

Figure 4.13. *Mid-fourteenth-century stone-lined Well 22: plan and section of the well, plus photographs of its upper shaft, facing northeast, and the central portion of the well, facing northeast.*

Case study 3: *Well 32* incorporating specialist information from Steve Allen, Richard Darrah, David Hall, Lorrain Higbee, Rosemary Horrox and Quita Mould

Wattle-lined *Well 32*, which was constructed in the mid-thirteenth century, was a relatively typical example of the period (Fig. 4.14). Its oval construction cut measured 1.75m by 1.55m in extent and over 1.0m deep, with steeply sloping sides and a flat base. In the base of this was a 0.7m-deep vertically sided circular shaft, which measured 0.7m in diameter. This lower shaft had a surviving wattle lining, with 14 sets of upright sails each consisting of one to three pieces of wood. The wood used was 12–27mm in diameter and principally three to seven years old. All of the horizontal woven rods and many of the upright sails were ash (21), while the uprights also included willow (nine), hazel (four) and oak (two). The collection of the wood took place over some time, with 18 pieces cut in autumn/winter, 10 in spring and eight in summer, with no correlation between cutting season and species or size. It appears that as long as the wood was of somewhere

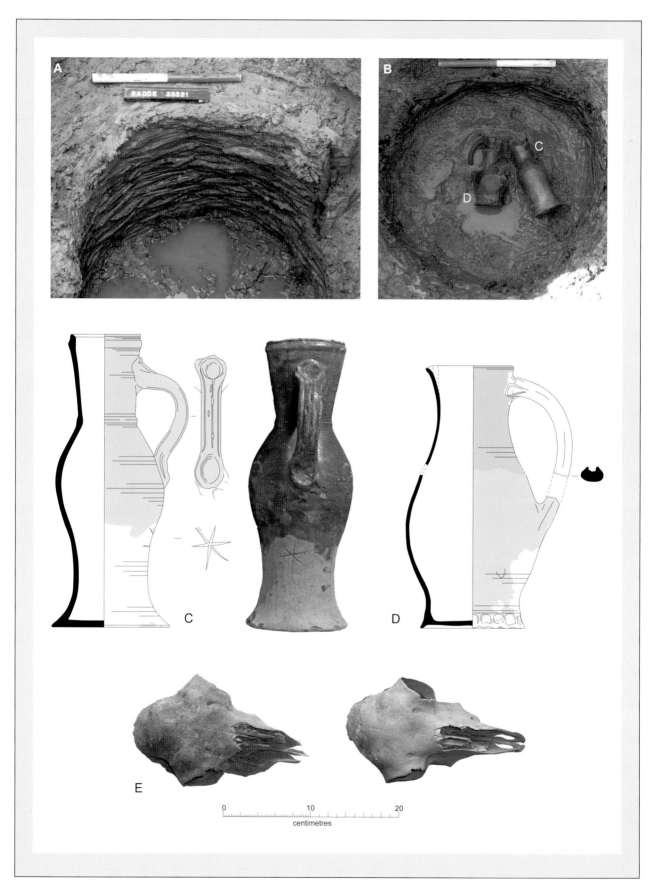

near the 'right' diameter, species was unimportant. This well would have naturally filled with water to a depth of *c.* 0.7m, holding *c.* 0.25 cubic m.

Although it lies beyond the realm of stratigraphic proof, *Well 32* was probably a replacement for twelfth-century wattle-lined *Well 14* and it in turn was later replaced by wattle-lined *Well 31*, which continued in use until the early fifteenth century. All these wells were broadly similar in form and survived in good condition, suggesting that they were abandoned during more general plot reorganizations. They all probably served Plot XV. By 1279, when *Well 32* was in existence, ownership of this plot had been acquired by Barnwell Priory but due to the dissolution of this institution in 1538 nothing is known of its lessees and occupants.

Well 32 was backfilled in the mid-fourteenth century, suggesting that it had been in use for around a century. Lying at the base of the well was a complete Grimston ware jug and a near-complete Essex Redware jug (Fig. 4.14B–D). This was the second fourteenth-century well backfilling to be excavated that produced groups of complete and near-complete jugs and it was initially believed that these might represent accidental losses, perhaps of vessels used as water containers. This interpretation derives in part from the archaeological fetishization of ceramics, as these items were carefully cleaned and recorded *in situ*. Yet what this practice obscured was the presence of large quantities of other domestic material in the same deposits, as these fragments were simply removed as part of the excavation process. This suggests that the redundant wells were used to dispose of groups of material including ceramics, and that the jugs therefore have no specific use-relationship to the wells. It has been noted that in antiquarian discoveries of complete or semi-complete medieval Ely ware vessels, jugs are over-represented in comparison to other vessel forms such as bowls (Spoerry 2008, 46–7, 51). This phenomenon is also recognizable at Grand Arcade and it appears that there was a greater propensity to discard jugs when they were slightly damaged, whereas other types of vessel continued to be used after they had suffered similar levels of impairment.

In the case of *Well 32*, the other material associated with the jugs included a fragment of a leather clump sole repair patch and a considerable number of animal bones. A total of 368 bones were recovered from the well; 58 were identified to species, 95 per cent of which were from the primary fill. Sheep bones dominate the assemblage (52 per cent NISP), with at least 12 joints (*c.* 20.3kg; see Table 4.3) and three partial skulls from naturally polled hornless sheep were also recovered (Fig. 4.14E).

Figure 4.14 *(opposite). Mid-thirteenth-century wattle-lined Well 32, plus material recovered from its mid-fourteenth-century backfilling. This shows: (A) photograph of the well, facing west; (B) photograph of in situ jugs in the base of the feature, facing west; (C) Grimston ware stabbed strap-handled baluster jug with a post firing non-decorative incised star-shaped graffiti below the handle ([34728]); (D) Essex Redware baluster jug with strap handle and thumbed base with lots of slip at the top, green glaze and metallic finish ([34729]); (E) sheep skulls, belonging to a naturally polled or hornless breed ([33325] (photograph E courtesy of Lorrain Higbee).*

Cattle and pig bones were comparatively rare (8.5 per cent and 15.5 per cent NISP respectively); however, most of the bones from these two species are from meat joints. At least three beef joints (*c.* 20.6kg) and seven pork joints (*c.* 30.6kg) are represented. It would therefore seem that this household ate more pork than beef or mutton. Fresh pork was generally consumed in winter (Albarella 2006, 84; Dyer 2006, 203); however, it can be preserved for later use as bacon joints and at least four of the pork joints (*e.g.* the leg and shoulder/hand joints) are traditionally cured for long term storage. A small number of chicken and pigeon bones were also recovered. All of the chickens were adults, but the two pigeon bones were from juvenile birds or squabs. These were primarily available during summer, and around Easter and Michaelmas, but not during the winter (Dyer 2006, 206; Stone 2006, 151).

The exigencies of developer-funded excavation meant that after the initial excavation of the upper *c.* 1.2m of deep features, such as *Well 32*, it was often necessary to postpone excavation of their lower portions until a later date, when the general area had been cleared (often by machine). As a result, different individuals excavated *Well 32* in two separate phases during early August and late September 2005. The dislocation between these phases created a 'fault line' in the excavation/recording process. It was also necessary to routinely auger such features, to determine how much remained to be investigated in the second phase. In the case of *Well 32*, this had an unfortunate side effect as the auger passed directly through the body of the Essex Redware jug.

Table 4.3. *Minimum number of butchery units and meat weights from Well 32.*

Species	Joint	Total no. of bones	MNBU	Estimated meat weight (kg)	Total estimated meat weight (kg) by meat type
Cattle	Neck & clod	1	1	7.4	20.6
	Shin	1	1	2.3	
	Chuck and blade	1	1	10.9	
Sheep	Leg	13	5	11.0	20.3
	Shoulder	20	2	5.8	
	Scrag	2	1	0.3	
	Loin	12	2	1.8	
	Best end of neck	11	2	1.4	
Pig	Leg	5	2	14.2	30.6
	Shoulder/ hand	4	2	9.2	
	Spare rib/ collar	4	1	4.6	
	Chump	8	2	2.6	
Chicken		12	1		
Pigeon		2	1		
Total		**96**	**24**	**71.5**	

Figure 4.15. *Photograph of pottery from mid/late fourteenth-century backfilling of early fourteenth-century wattle-lined Well 33.*

in form to those constructed during the preceding period, although the wood species used changed. In the thirteenth century, willow and ash were of roughly equal significance, while alder was prominent in one well and hazel, oak and maple were occasionally employed. But, by the fourteenth century, hazel had become the most commonly employed type of wood. This species is the most commonly used for wattle work in modern times, and would generally have come from a drier environment than the earlier willow. Willow was still relatively frequently employed, and oak was prominent in one well while alder, ash and maple were also occasionally used. In addition, a general shift took place from winter to summer felling.

With regard to specific features, *Well 25* is distinctive in that its upright sails were composed of a mixture of reused material – including a staff-like object (Fig. 4.17C) and two ladder rails (Fig. 4.17D–E) – rather than roundwood. These reused fragments would have been much more difficult to weave the horizontal rods

around than standard roundwood sails, of which there would have been no shortage, and it is unclear why they were selected. In the mid-fourteenth century the first stone-lined well, *Well 22* (Fig. 4.13), was constructed at the site. This utilized *c.* 100–110 carefully re-worked clunch blocks, including parts of a doorway arch and stairwell of *c.* 1270–1400, which were originally derived from a high status late thirteenth- or early fourteenth-century secular building. This structure was therefore unusual in being less than a century old when it was demolished; similar material was not commonly employed again until after the Dissolution. The quality of this well's construction, allied to its distance from the frontage, suggests that it may not have been intended solely or primarily for domestic use.

In addition to the above, earlier cask-lined *Well 6* was backfilled during this period and no additional cask-lined wells were created. The backfill of this feature contained numerous large

114

Figure 4.16. *Well 33: (A) Hedingham ware stamped strip-style globular jug of c. 1225–1300/25 ([34046]); (B) Medieval Ely ware globular jar or more probably jug – as thumbing around the base appears to be limited to jugs – that is relatively thin and hard for Medieval Ely ware and is probably a Spoerry type D jug; (C) photograph of well partway through excavation, facing west; (D) close-up detail of the well's wattle structure, facing east.*

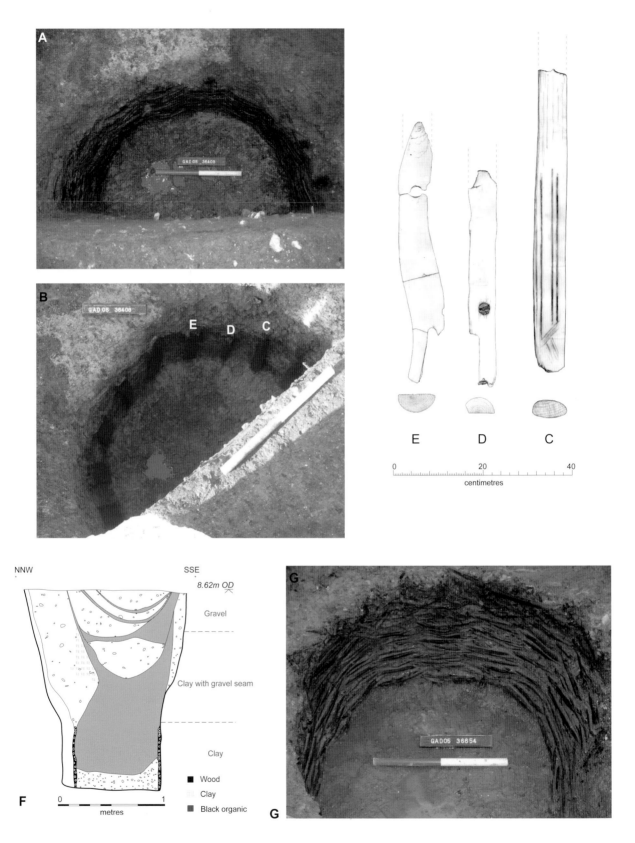

Figure 4.17. *Mid-thirteenth-century wattle-lined Wells 23 and 25: (A) photograph of Well 25, facing west; (B) photograph of the upright sails in Well 25 following the removal of the rods, facing northwest; (C) reused staff-like object in Well 25 ([36408]); (D–E) reused ladder rails in Well 25 ([36408]); (F–G) section and photograph, facing east, of Well 23.*

pieces of charcoal that were derived from a wattle structure, and it is possible that they represent elements of the upper portion or superstructure of the well that had collapsed into it. Finally, a number of other backfilled wells produced significant assemblages of material (including *Wells 5, 18, 20, 32 and 33*), although in most cases this appears to simply represent the *ad hoc* reuse of a redundant feature. There are several instances of groups of complete or semi-complete pottery vessels, however (*Wells 32–33*; Figs. 4.14–4.16), and this pattern was also repeated during the fifteenth century (*Well 22*; see Figs. 4.24 (lower) and 4.33). Whilst these could represent accidental losses, perhaps of vessels used as water containers, in both instances the finds were associated with other contemporary material, suggesting that they were most likely introduced as domestic refuse.

Cesspits

No thirteenth–fourteenth-century cesspits were positively identified, the only exception being a possible fourteenth-century square example that was investigated in 1959 (*Cesspit AB1*). Although wattle-lined cesspits almost certainly continued in use during this period, it is likely that their relative shallowness resulted in their extensive truncation. Other contemporary features do appear to have been used for the *ad hoc* disposal of cess-rich material, however, such as *Pit 14*. In London, by the late thirteenth century stone-lined cesspits had frequently replaced their timber predecessors, although many timber examples did continue, often in same location (Schofield & Vince 2003, 82). There is no evidence for stone-lined cesspits of this date in Cambridge, however, presumably due to the relative paucity of local stone.

Buildings

It is likely that the buildings of the street block, particularly the structures situated within the plot heads, underwent major changes during the thirteenth century, as it was around this time that timber-framing technology was widely adopted (see Pearson 2005; Rees Jones 2008). Unfortunately, little archaeological evidence was recovered from the present site to confirm this pattern and it is difficult to reconstruct specific building plans from the paucity of surviving elements. The water-filled features (see below) contained a number of pieces of reused timber derived from nearby twelfth–thirteenth-century buildings, and it is conceivable that the poorly preserved mid-fourteenth-century *Building 7/8* is a dovecote mentioned in a document of 1369. More extensive structural evidence was recovered from the nearby Christ's Lane site (see Chapter 6).

Gullies

A significant number of twelfth-century gullies continued in use into the thirteenth and even the fourteenth centuries, often with evidence for recutting. This indicates a substantial degree of continuity within the layout of the properties. In addition, a number of new gullies were also created, although the general impression is that gullies declined in significance during the thirteenth–fourteenth centuries. Whilst this may simply be a product of their reduced archaeological visibility, this decline is also paralleled elsewhere both locally (Cessford with Dickens 2004) and nationally (Hall & Hunter-Mann 2002, 807–10), suggesting that the phenomenon is genuine.

Water-filled features (incorporating specialist information from Richard Darrah)

From the thirteenth century onwards a range of features were dug in to the underlying clay natural that would have naturally filled with water, but whose primary function does not appear to have been as wells to supply water for domestic purposes. Such features have been grouped together as 'water-filled features' (Figs. 4.18–4.20 and 4.22), although they are a disparate group that undoubtedly fulfilled a wide range of functions. They were of variable shape and

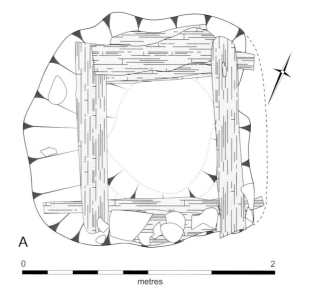

A

0   2

metres

Figure 4.18. *Fourteenth-century WFF 7: (A) plan; (B-C) photographs of its* in situ *timber lining, facing east and south.*

Case study 4: *Water-filled features 3–5*
incorporating specialist information from Steve Allen, Steve Boreham, Richard Darrah, David Hall, Rosemary Horrox and Ian Tyers

Water-filled features are an amorphous and enigmatic category of thirteenth–fifteenth-century features. A group of three, *WFF 3–5*, were created in the mid-fourteenth century and were all probably

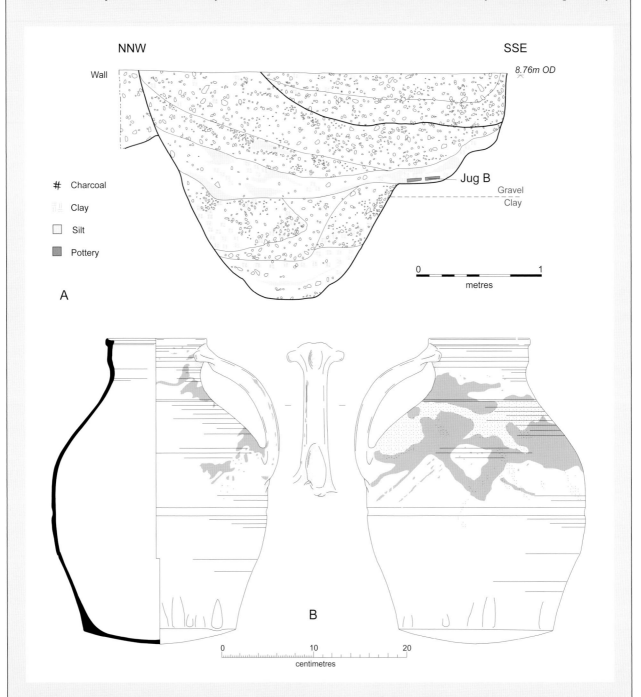

Figure 4.19. *Mid-fourteenth-century WFF 3, plus material recovered from its late fourteenth-century backfilling: (A) section; (B) Medieval Ely ware rounded or globular jug with rod handle, probably a Spoerry type E small rounded jug ([36814]).*

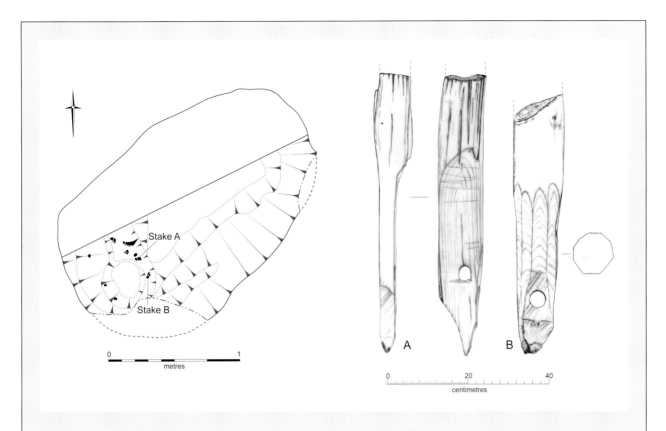

Figure 4.20. *Plan of mid-fourteenth-century WFF 4, plus (A) stake made from a reused piece of ash with tusked tenon ([36737]); (B) stake made from a reused piece of Scots pine with a tusked tenon ([36735]).*

in use together in the same plot for a few decades. The first, *WFF 3* (Fig. 4.19), was sub-rectangular in form and measured 3.3m long by 3.0m wide and over 1.0m deep, with a step at its northern end over 1.95m deep. It would have naturally filled with water to a depth of *c.* 0.8m, and held *c.* 0.3 cubic m. It seems likely that individuals climbed into the shallower, dry southern end of the feature in order to conduct activities linked to the deeper, wet northern portion. Nearby, *WFF 4* (Fig. 4.20) measured 4.1m by 1.9m in extent and over 1.3m deep, with steep sides and a moderately flat base; it would have naturally filled with water to a depth of *c.* 0.8m, holding *c.* 3.0 cubic m. Finally, *WFF 5* was a substantial steep-sided flat-bottomed rectangular feature with rounded ends that measured over 5.7m long, 3.0m wide and over 1.4m deep; it would have filled naturally with water to a depth of *c.* 0.9m, holding *c.* 10 cubic m.

The creation of these three features can only be broadly dated to the mid-fourteenth century. It is therefore impossible to tell if they pre- or post-dated the Great Mortality of 1348–9,

which profoundly altered life in medieval Cambridge and far beyond. On a more local scale, it is likely that they were in existence on 25 December 1369 when Margaret, prioress of the Benedictine priory of St Mary and St Radegund, leased the tenement Plot IX where *WFF 3–5* were almost certainly located to John Berlee, a carter, for 18s a year (which in modern terms corresponds to around £285 using the retail price index or £5000 using average earnings). This lease ran until 1409, although we do not know if it ran for its full term. Berlee appears to have become a draper by 1363, and is mentioned as a witness in other leases of the Benedictine priory in 1363, 1370 and 1376, suggesting that he occupied Plot IX until 1376. More generally, it is not known when Berlee was born – although his toponymic surname suggests he or his family came from Barley (*Berlei*) in Hertfordshire, some 21km southwest of Cambridge – or when he died.

The frontage buildings of Plot IX are enumerated in some detail in the lease (Fig. 4.11). Berlee was 'to maintain all the houses and walls, *viz* a hall, a solar at the front, two cellars and a gateway below the solar, all under one roof'. The hall was 21ft (6.4m) long by 18ft (5.5m) wide and the solar, which was located on an upper floor at the front, was 23ft (7.0m) long and 15ft (4.6m) wide. There was also a chamber on the west side of the hall under another roof 33ft (10.1m) long by 20ft (6.1m) wide. In addition, 'three chambers at the front of the tenement are annexed to the said solar and cellars, but under another roof', and there was also a dovecote. Unfortunately these buildings, with the possible exception of the dovecote, were

119

Figure 4.21. *Photograph of cleaning of fragments of a willow eel grig ([36554]) from late fourteenth-century backfilling of mid-fourteenth-century WFF 5, plus drawings of grig.*

entirely removed by nineteenth–twentieth-century cellars. In contrast, the features that did survive in the backland – such as *WFF 3–5* – were too insignificant to be mentioned in the lease.

One of the three features, *WFF 4*, had two lines of parallel stakes and some collapsed timbers in its base, indicating some form of relatively lightweight structure. One of the collapsed timbers was a piece of oak from a 0.5m-diameter tree, which had been radially split into eighths. This piece produced a 143-year tree-ring sequence with sapwood and bark edge, which matched a range of English oak reference data with the closest results being from various sites in London. The tree began to grow in 1156, when Henry II (1154–89) was on the throne. At this time the Grand Arcade street block had only been intensively occupied for around half a century, and the Barnwell Gate suburb proper had only come into existence a few years before, if the King's Ditch was created in *c.* 1143–4 (Chapter 3). The tree was felled in the winter of 1298 in the reign of Edward I (1272–1307); however, the timber had an angled auger hole with an intact peg indicating reuse, suggesting that *WFF 4* dates instead to the mid-fourteenth century in the reign of Edward III (1327–77). The seven stakes were oak (3), ash (2), willow (1) and Scots pine (1), the last of which was probably imported from Scandinavia or the Eastern Baltic. The stakes measured 50–60mm in diameter and included two pieces with redundant peg holes near their ends (Fig. 4.20A–B).

Peg holes near reshaped ends tend to indicate the end of the original worked piece of wood. In both cases, the earlier shaping reduced the cross section near the peg holes. This suggests that the peg holes and reduced sections of timber may have been a tusked tenon at the end of a pole. If the original pole had tusked tenons at both ends it could have been a tie beam across a small building, a piece of a large frame or a stretcher for a bench. These points had been cut with a blunt tool, unlike the earlier work on their sides that was cut with a sharp tool. One squared pole had been burnt on one side before it was pointed, as the pointing tool marks cut through the burnt wood. Pine is not known to be a native species in Cambridgeshire at this time, suggesting that this was imported (Rackham 1980, 151). It was slow grown and the last five rings were each less than 1mm in diameter. Because of its careful working with the fine taper to the end it could have been imported as part of a boat, or as a pine pole. The other poles may have been reused and had different growth rates. The range of species and reused

material indicates that this structure was built from a varied collection of material that happened to be available at the time.

These water-filled features were only in use for a few decades. When they went out of use in the late fourteenth or early fifteenth century, relatively little material was included in their infilling. There were, however, two items that appear to relate to the use of the features. Firstly, lying broken on the base of a step in *WFF 3* was most of a medieval Ely ware rounded or globular jug with rod handle, potentially representing *in situ* breakage (Fig. 4.19B). This is probably a Spoerry type E small rounded jug; a long-lived form of vessel produced at Ely, 23km northeast of Cambridge, between the late twelfth/early thirteenth and fifteenth centuries (Spoerry 2008, 56). Secondly, in the base of *WFF 5* was part of a woven willow object (Fig. 4.21); this was identified by Peter Carter, the last surviving traditional Fenland fisherman (whose family has been catching eels locally since 1470) as an eel grig. A grig is a long basket with a funnel neck that is laid under waterweeds where eels tend to lurk.

Originally, there would have been an opening with a wooden bung at one end of the grig while at the other there was a chair, which would have stopped the eels escaping. As the willow was still pliable enough to collapse without snapping it must have been of relatively new construction. This item had presumably been used on the river Cam. It may simply have been discarded in *WFF 5*, or it is possible that the feature was used to store live eels, caught as elvers, which were kept until they had grown large enough to consume. The grig is virtually identical to both the earliest identified Bronze Age woven willow grig, from Must Farm in Cambridgeshire dating to *c.* 1100 BC (Knight & Murrell 2010), and also to those still in use locally. The water-filled features had probably gone out of use by 1408 when Plot IX was leased to Robert Pynnyngton, but it is just possible that they were infilled at this date. As part of his lease, Pynnyngton agreed to construct new buildings on the site by 1411, suggesting that the old ones were in poor condition. The priory was to supply him with one acre of wheat straw after the harvest, presumably for thatching, and he was allowed to cut down trees to effect necessary repairs, replanting others in their place. Pollen evidence confirms the presence of a few scattered trees in the area at this time, although much of the woody vegetation appears to be represented by hazel and privet scrub. If *WWF 3–5* had not been backfilled already then they almost certainly went out of use *c.* 1408–11.

measured between 2.0m and 5.7m by 1.2m and 3.0m in extent, with the exception of one much larger example, *WFF2* (Fig. 4.22), which measured 11.0m by 3.0m. They were originally *c.* 1.5–2.0m deep and appear to have been dug so that they would fill with water to a depth of 0.5–1.0m; again with the exception of *WWF2*, which would have filled to a depth of *c.* 1.5m or more.

The majority of these features were revetted with a mixture of reused timbers and off-cuts, suggesting *ad hoc* usage of whatever materials were readily available (Skov 2009, 153–4) with some woodworking taking place inside the actual features. Many of the resultant linings were therefore relatively flimsy, and it is likely that most of the water-filled features had a lifespan of only a few decades, although the more robust examples may have existed for half a century or more. The better-constructed features, however (such as *WFF 7*; Fig. 4.18), were effectively fully timber-framed structures. These were distinguished from wells because of their rectangular form, and appear most likely to have functioned as cisterns. (Although it has been suggested elsewhere that such features might have comprised wells (*e.g.* Murray *et al.* 2009; Skov 2009,

153–4), it appears unlikely in this context as the majority occurred in properties that already possessed a contemporary wattle-lined well.

Of the remaining water-filled features, the majority appear to have been used for the prolonged immersion of materials for craft or industrial purposes. In one instance this appears to have occurred on a relatively large scale (*WFF 2*; Fig. 4.22), and there is also the suggestion of a quite intensive zone of activity containing three contemporary examples that were apparently demarcated by a fence (*WFF 3–5*; see Case Study 4). Immersion also appears to have taken place on a much smaller scale, however, as indicated by two smaller pits (*WFF 8–9*), which had internal vertical wooden revetments that were backfilled on one side to create platforms to stand on reminiscent of some Bronze Age watering holes (Masefield *et al.* 2003; Webley & Hiller 2009, 15–17, 26–7). Although there is no direct evidence to reveal what material(s) were being immersed in these features, the faunal remains recovered from some contemporary pits suggest that activities might have included soaking cattle horns to remove the sheath. The retting of flax to make linen is also possible, as contemporary flax seeds were present

NNW

SSE

8.35m OD

Drain 7

Gravel
Clay

\# Charcoal

Clay

Silt

Sand

A

0   2

metres

C

B

Figure 4.22. *Early/mid-fourteenth-century WFF 2: (A) section, including nineteenth-century Drain 7; (B) photograph of the feature, facing east; (C) photograph of the base of the feature, facing east.*

in the King's Ditch (see Chapter 3). Finally, it is conceivable that some of the water-filled features were used to hold live fish or shellfish, a possibility suggested by the presence of an eel grig in *WFF 5* (Fig. 4.21).

Ovens

A number of fourteenth-century shallow oval or 'tear-drop' shaped clay-lined ovens were found, many with evidence of *in situ* burning. The better-preserved examples of these features, which frequently had evidence of up to three phases of relining, measured 1.2–2.4m long by 0.65–1.7m wide and survived up to 0.3m in depth. They appear to have had clay roofs and flues, and in one instance a nearby pit, *Pit 15*, contained the broken up remains of just such a superstructure. The majority of the ovens lay relatively far back within the properties, up to 50m from the frontage, and it is therefore unlikely that they were domestic in function. Indeed, in several cases they occurred in clusters (*e.g. Ovens 1–3* and *Ovens 4–5*; Figs. 4.23–4.24), thereby suggesting potential zones of craft activity. Although no clear evidence was recovered to demonstrate the specific nature of this activity, an association with the working of horn sheaths is possible. As it is likely that the ovens would have had to be frequently relined and replaced, the numbers involved appear to represent only small-scale intermittent activity.

Animal disposal pits (with Lorrain Higbee)

From the fourteenth century onwards, there is evidence to suggest that pits were dug specifically to dispose of the bodies of dead animals that had not been butchered or eaten. Initially, this practice related principally to horses, which were not generally eaten, but also included species such as pigs where individual animals were apparently deemed unfit for human consumption. Some pigs and dogs were also disposed of in larger features, such as the King's Ditch (Chapter 3) or general refuse pits, rather than in specially dug disposal pits. The lack of twelfth–thirteenth-century examples of this behaviour implies that a change in practice occurred. This may have related to a change in disposal practices, or could indicate a shift in the standards for determining whether animals such as pigs were edible; horse carcasses might also have been more fully utilized during earlier centuries.

Specialized pits

There were a number of pits that appear to have been 'tailor-made' for a specific purpose such as *SP 1* (Fig. 4.25); although it is usually impossible to determine precisely what this purpose was. As a group, these features are so heterogeneous that no generic description is possible. They are distinguishable from the more generic pits of unknown function by the apparent level of care that was taken in

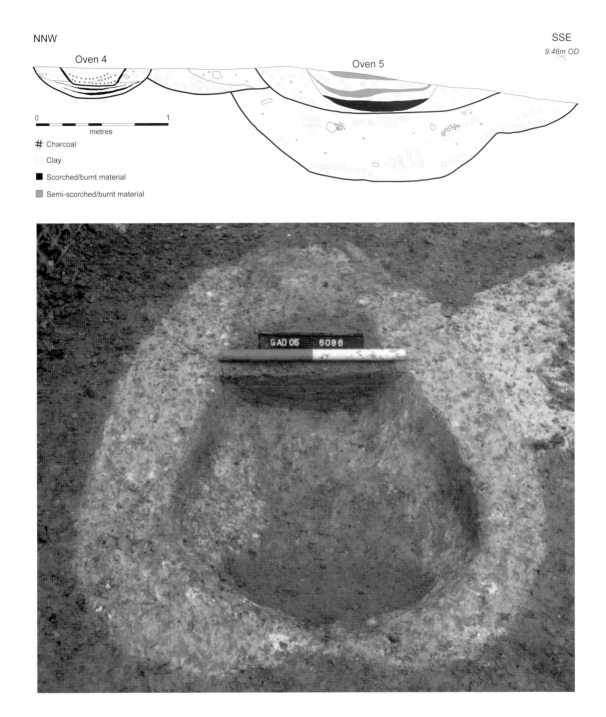

Figure 4.23. *Mid–late fourteenth-century Ovens 4–5, with section of the ovens and photograph of Oven 4, facing east.*

their creation, and also by their unsuitability for use as recognizable quarry pits, cesspits or water-filled features. They first appeared in the thirteenth century and the majority were short-lived, with some perhaps being used for only a single event.

Surfaces
Very few surfaces survived from this period. There was a clay and gravel *Surface 1* that comprised either a yard or a path, and some general spreads of trampled and accumulated material *Surface 2* indicative of a yard.

Pits
Both gravel quarry pits and pits of unknown function continued to be dug throughout the thirteenth–fourteenth centuries (Figs. 4.7 and 4.26–4.27). The gravel quarry pits were widely scattered, although there were some possible clusters and a few areas where they were absent. In general, they tended to be situated further back from the frontage than in the twelfth century, presumably because the properties were now more densely used and much of the gravel had already been extracted. In contrast, the pits of unknown function tended to be smaller and were located closer to the frontage than

Figure 4.24. *Photographs of mid–late fourteenth-century Ovens 4–5 over earlier pit, facing northeast; (upper) and in situ Essex Redware baluster jug in Well 36, facing north.*

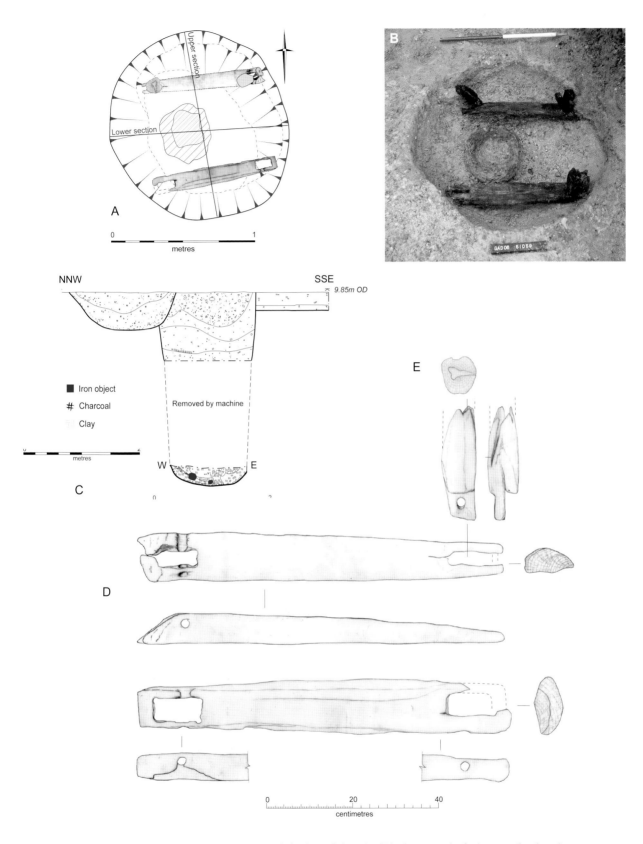

Figure 4.25. *Mid/late fourteenth-century SP 1: (A) plan of the pit; (B) photograph, facing north, showing remnants of the feature's timber-lining plus an iron vessel situated in its base; (C) composite section of the pit; (D) oak baseplate timbers ([51064], [51079]); (E) oak upright ([51060]).*

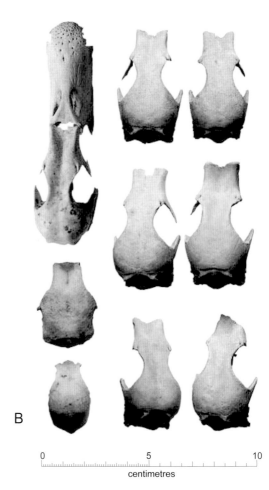

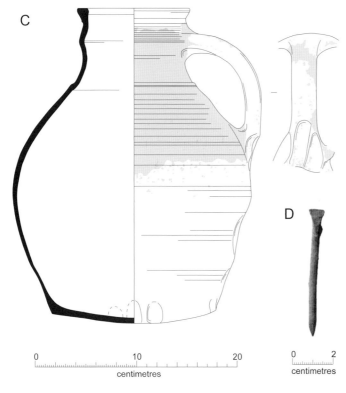

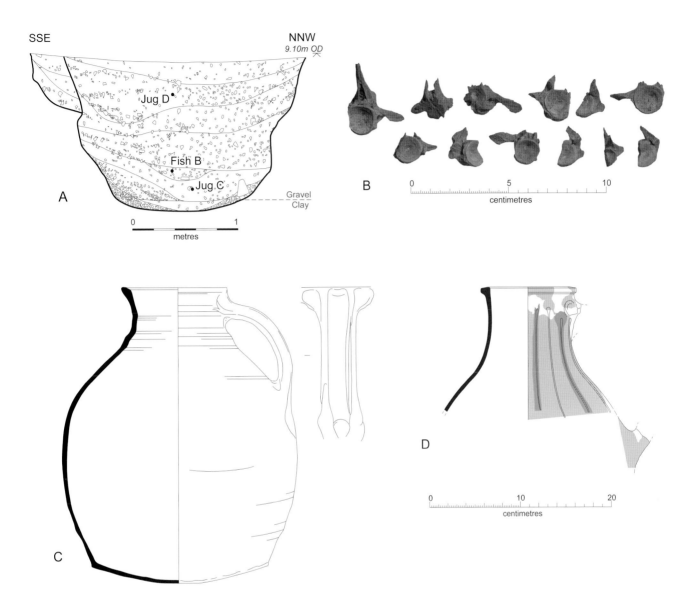

Figure 4.27. *Fourteenth-century gravel quarry Pit 23: (A) section of the pit; (B) butchered cod vertebrae ([33349]); (C) Medieval Ely ware unglazed rounded jug with strap handle, of relatively good quality ([33350]); (D) jug, probably a Brill-Boarstall product, with green glaze over its entire upper portion and alternating plain and brown striped decoration ([33333]) (photograph courtesy of Jen Harland).*

Figure 4.26 *(opposite). Material recovered from fourteenth-century Pits 20 and 29 of unknown function: (A) photograph of a fragmentary jug in situ in Pit 20, facing northwest ([34898]); (B) group of chicken and duck skulls ([30571]) from Pit 29; (C) Medieval Ely ware rounded jug with strap handle, of Spoerry type D from Pit 20; (D) iron stylus with opposing pointed and flattened triangular ends from Pit 20 ([34898]) (photograph B courtesy of Lorrain Higbee).*

the gravel quarries. The vast majority of both types of pit contained very little material culture, although in a minority of cases there was evidence for the rapid deposition of refuse.

In the mid–late fourteenth century part of the street block also began to be exploited for clay extraction. This occurred in an area where the gravel was relatively thin, and the clay therefore more readily accessible. Here, a series of six intercutting large oval to sub-rectangular clay quarry pits, measuring 4.5–5m long, 2–3m wide and over 2m deep, were excavated between the mid–late fourteenth and mid-fifteenth centuries. Each pit would have produced *c*. 15 cubic m of clay, suggesting a relatively substantial requirement (perhaps linked to building work), although extraction appears to have been undertaken only on an intermittent basis, with gaps of perhaps decades between each pit being dug. Two of

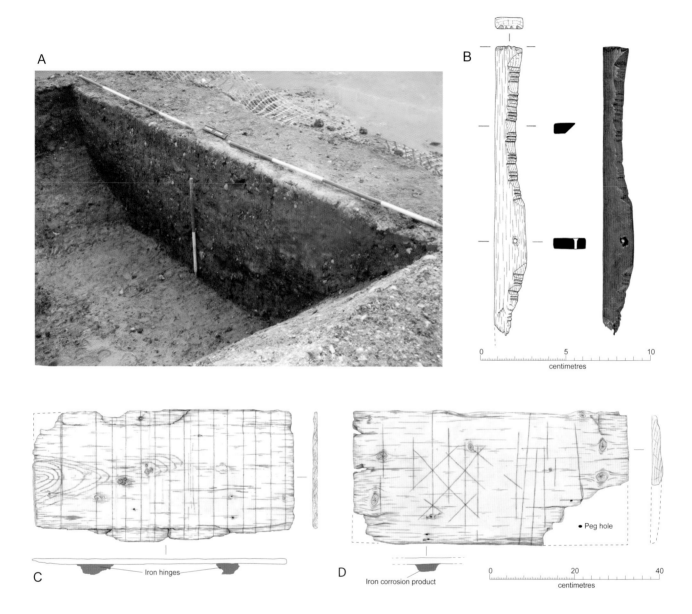

Figure 4.28. *Mid/late fourteenth-century clay quarry Pit 16: (A) photograph, facing southwest; (B) part of a notched wooden frame ([33329]); (C) the top of a pine chest ([33975]); (D) the back of a pine chest ([33974]).*

the clay quarry pits dated to the mid/late fourteenth century; these comprised *Pit 16* (Fig. 4.28), which contained a range of material including parts of a chest (Fig. 4.28C–D), and *Pit 17*.

Fifteenth–sixteenth centuries

Archaeologically, the early/mid-fifteenth century represents a period of broad continuity with the preceding thirteenth–fourteenth centuries. From the mid/late fifteenth century onwards, however, it appears that the number of features within the street block gradually declined, suggesting a commensurate decrease in the intensity of occupation at the site. Yet, counterbalancing this, a range of new material culture was introduced

and the overall standard of living appears to have risen. Off-stage, the maintenance of the King's Ditch became markedly poorer around the mid/late fifteenth century and a significantly greater quantity of refuse was deposited within it (Chapter 3).

In Cambridge more generally, colleges continued to be founded throughout the fifteenth–sixteenth centuries. King's College was founded by Henry VI in 1441 and although initially modest in scale, by 1445 it had become the recipient of a massive display of royal patronage. In 1443 this resulted in the movement of God's House (originally founded 1437, re-founded as Christ's College in 1505) – to the Barnwell Gate suburb.

Soon after came the Wars of the Roses (1455–85) and the eventual establishment of the Tudor dynasty (1485–1603). The decline of earlier religious institutions in the town is attested by the transformation of the Priory of St Mary and St Radegund into Jesus College in 1497 and the Hospital of St John the Evangelist into St John's College in 1511. The Dissolution in 1534–8 then saw the closure of many of Cambridge's remaining monasteries, including the Dominican friary located in the Barnwell Gate suburb (Chapter 6), but ultimately the Colleges of the University were spared in 1545–6 (Loewe 2009).

The end of the sixteenth century also witnessed the foundation of Emmanuel College on the site of the former Dominican friary (1584), and Sidney Sussex College relatively close by on the site of the former Franciscan friary (1589). Altogether, therefore, by the close of this period a significant collegiate presence existed in and around the Barnwell Gate suburb (see Chapter 6).

The documented plots Rosemary Horrox with Craig Cessford

During the fifteenth–sixteenth centuries the surviving documentary sources provide a more detailed view of the street block than was possible during earlier periods; especially by the late sixteenth century, when a relatively extensive array of documents is available. This evidence reveals that a gradual increase in collegiate ownership took place at the site, although the majority of plots only appear to have been purchased as investments and had little or no direct association with the respective institutions. Plots I–II, however – which were owned by Christ's College – represent a notable exception to this pattern. Here, a considerable number of the college's staff – particularly beadles, who performed various functions as executive officers – came to lease these plots. This difference is probably attributable to the close proximity of Christ's College to the Grand Arcade street block (Chapter 6).

Elsewhere within the street block there is relatively little evidence for the origins of any of the lessees of plots, especially as by now surnames had ceased to be reliable indicators of either origin or occupation. At least four plots were occupied by inns during this period – the Brazen George (Plots I–II), the Sword on the Hope (Plot IX), the Chalice (Plot XI) and the Birdbolt (Plot XX) – although no evidence of this was encountered archaeologically. The trades of other probable occupants included apothecary, baker, basket maker, brewer, carpenter, draper, glazier and glover. This represents a broadly comparable range of artisanal occupations to those recorded during the thirteenth–fourteenth centuries.

Usefully, the first detailed maps of Cambridge were produced in the late sixteenth century (Baggs & Bryan 2002; Clark & Gray 1921). The earliest cartographic depiction of the Grand Arcade street block was made by Richard Lyne in 1574 (Fig. 4.29A). But although Lyne's map provides a useful overview, it is too schematic and inaccurate to be considered reliable. Over the next two decades several additional maps were produced, yet each of these was directly based upon Lyne's original plan and none increased its accuracy. The situation changed in 1592, when John Hammond produced the first detailed and relatively reliable map of Cambridge. Unfortunately this only survives in poor, fragmentary condition, but it did serve as the basis for a later plan drawn by John Speed in 1610. In this map, a more accurate depiction of the Barnwell Gate suburb is revealed (Fig. 4.29B).

Archaeological remains

In archaeological terms the division between the thirteenth–fourteenth centuries and the fifteenth–sixteenth centuries is largely an arbitrary one, with at least the early/mid-fifteenth century representing broad continuity with the preceding century (Fig. 4.30). Initially, the number of properties within the street block appears to have remained relatively stable. There was also a broad correspondence between the archaeologically identified properties and the historically documented plots (Fig. 4.31). Over the course of the fifteenth–sixteenth centuries, however, several important changes did occur. Perhaps most notably, the overall number of features at the site began to decline. Whilst it does not appear that any of the properties were abandoned at this time, as in each instance features continued to be created within them, some plots may have ceased to be used for domestic occupation. Consequently, it is likely that the population of the street block fell to around 20 households with perhaps 80 inhabitants. This was a gradual rather than a rapid process, which in particular instances later appears to have been reversed (Chapter 5).

The decreasing numbers of wells, water-filled features, ovens and specialized pits between the mid-fifteenth and mid-sixteenth centuries indicates a decline in the various types of specialized industrial activities that had been taking place in the property tails, commensurate with the reduction in domestic occupation. Even the digging of gravel pits and pits of unidentified function declined. Although the reduction in feature numbers may in part be attributable to issues of archaeological visibility, the overall process of decline nevertheless appears to have been systemic. Yet this was also a period of significant change and innovation. New material-types appeared for the first time – such

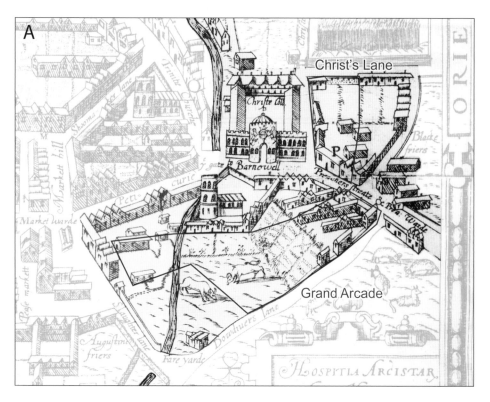

Figure 4.29. *Late sixteenth-century cartographic sources, comprising: (A) plan of the area published by Richard Lyne in 1574; (B) plan of the area published by John Speed in 1610, primarily based upon a map published by John Hammond in 1592, of which no complete copy now survives.*

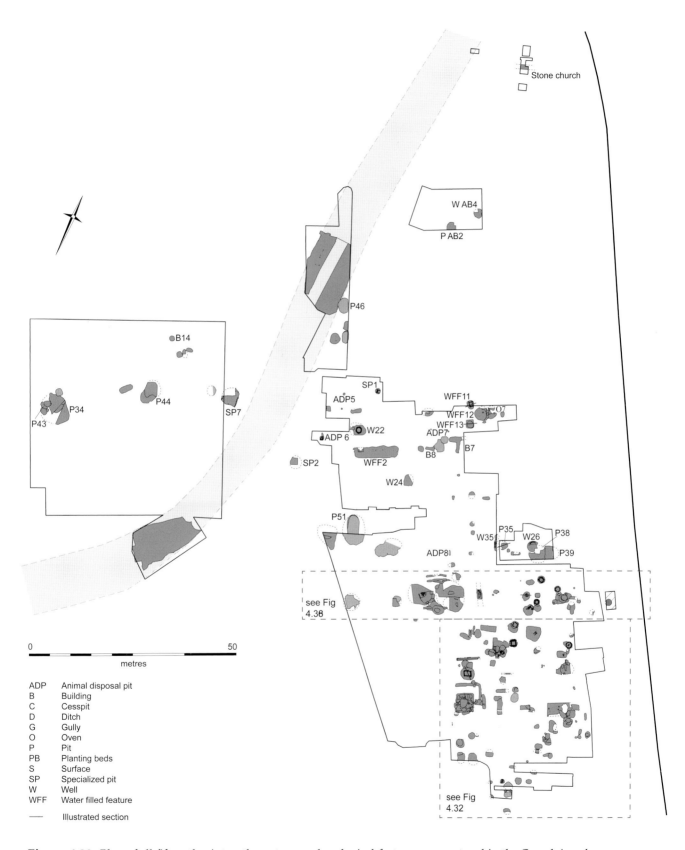

Figure 4.30. *Plan of all fifteenth–sixteenth-century archaeological features encountered in the Grand Arcade street block.*

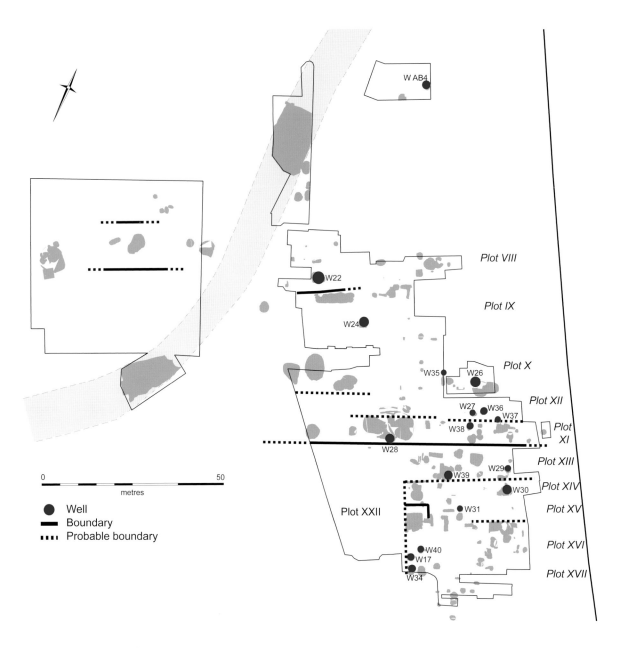

Figure 4.31. *The layout of putative fifteenth–sixteenth-century property boundaries in relation to contemporary wells.*

as brick-, cask- and reused moulded stone-linings – as well as new feature-types – such as planting beds – while the range of material culture in use at the site increased significantly. It would be overstating the case, and potentially misleading, to group these disparate phenomena together and label them a post-medieval or Tudor 'revolution'. Nevertheless, between *c.* 1400–1600 – and predominately between *c.* 1450–1550 – significant changes took place in the lives of many of the street block's inhabitants; arguably perhaps, the most significant changes to have occurred since the suburb's foundation in the mid-twelfth century.

Wells (incorporating specialist information from Richard Darrah, Lorrain Higbee, Mark Samuel and Ian Tyers)

During this period, both the number and lining-type of the wells in use within the street block changed markedly. Firstly, both stone- and cask-linings became increasingly common. Of particular note were *Well 36*, which contained a significant group of stone mouldings derived from a late thirteenth–early fourteenth-century religious house (see Fig. 4.34), and *Well 38*, which contained a reused Ottoman cask from Greece (Case Study 5). Secondly, a clear decline in the overall number of wells occurred during the fifteenth–sixteenth centuries. At the start of the fifteenth century 10 wells were present in the main excavated area, for example, while by the start of the sixteenth century there were just six and by the end of the sixteenth century the number had fallen to just three. Although some of the cistern-like water-filled features discussed below may also have

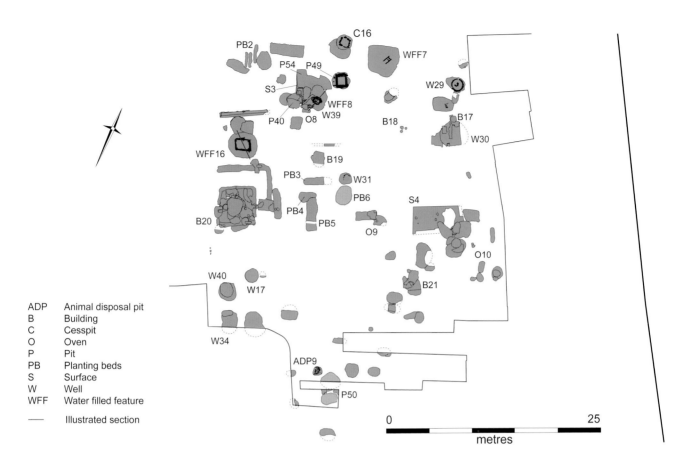

Figure 4.32. *Plan of southeastern area of main excavation area at Grand Arcade in the fifteenth–sixteenth century.*

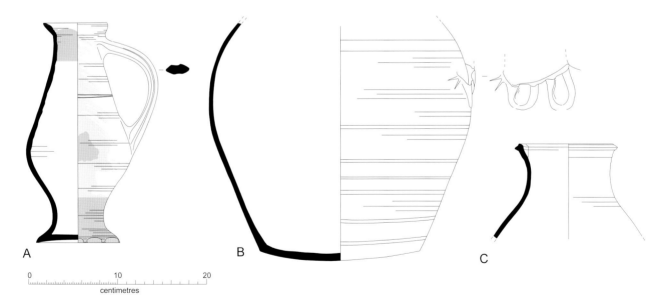

Figure 4.33. *Vessels recovered from the mid-fifteenth-century backfilling of stone-lined Well 22: (A) Essex Redware baluster jug, probably Colchester-type ware, with thumbed base and red painted wash on the inside of its neck. Similar to the Late Medieval 'metal copy' baluster jugs produced c. 1400–1550 (Cotter 2000, 118 and 128) ([51137]); (B) large buff coarseware globular jug with strap handle and occasional rilling, its fabric is sandy with occasional white grits ([51136]); (C) Essex Redware jug, probably Colchester-type ware, with a metallic glazed finish ([55135]).*

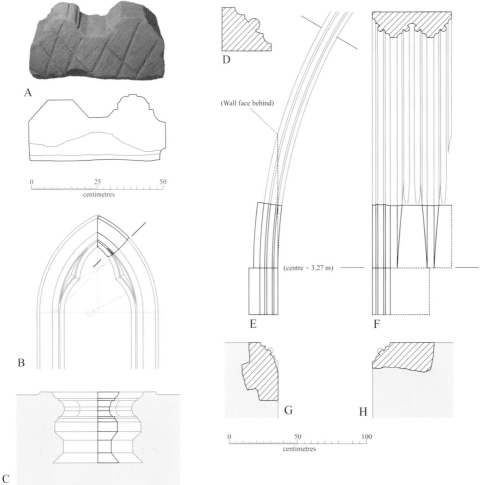

Figure 4.34.
Photograph of mid-fifteenth-century stone-lined Well 36, facing south, plus reused blocks from Clunch piscina of c. 1320–50 ([35687]) and Clunch spiked hollow moulding arch respond of c. 1290–1320 ([35774]): (A) keying for mortar on piscina; (B) the restored elevation of the piscina arch; (C) the restored plan of the piscina (reversed): (D) the restored moulding of the arch respond; (E) elevation detail with elements restored of the arch respond; (F) elevational section detail with elements restored of the arch respond; (G) angle moulding showing reveal of the arch respond; (H) springer moulding of the arch respond (A–H based upon illustrations by Mark Samuel).

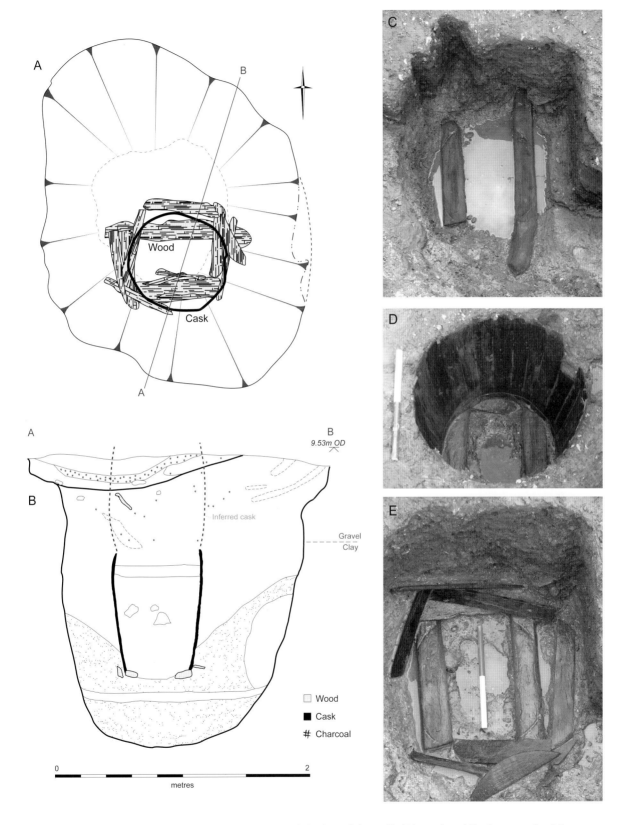

Figure 4.35. *Mid-fifteenth-century cask-lined Well 39: (A) plan of the well; (B) section; (C) photograph of the supporting oak beams, facing west; (D) photograph of the cask-lining, with the supporting beams also visible, facing east; (E) photograph of the packing timbers, with the supporting beams also visible, facing west.*

Figure 4.36. *Photograph of fourteenth–fifteenth-century jugs, including a Grimston ware stabbed strap handled baluster jug from the mid-fourteenth-century backfilling of Well 32 (left), an Essex Redware baluster jug from the mid-fifteenth-century backfilling of Well 22 (centre) and a Hedingham ware globular jug from the mid/late fourteenth-century backfilling of Well 33 (right).*

acted as surrogate wells in addition to fulfilling other functions, their presence alone cannot account for the entire decline.

One possibility is that the reduction in the number of wells corresponded to declining levels of occupation in the street block. Alternatively, their reduction might indicate that unlike earlier wells, which had primarily been associated with individual properties, the new cask- and stone-lined features were communal, serving a number of properties. There is certainly some evidence for plot vacancy that might explain the decline; Plots VII–VIII, for instance, comprised 'empty ground' between 1408 and 1479 and a 'waste messuage lately built upon' in 1528. This period of at least relative abandonment may correspond with the backfilling of stone-lined *Well 22* in the mid-fifteenth century, after around a century of use. *Well 22* showed no signs of structural failure and was in many respects superior to any of the other fifteenth–sixteenth-century wells in the street block. The abandonment of such an expensive and well-constructed feature is striking, and requires some explanation. In this regard, it is notable that the infill of the feature contained a relatively large quantity of domestic refuse including three jugs (Fig. 4.33; see also Fig. 4.36), two shoes and a large animal bone assemblage. Included amongst the latter were eight dogs, four cats and one pig, perhaps as a result of an outbreak of a disease such as Yersinia or Aujeszkys Disease, which affects all three species. Such an outbreak could potentially have caused a panic that led to the well being backfilled. Other evidence for plot vacancy pertains to Plot XVII, which was referred to as 'garden ground' in 1539–80, while

cartographic sources of 1592/1610 indicate that the frontage of Plots XIV–XIX was unoccupied, although a large building lay to the rear.

The last wattle-lined well to be constructed at the site was *Well 35* in the fifteenth century, and only three wattle-lined wells survived in use into the sixteenth century. Two of the latter went out of use in the early sixteenth century (*Wells 1* and *35*) while the last was backfilled in the late sixteenth century (*Well 28*). They were replaced instead by cask-lined (Figs. 4.35, 4.39 and 4.41–4.42) and stone-lined (Figs. 4.34 and 4.38) wells, which came to dominate the area from the mid-fifteenth century onwards. Both of these well-types would have been significantly more expensive to construct than a wattle-lined feature. Moreover, casks did not offer any significant structural advantages over wattle and their increased usage probably relates instead to availability. At least one of the reused casks was quite old and no longer serviceable as a container for liquids, for example, but was still perfectly functional as a well lining. Another from Ottoman Greece (*Well 38*; Case Study 5) was of a different size to local British casks, making it less useful as a container. For various reasons the supply of cheap casks that were not wanted for other purposes increased in the fifteenth–sixteenth centuries, making them a more attractive option than wattle. In some cases, the casks were placed upon a timber base and had other timbers placed around them as packing, whereas others wells used only the cask. All the cask-lined wells at Grand Arcade had only one surviving cask and probably originally contained two, with the uppermost cask protruding above the ground surface.

Figure 4.37. *Photographs of: (A) oak lid in Well 38 ([35419]); (B) leather drinking vessel recovered from the backfilling of Cesspit 16 ([34895]); (C) a leather sheet fragment with stamped and tooled decoration, including stamped fleur-de-lis motif in lozenges from Well 38 ([35392]); (D) detail of (C).*

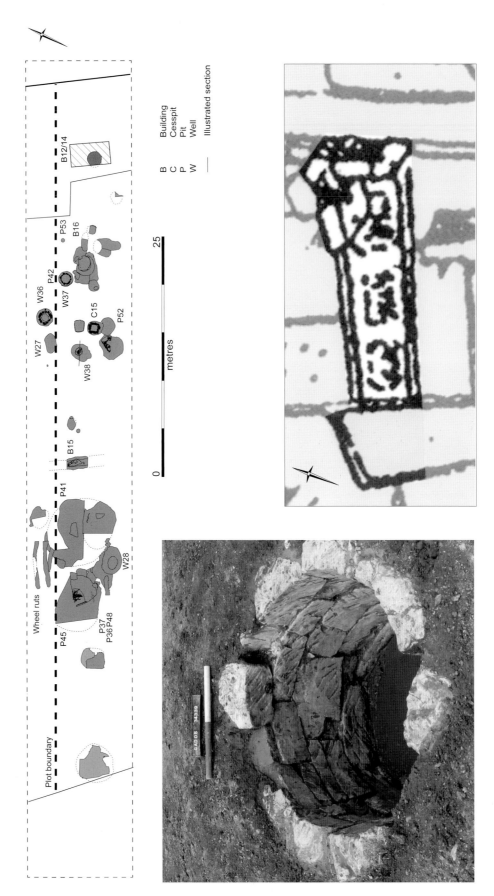

Figure 4.38. *Plan of fifteenth–sixteenth archaeological features in what is probably one plot, detail of that plot from the Speed map of 1610 and photograph of late sixteenth-century stone-lined Well 37, facing west.*

Case study 5: *Well 38* incorporating specialist information from Richard Darrah, David Hall, Lorrain Higbee, Quita Mould and Ian Tyers

By the sixteenth century new wells were predominately constructed from reused casks rather than wattle, due to the increased availability of cheap second-hand casks. A relatively typical example of this feature-type was late sixteenth-century *Well 38* (Figs. 4.39–4.40). Its oval construction pit measured 2.1m by 1.9m in extent and over 1.8m deep and it would have naturally filled with water to a depth of *c.* 0.8m, holding *c.* 0.6 cubic m. The cask itself had 27 staves and measured 1.39m high (1.30m

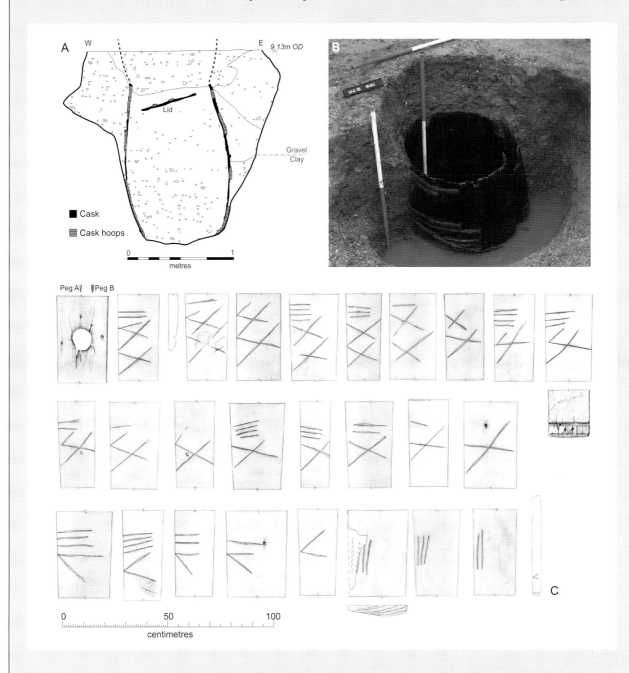

Figure 4.39. *Late sixteenth-century cask-lined Well 38: (A) section of the well; (B) photograph, facing northeast; (C) the 'mirror image' Roman numerals employed when rebuilding the cask, in the order they were found ([35462]).*

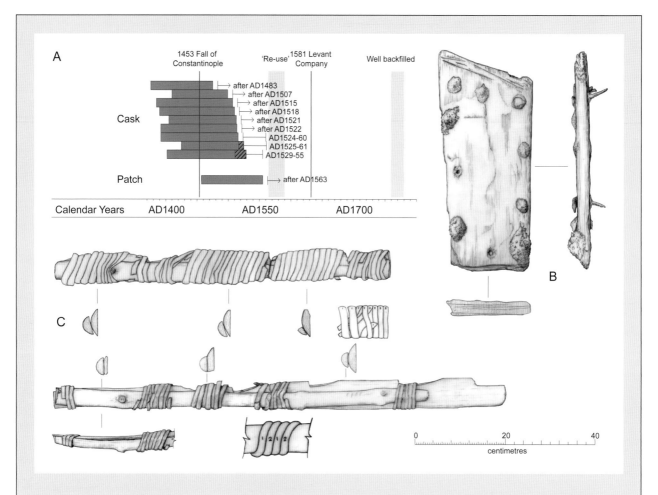

Figure 4.40. *Late sixteenth-century cask-lined Well 38: (A) dendrochronology plot for the cask's constituent staves and associated patch; (B) the Eastern Baltic oak patch ([35462]); (C) the oak, ash and hazel lashed hoops ([35462]).*

between the croze grooves), with a croze diameter of 0.815m and a maximum diameter of 1.105m; it would originally have held 0.77 cubic m. This cask had a 4mm deep croze groove, tapering from 9–7.5mm wide, which was distinct from the other casks at the site. There were also some subjective features, including the timber seeming denser and the sapwood being harder, that suggested the possibility of a more exotic origin.

The tree ring sequences of 13 of the 27 staves could be inter-correlated to produce a 174 year composite sequence, which initially proved impossible to match with central, western and northern European oak reference data. Subsequently, it was matched to two regional oak tree-ring chronologies from Greece, with the sequence from the Central and Western region having a slightly stronger correlation than the Thessaloniki and Thrace region,

with *t* values (Baillie & Pilcher 1973) of 8.03 and 7.92 respectively. This appears to be the first time that oak from Greece has been identified through dendrochronology in Britain. The tree began to grow in 1368 and the last ring dates to 1542, with sapwood suggesting a felling date of 1542–55 (Fig. 4.40A). A piece of a reused oak stave nailed on to the cask as a patch (Fig. 4.40B) proved to be made of eastern Baltic oak with a 98 year sequence ending in 1555, which cannot have been felled prior to 1563. As the main cask only had a single bung hole and was a non-standard size it may not have been reused in Britain, suggesting a relatively short delay between felling and well construction in *c.* 1563–90. One of the staves that matched the Greek sequences had a burnt cooper's or merchant's mark at its base in the form of a star, although there is no way to determine when this mark was added.

The well-built cask could have contained a range of products, including figs (which have been recovered from deposits in Cambridge from the thirteenth/fourteenth centuries onwards), grapes (which occur in deposits from the sixteenth century onwards) or olives (which have not been recovered archaeologically in Cambridge). Cultivation of English grapes had declined by the Elizabethan period and although figs were grown locally it is difficult to get a good crop so many figs and grapes, which are quite common archaeological discoveries, were probably imported (Giorgi 1997, 203–4). A more likely content, however, is wine, as the quality of the cooperage indicates that the cask probably held liquid. Compared to northern European wines Mediterranean wine was sweeter, heavier and had a higher alcohol content. It also travelled better, lasted longer and was more valuable (Unwin 1991, 185). Trade in Mediterranean wine to England began around the thirteenth century and increased in the fourteenth century; it was largely conducted by Genoese and Venetian merchants, with some Byzantine involvement, and was principally focused on London and Southampton (Harris 2007).

The wood for the cask was felled 89–102 years after the Fall of Constantinople to the Ottoman Empire under Sultan Mehmed II in 1453. More significantly in terms of the cask itself, the Ottoman Empire had begun to expand into the Balkans from the mid-fourteenth century and by 1430 controlled much of Greece. There is a general perception that the Ottoman expansion had a negative impact on the wine trade, with vineyard destruction and a reorientation of trade (Unwin 1991, 186), although this cask challenges this assumption somewhat. During his time as Lady Margaret's Professor of Divinity in Cambridge the Dutch humanist and theologian Desiderius Erasmus Roterodamus (1466/69–1536) sent for Greek wine from London (Thomson & Porter 1963, 85–6, 108, 176). In 1511–13 Erasmus obtained four casks of Greek wine from London, with the empty casks being returned. The implication is that the Greek wine available in Cambridge was of inferior quality, although there were also problems with some of the wine he obtained from London.

There are also references in a Cambridge vintner's accounts of c. 1511 to the selling of Greek wine, including Malmsey wine from the Greek mainland and Rumney from the western Greek islands (Minns 1934, 51). In the early sixteenth century there is some evidence of direct English trade with the Ottoman Empire, a practice which appears to have come to an end by the middle of the century when trade was controlled by Venetians via Antwerp (Willan 1955, 400). Archaeologically this is represented by silver coins, such as a Venetian soldino of Leonardo Loredan (1501–21) found during excavations at Jesus College, which is of a type that was imported into England in large quantities for use as the equivalent of the halfpenny that remained in circulation until the 1540s (Challis 1978, 214–15; Daubney 2010; Spufford 1963, 137–8).

The well was constructed during the first half of the reign of Elizabeth I (1558–1603). This period spans the reigns of several Ottoman emperors, beginning with the last years of Suleiman I (the Magnificent or the Lawmaker; 1520–66) the longest-reigning sultan of the Ottoman Empire, who presided over the height of the empire's military, political and economic power. Alternatively it may have been manufactured during the reign of his successor Selim II (the Sot; 1566–74), who – rather appropriately given the context – was notorious for his love of wine and allegedly invaded Cyprus in 1571 in part for its wine, which was his favourite. He died after drinking a whole bottle of Cypriot wine at a single draft. The last possibility is Murad III (1574–95), under whom England and the Ottoman Empire established diplomatic relations in 1578 and signed a treaty of

commerce in 1580. The Levant Company was then formed in 1581 (Epstein 1908; Horniker 1942; Mather 2009; Rawlinson 1922; Skilliter 1977; Wood 1935). Judging by the taxation that was applied to it, wine, along with currants and oil, appears to have been amongst the most significant items the company traded. A shipwreck in the Straits of Rhodes, identified as an armed English merchantman of c. 1560–90 (Royal & McManamon 2010), may represent one of the vessels used in this trade. Documentary sources refer to malmsey, muscadet and other wines and indicate that the main source was Candia (Crete) and to a lesser extent Zante (Zakynthos) (Skilliter 1977) and mention casks that held 29ft^3 (0.82 cubic m) or 108–40 gallons (Skilliter 1977, 114); which is close to the 0.77 cubic m volume of the cask in *Well 38*.

The most famous reference to Greek wine in medieval England is when Shakespeare refers to the Duke of Clarence (1449–78) being drowned in a butt of malmsey (Richard III, Act I Scene IV). It is unclear what if any truth there is in the story, but as the play was written c. 1591 it suggests that Shakespeare expected his audience to be familiar with Greek wine. The development of late sixteenth-century trade with the Ottoman Empire, although primarily economically motivated, was also in part a political and Protestant endeavour, with explicitly anti-Catholic connotations. It broadly coincided with the origins of the 'First British Empire' in 1583–4 when Humphrey Gilbert travelled to Newfoundland and his half-brother Walter Raleigh founded the colony of Roanoke. The Levant Company, in contrast to these colonial ventures, created bases in pre-existing commercial centres within a well-established powerful empire. Indeed, the Ottoman Empire was a much more significant economic, military and political power than England and in some respects was the most globally significant state of its day. The Levant Company sold wool and tin in return for silks, spices, indigo and currants and by the end of the seventeenth-century trade with the Ottoman Empire accounted for a quarter of English overseas trade. In sharp contrast to later periods it was the English who had to conform to local traditions and mores, rather than imposing them on others.

The cask was specifically rebuilt to line the well, incorporating staves from more than one cask and all but one of the staves had vigorously cut race knife 'mirror image' Roman numerals (Fig. 4.39C). This probably occurred locally as the hook-bladed race knife was a common English tool for numbering in the fifteenth and sixteenth centuries. Number I was represented by the single bunghole, and flanked by IIVXX and II; IIXX was missing and a new stave had been inserted between XXIV and XXIII. This new stave was made from fast grown oak with only 38 rings. It is of such poor quality that it was probably only ever used in the well lining and was potentially produced specifically for this. The hoops on the cask were complete and must have been fitted after the rebuild (Fig. 4.40C). They were made from 3.5m-long coppice poles of oak, ash and hazel lashed for 0.37–0.45m with bark – probably willow – which had been cut from a narrow stem. No pegs or nails were used to hold the hoops to size and they relied on lashings alone.

A set of short notches was cut on one side of the prepared hoops near the ends, while the opposite side of the half round hoop had a sharp angle on it so that once bent around the lashing could not slide. The presence of notches meant that some of the lashings were shorter than others; these short lashings stopped the half round pieces of hoop from sliding over each other. The hoops were attached via the lashings, although some nails had also been added to the structure when it was used as a well; these were driven through the hoops into the staves. The nails had split the hoops and would have prevented the cask from retaining liquid. Where pegs were found some were pine and were used to hold the hoops together. The absence of pine pegs in the staves means that the function of these pegs was to hold the hoops together rather than to attach the hoops to the staves. The lashings were up to 9mm wide and 540mm long but each lashing was only six or seven turns, the ends being trapped in between the rods or caught under the next lashing. There was a hint that all the lashings were kept on the same side of the cask, as also occurs in York (Morris 2000, fig. 1089). Opposite the bung hole in stave XV was a small 11mm-diameter spile or vent peg.

Well 38 continued in use until the eighteenth century, when it was backfilled (Chapter 5). Although the small pottery assemblage initially suggested a sixteenth- or early seventeenth-century date for the its backfilling, subsequent analysis of the shape and nature of the seam of the welted soles of two leather shoes from the infill indicted a date no earlier than the eighteenth century. The faunal remains, which included some leather-working waste, were probably derived from the same source as an adjacent feature dated *c.* 1760–80, suggesting that this was the period when *Well 38* went out of use. The backfilling material also included part of an oak lid (Fig. 4.37A). This was not a cask lid, as the battens do not go all the way to the side, and it may comprise a specially constructed seal for the top of the well. Also present was a fragment of decorated leather derived from a piece of upholstery or other furnishing (Fig. 4.37C–D).

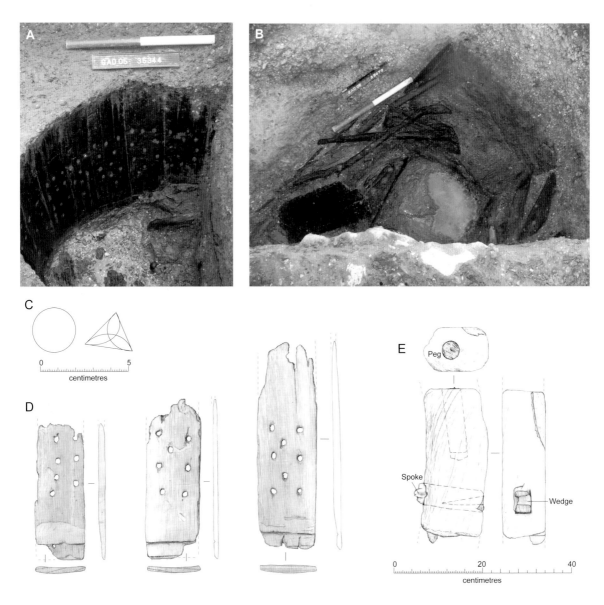

Figure 4.41. *Fifteenth-century cask-lined Cesspit 14: (A) photograph of the cask, facing east; (B) photograph of the packing timbers, facing north; (C) cooper's or owner's marks incised onto the cask head (based upon an original drawing by Richard Darrah); (D) cask staves with augured holes ([35344]); (E) beech felloe and an oak spoke ([35504]).*

Stone-lined wells potentially had a significantly longer lifespan and, due to their increased structural integrity, were also typically deeper than most of their wattle- and cask-lined equivalents. Although more costly to create, there was probably a large increase in the availability of stone locally immediately after the Dissolution, although some stone-lined wells were constructed prior to this and only one stone-lined well was constructed in the half-century or so immediately following the Dissolution (*Well 37*; Fig. 4.38). It is notable that this latter well incorporated ashlar blocks without mouldings. Whilst this lack of diagnostic elements makes the blocks archaeologically less interesting, it does suggest that the relative value of stone had decreased, since the earlier stone-lined wells had utilized moulded elements that could not readily be reused in above-ground contexts. Unlike later examples at the site (Chapter 5), the stone-lined wells constructed between the mid-fourteenth and late sixteenth centuries (*Wells 22, 36, 37*) did not have timber baseplates. Contrastingly, at Chesterton stone-lined wells with baseplates have been investigated that dated to the mid–late fourteenth (Newman 2015) and early fifteenth centuries (Cessford with Dickens 2004) respectively; thirteenth–fourteenth-century examples with baseplates are also known from London (Burch *et al.* 2010, 317–18). The absence of contemporary baseplates in the wells at Grand Arcade may therefore be associated with a difference in construction-technique as opposed to a lack of available technology.

Cesspits (incorporating specialist information from Richard Darrah and Mark Samuel)

Due to their increased depth and more robust linings, which resulted in a higher degree of archaeological visibility, three cesspits belonging to this period were identified (Figs. 4.41–4.43). Nevertheless, this low number – allied with the expense of the surviving examples – suggests that the majority of cesspits continued to be wattle-lined and were consequently removed by later truncation. An additional factor is that some latrines are known to have been constructed out over the King's Ditch during the fifteenth–sixteenth centuries (Chapter 3); once again, these features did not survive to be represented archaeologically. The extant cesspits contained no primary deposits that could be linked to their usage.

The staves of the cask that formed the lining of *Cesspit 14* had had numerous holes augured through them to assist drainage, and – in common with several contemporary wells – the cask was placed upon a wooden base and had other timbers placed around it as packing (Figs. 4.41–4.42). Meanwhile, the reused moulded stone employed in the lining of *Cesspit 16* (Fig. 4.43) hints at the demolition of a late thirteenth–early fourteenth-century high status, probably secular, building (see further below). In London the Assize of Nuisance stipulated that the mouth of a cesspit walled in stone could be located as little as 2½ft (*c.* 0.75m) from an adjacent property rather than the 3½ft (*c.* 1.05m) required for other lining-types (Chew & Kellaway 1973). Archaeological evidence suggests that similar rules also applied in Cambridge.

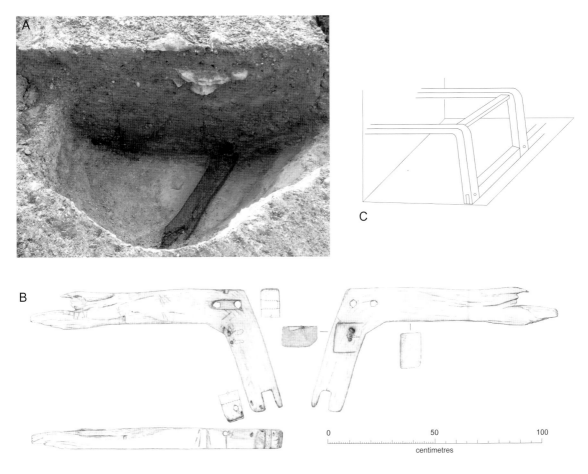

Figure 4.42. *Fifteenth-century cask-lined Cesspit 14, showing (A) photograph of the oak framed baseplate in situ, facing south; (B) the baseplate's constituent timbers ([35497]); (C) reconstruction of the original oak frame from which the timbers were derived (based on an original drawing by Richard Darrah).*

Figure 4.43. *Photographs of late sixteenth-century stone-lined Cesspit 15, facing north (top), and mid-sixteenth-century stone-lined Cesspit 16, facing north (bottom).*

Buildings

In common with preceding centuries, relatively few fifteenth–sixteenth-century buildings were identified at the site and many of those that were present were highly fragmentary in nature. Little could be determined of *Building 12/14*, for example, beyond the fact that it was situated in close proximity to the street frontage and underwent several phases of rebuilding/redevelopment. Within the property tails the relatively scarce structural evidence indicates the existence of a number of plot accessory buildings, but again reveals little of their size, form or nature. In several instances reused moulded stone was used to construct sill walls, indicating that all of these structures post-dated the Dissolution.

The best-preserved, and certainly the most intriguing, structure was *Building 20* (Fig. 4.44). In its initial mid-fifteenth-century form this comprised a square building that measured 4.4m by 4.5m in extent. In its centre was situated a large timber-revetted

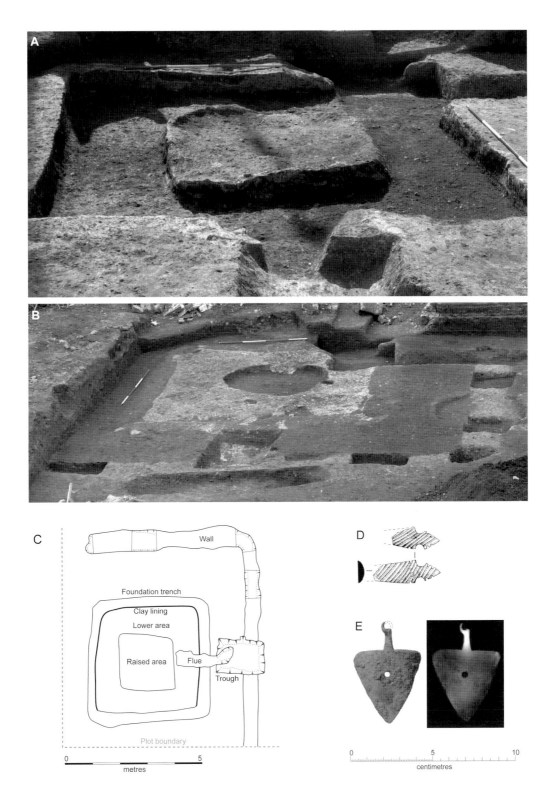

Figure 4.44. *Mid-fifteenth–mid-sixteenth-century possible malting kiln Building 20: (A) photograph of the building's upstanding central island and associated wall footings, facing west; (B) photograph of the building's foundation trenches, facing west; (C) plan of the building; (D) finely worked decorative object – probably made from mammal long bone rather than antler – which may have comprised the side plates of a comb or possibly furniture fittings, recovered from early sixteenth-century modifications ([30699]); (E) shield-shaped copper alloy horse pendant with gilt decoration, recovered from mid-sixteenth-century demolition deposit ([30513]).*

square pit, which in turn contained an upstanding central island. Around the perimeter of the pit were arranged a series of clay-filled foundation trenches, while on its eastern side the building also possessed a clay-lined flue-like structure. The result was a square building with raised floors, under which air from the flue could circulate. As there was no evidence of *in situ* scorching or burning, the air appears to have been warm rather than hot. *Building 20* went through a series minor rebuilds and repairs during the early sixteenth century, when a clay-lined trough was added. At around the same time additional wall footings were constructed to the north and east of the building, enclosing it and creating a 1.7–1.8m-wide strip around the structure.

Subsequently, after a further period of use, the flue and other sunken areas were backfilled and a clay floor was laid over the area. *Building 20* thereby lost its specialized nature and became instead a simple square structure. No definitive evidence pertaining to the function of *Building 20* was recovered. It clearly served a specialized function and the most likely explanation is that it was a malting kiln used to produce malt for beer, where cereal grains that had been made to germinate by soaking them in water are then heaped on a warm, heated floor. Although no charred grains were found, this situation is paralleled at other sites and simply indicates that if it was a malting kiln the roasting was done with care and the structure regularly cleaned.

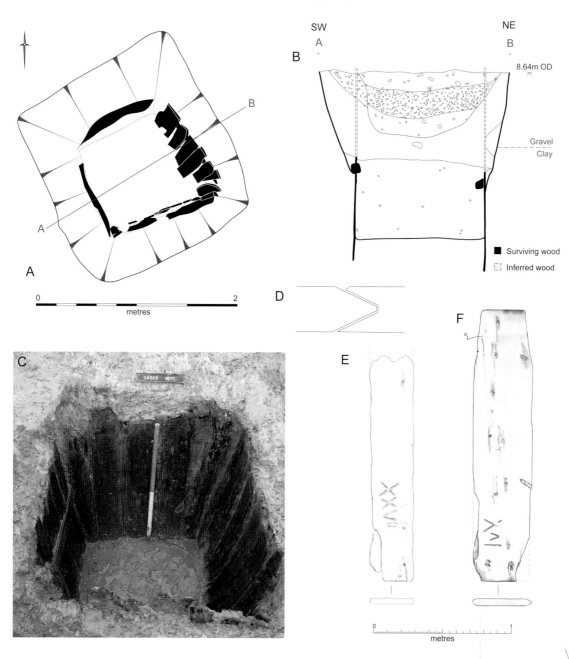

Figure 4.45. *Mid/late fifteenth-century WFF 13: (A) plan; (B) section; (C) photograph of the timber-lining facing south; (D) tongue-and-grooved board joint (based upon an original drawing by Richard Darrah); (E–F) numbered cask staves XXVll and lVX ([37050], [37051]).*

Water-filled features incorporating specialist information from Richard Darrah

Water-filled features continued to be constructed during the fifteenth and early sixteenth centuries (Figs. 4.45–4.49). Two examples, *WFFs 11* and *13*, both appear to have functioned as cisterns and were located close together in the same property. They were nevertheless of quite different construction. *WFF 11* relied for strength on heavy durable timbers and massive joints (see Case Study 6), whereas *WFF 13* relied on nails and a light

frame that was primarily constructed from non-durable pine (Fig. 4.45). This lightweight structure had a relatively short life-span as it failed within a few decades. Consequently, it is possible that *WFF 11* may have been a direct replacement for *WFF 13*. *WFF 11* was constructed using reused twelfth-century timber derived from a substantial oak trough (Case Study 6). Also notable were *WFFs 14* and *15*, which were located close together and backfilled around the same time in the mid-sixteenth century; both contained an *in situ* ladder (Figs. 4.46 and 4.48).

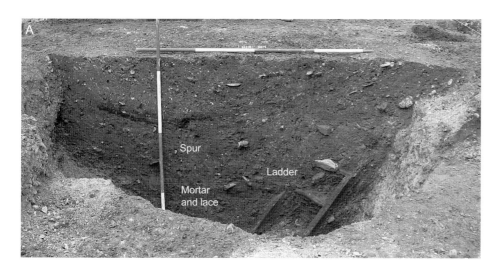

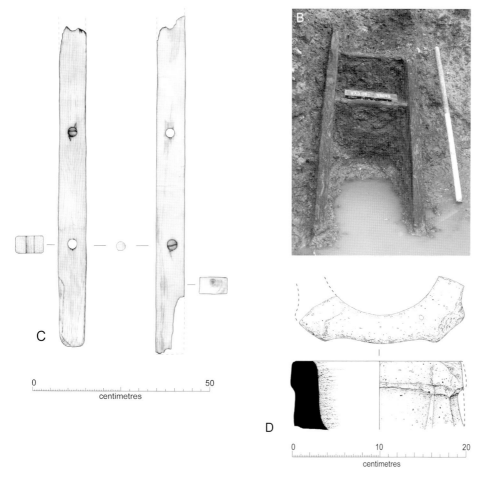

Figure 4.46. *Mid/late fifteenth-century WFF 14, plus a ladder recovered from its mid-sixteenth-century backfilling: (A) photograph of the feature with a portion of the ladder visible, facing north; (B) photograph of the ladder in situ, facing northeast; (C) the ash ladder ([35082]); (D) finely carved limestone mortar ([35073]).*

147

Case study 6: *Water-filled feature 11*
incorporating specialist information from
Richard Darrah, David Hall and Ian Tyers

WFF 11 (Fig. 4.47) was located on the extreme
northern edge of the area of archaeological investigation. Because this area was covered by a site
walkway it could not be investigated until the end
of the excavation phase in mid-December 2005. Its
depth then meant that the lower portion had to be
left until mid-January 2006, by which time the rest
of the area had been lowered some 6m and a 45°
batter created, leading to challenging excavation
conditions. *WFF 11* was created in the mid/late
fifteenth century, possibly as a direct replacement
for nearby less substantial structure *WFF 13*.

WFF 11 had a circular construction pit that
measured 2.1m in diameter and over 2.1m deep.
Within the construction pit was situated a square
timber-lined structure that measured 1.3m in extent.
It was composed of four heavy-jointed frames of
oak planks stacked vertically on edge, thereby
creating a robust timber-lined cistern with internal
dimensions of 0.96m by 0.98m. This cistern would
have naturally filled with water to *c.* 1.6m, holding
c. 1.6 cubic m. The individual planks of the upper
two frames consisted of tusked tenoned planks
up to 1.4m long, 0.54m wide and 0.05m thick (Fig.
4.47E–F). One side of the higher and middle frames
and three sides of the lowest frame were made up
from narrower heavy boards held in place with
vertical timbers. Dendrochronology confirmed that
six of the planks came from a single tree *c.* 1.0m in
diameter, while another came from a radially cleft
eighth of a different *c.* 0.6m diameter oak trunk.

The mortices and tusked tenons were cut to fit on plank lengths
varying between 1.11–1.40m long and 0.36–0.54m wide; the
thickness varied between 35–65mm, while the tenons were
110–145mm long and up to 115mm deep. The mortices were
predrilled at the four corners from both sides with 18mm or
24mm diameter holes and varied in cross section between
125mm by 60mm and 160 by 82mm. There was no evidence
of packing to fill gaps in the frames, but the heavy boards had
not been trimmed to fit tightly. The tenons had 18mm-diameter
auger holes for a peg outside to form tusked tenons. Each board
had either two mortices or two tenons. The remaining pieces
were fast grown slab wood and had too few rings to date. The
main group of planks produced a 123-year composite tree
ring sequence dated by comparison to English sequences to
1035–1157. There was a complete absence of surviving sapwood,
but the reasonable clustering of end-dates indicates that this
material is near to the original sapwood surface of the tree.

In addition, two of the samples had curved and
discoloured outer edges, perhaps indicating the heartwood/

sapwood transition zone. Allowing for the minimum amount
of absent sapwood the tree was felled 1167–95. The plank from
the other oak tree produced a sequence of 1047–1136, and must
have been felled after 1146. The similarity in dates suggests that
it derives from the same original item as the other timber, which
was *c.* 250 years old when it was reused. Most of the surfaces of
these timbers were worn, but there were fresh splits along one
edge of three of them and one of these splits was associated
with a lip on the timber. This, together with the absence of saw
marks on these outer axe-dressed tangential timbers, indicates
that the timbers had formed part of a larger hewn object with
flat sides that had been broken up into planks. The most likely
original object is a trough (see Morris 2000, 2273–5, 2413). At least
seven of these planks survive. If both the base and two sides of
the hewn trough are present then it was three times the length
of the planks, making it over 4m long. The evidence from the
surviving pieces is that the original trough was *c.* 0.75m wide
and 0.4m high (Fig. 4.47D). It could have been made from a
0.9m-diameter tree.

Allowing for losses in axe cutting, the trough must have
been over 4m long and is unlikely to have been over 7m long,
as timber of this size would have been too valuable. With
ends missing, as only the straight central part of the structure
is present, this trough would have been both long enough
and stable enough to have been a dugout, as some medieval
examples were flat-sided such as the Clapton dugout (Goodburn
2008), although there is no surviving evidence to indicate that
it was anything other than a trough. A trough with internal
measurements of 4.0m by 0.65m by 0.35 would hold *c.* 0.9 cubic m
of water. It was probably shaped where the tree was felled, as
the trunk would originally have weighed three tonnes. Most
of the wood would have been hewn off the outside, split out
probably in 0.5m lengths that were useable only as firewood.
Hewing would produce chunks 200mm by 200mm by 100mm
by notch and chop.

A number of stakes were used to hold this structure in
place during construction; these included nine made from ash,
three of oak and one each of field maple, beech and willow.
This structure is similar in form and construction, but much
smaller than, a cistern in use between the fourteenth–sixteenth
centuries at Oyster Street, Portsmouth, believed to have been
used for supplying ships (Fox *et al.* 1986, 46–50). The Oyster
Street cistern was covered by a floor of planks with gaps. In
the backfilling of the Grand Arcade cistern there were several
pieces of timber including a slow grown backed and hollowed
coopered stave with a damaged croze groove and a cask stave
that could have derived from such a floor.

In sum, mid/late fifteenth-century *WFF 11* was constructed
by breaking up a substantial 4–7m long trough that was made
from a tree felled *c.* 1167–95. It seems unlikely that this trough
had travelled far, and if it had been in the Grand Arcade street
block since it was made this would take it back to the earliest
phase of the suburb's existence. As this tree from which it was
made began to grow somewhere relatively locally in 1035, this
in turn takes us further back before the beginning of dispersed
occupation of the site to when the area was ploughed as open
fields.

WFF 11 went out of use and was backfilled in either
the late fifteenth or early sixteenth century; the backfilling
contained few objects apart from three sherds weighing 1334g
which refitted to form the lower two-thirds of a buff coarseware
shouldered jug (Fig. 4.47C). This appears to be a Hertfordshire
Fineware vessel dating to the thirteenth century, suggesting
that it was *c.* 200–250 years old when deposited. Whilst the

apparent archaeological 'default position' of regarding pottery that is older than the context in which it is found as residual should be challenged, as there is evidence that some medieval jugs were relatively long-lived heirlooms (Gilchrist 2012, 238–9), this seems improbable for such a long period. It is perhaps more likely that the material used to backfill *WFF 11* was excavated from somewhere nearby, perhaps to create a replacement for it. If this was the case then the most likely context to have produced such a semi-complete jug would be the base of a well backfilled in the thirteenth century, suggesting that such a feature was effectively re-excavated in the late fifteenth or early sixteenth century. The most likely candidate for this hypothesis is a nearby feature *WFF 12*, constructed in the mid/late fifteenth century, which consisted of an unusual circular 3.2m-diameter and 3.8m-deep vertically sided shaft that could easily have removed all traces of an earlier well.

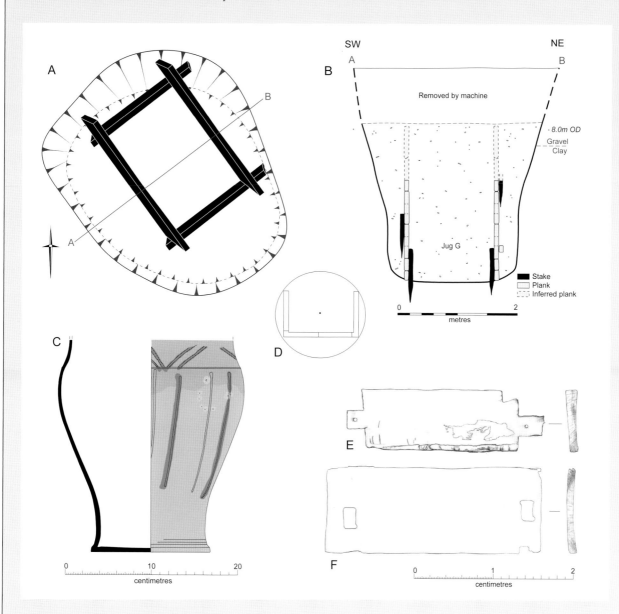

Figure 4.47. *Mid/late fifteenth-century WFF 11, plus material recovered from its late fifteenth- or early sixteenth-century backfilling. This shows: (A) plan; (B) section; (C) buff coarseware shouldered jug with applied vertical brown and self-coloured strip decoration, plus zigzag strips on the shoulder – possibly Hertfordshire Fineware and probably dating to the thirteenth century ([37128]) (D) reconstruction of the probable trough from which the planks were derived (based upon an original drawing by Richard Darrah); (E–F) morticed and tusked tenoned planks ([37088], [37121]).*

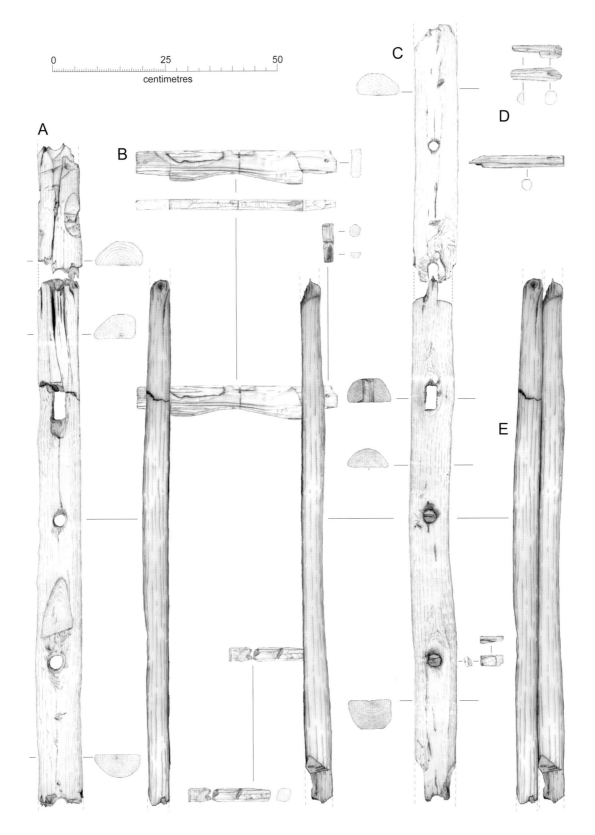

Figure 4.48. *Ladder from mid-sixteenth-century backfilling of mid/late fifteenth-century WFF 15: (A) an elm rail ([34590]); (B) ash 'makers rung' ([34591]); (C) elm rail ([34590]); (D) ash rungs ([34590]); (E) refitted elm rails, forming an original pole ([34590]).*

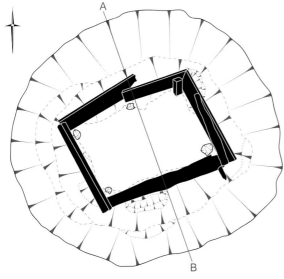

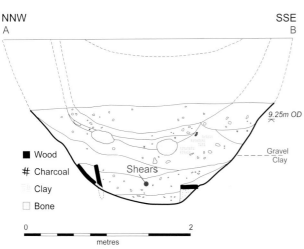

Figure 4.49. *Mid-fifteenth-century WFF 16: (A) plan; (B) section; (C) photograph, facing north.*

Ovens incorporating specialist information from Rachel Ballantyne and Anne de Vareilles

While one group of fifteenth–sixteenth-century ovens (*Ovens 7*) represents a continuation of the earlier, fourteenth-century clay-lined tradition, brick-built *Oven 8*, which dated to *c.* 1580–1600, represents instead the introduction of a new type. A rather different type of oven again was present in *Building 12*, which was situated significantly closer to the frontage than the other ovens and may even have comprised the plot dominant building. This was a large circular oven, measuring *c.* 1.55m diameter, which did not possess a permanent superstructure. Charred plant remains associated with the abandonment of the oven in the sixteenth century contained few grains or wild plant seeds, but rather a rich mix of barley, free-threshing wheat and rye chaff, along with cereal and great-fen sedge straw and common reed (*Phragmites* sp.). This material represents a mix of crop processing waste that was added to great-fen sedge and reed and used as oven fuel.

Animal disposal pits with Lorrain Higbee

The fifteenth–sixteenth-century animal disposal pits were similar to those of the fourteenth century. During this period animals also continued to be deposited into the King's Ditch (Chapter 3) along with wells and pits dug for other purposes. It is notable that sixteenth-century *ADP 8*, which contained a pig, was located in close proximity to fourteenth–fifteenth-century *ADP 2*, which also contained a pig that had suffered similar health problems. A rather different phenomenon is represented by a horse skeleton in *ADP 9* (see Fig. 4.70), as its body may have been utilized prior to its disposal and other waste was also deposited in the pit. In addition, this latter feature also contained the skeleton of a toad; although this could represent an animal that fell into an open feature (Piper & O'Connor 2001) there were indications that the toad may have been deliberately placed. It could therefore relate to local beliefs, as Cambridgeshire folklore records a figure known as the 'Toadman' who could make horses stay perfectly still (Porter 1969, 56–7). The 'Toadman' had to catch a toad and kill it; the bones were then kept until perfectly dry, thrown into a river and any that moved or pointed upstream would be kept.

A town ordinance of 1575 stated that most dead animals could be either buried on the owner's property or disposed of on common dunghills, but that larger animals such as horses and bullocks had to be removed to the one of the common dunghills or other places further from the town (Cooper 1843, 336). This ordinance appears to have been effective as it seems to have marked the end of burying horses in the Grand Arcade street block. Smaller animals such as dogs continued to be disposed of, however; most commonly within larger pits that were initially dug for some other purpose.

Specialized pits

There were fewer specialized pits than in the thirteenth–fourteenth centuries, although a few clay-lined examples were created in the fifteenth–sixteenth centuries; presumably for some purpose that involved holding liquids.

Surfaces

Surviving surfaces continued to be rare. A sequence of gravel surfaces and accumulations, *Surface 3*, are suggestive of an external yard over 4.7 by 2.1m in extent. As well as over 1kg of pottery these surfaces also contained a clay tobacco pipe bowl of *c.* 1580–1610 and two Rose/Orb-type jettons of 1586–1635. In another area mid-fifteenth-century *Surface 4*, which was composed of firm light greyish brown clay extending over 6.0m by 3.1m in extent and 0.07m thick, suggests the construction of a formal yard area.

Pits

During the fifteenth–sixteenth centuries gravel quarry pits gradually became less common, although they continued to be dug until the mid-sixteenth century (Figs. 4.50–4.53); following this date, there is evidence for more intensive quarrying in parts of the East Fields (see

151

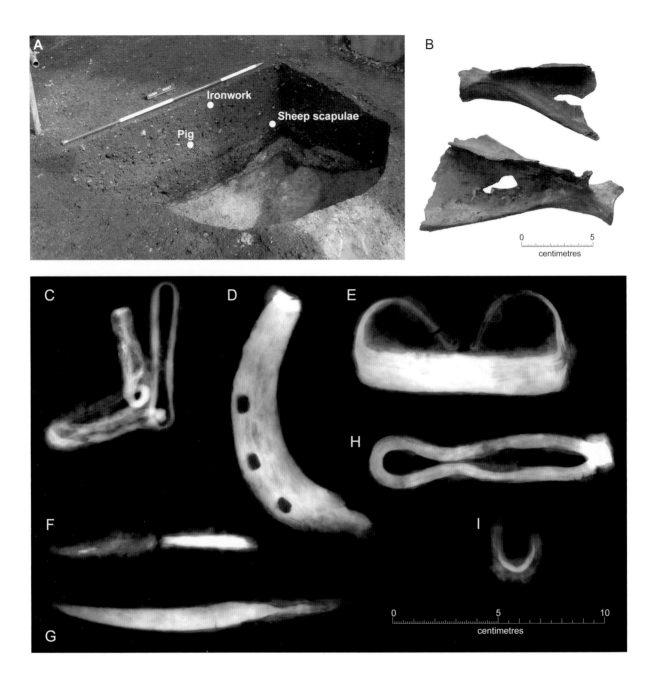

Figure 4.50. *Mid-sixteenth-century gravel quarry Pit 46: (A) photograph of the pit, facing northeast; (B) sheep scapula with butcher's hook damage to the blade ([50295]; (C) three interconnecting figure of eight-shaped iron loops, probably looped hasps ([50274]); (D) iron horseshoe arm with rectangular nail holes ([50274]); (E) iron fire steel with rectangular blade and curved arms ([50274]); (F–G) whittle-tanged iron knives, (G) is a Goodall type J with concave back, none of which are complete or closely dated (Goodall 2011, 107, fig. 137) ([50274]); (H) figure of eight-shaped iron looped hasp ([50274]); (I) simple U-shaped iron staple ([50274]) (photograph B courtesy of Lorrain Higbee).*

Chapter 6). Pits of unknown function also continued to be dug on a fairly regular basis until around the mid-sixteenth century, after which their incidence declined. Unlike in earlier periods, a significant number of these latter pits were dug slightly into the underlying clay and they would consequently have held a small quantity of water in their base, filling to a depth of *c.* 0.1–0.2m. Whilst not enough to categorize them as true water-filled features, this circumstance has led to some organic preservation (Figs. 4.51D and 4.53).

Clay quarry pits continued to be dug in the same area as in the fourteenth century, gradually spreading outwards to both the west and east from the highest point of the clay. The original pits do not appear to have been fully backfilled as there was sixteenth-century pottery in their upper portions, suggesting that this 13m long zone had remained a relatively messy damp hollow for a considerable period. A number of the items recovered from the clay quarry pits, such as wooden battens and possibly also thatch (see further below),

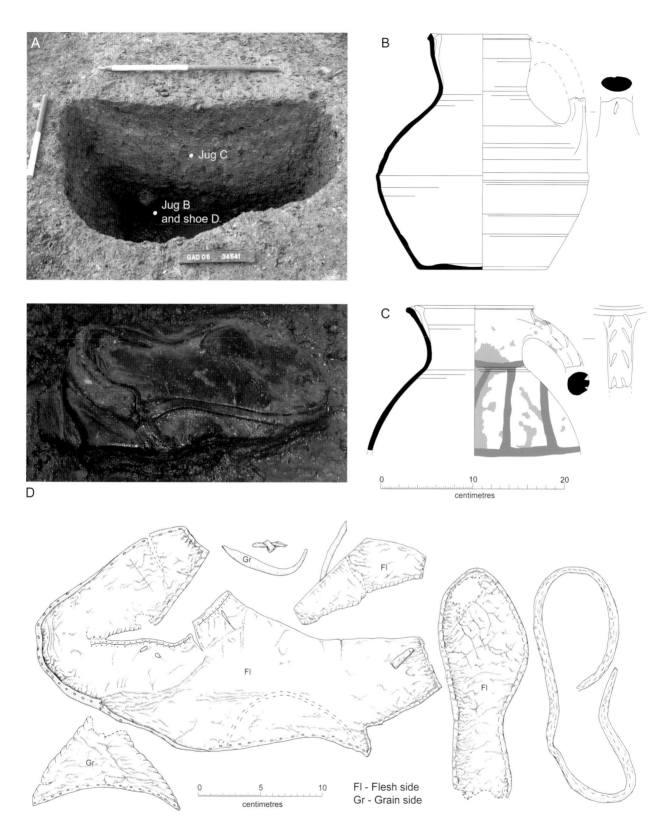

Figure 4.51. *Fifteenth-century pit of unknown function Pit 49, plus material from its backfilling: (A) photograph of the pit, facing south; (B) grey coarseware rounded jug with strap handle ([34525]); (C) Surrey Borders ware jug with painted decoration and slashed rod handle ([36774]); (D) turnshoe ankleshoe with knotted lace fastening, child's right foot ([34525]).*

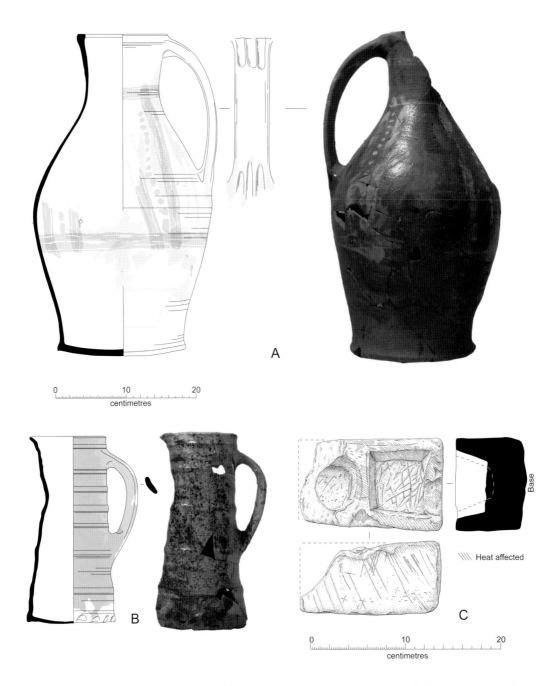

Figure 4.52. *Material recovered from early/mid-fifteenth-century clay quarry Pit 36: (A) large Essex Redware rounded jug with strap handle and thumb-pinched base, decorated with applied strips and blobs ([34263]); (B) Essex Redware slender conical jug with a strap handle that has become rather deformed in the kiln and is clearly a second. It has cordon decoration and a thumb-pinched base, while the body is almost entirely covered by an all over slip, green glaze and brown/iron splashes ([34831]); (C) broken rectangular stone object, perhaps a cresset or a heating tray ([34456]).*

suggest that the digging of clay quarry pits was directly linked to construction activities on the frontage. Although most of the clay quarry pits contained some quantity of material there was little in the way of substantial domestic refuse. This is true for almost all the pits at the site, contrasting strongly with a number of sites in central Cambridge where most sixteenth-century pits contained significant assemblages of material (*e.g.* Cessford 2005; Edwards & Hall 1997).

Material culture

Substantial assemblages of eleventh–sixteenth century artefactual, ecofactual and environmental remains were recovered from the Grand Arcade street block. Smaller, but nevertheless highly comparable, assemblages of the

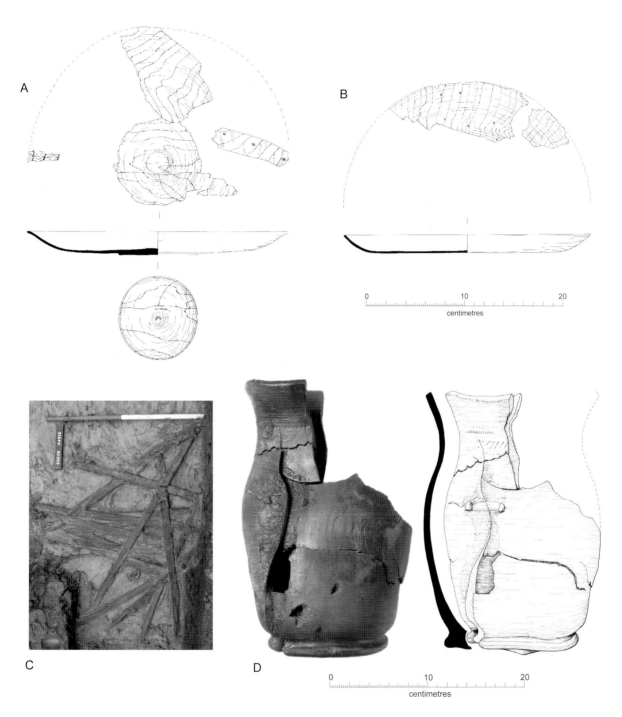

Figure 4.53. *Wooden items recovered from early/mid-fifteenth-century clay quarry Pits 36–7, including: (A–B) two fragmentary wooden bowls ([34264], [34555]) from Pit 36; (C) photograph of the oak battens in the base of Pit 36, facing south ([34518]); (D) European maple jug from Pit 37 ([34481]).*

same date were also recovered from the nearby site at Christ's Lane (Chapter 6); to avoid unwarranted repetition, the two groups are presented here together. For the same reason, the medieval material recovered from the King's Ditch (Chapter 3) has also been incorporated below. Because of the extensive nature of many of the assemblages that are discussed, the following reports primarily present a general overview, illustrated by a selection of the most pertinent examples; additional information – including methodological statements and detailed discussions as well as further tables and figures – can be found within the digital-only volume.

Structurally, due to the problematic nature of distinguishing between diagnostically eleventh- and diagnostically twelfth-century material, the two are considered here together, despite the fact that relatively discrete phases of eleventh- and early twelfth-century (Chapter 2) and mid–late twelfth-century activity have been identified. Similarly, while an effort has been made to structure the discussions around the arbitrary temporal sub-divisions utilized above in relation to the period's archaeological remains (thirteenth–fourteenth century and fifteenth–sixteenth century), this has not always been possible. Where a more precise, or directly relevant, sub-division can be identified, this has been adopted in preference. One consequence of this approach is that in certain instances – as with ceramics, for example – seventeenth-century material has been included in the following discussion outside its nominal position in the chapter sequence.

Finally, it should also be noted that in some instances, where a substantial proportion of the recovered assemblage of a certain material-type is sixteenth-century or earlier in date – as is the case with faunal and environmental remains, for example – a general discussion of the overall sequence and patterning is presented here; a more limited discussion of the remains directly pertaining to any later periods is included in Chapter 5. Conversely, where a material-type first appeared in the present period but is more substantively represented in later centuries – as is the case with clay tobacco pipes and ceramic building materials, for instance – a broader discussion of the assemblage is instead to be found in the succeeding chapter.

Jettons Martin Allen

Seven jettons of thirteenth–sixteenth-century date were recovered from Grand Arcade and Christ's Lane, but no coins of this date were recovered. This relative paucity contrasts with other areas of Cambridge, such as the town centre and Trumpington and Castle Hill suburbs, where contemporary coins and jettons comprise more regular archaeological discoveries.

Two copper alloy English jettons of *c.* 1280–1350 were recovered from Grand Arcade. One had a five-petalled barbed rose with a pseudo-inscription +BA+BO+BA+BOS+BA+[BO]S in the border on the obverse and an arcuate cross with crosslet and two rosettes at each end and a border of pellets on the reverse (Mitchiner 1988, nos. 186, 244). The other had an illegible obverse and what appears to be a triple-stranded cross fleury on the reverse (Mitchiner 1988, nos. 90–1, 178–80). Elsewhere, a ditch in the East Fields at the Former Marshall Garage site produced a jetton with a sterling bust obverse, possibly of class 15 (*c.* 1319–43), whose reverse bore a cross moline with a quatrefoil in each quarter (similar to Mitchiner 1988, no. 192; see further Chapter 6).

Five late fifteenth–early sixteenth-century jettons were recovered, two of which were from Christ's Lane. These were predominantly from Nuremberg, but with single English and French examples. The Nuremburg jettons are all of rose/orb-type; one is anonymous (*c.* 1550–90), whilst certainly one and probably both of the others are by Hans Krauwinckel II (master in 1586, died 1635). This type of jetton and maker are the commonest type found locally and have a widespread international distribution. There was also an English lead-alloy (pewter) 'Lyon counter' jetton of 1574–1600 with a rampant lion left, within garter, crowned on the obverse and a crowned oval French arms of three *fleur de lis* between two crowned pillars on the reverse (Mitchiner 1998, nos. 4584–672). The final example was a late fifteenth-century copper alloy French jetton with [+VIVE]:LE:RO[I:VIVE:L.E:ROI] and four *fleur de lis* in a lozenge on the obverse and an illegible reverse (Mitchiner 1998, nos. 584–600). Dies for jettons with this design were ordered from the engraver of the Paris mint in 1488, but this may not have been the first occasion on which they were produced (Mitchiner 1998, 206). The function of these jettons is unclear; they may have been used as counters but it is also possible that they acted as unofficial coinage at a time when the government was failing to strike enough low value coins to satisfy demand.

Metalwork and metalworking Craig Cessford, Andrew Hall and Simon Timberlake

A total of 234 eleventh–sixteenth century copper alloy objects, weighing 1.1kg, were recovered from Grand Arcade, plus 24 items weighing 105g from Christ's Lane. Although there are a number of individually interesting items, there are no exceptional objects or assemblages. The lead/lead-alloy assemblage from Grand Arcade consists of 91 objects weighing 5.6kg plus three items weighing 95g from Christ's Lane; there are also 1747 iron objects weighing 74kg from Grand Arcade plus 90 items weighing 2.8kg from Christ's Lane. Once again, no exceptional objects or assemblages were identified and the overall metalwork assemblage is relatively modest.

In addition, almost 20kg of ironworking slag was recovered from Grand Arcade (161 pieces, weighing 19,923g) plus a small amount from Christ's Lane (four pieces, weighing 193g). The Grand Arcade slag was identified in hand specimen with the aid of an x10 illuminated magnifying lens and a magnet to help estimate the free iron content. Ironworking material was identified throughout the occupational sequence, however the volume of ironworking debris is rather small for a site of this size, and there is no particular evidence suggesting that this was a major area of workshops or smithies. The distribution of slag on site was fairly widespread, with only a few minor localized concentrations of material.

The most significant eleventh–twelfth-century iron object was a complete scythe head from *Pit 6* (Fig. 4.9). This example is typical of scythes of the period consisting of a straight parallel-sided triangular sectioned blade with thickened back rib that curves gently to the tip and a short clenched tang at right angles to it (Edwards 2002, 113–15; Goodall 2011, 82; Leahy 2013, 225–7). Many of the Late Saxon scythes in particular come from hoards and may represent 'special' deposits. Other items include numerous nails, seven whittle-tanged knives (Fig. 2.4D), parts of four horseshoes, a rectangular staple, a small

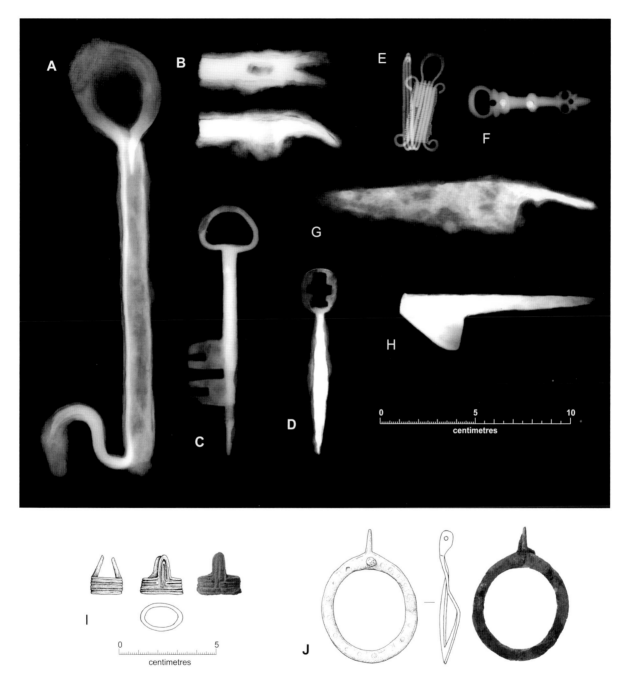

Figure 4.54. *Thirteenth–sixteenth-century metalwork, including: (A) thirteenth-century iron key with ring bow, hollow stem with projecting tip, Goodall type B although this has an atypical bow and is unusually large (2011, 241) from Well 6 ([36578]); (B) fourteenth/fifteenth-century iron claw hammer head with gently curving claw, rectangular hole and square sectioned butt (Goodall 2011, 26–7) ([50969] F.5134); (C) fourteenth/fifteenth-century iron key with D-shaped bow, solid stem with projecting tip and symmetrical bit, Goodall type G1 (2011, 241–2); (D) the head and shank of a fourteenth-century iron padlock key with bit, stem and terminal in line, Goodall type 1a with twelfth–thirteenth-century parallels (2011, 237) ([34328] F.3784); (E) sixteenth-century copper alloy chatelaine with a decorated front plate ([32355] F.6353); (F) sixteenth-century copper alloy buckle with sub-oval frame and integral rigid D-sectioned composite plate, with two perforations for attachment of strap and foliate terminal ([50197] F.5117); (G) sixteenth-century iron blade from a set of shears, from Pit 51 ([40400]); (H) sixteenth-century iron latch rest ([33144] F.3562); (I) copper alloy shoulder bolster for a knife from sixteenth-century pit, typologically Late Medieval ([32353]); (J) fifteenth-century copper alloy circular suspension loop with ring and dot ornament from Pit 44 (evaluation GAD02 [041]/[042]).*

hook and several unidentified objects. There is some evidence for ironworking; however, this was largely limited to shoeing horses.

Copper alloy objects were relatively rare and the earliest examples came from fourteenth-century contexts. There were parts of three buckles, including a fragment of a buckle plate, an oval-shaped gilt buckle frame and a slightly trapezoidal frame with plate. There was also a possible fragment of horse harness and a wire hook and eye fastener. No lead objects were recovered, although two writing leads were found in fourteenth-century contexts in 1959 (Addyman & Biddle 1965, 127, figs. 21.6–21.7).

There were relatively few identifiable iron objects from fourteenth-century contexts and included three whittle-tanged knife blades, three keys (Fig. 4.54A, 4.54C–D), two simple U-shaped staples, a claw hammer (Fig. 4.54B), a stylus (Fig. 4.26D), a hook, a horseshoe fragment and some unidentified tools. There was also a small quantity of ironworking slag. The apparent presence of high temperature fuel ash and possible coal shale within this latter material suggests that coal may have been reaching Cambridge by the fourteenth century. There was a trade in coal from Newcastle along the east coast during the thirteenth–fourteenth centuries that certainly reached King's Lynn (Hatcher 1993), so the presence of coal in Cambridge is plausible although it is not documented until the 1480s and did not become a common fuel until the late sixteenth century (Lee 2003; Lee 2005, 161).

From around the mid/late fifteenth century there was a significant increase in the range and quantity of metalwork deposited at both Grand Arcade and Christ's Lane. The most common copper alloy items were 18 copper alloy sheets bent into tubes known as lace-tags or *aiglets* from fifteenth–sixteenth-century contexts (seven from Christ's Lane). These were used on the end of laces to aid threading and prevent fraying and are found in large numbers on fifteenth–seventeenth-century sites (Egan & Pritchard 2002, 281–90; Margeson 1993, 22–4; Richards in Gardiner with Allen 2005, 94–5). There were nearly as many pins (16; eight from Christ's Lane) and parts of four copper alloy and five iron buckles (Figs. 3.17B, 3.21E, 4.54F and 6.11F). These include one ornate example that is similar to a fifteenth-century buckle from York (Ottaway & Rogers 2002, 2889–90, 3089, no. 13336) (Fig. 4.54F) and one decorated with groups of grooves set slantwise, similar to examples from Colchester dated 1250–1400 (Crummy 1988, 15–16, no. 1744) and London of 1350–1400 (Egan & Pritchard 2002, 97–8, no. 447).

In addition, there were single examples of a copper alloy arched pendant mount, wire hook and eye, a strap end plus an iron strap end with a terminal loop, a hooked tag and a child's thimble decorated with a border of stamped roundels containing *fleur de lis* on lower band with parallels from Norwich (Margeson 1993, 187, no. 1464). Other finds included a purse frame, part of a strap mount, two book clasps, a spoon, a shoulder bolster for a knife (Fig. 4.54I), a locking buckle from a barrel padlock similar to an example from Southwark (Egan 2005a, 47–8, no. 117) and half of a rigid balance arm for weighing. The most impressive items were a sixteenth-century chatelaine similar to an example dated 1500–50 from Southwark (Egan 2005a, 64) (Fig. 4.54E) and a fifteenth-century circular suspension loop with ring and dot ornament; this item does not appear to be either the rim of a vessel or a pocket sundial (Fig. 4.54J). A similar object from Winchester has been interpreted as a harness pendant (Hinton 1990, 1049) although this is not entirely convincing and a close parallel was found at Capel St Mary, Suffolk (Hall in Tabor 2010). Also worthy of note was a shield-shaped horse pendant with gilt decoration (Fig. 4.44E; Ashley 2002). This was found in a sixteenth-century context, but typologically appears to be twelfth–fourteenth-century.

Identifiable fifteenth–sixteenth-century iron objects included nine whittle-tanged knives (Fig. 4.50F–G), three U-shaped or rectangular staples (Fig. 4.50I) and three horseshoes (Fig. 4.50D). There were also a prick spur and a nearly complete rowel spur

(Margeson 1993, 220–3; Ottaway & Rogers 2002, 2956–7) with a non-ferrous coating, probably tin, which was often used to protect and enhance the appearance of iron spurs (Jope 1956). One complete set of iron shears and a blade from another set (Fig. 4.54G) were found; these appear to be common at this date (Margeson 1993, 133–5; also Ottaway & Rogers 2002, 2749–51). There were also two latch rests with tapering tangs (Fig. 4.54H), two hinge pivots, a fire steel used for striking with flint to produce a spark for igniting fires (Fig. 4.50E; Egan 2005a, 79–80; Goodall 2011, 300), a key, an awl with two tapering arms for leatherworking, although a range of other uses are possible (Ottaway & Rogers 2002, 2728–9), a punch (Ottaway & Rogers 2002, 2720–2) and a circular-headed iron tack. There was more lead in the sixteenth century than in earlier periods, in part perhaps as a result of the reclamation of lead during the Dissolution. Although little of this was directly identifiable, items included twisted pieces of window caming and an unfired 19mm-diameter musket ball, while a fifteenth-century feature produced a trilobed mount that is possibly a piece of horse harness.

Although the quantity of slag remained low, as well as material associated with the repair or forging of small objects as found in earlier periods there was some sixteenth-century material that shows indications of serious forge work, including the formation of proto-hearth bases (part-molten slag detached from the end of a tuyère during the process of forging in order to unblock it) or else proper smithing hearth slag bottoms. The latter are formed within the base of hearths during the process of smithing and show evidence for complete melting and also the inclusion of re-melted hammer scale and glassy slag (English Heritage 2001). The presence of welded slag droplets is very typical of high temperature forging where sand is used to combine with hammer scale and iron waste in order to remove this and also reduce the level of oxidation. There is also evidence for partly vitrified tuyère (ceramic air pipe) debris and hearth linings. Although coal was used as a fuel the use of charcoal, both on its own and in conjunction with wood, continued into the sixteenth century although its use was restricted to activities such as farriering (shoeing).

The type of slag debris which has been identified at Grand Arcade is typical of small-scale medieval to post-medieval ironworking of the sort associated with small smithies, most of which would be associated with the repair or forging of small objects. A high percentage of this may be linked to the work of farriers, as there is both faunal and artifactual evidence for the presence of horses. A fair proportion of the medieval and post-medieval ironworking debris shows indications of serious forge work, including the formation of proto-hearth bases.

The presence of welded slag droplets is most common in the sixteenth-century slag, along with evidence for the partly vitrified tuyère debris and hearth linings; however, the use of clay linings (clay tempered with sand and flint grit) can also be seen in most of the earlier (twelfth–thirteenth-century) slag. The only possible evidence for the primary smithing of iron comes from a single piece of discarded possible iron bloom from a medieval context; all the other slag appears to be associated with secondary iron smithing. The most likely explanation is that in addition to farriers there was occasional small-scale ironworking on the site related to the requirements of building activities in the plots and temporary smithies were erected to deal with this.

The early use of coal as a fuel in smithing more or less accords with what is known of the introduction and use of coal in Cambridge Colleges from the fourteenth century onwards and a similarly early fifteenth-century use of coal was identified at the Corfield Court site (Timberlake in Newman 2008c). The ready availability of this fuel is supported by documentary sources, which suggest that Cambridge was involved in the east coast coal trade from Newcastle to King's Lynn during the fourteenth century (Hatcher 1993). Moreover, it would seem that coal was already being used domestically in Cambridge during the fifteenth century, and became common in the sixteenth century (Lee 2005, 161; see also Lee 2003).

It is difficult to date the earliest use of coal as a fuel in iron smithing at Grand Arcade, given the wide date range of some of the medieval features. However, wood and charcoal seem to be associated with all the twelfth–fourteenth-century slag, though coal mixed with charcoal and wood can still be seen within some of the slag dating to the fourteenth–fifteenth century. The small-scale use of charcoal and charcoal plus wood continues well into the sixteenth century, though in this case the use of charcoal could have been for farriering (shoeing) rather than for the more critical operations such as forging and welding for which a fuel burning at a higher temperature would have been favoured. Nevertheless, the presence of what appear to be high temperature fuel ash and shale (possibly coal shale) within some of the earlier (fourteenth-century or even pre-fourteenth-century slag) might suggest a still earlier date for the small-scale industrial use of this fuel.

Worked stone Simon Timberlake and Craig Cessford
A total of 35 worked stone objects were recovered from Grand Arcade and Christ's Lane, principally quernstones and whetstones/honestones. The material has subsequently been more thoroughly examined when

all stone was identified in hand specimen with the aid of a x10 illuminated magnifying lens.

Only small quantities of eleventh–twelfth century stone objects were recovered, consisting of fragments of Niedermendig Mülstein lava querns, Scandinavian whetstones/honestones and local limestone mortars. These items are all typical of sites of this period and the broad patterns present in the eleventh–twelfth centuries continued until the sixteenth century.

The majority of the thirteenth–fourteenth-century stone objects are querns, whetstones/honestones and mortars of similar types to those used during the eleventh–twelfth centuries. In addition, there is some evidence for the use of local chalk, including a possible loom weight and a further piece decorated with an incised cross (Fig. 3.12A). There is also evidence for the reuse of some stone; a number of quern fragments have sooting on their underside/grinding surface, suggesting that they were employed in an oven or on the side of a hearth. A small rounded square/rectangular block of limestone, originally a piece of building stone, appears to have been fashioned either to be placed in soft ground and used as a small anvil or to be used as a small hand-held mallet.

Most of the fifteenth–sixteenth-century worked stone objects, such as mortars (Fig. 4.46D), are broadly similar to those of earlier centuries, but there are some differences. Hones become less common by the sixteenth century, perhaps because it became more common for blacksmiths to sharpen tools or for steels to be used (Rees *et al.* 2008, 397). Several of the sixteenth-century querns were of different forms to earlier examples and there was an object from an early/mid-fifteenth-century context that may be a cresset, heating tray or multiple-welled lamp (Fig. 4.52C).

Pottery David Hall and Craig Cessford
In total 20,852 sherds of eleventh–seventeenth-century pottery, weighing 350kg, were recovered from Grand Arcade plus 3402 sherds weighing 57kg from Christ's Lane. In addition, there were small assemblages from the various phases of evaluation and the pottery from various earlier excavations was also re-examined. The overall assemblage includes small quantities of Prehistoric, Roman and Middle Saxon pottery, but the bulk of the material spans the eleventh–twentieth centuries (Table 4.4). To facilitate analysis the assemblage has been broadly divided into several categories, which comprise: Saxo-Norman (tenth–twelfth centuries); medieval (thirteenth–fifteenth centuries) and post-medieval (sixteenth–seventeenth centuries). The modern

Table 4.4. *Overall pottery assemblage from Grand Arcade and Christ's Lane.*

Period	Grand Arcade no.	Grand Arcade weight (g)	Christ's Lane no.	Christ's Lane weight (g)	Total no.	Total weight (g)
Prehistoric	7	28	-	-	7	28
Roman	121	1237	13	108	134	1345
Middle Saxon	7	215	4	46	11	261
Saxo-Norman	3558	62,273	435	6281	3993	68,554
Medieval	12,755	178,409	1374	17,601	14,129	196,010
Early Post-Medieval	4539	109,117	1593	33,456	6132	142,573
Modern	22,889	496,799	501	8390	23,390	505,189
Total	**43,876**	**848,078**	**3920**	**65,882**	**47,796**	**913,960**

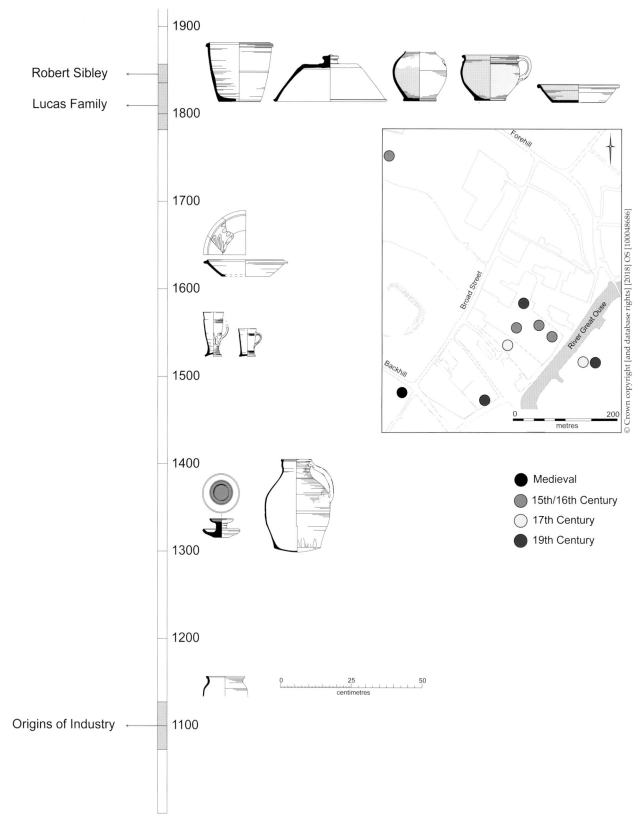

Figure 4.55. *Timeline for the Ely pottery industry showing selected products and map of where kilns, waster dumps etc. have been discovered.*

Table 4.5. *Saxo-Norman pottery from Grand Arcade and Christ's Lane by count and weight.*

	Grand Arcade Thetford-type	Grand Arcade St Neots-type	Grand Arcade Stamford	Grand Arcade Total	Christ's Lane Thetford-type	Christ's Lane St Neots-type	Christ's Lane Stamford	Christ's Lane Total
No. count	1438	2037	83	3558	179	228	28	435
No. %	40.4	57.3	2.3		41.1	52.4	8.7	
Weight (g)	32,686	28,859	728	62,273	3407	2723	151	6281
Weight %	52.5	46.3	1.2		54.2	43.4	2.4	
Mean sherd weight (g)	22.7	14.2	8.8	17.5	19.0	11.9	5.4	14.4

material (eighteenth–twentieth centuries) is considered separately in Chapter 5.

A detailed discussion of the changing patterns of ceramic use over time is presented in Chapter 7, and will not therefore be repeated here. Two points are worth noting, however. The first is that certain long-lived ceramic industries cut across the temporal boundaries by which this report has been organized; most notably in a local context that of the Isle of Ely (Fig. 4.55). This issue is explored further in Chapter 7. The second is that the sources of the various wares alter on a period-by-period basis; these changes have been represented here graphically (Fig. 4.56) and are also discussed further in Chapter 7.

At both Grand Arcade and Christ's Lane the tenth–twelfth-century pottery is dominated by the typical triumvirate of wares found in southern Cambridgeshire (Spoerry 2016, 26–34); with Thetford-type ware probably principally from Thetford itself (Figs. 2.3A–B, 4.57A and 4.57C–E; Hurst 1957; Hurst 1976, 314–20; Rogerson & Dallas 1984, 117–23) and St Neots-type ware from a range of unidentified sources (Figs. 2.3C–D, 2.4B, 4.9 and 4.57F–G; Denham 1985; Hurst 1956; Hurst 1976, 320–3) dominant plus a small proportion of Stamford ware (Fig. 4.57H; Hurst 1958; Hurst 1976, 323–36; Kilmurry 1980) (Table 4.5). Most of the forms and fabrics are typical of these wares; the only slightly unusual piece was a Thetford-type ware jar with a rather atypical strap handle form (Fig. 4.57A), paralleled from the Castle Kiln site (McCarthy & Brooks 1988, fig. 76.107). There were only two significant assemblages, from *Cesspit 1* and *Pit 2* both dated to *c.* 1100, which have already been discussed (Chapter 2). In common with other excavations in Cambridge there was no imported Continental material.

Other wares began to be used in small quantities in the late twelfth century; these included Early Ely ware (Fig. 4.57I; Spoerry 2008) and grey and pink coarsewares of various origins (Fig. 4.57B, 4.57J–L). These fabrics all continued in use into the thirteenth century and distinguishing specifically late twelfth-century material is usually impossible. These late twelfth-century wares are rarely found in direct association with the earlier fabrics, suggesting a relatively abrupt ceramic transition.

The thirteenth–fifteenth-century assemblage consists of a range of coarsewares, finewares and material that is intermediate between the two (Table 4.6). The coarsewares found in Cambridge are not all well understood; they include sandy coarsewares from Essex whilst other fabrics were either manufactured in or near the town or derive from the Bedfordshire–Cambridgeshire border (Figs. 3.13A–B, 4.33B, 4.47C, 4.51B and 458A–C; Spoerry 2016, 49–82). The main coarseware that can be identified is medieval Ely ware (Figs. 4.16B, 4.19B, 4.26C, 4.27C and 4.58D–H), which was made at Potters

Lane and elsewhere in Ely from at least the early twelfth century onwards (Hall 2001; Spoerry 2008). This material has been sub-divided into three categories: Early Ely ware, which dates to the twelfth–early thirteenth century; medieval Ely ware, which constitutes the bulk of the material, and Ely-Grimston ware, which is rather higher quality material that deliberately imitates Grimston ware. A distinction has also been made between thirteenth–fourteenth-century medieval Ely ware and fifteenth-century Late Medieval Ely ware (Spoerry 2008); however, the distinction is of limited applicability and has not been adopted here. Medieval Ely ware does occur in some fifteenth-century contexts, but appears to decline in significance after the fourteenth century.

In total, medieval Ely ware constitutes 16–20 per cent of the thirteenth–fifteenth-century pottery from Grand Arcade and 23 per cent from Christ's Lane. This contrasts with the only previously published assemblage from Cambridge, where it totalled only eight per cent (Edwards & Hall 1997, 157). Values in the range of 20 per cent accord well with Spoerry's suggestion that Cambridge was a key market for medieval Ely ware, and is in line with other sites on the South Cambridgeshire fen edge (Spoerry 2008, 70). Cambridge appears to represent something of a transitional zone for medieval Ely ware, as further south it is much less common and indeed is absent entirely from some sites (Spoerry 2008, 72). Ely's population was around three-quarters the size of that of Cambridge throughout the medieval period, but as medieval Ely Ware was much more common in Ely, at *c.* 70 per cent or higher (Spoerry 2008, 67), it is likely to have been the more significant market, perhaps 2.5 times larger than Cambridge assuming similar levels of pottery usage. Similarities in fabric and glaze suggest that, as with a number of pottery industries (*e.g.* Chapman *et al.* 2008, 255–7), the Ely potters also produced the various relatively ornate types of tile that were used locally, although some of this material may derive from elsewhere in the Fenland (see below). In terms of overall weight and volume, it is likely that such tiles were the 'potters' most significant products. Ceramic water pipes may also have constituted another important product.

A significant number of the complete or semi-complete medieval Ely ware vessels are jugs, a figure which is disproportionate

Table 4.6. *Thirteenth–fifteenth-century pottery by broad ware types.*

Types	Grand Arcade no.	Grand Arcade weight (g)	Christ's Lane no.	Christ's Lane weight (g)
Coarseware	9200 72.1%	122,138 68.5%	911 66.3%	12,264 69.7%
Intermediate	410 3.2%	9130 5.1%	12 0.9%	189 1.1%
Fineware	3146 24.7%	47,143 26.4%	451 32.8%	5148 29.2%
Total	12,755	178,409	1374	17,601

161

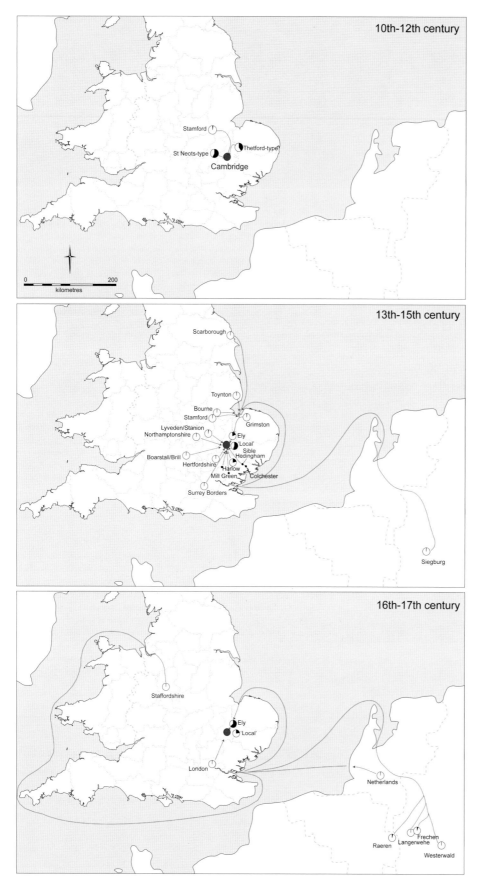

Figure 4.56. *The sources of ceramics used at Grand Arcade during the tenth–seventeenth centuries, see Fig. 5.96 for later sources.*

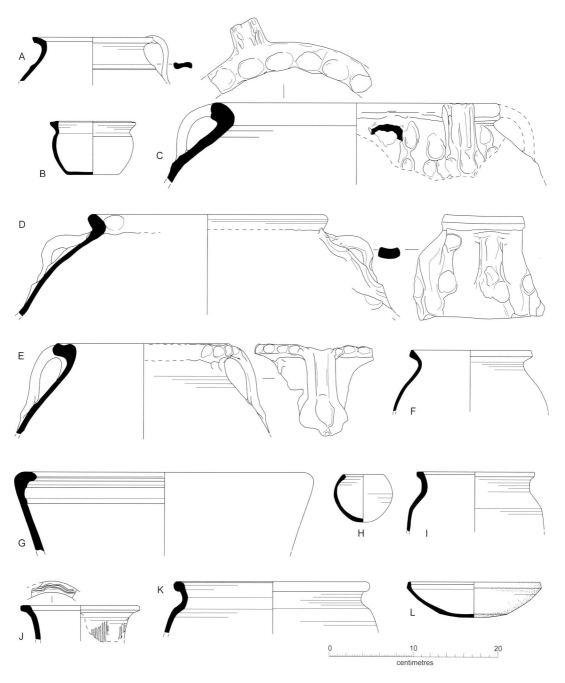

Figure 4.57. *Twelfth-century pottery, including: (A) Thetford-type ware jar with strap handle, a rather atypical form, from Well 12 ([35641]); (B) Thetford-type ware handled jar with heavily thumbed rim and body, from Well 15 ([31339]); (C) pink coarseware small rounded squat jar with everted rim of unknown origin, with signs of external sooting, from Ditch 1 ([35041]); (D) Thetford-type ware handled jar with thumbed body ([34439] F.3609); (E) Thetford-type ware handled jar with thumbed rim and body ([33647] F.3647); (F) St Neots-type ware jar with everted rim ([34685] F.3830); (G) St Neots-type ware bowl with inturned rim, from Cesspit 13 ([33395]); (H) small Stamford ware hemispherical bowl, these could be used as either lamps or crucibles although this was probably a lamp ([32948] F.6360); (I) Early Ely ware jar with everted rim, a form very similar to St Neots-type ware ([40478] F.4052); (J) grey coarseware jug with wavy decoration on rim and body, probably from North Essex, with some feldspar and mica in the fabric, from Building 3 ([70070]); (K) grey coarseware jar with clubbed rim, of unknown origin ([33203] F.3578); (L) grey coarseware small shallow hemispherical bowl of unknown origin that may have been used as a lamp or a lid, moderately sandy fabric with few grits, from the King's Ditch ([50383] F.5192).*

163

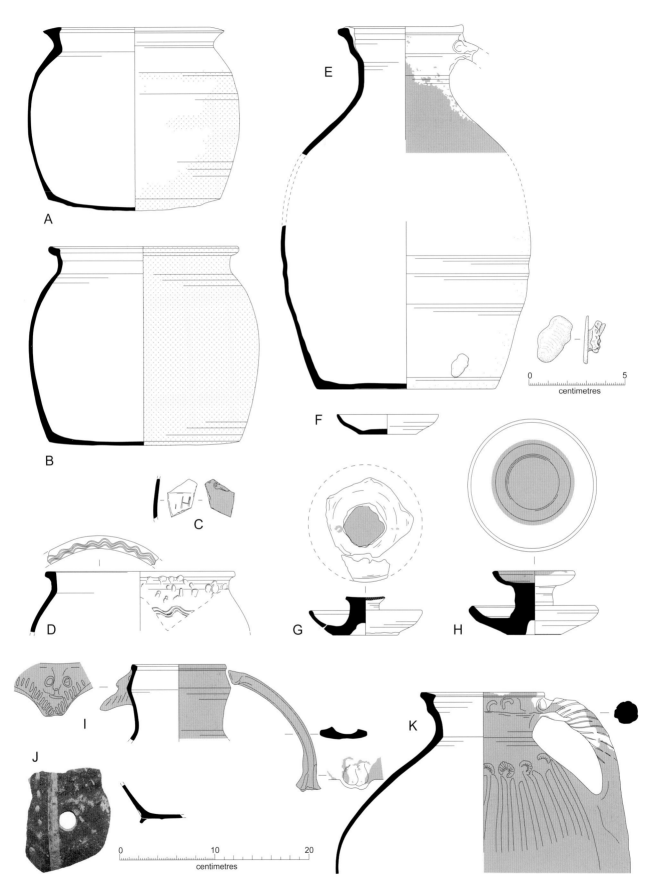

Table 4.7. *Thirteenth–fifteenth-century intermediate pottery.*

Ware	Grand Arcade no.	Grand Arcade weight (g)	Christ's Lane no.	Christ's Lane weight (g)	Date range	Source
Grimston	244	6256	6	151	12th–15th century, 14th century *floruit*	Norfolk
Ely-Grimston	99	1997	1	10	14th century	Cambridgeshire
Pink shelly	36	428	3	22	13th century	Northamptonshire
Developed Stamford	31	449	2	6	13th–14th century	Lincolnshire
Total	**410**	**9130**	**12**	**189**		

to their relative frequency in the assemblage. A similar disparity has previously been noted with regard to largely antiquarian discoveries (Spoerry 2008, 46–7, 51) and it appears that there was a greater propensity to discard slightly damaged jugs than other types of vessel, upon occasion by throwing them down wells (*e.g. Wells 32 and 33*, plus fifteenth-century *Well 22*; Figs. 4.14–4.16 and 4.36). In addition to the jugs, a number of medieval Ely ware saucer lamps (MNV 10)

Figure 4.58 *(opposite). Thirteenth–fourteenth-century pottery, including: (A) thirteenth-century grey coarseware small rounded jar with bevelled rim and external sooting. Its fabric contains very little sand. From SP 5 ([34349]); (B) thirteenth-century grey coarseware rounded wide jar with flanged rim and external sooting. The fabric contains relatively little sand and occasional white grits. From a beamslot belonging to Building 6 ([33285]); (C) fourteenth-century grey coarseware sherd with post-firing incised letter H on the inside of the vessel and external sooting, indicating that it comes from a jar. The incised letter is probably post-breakage and therefore a piece of graffiti that has nothing to do with its use ([31234] F.3270); (D) thirteenth-century medieval Ely ware handmade jar with flat topped clubbed rim. It has wavy line decoration on the rim and body and belongs to Spoerry type B/Hall type CP2. Decoration on medieval Ely ware jars is rare, but wavy line decoration is paralleled on bowls from WFF 1 ([36944]); (E) fourteenth-century medieval Ely ware shouldered jug with rod handle of Spoerry type C, which has in situ sub-oval lead repair plug close to the base (25mm by 8mm) ([34164], [34167] F.3737); (F) fourteenth-century medieval Ely ware saucer lamp, from Building 13 ([33466]); (G) fourteenth-century medieval Ely ware saucer lamp, consisting of a small bowl on a pedestal base above a drip tray ([36326] F.6180); (H) composite reconstruction of the Medieval Ely ware saucer lamp; (I) fourteenth-century Grimston ware face jug with strap handle ([34781] F.3832); (J) fourteenth-century Essex Redware sherd, probably a Colchester-type ware jug, decorated with applied strip and blobs that had been turned into a cistern ([34231] F.3761); (K) Hedingham ware stamped strip style jug of c. 1225–1300/25, from Well 5 ([36999]).*

were also discovered (Figs. 4.58F–H and 4.59A). These consisted of a small bowl carried on a pedestal base above a drip tray. There is no evidence that these lamps had handles or spouts, and no more elaborate lamp forms or candlesticks were found. Medieval Ely ware lamps were recovered from sites in Cambridge by Hughes and these 'double shelled lamps' were discussed by Lethbridge (1949, 6, pl. 2), but they appear to be rare at Ely, with only a single lamp/candlestick base or lid identified (Spoerry 2008, 19, no. 26). Thirteenth–fifteenth-century pottery lamps are generally rare, and at Oxford there are suggestions that the high percentages of thirteenth–fourteenth-century pottery lamps at some sites may be linked to the presence of student lodgings or academic halls (Naton & Cockin 2008, 168, 171–3, 183–4; Poore *et al.* 2006, 263). The quantities at Grand Arcade are not high enough to suggest a University presence; however, the recognition that the Ely industry manufactured such relatively rare products may indicate that this was linked specifically to the scholarly/religious Cambridge market. There was also a single fragment from an Ely-Grimston ware face jug, a few examples of which have been found at Ely and Swavesey (Spoerry 2008, 76).

The only intermediate ware (Table 4.7) of any note was Grimston ware (Figs. 4.14C, 4.36, 4.58I and 4.59B) (Leah 1994), which constituted 1.9–3.5 per cent of the thirteenth–fifteenth-century assemblage at Grand Arcade and 0.5–0.9 per cent at Christ's Lane. Fragments of at least four Grimston ware face jugs were found. These have long been recognized from Cambridge (McCarthy & Brooks 1988, 268–9) and it has been argued that Cambridge lay 'outside the marketing boundary' for Grimston ware 'but fragments of these very distinctive face jugs have been found' (Leah 1994, 117). In fact, a range of Grimston products including lamps, skillets, bowls and jars occur, and while jugs are common the majority are not face jugs. A single Grimston ware saucer lamp, which is similar to the medieval Ely ware lamps, was also identified. A single sherd from a lamp was previously identified at Grimston itself, although its form is not stated (Leah 1994, 80, 87). There was also a baluster jug (Figs. 4.14C and 4.36), a form that does not appear to have been discovered at Grimston itself (Leah 1994), with an incised star-shaped graffiti below the handle. An extremely similar jug from Cambridge with the same form of graffiti in the same location was published as a 'Cambridge-type baluster jug' (Rackham 1948, no. 27). This similarity makes it unlikely that the graffiti is an owner's mark and it is probably a maker's mark, which could have functioned as a trademark or recorded particular batches or consignments of pots (Pearce 1992, 35). A similar post-firing five line star-shaped graffito was found on a fourteenth-century grey coarseware jug from Corfield Court, Cambridge (Newman 2008c, 192).

The thirteenth–fifteenth-century finewares (Table 4.8) consist principally of relatively high quality jugs from a range of sources. In the thirteenth century the most common material was from Lyveden/Stanion (Bellamy 1983; Bryant & Steane 1969; Chapman *et al.* 2008; Steane 1967), and there was also some Hertfordshire fineware (Fig. 4.47C) (Turner Rugg 1995) plus Boarstall/Brill ware (Fig. 4.27D) (Farley 1982; Ivens 1981; Ivens 1982; Jope 1954; Jope & Ivens 1981). The most distant source was Scarborough, which has long been

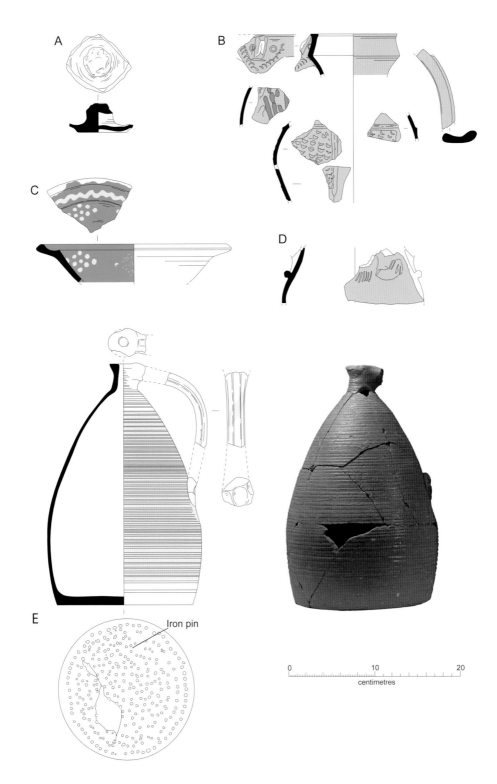

Figure 4.59. *Fifteenth–sixteenth-century pottery, including: (A) fifteenth-century Medieval Ely ware saucer lamp ([33693] F.3658); (B) mid-fifteenth-century Grimston ware face jug with strap handle and panels of decoration, from Well 29 ([34512]). The presence of spots of yellow glaze indicates that it is of early fifteenth-century date; (C) sixteenth-century Glazed Red Earthenware small slip-decorated rounded shallow bowl with dots and zigzag lines. The fabric and glaze suggest that it is probably not an Ely product ([31727] F.3334); (D) mid-fifteenth-century Scarborough ware face jug, from Well 34 ([31830]); (E) fifteenth-century red coarseware strap handled sprinkler watering pot, upper part glazed and all over rilled decoration ([20242] F.1088).*

Table 4.8. *Thirteenth–fifteenth-century fineware pottery. * denotes a ware only recognized partway through analysis.*

Ware	Grand Arcade no.	Grand Arcade weight (g)	Christ's Lane no.	Christ's Lane weight (g)	Date range	Source
Essex Redware	2520	36,320	351	4082	Late 13th–15th century, 15th century *floruit*	Essex
Essex Greyware	74*	881*	26	335	15th century	Essex
Cambridge-type Sgraffito	53	696	1	4	14th–15th century	North Essex or South Cambridgeshire
Lyveden/Stanion	204	2947	54	507	13th–14th century, 13th century *floruit*	Northamptonshire
Surrey Borders	90	1838	4	44	14th–15th century, 14th century *floruit*	Surrey
Hertfordshire Fineware	51	1981	6	48	13th–15th century	Hertfordshire
Scarborough	35	350	2	6	13th–14th century	Yorkshire
Boarstall/Brill	53	970	4	22	13th–15th century, 13th century *floruit*	Buckinghamshire
Toynton	7	192	-	-	14th century	Lincolnshire
Siegburg	7	203	-	-	15th century	Germany
Bourne	8	134	-	-	15th–16th century	Lincolnshire
Potterspury	3	12	1	5	14th century	Northamptonshire
Unidentified	41	619	2	95	13th–15th century	Unknown
Total	**3143**	**45,809**	**451**	**5148**		

recognized in Cambridge, with the most well-known example being the top and most of the body of a knight jug with a stag motif and antlers running up the spout in a Phase II fabric of *c.* 1225–1350 (Farmer & Farmer 1979, 25, 35, 56, 68; also Farmer & Farmer 1982). This ware was found in quite widely scattered contexts at Grand Arcade, suggesting at least eight separate vessels were present. With the exception of a single bearded mask jug (Fig. 4.59D), all the Scarborough ware appeared to be from relatively simple jugs. All of these finewares continued in use into the fourteenth century, although Lyveden/Stanion ware declined in significance at this time.

By the end of the fourteenth century Essex redwares (Figs. 4.14D, 4.16A, 4.24, 4.33A, 4.33C, 4.36, 4.52A–B and 4.58J–K), and to a lesser extent Essex greywares, had become the most common types of fineware in use at the site. The growth in this industry reflects its significant role in supplying London (Pearce *et al.* 1982) and there is evidence that redwares were reaching Cambridge prior to *c.* 1370 (Newman & Evans 2011, 190). The most common fabric is the rather generic Colchester-type ware (Cotter 2000, 107–80) or similar material, which included a piece of a jug with 'Rouen-style' decoration (Cotter 2000, fig. 81) that had a post-firing perforation which turned it into a cistern (Figs. 4.33A, 4.33C and 4.58J). There were also at least four distinct Hedingham ware (Cotter 2000, 75–80; Walker 2012) rounded stamped strip style jugs of *c.* 1225–1300/25 with twisted rod handles and rows of cartwheel stamps and applied strip decoration (Figs. 4.16A, 4.36 and 4.58K) (Walker 2012, 43–4), plus small quantities of material from Harlow (Davey & Walker 2008) and Mill Green (Pearce *et al.* 1982; see also Cotter 2000, 180–2). Cambridge-type Sgraffito ware (Fig. 3.16A) is broadly a form of Essex redware; it is relatively uncommon (53 sherds, weighing 696g, from Grand Arcade), and its fabric and inclusions do not match known Essex fabrics (Cotter 2000, 166–70). Although it is unlikely to have been produced in Cambridge, this is the location where it was initially identified and from which it is best known (Bushnell & Hurst 1952; Dunning 1950; Edwards & Hall 1997, 158). Its distribution suggests a North Essex or South Cambridgeshire origin.

Surrey Borders ware (Figs. 3.13C and 4.51C) also appears in the fourteenth century (Pearce 1992), and small quantities from Potterspury (Jope 1950; Mynard 1970) and Toynton were present. Most of these wares continued in use into the fifteenth century. At this time, Essex Redware retained its dominant position and there were also small quantities of material introduced from Bourne (Healey 1969; Healey 1975). Stoneware from Siegburg marks the first appearance of Continental imports. Although it occurs in Cambridge by *c.* 1370 (Newman & Evans 2011, 190), the majority dates to the late fifteenth century and it only occurs in small quantities.

Most thirteenth–fourteenth-century features produced relatively small quantities of pottery that can be broadly interpreted as the inherent 'background noise' of medieval urban occupation. There were however some exceptions where complete or semi-complete vessels were recovered. There appear to be two apparently exclusive groups, with several examples of two or more jugs in wells (*Wells 32–33*) or pits (*Pits 23, 29*), whereas substantial proportions of one or more coarseware jars were deposited in a beamslot (*Building 6*) and in specialized pits (*SPs 4–6*). This suggests, perhaps unsurprisingly, that the use of jars for cooking and jugs for serving liquids took place in different contexts. There was also an unusual group of deliberately fragmented coarseware jars in *Pit 26*.

During the early sixteenth century Essex Redware continued to be a significant source of jugs and there are some Surrey Borders jugs, which is significant considering their later influence (see below). Medieval Ely ware saucer lamps (Fig. 4.59A) and Grimston ware face jugs both continued in use into the fifteenth century, while Cambridge-type Sgraffito ware continued rather longer than has previously been recognized into the first half of the sixteenth century. In the first half of the sixteenth century the pottery in use went through what had been termed the 'post-medieval ceramic revolution' (Gaimster 1994; Gaimster & Nenk 1997; Pearce 2007b), with radical changes in form, fabric and glaze. The local products from Ely changed markedly and were supplemented by significant

167

Table 4.9. *Sixteenth–seventeenth-century pottery by broad ware types. * denotes wares that continued after the seventeenth century, but values are for material believed to be sixteenth–seventeenth century in origin.*

Type	Grand Arcade no.	Grand Arcade weight (g)	Christ's Lane no.	Christ's Lane weight (g)
Coarsewares	804	20,146	489	9179
Ely-type wares	3070	77,157	717	14,038
Dutch Glazed Red Earthenware	27	618	-	-
German Stoneware*	315	8885	328	9716
Tin-glazed earthenware*	38	274	48	366
Staffordshire-type slipware*	57	1661	7	73
Other	48	376	4	84
Total	**4359**	**109,117**	**1593**	**33,456**

quantities of German stoneware, plus smaller amounts of tin-glazed earthenware and a few other wares (Table 4.9).

Coarsewares were produced at a range of relatively local sites; forms are mainly jars, jugs and bowls (Fig. 6.11A) with some cisterns and skillets and a single watering pot (Fig. 4.59E), which had an iron pin poked through one perforation indicating an attempt to unblock it. A substantial proportion of the pottery was either produced at kilns near the river Great Ouse in Ely (Cessford *et al.* 2006, 46–71, 81–5) or is of similar forms and fabrics and presumably produced relatively locally (Table 4.10). Broad Street Gritty Red Earthenware dating to the late fifteenth and early sixteenth centuries was the earliest of these products (Cessford *et al.* 2006, 46, fig. 30). This ware is intermediate between the medieval and post-medieval Ely traditions, as it contains quantities of white quartzose grits similar to medieval Ely fabric and is softer than the later wares, but the forms are post-medieval. Broad Street Gritty Red Earthenware appears to be relatively short-lived and has quite a restricted distribution at the sites. Vessels included a bunghole jar or cistern (Fig. 3.21A), a form not recognized at the production site (Cessford *et al.* 2006, 46).

Broad Street Gritty Red Earthenware was effectively succeeded by Glazed Red Earthenware in the early/mid-sixteenth century; this is a red bodied coarseware with a shiny glaze and was the commonest form of coarse pottery regionally during the sixteenth to mid-nineteenth centuries (Cessford *et al.* 2006, 53–4, figs. 39–46). It occurs in a wide range of forms; the products found include bowls, jugs, cisterns, pancheons, skillets, basting dishes, candlesticks, lids and pipkins. Whilst much of the material from Cambridge was produced at Ely, a significant proportion derives from other unidentified sources (Fig. 4.59C). Some of the material produced in Ely had a green glaze on the outer surface and clear glaze inside making it a bichrome (Cessford *et al.* 2006, 56, fig. 48), and a piece decorated with the royal coat of arms of 1406–1603 was found at Christ's Lane (Fig. 6.11B). Armorial style decoration has previously been recognized on sixteenth-century vessels produced at Ely (Cessford *et al.* 2006, fig. 50.11), but this is the first time that the royal coat of arms has been found.

Glazed Red Earthenware may have been inspired by late fifteenth- and early sixteenth-century Dutch Glazed Red Earthenware, although this relates mainly to colour and texture rather than specific forms (Cumberpatch 2003; see also Baart 1994). This ware does occur in small quantities in Cambridge and a significant group was discovered in 1959 in *Pit AB1*. Babylon-type ware is a red earthenware with a black iron based glaze; much of the material from Cambridge was manufactured in Ely (Cessford *et al.* 2006, 56–8, fig. 49), but a

significant quantity with a browner fabric and a lighter, browner coloured glaze indicates that it comes from a different source. Forms found include tygs, cups and small jugs. Babylon ware is a local variant of the Cistercian ware tradition which developed in the late fifteenth century at sites such Wrenthorpe in West Yorkshire and Ticknall in Derbyshire, although Babylon ware production only began in the early/mid-sixteenth century and is not as hard fired as most Cistercian ware and is an earthenware rather than a vitrified pseudo-stoneware.

Broad Street Fineware was made from clay that fired off-white or light pink and was used to produce fine thin-walled delicate vessels (Cessford *et al.* 2006, 58, fig. 50). The vessels were lead glazed, usually with copper added to give a specked green colour and some were bichrome. This ware is visually very similar to those of the Surrey white-ware industries (Pearce 1999; Pearce & Vince 1988). In the early sixteenth century there was a peak of production of fine drinking vessels (Pearce & Vince 1988, 17, 88–9). Products identified include cups, jars, jugs, strainers, platters, chafing dishes, bowls and candlesticks.

It is only in the sixteenth century that significant quantities of German stoneware appear in Cambridge, although only jugs were recovered (Table 4.11). In the early sixteenth century products from Langerwehe and particularly Raeren began to arrive, while later in the sixteenth century Frechen overtook these sources in significance. Tin-glazed Earthenware is a mixture of Netherlandish, Anglo-Netherlandish and English material and occurs in small quantities from the late sixteenth century onwards. Other material found in small quantities in the late sixteenth to mid-seventeenth centuries includes bowls and dishes with a fine off-white to pale buff fabric and golden yellow glaze (Fig. 6.11C–D). These are part of the Midlands

Table 4.10. *Sixteenth–seventeenth-century Ely-type products.*

Ware	Grand Arcade no.	Grand Arcade weight (g)	Christ's Lane no.	Christ's Lane weight (g)
Broad Street Gritty Red Earthenware	144	4592	-	-
Glazed Red Earthenware	2122	61,119	539	12,033
Broad Street Bichrome	86	2293	3	34
Babylon-type	499	7006	149	1809
Broad Street Fineware	219	2147	45	250
Total	**3070**	**77,157**	**717**	**14,038**

Table 4.11. *Sixteenth–seventeenth-century German stoneware * denotes wares that continue after the seventeenth century but values are for material believed to be sixteenth–seventeenth-century.*

Ware	Grand Arcade no.	Grand Arcade weight (g)	Christ's Lane no.	Christ's Lane weight
Langerwehe	7	409	24	179
Raeren	110	2480	23	464
Frechen*	198	6152	129	2273
Westerwald*	9	45	1	32
Total	**315**	**8885**	**328**	**9716**

Yellow-ware tradition (Brears 1971, 31–6). Other discoveries include an unidentified Continental import with a hard off-white fabric with a green glazed relief picture of a castle and trees plus some possible Saintonge ware.

Ceramic building material Philip Mills, incorporating specialist information from Alan Vince

There is a small quantity of residual Roman material, consistent with the levels found away from the main foci of Roman settlement. The earliest medieval ceramic building materials are small quantities of thirteenth–fourteenth-century glazed roof tile and impressed decorated floor tiles. These would have come from a high status ecclesiastical building, the most likely candidate being the nearby Dominican Friary (Dickens 1999a). There are a number of bricks that were imported from the Low Countries into the east coast of Britain in the fourteenth/fifteenth centuries, particularly at Christ's Lane, plus some early handmade sandy bricks of uneven dimension, although there is little evidence to suggest the presence of major brick buildings at Grand Arcade prior to the seventeenth century. For this reason, the overall assemblage will be discussed in greater detail in Chapter 5.

During this period, brick supply is dominated by the area around Ely, which was a significant regional centre, with some other 'Eastern Counties' material of unknown origin that occurs infrequently between the fourteenth–sixteenth centuries. Slop moulded bricks are introduced in the sixteenth century, as in other parts of the country. Roof tiles are predominantly peg tiles, mainly with two rounded peg holes; there are some experiments in form in the fifteenth/sixteenth centuries, involving single peg holes and square peg holes. Tile supply is also dominated by the Ely area, as is the rest of the region. It appears that different plots may have obtained their bricks from different sources, although the limitations of the data make this conclusion problematic. Finally, the levels of burning of brick and tile for the eleventh–fifteenth centuries are typical of those found on rural sites (2–3 per cent); while by the sixteenth–seventeenth centuries they rise to the normal range for urban sites (5–8 per cent) (Table 4.12).

Although there is no contemporary evidence for the use of brick in the suburb, a small number of thirteenth–fourteenth-century imported Low Countries bricks, along with more local handmade sandy bricks of uneven dimension, were recovered residually from later contexts. These were largely produced in the area around Ely, which was a significant regional centre, with some less common 'Eastern Counties' material of unknown origin also present. The earliest surviving brickwork in Cambridge is in the vault of the bone-hole of St Mary the Less, dated to *c.* 1350, and there is additional documentary evidence for the use of brick at King's Hall in 1375–6 and Gonville & Caius College *c.* 1390 (RCHM(E) 1959, c).

Although some thirteenth–fourteenth-century decorated floor tiles were recovered, these were almost certainly used elsewhere and arrived at the street block after the Dissolution. Some plain

Table 4.12. *Percentage burning of ceramic building material by date. MT - Minimum number of Tiles per context, derived by dividing the number of corners present by the number of corners for a complete piece. TE - Tile Equivalent, a percentage based on the number of corners present.*

Date	No.	Weight	Corner	MT	TE
11th–12th	3.23	12.41	-	-	-
14th–15th	2.66	3.36	2.56	3.30	3.19
13th–15th	0.24	1.99	1.89	6.25	3.23
16th–17th	7.08	8.44	10.51	4.98	8.74

floor tiles were in use at the site, however, as five nearly complete plain green glazed floor tiles, measuring 0.10m by 0.10m in extent and 0.02m thick in a single fabric, were recovered from the Birdbolt site in 1905. These suggest the presence of a relatively high status thirteenth–fourteenth-century building with a tiled floor. There were also small quantities of glazed ridge tiles from Ely. The production of brick and tile in Ely is partially related to the pottery industry (see above) and excavations at Potters Lane have revealed evidence for peg tile production in the thirteenth–fourteenth centuries, with production of crested ridge tiles and small thick floor tiles in the fifteenth century (Spoerry 2008, 27–9, 64). There is also evidence for medieval brick and tile production at Shippea Hill Farm, where stacked bricks and tiles were recorded (Cra'aster *et al.* 1965, 147). Bricks that were 9in long, 4in wide and 2in thick were found in large regularly laid 10ft-square stacks, while 11in long by 6 1/6in wide tiles with two holes were found stacked on edge lengthways in 15ft-long rows. Thin section and ICPAES of tile fabrics that are visually similar to medieval Ely ware pottery indicated that they are in fact more similar to Colne and Huntingdon wares.

In the mid/late sixteenth century in particular there is a great increase in the quantities of brick and tile recovered. The majority of this comes from the backfilling of features, so the material relates not to the sixteenth-century use of brick and tile but to demolished fourteenth–fifteenth-century buildings. Even when brick and tile is found in structures there is often evidence from mortar *etc.* that the material is reused. The period does also, however, witness the earliest features at Grand Arcade that appear to represent the use of contemporary brick, notably *Oven 8* and some associated but poorly preserved structural remains. Contrastingly, at Christ's Lane frontage *Building 9* was rebuilt in brick in the late fifteenth or early sixteenth century, utilizing bricks imported from the Low Countries (although some of these may have been reused). A substantial brick-built oven was also constructed within adjacent *Building 10* at this time; this may have functioned as a commercial premises (see Chapter 6). Such variations in date, as well as the extent to which brick was used, may correspond to a difference in status between the two sites during this period.

In general, most of the brick and tile in use during this period appears to derive from Fenland sources, located on or near the Isle of Ely. The earliest documentary evidence for production in Ely dates to the second half of the fifteenth century, when there was a 'tyle kylne close' at Barton Farm (Lucas 1993, 157). The fine quality of brickwork veneer with traces of diamond or diaper patterning at Queen's College of 1448–9 represents the earliest extensive use of exposed brickwork in Cambridge (RCHM(E) 1959, c), while Bishop Alcock's work at Jesus College started in 1496 and dated *c.* 1500 including the diaper work near the top of the gatehouse represents the earliest 'conscious' use of 'white' brickwork, although some is suffused with pink (RCHM(E) 1959, c). When St John's College First Court was being built in 1511–16 the brick maker was one Recluver of Greenwich and the College paid his travelling expenses, suggesting an absence of local expertise. The bricks appear to have been purpose made and were fired using wood from Coton (RCHM(E) 1959, c). The use of brickwork by colleges became common in the sixteenth century, some of which – including that for the Great Gate of King's Hall – was bought at Ely in 1528–9 (Lucas 1993, 158; RCHM(E) 1959, c). As well as its use by the colleges there are sixteenth-century documentary records of brick boundary walls around plots in 1546 and 1574–5, and named bricklayers are first attested in the 1540s (Richard Mason in 1544, Charles Palmer who lived in St Andrew's parish in 1546).

Worked bone Craig Cessford and Lorrain Higbee
A total of 48 worked bone items of eleventh–sixteenth century date were initially identified from Grand Arcade and Christ's Lane, while a further three have been subsequently identified. It is likely that a few additional items remain unrecognized in the unstudied animal bone. There were only two relatively small assemblages of note: three double-ended implements from the twelfth-century construction of *Well 18* and a decorated item, a scoop, a point and a stamp or rough-out from late eleventh–early twelfth-century *Pit 2*.

A range of eleventh–twelfth-century worked bone objects were recovered. These are all of typical types of the period and include eight double-ended implements (Fig. 4.5), three whistle/flute fragments (Fig. 4.60A), two toggles/buzz bones, two points, a scoop, a square-sectioned rod decorated with dots (Fig. 2.4C), a possible stamp or handle rough-out, a needle, a ring and possibly part of a comb case. The worked bone objects were scattered across the site and do not indicate any specialized activity zones.

Despite considerable evidence for bone-working activity at the site (Fig. 3.14), relatively few thirteenth–fourteenth-century worked bone objects were recovered. The identified artefacts included a pen or possibly a knitting needle made from a goose radius (Crummy 1988, 97), a spatula made from a pig fibula, a decorated stylus or point (Fig. 4.60B), a tuning peg and a possible side-plate from a composite comb or handle. The only more frequently occurring objects were five fourteenth–fifteenth-century 'parchment' prickers or styli (Margeson 1993, 69–70; MacGregor 1985, 122–5). These were lathe turned with an ovoid or spherical head and a short tapering or parallel-sided shank; two had bone points and two holes that originally held iron points. Such objects may have been used for a range of domestic purposes, including transferring patterns onto embroidery.

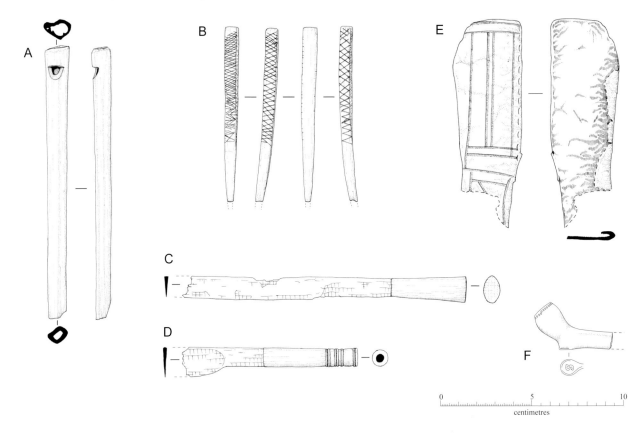

Figure 4.60. *Miscellaneous twelfth–sixteenth-century items: (A) twelfth-century flute made from roe deer metatarsal with shaft shaped to produce smooth surface, the proximal articulation removed and a perforation in the proximal shaft ([36173] F.6143); (B) fourteenth-century square-sectioned bone object that tapers towards one end made from a large mammal long bone, decorated with cross hatch lines on three sides, may be some form of stylus or point ([31233] F.3270); (C) sixteenth-century bone-handled whittle-tanged iron knife, from Pit 50 ([32050]) with handle is made from a mammal long bone; (D) sixteenth-century bone-handled scale-tanged iron knife ([32118] F.3413) with handle made from a medium-sized mammal, probably sheep, long bone with lathe-turned line decoration; (E) fourteenth-century leather back section of a knife sheath, broken off from the blade section. From Pit 18 ([34266]); (F) Type 1 clay tobacco pipe bowl of c. 1580–1600 with incuse letter S on the base of the heel, probably manufactured in London ([32704] F.6472).*

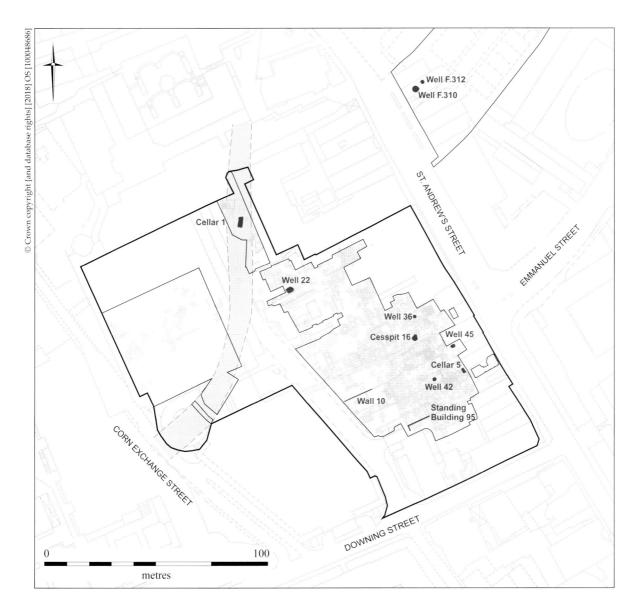

Figure 4.61. *The distribution of significant assemblages of stone mouldings, showing their wide dispersion across Grand Arcade and Christ's Lane.*

There is continued evidence for bone-working in the Barnwell Gate suburb in the fifteenth–sixteenth centuries; the quantity of worked bone objects remains low but in the sixteenth century a range of new artefacts types appear. The most common are four implement handles principally for whittle-tanged knives (Fig. 4.60C–D), one of which is highly decorated (Fig. 3.17C). Other items include a skate plus a possible rough-out for a skate made from a cattle metatarsal, a gaming piece or button, a comb and a possible side plate from comb or comb case.

Stone mouldings Mark Samuel, incorporating specialist information from Kevin Hayward
A large quantity of moulded stone was recovered from the Grand Arcade excavations; of these 242 pieces that were deemed significant enough to warrant consideration were retained and assessed. Five pieces from

Christ's Lane were also examined. Subsequently, around 70 stones were subject to further analysis. None of the moulded stone was found *in situ* and all of it was reused in a variety of structures such as well linings and wall foundations. As the main interest in the material relates to its primary architectural context rather than its secondary or even tertiary archaeological context, the moulded stone has not been as thoroughly integrated into the site narrative as the other material.

The reused stone was widely dispersed across a number of plots (Fig. 4.61) and had been employed in structures that were constructed in several different centuries. While the stone mouldings from individual features often have a degree of coherence, those from

171

the site as a whole do not and in most respects they should not be considered a meaningful assemblage at any level greater than the feature. In all cases it is impossible to determine the precise origin of the stonework, as Cambridge was home to a significant number of medieval churches and religious houses. Moreover, documentary evidence indicates that after the Dissolution stonework from a number of religious houses in the fens was transported to Cambridge for reuse. It appears that the 'best' stonework in terms of reuse was utilized in above ground contexts that do not survive and that the stonework that was reused in well linings

and wall foundations consists principally of pieces that were awkwardly shaped for reuse. These limitations mean that the overall assemblage of stone mouldings from the site is a relatively meaningless entity and the main focus of the material must be on the individual feature assemblages; their interest lies not so much in their origins *per se* but in their contexts of reuse.

By considering the date range of stone mouldings using decade incidence it is possible to determine that there is a gradual increase from about 1100, rising sharply in the early thirteenth century and eventually peaking in 1310–20 (Fig. 4.62A). The numbers fall off gradually after that date, prior to a drastic decline after 1400.

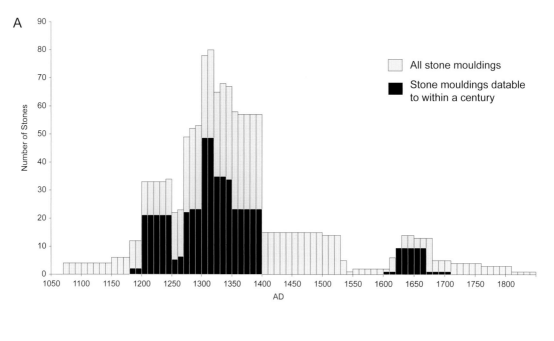

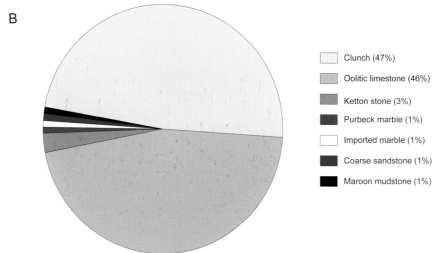

Figure 4.62. *Stone mouldings: (A) cumulative date ranges of stone mouldings from Grand Arcade using decadal incidence of all moulded stones and those datable to within a century; (B) relative proportions of building stone types used at Grand Arcade.*

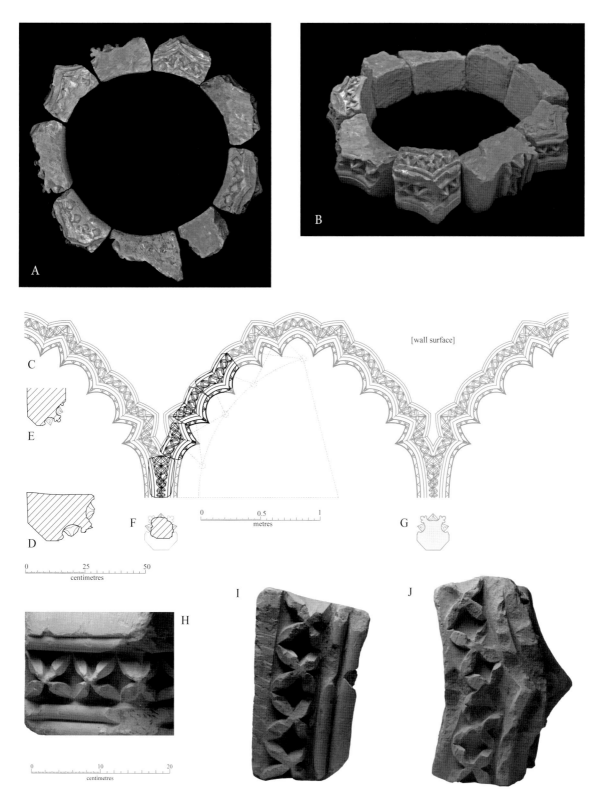

Figure 4.63. *General views of the stone mouldings from a dogtooth triforium blind arcading of c. 1250 reused in the lining of Well 42 in the 1620s ([34586]): (A–B) reconstructed as found; (C) conjectural reconstruction of elevation of blind arcade arches, showing geometry (indicative only); (D) moulding of typical voussoir, showing recutting damage; (E) restored moulding at arch apex; (F) restored moulding at springing line, showing extant arch details; (G) elevation of dogtooth ornament; (H–J) detail of lateral dogtooth ornament (C–G based upon illustrations by Mark Samuel).*

A near-complete break at 1530 gives way to a separate concentration in the post-medieval period. A more 'refined' dating, although based on a smaller sample, can be created by selecting only those items with a date span of a century or less (Fig. 4.62A). This indicates two peaks of construction, the largest in the late thirteenth–early fourteenth century and an absence of building campaigns after the fourteenth century. Assuming that most of the reused stone derives from institutions in Cambridge, rather than the being post Dissolution 'imports', these patterns can perhaps be viewed as delineating the overall pattern of building in stone in medieval Cambridge, although not of individual institutions.

The majority of the stone used was visually identified as Clunch (47 per cent) and Oolitic limestone (46 per cent), with smaller amounts of Ketton stone (3 per cent) and single stones of Purbeck marble, coarse sandstone and maroon mudstone (Fig. 4.62B). Petrological analysis using thin section was undertaken on 10 stones; samples were identified as Clunch Weldon stone, Barnack stone, Ancaster freestone, Alwalton marble and possibly Derbyshire Fossil Limestone. In some cases these samples derive from elements that predate the earliest use of a type of stone known from surviving buildings or documentary sources (Purcell 1967).

Clunch (also known as Burwell stone and Totternhoe stone) is a greyish white chalk, often with a greenish tinge, which was quarried at Barrington, Burwell, Cherry Hinton, Eversden, Haslingfield, Isleham, and Reach (Fig. 7.2E). Excavations at Isleham have revealed evidence for eleventh–sixteenth-century clunch extraction and

processing with quarry pits and associated tanks to soak the stone, which is cut into blocks with a large two-handled saw when wet, plus wells to provide water (Newton 2010). Clunch was referred to locally as 'white stone' and was used in most stone buildings at Cambridge prior to the fifteenth century (Purcell 1967, 24–8). Its fine grain means that it is capable of taking very delicate carving and although its high porosity and high water absorption means that its resistance to weathering is limited, its performance is strongly related to its depth in the bed, the way the stone is extracted, seasoned, and laid in the building so that some clunch can acquire a remarkable toughness. It is suitable for external work where not exposed to dripping water or damp and it lasts well if whitewashed.

Clunch was used for the richly carved tracery at the Lady Chapel of Ely Cathedral and for internal work at Barnwell and Barrington churches (Hughes & Hughes 1909, 113–14). One piece was examined petrologically. In hand specimen this soft freestone resembles Reigate stone from Surrey, both with its green colour and very low density. It differs from Reigate stone as it does not contain mica flakes and has a much paler muddy grey-green colour. In thin-section it can be described as a limestone rather than a sandstone; this is because the chemical test for ferroan calcite has brought out a deep pink colour in the section, a feature of a rock with a high percentage of calcium carbonate. It is fine enough to be considered a chalk-rock.

The majority of the Oolitic limestone used was Barnack stone (Alexander 1995, 115–16), a hard crystalline pale yellow limestone, which is robust enough for external purposes but whose hard coarse

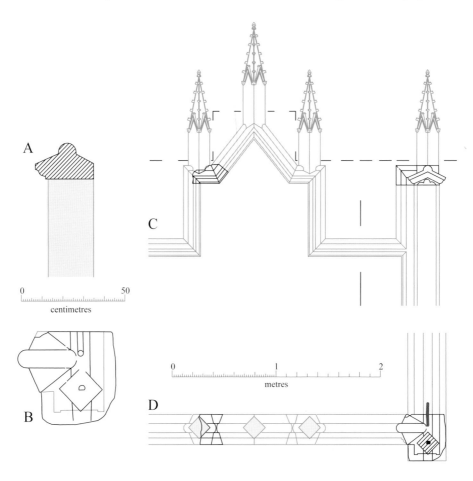

Figure 4.64. *Elevation and plan of parapet crenellation junction with narrow coping made of Weldon stone c. 1350, reused in Wall 10 c. 1720–50 ([40123]). Showing: (A) moulding of coping; (B) plan of junction element as recorded; (C) detail of elevation; (D) plan at base of finials (based upon illustrations by Mark Samuel).*

texture makes it unsuitable for delicate or detailed mouldings (see Fig. 7.2F). Barnack stone was used in Cambridge from the first half of the twelfth century onwards (RCHM(E), 1959, xcix) and was frequently employed from the late thirteenth century onwards (Purcell 1967, 29–34). The evidence from Grand Arcade indicates that it was being used in the late twelfth and early thirteenth centuries.

Detailed descriptions of the individual assemblages are provided in the digital-only volume and illustrated there. There are five assemblages of stone mouldings that are of particular significance. In chronological order of features that they were ultimately incorporated into the earliest is the lining of *Well 36* constructed in mid-fifteenth century, which contained range of elements including the rear arches of windows, angle roll mouldings and spiked hollow moulding arch plus a probable piscina from a late thirteenth–early fourteenth-century church of a religious house (Figs. 4.34 and 7.2J). The lining of *Well 42* constructed in the 1620s contained a triforium arch and associated lancet window from a high status thirteenth-century religious building (Fig. 4.63). *Well 45* constructed *c.* 1723 included material from two domestic windows of *c.* 1570–1640, which themselves incorporated reused thirteenth-century stone. The foundations of *Wall 10* constructed *c.* 1720–50 contained a heterogeneous assemblage; the bulk of the stone, however, relates to a complex crenelated parapet from a fourteenth-century religious building (Fig. 4.64). Finally *Well F.312* constructed at Christ's Lane in the 1830s contained material from a religious institution that appears to have originated in the late twelfth century and had a phase of major building in the first half of the fourteenth century (Fig. 6.14).

Wood and timber Richard Darrah, incorporating specialist information from Steve Allen and Ian Tyers

Wood and timber only survived in the anaerobic waterlogged conditions of features cut into the Gault Clay, but assemblages from over 70 eleventh–sixteenth-century features were studied with dendrochronological analysis undertaken by Ian Tyers and species identification by Steve Allen. The only timber of note at Christ's Lane was a single cask-lined well. Subsequently, further analysis has been undertaken as well as additional dendrochronology and species identification of outstanding material.

The majority of the pieces of wood and timber recovered had been used to line features, including wattle-lined wells (26), cask-lined wells and cesspits (six), square or rectangular timber-lined features referred to as water-filled features (11) and internally revetted pits (three). There was generally very little 'stray' non-structural wood in features, presumably the vast majority of wood that became available was used as firewood rather than being disposed of in below-ground features. Much of the timber showed signs of reuse and it is likely that the assemblage represents a biased sample, as with a few exceptions the timber used to line underground features appears to be relatively poor quality material that was often no longer fit for its original purpose, with better quality material presumably utilized above-ground.

There was a timber market at Cambridge market place by 1377, although it appears that over time the emphasis for large structural timbers shifted to Stourbridge Fair and the role of the central market was as a 'shaggery' where smaller pieces of wood such as kindling and stakes were sold (Bryan & Wise 2002, 85). Timber for building was in short supply locally and in the fifteenth–sixteenth centuries was acquired from Essex, Norfolk, Suffolk, London, King's Lynn and at local fairs (Lee 2005, 189).

The only wooden object from a twelfth-century feature was part of a carbonized ash hay rake head with field maple tines from *Pit 5* (see Case Study 2). Later features also produced some twelfth-century wooden objects that had been broken up and reused; this included some parts of a chest in mid/late fourteenth-century *Pit 16* (Fig. 4.28C–D) and a trough in mid/late fifteenth-century *WFF 11* (Fig. 4.47D; Case Study 6). Unfortunately, there is no way to know whether these items had been present in the Grand Arcade street block since the twelfth century or not.

Relatively few wooden objects were recovered from thirteenth–fourteenth-century contexts. Items that were present included several reused ladder rails (Fig. 4.17D–E) and part of a notched frame (Fig. 4.28B), but the most significant pieces were a staff-like object, two boards from a chest and an eel grig (see Case Study 4). The incomplete staff-like object (Fig. 4.17C) was reused as an upright sail in mid-thirteenth-century *Well 25* and had been carefully shaped from an eighth-section of a field maple trunk into an almost round cross section with two 'parallel' curved mouldings with grooves on either side cut along the length. It is unclear what exactly the original object was; it is unlikely to be a bow as it was not made from yew. It may well be a staff, although it is different from those recovered from medieval burials; these were purely symbolic mortuary items created just to be put in the grave (Gilchrist 2008, 126–8; Gilchrist and Sloane 2005, 126–7, 169–75). The staff-like object was a high status item that had been shaped out of a much larger piece of wood and was not just a straight rod that had been cleaned up. The object was cut down for use as a sail, presumably when it had ceased to be useable in its original function as it had been attacked by boring insects. Also reused in *Well 25* were two ash ladder rails (Fig. 4.17D–E), while a piece of half-round ash with a single hole from *WFF 2* is possibly a ladder rail and could either have been reused or have broken off *in situ*.

Two pine boards from a chest were deliberately placed lying horizontally in mid/late fourteenth-century clay quarry *Pit 16* after it was partially backfilled, possibly to create a stable surface. The original chest appears to have been a personal item that was imported by its owner from Scandinavia during the twelfth century. The boards were decorated with a scored set of parallel lines, and represent the back and top portions of a chest over 0.65m long and 0.31m wide and deep (Fig. 4.28C–D). The top can be identified by the presence of iron hinges, while the back can be identified because an original peg hole from its use as a box survived at the bottom edge of back board. The boards are a distinct type, different to the standard pine boards found elsewhere at Grand Arcade. Both were inner tangential boards, made from trees with distinct growth patterns. The lid came from a 0.35–0.4m-diameter trunk, while the back was made from a 0.32m-diameter trunk. Both had been shaped in a similar way, so that the boards were thicker to the centre of the tree.

Broad axe marks were visible on the lid, made with a blade more than 130mm long that was quite curved for a broad axe. Five mm over the blade length survived as a stop mark on the face of the timber, and there were a set of these stop marks at 45° to the pith line. The fact that these tool marks remained visible means that although the boards were effectively finished spilt boards, they were not up to the standard of the finest coopers work or later imported Baltic boards. As the boards were joined together with iron hinges, presumably at some expense, it might be expected that the finish of the boards would reflect this cost and would have been of better quality. This suggests that the chest may be the work of a skilled amateur, and that the item was made by an individual either to hold their own belongings or as a gift. If the box had been produced commercially, it would either have had cheaper hinges or better-finished boards. As pine was used, it is likely to have been imported from Scandinavia as a personal object. The boards have a set of evenly spaced parallel lines scored on their faces; this pattern was on both the inside and outside of the back suggesting that it was decorative and not for a later board game. There was some damage to both boards at one end where a secondary chamfer had been cut through insect channels. A single nail hole at the front edge of the lid may have held a hasp and staple.

The only evidence of the way the box had been fitted together was a single central peg hole at the bottom of the back of the chest. The absence of peg holes at the ends of the bottom edge of the back, and on the ends of the back, indicate that there had been some reduction of length of the timber prior to its deposition. This chest is similar to another reused as a child's coffin at Barton-upon-Humber in the twelfth century (Waldron 2007) and can also be compared to examples from York (Morris 2000, 2298–9). Given the state of the timber, it is probable that the chest was constructed around the twelfth century and a bevelled end suggests that the timber may have been reworked for use in the pit.

Chests, as well as being functional containers, may have played a significant role as family heirlooms, with other examples being recovered from contexts that indicate that were of considerable age (Gilchrist 2012, 241). This example, which was perhaps 200 years old when deposited, may have passed through around 10 generations and the fact that it may have been personally made by a Scandinavian immigrant would have made it particularly well suited to becoming an heirloom to which a story of familial lineage became attached. This heirloom status was eventually rejected and the chest broken up and discarded, although what caused this rejection is unknown.

Wooden objects remained rare in the fifteenth–sixteenth centuries, but did include some significant pieces. Casks were reused in wells and cesspits (see Case Study 5, for example) and a trough was broken up and reused in the lining of a water-filled feature (see Case Study 6). Early/mid-fifteenth-century *Pit 36* had group of 22 oak and one ash battens, placed there to create a less slippery surface (Fig. 4.53C). The most complete were 0.8–0.9m or around 3ft long and 39–49mm or 1.5–2in wide. They had been radially split and had had their sides trimmed so that they were straight. As plaster laths were used as split, the trimming suggests that these were roofing battens. The split surfaces were uneven with the split stepping at annual rings; this happens occasionally on splitting and is indicative of brittle oak. The battens' thickness varied between a maximum of 6–8mm and a minimum of 4–2.5mm; the variation in thickness and the brittleness of the timber both suggest that they were too irregular and brittle to use. These battens were much thinner than the minimum thickness of half an inch mentioned as common in the reign of Edward III (1330–77) (Salzman 1952, 240), although this may be for a specific type of batten. An assize of 1528 states that laths should be 5ft long, 2in wide and half an inch thick and in 1607 they were supposed to be 4–5ft long, 1in wide and 1/3in thick, while some lath fragments from the late sixteenth-century Rose Theatre were 30–40mm wide and 9–12mm thick (Goodburn in Bowsher and Miller 2009, 222–3). Most surviving post-medieval buildings were battened with 9–10mm thick battens.

The battens from *Pit 36* lack nail holes and had therefore not been used. It appears that they were discarded by the tiler who would have been unwilling to risk his life by kneeling on them while he was working on the roof, making this a rare discovery of unused Late Medieval building materials. As the battens were discarded as unusable they should be regarded as substandard and atypical of the hundreds that would have been used in a roof. This raises the question of whether other archaeologically recovered timber can be assumed to be representative of materials used in the past, or whether it represents a biased sample. A slightly later instance is some poor quality small wooden pegs in *Cesspit 16* which are also unused. The rejected battens would have made excellent kindling and are unlikely to have survived long; this suggests that the clay was being extracted for some building purpose, such as daubing, at the same time as the tile battens were being fitted on a roof.

Pit 36 also contained two wooden bowls (Fig. 4.53A–B), while slightly later mid-fifteenth-century *Pit 37* contained a much more unusual wooden jug (Fig. 4.53D). The jug, which parallels pottery, pewter and leather forms, is made of European maple and has been repaired with rivets or staples. The grain runs vertically and may be a German import, as it is broadly similar to spindle turned (vertical grain) vessels from Freiburg, Windsheimer and Lübeck. It may also be British, in which case it would be made from field maple (*Acer campestre*), but if it was an import it may be made from Norway maple (*Acer platanoides*), which was the standard maple in Novgorod and probably Germany. Perhaps the nearest equivalents in wood are some common seventeenth–eighteenth-century Irish drinking vessels called *lamhog*, made in exactly the same way from willow or poplar. The vessel has turning marks either side of the handle, indicating that it was turned on a pole lathe. The lathe was not being turned a complete revolution, but going backwards and forwards through around 340° and stopping at the handle, which is a difficult technique. Hollowing a large vessel through a small opening is also difficult, as a core of wood has to be left up the middle until the end so there is only a narrow aperture to work through. This jug form is a technically difficult piece to produce in wood and much easier to make in other materials such as pottery, pewter or leather.

A late fifteenth-century iron knife from the King's Ditch (Fig. 3.16B) had part of a desiccated wood handle surviving. This was the only surviving wooden handle from the site, but as bone handles do not occur prior to the sixteenth-century wooden handles were presumably common. In Late Medieval London wood was the most common material for knife handles (61 wood, 10 bone, five other; Cowgill *et al.* 2000, 25, table 6) and the situation was similar on the Mary Rose (50 wood, five bone; Every & Richards 2005, table 3.5).

The construction of *Cesspit 14* in the fifteenth century provides a useful snapshot of the wood available in a property at one point in time. The material used as a baseplate and as packing around the cask appears most likely to derive from a stockpile kept in the rear of a property, probably for a mixture of reuse and as firewood. It included branches from clearing or trimming an elder bush and an oak tree, both of which may well have been growing in the plot tail. There was also a collection of pieces of old objects including two curved oak timbers from a heavy frame (Fig. 4.42B–C) and part of the beech felloe from a wheel with an oak spoke that was probably not of local origin (Fig. 4.41E). Other pieces included a fluted trunk of field maple, an aspen or poplar board and fragments from two oak cask heads (Fig. 4.41C). Such stockpiles were presumably a common feature of medieval properties, and were a relatively frequent source of complaint in the London Assize of Nuisance (Chew & Kellaway 1973), but are usually archaeologically invisible.

Two *in situ* ladders were found associated with the mid-sixteenth-century backfilling of *WFFs 14–15*. The ladder from *WFF 14* (Fig. 4.46A–C) was made entirely from ash, including the wedges in the rungs on the outside of the rails. One side was square in section and made from a halved pole, the other was a small squared-up trunk. The rungs were a split quarter of a pole shaped into a D-shaped or sub square cross-section. It is unclear whether the rungs were wider in the centre, but the rungs were 30mm-diameter where they met the rails; as the holes in the rails were only 27mm-diameter the rungs may have tapered. One rung still attached to the rail had the grain vertical; the second had the grain horizontal. Surprisingly they had used ash with some very narrow rings; this wood is both less strong, and less durable, a very dangerous thing to have in a ladder rung. The ladder from *WFF 15* (Fig. 4.48) had two sinuous rails made from a single elm pole, sawn in half down its length.

The ash rungs at 330mm intervals had been set centrally in the rails so that they did not run in a flat plane. Most of the rungs were made from cleft and drawn ash and were almost round in cross section. The rungs were wedged on the outside of the rails; one wedge was ash, another was oak. In contrast medieval ladders from York had rails made of oak and alder, while rungs were made of oak and possibly maple and hazel (Morris 2000, 2320–1, 2416). Unusually one of these rungs was a flat ash board with tusk tenons with round pegs outside the rails (Fig. 4.48D). As the underside of this rung had been shaped, the ladder could only have been used one way up with this rung at least the fourth rung up the ladder. It was not clear whether this rung's function was to hold the sides of the ladder together when there may have been several on one ladder, or to identify the ladder from a distance when only one shaped rung would be required. A similar 'maker's rung' can be seen on a late nineteenth-century photograph from Yorkshire (Winter 1973, 30).

These ladders were presumably used for access to the pits in which they were found in order to dismantle and retrieve their timber linings; the pits were then carefully backfilled and the ladders would allow the backfilling material to be tamped down to ensure that it was compressed as much as possible. These were the only ladders that were abandoned in this manner at the site, and at the time did not occasion particular comment as their presence appeared completely natural and the use of ladders to enter pits must have been an everyday occurrence. However, when we consider the hundreds of waterlogged Roman and later features excavated in Britain every year the recovery of such ladders is rare, because of course ladders are removed and the few rung and rail fragments found in earlier features at the site are comparable to what is typically found at other medieval sites such as York (Morris 2000, 2320–1, 2416). Both ladders were apparently still in good and usable condition and there is no evidence for any instability or collapse in either pit that might have necessitated 'emergency' abandonment. There is no clear reason why these two ladders were abandoned, however the rarity of the phenomenon and its occurrence, combined with the proximity of the two features in the same property, suggests that they may be contemporary and hints at extremely atypical behaviour.

A mid-sixteenth-century recut of the King's Ditch contained a badly compressed woven round-based basket (Fig. 3.18) similar to examples from the Mary Rose (Hurcombe & Lemieux 2005, 400–8) and a complete bowling ball or wood with the standard incised pattern of lines and dots, which was 100mm in diameter by 81mm thick (Fig. 3.17D) and is similar to other fourteenth–seventeenth-century English examples (Egan in Grainger 2000, 35; Morris 2007, 59–65). There was a fragment of a double-sided simple comb carved in one piece from mid/late sixteenth-century *Pit 38*; this is similar to an example from York (Morris 2000, 2309–12, 2415) and the large assemblage from the Mary Rose (81 of boxwood and one of alder; Richards & Maddocks 2005, 156–9).

Species

Quantifying the wood species used is highly problematic given issues of survival, sampling and comparability between different types of item. What is clear is that oak was the most common species, occurring in around half of the features that contained wood and timber. Other identified species in declining order of occurrence were *Fraxinus excelsior*

L. (ash, 36 features), *Salix* spp. (willows, 36 features), *Corylus avellana* L. (hazel, 20 features), *Alnus* spp. (alder, 12 features), *Pinus sylvestris* L. (Scots pine, 10 features), *Ulmus* spp. (elms, 10 features). Rather less common were *Acer campestre* L. (field maple, seven features) and *Sambucus nigra* L. (elder, six features), *Fagus sylvatica* L. (beech, three features) and *Populus sp.* (aspen, white or black poplar, two features). *Abies alba* L. (silver fir), *Ilex aquifolium* L. (holly), *Pomoideae* spp. (includes apple, pear, hawthorn, quince), *Prunus avium* L. (cherry), *Prunus spinosa* L. (blackthorn) and *Rosa* spp. (rose) were only found in one feature apiece.

Roundwood

The majority of the roundwood occurred as woven cylindrical well structures with multiple sails, built using a number of sharpened upright sails around which a series of horizontal rods were woven to create a basket-like structure (Table 4.13), plus a few examples of linear hurdle structures. Much of the roundwood was 10–30mm in diameter and had the typical chisel points of wood cut from a stool with a single blow of an axe or bill hook by a skilled worker. This suggests that the wood was cut by people who knew how to use the tools they were employing and it is likely

Table 4.13. *Species and felling season of roundwood from twelfth–fifteenth century wattle-lined wells.*

Well	Date	Species							Season		
		Alder	Ash	Maple	Hazel	Oak	Willow	Other	Autumn/winter	Spring	Summer
Well 18	12th	-	2	-	4	1	2	-	5	3	-
Well 13	12th	-	22	1	-	-	77	-	72	19	9
Well 8	12th	-	-	-	5	-	-	-	2	-	3
Well 4	12th	6	-	-	-	-	18	-	5	9	8
Well 5	12th	-	61	-	6	5	12	-	48	28	10
Well 7	12th	3	-	-	-	-	33	-	-	-	7
Well 32	13th	-	22	-	4	1	9	-	18	-	8
Well 25	13th	2	4	1	-	-	-	-	-	-	-
Well 23	13th	20	-	-	-	-	16	-	11	21	4
Well 33	14th	2	3	-	37	-	15	-	18	2	35
Well 31	14th	-	1	-	3	-	2	1	-	-	-
Well 29	14th	2	-	2	70	-	10	-	16	28	32
Well 21	14th	-	-	-	-	41	-	-	-	-	-
Well 26	14th	1	2	-	22	-	3	-	9	14	5
Well 35	15th	-	11	-	-	13	-	-	14	2	2
Total		36	128	4	151	61	197	1	218	126	123

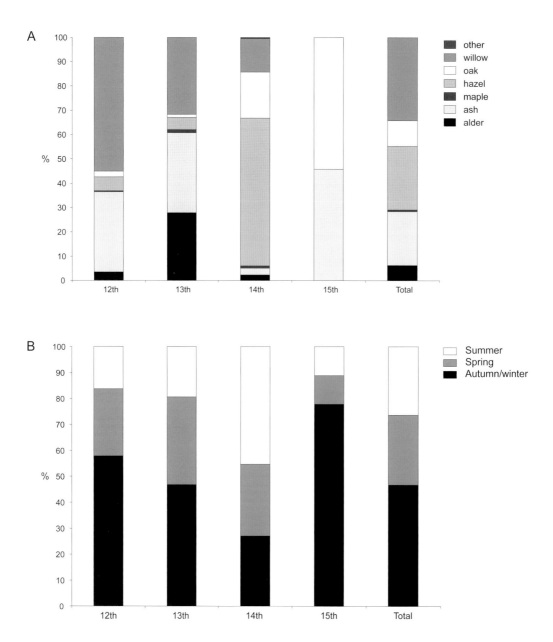

Figure 4.65. *The species (A) and felling seasons (B) of coppiced roundwood utilized in twelfth–fifteenth-century well linings.*

that every adult in a peasant population could use a bill hook. If skilled people were cutting stools they would be likely to cut a whole stool at once, clean it (cut off side branches) and bundle it up and stack it, or draw felling selecting and taking single branches of the correct size.

Cutting any rod takes less than one minute per 10–25mm rod, so no stool would take more than an hour to cut. A typical tightly woven wattle-lined well would require around 240 rods plus 40 sails weighing *c.* 120kg or one tenth of a cart load. Cutting 60 rods per hour equates to less than five hours to cut and bundle

the rods for one well, substantially less than one day. With hazel trees the rods per stool varies between nine and 36, averaging 19, which means that if all the wood from stools was used then 14 stools would be required to line a well. The wood would be bundled soon after cutting, as by summer rods would be hidden in new growth if left lying and it cannot easily be transported before bundling. Despite this many wells employed wood cut during different seasons spanning autumn/winter, spring and summer.

There appear to be two distinct features about the selection and cutting of coppice rods used for the construction of wells. The species utilized change over time (Fig. 4.65A). Initially in the eleventh–twelfth centuries willow is dominant. Ash is also significant in the twelfth and especially thirteenth centuries, while alder is significant in one thirteenth-century well. By the fourteenth century hazel has become the most significant species, although one well solely employed oak. In recent times hazel is the most commonly species used for wattle work; willow is also common but must not be used where structures are backfilled with soil as it might take root and grow, which is not a factor with regard to wattle-lined wells. Secondly there is more summer felling in the fourteenth century, hinting at a longer cutting season (Fig. 4.65B).

The coppice products in most wells were felled over several months; this pattern is counter-intuitive as the process of cutting rods takes less than one day. Even if some re-selection for size took place, this should have happened over a short term of perhaps a week rather than four months of harvested rods. Added to this is the fact that the rods and sails found survive at the bottom of the wells, the part built first when the first few bundles of rods were opened, not the part built of the odds and ends left over. This means we have to look to a distinct mechanism where we find winter, spring and summer wood harvested or sold together. Clearly different shrubs of the same species come into leaf at distinct times, so we should expect some variation in growth pattern from stool to stool. If we add to this the stools growing on woodland edge with unrestricted sun light coming into leaf early and in shade under the canopy of trees coming into leaf late we may get a variation of spring to summer.

It may simply be that when they selected two bundles for the sails – one winter plus one spring and summer combined – then the remains of these two bundles were used for the rods at the bottom of the wells. As the rods and sails could all have been cut in one day this suggests several possibilities. The material could represent purchases at different dates from a market, separate cutting events or purchases from a wholesale market where large quantities of coppice have been bought by a merchant who resold material cut at different seasons together at a later date. Another alternative is stealing wood in small quantities over a long period, or 'cut-it-yourself' wood sales (Rackham 1980, 156).

Twelfth-century *Well 5* differs from the other rod sets in that the rods coppiced in summer were larger than those at other periods, suggesting that a bundle of larger late felled rods had been acquired. Some wells have a set of individual rods that lie outside the average growth rate being slower grown; these were usually used as uprights and were larger in size and clearly some selection had gone on. In later woodland management the different sizes of roundwood were bundled separately (Trust 1956). This selection may represent either this, or the selection by draw felling but this would not explain the spread of wood over three seasons if all the rods were purchased directly from a wood man. The evidence for coppice rotation is not clear, but most of the rods were felled at five to nine years.

Casks

Casks were reused as linings for wells and cesspits, while staves from casks were used to line water filled features and a number of individual staves and parts of cask heads were also recovered from the fills of features. Relatively few of the casks were intact enough to provide substantive information (Table 4.14). One cask was of Greek origin and a number of others whose tree ring sequences could not be matched may also be of Mediterranean origin. Whilst this could suggest that Mediterranean casks were relatively common, it is more likely that they were selected for reuse as they did not correspond to accepted local sizes.

Table 4.14. *Casks repurposed as feature linings that survived well enough for accurate measurement. Height measured from croze groove to croze groove length, not the full length of the stave.*

Feature	Date	Height (m)	Max dia. (m)	Croze dia. (m)	Volume (cubic m)	Stave thickness (mm)	No. of staves	Origin
Well 6	12th	1.12	0.68	0.67	0.4+	18	18	Unknown, possibly Mediterranean
Cesspit 14	15th	-	0.76	0.73	1.0	12.25	20	English
Well 40	Early 16th	-	-	0.85	1.0	24	35	Unknown, possibly Mediterranean
Water Filled Feature 13	Mid/late 15th	1.085	-	-	0.23	17	Unknown	Unknown
Well 39	Mid-15th	0.93	0.79	0.72	0.4+	10	27	Unknown
Well 38	Late 16th	1.300	1.015	0.815	0.77	23	27	Mainland Greece

Boards

There is evidence for the use of a wide range of types of boards from continually changing timber sources, but also long term evidence of imports from the Baltic and Scandinavia. There is evidence for eight distinct types of board, excluding cask staves, being used in the medieval period and six more in the post-medieval and modern periods. The conversion and origin of the medieval boards were:

1) Radially cleft East Anglian oak, finished by axe to parallel sided boards.
2) Tangentially cleft East Anglian oak, finished by axe to parallel sided boards.
3) Cleft and hand hewn tangential pine boards that are thicker in centre of board.
4) Imported tongue and grooved pine boards with parallel faces.
5) Imported pine boards with parallel faces and straight edges.
6) Tongue and grooved Baltic oak boards with radial faces.
7) Baltic oak boards without tongue and groove.
8) Tangentially sawn oak, ash, poplar and elm.

Notably absent from the types of medieval board are the very wide slow grown oak boards used in the fittings of prestigious buildings like King's College Chapel, whose use was presumably restricted to high status buildings. Also absent is the type of roughly hewn pine boards used in the twelfth-century Newton Culvert. The conversion and origin of the sixteenth–nineteenth-century boards were:

1) English tangentially sawn thin oak boards, which were planed up.
2) Radially sawn panel boards, which were planed up.
3) Pine boards sawn from a squared baulk from Norway.
4) Reciprocating saw pine boards, from the hinterland of Trondheim.
5) Similar pine boards cut with a circular saw.
6) Over-thick hand-sawn pine floorboards, notched to fit over joists.

There was clearly a very diverse trade in boards in the medieval period, which occurs as the English supplies of slow grown cleavable oak were used up. It is difficult to track this change as most fast grown timber that was sawn up had too few rings to date, so it is unclear how much fast grown timber was English and how much was imported. What is interesting is the absence of Scottish pine from the Caledonian forests that were felled in the eighteenth century and American pine from the nineteenth century. This may be because East Anglia had traditionally traded with the Baltic and this tradition continued.

Leatherwork Quita Mould

A large assemblage of over 235 leather items of eleventh–sixteenth-century date was recovered from Grand Arcade. The bulk of the material was re-examined following treatment. The material consisted principally of shoes, but there were also some straps and other items as well as a small quantity of leatherworking waste. The only significant assemblage, of late fifteenth–mid-sixteenth-century material, was recovered from the King's Ditch, although, as this group was deposited over a period of several decades and may have originated from a wide variety of sources, it can only loosely be defined as an 'assemblage'.

Documentary sources attest to a Lorimers' (harness makers) Row in Cambridge in 1299, a Cordwainers' (shoemakers) Row in 1322, a Leather Market in 1362 and a Saddlers' Row in 1370 (Bryan & Wise 2002, 83–5). Several individuals associated with these trades were living in the Grand Arcade street block and there is considerable animal bone evidence for related trades. The waste leather spanned the thirteenth–sixteenth centuries; this is principally secondary cattle hide waste from the cutting and trimming of pattern pieces during the manufacture of leather goods or their repair, plus a single piece of primary waste. The majority comprised trimmings and it is likely that they derive from the small-scale repair of footwear (cobbling) rather than shoe manufacture.

Although overall there was a large leather assemblage from the site it should be noted that no leather was found in roughly three quarters of the features where it would have survived and most features that did contain leather produced only a few pieces. This indicates that the disposal of leather was relatively uncommon. One potential factor is suggested by an ordinance of 1575, which stated that 'no person shall hereafter willingly burn within his house or chimney, any shreds of cloth or leather' (Cooper 1843, 336). The word 'shreds' possibly suggests that leather off-cuts were being burnt by local leatherworkers; these are unlikely to have been a particularly useful source of fuel so it is probable that they were simply disposing of inconveniently large accumulations of waste material.

The only significant eleventh–twelfth-century leather item was a turnshoe recovered from the King's Ditch and dated stylistically by parallels from London and York to the early twelfth century (Chapter 3; Fig. 3.8). There was also a fragment of leather with one surface coated in pitch, likely to be broken from a container for liquids in *Pit 12*. The small thirteenth–fourteenth-century leather assemblage consisted primarily of fourteenth-century turnshoes from the King's Ditch (Chapter 3; Fig. 3.12D–F). There was also the back panel from the handle section of a torn knife sheath, with linear tooled decoration comparable to that on sheaths from early–mid-fourteenth-century contexts in London (Cowgill *et al.* 2000); this was recovered from fourteenth-century *Pit 18* (Fig. 4.60E). A small amount of thirteenth–fourteenth-century leather waste, consisting mainly of cattle hide trimmings, was also present at Grand Arcade; this represents the small-scale repair of footwear.

The fifteenth–sixteenth-century leather consisted largely of shoes/boots, plus some straps, a fragment of a decorated panel, a disc, part of a scabbard and waste. The sixteenth-century footwear (Figs. 3.16C–D, 3.19 and 3.21B) was of welted construction with distinctive broad toes and a single straight-toed example, both indicative of the Tudor period. Examples of low-sided shoes with square throats, one fastening with a buckle and strap over the instep and high-throated shoes were present. There was also the leg cut from a tall boot and an annular buckle of tinned iron with strap knotted around the frame, likely to be a shoe buckle. The proportion of shoe bottom parts and the presence of two soles cut to salvage reusable leather suggest that cobbling waste is present.

A small number of fifteenth–sixteenth-century straps were recovered; all were of cattle hide, around ¾in to 1in thick. The majority of the straps were plain and may well come from harness, none appear to be spur leathers. A single example (Fig. 3.21D), from the King's Ditch, had two buckle holes with lead alloy eyelets suggesting it may come from a girdle or belt. An impressive piece of decorated leather from a piece of upholstery or other leather furnishing came from the King's Ditch (Fig. 3.20). Also from the King's Ditch was a circular disc clearly cut from an old shoe sole (Fig. 3.21C); spare discs to replace worn out pump valves must have always been required. A piece cut from an undecorated sword scabbard was recovered from fifteenth-century *Pit 39*.

A small amount of fifteenth–sixteenth-century waste leather was recovered, the majority comprising trimmings of cattle hide and it is likely that they derive from the small-scale repair of footwear, that is cobbling, not shoe manufacture. A single piece of primary waste from a sixteenth-century fill of the King's Ditch appears to be a thick shaving or other unusable area of hide. Although the majority of the waste material comes from the King's Ditch, waste leather was also found in a number of other pits whose distribution indicates that the activity was widespread.

Miscellaneous materials Craig Cessford

A total of 26 pieces of flint weighing 299g were recovered from Grand Arcade; none was recovered from Christ's Lane. This was all residual Prehistoric material, with the exception of a single gunflint (Fig. 5.57L). In addition, 103 pieces of baked clay weighing 461g were recovered from the Grand Arcade excavations, while no baked clay was recovered from Christ's Lane. The only identifiable object was a spindle whorl from a thirteenth-century context. A few fifteenth/sixteenth century fragments of textile were recovered.

The use of clay tobacco pipes begins in the late sixteenth century, and one bowl of *c.* 1580–1600 and another of *c.* 1580–1610 (Fig. 4.60F) were recovered. These were both probably produced in London and the latter has an incuse letter S on the base of the heel, which is paralleled by discoveries from London (le Cheminant 1981, fig. 1, no. 3; Oswald 1975, fig. 2, no.

7). Clay tobacco pipes became much more common from the seventeenth century onwards (see Chapter 5).

Economic and environmental data

Mammal and bird bone Lorrain Higbee

In total, 57,942 fragments of faunal material weighing 959.4kg were recovered from Grand Arcade and 2963 fragments weighing 37.3 kg from Christ's Lane. Approximately 65 per cent of the assemblage (39,555 fragments) was selected for analysis; this includes all of the Christ's Lane assemblage, any large securely dated and/or particularly interesting groups from Grand Arcade, plus the entire assemblages from King's Ditch and the areas identified as four discrete plots (Plots VIII, XI, XIII, XVI). Overall, 16,412 fragments were identified; this includes 7095 bones from 61 complete and partial skeletons and a deposit of four horse skulls (see Table 4.15). This material was divided into five periods for analysis: eleventh–twelfth century (of which the bulk is late eleventh–twelfth century), thirteenth century, fourteenth–fifteenth century, sixteenth–seventeenth century (of which the bulk is early–mid-sixteenth century) and eighteenth–nineteenth century (effectively *c.* 1760–1850). Although the material belonging to the last of these periods is discussed separately in Chapter 5, the overall pattern – including changes in species frequency, industrial deposits, mortality profiles, biometry and butchery over time – is discussed here.

Of the 5554 eleventh–twelfth-century bones studied, the bulk of which are twelfth century, 1051 (18.9 per cent) were identified as mammal (832), bird (171) and amphibian (48) (Table 4.15). The animal bone is dominated by the principal livestock species, with sheep the most common followed by cattle and then pig, although cattle provided the most meat (Fig. 4.66A–B). The relatively high sheep bone and low cattle bone frequency is probably due to the dominance of sheep farming locally after the Norman Conquest. Goat does not appear to have been eaten, but there are a small number of fallow and roe deer bones suggesting poaching. The assemblage is a mixture of principally primary butchery of animals or the processing of by-products (*e.g.* horn) from the butchery trade, plus a small amount of domestic waste indicating that animals arrived on-the-hoof for slaughter.

The cattle are a mixture of prime beef cattle plus animals that had been managed for milk and traction. The sheep included animals slaughtered for prime mutton, plus younger animals culled for meat and older animals managed primarily for wool, while the pigs may have been kept locally. There is no evidence that live sheep were ever kept at the site, unlike some contemporary suburbs such as the Hamel in Oxford (Palmer 1980, 204–5, 208–9) and even more central parts of Cambridge where there was a partially articulated neonate at Hostel Yard indicating the presence of live animals in the vicinity as late as the early/mid-fourteenth century (Swaysland in Cessford 2005). Horse, dog and cat were present in small numbers, whilst chicken was relatively common with goose, duck and a few wild species present in smaller numbers. Although most features produced only small quantities of bone there were two larger groups (*Pits 10* and *12*).

Table 4.15. *Number of specimens identified to species (or NISP) by period. Identified fragments are POSACs following Davis (1992); all other fragments have been assigned to either a general size or taxonomic category. The POSACs of fragments from complete/partial skeletons and a deposit of horse skulls are counted as one specimen each, whilst nonPOSACs are included in the unidentified counts (see digital-only volume). Poorly dated material that was analysed is excluded, as is fish bone.*

Species		11th–12th	13th	14th–15th	16th–17th	18th–19th	Total
Bos f. domestic	Cattle	217	77	903	808	215	2220
Caprovid	Sheep/goat	368	57	472	1220	331	2448
Ovis f. domestic	Sheep	104	18	260	738	205	1325
Capra f. domestic	Goat	4	4	15	10	-	33
Sus f. domestic	Pig	86	24	183	270	143	706
Equus f. domestic	Horse	19	14	70	97	7	207
Canis f. domestic	Dog	16	5	93	103	19	236
Canis/Vulpes	Dog/fox	-	-	2	1	-	3
Felis f. domestic	Cat	14	6	50	37	50	157
Dama	Fallow deer	1	-	5	18	1	25
Capreolus	Roe deer	1	-	-	1	-	2
Cervus elaphus/Dama dama	Red/fallow deer	-	-	2	-	-	2
Lepus sp.	Hare	-	-	-	-	16	16
Oryctolagus cuniculus	Rabbit	1	-	4	23	29	57
Lepus/O. cuniculus	Hare/rabbit	-	-	-	2	3	5
Microtus agrestis	Field vole	1	-	-	-	-	1
Rattus norvegicus	Brown rat	-	-	-	-	3	3
Rattus sp.	Rat	-	-	1	1	3	5
Talpa europaea	Mole	-	-	-	-	1	1
Gallus f. domestic	Chicken	144	18	147	137	190	636
Anser sp.	Goose	19	-	43	34	23	119
Anas cf. *platyrhynchos*	?Mallard	-	-	17	33	53	103
Columbidae	Pigeon/dove	3	-	101	53	38	195
Meleagris gallopavo	Turkey	-	-	-	-	4	4
Pavo cristatus	Peafowl	-	-	-	1	-	1
cf. *Anser*	?Greylag goose	-	-	2	-	1	3
cf. *A. albifrons/A. brachyrhynchus*	?White-fronted goose/ pink-footed goose	1	-	-	-	-	1
cf. *A. crecca/A. querquedula*	?Teal/garganey	-	-	-	3	5	8
Anas sp.	Duck	1	1	11	8	6	27
Phasianus colchicus	Pheasant	-	-	-	-	3	3
Perdix	Grey partridge	-	-	1	-	16	17
cf. *Pluvialis squatarola*	?Grey plover	-	-	-	-	1	1
cf. *Pluvialis apricaria*	?Golden plover	1	-	-	-	-	1
Pluvialis sp.	?Plover	-	-	1	-	-	1
cf. *Lagopus*	?Red grouse	-	-	-	-	3	3
Gallinago	Snipe	-	-	-	-	2	2
small wader sp.	Small wader	-	-	15	-	5	20
cf. *Rallus aquaticus*	?Water rail	-	-	1	-	-	1
Vanellus	Lapwing	1	-	3	-	1	5
Cygnus cf. *olor*	?Mute swan	-	-	4	1	2	7
Botaurus stellaris	Bittern	-	-	2	-	-	2
Ardea cinerea	Grey heron	-	-	-	-	1	1

Table 4.15 (*continued*).

Species		11th–12th	13th	14th–15th	16th–17th	18th–19th	Total
Corvus corax	Raven	-	-	15	6	-	21
C. corone/C. frugilegus	Crow/rook	-	-	1	5	11	17
Corvus monedula	Jackdaw	-	-	-	31	1	32
Larus cf. *argentatus*	?Herring gull	-	-	-	-	5	5
Haliaeetus albicilla	White-tailed eagle	-	-	-	1	-	1
Tyto alba	Barn owl	1	-	-	-	1	2
Strix aluco	Tawny owl	-	-	-	4	1	5
Milvus	Red kite	-	-	-	1	-	1
Turdidae	Blackbird family	-	-	1	4	6	11
Rana temporaria	Common frog	48	6	182	19	2	257
Bufo	Common toad	-	1	8	1	1	11
Cancer pagurus	Edible crab	-	-	-	-	1	1
Total identified		**1051**	**231**	**2615**	**3671**	**1409**	**8977**
Large mammal (cattle/horse/deer)		1126	211	3552	3290	717	8896
Medium mammal (sheep/goat/pig/dog)		2252	324	2849	4219	1691	11,335
Small mammal (cat/rabbit/hare/rodent)		25	5	71	54	165	320
Mammal indeterminate		968	211	2518	2581	906	7184
Bird indeterminate		131	26	404	285	460	1306
Amphibian indeterminate		1	7	8	-	-	16
Total unidentified		**4486**	**784**	**9349**	**10,221**	**3891**	**28,731**
Grand Total		**5571**	**1015**	**12,090**	**14,308**	**5396**	**38,380**

Due to issues of comparability with other Cambridge sites, the thirteenth–fifteenth-century animal bone assemblage was divided into two groups, one thirteenth-century and one fourteenth–fifteenth-century in date. The results from analysis of both groups are presented here. In the first instance, a total of 231 thirteenth-century mammal (205), bird (19) and amphibian (7) bones out of 1015 (22.8 per cent) were identified (Table 4.15). The mammal bone was dominated by the principal livestock species (Fig. 4.66C–D), with cattle and sheep the most common. Cattle provided the most meat, followed by pigs, which were probably being raised on site as their bodies were occasionally disposed of. This was a common medieval phenomenon, with urban pig sties featuring repeatedly in the London Assize of Nuisance (Chew and Kellaway 1973). Whilst some cattle were apparently raised for beef, a significant proportion were probably kept principally for secondary products and traction, whereas a large proportion of the sheep was raised primarily for meat. There was also some goat, horse, dog and cat, with birds represented by chicken and duck.

In the second group, a total of 2615 fourteenth–fifteenth-century mammal (2060), bird (365) and amphibian (190) bones out of 12,037 (21.7 per cent) were identified (Table 4.15). This assemblage was again dominated by the principal livestock species (Fig. 4.67A–B), with sheep the most common followed by cattle and pig, but with cattle supplying the most meat. The dominance of sheep is unusual nationally, and reflects the strong regional tradition of sheep farming in East Anglia. The cattle bone was dominated by horn-working waste (*e.g.* Fig. 3.14A), but also included a significant quantity of primary butchery waste and domestic refuse from the consumption of good quality meat joints. The cattle represent a mixture of animals culled for prime beef and others that were

primarily managed for milk and possibly traction. The sheep bones appear to be a mixture of primary butchery, industry and consumption, often from animals that had provided some fleeces but were then slaughtered for prime mutton.

Pigs were still being raised at the site for pork and a small amount of goat meat was consumed, although the majority of the goat remains relate to skins or horn-working. A small quantity of fallow deer bones were present, probably representing either poached venison or rewards passed on by those with access to it, and rabbit was also consumed. In addition, horse, dog and cat bones were relatively common and several complete and partial skeletons were present, as well as disarticulated remains and evidence for the working of horse bone. Chickens were eaten, but were probably kept primarily for their eggs, as were geese, which may have been kept principally for their feathers. Duck was rare but pigeon was relatively common. Wild birds were relatively uncommon, but included ravens and crows (or rooks), which were probably local scavengers, plus small waders, mute swan and bittern that were probably eaten.

In the fourteenth century horses and possibly pigs were disposed of in specifically dug animal disposal pits and pigs and dogs were disposed of in reused features as has already been discussed. In addition parts of a cow were disposed of in a backfilled beamslot of *Building 6*. There were also some individual fourteenth-century assemblages that provide more specific 'snapshots' of contemporary meat consumption. The contents of three pits in particular appear to relate to individual high-status meals, for example; these include the spit roasting of two immature pigs perhaps as a Christmas feast for a large group (*Pit 19*), a meal consisting of 21 adult pigeons plus some other birds and over 400 garden snails (*Pit 20*) and a haunch of venison plus a whole roasted chicken (*Pit 21*). Another rather

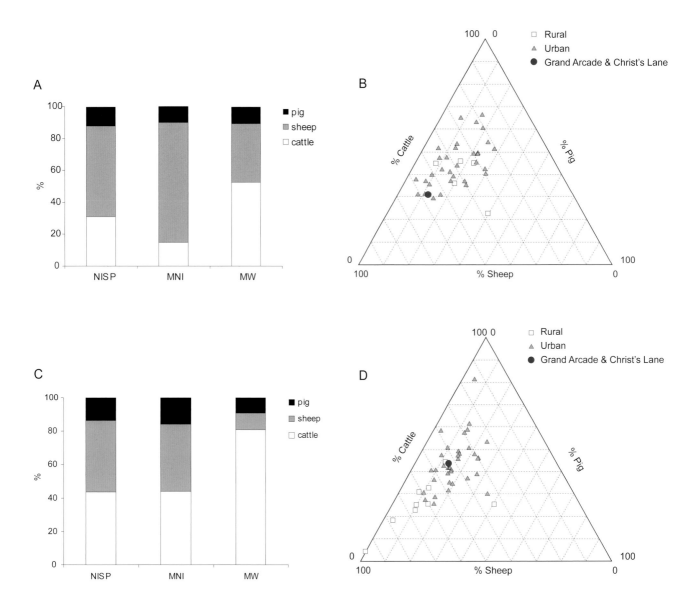

Figure 4.66. *The relative frequency of livestock species, excluding large industrial deposits, by number of specimens identified to species (NISP), minimum number of individuals (MNI) and meat weight (MW) plus the relative frequency of livestock species (by NISP) compared to contemporary sites. These cover the eleventh–twelfth century (A–B) and thirteenth century (C–D).*

different group, from *Pit 22*, represents nearly 700kg of meat (cattle *c.* 519.4kg, sheep *c.* 68.8kg, pig *c.* 102.2kg and fallow deer *c.* 7.5kg). This material was deposited over a short period and equates to *c.* 2550 person days of meat consumption, suggesting that it represents a combination of material from a considerable number of households.

The sixteenth–seventeenth-century animal bone is considered as a single group, although the overwhelming majority is sixteenth-century. Out of 14,100 bones studied 3671 (26.0 per cent) were identified as mammal (3329), bird (322) and amphibian (20) (Table 4.15). The animal bone is dominated by the principal livestock species; sheep is the most common species, followed by cattle and then pig, although cattle provided the bulk of the meat (Fig. 4.67C–D). The relative frequency is similar to the fourteenth–fifteenth centuries and reflects the continued regional importance of wool. The cattle bone is a mixture of domestic, butchery and light tanning

and horn-working refuse, as is the sheep bone, much of which is leatherdressers' waste. The cattle were killed at different ages than in the fourteenth–fifteenth centuries; this is linked to the growing importance of the dairy industry, which resulted in an increase in both veal calves and older cattle that were slaughtered after they had become barren or because their milk yields were too low.

There were also some prime beef cattle, so at least some of the meat came from sources other than the dairy industry. Sheep were slaughtered at a slightly older age than in the fourteenth–fifteenth centuries, due to the continued importance of wool. Pigs still appear to have been raised locally for meat and the pattern is similar to the fourteenth–fifteenth centuries. Rabbits, fallow deer and roe deer were also eaten at the site. A few goat bones are present, but these represent skins and raw materials rather than consumption. The horse bones probably largely derive from the light tanning industry, although it

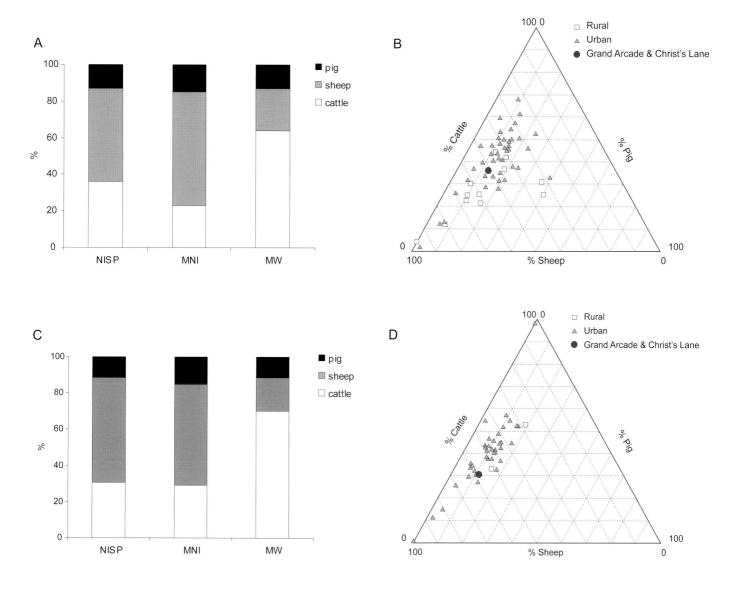

Figure 4.67. *The relative frequency of livestock species, excluding large industrial deposits, by number of specimens identified to species (NISP), minimum number of individuals (MNI) and meat weight (MW) plus the relative frequency of livestock species (by NISP) compared to contemporary sites: (A–B) the fourteenth–fifteenth century; (C–D) sixteenth–seventeenth century. For eighteenth–nineteenth frequencies see Fig. 5.99.*

is probable that some animals were present to provide transportation and pull carts. Dogs and cats appear to represent animals that lived in the area and were relatively casually disposed of after they died.

Chicken is the most common bird species; these were kept as much for eggs as meat. Geese and duck were also present, with duck increasing in importance. Pigeon was relatively common and many birds probably came from a managed breeding population, while peafowl (or peacock), mute swan, teal/garganey and thrush were also eaten occasionally. There were also species that were probably scavenging on domestic refuse; the most common are corvids (raven, crow/rook and jackdaw) and there were also red kite and white-tailed eagle. The sixteenth-century robbing of *Building 16* produced four tawny owl bones, including bones from both wings. It is possible that there were suitable nesting sites nearby and that the bones represent discard of a bird that died locally. Alternatively,

they could represent broth made with owl meat, a contemporary remedy for whooping cough presumably because the birds' calls sound similar to the symptoms of the ailment (Rolleston 1942).

In contrast to the preceding thirteenth–fifteenth centuries, a number of large sixteenth-century groups were recovered (*Well 40, WFFs 14, 16, Pits 46, 47, 51, PB 4*).

Species frequencies

Livestock species dominate the assemblages from each period and the pattern of relative importance is remarkably similar between periods (Table 4.15, Fig. 4.68). Sheep is the most common species in all periods except the thirteenth century, which has near equal proportions of sheep and cattle, although the results for this period might not be truly representative since the sample is extremely small. Sheep bone frequencies range from 43–58 per cent NISP (40–75 per cent MNI), with the highest frequency in the eleventh–twelfth-century assemblage. Cattle bone frequencies range from 31–44 per cent NISP (14–44 per cent MNI) and pig bone frequencies range from 12–21 per cent NISP (10–17 per cent MNI). The most obvious change to have occurred throughout the sequence is a general increase in the proportion of pig during the eighteenth–nineteenth centuries.

It has been suggested that the East Anglian fenlands were dedicated to sheep farming during the Saxo-Norman period (Sykes 2007, 29), so it is unsurprising that this species dominates. However, despite the relative abundance of sheep bones it is clear that cattle were the most important source of meat in all periods (53–81 per cent), whilst the importance of sheep as a source of meat declines from 36 per cent in the eleventh–twelfth centuries to *c.* 20 per cent in later periods (Table 4.16; Fig. 4.68). The fact that fewer sheep were eaten in later periods reflects their greater significance as wool producers. The dominance of this species throughout the occupation sequence indicates that established local farming practices continued and became more important due to the rise of the wool industry. Pig meat is of minor importance (9–14 per cent) throughout the sequence, but this does not mean that pigs were not an important and inexpensive source of meat for households that raised them in their plot tails.

Other noticeable trends include an increase in the consumption of wild birds from the fourteenth–fifteenth century onwards and an increase in the consumption of duck meat from the sixteenth–seventeenth century onwards. This first trend has been noted nationally (Serjeantson 2006, 145) and represents an attempt by the wealthy in society to further distinguish themselves from the lower classes (Albarella & Thomas 2002, 29). The second trend has also been noted elsewhere (Higbee in Alexander 2003) and reflects changing attitudes to duck meat, which was generally considered unhealthy throughout the Saxo-Norman and medieval periods (Albarella *et al.* 1997, 50; Sykes 2007, 28).

Industrial deposits
A range of industrial deposits were identified in a number of plots (Tables 4.17–4.20; Fig. 4.69). No eleventh–twelfth-century industrial deposits were identified and only one thirteenth-century pit produced a small amount of horn- and bone-working waste. It is not until the fourteenth–fifteenth centuries that

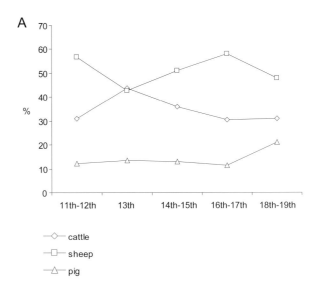

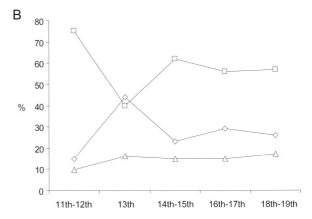

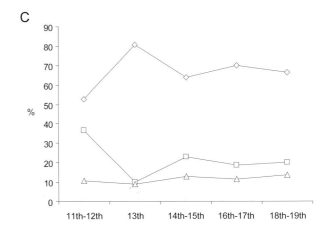

Figure 4.68. *The relative frequency of eleventh–nineteenth-century livestock species by number of specimens, excluding large industrial deposits, over time: (A) identified to species (or NISP); (B) minimum number of individuals (or MNI); (C), meat weight (or MW).*

Table 4.16. *Estimated meat weights for livestock species based on MNI by period, excluding large deposits of industrial waste; % = relative frequency. Meat weights calculated from mid-range of Manching data (Boessneck et al. 1971); cattle 275kg, sheep/goat 37.5kg and pig 85kg.*

Period	Cattle		Sheep/goat		Pig		Total meat weight kg
	Meat weight kg	%	Meat weight kg	%	Meat weight kg	%	
11th–12th	3300	52.6	2287.5	36.4	680	10.8	6267.5
13th	3025	80.9	375	10.0	340	9.1	3740
14th–15th	6600	63.7	2400	23.1	1360	13.1	10,360
16th–17th	10,450	70.0	2775	18.6	1700	11.4	14,925
18th–19th	2475	66.3	750	20.1	510	13.6	3735
Total	**25,850**	**69.2**	**8587.5**	**19.8**	**4590**	**10.9**	**39,027.5**

substantial deposits of industrial material were deposited. The most prominent industry during this period appears to be horn-working. Large concentrations of horn-working waste were recorded from the King's Ditch and a small concentration was noted from a pit in Plot VIII, which also included a number of off-cuts from bone-working that probably originated from the same source. This suggests that there may have been a workshop located at Plot VIII, which processed horn and produced a small number of bone objects. Small deposits of leatherdressers' waste were also identified from fourteenth–fifteenth-contexts in the King's Ditch and from Plot X.

In later periods the horn-working industry is still present; however, the emphasis appears to shift and deposits of leatherdressers' waste become more frequent. Leatherdressers process mainly sheep and goat hides, which they treat with oil or alum to produce light coloured leather (Yeomans 2007, 99). The process is technically different from the heavy tanning industry and there are fewer constraints on locating this type of industry, since it does not require a plentiful supply of water and is generally less noxious. It would appear that this industry was well established in the area during the seventeenth century, as a large deposit of leatherdressers' waste was identified from a nearby site at Emmanuel College (Luff in Dickens 1994). Some of the sixteenth-century deposits of leatherdressers' waste are directly associated with the semi-articulated remains of old workhorses, and it appears that knackered horses were occasionally exploited by the light tanning industry (Yeomans 2005, 75). By the

Table 4.17. *Size and general character of deposits of horn-working waste by period.*

Feature	Period	Species	Side			MNI
			Left	Right	Indeterminate	
Christ's Lane cesspit (F.137)	13th	Cattle	3	4	3	5
		Sheep	1	1	-	1
		Goat	1	1	-	1
Well 20	Early 14th	Cattle	17	37	24	39
King's Ditch F.5085	14th	Cattle	16	32	14	32
King's Ditch F.5198	14th	Cattle	82	82	44	104
		Goat	-	-	4	2
King's Ditch F.1073	Early/mid-16th	Cattle	5	8	2	8
		Sheep	2	1	12	8
Pit 51	16th	Cattle	2	-	-	2
		Sheep	-	1	1	1
WFF 16	16th	Cattle	1	-	2	2
		Goat	-	1	1	1
		Sheep	4	-	4	4
King's Ditch F.1104	16th	Cattle	4	6	1	6
		Goat	-	-	1	1
		Sheep	1	1	5	4

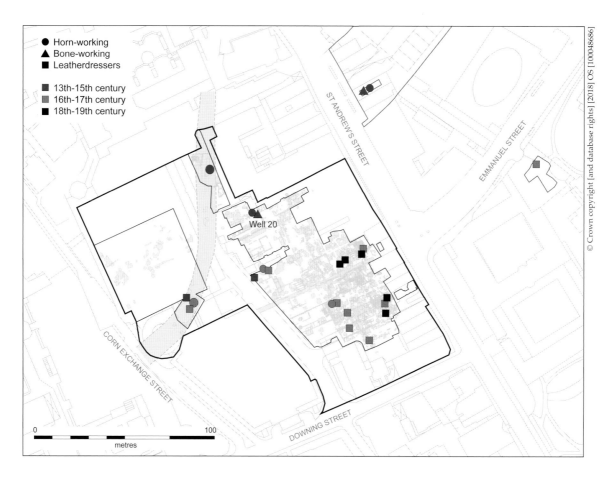

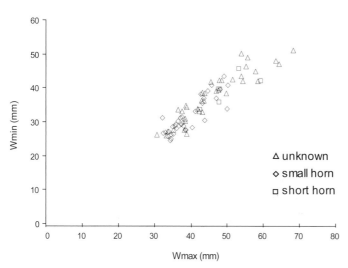

Figure 4.69. *The distribution of thirteenth–nineteenth-century assemblages of horn-working, bone-working and leatherdressing waste plus animal bone from early fourteenth-century backfilling of Well 20 showing size variation of cattle horn cores based on their minimum (Wmin) and maximum (Wmax) basal diameter measurements and photograph of horse bones that are off cuts from bone-working ([50070]) (photograph courtesy of Lorrain Higbee).*

188

Table 4.18. *Size and general character of deposits of bone-working waste by period, L = left, R = right, I = side indeterminate.*

Feature	Period	Species	Metacarpal L	Metacarpal R	Metacarpal I	Metatarsal L	Metatarsal R	Metatarsal I	Metapodia I	Radius L	Radius R	Radius I	Tibia L	Tibia R	Tibia I	MNI
Christ's Lane cesspit (F.137)	13th	Cattle	1	-	-	1	-	2	-	-	-	-	-	-	-	2
		Horse	-	-	-	1	-	-	-	-	-	-	-	-	-	1
		Sheep	-	-	-	1	-	1	-	-	-	-	-	-	-	1
Well 20	Early 14th	Cattle	-	-	1	-	-	-	-	1	1	-	-	-	-	1
		Horse	1	-	-	1	-	-	8	1	2	-	4	4	-	4

Table 4.19. *Size and general character of deposits of leatherdressers' waste by period, L = left, R = right, I = side indeterminate. For Emmanuel College see Luff in Dickens 1994.*

Feature	Period	Species	Metacarpal Side L	Metacarpal Side R	Metacarpal Side I	Metatarsal Side L	Metatarsal Side R	Metatarsal Side I	Metapodia I	Phalanges p1	Phalanges p2	Phalanges p3	MNI
Pit 27	14th–15th	Sheep	6	4	3	9	3	8	3	2	-	-	10
King's Ditch F.1075	Late 15th	Sheep	5	6	-	5	9	-	-	1		1	9
Well 40	Early 16th	Sheep	14	13	23	10	9	33	4	4	-	2	27
King's Ditch F.1073	Early/mid-16th	Sheep	10	5	1	10	12	1	-	3	-	-	13
		Cattle	2	2	2	-	4	-	3	3	2	1	4
Pit 51	16th	Sheep	14	9	4	12	11	4	1	2	-	-	14
Pit 53	16th	Sheep	5	4	36	4	1	21	-	5	-	1	23
WFF 16	16th	Sheep	18	22	1	35	44	4	1	19	2		46
PB 4	16th	Sheep	7	8	6	4	3	-	-	6	1	-	11
Pit F.3658	16th	Sheep	-	-	6	2	1	8	-	6	1	-	6
ADP 8	16th	Sheep	12	14	9	-	7	-	2	61	21	14	19
King's Ditch F.1104	16th	Sheep	3	8	-	10	7	-	-	-	1	-	10
EC garden feature	17th	Sheep	174	190	150	-	-	5	-	-	-	-	265
Buildings 25	1700–60	Sheep	2	4	4	7	4	3	2	-	-	-	9
PB 10	1760–80	Sheep	11	10	7	3	3	2	1	4	-	-	15
Well 38	1760–80	Sheep	21	13	19	20	12	13	-	5	2	-	31
Well 41	1840–60	Sheep	8	5	6	-	3	1	-	1	-	-	11
Well 43	1882–85	Sheep	8	3	2	-	2	3	1	18	5	3	9

Table 4.20. *Number and type of industrial deposits of animal bone by period.*

	13th	14th–15th	16th–17th	18th	19th	Total
Horn-working	1	3	4	-	-	8
Bone-working	1	1	-	-	-	2
Leatherdressers' waste	-	2	9	4	1	16

eighteenth–nineteenth centuries most of the evidence for this industry is concentrated in only a few plots and the largest number of deposits are from Plot XI.

All of these industries rely on the availability of carcass by-products and are usually spatially associated within suburban areas, partly as a result of the trade networks that supply them with raw materials (Yeomans 2005, 81; Yeomans 2007, 99). The industries do not, however, appear to have been exclusively suburban, as smaller groups of light tanning and bone-working waste have been found at sites in the centre of town (Higbee in Newman 2008c). The nearby Fair Yard was associated with slaughtering animals from the Late Medieval period onwards and St Andrew's Hill retained this association until 1842. There is also documentary evidence that various plots were associated with skinners (Plot II, 1375), tanners (Plot II, 1375; Plot XXII, 1608–20), fellmongers (Plot II, 1647; Plot IX, 1622–48, 1665–77), a cordwainer (Plot I, 1717) and tallow chandlers (Plot XIII, 1751–1841).

Some of the links between these different trades are apparent in the bone assemblage. For example, the butchery waste from some sixteenth-century pits contained several sheep skulls that had their horn cores removed by the butcher, presumably so that these elements could be sold on to the horn-worker for an extra profit (see Yeomans 2005, 73). Similar scenarios can be suggested for other stages in the carcass reduction sequence, for instance leatherdressers purchasing skins with the horns and feet still attached might assume the role of supplier to the horn-worker, tallow chandler and neatsfoot oil producer. These examples demonstrate how the supply network was central to the spatial association of related industries in the suburbs of Cambridge.

Skeletons

A local ordinance of 1575 stated that no 'dead beasts, hogs, cat, dog, rat, fowl, vermin, or fish, as carrion' were to be dumped 'in any common street, lane, or churchyard within the town' or within a quarter mile of the town or dumped in the river. Instead they shall 'either bury the same within his own ground, or 3ft (c. 0.9m) within the ground in one of the places appointed for common dunghills, except dead horses and bullocks, to be carried to one of the common dunghills or other place further from the town' (Cooper 1843, 336). A total of 65 complete and partial skeletons were identified (Tables 4.21–4.22; Fig. 4.70). The most commonly occurring skeletons are those of cats and

dogs; cats were generally discarded with the rubbish into middens, whilst dogs were buried in small pits or dumped into larger pits and the King's Ditch.

The number of disarticulated bones from these species is also quite high and this suggests that not only was the overall number of skeletons much greater, but that buried cats and dogs were often disturbed and re-deposited. The pattern of disposal is similar to that recorded at other sites; for example, in Exeter dogs and cats were generally 'buried in or cast upon rubbish heaps' (Maltby 1979, 62). 'The predominance of partial dog and cat skeletons, in rather ignominious locations, is more representative of a functional method of disposal than careful, reverential burial' (Thomas 2005, 98) and this certainly appears to the case in the Barnwell Gate suburb.

Pigs were also frequently buried as whole or partial skeletons, particularly during the fourteenth–sixteenth centuries. This is perhaps unsurprising as these animals were raised in the plot tails throughout the sequence of occupation, although it does represent the discarding of significant quantities of meat. This appears to have included animals that died soon after birth or were culled and discarded due to disease. Other partial skeletons are clearly the remains of pigs that have been eaten, such as a rack of pork ribs from the King's Ditch (F.5195) or two spit-roasted porkers from *Pit 19*.

Table 4.21 *(continued opposite). Complete and partial animal skeletons and unusual deposits (in Table 4.15 each entry has been counted as one specimen, so as not to over-inflate NISP counts).*

Feature	Disposal context	Date	Species	POSACs	Non POSACs	Comments
Well 22	RF	Mid-15th	Cat	26	37	At least 4 cats, 1 immature, 3 adults
Cellar 5	RF	1770–90	Cat	16	10	At least 4 cats, 2 immature, 2 adults
Cellar 7	RF	1820–30	Cat	12		Partial skeleton, adult
Cellar 7	RF	1820–30	Cat	14	66	Partial skeleton, adult
Cellar 7	RF	1820–30	Cat	7		Partial skeleton, immature
Building 6	RF	13th	Cattle	5	75	Partial skeleton, immature
ADP 10	ADP	1680–1720	Cattle	48	288	Complete skeleton, young adult
ADP 10	ADP	1680–1720	Cattle	34	594	Complete skeleton, young female adult
ADP 10	ADP	1680–1720	Cattle	38	467	Near-complete skeleton, young adult pregnant cow with associated foetus
ADP 10	ADP	1680–1720	Cattle	39	161	Partial skeleton, young female adult
ADP 10	ADP	1680–1720	Cattle	14	161	Complete skeleton, foetus associated with adult
ADP 11	ADP	1680–1720	Cattle	14	20	Partial skeleton, foetus associated with adult
ADP 11	ADP	1680–1720	Cattle	45	294	Complete skeleton, young adult
ADP 12	ADP	1680–1720	Cattle	46	262	Complete skeleton, elderly pregnant cow with associated foetus
ADP 12	ADP	1680–1720	Cattle	14	111	Complete skeleton, foetus associated with adult
Pit 21	Meal remains	14th–15th	Chicken	10	2	Partial skeleton, immature
KD F.5198	Ditch	14th	Dog	6	2	Partial skeleton, adult

Table 4.21 (continued).

Feature	Disposal context	Date	Species	POSACs	Non POSACs	Comments
KD F.5198	Ditch	14th	Dog	7	10	Partial skeleton, adult
KD F.5192	Ditch	14th	Dog	7	21	Partial skeleton, adult
Well 22	RF	Mid-15th	Dog	8	57	Partial skeleton, immature
Well 22	RF	Mid-15th	Dog	8		Partial skeleton, immature. Poodle-like skull morphology (domed head and no sagittal crest)
Well 22	RF	Mid-15th	Dog	17		Partial skeleton adult. Terrier-like skull morphology
Well 22	RF	Mid-15th	Dog	12		Partial skeleton, immature. Terrier-like skull morphology
Well 22	RF	Mid-15th	Dog	19	-	Partial remains of 2 adults and 1 immature
Well 30	RF	Mid-15th	Dog	15	151	Complete skeleton, adult male
KD F.1081	Ditch	Late 15th	Dog	13	34	Partial skeleton, adult. Terrier-like skull morphology
KD F.1073	Ditch	Early/ mid-16th	Dog	1	4	Partial skeleton, includes 3 lumbar vertebrae, sacrum and pelvic girdle
ADP 6	ADP	16th	Dog	8	28	Partial skeleton, adult
ADP 6	ADP	16th	Dog	6	115	Partial skeleton, adult male
ADP 6	ADP	16th	Dog	36	196	Partial skeleton, adult
Building 16	RF	16th	Dog	13	65	Partial skeleton, immature
Pit 50	RF	16th	Dog	28	227	Complete skeleton, immature
ADP 5	ADP	16th–17th	Dog	4	185	Partial skeleton, adult
Well 38	RF	1760–80	Dog	12	30	Partial skeleton, adult male
ADP 14	ADP	1830–45	Dog	24	12	Partial skeleton, adult
ADP 1	ADP	Mid/late 14th	Horse	11	4	Partial disarticulated skeleton, includes some long bones and phalanges
ADP 4	ADP	14th–15th	Horse	26	434	Partial skeleton, young adult male
KD F.1073	Ditch	Early/ mid-16th	Horse	7	22	Partial skeleton, includes hind limbs, thoracic and lumbar vertebrae
ADP 6	ADP	16th	Horse	5	-	Partial skeleton, articulating lower hind limb
ADP 9	ADP	16th	Horse	5	304	Partial skeleton, adult
Pit 56	Ritual	Early 17th	Horse	4	662	4 complete but fragmented skulls
C L (F.212)	RF	13th	Pig	26	24	Partial skeleton, neonate
Pit 19	RF, meal remains	14th	Pig	9	16	Partial skeleton, immature
Pit 19	RF, meal remains	14th	Pig	12		Partial skeleton, immature
KD F.5195	Ditch	14th	Pig		18	Articulating cervical and thoracic vertebrae
Pit 27	Pit fill	14th–15th	Pig	6	67	Partial skeleton, adult
ADP2	ADP	14th–15th	Pig	10	210	Partial skeleton, immature
Well 22	RF	Mid-15th	Pig	19	53	Partial skeleton, immature male
ADP 8	ADP	16th	Pig	67	345	Complete skeleton, immature male
Pit 52	RF, meal remains	16th	Pig	12	21	Partial skeleton, perinatal
Pit 46	Pit fill	Mid-16th	Pig	37	208	Partial skeleton, immature
ADP 13	ADP	Early 19th	Pig	13	79	Partial skeleton, immature
Pits 54	RF	Mid/late 16th	Small bird	16	-	Partial skeleton *Turdidae*, blackbird family
ADP 9	ADP	16th	Toad	8	24	Complete skeleton, adult female
Total				**919**	**6176**	

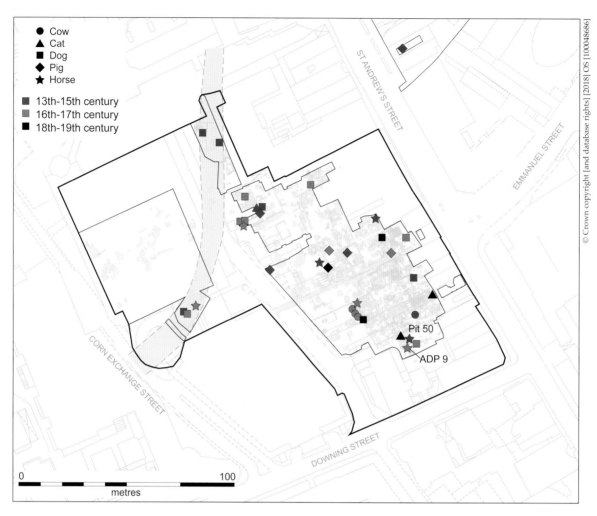

Table 4.22. *Number of complete and partial skeletons by period.*

Species	13th	14th–15th	16th–17th	18th–19th	Total
Cattle	1	-	9	-	10
Pig	1	6	3	1	11
Horse	-	2	7	-	9
Dog	-	12	7	2	21
Cat	-	4	-	11	15
Other	-	1	2	-	3

A number of fourteenth–sixteenth-century horse skeletons were also identified; the horses represented are generally adults and many show signs of pathological changes consistent with heavy work. A few are directly associated with deposits of leatherdressers' waste and show signs of utilization consistent with skinning and butchery as already discussed. One of the more interesting deposits is an early seventeenth-century foundation deposit of four horse skulls in *Pit 56*.

Most of the seven cattle skeletons deposited on the site come from a group of three pits (*ADPs 10–12*) of *c.* 1680–1720, which includes one immature animal and five adults, three of which were pregnant at the time of death. The nature of the deposit and the pathological changes strongly suggest that they all died in an outbreak of milk fever.

It is worth noting that no sheep burials were present. Such deposits are rare, but a foetal lamb was recovered from early–mid-fourteenth-century pit in central Cambridge (Swaysland in Cessford 2005) and there is evidence from other towns for the presence of sheep in early suburbs (Palmer 1980, 204–5, 208–9). Toad and frog bones were found in a range of features, occasionally in considerable numbers, and represent animals that fell into open features (Piper & O'Connor 2001), although there is one possible case where the toad may have been included deliberately (*ADP 9*).

Mortality profiles
The mandible wear stage data and epiphyseal fusion data from all periods is presented within the associated digital-only volume. The following comparison between periods is based entirely on the mandible wear

Figure 4.70 (*opposite*). *The distribution of thirteenth–nineteenth-century animal skeletons, excluding those interpreted as food remains or incidental inclusions, plus photograph, facing north, of a horse buried in sixteenth-century ADP 9 (lower left) and photograph, facing northwest, of dog in sixteenth-century gravel quarry Pit 50 (lower right) ([32025]).*

stage data. Composite mortality profiles of this data have been plotted in order to assess any changes in husbandry regimes over time in the digital-only volume. The mortality profile for cattle shows a remarkable consistent pattern between the eleventh–twelfth and fourteenth–fifteenth centuries. It is only in the sixteenth century that the strategy changes significantly with higher rates of mortality amongst calves and immature cattle. There is also a notable increase in the culling of adults (wear stage G) compared to the fourteenth–fifteenth centuries. These changes reflect a move towards dairying that began in the Late Medieval period (Sykes 2006, 59) and intensified during the post-medieval period (Albarella & Davis 1996, 34; Trow-Smith 1957).

The main mechanism that facilitated this shift is thought to be the gradual introduction of the plough-horse; this innovation diminished the number of adult cattle required for traction (Langdon 1986) and allowed more calves to be slaughtered for meat, which in turn freed up milk for human consumption (Albarella 1997, 22). Similar mortality patterns have been recorded for a number of post-medieval urban assemblages (Albarella *et al.* 1997, 25; Dobney *et al.* 1996, 31; Gidney 2000, 176–7; Luff 1993, 58; Maltby 1979, 32; O'Connor 1984, 11–12). The mortality profile for modern cattle generally reflects the intensification of this process, with high rates of mortality amongst calves and immature cattle; however during this period the emphasis was on meat production (Albarella *et al.* 1997, 25) rather than dairying (Albarella & Davis 1996, 34–5; Campbell & Overton 1992; Campbell & Overton 1993).

The sheep mandible wear stage data from each period has been compared to Payne's (1973) theoretical models for specialist production. Although there is some variation between early and late periods the basic pattern suggests that sheep were principally exploited for wool and that meat production was a secondary consideration. The mortality profile for thirteenth-century sheep, based on a small and possibly unreliable sample, shows a higher rate of mortality amongst 2–3 year old animals (wear stage E) than the other periods. The most significant difference is between the earlier periods and the sixteenth century. The mortality profile for this period closely mirrors those for the earlier periods; however it is clear that considerably less sheep were slaughtered in the youngest age classes than in previous periods.

This trend towards the culling of older animals has been consistently recorded for many post-medieval urban assemblages (Albarella *et al.* 1997, 33; Dobney *et al.* 1996, 40; Gidney 1991; Gidney 1992; Luff 1993, 72) and indicates that wool continued to be an important commodity throughout the post-medieval period and well into the eighteenth century (Bond & O'Connor

1999, 388). The relatively high rate of mortality noted amongst lambs during the modern period suggests that although the urban demand for tender meat increased during this period the importance of wool did not decrease (Albarella *et al*. 1997, 33; Trow-Smith 1957).

The mortality profiles for pig also show a remarkably similar pattern between periods. The high rates of mortality amongst animals in wear stages C–D reflects the fact that pigs are essentially meat animals and are generally killed at a younger age than other livestock. Pigs killed in the youngest age class represent the best porkers (Markham 1614; quoted in Albarella & Davis 1996, 38), whilst the slightly older animals provided the best bacon (Mortimer 1712; quoted in Davis 2002, 56). The most significant change to this general culling pattern occurred between the sixteenth century and the eighteenth–nineteenth centuries, when there is a noticeable increase in the culling of younger animals. A similar trend has been recorded at other sites (Albarella *et al*. 1997, 38–9; Dobney *et al*. 1996, 44; Maltby 1979, 57), however this change usually occurs in the post-medieval period and is generally linked to the selection of improved, and faster growing breeds.

Most of the chickens and geese that were consumed were adults and it is not until the eighteenth–nineteenth centuries that a significant change occurs in their exploitation. The higher incidence of juvenile chickens and geese in the eighteenth–nineteenth-century assemblage marks a general shift away from egg production and towards meat production; this occurs much later than at other sites (Albarella 1997; Albarella *et al*. 1997, 49; Serjeantson 2006, 145), although this is in part due to the relative lack of late sixteenth–mid-eighteenth-century animal bone from the site.

Biometry
Chronological changes in the size and shape of livestock species were assessed using three different methods, reconstructed withers heights, percentage difference between mean values and Students t-test (assuming equal variance). The 'standard' mean values used in the percentage difference analysis for cattle and sheep are the means for the eleventh–twelfth-century assemblage, however due to the small sample of biometric data for eleventh–twelfth-century pigs, the 'standard' values used are the means for the fourteenth–fifteenth-century assemblage. The Students t-test was carried out on all of the measurements used in the percentage difference analysis and small samples of measurements from certain periods (*e.g.* eleventh–twelfth century and thirteenth century) were combined where necessary.

Cattle from the eleventh–twelfth-, thirteenth- and fourteenth–fifteenth-century assemblages were of similar size; their mean withers height ranges from 1.06–1.12m, whilst sixteenth–seventeenth-century cattle were generally much larger. The mean withers height of sixteenth–seventeenth-century cattle is 1.18m and the range of values of 0.95–1.48m is far greater than for all other periods. The results of the percentage difference analysis for cattle bone measurements show an interesting pattern and confirm the much larger size of sixteenth–seventeenth-century cattle and the even larger size of eighteenth–nineteenth-century cattle. It is noteworthy that lower third molars are larger than the standard and that the biggest difference is between the eleventh–twelfth centuries and the thirteenth century.

Teeth are less affected by age, sex or environmental factors (*e.g.* nutrition) than post-cranial bones, therefore the increase in size of third molars is genuine and this suggest that larger cattle were present from the thirteenth century onwards. However, the results of a Students t-test indicate that this difference is not statistically significant. The changing size and shape of cattle is also attested by the post-cranial bones and several statistically significant differences were noted between periods. The greatest differences were recorded for the humerus, tibia and astragalus, and the most significant increases occurred between the fourteenth–fifteenth centuries and the sixteenth–seventeenth centuries. The larger size of sixteenth–seventeenth-century cattle is also apparent from basal measurements on horn cores. It is also clear from the results of the statistical analysis for the astragalus that there was also an increase in the size of cattle during the fourteenth–fifteenth centuries.

A gradual increase in the mean withers height of sheep was noted. The mean withers height for eleventh–twelfth-century sheep is 0.55m and this increases to 0.59m for modern sheep. The results of the percentage difference analysis for sheep bone measurements indicate a general increase in the size and conformation of sheep. For example, bones from the forequarter show the least amount of size difference in comparison to the eleventh–twelfth centuries and there is even a size decrease during the fourteenth–fifteenth centuries, whilst bones from the hindquarter differ greatly from the standard. Many of these changes, including the apparent size decrease noted for fourteenth–fifteenth-century forelimb bones, are highly statistically significant. The most change occurs between the fourteenth–fifteenth centuries and sixteenth–seventeenth centuries, and again between the sixteenth–seventeenth centuries and eighteenth–nineteenth centuries. Several authors have commented on the general homogeneity of English medieval sheep (Grant 1988; O'Connor 1995; Trow-Smith 1957); however, these results suggest that significant size increases also occurred between the earliest periods and the fourteenth–fifteenth centuries.

It was only possible to estimate withers heights for six pig bones, five from the fourteenth–fifteenth centuries and one from the sixteenth–seventeenth centuries. Fourteenth–fifteenth-century pigs have a means withers height of 0.77m, whilst the single sixteenth–seventeenth-century specimen is taller at 0.87m. The results of the percentage difference analysis indicate that on the whole eleventh–twelfth-century and thirteenth-century pigs were smaller than fourteenth–fifteenth-century pigs, whilst sixteenth–seventeenth-century and eighteenth–nineteenth-century pigs were generally much larger. The most striking change is the increase in the mid-shaft diameter (or SD) of tibiae between the fourteenth–fifteenth centuries and the sixteenth–seventeenth centuries. This increase is highly statistically significant; several other significant results were recorded for molar teeth and this generally confirms the larger size of sixteenth–seventeenth-century and eighteenth–nineteenth-century pigs.

The analysis of the biometric data indicates that livestock significantly increased in size between the fourteenth–fifteenth centuries and the sixteenth–seventeenth centuries. It is possible to pin down more precisely the timing of these changes since the bulk (c. 96 per cent) of the sixteenth–seventeenth-century assemblage is from securely dated early/mid-sixteenth-century contexts. Similar size increases have been noted elsewhere, for example, at Launceston Castle (Albarella & Davis 1996, 57). Cattle appear to have increased in size quite rapidly between the fifteenth and sixteenth/seventeenth century, whilst sheep changed size more gradually between the fifteenth and eighteenth/nineteenth century. Pigs also showed a continuous trend towards increased size and a large increase in the size of hind-limb bones was also noted. This is thought to reflect a general change in conformation that might be linked to the import of Chinese stock during the eighteenth century.

Similar trends have also been recorded at Norwich (Albarella et al. 1997, 26–7, 33–5, 40–1) and Lincoln (Dobney et al. 1996, 60). These size increases and changes in the conformation of livestock are thought to be the product of improvements in husbandry techniques brought about by the 'agricultural revolution' (Albarella & Davis 1996, 58; Albarella et al. 1997, 57), which some historians suggest was an earlier and more gradual processes than is often claimed (Kerridge 1967). It is widely accepted that the agricultural revolution commenced in the sixteenth–seventeenth centuries, and the evidence from the current assemblage generally supports this view.

Analysis of the biometric data for chicken suggests that sixteenth–seventeenth-century and eighteenth–nineteenth-century chickens were generally larger

than those from earlier periods; analysis of greatest length measurements for selected bones confirms that this difference is statistically significant. It is possible that this size increase can also be ascribed to improvements brought about by the agricultural revolution (see Albarella et al. 1997, 49).

There is a slight increase in the mean withers height of horses and more variation in the size range between early and late periods. Unsurprisingly there is also considerable variation in the size of dogs. The fourteenth–fifteenth-century assemblage includes small lap-dogs; the fashion for keeping these animals is thought to have reached unprecedented levels of popularity by the sixteenth century (Serpell 1996, 49; Thomas 2005, 96). It is also noteworthy that the largest dogs are from the sixteenth century; the animals represented here are intermediate in size between a mastiff and Irish wolfhound. However, shoulder height estimates provide only a rough guide to the general size of dogs, whilst the robusticity of limb bones is a better guide to breed type. With this in mind the mid-shaft index of tibiae was calculated and plotted against the greatest length measurement. There are few direct correlations with dogs of known breed. The closest parallels are that one of the fourteenth–fifteenth-century dogs has a similar conformation to a Setter, whilst one of the sixteenth-century dogs is similar to a Doberman or Pointer. The largest sixteenth-century dog is similar to a Saint Bernard, but slightly more gracile.

Butchery

Chop marks were frequently recorded on the bones of livestock species and cut marks were generally more frequent on sheep and pig bones. This variation is a product of size-related butchery techniques (see also Swaysland in Cessford & Mortimer 2004; Moreno Garcia in Regan 1997). Medieval butchery techniques were more refined than in previous periods, with minimal use of cleavers to disarticulate carcasses and a greater reliance on knives (Seetah 2007, 28). However, in Cambridge and other towns in the region such as Norwich (Albarella et al. 1997, 28, 36) cleavers appear to have been extensively used, particularly to dismember cattle carcasses (see also Sykes 2006, 69). The use of tools with serrated blades appears to have been largely restricted to craft-type activities (i.e. horn- and bone-working) during the fourteenth–fifteenth centuries and sixteenth century, whilst during the eighteenth–nineteenth centuries this type of tool appears to have been used to reduce meat joints. A similar trend was noted in Norwich (Albarella et al. 1997, 36).

In general, there is very little variation in butchery techniques between periods. Carcasses were split into sides by chopping through the mid-line of the vertebral column before further division into joints (*e.g.* Fig. 3.12C). This method of dividing carcasses was uncommon in Exeter before the post-medieval period (Maltby 1979, 39), although standardized butchery techniques, including the splitting of carcasses into equal sides, emerged during the Saxo-Norman period and this type of evidence is frequently recorded on Saxo-Norman and medieval bones from towns (Sykes 2006, 69). Sagittally split vertebrae were common in all periods at the current sites, and similar evidence has been recorded from other areas of the town (*e.g.* Luff in Dickens 1994). A notable exception to the standardized pattern is a small group of sixteenth-century sheep scapulae (Fig. 4.50B), all of which have a hole in the blade on the caudal side of the spina caused by the insertion of a butcher's hook. The most significant change in butchery techniques occurred during the modern period. Serrated blades were more readily used to reduce joints into portions and for the first time it is possible to clearly distinguish 'modern' cuts of meat (or units of acquisition after Huelsbeck 1991), such as rump steak (Fig. 3.25E) and thick flank.

Pathology and non-metric traits

The most noteworthy trend is the much higher incidence of penning elbow in eighteenth–nineteenth-century sheep, suggesting that stocking densities were much higher during this period.

Conclusions

The animal bone assemblage is fairly typical of urban assemblages from contemporary sites in England. It includes a mixture of waste from different stages in the carcass reduction sequence (O'Connor 1993), from butchery through to domestic consumption, and the use of carcass by-products (*e.g.* hides, horn and bone). Horn-working, and to a lesser degree bone-working and light tanning, were the principal types of industrial processes being carried out in the area during the medieval period. In the post-medieval and modern periods the emphasis is largely on light tanning; although some horn-working was also taking place, it was not on the scale seen in the Late Medieval period.

The type of animals identified from the assemblage and the husbandry techniques employed are generally consistent with other sites and with information from historical sources. The main innovations in the use of animals to have occurred over the sequence of occupation are summarized in Table 4.23. Sheep, which are the dominant species in all periods, were primarily managed for their wool and it is only in later periods that meat production also became an important secondary consideration. Cattle were principally used for traction during the eleventh–twelfth and thirteenth

centuries; it is only with the gradual introduction of plough horses that the emphasis shifted towards a more intensive husbandry regime focused on beef, veal and dairying (Albarella & Davis 1996, 34). Pigs do not provide any secondary products and were consistently slaughtered at a young age to provide pork, bacon and fat. The exploitation of chicken and goose shifted from secondary products (*i.e.* eggs and feathers) to meat production in the modern period and this shift occurs at a slightly later date than at other sites (Albarella 1997; Albarella *et al.* 1997, 49; Serjeantson 2006, 145).

Changes in mortality patterns, and the size and shape of livestock species and domestic poultry are summarized in Table 4.24. It would appear that changes in the size and shape of cattle and sheep were generally preceded by variations in the mortality profile and a similar pattern has been noted at other sites (*e.g.* Albarella *et al.* 1997, 58). These changes reflect a shift toward the selection of larger animals for meat production. In the case of sheep, the shift towards the culling of older animals reflects the continued importance of wool production, whilst the increase in size suggests that larger animals capable of producing more mutton were also being selected (Albarella *et al.* 1997, 58). A slightly different pattern was recorded for pigs, where it is only after a size increase during the post-medieval period that the mortality pattern changes. The shape of pig post-cranial bones also alters at about the same time, suggesting that the increase in productivity was achieved through the import of new stock, which were larger, faster growing and could therefore be slaughtered at a younger age. A similar trend was noted for chicken and this reflects the selection of larger birds in order to increase meat production.

These trends in mortality, size and shape can generally be ascribed to improvements brought about by the agricultural revolution, which allowed a much greater emphasis to be placed on meat production. The

Table 4.23. *Main innovations in the use of livestock species, horse and domestic poultry by period. Products or uses of greater importance are capitalized.*

Species	11th–13th	14th–16th	18th–19th
Cattle	TRACTION, meat, milk	MEAT, milk (traction in limited areas)	MEAT, milk (traction in limited areas)
Sheep	WOOL, meat, milk	WOOL, MEAT, milk	WOOL, MEAT, milk
Pig	MEAT, fat	MEAT, fat	MEAT, fat
Horse	traction	TRACTION	TRACTION
Chicken	EGGS, meat	EGGS, meat	MEAT, eggs
Goose	FEATHERS, meat	FEATHERS, meat	MEAT, feathers

Table 4.24. *Summary of main changes in the age, size and shape of livestock species and domestic poultry by period.*

Species		11th–12th	13th	14th–15th	16th–17th	18th–19th
Cattle	Age	Stable	Stable?	Stable?	Decrease	Decrease
	Size	Stable	Stable?	Increase??	Increase	Increase
	Shape	Stable	Stable?	Change??	Change	Change
Sheep	Age	Stable	Stable?	Stable	Increase	Stable
	Size	Stable	Stable?	Stable??	Increase	Increase
	Shape	Stable	Stable?	Change	Change	Change
Pig	Age	Stable	Stable?	Stable	Stable	Decrease
	Size	Stable	Stable?	Stable??	Increase	Increase
	Shape	Stable	Stable?	Stable	Change	Change??
Chicken	Age	Stable	Stable?	Stable	Stable	Decrease
	Size	Stable	Stable?	Stable	Increase	Increase
Goose	Age	Stable	Stable?	Stable	Stable	Decrease

data from Cambridge and other contemporary sites in England (Albarella & Davis 1996, 57–8; Albarella *et al.* 1997, 26–7, 33–5, 40–1, 57; Dobney *et al.* 1996, 60) suggests that these changes were well under way by the sixteenth century (Kerridge 1967) and that some changes may even have occurred slightly earlier. The main catalyst for these innovations was urban population growth and the need to produce increasingly larger supplies of meat.

Fish bone Jen Harland

The fish bone from Grand Arcade was subject to an initial assessment and a total of 3697 identified bones from sieved features plus 93 hand-collected bones were then analysed (Tables 4.25–4.26). In general most features produced only small assemblages of fish bone, the exception being fourteenth-century *Pit 23*. The fish are a diverse range of freshwater and marine species, some of which were probably caught in local river systems, some in the southern North Sea, and some of which were imported as preserved fish, probably from Northern European regions. Cod and marine cod family fish were present only from the fourteenth century, and then only at low levels, which is surprizing given comparative material. Freshwater fish made up about half of all fish from the small twelfth-century assemblage, decreasing to about 10 per cent by the fourteenth century. This indicates a greater reliance on freshwater fish, and corresponding low levels of cod consumption, compared to many other English sites. However, the large sieved fourteenth-century deposits indicate a reliance on herring and whiting, both caught in local North Sea waters.

Only a small number of eleventh–twelfth-century fish bones were recovered. Approximately half the identified bones are herring and a third are pike, with small quantities of eels, carp family and

a single burbot. Unusually for British sites of this period, cod and cod family fish are entirely absent. Most thirteenth–fourteenth-century features produced only small assemblages of fish bone. Cod and marine cod family fish were present only from the fourteenth century onwards, and then only at low levels, which is atypical for English sites of the period. Whiting, in contrast, were found in very large quantities (44 per cent), a pattern paralleled at other contemporary sites in London (Serjeantson & Woolgar 2006). Herring were the second most common species (42 per cent), which is typical of English sites of this date (Barrett *et al.* 2004a; Barrett *et al.* 2004b). Both of the latter species were caught in local North Sea waters, with the herring perhaps being lightly cured and used as a seasonal resource during the autumn and early winter. Freshwater fish decreased in occurrence to about 10 per cent of the overall assemblage by the fourteenth century; species identified included those of the carp family (seven per cent), plus small quantities of eels and perch, a range that is typical for English sites of the period. The one significant assemblage of this date, from fourteenth-century gravel quarry *Pit 23* (Fig. 4.27B), contained bones from at least 124 fish. Around a third of these were Atlantic herring, a third whiting and a sixth of the carp family, whilst a number of other species were also present.

In the sixteenth century eels became common for the first time, representing about two thirds of the sieved material, while herring were still frequently consumed. Other fish make their first appearance, including a single specimen from the ray family, the first flatfish from the halibut family and a single haddock. The hand collected assemblage is dominated by cod, ling and cod family specimens, with a few flatfish appearing for the first time, including turbot, turbot family and halibut family specimens. These indicate exploitation of a wider range of fish, perhaps in response to demand for fresh marine fish of higher value (Serjeantson & Woolgar 2006). The absence of eels from earlier deposits is surprising. These tend to be common finds from many English sites (Serjeantson & Woolgar 2006) and the bones from three whole European Eels have been found in a bowl in a seventh-century grave in Cambridge (Dodwell *et al.* 2004, 98). The Cambridgeshire fenland was an ideal habitat for eels, and their prevalence likely gave the name to nearby Ely (Fort 2003). A thirteenth-century merchant's poem mentions 'Eels of Cambridge...Herring of Yarmouth...Cod of Grimsby' (Kowaleski 2000), implying their importance in the city. They were probably a low status fish, commonly and cheaply available in the fens and the River Great Ouse, which is joined by the River Cam (Lucas 1998; Pinder *et al.* 1997); their absence may therefore indicate wealthy, or at least, not poor, consumption patterns.

Table 4.25. *Number of identified fish specimens (NISP) by species from >2mm sieved material; P = present but unidentified.*

Family	Taxa	12th	14th		14–15th	15–16th	16th	Total	
Rajidae	Ray Family	-	-	-	-	-	1	1	<0.1%
Anguillidae	Eel	6	32	1%	2	-	24	64	1.7%
Clupeidae	Atlantic Herring	17	1513	42%	2	5	7	1544	41.8%
Cyprinidae	Carp Family	2	245	7%	-	-	-	247	6.7%
	Rudd	-	-	-	1	-	-	1	<0.1%
	Roach	-	10	<0.1%	-	-	-	10	0.3%
	Dace	-	1	<0.1%	-	-	-	1	<0.1%
Esocidae	Pike	10	17	<0.1%	-	-	1	28	0.8%
Gadidae	Cod Family	-	23	1%	-	-	-	23	0.6%
	Cod	-	130	4%	-	-	-	130	3.5%
	Haddock	-	-	-	-	-	1	1	<0.1%
	Whiting	-	1602	44%	-	-	1	1603	43.4%
	Burbot	1	-	-	-	-	-	1	<0.1%
Triglidae	Gurnard Family	-	P	-	-	-	-	P	-
Percidae	Perch Family	-	2	<0.1%	-	-	-	2	0.1%
	Perch	-	40	1%	-	-	-	40	1.1%
Pleuronectidae	Halibut Family	-	-	-	-	-	1	1	<0.1%
Total identified		36	3615		5	5	36	3697	
Unidentified (QC0)		0	978		2	0	5	985	
Total >2mm sieved		**36**	**4593**		**7**	**5**	**41**	**4682**	

Table 4.26. *Number of identified fish specimens (NISP) by species.*

Family	Taxa	11–12th	12th	14th	13–15th	14–15th	15–16th	16th		18th	19th	Total	
Clupeidae	Atlantic Herring	-	1	-	-	-	-	-	-	-	2	3	3%
Esocidae	Pike	-	-	-	-	-	-	1	2%	1	-	2	2%
Salmonidae	Salmon/ Trout	-	-	-	-	-	-	-	-	1	-	1	1%
Gadidae	Cod Family	-	-	-	-	-	-	1	2%	-	-	1	1%
	Cod	-	-	1	-	1	9	42	82%	-	7	60	65%
	Ling	-	-	-	-	-	-	3	6%	-	-	3	3%
Bothidae (Scophthalmidae)	Turbot Family	-	-	-	-	-	-	1	2%	-	-	1	1%
	Turbot	-	-	-	-	-	-	2	4%	-	-	2	2%
Pleuronectidae	Halibut Family	-	-	-	-	-	-	1	2%	-	6	7	8%
Soleidae	Sole Family	-	-	-	-	-	-	-	-	-	13	13	14%
Total identified		0	1	1	0	1	9	51		2	28	93	
Unidentified (QC0)		2	13		4	4	1	87		6	14	131	
Total hand collected		**2**	**14**	**1**	**4**	**5**	**10**	**138**		**8**	**42**	**224**	

Even in the sixteenth century, when eels were found in quantity for the first time, contemporary deposits of large, expensive flatfish indicate the continuing probable wealth. Much of the cod was probably imported as prepared, preserved fish. Different sources were used in the fourteenth and sixteenth centuries, each with distinctive sizes and butchery strategies. The freshwater species were caught with hook and line, or with fish traps or nets, and some of the smallest fish may have been bait or stomach contents of the larger ones like pike. The marine fish were caught by long lining (particularly the cod and marine cod family fish) or by netting or with hook and line. Some of the freshwater species, including the cyprinids and possibly the pike, may have originated in managed fishponds. These were reserved for high-status consumption and thus had status correlations, but they are difficult to distinguish from wild fish. There is some evidence for an increase in local river pollution, possibly linked to increasing urbanization and more intensive agriculture around Cambridge, as well as the draining and management of the fen river systems.

The herring were probably lightly cured, and were thus a seasonal resource focussing on the autumn and early winter. In the sixteenth century, eels became common for the first time, as do the flatfishes, the latter suggesting that there was an expansion in fishing grounds exploited compared to earlier phases. The absence of eels from earlier deposits, despite evidence of their ubiquity, may indicate the relative wealth of the inhabitants. Even in the sixteenth century, when eels were found in quantity for the first time, contemporary deposits of large, expensive flatfish indicate the continuing probable wealth associated with the Grand Arcade deposits. Much of the cod was probably imported as prepared, preserved fish. Different sources were used in the fourteenth and sixteenth centuries, each with distinctive sizes and butchery strategies. The freshwater species were caught with hook and line, or with fish traps or nets, and some of the smallest fish may have been bait or stomach contents of the larger ones like pike.

The marine fish were caught by long lining, particularly the cod and marine cod family fish, or by netting or with hook and line. Some of the freshwater species, including the cyprinids and possibly the pike, may have originated in managed fishponds. These were reserved for high status consumption and thus had status correlations, but they are difficult to distinguish from wild fish. There are some indication of freshwater environmental change, albeit based on very small quantities of fish. The carp family fish shift towards fish preferring slow moving rivers by the sixteenth century, and the pollution sensitive burbot was last seen in the twelfth-century Grand Arcade deposits, although they were found in very small quantities in sixteenth-century deposits at Hostel Yard, Corpus Christi. Together these imply an increase in local river pollution, possibly linked to increasing urbanization and more intensive agriculture around Cambridge, as well as the draining and management of the fen river systems.

Preliminary results of stable isotope analysis of cod from Grand Arcade and other sites in Cambridge indicate that in the thirteenth–fourteenth centuries the cod studied came exclusively from the southern North Sea (Barrett *et al.* 2011). By the fifteenth–sixteenth centuries about half of the sampled cod was from the southern North Sea, about a third was from Arctic Norway or the Northeast Atlantic and a few were from the Kattegat or Western Baltic. By the sixteenth century there were also a few from the waters of the Grand Banks off Newfoundland. The Grand Banks may have been fished by Europeans in the fifteenth century, however it was only after the voyage of John Cabot in 1497 that the existence of these fishing grounds became generally known in Europe. The waters were fished by French, Spanish, Portuguese and English

vessels, with the English becoming dominant in the second half of the sixteenth century, as its maritime power increased and Spanish power declined.

Plant macrofossils Rachel Ballantyne and Anne de Vareilles

This report presents the waterlogged, charred and mineral-replaced macro-botanical evidence for past activities and local environment at Grand Arcade and Christ's Lane. With the exception of a single Iron Age sample, the majority date from the eleventh–early seventeenth centuries and so provide a rare opportunity to address the historical development of Cambridge (Table 4.27). Due to the size of the assemblages, full tabulated data is not presented here; it can be found instead within the associated digital-only volume. At both sites, the charred and mineral-replaced plant assemblages are richest during the twelfth–fourteenth and sixteenth centuries, the former associated particularly with possible oven ash, and the latter with refuse and cess. Waterlogged plant remains are present from deeper features throughout the eleventh–sixteenth centuries; their distribution is a direct reflection of water-table height rather than activity patterns. The incidence of waterlogged food seeds (indicative of human faeces) does, however, also appear to peak during the twelfth–fourteenth and sixteenth centuries.

Most food plants were locally available cultivated or wild types. Cereal and legume staples included hulled six-row and two-row barley (*Hordeum vulgare*), bread wheat (*Triticum aestivum sensu lato*), rivet/durum wheat (*Triticum turgidum sensu lato*), rye (*Secale cereale*), oats (*Avena sativa* type), peas (*Pisum sativum*), Celtic bean (*Vicia faba* var. *minor*) and flax (*Linum*

Table 4.27. *Numbers of fully analysed environmental samples from Grand Arcade and Christ's Lane.*

Period	Grand Arcade				Christ's Lane			
	Waterlogged	'Rich' charred	Mineral-replaced	Total	waterlogged	'Rich' charred	Mineral-replaced	Total
Iron Age	-	1	-	**1**	-	-	-	**-**
11th–12th	6	6	3	**13**	1	-	2	**3**
13th–14th	11	4	-	**14**	1	-	2	**3**
15th–16th	16	2	3	**20**	2	1	2	**3**
17th	1	-	-	**1**	-	-	-	**-**
18th	-	-	1	**1**	-	-	-	**-**
Total	**34**	**13**	**7**	**50**	**4**	**1**	**6**	**9**

usitatissimum). There is good evidence that fruits and nuts were also frequently consumed, including hazelnuts (*Corylus avellana*), wild plums/cherries/sloes (*Prunus* spp.), apple/pear (*Malus/Pyrus* sp.), blackberries (*Rubus* subgen. *Rubus*), strawberries (*Fragaria* sp.) and elder (*Sambucus nigra*). Herbs and condiments included hops (*Humulus lupulus*) and the seeds of poppy (*Papaver somniferum*), celery (*Apium graveolens*), coriander (*Coriandrum sativum*), fennel (*Foeniculum vulgare*) and perhaps also mustard (*Brassica/Sinapis* sp.). Evidence is very limited for exotic plants, almost all of which date from the sixteenth century onwards: fig (*Ficus carica*), grape (*Vitis vinifera*), cucumber (*Cucumis sativus*) and grains-of-paradise (*Aframomum melegueta*).

The plant remains are dominated by specific refuse-generating activities: charred items are dominated by ash from corn-drying/bread ovens, mineral-replaced items by human faeces and fibrous fodder/dung/other, and waterlogged items by debris from the local environment, which includes cooking and the previously listed activities. During the eleventh–fourteenth centuries, many of the waterlogged wild plant seeds indicate nearby open grazing pasture and disturbed/cultivated land. By the sixteenth century, almost all the wild plants are characteristic of disturbed and nutrient-enriched land, as could be expected with an increasingly refuse-rich and built environment.

Charred, waterlogged and mineral-replaced plant remains were all present in eleventh–fifteenth-century features, although the survival of waterlogged remains and the presence of mineral replaced remains were both sporadic. There is relatively little spatial or temporal patterning apparent in the charred plant remains and the majority are consistent with bread/corn-drying oven ash. The waterlogged seeds are probably from nearby plants and human cess, while the mineral-replaced fragments are from human faeces and a range of ingested seed types. The grain to chaff ratios for both barley and wheat are highly variable, as might be expected if grain was introduced separately to a chaff and straw mixture for kindling or oven bedding. The only exception is rye, which is almost always dominated by chaff. There is no clear spatial patterning across the different properties at Grand Arcade, which suggests that the ash derives from a particular activity that was widespread and that the waste from that activity was freely discarded.

The major charred economic species are all cereals. Wheat was the most abundant and frequently charred grain, and chaff fragments reveal a mixture of breadwheat and rivet wheat types. Both are free-threshing forms consistent with medieval to post-medieval England (Moffett 1991), and it appears that both types were present from the eleventh–twelfth centuries with breadwheat favoured. Most of the barley grain is hulled, but of ambiguous form. The rarity of twisted grains compared to straight grains suggests that much was two-rowed (*Hordeum vulgare* ssp. *distichum*), although it is only conclusively identified in the early seventeenth century. Other cereals are rye and oats; unfortunately, no chaff has been recovered to confirm whether the latter was wild or cultivated.

A small number of other charred edible plants are present; these could be weeds of the cereals and/or refuse from other activities such as cooking. Diverse charred edible plants do co-occur in two contexts, suggesting that refuse from cooking is a more likely source.

Perhaps the most unusual charred economic plant resource is great fen sedge (*Cladium mariscus*), which occurs sporadically across the site and is abundant in several twelfth–sixteenth-century features. This fen-edge plant was managed and harvested from at least the Late Saxon period onwards as an oven fuel and strewing material (Ballantyne in Mortimer *et al.* 2005; Rowell 1986). The leaves are rich in volatile oils, which burn intensely and rapidly, although the sharply serrated leaf edges must be handled with care.

The charred wild seed assemblage is dominated by heavy grain-sized seeds that would be expected to be retained with grain, and not removed during threshing and raking. If intact sheaves or the waste from threshing was charred, one would expect numerous large light seeds (Jones 1984). Although the seeds of stinking mayweed (*Anthemis cotula*) are tiny and might require sieving for their removal, its seed heads are large and can be removed with straw and chaff, as illustrated by a very well-preserved thirteenth–fourteenth-century oven ash at Fitzbillies, Cambridge (Ballantyne in Whittaker 2001a).

Overall, the cereals and weed seeds from Grand Arcade might be characterized as having more of a rural/producer than an urban/consumer feel to them. This was not apparent at Christ's Lane; however, this was a more constrained and densely occupied site with a more 'urban' character to it. Peas, apples, pears, strawberries, raspberries, black mustard, opium poppy, sloe (*Prunus* cf. *spinosa*), small plums and possibly other types of cherry varieties are all present in eleventh–fifteenth-century features.

In the sixteenth century intensification of space use can be inferred from both the decline in 'natural' grassland flora and an increase in plants associated with bare, nutrient-enriched land. The very high amounts of Brassicaceae pollen (Cabbage Family) are likely to indicate cultivation, and so perhaps may some of numerous waterlogged black mustard seeds. The lower incidence of oven ash suggests that crop processing and baking may have become less important activities.

The eleventh–fourteenth-century range of foodstuffs and activities compares well to those reported from other towns across southern Britain, such as Stafford (Moffett 1994), Huntingdon (Clapham in Clarke 2006; Ballantyne in Clarke 2009) and Norwich (Ayers & Murphy 1983; Murphy 1998). One distinctive local trait is the presence of great fen sedge ash (*Cladium mariscus*), which was favoured as a medieval to early modern oven fuel along the East Anglian fen-edge (Rowell 1986) and has been found in large quantities elsewhere in Cambridge (Ballantyne in Whittaker 2001a; de Vareilles in Newman 2009b) and at Ely (Ballantyne in Mortimer *et al.* 2005; Ballantyne in Cessford *et al.* 2006) and Cherry Hinton (Roberts in Cessford & Mortimer 2004). Although it occurs from the ninth century onwards, charred great fen sedge only becomes frequent in Cambridge from the eleventh–twelfth centuries, suggesting that sedge fuel may have been a fenland innovation that spread to the wider region.

This may also represent the increased use of fen resources as time passed (Ballantyne 2004). However, as very few ninth–tenth-century features have been excavated in Cambridge, evidence for earlier sedge fuel use may still await discovery. Further afield, recent extensive excavations within Huntingdon (Clapham in Clarke 2006; Ballantyne in Clarke 2009) show charred cereal by-products are frequent, but great fen sedge ash is again found only from the eleventh–twelfth centuries onwards; suggesting wider, medieval regional patterning to the redistribution and use of sedge fuel. The sixteenth-century presence of cucumbers and grains-of-paradise is relatively early for a small town, and is comparable to the large centres at Norwich (Murphy 1997) and London (Giorgi 1999; Malcolm 1999).

The assemblages from Grand Arcade and Christ's Lane are the largest and most diverse so far recovered from Cambridge, due both to the size of the excavated areas and the numerous waterlogged contexts that include plants from a much wider range of activities than usually occurs with charring or mineral-replacement. The role of preservation pathways in the survival of biological evidence means that it is always very difficult to tell whether patterns of plant recovery show the past distribution of activities and diet types (Green 1982; Keene 1982). Charring is not dependant on a particular type of burial environment and so is most likely to reflect patterns of space-use, although associated with only a narrow range of activities. Calcium phosphate mineral-replacement is broadly linked to human activity as it reflects concentrations of organic matter, such as refuse pits and latrines (Green 1979; McCobb et al. 2001).

Waterlogging is dependent upon continuously wet natural or man-made settings, and usually preserves a complex mixture of refuse and local biota (Jones et al. 1991). Due to practical difficulties, at present no waterlogged contexts have been sampled within the urban core of Cambridge, unlike the suburban area which consequently has much better evidence of human diet and activities. A further complicating factor may be the practice of night-soiling, as it is likely that the most urbanized areas of Cambridge would have had a system in place for the removal of faeces and other more noxious waste types. If so, then it might be expected that the less-formally organized suburban areas would be more refuse-rich. An interesting trait in Cambridge is that untransformed seeds are associated with sixteenth–eighteenth-century contexts; over a longer timescale these seeds may have become waterlogged or mineral-replaced, or it may be that a residual toxicity in these urban soils has slowed the decay process. Untransformed elder seeds, confirmed by radiocarbon dating as Roman in origin, have been reported from Leicester (Monckton 1999).

Living environment and space-use

The King's Ditch sequence contains the most reliable evidence for local environment in the Barnwell Gate suburb; its recutting and gradual infilling over the twelfth–sixteenth centuries has produced strata of differing waterlogged biota (pollen, seeds, insects) that reflect changes in nearby human activities and associated vegetation communities. Wells have acted as local pit-fall traps, with surface debris entering sporadically during (dis)use.

The distribution of plant types and preservation pathways appears to reflect the backland–innerland–frontage zoning. During the eleventh–fifteenth centuries, waterlogged seeds from the King's Ditch suggest the backland was open, seasonally damp grazing land that was relatively undisturbed and there is very little refuse or evidence of activities. In contrast, the innerland contained numerous likely bread/corn-drying ovens, with evidence for ash and faeces deposited into quarry pits. The plant remains compare well to pollen and insect evidence from the King's Ditch, which indicate damp riparian meadow and grazing land. High levels of cereal pollen also suggest nearby arable land or waste laden with cereal pollen that was dumped into the ditch. The lack of waterlogged cereal macrofossils leaves open the interpretation of the abundant cereal pollen, however widespread chaff and straw ash from the nearby eleventh–fourteenth-century bread ovens show that large quantities of cereal by-products were on-site and this may have been the pollen source.

A thirteenth–fourteenth-century waterlogged ditch base and 'tank' at nearby Emmanuel College (Fryer & Murphy in Dickens 1994) included a limited range of ruderal and grassland plant seeds, suggesting that open rough grazing characterized much of the Barnwell Gate suburb. The environmental remains at the Grand Arcade support the interpretation of processing activities associated with the ribbon of properties along the road, which at this date passed through grazing and rough open land. Few other sites in Cambridge have waterlogged plant remains, with the exception of riverside sediments that are dominated by naturally occurring riparian plants, such as at Trinity Hall Library (Stevens in Alexander 1997b) and Thompson's Lane (de Vareilles in Newman 2008a).

The sixteenth century is associated with marked changes in the intensity of space use and refuse discard at Grand Arcade, with the innerland more formally subdivided, processing activities encroaching further upon the backland area and the King's Ditch being increasingly used as a latrine. Intensification of space use can also be inferred from both the decline in 'natural' grassland flora and an increase in plants associated with bare, nutrient-enriched land. However, the lower incidence of oven ash reveals that crop processing and baking may have become less important activities compared to the earlier thirteenth–fourteenth centuries.

The deep, dark 'garden earth' found widely across the Grand Arcade site suggests that during the twelfth–seventeenth centuries small-scale cultivation was taking place quite extensively across the plot tails. Despite this the presence of gardens or cultivation plots is extremely difficult to demonstrate from the plant assemblage. A wide range of plants tolerant of very high levels of soil nutrients, such as nettles (*Urtica dioica* and *U. urens*), Chenopodiaceae (oraches *Atriplex* spp.; goosefoots *Chenopodium* spp., fat hen *C. album*) and Solanaceae (henbane *Hyoscyamus niger*; nightshades *Solanum dulcamara, S. nigrum* and *Atropa belladona*) are consistent with rich garden soils, but are also naturally found in association with densely occupied urban areas. The very high amounts of Brassicaceae pollen within a mid-sixteenth-century recut of the King's Ditch are, however, likely to indicate cultivation, and so perhaps some of numerous waterlogged black mustard seeds may also derive from crops rather than human faeces.

Other evidence for cultivation plots is very limited; waterlogged seeds of carrot (*Daucus carota*) in an early sixteenth-century context (*Well 40*) could be from wild or cultivated plants. Almost all other waterlogged seeds of food plants are, like the cabbage/mustard seeds, potential condiments in their own right such as celery, fennel, and poppy. The only possible garden plant may be cotton thistle, a probably introduced species which was also found in a late sixteenth–early seventeenth-century cesspit at Pembroke College (Ballantyne in Hall 2002). However, the plant is known to have been widely naturalized in East Anglia from the post-medieval period (Stace 1997) and so this interpretation is by no means secure. The absence of 'showy' or introduced plants clearly associated with leisure gardening (*contra* Murphy & Scaife 1991), does suggest that cultivation and soil improvement at the Grand Arcade was largely mundane and linked to food cultivation.

Economic activity

The following discussion is tentative in light of the biases noted earlier for different plant preservation pathways. By far the most consistent evidence for processing is provided by charred remains as their survival is not reliant upon particular burial conditions. At Grand Arcade, charred plant remains are strongly associated with the innerland, particularly as ash redeposited into quarry pits and other negative features. It is striking that despite the abundance of ash, it is never found in quantity in the wells – providing further circumstantial evidence that water sources were covered and/or had raised edges that prevented surface debris and refuse from entering.

The thirteenth–fourteenth-century peak in probable oven ash at Grand Arcade is part of a wider pattern of occurrence across both urban and suburban Cambridge. Similar ash, very rich in cereal chaff and straw,

and occasionally great fen sedge leaves, cereal grain and large weed seeds, has been found at numerous sites in Cambridge (Roberts in Cessford 2003a; Simmons in Cessford 2005; de Vareilles in Newman 2008c; Ballantyne in Whittaker 2001a). As noted earlier, the waste contrasts very well to *in situ* oven ash found at Late Saxon Stafford (Moffett 1994) and shows that cereal by-products were also treated as resources. At Grand Arcade, over 18 ovens have been identified; these are mostly fourteenth–fifteenth century or later, although the characteristic ash occurs in features from the twelfth century onwards. The excavated ovens appear to have been relatively short-lived and lack ash accumulations, suggesting they were raked out frequently.

Although ovens are today commonly associated with bread baking, their use for grain-drying was also widespread in medieval and post-medieval Britain, particularly in regions of the west and north with damper climates (Gailey 1970; Scott 1951). Grain-drying could take place between harvest and storage, to halt fungal growth, germination or decay, which required large ovens to cope with the volume of material; these have provided the more dramatic archaeological finds (*e.g.* Monk 1986). An additional or alternative drying stage would be between storage and milling, to harden the grain and so improve milling efficiency. Smaller ovens would be required as the process was conducted on a daily basis, and it is suggested that the remains at Grand Arcade and Christ's Lane could derive from this type of grain-drying and/or bread making itself. Small ovens would often be multipurpose, in addition to generating ash that was a mixture of both the fuel and processed items (Monk 1981; van der Veen 1989).

Widespread thirteenth–fourteenth-century grain-drying and baking in Cambridge leaves open to conjecture the identity of the consumers. Religious institutions and colleges could be expected to have had their own bakehouses, so in the Barnwell Gate suburb the properties that fronted onto the street may have sold their produce. The decline in evidence for oven ash from the sixteenth century onwards, when intensity of space use and refuse otherwise increases, suggests that commercial activity in this suburb may have shifted away from grain processing and baking. An alternative explanation would be that evidence is lacking as, instead of being deposited into quarry pits and other negative features, oven ash was mixed as a soil improver within the extensive garden earth.

Diet and status

The waterlogged plant remains from Grand Arcade provide evidence for a very wide range of foodstuffs (fruits, nuts and condiments), whereas the mineral-replaced remains at both Grand Arcade and Christ's

Table 4.28. *Summary of medieval and post-medieval economic plant species recovered from sites across central Cambridge. Urban sites are a. Corfield Court (22 samples), b. Hostel Yard, Corpus Christi (11 samples), c. Fitzbillies (four samples) and d. ADC Amateur Dramatic Club (three samples). Suburban sites are e. Grand Arcade (50 samples), f. Christ's Lane (nine samples), g. Emmanuel College (seven samples), h. Pembroke College (two samples), i. Chesterton Lane Corner (eight samples) and j. Cambridge & County Folk Museum (seven samples).*

Date and preservation type	1st–5th	9th–10th	11th–12th	13th–14th	15th–16th	17th	18th	Charred	WL	Min-replaced	Untrs	
Number of samples (urban/suburban)	12	8 (0/8)	25 (9/16)	29 (5/24)	42 (18/24)	3 (0/3)	3 (2/1)	70	44	22	5	**Total number of cases**
	Number of occurrences in samples							Number of occurrences by preservation type				
FRUIT AND NUTS												
Walnut	-	-	-	-	-	1h	-	-	1sub	-	-	1
Hazelnut	-	1j	2a **3e** 1i	1c **1e** 1j	4a 1b **1f**	-	-	8urb 5sub	2sub	-	1urb	16
Raspberry	-	-	**2e**	-	2a	-	2a	-	2sub	1urb	3urb	6
Blackberry	-	-	1a **2e** **2f**	**1e 1f**	1a **2e** **1f**	2a **1e**	**1e**	1urb	10sub	1urb 1sub	2urb	15
Wild/Hautbois Strawberry	-	-	1a **1e**	-	6e	**1e**	3a	-	8sub	2urb	2urb	12
cf. Domesticated Plum	-	-	-	**2e**	**1e**	1f 2h	-	-	6sub	-	-	6
cf. Bullace/Damson	-	-	**2e 1f**	-	**1e**	2h **1e** **1f**	-	-	7sub	1sub	-	8
Wild or Cultivated Cherry	-	-	-	**1e**	2e	**1e** 1h	-	-	5sub	-	-	5
Sloe	-	-	**1e**	**1e**	2f	-	-	1sub	3sub	-	-	4
Wild or Cultivated Pear/Apple	-	-	1a **1e** **1f**	**2e 1f**	2e	**1e**	**1e**	1urb 1sub	3sub	5sub	-	10
CONDIMENTS												
Opium Poppy (poppy seed)	-	-	2a**2e**	1c **3e**	**1e**	-	-	1sub	4sub	2urb	2urb	9
Black Mustard seed	-	-	**2e 1f**	**1e 1f**	**5e 1f**	-	-	-	11sub	-	-	11
Wild or cultivated Cabbage/Mustard seed	1i	-	**5e** 1i	1c **5e** **1f**	**5e 1f**	1e	1a **1e**	1r	15sub	1urb 5sub	1urb	23
Coriander seeds	-	-	-	-	**1e**	-	-	-	1sub	-	-	1
Fennel seeds	-	-	-	**1e**	**1e**	-	-	-	2sub	-	-	2
Celery seeds	-	-	**1e** 2g	-	-	-	-	-	1sub	2sub	-	3
'EXOTIC' FOODS												
Grapes	-	-	-	-	2e	**1e**	2a **1e**	-	3sub	1sub	2urb	6
Fig	-	-	-	**2e**	2a **8e**	**1e**	3a **1e**	-	11sub	2urb 1sub	3urb	17
Cucumber	-	-	-	-	-	**1e**	-	-	1sub	-	-	1
Grains-of-paradise	-	-	-	-	-	**1e**	-	-	1sub	-	-	1
GRAINS AND PULSES												
Six-rowed Barley	**1e** 2i 1j	4j	**3e** 1f1i	1c **2e**	**1f**	-	-	4r 1urb 12sub	-	-	-	17
Two-rowed Barley	-	-	-	-	**1e**	-	-	1sub	-	-	-	1
Bread wheat type (hexaploid)	-	2j	2a 1c **6e** 1i	1b **4e** 1j	**4e 1f**	-	-	4urb 19sub	-	-	-	23
Rivet wheat type (tetraploid)	-	3j	1i **3e**	1c **2e**	**1e 1f**	-	-	2urb 10sub	-	-	-	12
Glume wheats	1a 3d 5i 1j	1j	1c	-	-	-	-	10r 1urb 1sub	-	-	-	12

Table 4.28 (continued).

Date and preservation type	1st–5th	9th–10th	11th–12th	13th–14th	15th–16th	17th	18th	Charred	WL	Min-replaced	Untrs	
Number of samples (urban/suburban)	12	8 (0/8)	25 (9/16)	29 (5/24)	42 (18/24)	3 (0/3)	3 (2/1)	70	44	22	5	Total number of cases
	Number of occurrences in samples							Number of occurrences by preservation type				
Rye	1j	1j	3a 4e 1i	2c 3e 1j	1a 2e 1f	-	-	1r 6urb 13sub	-	-	-	20
Cultivated Oats	1j	-	-	1c	-	-	-	1r 1urb				2
Lentil	-	-	1a	-	-	1b	-	1urb	-	1urb	-	2
Garden Peas	1d	-	1a 1e 1i	1e	1e	-	1e	1r 1urb 5sub	-	-	-	7
Celtic Beans	1d	-	-	1e	-	-	-	1r 1sub	-	-	-	2
OTHER PLANT RESOURCES												
Hops	-	-	-	-	1e	1e	-	-	2sub	-	-	2
Hemp	-	-	-	-	3e	-	-	-	3sub	-	-	3
Flax (for linseed or linen)	-	-	2a	3e	-	-	-	2urb 2sub	1sub	-	-	5
Common Club-rush	-	-	1e	1j	-	-	-	1sub	1sub	-	-	2
Great Fen-sedge leaf ash	-	-	3e	1c 2e	3a 1c 5e 1f	-	-	5urb 10sub	-	1sub	-	16

Lane are strongly biased towards fruit seeds and stones. Cereals and pulses are only represented when charred. These trends in recovery are well known (Giorgi 1997; Green 1982), and the use of archaeobotany to interpret past diet is a challenge, particularly for historic periods where documentary evidence often provides much greater detail (Green 1984; Greig 1996). For early Cambridge, the greatest value of the archaeological plant remains is for identifying general trends in access to different food types through time, as the present absence of urban waterlogged samples renders spatial analysis of limited value.

The summary of plant types found across Cambridge (Table 4.28) shows growth through time in the evidence for a range of edible plants. Within this trend, 'exotic' types that would require specialist cultivation or importation are particularly evident from the fifteenth–sixteenth centuries onwards; evidence is limited, however, to waterlogged contexts at Grand Arcade and mineral-replaced/untransformed seeds at Corfield Court (de Vareilles in Newman 2008c). The range of native, and probably locally grown, plants increases dramatically in the eleventh–twelfth centuries, corresponding to the greater number of excavated archaeological remains. Although far more limited than finds from London (Giorgi 1997) the broad trend of growing diversity in diet is comparable, particularly the increasing evidence for traded imports during the early modern era.

The 'exotic' types of fig, grape, cucumber and grains-of-paradise are perhaps a little deceptive. All would have been widely available by the dates they occur in Cambridge, and by the seventeenth century cucumbers could easily have been grown locally. Grains-of-paradise, an import from West Africa, have been recorded from the fifteenth century or later in urban latrines/rubbish deposits at Worcester, Taunton, Oxford and Shrewsbury (Greig 1996). At present, the plant remains from Cambridge do not therefore show clear evidence of wealth or status beyond that found in communities across the provincial urban centres of medieval and early modern England (Murphy 1997).

Conclusions
The Grand Arcade project has provided the first opportunity to collate direct, biological evidence for life-ways and environment across Cambridge. These results reveal a diverse range of suburban activities, from stock grazing, small-scale cultivation, grain-drying and bread baking to formal and informal latrines. Although plots became increasingly demarcated with time, the distribution of ash across the innerland area at Grand Arcade suggests that space-use may have been more tightly controlled for some activities than others. The presence of sedge ash hints at the position of Cambridge as a hub for trade of fenland products in addition to the more usual agricultural and hunted/gathered natural products. The limited comparison of

plant remains that is currently possible from urban and suburban excavations in Cambridge highlights that there are significant areas still open to new research; environmental sampling and waterlogged contexts should be a priority for all periods.

Insects David Smith

Initially, the insect remains from seven samples from Grand Arcade and Christ's Lane were analysed, with two more samples and additional analysis being undertaken later (Table 4.29–4.30). This represents the first successful analysis of insect remains from Cambridge and contains significant evidence of ecological and synanthropic groupings. The samples span the thirteenth–sixteenth centuries and the insect remains suggest that the features were filled with a mixture of urban rubbish, waste and cess. The insects also shed some light on the nature of the surrounding environment, indicating that some areas were periodically flooded and also providing evidence for slow moving or stagnant water in the King's Ditch. One sample suggests that dry roofing thatch or a similar material was deposited in early/mid-fifteenth-century *Pit 41*.

A single twelfth-century sample was analysed from *Pit 5* (see Case Study 2). Insects from the King's Ditch and a number of thirteenth–fourteenth-century pits were studied. The insect remains from the

King's Ditch showed clear evidence for slow moving or stagnant water, most clearly indicated by the hydrophiliid 'diving beetle'. There appears to have been little surface or marginal vegetation present, as only single individuals of species that feed on duckweed and water reed were recovered. Additional indications from ground beetles and phytophage weevils suggest that a weedy and grassy area surrounded the ditch. A large amount of settlement waste was present, as a high proportion of the insects consisted of 'house fauna' and a range of other synanthropic species, while fly pupae suggest the presence of human cess. From Christ's Lane, thirteenth-century *Pit 24* produced a moderately sized insect fauna that suggests settlement waste, in a variety of conditions, entered this deposit. A number of the beetles that were recovered are directly associated with human settlement, including species usually associated with dry materials such as hay or straw, others normally associated with very decayed settlement waste and rubbish and decaying and wet settlement waste as well as animal dung or human cess. Species indicative of the general environment included those associated with stinging nettle, clover and vetches and cultivated peas or vetches. Another thirteenth-century pit, *Pit 25* from Christ's Lane, produced a similar but very small fauna of insects, as did fourteenth-century *WFF 10* from Grand Arcade.

A sample from early/mid-fifteenth-century clay quarry *Pit 41* produced a very unusual, although small, insect fauna. The sample came from a highly compacted tan brown organic deposit up to 0.47m thick and 3.75 by 2.0m in extent, covering *c.* 2.25 cubic m. This was initially interpreted as being dumped material from the clearance of stables or flooring material. When processed the sample consisted of a dense mat of material and produced huge amounts of frass (insect debris). The fauna recovered is dominated by the small 'fungus beetle' *Mycetea hirta* along with *Cryptophagus* and *Lathridius* species with a single individual of the 'woodworm' *Anobium punctatum*. Similar insect faunas have been found to be associated with the interior of dry roofing thatch (Smith 1996a; Smith *et al.* 1999; Smith *et al.* 2005).

Table 4.29. *Percentages of the ecological grouping of Coleoptera.*

Sample	207	401	3053	3070	3132	3149	5002	5006	1083
Feature	Pit 24	Pit 25	Pit 41	WFF 10	Pit 38	Pit 5	King's Ditch F.5191	King's Ditch F.5192	King's Ditch F.1073
Date	13th	13th	14th	14th	Mid/late 16th	12th	14th	14th	Early/ mid-16th
No. of individuals	12	67	31	38	154	218	34	199	173
No. of species	8	34	14	21	76	84	22	66	77
oa (will not breed in human housing)	66.7	37.3	16.1	18.4	53.2	64.2	61.8	15.6	45.1
w (aquatic)	16.7	1.5	-	-	19.5	30.7	23.5	6.0	24.3
d (damp watersides and river banks)	-	-	-	-	1.9	5.0	8.8	1.5	1.7
l (timber)	-	1.5	-	5.3	3.2	1.8	-	1.5	1.7
rd (drier organic matter)	-	9.0	35.5	2.6	5.8	5.5	2.9	5.0	5.2
rt/ (decaying organic matter)	25.0	38.8	48.4	60.5	24.7	20.2	17.6	54.8	27.2
rf (foul organic matter often dung)	-	-	-	2.6	1.9	3.7	2.9	7.5	4.6
g (grain)	-	-	-	-	3.9	0.5	-	1.0	1.2
p (waste areas or grassland and pasture)	-	1.5	6.5	2.6	10.4	12.8	8.8	1.5	5.8
pu (pulses)	-	-	-	-	-	-	-	0.5	
h ('house fauna')		11.9	38.7	7.9	8.4	7.8	2.9	6.5	6.4

Table 4.30. *Percentages of the synanthropic groupings of Coleoptera.*

Sample	207	401	3053	3070	3132	3149	5002	5006	1083
Feature	Pit 24	Pit 25	Pit 41	WFF 10	Pit 38	Pit 5	King's Ditch F.5191	King's Ditch F.5192	King's Ditch F.1073
Date	13th	13th	14th	14th	Mid/late 16th	12th	14th	14th	Early/ mid-16th
ss (strong synanthropes)		1.5	29.0	-	3.9	1.4	-	3.0	2.3
sf (facultative synanthropes)	25.0	19.4	35.5	15.8	10.4	12.4	5.9	40.2	9.2
st (typically synanthropes)	8.3	10.4	9.7	15.8	7.8	7.8	2.9	6.0	8.7

Archaeologically such discoveries are rare, although it has been suggested that there is circumstantial evidence that a late fifteenth/early sixteenth century deposit at Stone, Staffordshire, consisted of roofing thatch (Moffett & Smith 1997, 172–3). This group of taxa could potentially occur in a range of other settlement deposits, including drier stabling matter and hay residue. The deposit contained no charred material and very few waterlogged seeds, plus a small quantity of domestic debris. *Pit 41* is one of a series of such clay quarries and evidence for the others indicate that they are linked to nearby construction activities. One of the others, *Pit 36*, contained unused roofing battens (see above) and on balance it appears highly probable that the insects in *Pit 41* derive from thatch discarded from an old roof on a building that was being demolished or repaired.

As well as a sample from a sixteenth-century recut of the King's Ditch (see Chapter 3), there was a sample from a sixteenth-century *Pit 38*. This contained essentially similar insects to those of twelfth-century *Pit 5*, with 'house fauna' species that imply the presence of rotting settlement waste and decayed grain. There were also species that derive from the surrounding environment, with evidence for open and grassy areas with stinging nettle, Sheppard's purse, vetches, clover and dock plus animal dung. The insects also indicate that *Pit 38* was seasonally flooded.

Pollen Steve Boreham

A total of 24 pollen samples from three sequences of the King's Ditch spanning the early/mid-twelfth to mid-sixteenth century were analysed. Although earlier attempts were made to undertake pollen analysis from sites in Cambridge in the 1990s, none of these were successful. The samples were prepared using the standard hydrofluoric acid technique and counted for pollen using a high-power stereo microscope. Whilst the relative order of the samples within the three sequences is clear, the lack of stratigraphic links between the sequences makes it impossible to place all the samples in a definite sequential order, although the dating of the various recuts of the King's Ditch means that they can be placed in a broad order. The taphonomy of pollen from such contexts is complex and relatively few comparable contexts have been examined, although work has been undertaken on the London city ditch, the results of which show some similarities (Scaife in Butler 2001, 94–9). Detailed results can be found in the associated digital-only volume.

The pollen provides evidence about the environment of the ditch itself and the surrounding vegetation and land use. It is clear that arable activity was taking place close to the ditch throughout the period of its infilling. There is a little evidence for scattered trees (oak, lime, beech) in the vicinity, although much of the woody vegetation appears to be represented by hazel and privet scrub or hedgerow. It seems the ditch itself was treeless, although it is possible there may have been the occasional alder that became established in wetter areas. At some times the ditch was essentially dry for at least the summer months, while at others there is a little evidence for standing water for a time. The vegetation of the King's Ditch in general was a damp riparian meadow with tall herb communities, but particular plant communities developed at the base of the channel in response to specific local conditions at different times.

It seems that the vegetation of the ditch can be envisaged as a continuum with four main types of plant communities. A relatively dry and low nutrient channel would give rise to the ubiquitous damp riparian meadow, whose signal appears in almost every sample. Discharge of nutrient-rich cess onto the channel floor might engender the development of goosefoot-dominated communities. Later infillings without these particular characteristics may have promoted cabbage family-dominated communities of the channel floor. Finally, elevated water levels within the channel would have given rise to small stands of emergent aquatic vegetation such as reedmace and bur-reed. These vegetation types must have co-existed as a mosaic within the channel. It is likely that aquatic dominated communities were more common nearer the river whilst at Grand Arcade; the higher and drier channel was more often damp meadow. The recutting and then infilling of the ditch resulted in a cyclical pattern of vegetation communities, where repeated cut and fill sequences show the same pattern of vegetational succession.

Discussion

The period between the mid–late twelfth century and the sixteenth century is predominantly characterised by archaeological continuity and gradual change in the Barnwell Gate suburb of Cambridge. For ease this discussion will, however, be sub-divided into the three sections.

Mid–late twelfth century
The mid–late twelfth century was a period of major urban growth in England, as typified by the substantial expansion of most existing towns and the foundation of many new settlements, particularly after *c.* 1180. The

archaeological evidence from Cambridge, both overall and specifically from Grand Arcade, corresponds to this broader national pattern. Cambridge grew considerably during this period, maintaining its position as the dominant county centre even as numerous smaller towns sprang up throughout Cambridgeshire. Whilst the precise form of the twelfth-century property layout at Grand Arcade cannot be determined with any degree of certainty there is nothing to contradict, and a considerable degree of circumstantial support for, a pattern of long-lived continuity, wherein the newly established properties formed the basis for spatial divisions that persisted for many centuries; in some instances, surviving into the early twenty-first century.

It appears that around 20 to 25 properties were present in the Grand Arcade street block during this period, housing *c.* 90–110 inhabitants. These individuals resided in timber-built plot dominant buildings located in the property heads that have not survived, while to their rear the innerland areas of the property tails each contained a well and a cesspit as well as a small number of plot accessory timber buildings. A certain amount of pit digging, some of it for gravel, also took place in these areas. Finally, at the rear of the properties were situated large open backland spaces that were used for horticulture and grazing. Such activities led to the formation of substantial garden soil deposits. This rather generic picture only occasionally comes in to sharper focus. The most notable example of a more intimate event is the evidence for a rather unsuccessful bonfire to dispose of rotting settlement waste, human cess, decayed grain and a broken rake, the partially burnt residue of which was dumped into *Pit 5* (Case Study 2).

Some evidence survives for the range of activities that took place in the street block, although most of those that can be identified occurred on such a limited scale that they need not have been particularly common. There is nothing to suggest that the area fulfilled any particularly specialized role or function, unlike the suburbs of some contemporary towns. Activities that may have been relatively common include grazing animals – as suggested by insects associated with dung that was left in the open – the primary butchery of animals and the processing of their by-products as well as weaving, smoothing, or burnishing using double-ended worked bone implements (see below).

Archaeologically, one of the most significant interpretive considerations concerns the relative position of Grand Arcade along the broad spectrum of medieval occupation-types, which ranged from 'urban' at one extreme to 'rural' at the other. At a broad level, the mid–late twelfth-century remains demonstrate a range of both typically urban and rural characteristics.

Firstly, the properties were generally larger than those located in the urban core of Cambridge, with the result that many features such as gravel quarries were more dispersed than in the town centre. Secondly, the number of wells also appears to be higher than in the more congested urban core, with each property apparently having its own individual water supply. Both these factors appear rather rural, although the lack of substantial ditches defining individual property boundaries could be considered urban. A few items, such as the scythe and hay rake (Case Study 2) are potentially farming tools; these are generally rarer in towns, although they do occur and could be used for various purposes in an urban context (Egan 2005b, 199–200). Nevertheless, their presence may indicate that the inhabitants of the property were involved in cultivating the nearby fields. A single fragment of field vole maxilla may also be linked to the proximity of nearby agriculture.

The occasional presence of 'cut-it-yourself' wood and poached venison may suggest slightly laxer controls in the suburb, and a greater opportunity for certain forms of petty larceny compared to the town centre. There was also a lower density of refuse in most pits than at urban sites in central Cambridge. Although problematic, due to different intensities of investigation, the densities of eleventh–twelfth-century pottery within the Grand Arcade street block were broadly similar to those in nearby villages and the West Fen Road 'suburb' of Ely. Those at nearby Christ's Lane were somewhat higher, and appear to be similar to those in the Castle Hill suburb, whilst still falling well below the level of the town core (see Chapter 6). The grazing of animals appears 'rural' and the botanical remains were more akin to those of a rural 'producer' site, with evidence that certain processing activities took place in the immediate vicinity (see further below). Overall, the impression is that the mid–late twelfth-century street block was rather more 'rural' than 'urban' in character, having more in common with the results of investigations in nearby villages than those in the urban core (see Chapter 7).

There is little evidence from the features or associated artefactual and environmental evidence for any pronounced differences between the various properties, either in terms of status or other aspects. Although the greater depth of *Well 7* and the reuse of a probable Mediterranean cask in nearby *Well 6* may suggest that the property within which they were located was in some sense 'special', there is no reason to assume that the inhabitants had necessarily consumed the original contents of the cask. A broad distinction can be drawn between the properties located to the north of *Ditch 1*, which seem to have extended all the way to the King's Ditch, and those to the south, which only extended as far back as *Gully 4*. The impression is that levels of activity were similar in both sets of properties despite their different sizes, but that this resulted in those located to the south of *Ditch 1* having a markedly denser pattern of activity (Fig 4.2). This difference may well have had a substantial impact upon how activities took place within the smaller properties.

Prior to this period, early–mid-twelfth-century developments in the area had included two profoundly significant 'top down' initiatives imposed from above; the large-scale planned layout of the area (Chapter 2) and the creation of the King's Ditch (Chapter 3). In contrast, the succeeding mid–late twelfth-century pattern was principally one of 'bottom up' outcomes created by the actions of those who occupied the site. In many respects this sets the scene for the subsequent occupation of the street block, as 'bottom up' outcomes initiated by occupiers and lessees rather than the 'top down' actions of landowners were to dominate the sequence until the early twenty-first century.

During the second half of the twelfth century, under the reigns of Henry II (1154–89) and Richard I (1189–99), the Barnwell Gate suburb developed into a well-established entity. It has been suggested that suburbs generally reached their maximum extent during the eleventh–twelfth centuries (Keene 1976, 78–9) and the evidence from Grand Arcade indicates that, although Cambridge was a relative latecomer in terms of English towns, its suburbs nevertheless conformed to this general pattern. In 1156 the sheriff who had failed to collect all the money due from the borough was pardoned for this by the Crown (Cooper 1842, 27). This implies that the town was then in relatively poor economic condition, perhaps due to the effects of the Anarchy (1135–53), and its expansion is therefore likely to have post-dated this event. In 1174 there was also a major fire (Cooper 1842, 27), although this appears to have had no discernible impact on the Barnwell Gate suburb.

Thirteenth–fourteenth centuries
As far as now can be determined, given the retention of the standing frontage buildings, during the thirteenth–fourteenth centuries the plot heads remained relatively unchanged. Nevertheless, it is likely that the nature of some of the plot dominant buildings altered during the thirteenth century. While eleventh–twelfth-century urban buildings were often comparatively small and insubstantial single-storey structures, this pattern changed with the appearance of timber-framing, which first emerged in London in *c.* 1180–1220 (Milne 1992) and then developed nationally over the course of the thirteenth century. The adoption of this new

technology led to the proliferation of larger and more durable homes, often of more than one storey. Behind these structures, many of the innerland zones of the property tails also appear to have expanded somewhat during this period, taking advantage of the open areas at their rear that may previously have been used as common grazing land.

The innerland zones were also being used for a wider range of specialized activities during this period, although these only appear to have occurred on a relatively sporadic basis. The majority of the backland areas remained open and this zone is likely to have still been used for gardening/horticulture, raising pigs and various other domestic activities. There is little evidence for significant differences between the various properties at this time, either in terms of their status or usage, although the level of investment represented by stone-lined *Well 22* is not paralleled elsewhere. The fourteenth-century documentary evidence broadly corroborates this picture. The main area of archaeological investigation corresponds quite closely to documented Plots VIII–XV and XVIII (Fig. 4.11), and it is possible to broadly correlate the two types of evidence in a manner that appears probable, although a degree of uncertainty remains (this is because any such interpretation is, at least in part, based upon assumptions of continuity that appear plausible but are unproven).

In terms of the distinctively 'suburban' nature of the Grand Arcade street block (a topic that is discussed further in Chapter 7), many of the more rural aspects that were previously identified during the twelfth century – particularly in relation to the botanical and faunal remains – persisted into the thirteenth–fourteenth centuries. With regard to the ceramics and other common types of material culture in use at the site, however, few differences were apparent to distinguish this area from sites situated in the town's urban core (although the density of these artefacts was relatively low, suggesting a dispersed pattern of disposal that is more commonly associated with a rural as opposed to an urban milieu). Furthermore, the lack of higher status artefacts such as coins and weights suggests that the street block's inhabitants were perhaps rather poorer and less engaged in mercantile activity than their urban counterparts, while vessel glass also appears to have been rarer; although this latter material was not especially frequent elsewhere in Cambridge at this time.

The practice of occasionally disposing of complete or near-complete jugs in wells is paralleled on urban sites of the period, whereas on rural sites it was more commonly bowls or dishes that were discarded in a complete or near-complete state – perhaps because they were contaminated dairying vessels (Wrathmell 1989, 264) – thereby suggesting an urban versus rural distinction. Quarrying activity, predominantly associated with the extraction of gravel but also undertaken for clay, also continued in parts of the street block throughout this period, whereas for largely practical reasons it had almost entirely ceased in the urban core by the fourteenth century. In general, the focus of such activity appears to have shifted to extramural areas such as the East and West Fields by this date (Chapter 6).

But perhaps the most the notable suburban discovery at the site comprised the repeated evidence, from the thirteenth century onwards, for industries linked to by-products derived from the carcasses of slaughtered animals. Residues from the working of horn and bone, as well as leatherdresser's waste, were identified. A similar pattern continued until at least the sixteenth century, and in the case of leatherdressing is apparent until the nineteenth century. The repeated evidence for bone- and horn-working – which occurred in a number of different properties, and continued over a period of several centuries – is distinctive. Indeed, although smaller groups of light tanning and bone-working waste have been found at sites in the town centre, these do appear to have comprised predominantly suburban industries. Such an association may in part be a reflection of the suburb's proximity to the beast market, however, from which the raw materials for bone- and horn-working were procured, as opposed to a direct result of the nature of the industries themselves.

Historically, the thirteenth–fourteenth centuries span the period from the rule of the Angevin King John (1199–1216) to the establishment of the House of Lancaster under Henry IV (1399–1413). These were tumultuous years and some of this tumult must have had a profound local impact. Events such as the First and Second Baron's Wars, which certainly affected the King's Ditch (Chapter 3), as well as the Great Mortality and the Great Uprising, would have had widespread repercussions across every level of society. Yet in contrast to local villages such as Chesterton, where there is evidence of fourteenth-century decline on the periphery of the settlement (Cessford with Dickens 2004), the population of the Grand Arcade street block appears to have remained relatively stable – at c. 100–120 – throughout this period. Indeed, in overall terms it appears that the level of activity being undertaken within the Barnwell Gate suburb may even have increased at this time (as occurred at Christ's Lane for example; see Chapter 6).

This does not preclude the possibility that short-term intermittent episodes of decline occurred during the fourteenth century, however, as discrete temporal events are almost impossible to identify archaeologically. Nevertheless, despite the undoubtedly high number of deaths during the Great Mortality, there were apparently enough new arrivals in the town – presumably attracted by the opportunities offered by Cambridge's expanding ecclesiastical and collegiate institutions – to counteract this trend. Similarly, the Great Uprising also had little discernible archaeological impact.

Occasionally, this slightly distanced overview of the general sequence of activity resolves into focus on a single event that occurred within a particular property at a specific moment in time. Examples of such events include the residues derived from occasional feasts, such as the consumption of two spit-roasted pigs (*Pit 19*) possibly at Christmas. But occasional gastronomic extravagances such as this are counter-pointed by the decision to dispose of an infected pig without eating it (*ADP 2*), which potentially had a profound impact upon the economy of that particular household. Other discrete events include the breaking up of a wooden chest, which was already perhaps two centuries old and had travelled as a personal possession from Scandinavia, to provide a firm footing on a slippery clay surface (*Pit 16*). This was a rather ignominious end for such a well-travelled and long-lived item, and the chest clearly had a substantial 'object biography' (Joy 2009), although it is probable that much of this had accrued outside the Barnwell Gate suburb.

While the majority of the deposited items had much shorter back stories, nonetheless occasional groups of material present intriguing 'snapshots', such as the two jugs – plus a clump sole repair patch and a faunal assemblage that suggests a preference for pork – which were recovered from *Well 32* (Case Study 3). What also stand out are some counter-intuitive acts, such as the use of reused timber rather than roundwood as sails in *Well 25*, which rendered its construction much more onerous. It seems highly unlikely that roundwood was sufficiently scarce to justify this choice, and it represents a highly idiosyncratic act.

Fifteenth–sixteenth centuries

Perhaps the most notable characteristic of the fifteenth-sixteenth century activity was the relatively low diminution in the overall level of activity being undertaken at the site. The topic of Late Medieval urban decline and decay in England is one that has received considerable attention from historians (*e.g.* Dobson 1977; Dyer 1991; Jervis 2017; Lilley 2015; Rigby 1979; Slater 2000) and has also been addressed using archaeological data (Astill 2000). Although there is clear archaeological evidence that some form of Late Medieval decline occurred in the Grand Arcade street block, this was much less marked than at many contemporary sites excavated in other towns and it is notable that no such pattern was identified at Christ's Lane (Chapter 6). Of course, such a process need not have manifested itself simplistically and apparent physical decline can in fact be accompanied by material improvement (Astill 2000); a situation that also appears to have occurred in the present instance. Yet the reasons for the pattern of mid-fifteenth–mid-sixteenth-century decline at Grand Arcade, an episode that was then followed by a period of relative stagnation during the seventeenth century (Chapter 5), remain unclear.

At a local level, one possible contributing factor may have been the establishment of a 'University quarter' in the town centre. The creation of this area, which lay between the main street and the river, began with the foundation of various Colleges and Halls in the fourteenth century, increased markedly with the creation of King's College in the 1440s and was solidified by the creation of Trinity College a century later. The establishment of the University quarter and its subsequent expansion had various impacts (Cooper 1842, 197), but the most notable change was a decline in the level of riverine trade being undertaken on the Cam upriver of the great bridge, although whether University quarter was a cause of this or a consequence of it is unclear. Similarly, the foundation of God's House in the Barnwell Gate suburb in the 1440s may also have had a negative impact on the area (see further Chapter 6). Yet this was counterbalanced to some degree by the increasingly affluent University providing a reliable and shock-resistant economic buffer for Cambridge, with the result that any localized detrimental effects were accompanied by the mitigation of broader patterns of decline.

In 1561 the suburbs of Cambridge were defined as extending 'one English mile around the town in every direction' (Cooper 1843, 168). Differences in treatment also appear to have emerged. In 1575, for example, it was stated that middens in the suburbs did not have to be cleared as frequently as those located in the urban core (Cooper 1843, 332). In addition, an act for paving the town of 1543–4 stated that paths should be 'well and sufficiently' paved with 'paving stone' (Cooper 1843, 409). Yet these pavements extended only partway along Preachers Street, as far as Emmanuel Street opposite Plots XI and XIII. It thus appears that there was an obvious transition at this point that would have clearly demarcated the boundary between town and suburb. Living on the 'wrong side' of this boundary may have had negative social as well as economic connotations.

In terms of specialized activities, both horn-working and leatherdressers' waste continued to be deposited in the street block, although there was no longer evidence for the less common practice of bone-working. These appear to have remained predominately suburban industries. Quarry pitting also continued to be relatively common in at least some properties until the mid-sixteenth century; in the urban core this practice had ceased centuries before. The eventual cessation of quarrying activity at Grand Arcade appears not to have resulted from the exhaustion of the resource, but rather because the depth of garden soil rendered it increasingly impractical to obtain. The density of material contained within the fills of most features also increased markedly during the sixteenth century, with the result that the principal difference between suburban deposits and those of the urban core was the absence of large groups of ceramics and other domestic materials.

It has been suggested that contemporary town dwellers ate more beef, with a possible rise in veal consumption in the fifteenth century, and produced more evidence for specialized butchery practices (Albarella 2005). A similar pattern can also be identified at Grand Arcade, although the evidence is somewhat equivocal. A further factor that might be considered predominately urban are the casks that were increasingly reused to line features during this period; it is only in towns that there would have been a ready supply of casks that were no longer useable as containers (Skov 2009, 154). Contrastingly, if *Building 20* was a malting kiln then this would qualify as a rural rather than an urban type of structure. It is also notable that Lyne's map of 1574 depicts animals grazing in open areas to the rear of the plots in a distinctly rural manner.

Occasionally this general picture of life in the street block can be resolved into focus on more specific events that shed light on a particular property at a single moment in time. Examples include the construction of *Cesspit 14*, which effectively involved clearing the property tail of a heterogeneous firewood pile consisting of detritus that had built up over a prolonged period. The clay quarry pits with their sub-standard battens employed to improve footing provide another instance (see below), while a further example is the backfilling of *Well 22*. This contained eight dogs, four cats and one pig – perhaps the victims of an outbreak of disease – as well as several pottery vessels. A catastrophic event such as disease potentially helps to explain the counterintuitive abandonment of such an expensive, well-built feature and its subsequent replacement by an inferior structure. Equally counterintuitive was the sacrifice of two perfectly useable ladders during the backfilling of *WFFs 14–15*; the lack of archaeological parallels for this action serve to further highlight its inexplicability.

The fifteenth-century wheel fragment in *Cesspit 14*, along with the presence of sixteenth-century wheel ruts at the site, emphasises how some properties were accessible from the rear by vehicles whilst others were not. Accessibility in this manner would have had a significant impact on how activities were carried out, making many tasks much easier for those properties where rear access was possible. Indeed, this remained an important facet of the development of many properties and is recognizable into the nineteenth and twentieth centuries at Plot XIII with the warehouse *Standing Building 70* (Chapter 5).

The reuse of a wine cask from Ottoman Greece as a lining for *Well 38* in *c.* 1563–90 is suggestive of the increased geographical reach of late Elizabethan England and may relate to the activities of the Levant Company that was formed in 1581 (Case Study 5). Isotopic analysis of cod bones from sites in Cambridge has revealed the presence of fish in late sixteenth-century deposits that were caught at the Grand Banks off Newfoundland, and in 1583–84 Humphrey Gilbert travelled to Newfoundland in an event that can be considered one of the formative events of the creation of the First British Empire (1583–1783). In contrast to the Newfoundland cod, which can be viewed as early archaeological evidence of colonialism, the cask represents contacts within the well-established Ottoman Empire, which at that time was a much more significant economic, military and political power than Elizabethan England and in some respects comprised the most globally significant state of its day. Ultimately the cod can be deemed to have been part of a more significant phenomenon, although this is only apparent with the benefit of hindsight. It is worth noting that these traces of long-distance contact were only detectable through detailed specialist analysis. Such linkages were not revealed by more everyday items like ceramics, which remained much more parochial in nature.

In some respects the medieval pattern of occupation at the site appears to have ended by *c.* 1550–60, when most of the feature-types that had characterized the preceding four centuries went out of use. Following this there were a few sporadic and rather different features of *c.* 1580–1600 – notably brick-built *Oven 8*, cask-lined *Well 38* and gravel *Surface 3* – that contained novel or relatively novel forms of material culture such as clay tobacco pipes and jettons. This newly established post-1580 pattern then in many respects continued into the seventeenth century (Chapter 5).

211

Chapter 5

From suburb to shopping centre: seventeenth to twenty-first century

Craig Cessford and Alison Dickens

Following on from the preceding pattern of medieval occupation in the Grand Arcade street block (Chapter 4), the seventeenth–twentieth-century material will now be discussed. This was a period of substantial change, which eventually saw the area transformed beyond all recognition. During the eighteenth century both the degree of occupation and the scale of commercial activity expanded markedly, while the nineteenth century witnessed a rapid escalation in the number of buildings and a commensurate decline in the amount of open space at the site. Commercial activities were now ascendant, although a strong residential component was retained. Moreover, by this date the area was no longer suburban but rather completely urban in character. Coeval with these developments, from the mid-eighteenth century onwards the range of material culture in use expanded significantly. Attitudes to such material also changed, as exemplified by the deposition of large 'feature group' assemblages on a hitherto unprecedented scale.

A major transformation occurred in the nature of the archaeological record from the seventeenth century onwards. Firstly, features no longer lay *beneath* the extensive deposit of garden soil at the site but were instead situated *above* it; the last feature to have been securely sealed beneath this horizon was constructed *c.* 1563–80, while the earliest to have conclusively truncated it dates to *c.* 1620–40. Consequently, although the garden soil still effectively formed the 'surface' for much of the street block – and, at the rear of many plots, continued to be utilized for horticulture and other purposes – it no longer impacted on the stratigraphic resolution of the archaeological remains to the same degree that it had during the preceding period (Chapter 4). Secondly, the degree of archaeological visibility during this period was greatly enhanced by the increasing prevalence of brick, which was utilized extensively in the construction of buildings, boundary walls, wells, soakaways and other features. Coinciding

with this development, pit digging as a discrete phenomenon largely ceased; whilst a few pits continued to be dug into the seventeenth century, the practice was much less frequent and in almost all cases the intended function of the feature is readily identifiable.

Concomitant with these changes in the nature of the archaeological record, the same period also witnessed a marked escalation in both the quantity and quality of associated documentary and cartographic sources. Although the seventeenth-century leases remained broadly similar to those of the sixteenth century, for example, the existence of parish registers for St Andrew the Great from 1635 onwards – as well as hearth tax returns between 1662 and 1689 – means that for the first time it is often possible to obtain additional information regarding specific individuals. Similarly, while the late sixteenth-century plans provide some basis for understanding the area in the early seventeenth century (Fig. 4.29), a much more accurate map was produced by David Loggan in 1688 (Fig. 5.1). Its vertical perspective and increased reliability mean that from this point on the contemporary cartographic and archaeological evidence can be much more firmly correlated. Moreover, into the eighteenth and particularly nineteenth centuries the extent, accuracy and reliability of both the documentary and cartographic material continues to increase; individuals can be traced via an expanding array of sources such as trade directories and census returns, thereby providing a previously unparalleled level of background information.

This combination of increased archaeological visibility, greater stratigraphic resolution and extensive, highly detailed documentary and cartographic evidence has a profound impact on the manner in which the archaeological remains can be presented. From the seventeenth century onwards, archaeologically identified 'properties' and documentarily recorded 'plots' can be unambiguously related to one

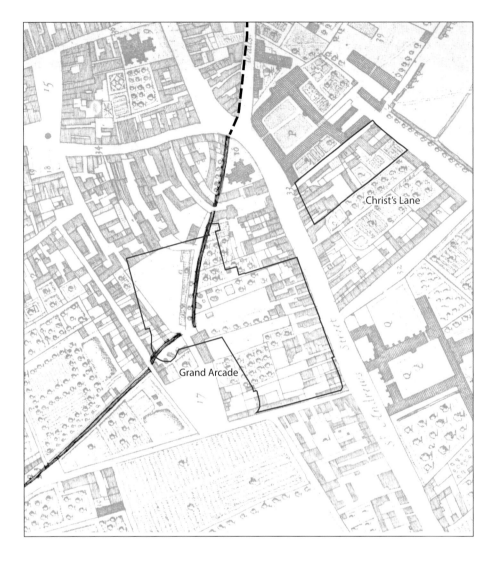

Figure 5.1. *Map of the area published by David Loggan in 1688.*

other. It is therefore no longer necessary to discuss patterns of development on a generic, site-wide basis (Chapter 4). Instead, the individual sequences generated within particular securely bounded plots can be adduced. This approach, which involves constructing a series of discrete 'tenement narratives' (Bowsher *et al.* 2007; Hall & Hunter-Mann 2002), has the benefit of introducing a level of subtlety and nuance that was previously unattainable. To maintain coherency, the boundaries of the various plot units remain consistent throughout this period – minor variations from this pattern at particular points in time are discussed on an individual basis – and an identical numbering system has been retained from previous chapters (Fig. 5.2; see also Chapter 1).

Equal quantities of information are not available in all instances. Some of the most well documented plots contained few if any archaeological remains,

for instance, and are thus treated in a relatively cursory manner. Similarly, from the eighteenth century onwards a number of standing buildings remained extant at the site; these structures were thoroughly recorded in 2005–6 (Baggs & Dickens 2005; Dickens & Baggs 2009), but the results of this work are not presented exhaustively here. Instead, the most interesting and/or representative examples have been selected and their discussion has been integrated with that of the contemporary below-ground remains. A similarly integrated approach has also been adopted in regard to the extensive feature groups that were recovered and the supplementary documentary, cartographic and – by the mid-nineteenth century – photographic sources that are available. Where multiple categories of evidence coincide, a more detailed treatment is presented. As in Chapter 4, a series of case studies are also presented in order introduce a level of thick

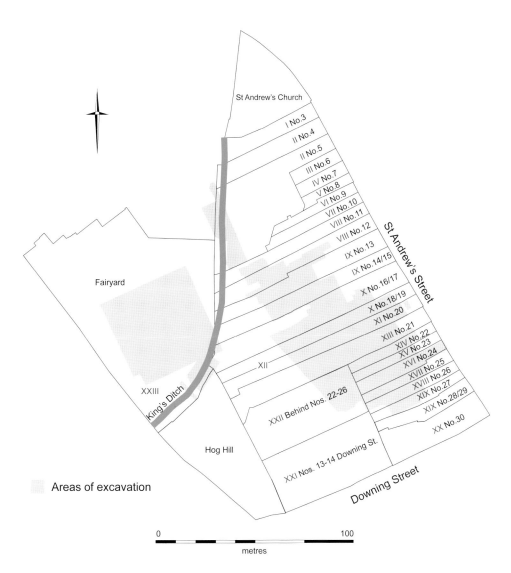

Figure 5.2. *The distribution of seventeenth-century and later plots within the Grand Arcade street block, based on a combination of documentary and cartographic evidence, with the 2005–6 excavations areas overlain.*

description which counterpoints the more general presentation of the majority of material.

Finally, it is notable that the discrete nature of many of the period's assemblages, allied with the wealth of documentary and cartographic information that accompanies them, means that they can make a substantive contribution to a wide range of research topics. Accordingly, a number of publications have been produced that address different aspects of the material's potential. These include: the contribution of Grand Arcade to the debate surrounding the relevance of post-medieval urban archaeology in a developer-funded context (Cessford 2009); material associated with life in an early twentieth-century department store (Cessford 2012); the materiality of writing (Cessford 2013a); a materialized biography of a nineteenth-century household (Cessford 2014a); the archaeology of

garden-related material culture (Cessford 2014b), the archaeology of nineteenth-century childhood (Cessford 2018a) and assemblages in general (Cessford 2017a). Many of these same subjects will also be addressed within the following account. In order to avoid undue repetition, in those instances where a full discussion exists elsewhere this will be referenced as appropriate.

This chapter adopts a similar structure to that previously employed in Chapter 4. It has been divided into two sections. The first presents a series of tenement narratives pertaining to the seventeenth–twentieth-century archaeological remains, the second the contemporary artefactual and environmental assemblages that were recovered. In addition, the first section has been further sub-divided into five parts, three of which – those pertaining to the seventeenth, eighteenth and nineteenth centuries respectively – contain two case studies each

215

(Case Studies 7–12). Further detailed information, including historical data, detailed feature descriptions and more extensive specialist analyses, can be found within the associated digital-only volume.

Due to the increased temporal resolution that is possible during this period, the following account of seventeenth–twentieth-century activity in the street block has been sub-divided by century, thus facilitating a more nuanced understanding of the pattern of development than could be achieved for the preceding period (Chapter 4). The principal exception to this presentational structure is the Robert Sayle department store. Because of its size, complexity and duration, this institution is considered independently of the other plots.

Seventeenth century incorporating specialist information from Steve Allen, Rachel Ballantyne, Richard Darrah, David Hall, Lorrain Higbee, Rosemary Horrox, Mark Samuel, Ian Tyers and Anne de Vareilles

The preceding pattern of medieval occupation that had predominated at the site since the mid-twelfth century came to an end *c*. 1550–60 (Chapter 4). By *c*. 1580–1600 sporadic examples of new feature-types had begun to appear, marking the beginning of a pattern that continued into the seventeenth century. During this period the King's Ditch declined significantly in both size and importance (Chapter 3); although it remained a major topographic presence, it no longer formed an effective boundary. Due to the extent of later truncation, no ditch deposits of this date survived to be investigated in 2005–6.

On the national stage the seventeenth century witnessed the establishment of the Stuart dynasty (1603), the Civil War (1642–9), the Commonwealth (1649–60) and the Restoration (1660). Locally, it is notable for the beginning of large-scale reclamation of the fens in 1631 and the fact that for the first time in centuries no University Colleges were founded. In addition, in 1616 and 1619 there were complaints of the building of 'unwholesome and base cottages' everywhere in Cambridge and the subdivision of plots into 'diverse small tenements' (Cooper 1845, 110, 126–7), indicating an increasing density of occupation.

Compared to earlier centuries, relatively few archaeological features of seventeenth-century date were present in the Grand Arcade street block (Fig. 5.3). Nevertheless, it appears that this was a period of considerable expansion; although only traces of this were detectable archaeologically, the features that do exist clearly point to considerable investment in certain properties at particular points in time. Furthermore,

documentary and particularly cartographic evidence indicates that the seventeenth century witnessed a considerable expansion in the density of occupation at the site (Fig. 5.1). In contrast to the map of 1592/1610 (Fig. 4.29), for example, by 1688 infilling meant that St Andrew's Street presented a relatively continuous frontage, broken only by narrow passageways between buildings. Despite the quality of the seventeenth-century documentary and cartographic evidence, however, its relative sparsity makes it difficult to shift the level of analysis beyond consideration of individual features to that of more cohesive archaeological properties; the principal exception is Plot XVI in the 1680s.

During this period the third of the street block closest to St Andrew's Street was densely occupied by buildings and yards, but the rear two-thirds remained predominately open garden/horticultural areas. Major changes had taken place along Downing Street and around Hogg Hill, and for the first time these areas represented genuine secondary foci of occupation. During the course of the seventeenth century the number of wells rose to five, although the fact that three of these were associated with a single plot renders the increase rather spurious in terms of overall levels of occupation and activity. Based on cartographic and documentary evidence, by the end of the seventeenth century there were around 30 households in the street block. As the mean household size in Cambridge at this time was 4.1 – with a substantial degree of variation based upon various modifying factors (Goose 1980, tabs. 4–5) – the estimated population of the street block was *c*. 120.

While isolated seventeenth-century features were identified in many plots there are only a few instances, most notably in Plots X and XVI, where anything approaching a meaningful pattern is apparent. There are, however, some individually significant deposits, foremost among which are a group of horse skulls in *Pit 56* in Plot XIV and a sequence of pits in Plot XIV that were dug to dispose of six cows (*ADPs 10–12*).

Plot IX
Archaeologically, little evidence relating to the northern plots in the street block survived (Fig. 5.3). In Plot IX, however, late seventeenth-century *Building 22* was encountered; this was represented by a series of brick-built footings situated at the eastern end of the area of archaeological excavation. This pattern closely corresponds to that shown on the 1688 plan, which indicates that the frontage was occupied by a series of building and yards while the rear two-thirds of the plot – which correspond to the majority of the investigated area – was covered by an orchard (Fig. 5.1).

Plot X/Plot XI
Plot X (incorporating Plot XI) was subdivided into three separately occupied messuages during this period. No features relating to the northern messuage survived and the only feature relating to the central messuage was late sixteenth-century stone-lined *Well 37*, which continued in use, although the 1688 plan suggests that it

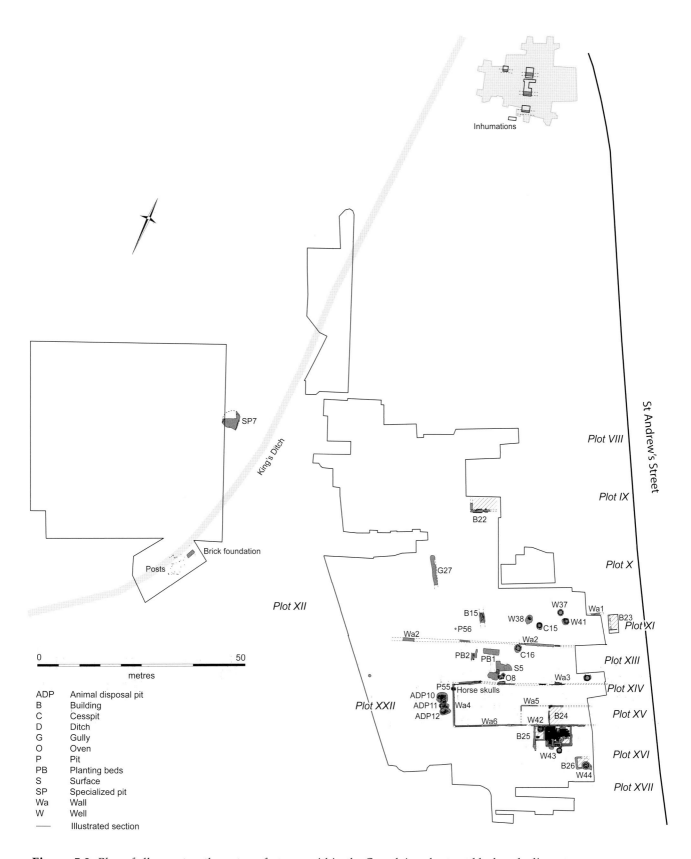

Figure 5.3. *Plan of all seventeenth-century features within the Grand Arcade street block and adjacent areas.*

acted as a communal water source serving more than one messuage. The southern messuage went through a major transformation in the second quarter of the seventeenth century, linked to it becoming an inn called *Le Chequor* that was first mentioned in 1637. This had an impact upon the frontage, where the pre-existing *Building 14* and an associated alleyway were sealed by a series of dumps. These deposits were then cut through by several postholes and sealed beneath a series of clay floors representing *Building 23*. There was

also a major impact at the rear, where the messuage expanded its plot tail behind the central messuage and became up to 13.0m wide.

Late sixteenth-century cask-lined *Well 38* and timber *Building 15* continued in use, but stone-lined *Cesspit 15* was backfilled and the southern messuage also gained access to pre-existing stone-lined *Well 37*. In addition, a new well, *Well 41* (Fig. 5.4), was constructed c. 1625–50; this had a rectangular oak baseplate made from four pieces of oak constructed using mortice and tenon joints. The oak

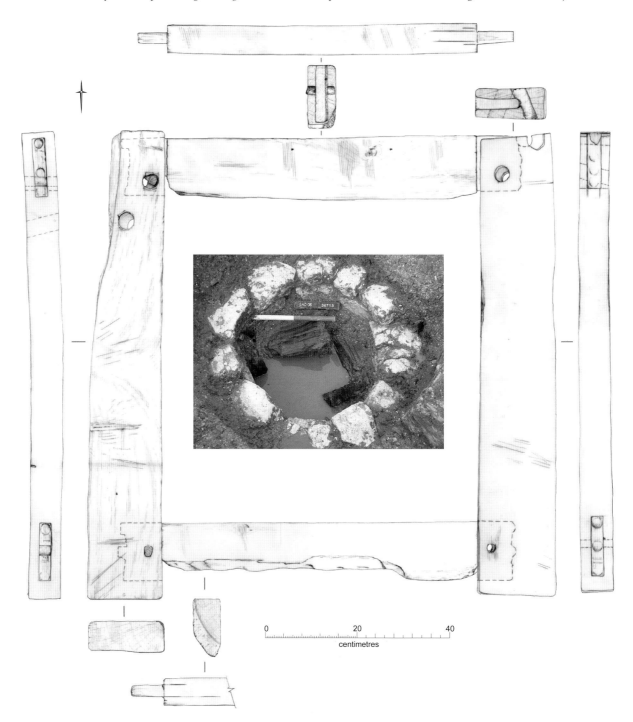

Figure 5.4. *Stone-lined Well 41, which was constructed c. 1625–42, showing plan of the oak baseplate ([35603]) and photograph of the well with oak boards in lower fill visible, facing north.*

Case study 7: *Cesspit 16* incorporating specialist information from Rachel Ballantyne, Richard Darrah, David Hall, Rosemary Horrox, Quita Mould, Mark Samuel, Simon Timberlake, Ian Tyers and Anne de Vareilles

Although constructed in the mid-sixteenth century (see Fig. 4.43), it is the backfilling of this feature that forms the focus of attention here. This event was initially dated to the mid–late sixteenth century on the basis of ceramic and dendrochronological evidence; however, subsequent analysis of the leather assemblage indicates instead an early seventeenth-century date. Overall, stratigraphic and other evidence suggests that the cesspit was most probably backfilled *c.* 1616–37, when the plot within which it was located was transformed from an inn into a chandlers.

There is no evidence for any primary deposits related to the use of *Cesspit 16*, suggesting that it was scraped clean immediately prior to its backfilling. All the material it contained had been deliberately dumped in a series of rapid episodes. Some of these items indicate contemporary building work was occurring on the plot dominant buildings, while the rest may relate to the disposal of unwanted material from the earlier inn. The building-related material indicates the removal of some timber-framing, which was achieved by sawing off the tenons (Fig. 5.5F). The building timber included an unidentified species other than oak, which was apparently a poor choice as it had been attacked by boring beetles. The timber-framing showed evidence of the use of a 25mm-wide plane, a saw whose *kerf* (width of cut) was 3mm and an auger. Some discarded, unused poor-quality small wooden pegs were intended to be used in a door or window, suggesting a rebuilding phase.

There were six large pieces of welded fuel slag (1.4kg) from a coal fired smithing hearth, which may derive from small scale smithing of structural elements. Hollows within the fused vitrified surface of the slag could have been caused by the pressure of the tuyère air blast, although at least one example was caused by the impression of the ends of a pair of blacksmith's tongs in the semi-molten plastic slag. Presumably this occurred when these pieces were broken off, picked up and pulled away as and when the accumulation of slag began to impede the air blast onto the hearth. Although we have no specific evidence for the form of the inn-related buildings that were demolished in 1637, the chandlers is described as having a substantial four-storey frontage building plus cellars and other structures; 'On the front, abutting the high street, one cellar, one hall, two chambers over the hall and two chambers over those, with a gallery all over; behind one hall and a chamber over, a kitchen with a chamber over, a barn and a hay house in the yard'.

Also present was a wide range of domestic refuse including over 9.6kg of relatively nondescript pottery, amongst which was an unusual Continental import similar to a piece from a late sixteenth–early seventeenth-century cesspit at Pembroke College (Hall in Hall 2002, 90). There was also some timber, including oak (10), ash (5), elder (2), alder (1) and willow (1). The oak and ash were derived from pieces of furniture and building

waste, consisting of pegs and dismantled structural timbers. There were five pieces of tangentially sawn oak board with rebates and nails, which originally formed the sides of boxes or drawers (Fig. 5.5A–D). There was also a piece of radially sawn oak panel with a polished face and candle burn mark, which had been reused as a box side (Fig. 5.5E). One board produced an English oak tree ring sequence of 1463–1548 from a tree felled after 1558.

Other wooden items included fragments from least two spoons (Fig. 5.5G–H); their bowls are 69mm long by 56mm wide and 15mm deep, whilst the handles are 8mm in diameter. Similar spoons are known from a late sixteenth–early seventeenth-century feature at Pembroke College (Taylor in Hall 2002, 95), King's Lynn (Carter 1977, 366), elsewhere in East Anglia (Rogers 2002), York (Morris 2000, 2267–9, 2412) and the Mary Rose (Weinstein 2005, 449–50). There was also a was an apple-corer or cheese scoop made from a sheep metatarsal with its shaft split axially, leaving a cross-section of the marrow cavity, which had some surface polish from use but no decoration. Such items may be a seventeenth-century innovation; the earliest published example appears to be from Norwich and dated *c.* 1620–50 (Margeson 1993, 120), broadly contemporary with this example.

Two leather shoes are late sixteenth- or early seventeenth-century in date. One was a latchet-fastening welted hobnailed shoe with a square toe and a high tongue, from an adult size 2 right foot whose shape, constructional details and style of upper all suggest a date at the end of the sixteenth century (Fig. 5.6A). A second welted shoe with the sole distinctly moulded to take a heel and a piece cut from a tie-shoe quarter with the stub of the fastening latchet present dates to the beginning of the seventeenth century. The shoe has a 'continuous' sole that passed down the breast and formed the top piece of the heel and was shaped for the right foot, both features that indicate a date early in the century. Heels were introduced in the 1590s and in order to accommodate them, shoes were made 'straight' and not shaped for a left and right foot. While some shoes continued to be made as lefts and rights into the 1620s, 'straights' quickly took over (Swann 1982, 7).

A near-complete moulded leather drinking vessel was also recovered (Figs. 4.37B and 5.6B). This type of object is rarely discovered archaeologically, but was common at the time. The majority of known examples are held in museums or private collections and have been preserved as a result of 'selective curation', being passed down through the generations. These vessels were made in a range of sizes; the larger known as bombards or beer jugs, the smaller back-jacks or drinking mugs (Waterer 1950, pl. xivb). They were used over a long time span from the medieval period onward, those in wealthy establishments being silver mounted. The vessel is made of two principal pieces, a circular base and a baluster-shaped body with an integral 'D'-shaped handle, with the body and handle cut from a single piece of leather. A separate strip of leather inside the handle and extending down to the base was added to provide extra support.

The seam has a double line of grain/flesh stitching, one line running along the edge of the body, the other diverging to run along the edge of the handle; a third line reinforces the handle edge. The two sides of the handle are broken and a hole has been knocked into the belly of the vessel. The circular base has the outer edge moulded upward for a distance of 15mm; this has a double row of grain/flesh stitching, stitch length 14mm, 7mm apart, forming a closed seam joining it to the body of the vessel. The base is moulded upward in the centre. No sign of pitch is visible on the interior, but solidified droplets

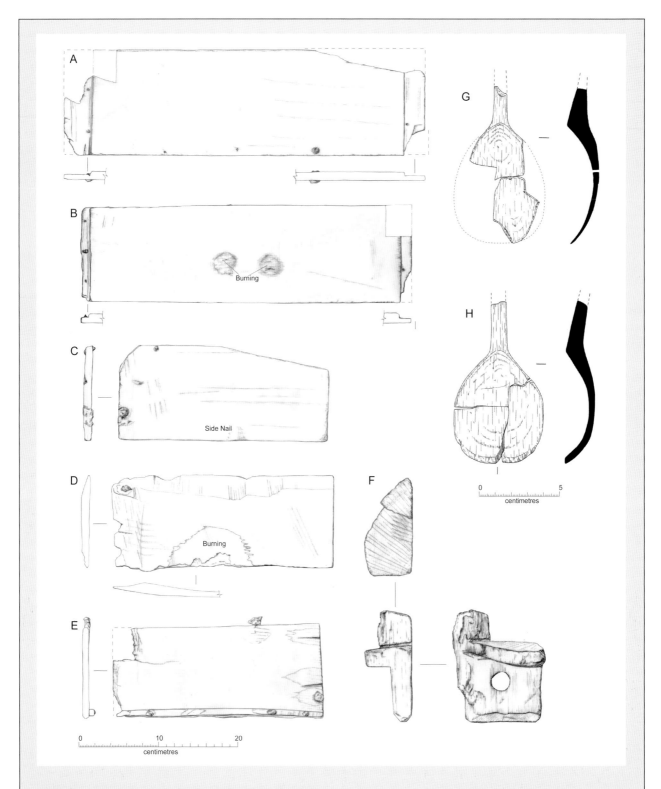

Figure 5.5. *Wooden objects recovered from the backfilling of Cesspit 16 in c. 1616–37 ([34718]): (A–D) tangentially sawn oak boards with rebates and nails, which formed the sides of boxes or drawers; (E) radially sawn oak panel with a polished face and candle burn mark, reused as a box side; (F) sawn off oak tenon from a rail in a timber framed wall; (G–H) parts of two or possibly three wooden spoons.*

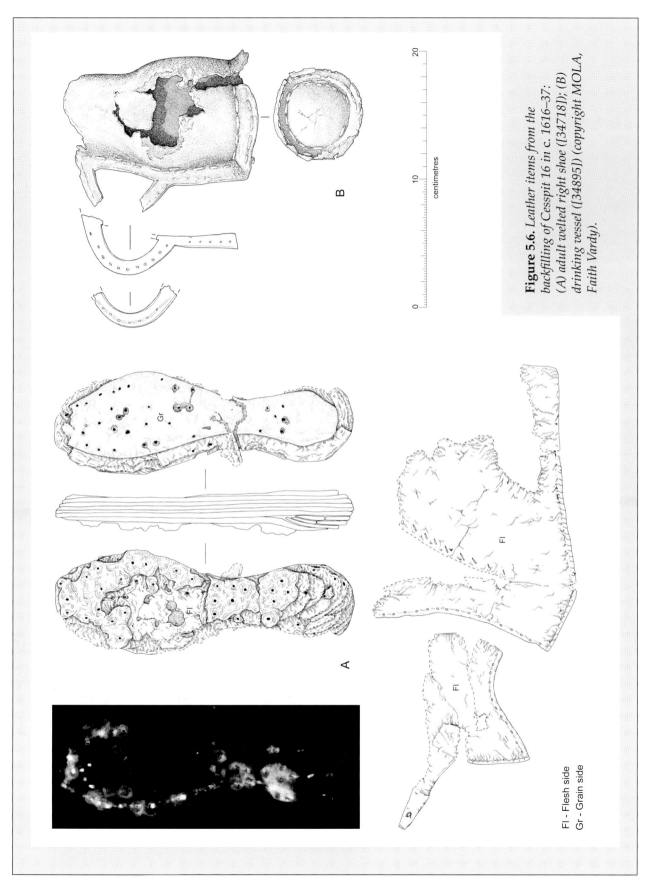

Figure 5.6. *Leather items from the backfilling of Cesspit 16 in c. 1616–37: (A) adult welted right shoe ([34718]); (B) drinking vessel ([34895]) (copyright MOLA, Faith Vardy).*

Fl - Flesh side
Gr - Grain side

of a wax-like substance are visible on the outer face. The body has a baluster shape, flaring at the foot to encompass the base, expanding at the belly and narrowing to a straight neck. The top edge is broken and the shape of the mouth is slightly distorted. The body is made in one piece with a single vertical, closed seam projecting outward as a flange *c*. 15mm from the vessel. A simple 'D'-shaped handle cut in one piece with the body projects from the top half. The body has a single, vertical, closed seam projecting outward as a flange 15mm from the vessel. A separate strip of leather shaped to fit the handle and extending down to the base was placed within the seam as a bead or welt to support and strengthen this potential site of weakness

A double line of grain/flesh stitching runs along the closed seam; one runs along the edge of the vessel, the other diverges to run along the edge of the handle. A third line reinforces the internal edge of the handle. It is made of cattle hide 4mm thick, its surviving height is 140mm, at the mouth it is 62–58mm with a basal exterior diameter of 75mm and an internal diameter of *c*. 54mm. The drinking vessel seams have been stitched with a thread, identified by Penelope Walton Rogers as plied Z2S (2-ply, Z-spun, S-ply). The fibres were poorly preserved, but were relatively narrow, 14–20 microns in diameter and arranged in bundles which had occasional longitudinal lines of dark brown tissue; these details suggest a partially processed plant fibre. Thread made from partially processed plant fibre, especially flax (linen), became standard in the stitching of shoes in the Late Medieval period and seem to have displaced animal fibres by the thirteenth–fourteenth centuries (Walton Rogers 2003, 3260–1).

Environmental samples from the feature contained few charred plant remains but were rich in waterlogged seeds of food plants that presumably derive from human cess. These include species that are relatively common in sixteenth-century waterlogged contexts at the site, such as hops, fig, black mustard, blackberry, strawberry, bullace/damson, pear/apple and grape. There were also two more unusual discoveries: cucumber and grains-of-paradise. These suggest that the remains are associated with a relatively wealthy household and the combination of 'hot' grains-of-paradise and 'cool' cucumbers could indicate dietary balancing of the humours, as was popular until the advent of modern science and medicine (Secord pers. comm.).

Cucumbers are known from third-century Roman London (Willcox 1977) and are mentioned by the English scholar Alexander of Neckham (1157–1217) (Greig 1996, 223), but appear to have died out and were reintroduced in the sixteenth century. They have been recognized archaeologically from a range of sixteenth–eighteenth-century sites including London (Malcolm 1999, 50) and Worcester although they are relatively rare and would have required careful cultivation under glass (Secord 2007). Cucumber would have been eaten primarily in the summer, although it could have been pickled for winter consumption.

Grains-of-paradise (*Aframomum melegueta*) are a West African member of the ginger family. This spice is mentioned in European documents as early as the thirteenth century and became a fashionable substitute for black pepper during the fourteenth–fifteenth centuries; its popularity waned during the seventeenth century (Alsleben 2009, 70, tab. 2; Greig 1996, 227) and it was later used only as a flavouring for sausages and beer. Grains have been recovered from sixteenth–seventeenth-century deposits at London, Worcester (Greig 1996, 227), Taunton and Shrewsbury (Tomlinson & Hall 1996) and are also known from Continental sites (Arndt & Wiethold 2001; de Clerq *et al.* 2007). The initial importation of grains-of-paradise into Western Europe predates the First Atlantic slave trade, although its greater sixteenth–seventeenth-century archaeological prominence relates to the rise of the Second Atlantic slave trade. The initial Atlantic slave trade of *c*. 1502–80 consisted primarily of transportation of enslaved Africans to Portuguese and Spanish colonies in South America.

This was eventually replaced by the Second Atlantic system beginning in the 1620s, which was conducted on a larger scale with English, Dutch, French and Brazilian traders transporting enslaved Africans to Brazil, the Caribbean and North America. Although North America remained a significant focus of English interest, with Jamestown founded in 1607, the most significant area of colonial expansion, commercially at least, was the Caribbean. After several failures, in the early seventeenth century settlements were established in St Kitts, Barbados and Nevis in the 1620s. These islands soon adopted systems of sugar plantations based on slave labour, giving rise to the triangular trade, with much greater archaeological impacts in both the Caribbean (Hicks 2007) and Britain (Brooks 1983; Moore & Corbett 1975) than grains-of-paradise.

The backfilling of *Cesspit 16* took place over the course of a few hours or days, yet the 'back-story' of the material incorporated in its structure takes us back some centuries. Spatially, many of the finds can be linked to events a few dozen metres away, related to demolition and construction works occurring at the front of the plot, while others link the feature to the Continent and more unusually all the way to West Africa.

included pieces of high-quality timber from a tree that began to grow in 1431. The tree was felled in 1606 and the wood was initially used in a bench. Above the baseplate the well was lined with *c*. 200 blocks of reused clunch that were derived from a demolished early/mid-fourteenth-century structure. The blocks were minimally reworked and the shaft appeared to have been relatively poorly and crudely constructed. The construction backfill consisted of largely sterile clay, but towards the top there was a near-complete tyg, which was possibly used by those constructing the well and discarded when it was chipped. It also appears that there was a boundary wall along part of the northern side of the plot, *Wall 1*, while the southern side was delineated by *Wall 2*, which was constructed by the plot to the south.

Plot XII

Plot XII was leased separately to Plot IX and Plot X and not always to the same individual as the frontage. The only evidence for activity here was large *Gully 27* and some ephemeral pits, including *Pit 55*.

Plot XIII

At the turn of the seventeenth century Plot XIII was the *Chalice Inn*, which belonged to Emmanuel College and was occupied by an *aquae vitae* – strong distilled alcohol, literally water of life – seller in 1616. Although the name persisted until 1637, by this date it had ceased to be an inn and was occupied by chandler James Hawkes (1637) and later his widow Ann (1664–88); the buildings of the plot were described in detail in 1637 (see Case Study 7).

The transition from inn to chandlers that occurred *c*. 1616–37 appears to have been marked by all of the existing features going out of use and the yard area becoming less well-maintained (*Surface 5*). Stone-lined *Cesspit 16* was backfilled (see Case Study 7) and both the northern and southern boundaries of the plot tail were enclosed by *Walls 2* and *3*. These and other seventeenth-century walls represent the earliest evidence for wall footings that are not parts of buildings but instead freestanding and apparently boundaries. These wall foundations were all highly fragmentary and heavily disturbed by later phases of wall in the same location, but were composed of a mixture of brick and reused stone blocks. There were no contemporary structures or major features located between *Walls 2* and *3*.

The seventeenth-century chandlers who occupied Plot XIII may have been general dealers or traders in supplies and provisions or may have made or sold items of tallow or wax, such as candles and soap. A number of sixteenth–nineteenth-century assemblages of animal bones recovered from several nearby plots (see Fig. 4.70) indicate that hooves could have been removed from hides and sold on to a tallow chandler (Yeomans 2007, 112, fig. 8.11), suggesting that this plot may have been part of a larger local network of various industries based upon raw materials obtained from animal carcasses. The 1688 plan shows Plot XIII as being divided into a distinct plot head and plot tail. The plot head was around a quarter of the plot length (*c*. 24m); its northern part was occupied by a rectangular building with a passageway to the south and a small yard behind. The plot tail is depicted as a large empty yard area, suggesting that the barn and hay house of 1637 had gone, with a distinct 'step' getting wider at *c*. 48m from the frontage.

Plots XIV–XIX

The maps of 1592/1610 (Fig. 4.29) indicate that Plots XIV–XIX were effectively a single property with an open area on the frontage and a large building at the rear. This pattern changed in the early seventeenth century when the area was divided into a series of plots; archaeological evidence indicates that this was a piecemeal development rather than a single event. Documentary evidence indicates that this process had begun by 1610, while archaeological evidence dates part of it to the 1620s; it had been completed by 1688 (Fig. 5.1). Plot XIV became a tenement by 1637 and was eventually enclosed by brick- and stone- footed walls, and although the northern and southern walls (*Walls 3, 5* and *6* respectively) were built by

adjacent plots they were connected by *Wall 4* at the rear which was specific to Plot XIV. Placed in shallow *Pit 56* near the northern end of *Wall 4* were four carefully arranged horse skulls (Fig. 5.7). These skulls were all derived from mature adult animals (two aged 8 to 12 years and two aged 15 to 25 years), which probably died naturally or were killed as part of normal practices.

The skulls could have been obtained from a nearby slaughterhouse or knacker's yard. Over 30 horse skulls of broadly the same date were recovered nearby from fills of the King's Ditch in 1914 (Chapter 3), indicating that they were readily available locally. Even archaeologists of historical periods with a 'ritual phobia' (Merrifield 1987, 5) would be hard pressed to argue that this represents rational behaviour. In relatively recent times horse skulls were occasionally used as foundation deposits to protect against evil, fulfilling some 'vaguely protective function' (Merrifield 1987, 126, 185) and were typically placed beneath doorways (Wilson 1999, 300). A similar deposit is documented during the construction of the Primitive Methodist Chapel at Black Horse Drove, Littleport, in 1897 (Porter 1969, 181). The centre of the site was marked by a stake, the horse's head – which had been obtained from a knacker's yard – was placed in a trench, a bottle of beer opened and a glass thrown onto it, after which bricks and mortar shovelled over as part of an 'old heathen custom to drive evil and witchcraft away' (Porter 1969, 181). Horse skulls have been found in a number of other intriguing broadly contemporary contexts in East Anglia (*e.g.* Hooper 1989). There are also numerous other instances from further afield, such as six horse skulls from the base a seventeenth-century well in Islington that are usually prosaically interpreted as knackered animals but could also have ritual explanations (Pitt with Taylor 2009, 29, fig. 31).

The only archaeological evidence for activity within Plot XIV is a Staffordshire-type slipware bowl that appears to have been

Figure 5.7. *Photograph of early/mid-seventeenth-century horse skulls in Pit 56, facing northeast.*

deliberately placed in the bottom of a small hole in the garden, perhaps to form a base of some kind. The plan of 1688 shows a rectangular building on the frontage with a passage or yard to the south, a small narrower building behind with a yard area and to the rear a slightly irregular garden or orchard. This involved an extension that was *c.* 17m long by 3m wide, covering *c.* 51 sq. m.

Within Plot XV clunch and brick footings belonging to *Building 24* were encountered. These footings spanned the entire width of the plot and the building was at least 3.6m long. There were also traces of brick footings of boundary *Wall 5* behind this, which indicate that

the plot was *c.* 31.5m long covering *c.* 190 sq. m. The 1688 plan depicts a relatively short plot where the front half is entirely filled by the plot dominant building; there is then a small yard and the rear third of the plot is entirely filled by two buildings. *Building 24* relates to one or both of these two buildings situated at the rear of the plot.

In Plot XVI stone- and brick-lined *Well 42* was constructed in the 1620s; it went out of use *c.* 1680–8 (see Case Study 8). The abandonment of *Well 42* after such a short lifespan relates to the construction of two-roomed slightly sunken red brick *Building 25* on the northern side of the plot (Figs. 5.8–5.9), which appears to have

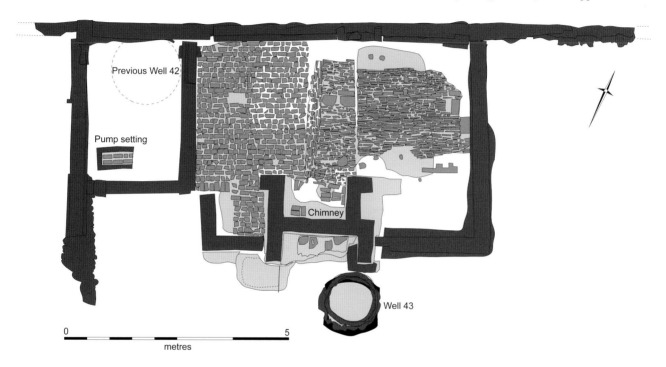

Figure 5.8. *Plan of Building 25 constructed in the 1680s, plus photograph facing west.*

224

Figure 5.9. *Photograph of Building 25 constructed in the 1680s, facing southwest.*

been a kitchen block. The larger room measured 7.0m long by 4.6m wide and had a brick floor and a chimney on its southern side. To the rear of this was a smaller room 3.3m wide and 2.5m wide that had a beaten earth floor and a brick-lined rectangular feature with a sloping base set into it. The latter would have housed a timber pedestal for a hand pump (Framework Archaeology 2008, 271–2), indicating that *Building 25* was an ancillary kitchen block.

To the south of *Building 25* was a *c.* 2.0m-wide passageway where stone- and brick-lined *Well 43* (Fig. 5.12) was built no earlier than *c.* 1680. *Well 43* had a layer of slate in its base, over which was placed a timber baseplate made of four pieces of oak connected using mortice and tenon joints and consisting of two curved halves of a single branch and two reused straight pieces. Above this was a course of tile, five courses of reused moulded stone blocks and then

Case study 8: *Well 42* incorporating specialist information from Richard Darrah, Mark Samuel and Ian Tyers

In Plot XVI stone- and brick-lined *Well 42* was constructed in the 1620s in a plot *c.* 48.5m long covering *c.* 290 sq. m. Due to its depth, *Well 42* had to be investigated in two separate stages in early August and late September 2005. The second phase was undertaken in challenging circumstances due to an abundance of groundwater; this was particularly problematic as it was only at this stage that the fact that much of the stone was intricately moulded was recognized. A timber baseplate was also recovered.

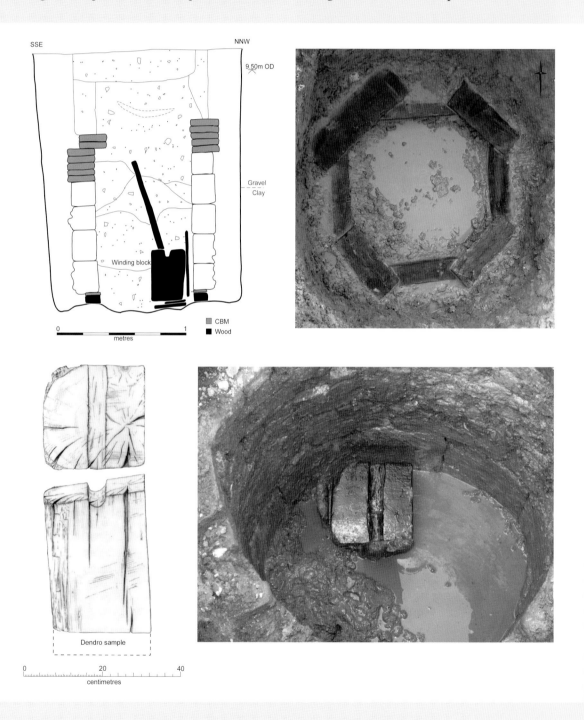

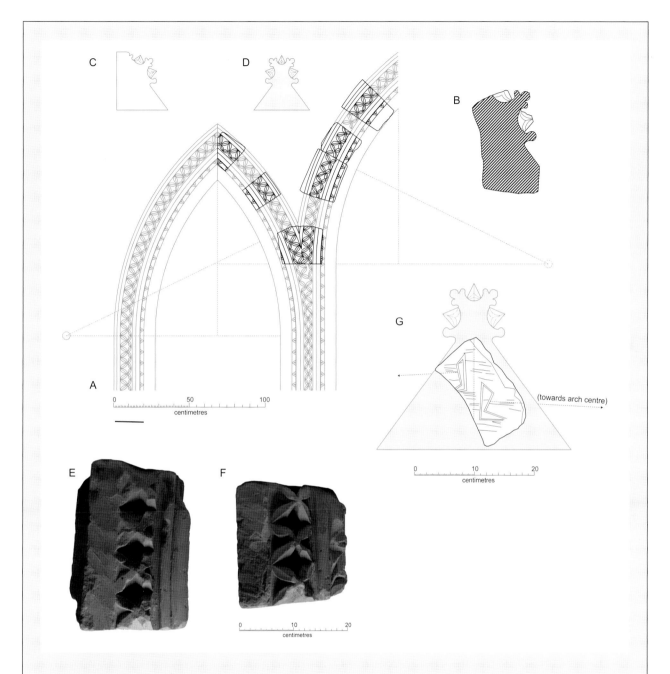

Figure 5.11 *(above). Dogtooth-ornamented rear arches from clunch lancet windows of c. 1250, reused in 1620s lining of Well 42 ([34586]) showing: (A) internal elevation (detail); (B) a typical voussoir as recovered; (C) restored scoinson; (D) restored mullion terminations; (E–F) elevations of dogtooth ornament; (G) setters' positioning marks (A–D and G based upon illustrations by Mark Samuel).*

Figure 5.10 *(opposite). Stone- and brick-lined Well 42, constructed in the 1620s and backfilled in the 1680s with section of the well, photograph of the timber baseplate, facing north, drawing and in situ photograph, facing north, of oak winding block ([34139]).*

At the base of the well was a square timber baseplate. This had been constructed from four pieces of oak slab wood with sapwood present, made from offcuts from the sawing of small beams of *c.* 8in by 6in (200mm by 150mm) (Fig. 5.10). Placed over the corners of these beams were four smaller pieces of oak, thereby creating an irregular hexagon. One of latter pieces had a sequence of 84 tree rings, which was matched to English oak reference data of

1527–1610 and comes from a tree felled no earlier than 1620. Two of the other pieces came from a complete width of tongue-and-groove board; this 202-year sequence matched the Eastern Baltic oak sequence of 1158–1359 and must have been felled after 1367. Felling occurred during the late fourteenth–mid-fifteenth centuries, making the board up to c. 250 years old when it was reused. The condition of the board indicates that it was initially used inside a dry building and its V-shaped tongue-and-groove is typical of much imported oak from the Baltic used in East Anglia. Some tiles were placed between the pieces of wood to fill the gaps.

Over the baseplate were placed four to five courses of clunch blocks (see Fig 7.2E), with a total of 40 blocks present; these blocks were then in turn surmounted by five to seven courses of brickwork. The stone was derived from a triforium arch and associated lancet window from a high status thirteenth-century religious structure constructed c. 350 years before the well (Fig. 5.11). The lack of weathering and abrasion on the blocks and the coherent and homogeneous nature of the group suggest that they come from a building in Cambridge. The deeply carved stone would have been difficult to reuse in most contexts; however it is extremely useful when lining a well as the carving allows the stone to be 'keyed in' to the clay. There is evidence that more than one type of arch was employed, but the survival of a paired springer block hints at a row of identical arches in an arcade. This arcade was whitewashed on several occasions, although no attempt to pick out the detail in polychromy was apparent, and the paint indicates that the arcade was free-standing but only to be seen from one side.

This stonework, and several other groups from the site, are significant architectural discoveries. Cambridge was home to a significant number of medieval religious houses and churches, and there is documentary evidence that stonework from a number of more distant religious houses in the fens was transported to Cambridge for reuse after the Dissolution. This makes it impossible to determine which particular thirteenth-century religious institution supplied the stone for *Well 42*. No other features were associated with the well and it is likely that contemporary buildings were restricted to the frontage of Plot XVI. Overall, the well lining had a shaft 0.8m in diameter that would have naturally filled with water to a depth of c. 0.8m, holding c. 0.4 cubic m of water.

Well 42 had a relatively short lifespan of perhaps half a century. Its backfilling contained three clay tobacco pipe bowls of c. 1660–80 and, based upon the features that succeeded it, it was backfilled c. 1680–8. In the base of the well was an oak winding block (Fig. 5.11). This consisted of a small baulk with a 50mm-diameter cylindrical hole cut through it with a 17mm-wide gouge. The gouged hole was sawn across; there were clear gouge marks inside but no evidence of wear. This was presumably the winding block for *Well 42* and it appears to have been accidentally lost whilst being removed for reuse. There were several oak and Scots pine boards placed around the block at steep angles, indicating an unsuccessful attempt to lever it out from the sticky mud in the base of the well where it had become embedded. The uppermost brick courses from *Well 42* were robbed, probably for reuse in *Well 43* which replaced it.

20 courses of red brick. The 45 reused stones were all carefully shaped and faced into curving blocks. No moulded elements survived and the curving blocks were cut down from larger rectangular blocks, suggesting the use of a considerable quantity of good-quality stone.

Given its location, the top of *Well 43* must have been sealed over to permit use of the passageway, possibly with a lead pipe connecting it to the pump setting in *Building 25* to the north. Intriguingly, *Building 25* lay directly over earlier backfilled *Well 42*, and there is no obvious reason why this latter well did not continue to be used as a source of water. The building range effectively formed part of the plot boundary and it appears that brick-built *Wall 6*, which incorporated some reused stone (see Fig. 7.2F, 7.2H), was constructed along the rest of the plot's northern edge at the same time. The 1688 plan shows a series of buildings stretching from the frontage for c. 39m, with a passageway to the south and a yard behind; it therefore appears that the *Building 25* complex was constructed c. 1680–8.

Between 1580 and 1610 Plot XVII changed from being referred to in abuttals as 'garden ground' to a 'tenement' and was established as a plot c. 48.5m long covering c. 260 sq. m. During the seventeenth century *Building 26* was constructed stretching back up to 19m from the frontage in the northern part of the plot, with a 1.0–1.5m-wide passageway to the south. Located within the rearmost of these structures was brick-lined *Well 44*. The 1688 plan shows a series of buildings situated along the northern part of the plot, with a passage to the south and a yard to the rear. Archaeologically there is no evidence relating to the southern Plots XVIII–XX, although the 1688 plan (Fig. 5.1) indicates that large-scale development occurred within this part of the street block.

Plot XXII

To the west, Plot XXII is shown on the 1688 plan as having been subdivided and partially developed. The excavated area was part of a garden/orchard roughly 33m by 33m in extent or c. 1090 sq. m,

with a small building on its southern side. By the end of the century part of its eastern boundary comprised the rear brick-built *Wall 4* of Plot XIV. During the late seventeenth century a series of three intercutting pits, *ADPs 10–12*, were dug in the north-eastern corner of the plot, located just inside the property boundary. The three pits appear to have been dug in quite rapid succession with *ADP 10* – which contained four cows – occurring first; as this feature contained a clay tobacco pipe bowl of c. 1680–1710, the group probably dates to c. 1680–1720. Overall, the pits contained six cows, at least five of which were female and three of which had associated *in utero* foetuses (Figs. 5.13–5.14), suggesting that the rear of Plot XXII was used for grazing.

These animals appear to have been milk cattle, and there is evidence they suffered from 'milk fever' caused by a lack of forage containing the right balance of minerals. This is perhaps unsurprizing given the small area that the cattle appear to have been kept in and they probably represent a 'flying herd', where animals were not bred at the site but were instead brought in from elsewhere whilst pregnant to give birth and then often culled or sold at the end of their lactation and cyclically replaced (pers. comm. A. Legge). The fact that the meat from these cows was not considered fit for human consumption, or even knackered for use as dog food (Thomas & Locock 2000; Wilson & Edwards 1993), combined with their unceremonious disposal supports the idea that the cattle died suddenly of a disease; potentially the rinderpest outbreak of 1714–15. Since 1575 such large animals should not have been buried in the

Figure 5.12 *(opposite). Stone- and brick-lined Well 43, constructed in the 1680s: (A) the stone and brick linings of the well, facing west; (B) the timber baseplate, facing northeast; (C) plan of the constructional sequence of well; (D) the timber baseplate ([34381]).*

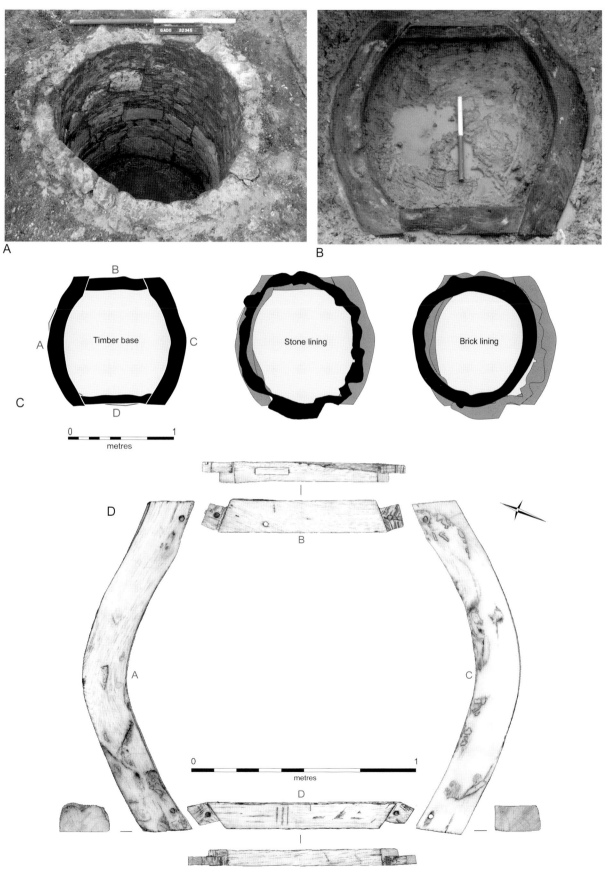

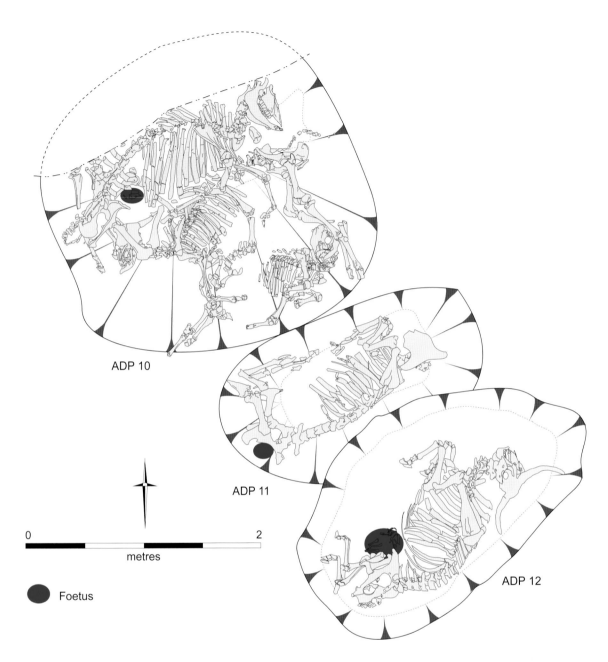

ADP 10

ADP 11

ADP 12

0   2
metres

● Foetus

Figure 5.13. *Plan of cattle ADPs 10–12, dug c. 1680–1720.*

plot, but taken to one of the common dunghills or other places further from the town (Cooper 1843, 336). This suggests that the pits represent a series of illicit acts, perhaps facilitated by the greater privacy provided by the erection of the nearby boundary wall.

The overall cattle bone assemblage from the site demonstrates that cattle were largely managed for milk throughout its occupation, while an inquisition at St Andrew the Great in 1274 records that tithes included milk (Cooper 1842, 54) and there was a documented milk market in Cambridge by 1360 (Bryan & Wise 2002, 84). In 1662 a student of Jesus College wrote that he went to an 'honest house' near the college to get a pint of milk boiled for his breakfast (Cooper 1845, 505) and it is likely that by the early eighteenth century the majority of milk was supplied on a commercial basis (Atkins 1977; Atkins 1980). The milk yield of these cattle is impossible to estimate accurately, but may have been in the region of three litres a day per cow. Although there are numerous factors that affect how much water animals require, lactating cattle generally need 50 to 80 litres per day whilst other cattle need 30 to 65 litres. This indicates that there must have been at least one well in Plot XXII located outside the excavated area.

The cattle would have been amongst the heaviest consumers of water in the street block. Working horses require a broadly comparable 45 to 80 litres while pigs only need around three litres, although a sow with a litter can require almost 30 litres. Human requirements are equally low, at two to three litres, while cats, dogs and chickens require negligible amounts. It should also be remembered that the cows and other animals known to have been present in the street block at various times would have required large amounts of fodder and produced large amounts of dung, presumably used as manure, as well as urine.

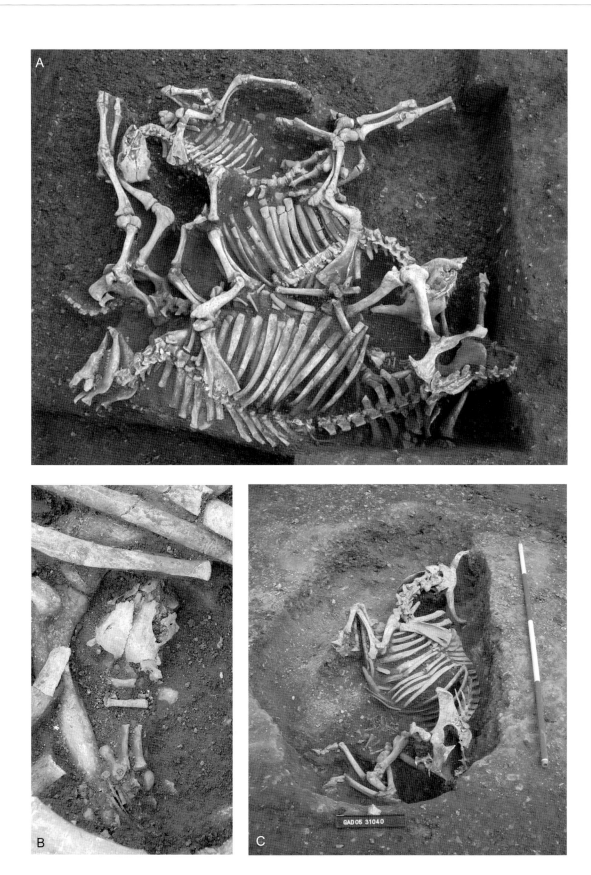

Figure 5.14. *Photographs of ADPs 10–12, which were dug c. 1680–1720: (A) ADP 10, facing north; (B) detail of nearly full term foetus found in womb area of cow in ADP 10, facing north; (C) ADP 12, facing east.*

Eighteenth century incorporating specialist information from Steve Allen, Tony Baggs, Rachel Ballantyne, Richard Darrah, Andrew Hall, David Hall, Vicki Herring, Rosemary Horrox, Mark Samuel, Ian Tyers and Anne de Vareilles

Although comparatively few seventeenth-century features were identified, there appears to have been an increase in the 1680s and this pattern of escalation subsequently continued into the eighteenth century (Figs. 5.15–5.17). There was also a substantial rise in the quantity of material culture that was deposited, although this did not occur until the 1760s. No eighteenth-century remains of the King's Ditch survived to be investigated in 2005–6 and by 1795 the feature had been legislated out of existence (Chapter 3). Nationally, the eighteenth century witnessed the rise of the British Empire, the Industrial Revolution, the American War of Independence and war with France. On a more local

scale, although no colleges were founded Senate House was constructed (1722–34), the bridges over the Cam were markedly improved (1754–56) and the University acquired the area to the west of Corn Exchange Street for a Botanic Garden (1762).

Over the course of the eighteenth century the archaeological evidence for occupation within the Grand Arcade street block markedly increased (Figs. 5.16–5.17). A significant component of this increase was an escalation in the number of brick-built structures that were constructed; moreover, for the first time several of these buildings remained standing to be recorded architecturally in 2005, thus providing a valuable source of additional information. Several other brick-built feature-types also appeared during this period, including boundary walls, cellars, soakaways and drains. Their presence does not simply indicate an increase in the visibility of the archaeological remains, but rather an expansion in the levels of activity that were taking place.

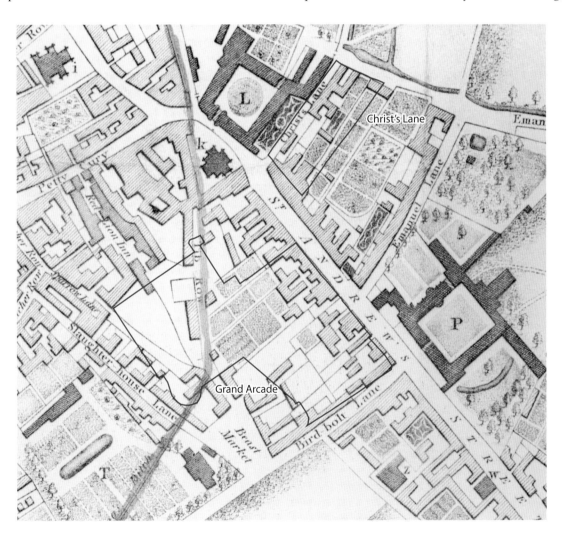

Figure 5.15. *Map of the area published by William Custance in 1798.*

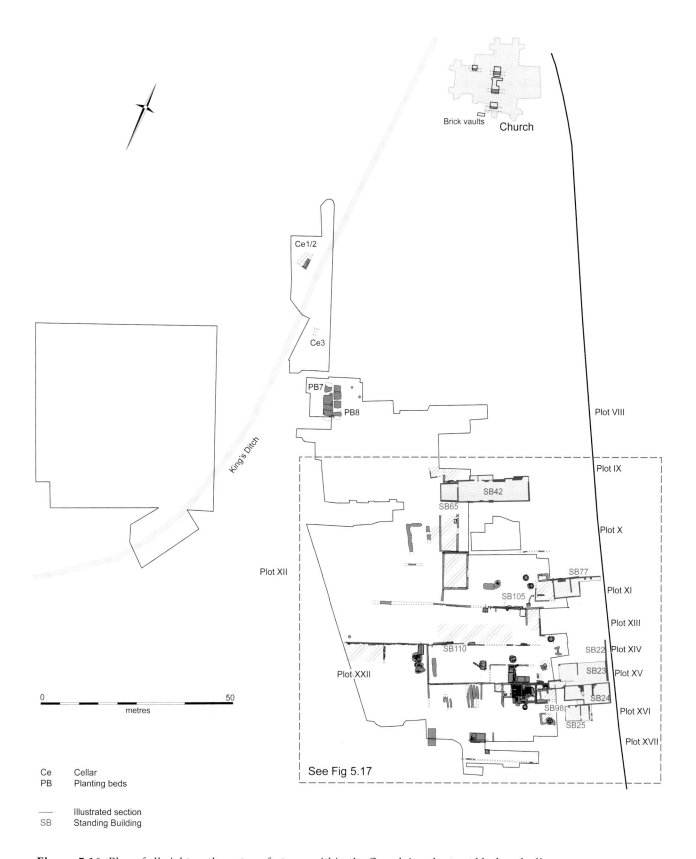

Ce   Cellar
PB   Planting beds

—   Illustrated section
SB   Standing Building

Figure 5.16. *Plan of all eighteenth-century features within the Grand Arcade street block and adjacent areas.*

233

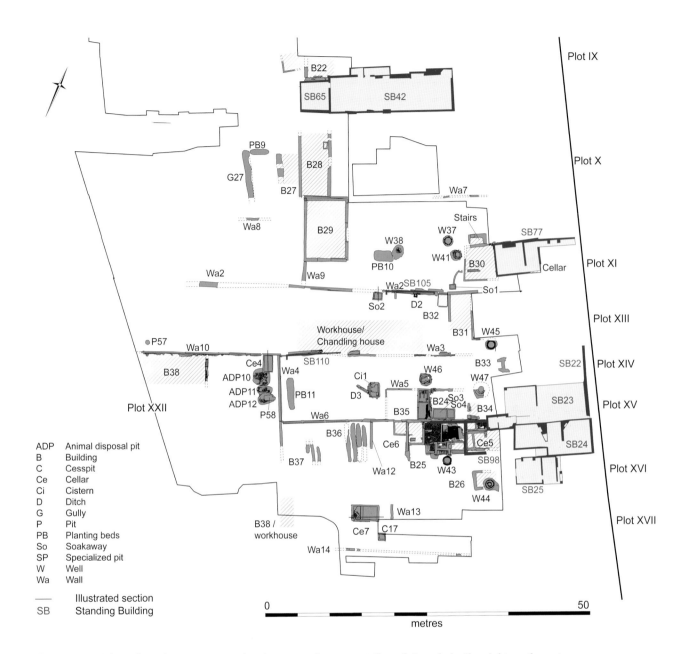

Figure 5.17. *Plan of southeastern area of main excavation area at Grand Arcade in the eighteenth century.*

A similar pattern is also represented cartographically. In the first instance, Loggan's 1688 plan (Fig. 5.1) provides a good overview of the area at the end of the seventeenth century, while a plan by William Custance of 1798 (Fig. 5.15) provides some evidence of the changes that took place over the course of the succeeding century, although it should be noted that the latter does not represent an entirely reliable depiction.

This period of expansion had a profound impact on the plot dominant buildings at the site, although only a few of these survived to be investigated architecturally. Its influence is much more visible archaeologically in the effective expansion of the plot heads, where a series of plot accessory buildings and other structures were constructed. A densely occupied zone was thus created that extended up to *c.* 40m from the frontage, rather than the *c.* 30m which had been typical during the seventeenth century. Despite this, the population of the street block appears to have remained relatively stable, numbering *c.* 130 individuals in the late eighteenth century. From *c.* 1760 onwards a further significant component of the archaeological sequence consisted of a number of large assemblages of material culture that were deposited on a scale not previously witnessed, primarily in the backfill of redundant features or as percolation fills in the base of planting beds.

The extensive array of archaeological features and material assemblages that pertained to this period, allied with the wealth of surviving documentary and cartographic sources as well as the architectural information that was recovered from contemporary standing buildings, means that more comprehensive tenement narratives can be constructed than were possible during the seventeenth century.

Plots I–VII

The northernmost plots were either not investigated archaeologically or produced no eighteenth-century remains. Evidence from the surviving frontage buildings indicates that many were rebuilt at around this time as two- or three- storey brick buildings with tile or slate rooves, paralleling contemporary developments occurring in the archaeologically investigated area.

Plot VIII

The only eighteenth-century archaeological remains in Plot VIII relate to two rows of planting beds (*PBs 7–8*) that were dug in the plot tail *c*. 1770–90 (Fig. 5.18). These features contained some material (MNI 87), mainly linked to dining and tea drinking, which was added as a percolation fill (Fig. 5.18I–M). The upper portions of the planting beds were single continuous trenches, but lower down they were discontinuous and were dug as three or four separate smaller square beds. The westernmost, *PB 7*, measured 8.0m long and 2.4m wide and contained two 0.5m-deeper sections that were 2.5m by 2.4m and 1.4m by 2.4m in extent. The easternmost, *PB 8*, measured 8.0m long and *c*. 1.9m wide and contained some 0.5–0.7m-deeper sections that were 1.1–1.9m long and 1.7–2.05m wide, one of which had a plank and stake revetment. In addition, a number of postholes and irregular shallow features were also present; these were probably for planting bushes. The layout of the planting beds indicates that there was a single garden behind the two plots, although it impossible to determine which frontage property it was associated with or who created them.

Plot IX

Seventeenth-century structure *Building 22* went through several phases of rebuilding and extension with red brick foundations (Fig. 5.19A). The messuage was divided into two *c*. 1778 and it appears that the plot went through a major rebuilding at this time, resulting in the layout depicted in a plan of 1792 (Fig. 5.19B). A large freestanding building, *Standing Buildings 42/65*, was constructed to act as offices, kitchens and a manufactory, indicating a considerable investment in the property. This may have occurred under the auspices of Francis Tunwell, who leased Plot IX in 1778 and also redeveloped Plot X.

Some of the pottery that was recovered from the demolition deposits of *Building 22* is very similar to material from another assemblage possibly linked to Tunwell (see Fig. 5.23G). Part of the late eighteenth-century building complex survived until 2005 in the form of four-storey freestanding *Standing Building 42*, which was 19m long by 6m wide, and single storey plus basement *Standing Building 65*, which was 4.5m long by 5m wide (Figs. 5.19–5.20). The two buildings were clearly integral to each other, with access to the staircase leading to the upper floors of *Standing Building 42* only possible from a staircase located inside the first floor of *Standing Building 65*. It seems likely, therefore, that the original function of the basement and ground floors of *Standing Building 42* was different to the upper floors, and that there was no direct access route between the two. *Standing Building 65* was described as offices in 1792 and 1862, whilst the lower floors of *Standing Building 42* were described as kitchens in 1862 and this may well

have been their original purpose. The function of the upper floors of *Standing Building 42* is unclear, but it may have been some form of manufactory. Overall, the construction of a four-storey building indicates a substantial investment in the plot.

Plot X (incorporating Plot XI)

In the early eighteenth century the frontage of Plot X was subdivided into five separate messuages, which subsequently underwent a series of developments. A substantial stable and another structure, which may have been a school associated with the northern messuage, were added to the rear of the built area in the early eighteenth century (*Standing Buildings 28* and *29*). At the same time, in the southern messuage the frontage building was rebuilt and several ancillary structures added. This latter messuage lost one of its wells in the late eighteenth century (*Well 38*), although two still remained (*Wells 37* and *41*) and a planting bed (*PB 10*) was dug. The most probable candidate for implementing the changes to the southern messuage was Francis Tunwell, the Christ's College cook and later a merchant who leased Plot X in 1769. Tunwell was mayor of Cambridge in 1768, 1777 and 1782 and then declared bankrupt by 1784 and was buried in the parish church in 1785 (Gray 1922, 50–1). Tunwell also leased Plot IX to the north in 1778, and may have been responsible for changes seen there.

The buildings at the rear of the complex were associated with the northern messuage and in 1726 Hugh Naish built a stable here, This was *Building 28*, which was aligned parallel to the street and measured 8.9m long by 5.0m wide. It contained a small brick-lined soakaway, presumably to dispose of liquid waste. It is likely that the stable originally had a more complex drainage system as well as a feeding trough, hay racks and stall dividers (Connah 2007, 123) that have not survived due to truncation. Modern stabling guidelines state that a standing stall should be 3.3m long with an additional 2.0m-wide passage; by these standards the building is slightly too narrow, but not excessively so. As stalls should typically be 1.7m wide, *Building 28* could have accommodated five or six horses. To the south of the stables was *Building 29*, a large structure that measured 9.3m by 6.8m in extent. Its original function is unknown but it was later used as a school.

At some point in the eighteenth century the southern messuage stopped being the Chequer Inn, although it remained the largest of the five messuages. Its frontage building, *Standing Building 20*, was rebuilt during the eighteenth century; the new structure measured 16m long by 7m wide and consisted of a basement and three storeys. The surviving core of the building had a traditional plan with a range parallel to the street and a short back wing. The street range had a ground-floor side passage at its southern end and a staircase was located in the east end of the back wing. A further structure – *Building 30*, which was represented by a series brick-built footings - measured 4.6 by 4.8m in extent and possessed a set of external stairs, indicating that the eighteenth-century building complex was originally more extensive. Attached to the rear of *Building 30* was brick-lined *Drain 1*, which led to the rectangular brick-lined *Soakaway 1* that collected rainwater from the roofs of *Standing Buildings 20* and *30*.

In the yard behind *Building 30* stone-lined *Wells 37* and *41* continued in use, but cask-lined *Well 38* went out of use *c*. 1760–80. The backfilling of *Well 38* contained part of an oak lid (Fig. 5.21C; see also Fig. 4.37A). This was not a cask lid as the battens do not go all the way to the side and it may have comprised a specially constructed lid to seal the top of the well. The backfilling also contained leather shoes, a fragment of decorated leather derived from a piece of upholstery or other furnishing (Fig. 5.21A; see also Fig. 4.37C–D), a knife (Fig. 5.21B), a dog, bones from a mixture of leather-working and food waste plus part of a horse. Immediately after the well's backfilling, *PB 10* was dug. This feature included a percolation fill that contained a range of material (MNI 52) including ceramics largely linked to dining, animal bone consisting of leatherdresser's and kitchen waste plus human cess.

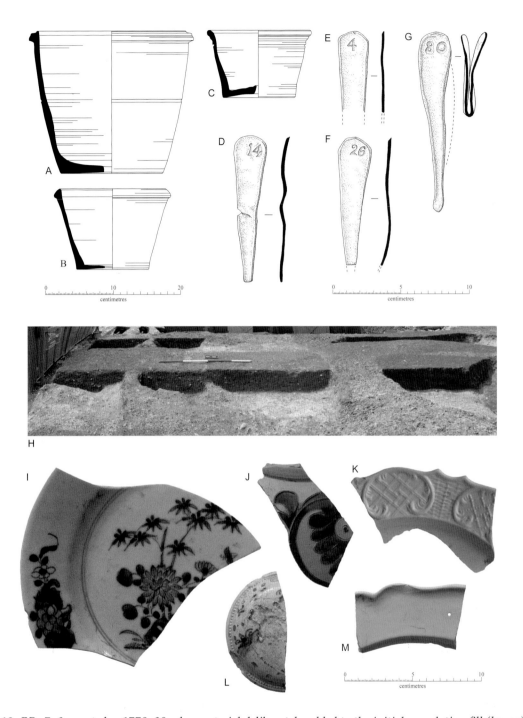

Figure 5.18. *PBs 7–8, created c. 1770–90, plus material deliberately added to the initial percolation fill (lower) and deposited during abandonment c. 1800–20 (upper) showing: (A) Late Unglazed Earthenware yellow flowerpot with rolled rim ([50245]); (B) Late Unglazed Earthenware red flowerpot with collared rim ([50244]); (C) Late Unglazed Earthenware yellow flowerpot with rounded rim ([50958]); (D) lead planting label, with the number 14 on one face ([50837]); (E) lead planting label, with the number 4 on one face ([50837]); (F) lead planting label, with the number 26 on one face ([51112]); (G) lead planting label with the number 80 on one face, which has apparently been deliberately bent over ([51112]); (H) photograph of PB 7, facing west; (I) Chinese Export porcelain plate with blue hand-painted floral and bamboo decoration, c. 1740–50 [50186]; (J) Westerwald stoneware vessel, probably a chamber pot ([50186]); (K) Staffordshire white salt-glazed stoneware dish or large plate with dot with diaper and basket pattern rim ([50193]); (L) creamware tea or coffee pot lid with blue hand-painted decoration ([50186]); (M) creamware dish or deep plate with Royal pattern rim, with a drilled hole from a repair ([50186]).*

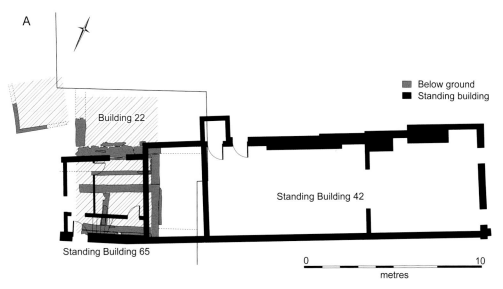

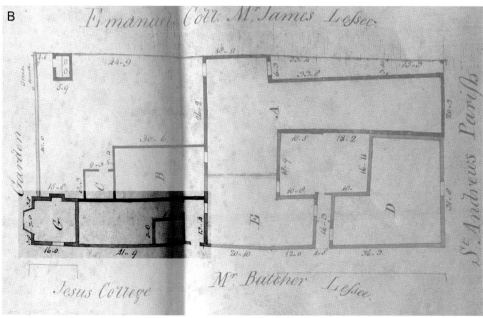

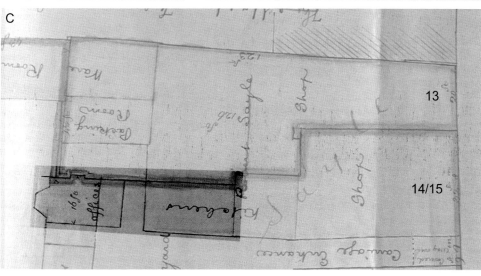

Figure 5.19. *Standing Buildings 42 and 65, plus Building 22: (A) the surviving standing buildings in 2005, plus below ground remains; (B–C) plans of Plot IX in 1792 and 1862 (plans B–C courtesy of the Master and Fellows of Jesus College Cambridge).*

Figure 5.20. *South elevation, cross-section and photograph, facing north, of Standing Buildings 42 and 65, also indicating footings of Building 22.*

Plot XII

In the large rear garden area of Plot XII limited evidence of a few minor structures was encountered (*Buildings 27, 28, Wall 8*) plus a planting bed (*PB 9*). Seventeenth-century *Gully 27* went out of use in the mid-eighteenth century. Its backfilling contained at least five clay tobacco pipes of *c.* 1740–80, including one manufactured by James Kuquit (active *c.* 1718–50) (Fig. 5.22A). Some gravel footings indicate that there was a lean-to structure situated behind *Building 28* (*Building 27*), while the brick-built footing of *Wall 8* indicates that it was either a freestanding wall or part of a small structure. There

238

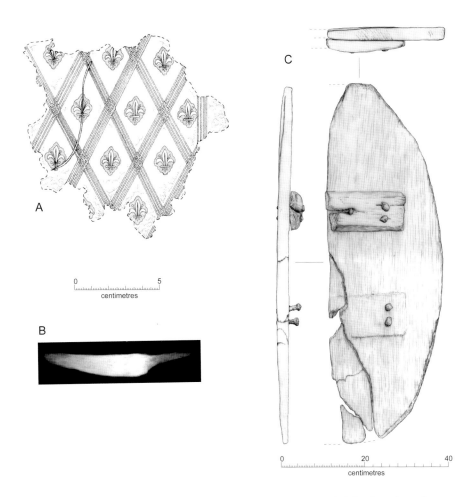

Figure 5.21. *Material recovered from the backfilling of Well 38 in c. 1760–80: (A) leather sheet fragment with stamped and tooled decoration, including a stamped fleur-de-lis motif in lozenges ([35392]); (B) iron whittle-tanged knife ([35392]); (C) oak lid ([35419]).*

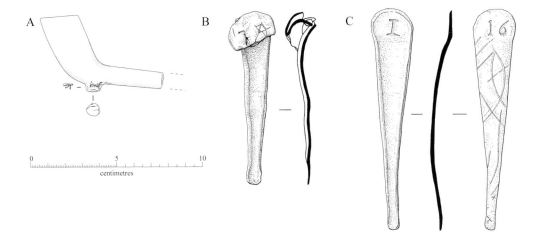

Figure 5.22. *Eighteenth-century material recovered from Plot XII: (A) type 10 clay tobacco pipe bowl of c. 1700–40 with initials IK on spur from Gully 27 ([32448]); (B) lead planting tag with the number 34 on its head, which has had notches pushed through it; found in association with a clay tobacco pipe bowl of c. 1730–80 ([31477] F.3296); (C) lead planting tag with the letter I on one side and number 16 on the other with line decoration; found in association with eighteenth-century pottery ([31427] F.6644).*

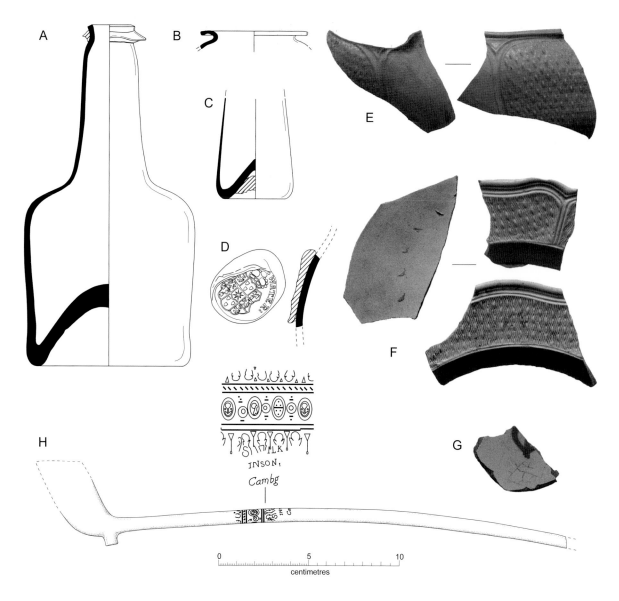

Figure 5.23. *Material recovered from the percolation fill of PB 9, dug c. 1760–80 ([32022]): (A) free blown squat cylindrical light green glass utility bottle with very thick patina, high rounded base kick with disc pontil scar and single applied collar below the lip, of c. 1750–60; (B) colourless free blown cylindrical glass phial with thin patina; (C) light green free blown conical glass phial; (D) rounded oval seal with part of body/neck of green free blown utility bottle, marked [PYRMONT] WATER around crowned shield with coat of arms; (E) Staffordshire white salt-glazed stoneware vessel, probably a sauce boat with seed pattern decoration on body; (F) Staffordshire white salt-glazed stoneware plate with 'barley' pattern rim and clearly visible stilt marks from firing; (G) English tin-glazed earthenware pedestalled bowl with decorated with a stylized leaf (Archer 1997, 179) on the inside of the base, probably an early–mid-eighteenth-century London product; (H) type 12 clay tobacco pipe bowl of c. 1730–80 with Wyer-style decoration of S WILK / INSON / Cambg.*

was also an oval or rectangular planting bed, *PB 9*, which was dug *c.* 1760–80 and possibly relates to the merchant Francis Tunwell. The percolation fill in its base (MNI 59) consisted mainly of glass bottles, principally for wine (Fig. 5.23A), but at least one contained imported mineral water from Pyrmont in Lower Saxony (Fig. 5.23D) which was popularized in England by George I (*r.* 1714–27), plus clay tobacco pipes (Fig. 5.23H) and coffee bowls. Two planting labels from 'garden soil' deposits attest to late eighteenth-century gardening activity (Fig. 5.22B–C).

Plot XIII

In 1723 Plot XIII was leased to Michael Headley, a tallow chandler and grocer, who appears to have been responsible for a phase of rebuilding including the construction of a well and two buildings in the plot head, plus the construction of a large building in the plot tail and substantial boundary walls. In the first instance, stone-lined *Well 45* (Figs. 5.24–5.26) was constructed in the plot head in a *c.* 2.3m-wide alleyway that lay to the south of the plot dominant building. *Well 45* had a timber baseplate made of Norwegian Scots

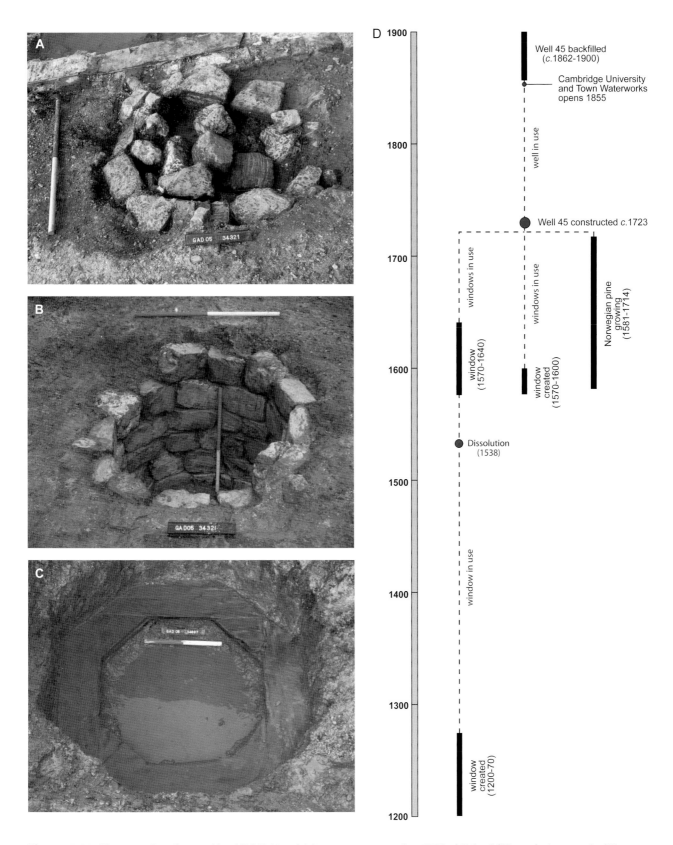

Figure 5.24. *Photographs of stone-lined Well 45, which was constructed* c. *1723: (A) backfilling, facing north; (B) stone-lining, facing south; (C) timber baseplate, facing south; (D) timeline of the well and the elements that it was constructed from.*

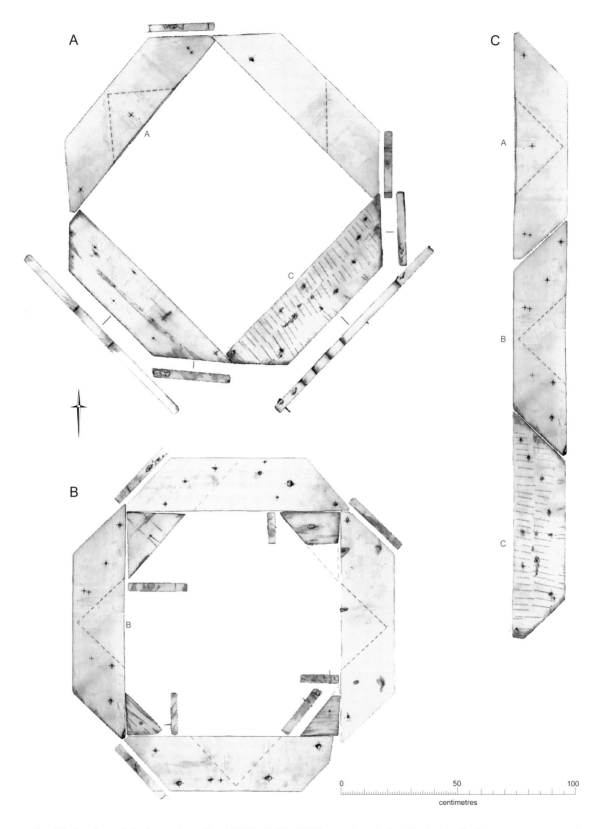

Figure 5.25. *Timber baseplate from stone-lined Well 45 ([34897]), constructed c. 1723: (A) the lower course of timber baseplate; (B) the upper course of timber baseplate; (C) reconstructed original board, which was used to form three boards in the baseplate.*

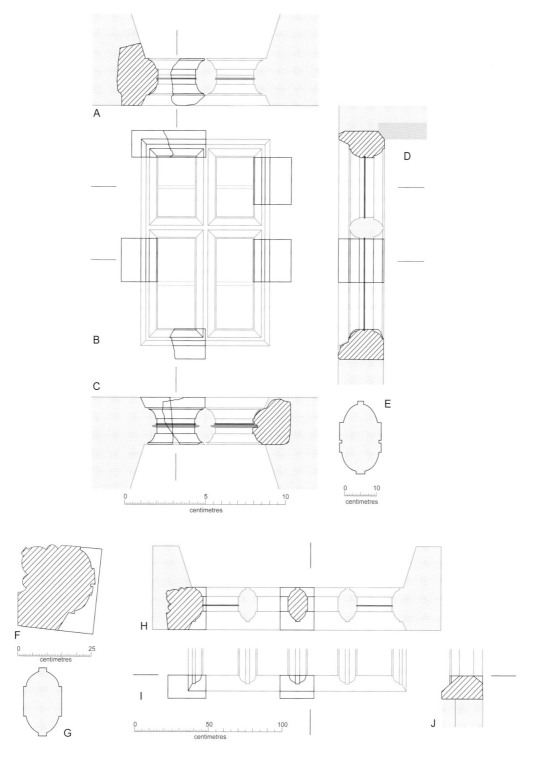

Figure 5.26. *Stone mouldings from windows reused in stone-lined Well 45 ([34897]), constructed c. 1723: (A)–(E) mullioned and possibly transomed domestic Clunch window of c. 1570–1600 showing: (A) plan of lower light; (B) external elevation of window; (C) reversed plan of upper light of window; (D) transverse sectional elevation of window; (E) restored mullion moulding of window; (F)–(J) Barnack stone sill from domestic window of c. 1570–1640: (F) recut stone, showing original thirteenth-century moulding in red; (G) restored central mullion moulding of window; (H) restored plan of sill showing partial fixed glazing of window; (I) restored elevation of sill of window; (J) transverse sectional elevation of central light sill of window (based on illustrations by Mark Samuel).*

pine felled after 1714 (Fig. 5.25) and its lining was composed of around 12 courses of reused moulded stone (c. 170 stones). This included blocks from two domestic windows of c. 1570–1640, which themselves reused thirteenth-century stone mouldings, and another piece of a thirteenth-century window (Fig. 5.26). One possibility is that these blocks derive originally from the nearby Dominican Friary (founded c. 1221–38) and were reused as part of a plot dominant building of Plot XIII constructed in the late sixteenth or early seventeenth century after the plot was acquired by Emmanuel College, which occupied the former site of the Dominican Friary in 1585.

On the northern side of the plot head two buildings were constructed. Firstly, stretching back up to 21m from the frontage were the fragmentary brick-built footings of *Building 31*, which measured 6.6m wide and c. 12.8m long. Abutting the rear of this structure were the brick-built footings and floor of small two-roomed *Building 32*, which measured 1.8m long by 1.55m long. *Buildings 31* and *32* formed the rear elements of the plot dominant building complex; their eighteenth-century function is unknown, although by the later part of the nineteenth century they comprised a kitchen plus office block and counting house respectively. Coeval with their construction a brick-built boundary wall – *Standing Building 105* – measuring 9in wide and 23 courses (c. 4ft) high with supporting pilasters, was constructed between Plots XI and XIII. Associated with the boundary wall were *Drain 2* and brick-lined *Soakaway 2* (see Fig. 5.46).

In 1744 a workhouse in the yard was mentioned for the first time. No trace of this structure survived archaeologically, but it can be correlated with a rectangular building depicted on a plan of c. 1815 that measured 67ft (20.4m) long by 16ft (4.9m) wide and

was divided into two rooms with some internal features, possibly fireplaces. Behind this another boundary wall, *Standing Building 110*, separating Plots XIII and XIV was constructed; this also measured 9in wide and 4ft high, with a wider (14in) return to the south at its western end. The Headley family continued to lease the plot for the rest of the eighteenth century; the only archaeological feature associated with their occupancy was *Pit 57* (see Case Study 9).

Plot XIV

In the eighteenth century a considerable amount of building work occurred at the front of Plot XIV, including a well of c. 1761 (*Well 46*), a cistern (*Cistern 1*) and a planting bed (*PB 11*) in the garden area behind. The plot dominant building was rebuilt c. 1730; it was described by the RCHM(E) (1959, 333, no.167) and was destroyed by fire in 1969, although the façade either survived or was recreated (see Fig. 5.30). *Standing Buildings 22–24* were described by Pevsner as 'a nice early eighteenth-century group, especially pleasant No.24 [Plot XIV] with keystone on the front' (2001, 246–7). A set of substantial 'H'-shaped brick footings, located at the rear are for a fireplace and chimney (*Building 33*). In the garden two substantial brick-lined features were constructed. The first, *Well 46*, was built c. 1761 with a baseplate made from wood felled in 1760 and was unusual in having a rectangular upper section and arched top with a circular shaft (see Case Study 10).

There was also rectangular *Cistern 1*, which had an arched roof fed by brick-lined *Drain 3*. Slightly later, c. 1770–90, *PB 11* was dug (Fig. 5.28A); possibly in association with a widow named Mary Ward. This consisted of a steep-sided, flat-bottomed rectangular trench with rounded ends that measured 4.45m long by 0.85m wide and over 0.65m deep. A considerable quantity of material

Case study 9: *Pit 57* incorporating specialist information from Craig Cessford and Andrew Hall

Pit 57 was initially recognized as a discrete 'cluster' of material during machining of the garden soil. Whilst no cut could be identified, it is assumed that the assemblage was contained within a small pit, although it is possible that it instead comprised the percolation fill of a small planting hole. The material appears to have been deposited c. 1760–80, when Plot XIII was occupied by the Headley family of grocers who resided there for around 90 years c. 1723–1815. The assemblage consisted almost entirely of pottery (MNI 18) plus a clay pipe (MNI one); in contrast to most late eighteenth-century assemblages, vessel glass and animal bone were conspicuous by their absence. The majority of the material appears to consist of some of the personal crockery belonging to Peter Headley and his wife/widow Frances, and its deposition was possibly related to the death of Peter in 1768. The group is not large and suggests *ad hoc* small-scale clearance of vessels that were no longer wanted, either because they were damaged or no longer fashionable.

The pottery (64 sherds weighing 1960g, MSW 30.6g) had an EVE of 4.55 (EVE per MNI 0.25) and was dominated by dining wares, consisting of plates (MNI five) (Fig. 5.27A–E) and bowls (MNI three). Tea and coffee drinking was also represented by tea bowls (MNI three), saucers (MNI one), a Sparrowbeak jug (MNI one) (Fig. 5.27F) and a coffee cup or can (MNI one). Tea drinking vessels included two pieces of English soft paste porcelain; a saucer (Fig. 5.27G) plus a tea bowl with a Chinosserie pattern that was manufactured in Worcester or Liverpool. A Chinese export porcelain coffee cup or can had Imari style decoration of c. 1710–30 (Fig. 5.27H), making it 30 to 70 years old when it was deposited and significantly older than the other material (none of which is likely to predate c. 1750). This material predates Peter and Frances Headley's occupancy and may have been inherited from Peter's uncle Michael Headley. There were substantial proportions of two chamber pots related to hygiene, one a piece of Westerwald stoneware from Germany decorated with floral roundels (Fig. 5.27I), the other a piece of tin-glazed earthenware with scenic decoration (Fig. 5.27J). A Nottinghamshire/Derbyshire stoneware jar would have been used for food storage and preparation. The clay tobacco pipe bore the stem mark of Samuel Wilkinson (active 1762, died 1787); the bowl can be typologically of c. 1730–80 and 115mm of stem survives, indicating rapid deposition (Fig. 5.27K).

Although the Headley family occupied Plot XIII for around 90 years and can be linked to a number of structural developments, there are only two assemblages that can potentially be linked to their occupancy, the other being *Soakaway 2* of c. 1813–23 (below). The grocery business was run by a succession of at least seven individuals, so the fact that only two associated assemblages were recovered indicates how most of their occupation has left few material traces.

Even these two groups are biased as they represent material deliberately selected for discard, probably a combination of damaged or chipped vessels and other pieces that were deemed too old-fashioned. This is apparent by the relative predominance of fabrics as it is likely that the dining and tea drinking vessels used by the Headley family at this date were dominated by creamware or possibly even pearlware, yet the vessels recovered are dominated by the old-fashioned Staffordshire white salt-glazed stoneware (MNI eight) with some creamware (MNI three) and no pearlware; it is likely that two-thirds of the deposited ceramic vessels (12 out of 18) were no longer current.

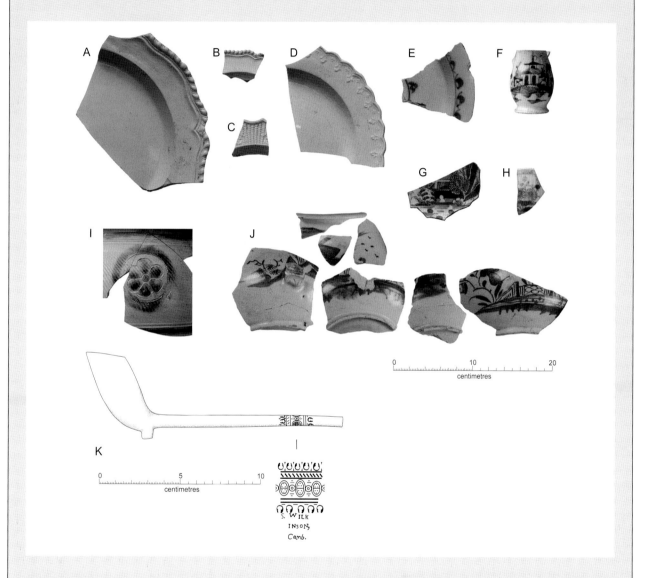

Figure 5.27. *Material recovered from Pit 57 of c. 1760–80 ([40408]): (A–B) Staffordshire-type white salt-glazed stoneware plates with 'bead and reel' pattern rims; (C) Staffordshire-type white salt-glazed stoneware plate with 'barley' pattern rim; (D) creamware plate with spearhead pattern rim; (E) English tin-glazed earthenware plate with simple floral or geometric decoration; (F) creamware sparrowbeak jug with hand-painted blue decoration showing oriental scene, of c. 1760–70; (G) English soft paste porcelain saucer with hand-painted blue cannonball pattern decoration with some old damage apparent, probably produced at Worcester; (H) Chinese Export porcelain coffee cup or can with Imari decoration, of c. 1710–30; (I) floral roundel from Westerwald stoneware chamber pot of c. 1740–60; (J) English tin-glazed earthenware chamber pot with hand-painted blue scenic decoration, probably produced in London; (K) type 12 clay tobacco pipe bowl of c. 1730–80 with Wyer-style decoration of S. WILK / INSON / Camb.*

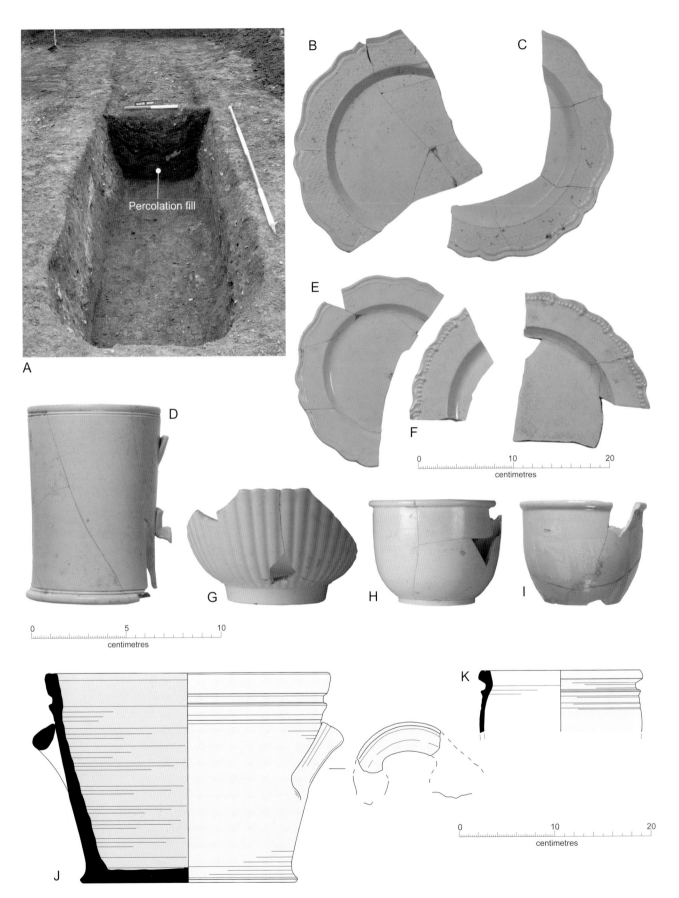

Percolation fill

A

B

C

D

E

F

G

H

I

J

K

0   10   20
centimetres

0   5   10
centimetres

0   10   20
centimetres

was introduced into its base to act as a percolation fill (MNI 60); this included quantities of ceramics mainly linked to dining and tea drinking (Fig. 5.28B–K), a considerable quantity of animal bone and some other material including a perfume bottle of Richard Warren of London. The animal bone mainly comprised domestic food refuse, which was dominated by mutton plus some beef, venison, rabbit, chicken, goose, duck and pigeon, but also included bones from a newborn pig suggesting that these animals were being raised in the plot.

Plot XV

During the early/mid-eighteenth century the frontage building in this plot was constructed, a well and two soakaways were built and an ancillary structure that appears to have formed a washhouse or laundry was appended. The frontage structure, *Standing Building 23*, had a basement and four storeys (Fig. 5.30). The eighteenth-century portion of the building had front and back ranges which both extended over the full width of the property. Between them a staircase ran from the basement to third floor, while a second service staircase occupied a slightly later turret (*Standing Building 106*). Some eighteenth-century full-height panelling survived, as well as other original features, and part of the building's constituent timber-framing was recorded (Fig. 5.31).

To the rear of *Standing Building 23* was a smaller structure, *Building 34*, which had brick-built footings that ended 19m from the frontage. In the passageway on the very northern side of the plot lay brick-lined *Well 47*; given its location, it could potentially have supplied water to Plots XIV and XV. Two rectangular brick-lined *Soakaways 3–4* were inserted into the southern side of seventeenth-century *Building 24* (Fig. 5.32A–B). One of the pair, *Soakaway 4*, had a relatively short lifespan and was backfilled *c.* 1780–90. Its infill did not contain a great deal of domestic material (MNI 13) but finds included a spills vase, a chamber pot with the initials GR for Georgius Rex (Fig. 5.32D), which probably refers to George III (*r.* 1760–1820), and a glass bottle (Fig. 5.32C). The second, *Soakaway 3*, is discussed further in Case Study 12. Behind *Building 24* narrow structure *Building 35* (Fig. 5.32A), which ran the width of the plot, was also added during this period. *Building 35* was divided into two by a relatively insubstantial internal wall and had a series of drains and related features in its northern half. These soakaways, drains and related features suggest that the plot tail buildings

Figure 5.28 *(opposite). PB 11, which was dug c. 1770–90, including the ceramics recovered from its percolation fill ([30200]): (A) photograph of the planting bed, facing south; (B–C) Staffordshire white salt-glazed stoneware plate with 'barley' pattern rim; (D) plain straight-sided Staffordshire white salt-glazed stoneware quart tankard with incised lines around the rim and base; (E) Queen's shape creamware plate; (F) feather-edged creamware side plate; (G) small creamware bowl with fluted body; (H) small plain creamware bowl with rolled over rim, probably for tea drinking; (I) small plain Staffordshire white salt-glazed stoneware bowl with rolled over rim, probably for tea drinking; (J) Late Glazed Red Earthenware flaring bowl with two horizontal side loop handles; and clubbed rim, glazed internally and externally; (K) Late Glazed Red Earthenware jar with clubbed rim, glazed externally.*

were used for some purpose that necessitated relatively large-scale water usage.

Plot XVI

A considerable amount of building work was conducted in Plot XVI during the early/mid-eighteenth century, affecting both the frontage building and the plot accessory structures to the rear. Plot dominant *Standing Building 24* was constructed in the early/mid-eighteenth century; it was of three storeys with a rear attic (Fig. 5.30). It also possessed a street range, which included the staircase, and a back wing with a few surviving original internal features. To the rear of the building a stretch of eighteenth-century boundary wall between Plots XV and XVI survived; it was 35 courses (7ft) high and had a return to the south at its western end. Behind this the existing *Building 25* was heavily altered. Its main room had several walls inserted, which subdivided it into four spaces and meant that the chimney was no longer in use, and there were also a number of internal features. Deposits associated with this phase included bone from a range of meat joints and a small amount of leatherdressers' waste.

It appears that after these alterations *Building 25* no longer functioned as a kitchen, although its new role is unclear. Several additional cellars and rooms were also constructed at this time, connecting *Building 25* to the plot dominant building on the frontage making this a continuous range of buildings. One of these, *Cellar 5*, employed reused pieces of stone moulding derived from a relatively high-status building of *c.* 1250–1400. Immediately behind *Building 25* lay *Cellar 6*, while further back *Wall 12* (see Fig. 7.2l) was constructed to separate off the plot tail. Behind this were two further relatively insubstantial structures, *Buildings 36–37*, which were represented archaeologically by rubble-filled linear footings that originally supported timber sill beams.

In *c.* 1780–90 *Cellar 6* was backfilled. The material that was deposited at this time represents the largest discrete late eighteenth-century assemblage from the site (MNI 123) and included pottery (Fig. 5.33B–D) mainly linked to dining and gardening, plus glass including two complete bottles (Fig. 5.33E–F) and animal bone. Some neonatal bones indicate that pigs were being raised on the plot. Four cats were also disposed of in the cellar and there were a range of birds. At the same time much of *Building 25* appears to have been used as a coal store as a substantial layer of coal dust containing a copper alloy triangular plate (Fig. 5.34B) accrued upon its floor.

Plot XVII

The frontage building of Plot XVII, *Standing Building 25*, consisted of three storeys and a basement. It was eighteenth-century in date, although most of the surviving eighteenth-century structural elements and fittings were limited to the rear wing and stairwell area. The underlying eighteenth-century structure originally had a street range and a back wing, which were separated by a staircase. Behind this seventeenth-century *Well 44* and *Building 26* continued in use, whilst in 1794 the rear of Plot XVIII was annexed as a 'necessary house'.

Plot XVIII

In the mid–late eighteenth century a phase of building occurred in the tail of this plot. This included brick-built dividing *Wall 13* which had brick and stone footings, brick-lined *Cellar 7* and square brick- and stone-lined *Cesspit 17* (see Fig. 7.2K). These changes may reflect the plot's transition from an inn, known as the *White Lyon* (1726) and the *Boar's Head* (1775), to a private residence by 1789.

Plots XIX–XXI

The only surviving archaeological remains in Plot XIX comprised a few fragmentary footings belonging to *Wall 14*; however, until the 1970s the southern part of the plot consisted of a 'little changed'

Case study 10: *Well 46* incorporating specialist information from Richard Darrah and Ian Tyers

Brick-lined *Well 46* had a baseplate constructed of two curving and two straight sections of oak, which were produced by a combination of sawing and hewing (Fig. 5.29B–D). The curving pieces came from a 1.5m long section of a 60-year old branch, which had its curved sides hewn before being sawn down its length into two halves. The straight pieces came from two different oak trees; one produced a 59-year tree ring sequence dated to 1702–60 inclusive

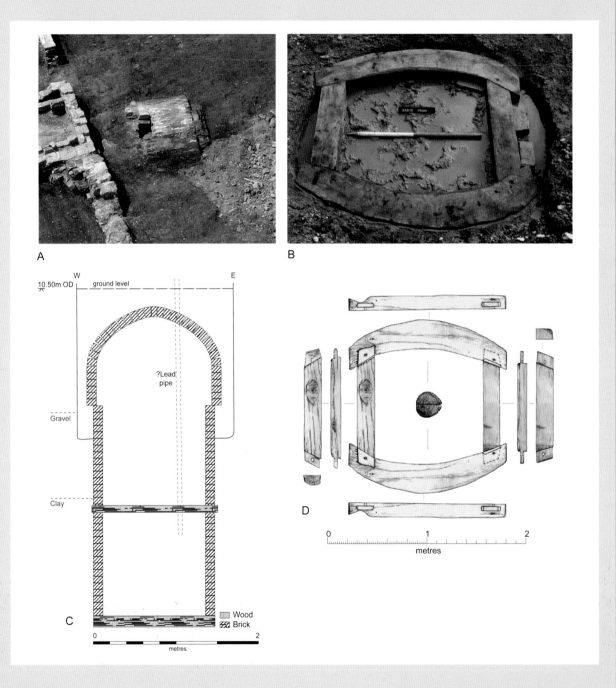

Figure 5.29. *Brick-lined Well 46, constructed c. 1761: (A) photograph of the arched top, facing northwest; (B) photograph of the timber baseplate, facing north ([35499]); (C) section; (D) timber baseplate ([35499]).*

by reference to English tree-ring data. This timber retained full sapwood and bark-edge, so the tree was felled in the winter of 1760. There is no evidence for re-use and as a halved log it is likely that it was sawn or selected specifically for this purpose, so the well was constructed in 1761 or soon after.

The four pieces of timber were connected by mortice and tenon joints, fastened by ash pegs. This relatively *ad hoc* use of material and traditional timber-framing techniques is similar to seventeenth-century well baseplates and differs from some eighteenth-century examples which used iron nails and boards purchased specifically for this purpose. The 1.45m-diameter

brick-lined shaft was built from a range of brick fabrics and was not mortared together. Around 1.6m up the brick-lined shaft, two squared sawn alder beams were set into holes between the bricks; these beams do not appear to have served any purpose other than to form a platform during construction. The uppermost part of the shaft broadened out to form a rectangular box measuring 1.6m by 1.3m in extent with an arched roof. A relatively small hole in the brickwork on the south-western side of this box indicates that the water was obtained through a lead pipe, which was eventually removed when *Well 46* went out of use. The well shaft was never backfilled and there is no clear evidence for when it went out of use; it almost certainly continued to function throughout most of the nineteenth century and possibly survived until a reorganization of the plot *c.* 1924–40.

four-storey building with basements of *c.* 1750 that was split into two houses, each with a front room used as a shop from an early date (Grey 1972, 20). By 1771 this part of the plot consisted of two houses with five cottages at the rear. Plot XX continued to be the Birdbolt Inn, lessees of which included Jonathon Pink (1750–5) who had some tin-glazed earthenware plates made, probably in London, that were marked *Pink at the/Birdbolt* (Fig. 5.34A). The extensive and impressive nature of this late eighteenth-century coaching inn is indicated by a plan of 1792.

Plot XXII

From 1723 onwards the investigated area of Plot XXII formed the rear portion of the Cock Inn. In the first half of the eighteenth century the plot was completely enclosed by substantial brick walls. The footings of one of these, *Wall 10*, contained a heterogeneous assemblage including large quantities of stone blocks derived from a medieval religious building plus earlier and later material. The overall impression of the reuse of unwanted reclaimed material from a builder's yard. Later in the century a cellar (*Cellar 4*), a timber-lined pit (*Pit 58*) and a building (*Building 38*) were constructed.

A series of three intercutting pits, *ADPs 10–12*, dug in the north-eastern corner of the plot may date to the either the late seventeenth or early eighteenth century; they have already been discussed above (see Figs. 5.13–5.14). Around 1720–50 Plot XXII was enclosed by substantial brick-built *Wall 10* along its northern side; this connected to the pre-existing eastern boundary, *Wall 4*, of Plot XIV, which was itself extended southwards behind Plot XV and probably further. The lowest foundation course of *Wall 10* consisted of large quantities of reused stone mouldings (Figs. 4.64 and 5.35–5.36). This was a heterogeneous group that had not been reshaped at all for reuse; the stones were simply placed in position and had mortar poured around them. The stone consists largely of pieces that were awkwardly shaped for reuse; they effectively represent the residue left after more useful building material has been removed. The bulk of the stone derived from a fourteenth-century religious building, but there was also some late twelfth-/thirteenth-century material and a few later pieces, one of which is no earlier than *c.* 1680.

Taken as a group the moulded stone could derive principally from a religious institution that originated in the twelfth century and where there was a major phase of fourteenth-century building, plus some later material. One possibility is that this material derives from the church of St Andrew the Great, which was rebuilt in the mid-seventeenth century (Chapter 6). Unfortunately, the few depictions of the church that pre-date this rebuilding are too generic to determine enough detail to confirm this hypothesis. If the more useful stone was reused in the rebuilding of the church this would mean that the

residue of less useful pieces remained unused for perhaps 75–100 years. The more recent pieces presumably represent accidental breakages, which were added to the existing collection of stone fragments. It is also possible that the material derives from elsewhere, although there are no particularly obvious candidates. There was some demolition of existing buildings at nearby Emmanuel College in the early eighteenth century, but Loggan's 1688 print indicates that these all post-dated the foundation of the College in the 1580s. Above the reused stone the wall foundations were made of brick, many of which also appear to have been reused as they were slop-moulded and this technique had been replaced locally during the sixteenth century. The construction of the boundary walls around the plot represents a relatively large investment and indicates a shift in function towards more intensive usage of the space.

In the mid-eighteenth century another boundary, *Wall 11*, was built along the eastern perimeter of the property just inside the earlier *Wall 4*. At the same time rectangular brick-lined *Cellar 4* (Fig. 5.37), which measured 2.45m (*c.* 8ft) long by 1.45m (*c.* 4ft9in) wide and over 1.2m deep was constructed. Located in the north-eastern corner of Plot XXII, this cellar incorporated a few pieces of reused medieval stone into its fabric. This cellar was cut down though the garden soil until the natural gravel was reached, partly truncating one of the buried cows (*ADP 10*). No floor was laid in the cellar; instead the firm natural gravel surface provided a base. The function of *Cellar 4* is unclear. There is no evidence for any particular entry point into it and it would not have made a useful place to undertake activities. It may have provided storage space, albeit rather damp, or it could be that the activity in the building above required substantial air circulation under the floor. To the south-southeast of the cellar was located rectangular *Pit 58*. This measured 1.5m by 0.75m in extent and *c.* 0.8m deep with vertical sides, indicating that it was originally plank-lined, and a flat base with a step in one end. In the late eighteenth century *Building 38* was constructed; only one wall foundation of this structure had survived. It was built from brick and employed some reused stone mouldings.

All of the above features relate to the Cock Inn, which was referred to in documentary sources from 1723 onwards. By 1798 the area was more built over than in 1688, with several substantial groups of buildings. The archaeologically investigated area of this plot lay at the end of a clearly defined lane with a dog-leg kink that ran from St Andrew's Hill. *Building 38* represents the eastern wall of a large building on the northern side of the lane that is shown on the plan of 1798 (Fig. 5.15). *Cellar 4* is not depicted on this plan, perhaps because the structure it formed a part of was not substantial enough to be included. Between 1753 and 1782 Plot XXII was owned by the Gibbons family, before passing into the hands of the Purchas family between 1782 and 1829.

No. 24   No. 23   No. 22

0 _____ 5
metres

Figure 5.30. *Elevation plus photograph, facing southwest, of the frontage of the 'nice early eighteenth-century group' Standing Buildings 22–4.*

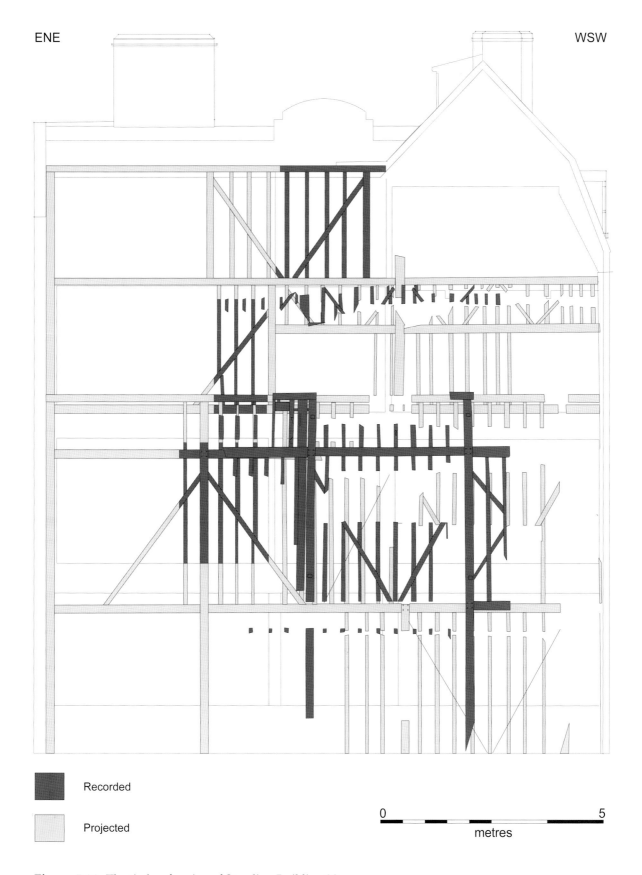

ENE

WSW

■ Recorded

▨ Projected

0   5
metres

Figure 5.31. *The timber-framing of Standing Building 23.*

251

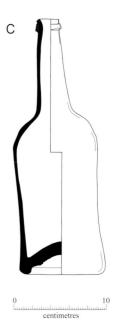

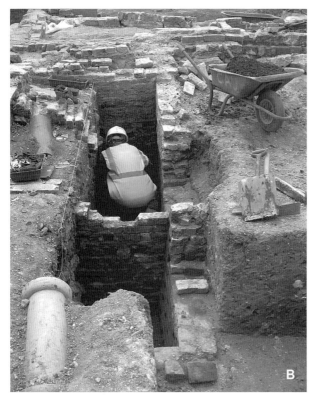

Figure 5.32. *Mid-eighteenth-century Soakaways 3–4 in Building 24, plus material from backfilling of Soakaway 4 c. 1780–90: (A) photograph of area, facing southwest; (B) photograph of Soakaways 3–4, facing west; (C) free blown cylindrical black glass utility bottle with thick patina, medium rounded base kick with glass tipped pontil scar and single applied collar below the lip, of c. 1780–1810 ([32702]); (D) scratch blue chamber pot with the initials GR (Georgius Rex) surmounted by a crown within a roundel ([32702]).*

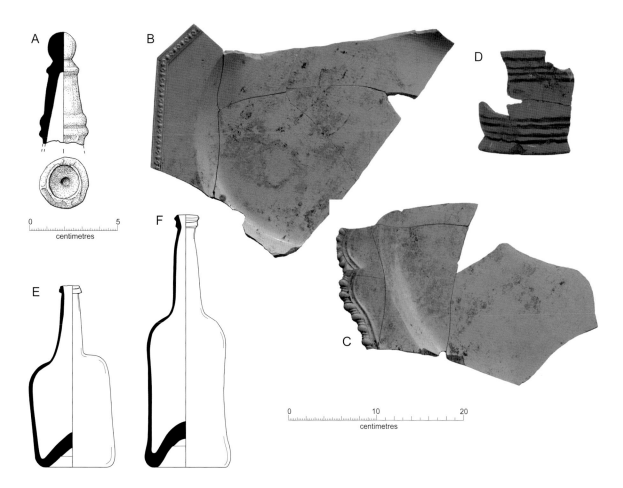

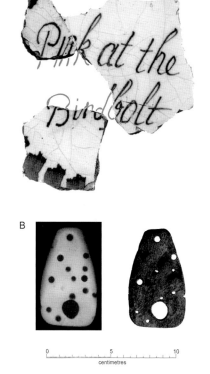

Figure 5.33 *(above). Material recovered from the backfilling of brick-lined Cellar 6 in c. 1780–90 ([32651]): (A) hollow cone-shaped pipeclay 'finial' with a ball on top of unknown function; (B) octagonal creamware serving dish or tureen stand with moulded diamond pattern decoration around edge; (C) Staffordshire white salt-glazed stoneware serving dish with 'bead and reel' pattern rim; (D) English tin-glazed earthenware storage jar or galley pot, of c. 1700–50; (E–F) two free blown cylindrical green glass utility bottles with patina. One has a high rounded base kick with disc pontil scar and long slender neck with single applied collar below the lip, of c. 1780–1820. The other has a high pointed base kick short body and neck and a single applied collar below the lip, of c. 1780–1820.*

Figure 5.34 *(right). Miscellaneous eighteenth-century items: (A) English tin-glazed earthenware sherds from plates marked Pink at the Birdbolt produced for the landlord Jonathon Pink, reconstructed from three sherds from separate vessels (originally recovered in 1905: see Hughes 1915, 425; (B) triangular copper alloy plate with drilled holes, probably a tool of some kind such as a leather worker's palm-guard, from Building 25 ([32692]) (photograph A courtesy of the Fitzwilliam Museum).*

253

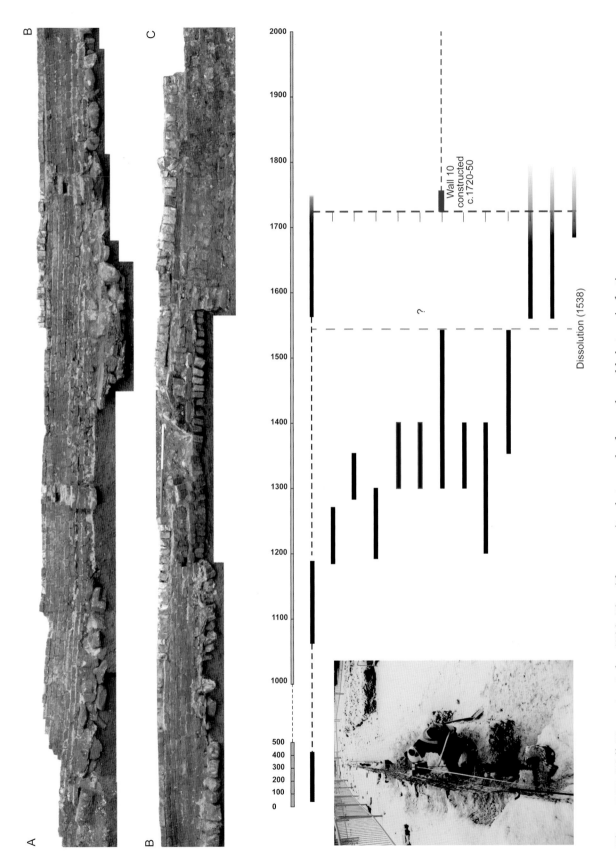

Figure 5.35. *Wall 10 constructed c. 1720–50, with composite photograph of reused moulded stone in footings ([40123]), facing north, and view of wall recording, facing east, and timeline of reused stone.*

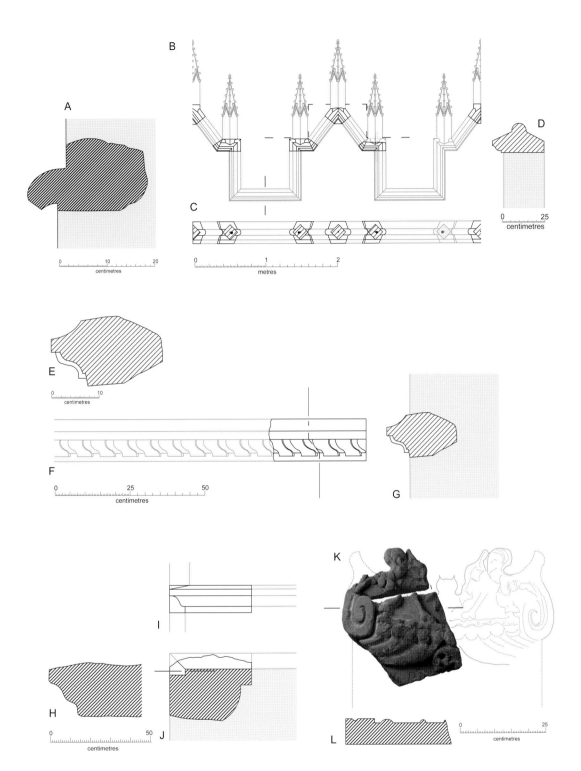

Figure 5.36. *Reused stone from footings of Wall 10 ([40123]) constructed* c. *1720–50: (A) chamfered beak of Barnack stone of* c. *1180–1270; (B–D) elevation and plan of parapet crenellation with wider coping made of Weldon stone* c. *1350 with: (B) elevation showing surviving elements; (C) plan showing surviving elements; (D) coping moulding; (E–G) Ketton stone cyma reversa cornice of* c. *1560–1800, showing: (E) composite section of moulding; (F) restored elevation detail; (G) moulding employed as string course; (H–J) Oolitic limestone Norman engaged column base with intermediate reuse as a cyma recta cornice* c. *1560–1750, showing: (H) weathered moulding as found; (I) elevation detail; (J) reversed plan showing ?primary Romanesque angle shaft (red); (K–L) Ketton stone gravestone of* c. *1680–1800 showing surviving fragments and partial reconstruction of elevation (K) and section (L) (based upon illustrations by Mark Samuel).*

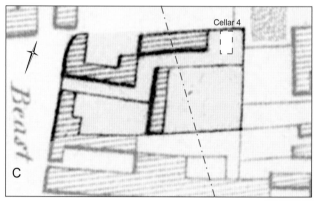

Figure 5.37. *Mid-eighteenth-century Cellar 4: (A–B) photographs of cellar, facing west and north respectively; (C) Plot XXII as depicted in a plan of 1798.*

Nineteenth century incorporating specialist information from Steve Allen, Tony Baggs, Rachel Ballantyne, Richard Darrah, Andrew Hall, David Hall, Vicki Herring, Rosemary Horrox, Mark Samuel, Ian Tyers and Anne de Vareilles

In many respects, the nineteenth century represents the period of greatest change to have occurred within the Grand Arcade street block since occupation first commenced in the eleventh century (Figs. 5.38–5.40). Moreover, this pattern was replicated all cross the Barnwell Gate suburb. The area as a whole underwent massive redevelopment, becoming largely built over and – for the first time – fully urban in character. Contributing to this transformation was the fact that the King's Ditch no longer existed as a discrete entity; infilled and sealed over, its former course was now followed by Tibb's Row (Chapter 3). Across the suburb the degree of building coverage, or proportion of the area covered by buildings (Conzen 1968, 123), rapidly expanded; at Grand Arcade many of the resultant structures survived to be recorded in 2005–6, either as

standing buildings or else as substantial below-ground foundations. The quantity of material being deposited within discrete feature groups – a practice that had first emerged in the 1760s – also escalated.

This increase in archaeological remains (Figs. 5.38–5.39) also coincided with a significant expansion in the quantity and quality of the associated documentary and cartographic evidence, although multiple occupancy and a high level of population mobility, both common features of nineteenth-century urban centres (Pooley 1979) do somewhat hinder attempts to link archaeological material to specific households. Nevertheless, the variety of newly available sources – which include in particular census returns and trade directories – provide a previously unparalleled level of detail. So much so, that, by the middle of the nineteenth century, there is if anything a *surfeit* of information. Asa Briggs has argued that it is 'tempting in considering Victorian things to treat them entirely archaeologically' (1988, 16) and whilst that approach will not be adopted here, it is important to introduce a greater degree of selectivity with regard to documentary and cartographic sources than was necessary in earlier centuries. Amongst the greatly increased body of cartographic sources that are available in relation to this period, the 1st Edition Ordnance Survey map (Fig. 5.40) – which was surveyed in 1885 – is of particular importance as it represents the first plan that can be unambiguously correlated with the archaeological remains.

The population of the street block increased significantly during this period, rising to 351 by 1881. This in turn stimulated an intensive programme of nineteenth-century building. These developments were of several types, whose forms varied depending on the nature of the plots within which they were constructed. The most spectacular took place in those locations where large open areas had survived into this period, such as Plot XXII, which was subdivided and exploited in several ways, and Plot XII, which became part of a department store. Another significant focus of activity were long plots which had effective rear access for vehicles and retained a significant proportion of open space; the only pre-existing example of this type was Plot XIII, which continued to develop successfully as a grocery business. In the nineteenth century this was joined by Plot XVII, which the Barrett family of ceramic retailers successfully expanded. The shorter, and commensurately smaller, plots that had no rear access were less easily developed, although it was still possible to exploit these. Examples of this include a photographic studio that was established in Plot X and a densely packed group of houses in Plot XIX.

Overall, the wealth of archaeological, architectural, documentary and cartographic information that is available for this period means that the nineteenth-century tenement narratives are the most complete – in terms of both range and nuance – of any century in the site's millennium-long history. A wealth of additional material can also be found within the associated digital-only volume. Excluded from the following discussion is the Robert Sayle department store, as its mid-nineteenth–twentieth-century development will be related separately (see below).

Plots I–VII

The northernmost portion of the street block, including Plots I–VII, was either not investigated archaeologically or produced no nineteenth-century remains, while a series of tail end plots linked to Tibb's Row are discussed elsewhere (Chapter 3). Plots I–VII were all heavily developed during the nineteenth century and several new plots were created through subdivision, including four on Post Office Terrace and eight small plots at the Blue Lion Yard.

Plot VIII

In this plot late eighteenth-century *PBs 7–8* went out of use *c*. 1800–20, probably due to a redevelopment that occurred prior to 1824. When the planting beds were abandoned a large quantity of material was deliberately dumped into them (MNI 109). Most of this assemblage was gardening-related in nature. It included 67 flowerpots (see Figs. 5.18A–C and 7.2P), two saucers and nine lead planting labels (see Fig. 5.18D–G). An iron peg and trowel may have been gardening tools and some window glass and caming could derive from a greenhouse. The disposal of so much material, particularly flowerpots, not affected by the vagaries of fashion suggests that this represents the end of intensive gardening in this plot (see also Cessford 2014b, 259). In 1856–60 Robert Sayle took over the plot, using most of it for his drapery business (see below), while the rear portion was carved out to become tail end plot 4 Tibb's Row (Chapter 3).

Plot IX

By the early nineteenth century Plot IX had been divided into two frontage plots, while the garden area to the rear had been amalgamated with the garden behind the plots to the south. In 1814 the southern plot was described as 'a capital brick-fronted house with a parlour, a good sized drawing room and several bedrooms'. These plots became part of the Robert Sayle premises in 1851 and around this time some domestic debris was deposited in *Pit 68* (MNI 39). The final stages of Plot IX as an independent entity are depicted on a plan of 1862.

Plot X

By the early nineteenth century there were five separate buildings along the frontage of Plot X. In 1814 the northernmost building comprised a 'substantial very well built residence' with two good parlours, a drawing room, seven bedrooms and servants' rooms. This plot utilized *Building 28*, which was a stables by 1862, and *Building 29*, which was converted to a coach house soon after 1814. Brick-lined *Well 48* was constructed by 1814; somewhat unusually it had no timber baseplate and it may have been a communal feature, located in a 'back room' accessible from several of the frontage plots. The buildings and well were demolished after Robert Sayle leased the plot in 1874 (below). As part of this same process the soakaway of *Building 28* was also backfilled. Its infill contained a substantial portion of a Willow pattern tureen cover and base. There are no remains relating to the second frontage building, which was occupied by Robert Sayle in 1878.

The frontage of the third and fourth plots from the north, *Standing Building 18/19*, still survives largely in its late nineteenth-century form. This was combined behind a single façade *c*. 1866–9 (Fig. 5.41A–B), when it was occupied by the chemist Henry James Church who occupied the northernmost building in 1866 and the combined 'newly builded' plot from 1869 onwards. The three-storey brick building, which retained earlier basements, is distinguished by three symbols on the keystones of the first floor window arches (Fig. 5.41C–E). The design on each of these is different; the southernmost is a foliage decoration with a stylized lotus flower at the top; in the centre is a Caduceus, two snakes entwined around the winged staff of Hermes, generally taken to be a symbol of the medical profession (Engle 1929; Friedlander 1992; Garrison 1920). Interestingly the true symbol of medical practice is generally accepted to be the single snake entwined around the unwinged staff of Aesculapius, both only coming into common usage in the twentieth century (Wilcox & Witham 2003). The northernmost symbol consists of a bunch of grapes flanked by vine tendrils. All of these symbols are closely paralleled by some of those in a more extensive series of seven on a nearby mid-nineteenth-century three-storied building at 41–45 Sidney Street, suggesting a local architectural tradition. Also associated with the 1866–9 rebuilding was *Pit 60*, which contained only glass bottles (MNI 20), 12 of them pharmaceutical.

The southernmost frontage structure, *Standing Building 20*, was modified in the early nineteenth century and in 1814 was described as a 'well built residence' with a 'handsome flight of steps and stone entrance'. Three planting beds were created in the rear yard in the

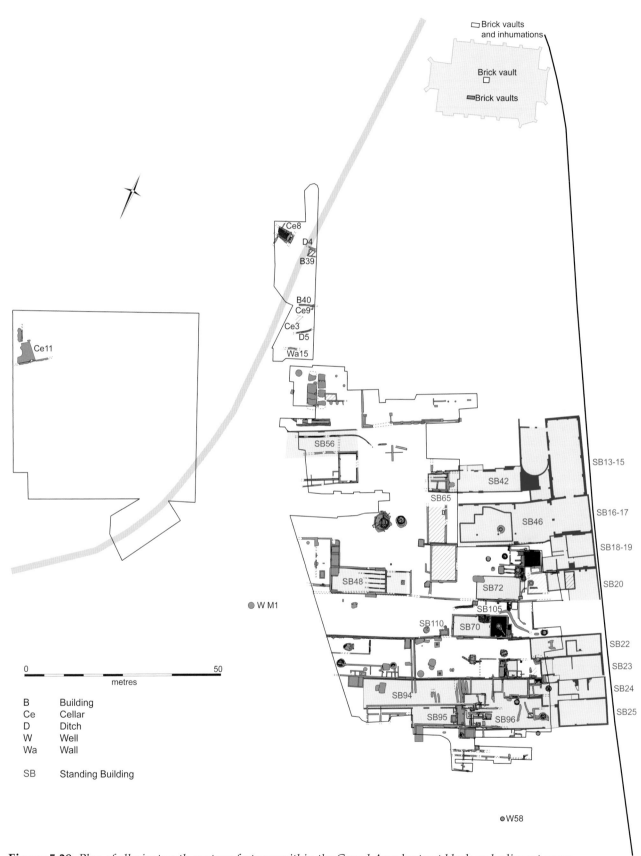

Figure 5.38. *Plan of all nineteenth-century features within the Grand Arcade street block and adjacent areas.*

ADP Animal disposal pit
B   Building
C   Cesspit
Ce   Cellar
Ci   Cistern
Dr   Drain
F   Foundation
P   Pit
PB   Planting beds
PH   Planting hole
S   Surface
So   Soakaway
W   Well
Wa   Wall
WC   Water closet

Illustrated section
Standing Building

0   25

metres

Figure 5.39. *Plan of main excavation area at Grand Arcade in the nineteenth century.*

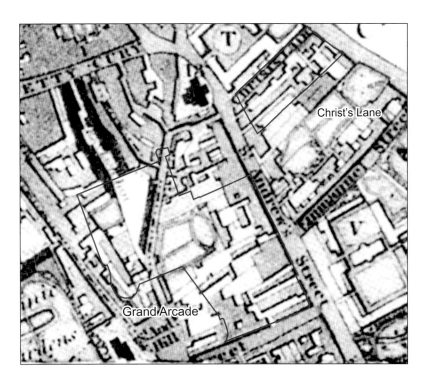

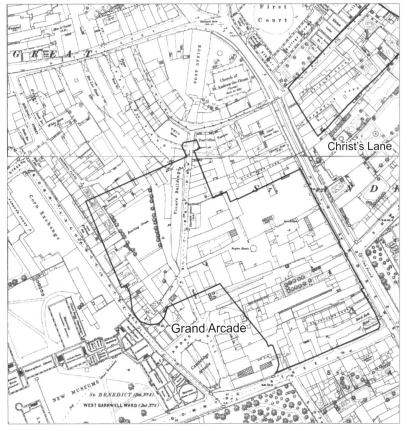

Figure 5.40. *Nineteenth-century maps of the area, including: (A) map published by Baker in 1830; (B) 1st edition Ordnance Survey map surveyed in 1885.*

Figure 5.41 *(opposite). The frontage of Standing Building 18/19, which was constructed c. 1866–9: (A) photograph of the frontage, facing west; (B) elevation of the frontage; (C–E) decorated stone keystones from window arches showing foliage decoration with a stylized lotus flower at the top (southern), caduceus with two snakes (central) and a bunch of grapes flanked by vine tendril (northern); (F) stone plaque over the door showing a pestle and mortar with an owl, the symbol of the Roman goddess of medicine Minerva, sitting on one edge holding a scroll in one claw. To either side are the dates 1851 and 1934; the scroll beneath has a Latin motto which appears to read SCIENDO ET C??ANDO.*

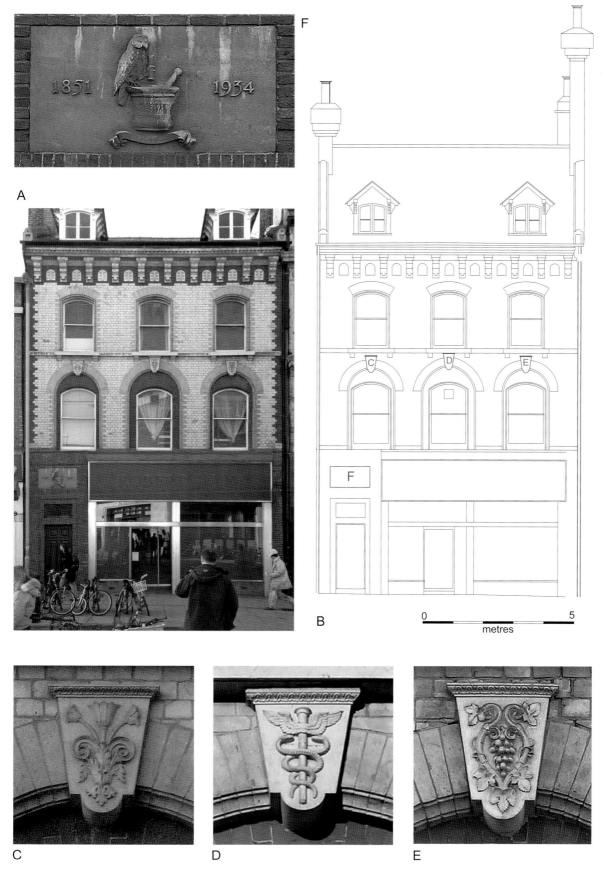

F

A

B

0 _____ 5
metres

C

D

E

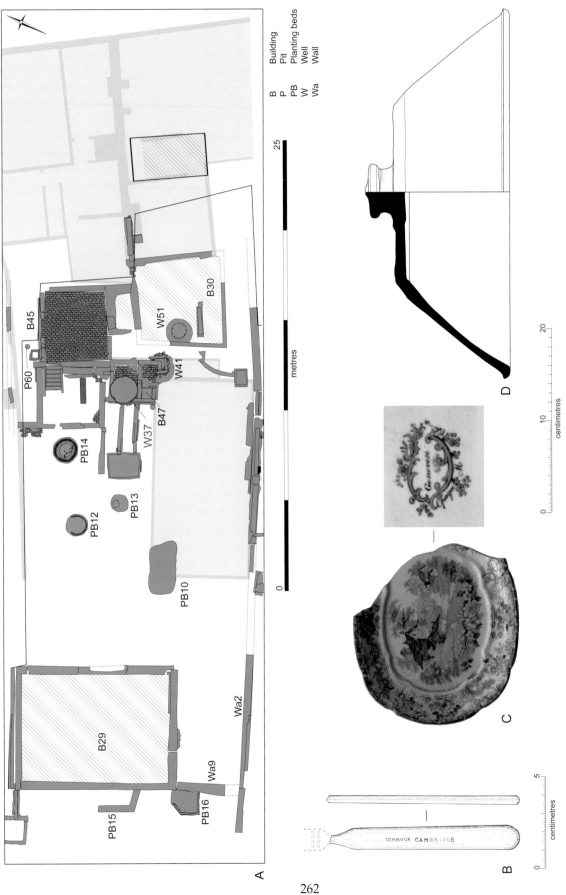

Figure 5.42. *Plan of Plot X in the nineteenth century plus material recovered from the initial backfilling of Well 37 in c. 1855–8 ([34524]): (A) Plan of nineteenth-century archaeological features; (B) brush handle, probably made from cattle long bone, likely to be a toothbrush and marked DIMMOCK CAMB[RIDG]E; (C) oval whiteware plate with blue transfer-printed decoration of Alpine chalets in a romantic setting, pattern mark Genevese, also Opaque M China; (D) large circular Late Unglazed Earthenware (red) cover with a knob-shaped handle, which may be a domed ceramic baking cloche used to bake bread.*

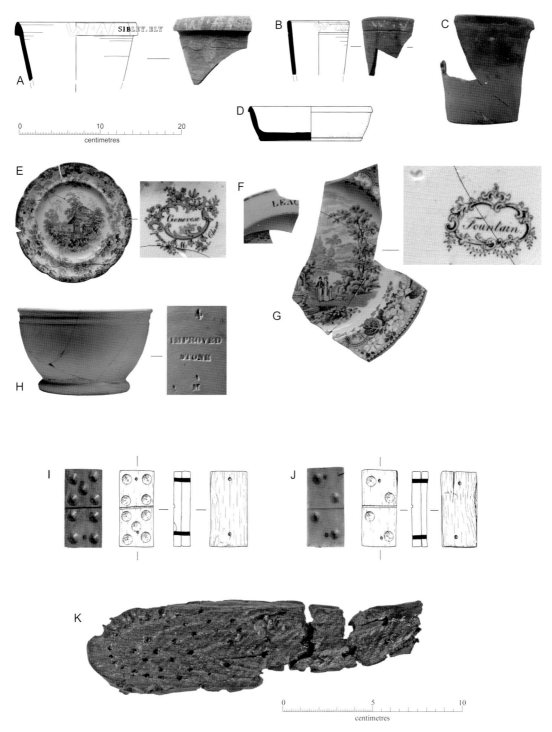

Figure 5.43. *Material recovered from the main backfilling of Well 37 in c. 1855–8 ([34338]): (A) Late Unglazed Earthenware (red) flowerpot with square-collared rim. Impressed roller stamp on rim SIB[LEY ELY] and white painted letters W·N; (B) Late Unglazed Earthenware (red) flowerpot with straight rim, and white painted letters W·N; (C) Late Unglazed Earthenware (red) flowerpot with square-collared rim, traces of red and black paint; (D) Late Unglazed Earthenware (red) saucer for flowerpot with square rim that has been painted red; (E) whiteware Genevese pattern plate; (F) whiteware plate with brown bands marked LEAC[H]; (G) a whiteware plate with blue transfer-printed decoration of a country garden scene, blue transfer pattern mark Fountain, in cartouche and impressed number 6; (H) a fine-grained white stoneware mortar marked 4/IMPROVED/STONE/M; (I–J) bone dominoes with wood plates, possibly of ebony, attached by pairs of copper alloy rivets; (K) willow brush back.*

early nineteenth century (*PBs 12–14*); *c.* 1840–60 these went out of use and *Wells 37* and *41* were backfilled. *Well 37* contained 139 items (MNI) (Figs. 5.42–5.43), which were probably deposited at a time of change and 'household succession' (Grover 2004). This could have been either in 1845, when William Newby a coal merchant died, or later *c.* 1852–58 when his widow Elizabeth Newby, a College servant, vacated the plot. As the backfilling of the well probably happened after the opening of the Cambridge University and Town Waterworks in 1855, the assemblage probably dates to *c.* 1855–8. Elizabeth moved to smaller premises without a significant garden at 18 Park Side, Parker's Piece, and all her children had left Cambridge by 1861 which may explain why the material was deposited. The assemblage therefore relates to a household of one or two adults, their four children, two servants and perhaps an additional visitor. The assemblage is dominated by dining related material, including a Genevese pattern dining service (Figs. 5.42C and 5.43E) showing Alpine chalets in a romantic setting, although they also had other services and possessed some relatively good quality Copeland and Garrett ceramics. This suggests that the family, and Elizabeth Newby in particular, subscribed to growing ideas of domesticity and gentility (Fitts 1999). There is also significant evidence for drinking alcohol, including imported wine.

Gardening is also prominent with 22 flowerpots (Figs. 5.43A–C and 7.2O) and two saucers for holding them (Fig. 5.43D). Some of the flowerpots were manufactured by the Ely potter Robert Sibley and two are marked with white painted letters WN, directly linking them to William Newby. The deposition of so much gardening-related material, combined with the abandonment of the planting beds, suggests that William and possibly Elizabeth Newby had a particular passion for gardening, but that the next occupants, the Price family did not and converted the yard so it could be used for other purposes (Cessford 2014b, 259). Uncommon vessels linked to food preparation, and presumably demonstrating the influence of Elizabeth Newby, included a large earthenware cover with a knob handle used to bake bread (Fig. 5.42D) and a white stoneware mortar (Fig. 5.43H). Other interests are indicated by the presence of two dominoes (Fig. 5.43I–J) and a probable bone gaming piece, while there were also some wooden brushes (Fig. 5.43K) and a worked bone brush handle from a toothbrush (Fig. 5.42B), inscribed DIMMOCK CAM… indicating that it was either made locally at Dimmocks Cote, or by a business in Cambridge run by someone with that surname.

Plot dominant *Standing Building 20* was rebuilt *c.* 1867–69, its most notable feature being the rather grand Romanesque-style doorway to the side passage (Fig. 5.44A–C). This has an ornate semi-circular arched top with three parallel layers, set on a group of round and squared pilasters with highly decorated capitals. In each of the spandrels above the arch is a recessed roundel, containing ornate intertwined letters WM (Fig. 5.44C). These initials can be linked to William Mayland or Maitland, a photographic artist who occupied part of Plot X *c.* 1864–69. This door and passage provided access via a staircase to the upper floors of *Standing Building 20*, which were used as offices, and to the rear yard area. As part of the same building campaign an unorthodox structure, *Standing Building 72* (Fig. 5.45), was also constructed in the rear yard as a purpose-built photographic studio for Mayland. There was no evidence for a ground floor doorway in the original two-storey structure.

Standing Building 72 measured 10.5m by 5.5m and had a timber frame infilled with lath and plaster set on brick dwarf walls four courses high. It appears to have been accessed solely by an external stairway which led to the first floor. This was an open studio space with large opening windows along the north wall designed to allow light to enter from the north, which would have been unimpeded as there was an adjacent open yard area. North light, also known as reflected or indirect light, is preferred by photographic artists as it negates the effect of the sun moving during the day and gives the artist much greater control. The pitched slate roof was not original, and it is likely that originally the northern side of the roof was paned with glass to allow more light to enter. The ground floor was entered

via an internal staircase and was divided into three spaces. None of the ground floor windows or doors that were ultimately present were original to the building and it seems likely that these ground floor spaces were used as darkrooms.

As Mayland had been based in Cambridge since *c.* 1858 and his initials are present above the passage doorway it seems likely that *Standing Building 72* was purpose-built for him and that he may have had a hand in designing it. In May 1869 the plot was described as including a 'photographic studio', but Mayland left soon after. The studio was then used by the figurative painter and engraver Robert Farren, the son of a local photographer, and members of his family including his daughter Amy, an artist and porcelain painter (*c.* 1869–81). It is unclear whether photography continued at the premises, although it appears that it may have been envisaged in 1875. By 1881 *Standing Building 72* had been converted into a school, so it had a relatively short use life for the function it was designed to fulfil. It was presumably at this stage, if not before, that windows were inserted into the ground floor to convert it from darkrooms to more useful space, although there is no evidence that a ground floor door was added.

Standing Building 20 had no basement and its rooms included a parlour, a good drawing room, several bedrooms, a convenient kitchen and a small walled garden. The second floor of the rear wing had a mansard roof, which may have been an addition of the early nineteenth century to convert the roof space into a usable room. In the rear yard eighteenth-century *PB 10* continued in use and three *PBs 12–14*, two of them brick-lined, were created in the early nineteenth century during the occupation of the plot by the coal merchant William Newby (1822–45). All of these features went out of use *c.* 1840–60 when the garden area underwent a major reorganization. At the same time two pre-existing stone-lined wells, *Wells 37* and *41*, were backfilled. One of these, *Well 41*, contained relatively little material, although there was leatherdressers' waste from the skins of 11 sheep and a bone from a tawny owl that may have lived nearby. The other, *Well 37*, contained much more material (Figs. 5.42–5.43).

Later in the century a new brick-lined well, *Well 51*, was built in the yard and two ancillary structures, *Buildings 46–47*, were constructed, indicating that the plot was being more intensively utilized. In 1867–69 the frontage building *Standing Building 20* was extended forward by about a metre and in May 1869 it was described as a 'part new builded brick built house' (Fig. 5.44). The cellar below the front room was largely infilled and the ground floor, which had been *c.* 0.5m above street level, was lowered to only *c.* 0.15m above. The old front wall of 2in brick was demolished and a new one of grey 3in brick was erected above a new glazed shop front with a central entrance and an elaborate doorway to the side passage.

Structurally, the extended upper floors were supported on nibs, formed by short lengths of the old front, which in turn held up the old floor plates which were strengthened by iron plates or flitches sandwiched between additional timbers carrying short joists to the new front wall. The structure of the old roof was retained but rafters to a lower pitch were added to the front to extend the roof over the extra metre. Internally there was some refitting. A white marble fireplace surround was put into the first floor front room and the small south room on the second floor front was given a corner fireplace.

The floor of the side passage was always close to street level. It was boarded and had heavy joists bridging a narrow brick-walled cellar. The rear wall above the ground floor was rebuilt in 3in brick, presumably in the 1880s. That was subsequently masked by the addition of service rooms containing sinks and WCs on each floor. The new back wall was timber-framed and weather-boarded. It is possible that until the second half of the twentieth century the old staircase existed to the ground floor and cellar and could be approached by a staircase from the side passage. The lower part of the stairs was removed to enable the shop to extend as a single room into the back wing and a new stair to the first floor was provided, parallel to the passage and taking part of the south side of the shop. The cellar below

A   B   C

Figure 5.44. *The frontage of Standing Building 20, which was constructed c. 1867–9: (A) photograph of the frontage, facing west; (B) elevation of the frontage; (C) photograph of intertwined initials WM in spandrels over a doorway arch; (D) plan of the property, based upon a plan of the mid-1870s and archaeological evidence.*

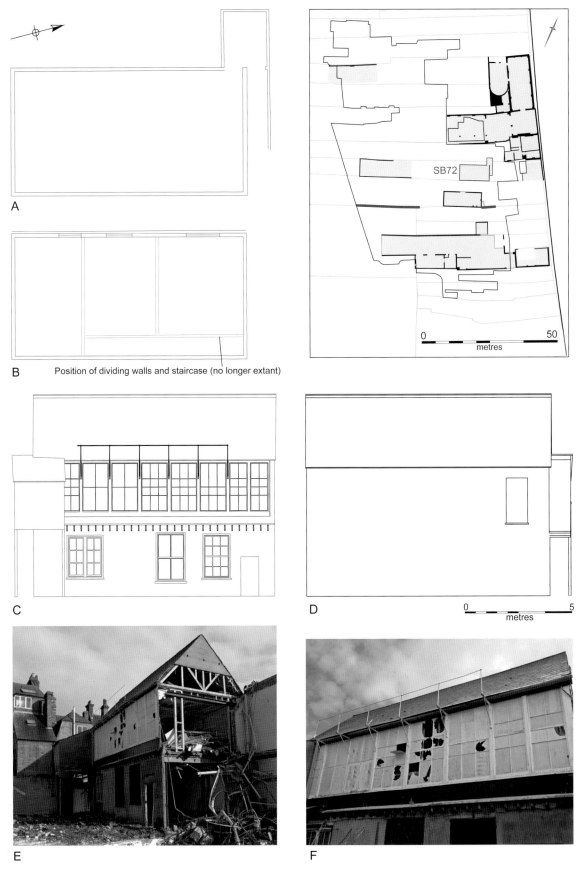

A

B

Position of dividing walls and staircase (no longer extant)

SB72

0   50
metres

C

D

0   5
metres

E

F

the stair was then reduced and could be approached only by a trap door. It may have been then that the cellar below the passage was partly infilled with loose rubble.

The ground floor of *Standing Building 72* (Fig. 5.45), which was open when recorded, was formerly divided into three rooms, each with a window to the north. A faint scar on the south wall indicated the position of a former internal staircase leading to the first floor. The west gable wall had been removed and an opening in the north wall was clearly a late insertion. Between the east and middle windows in the north wall was an area of brick infill that may represent an earlier door, but looks more likely to be a later insertion or repair. There was also a door opening in the east gable wall, which also appears to be a later insertion. The first floor was an open studio space with large opening windows along the north wall. It was also approached by a later covered external staircase against the northeast corner. Fragments of 'artistic' wallpapers survive beneath later decorations on both floors, including a scheme of foliage on the internal staircase and a variety of successive patterns on the ground floor. The first floor ceiling was tongue-and-groove. In the east end of the south wall was a blocked later doorway, possibly intended to provide access to a fire escape that no longer existed.

The external staircase, which accessed the first floor in its northeast corner, appeared from the outside to be a secondary feature. It was brick built rather than lath and plaster and was quite precariously supported on a late-looking red brick wall to the east and a wooden 'leg' on its northwest corner, which appeared modern and is likely to be a replacement. Internally, however, the picture was not as straightforward. On the first floor the pattern of windows ended with a 'half' window at the east end, however this was an opening casement in its own right rather than half of a blocked or removed larger window. It is possible that there were originally nine windows; there is certainly space to complete the run across the whole first floor, but if this is the case then no trace of the 'missing' windows survived. Additional evidence is present on what would be the outside wall of the studio, but within the staircase structure, where there are the remains of a dado rail and moulded skirting with decorated anaglypta wallpaper between. Truncation of this decoration suggests that the present door to the first floor was a later insertion, but that it is a replacement for an earlier door integral with the decorative scheme. The most likely interpretation is that there was always an external staircase attached to the building, but that the recorded structure was the replacement for an original feature. It appears that access to the building was at first floor level, with the internal staircase used to access the ground floor, explaining the apparent lack of a ground floor entrance.

Standing Building 72 appears to be have been a purpose-designed photographic studio for William Mayland, a photographic artist who occupied part of Plot X in 1864–69. Photography was still relatively novel in Cambridge; the earliest evidence dates to 1844 and it was only in the late 1850s that it became well-established. Mayland was born in London *c.* 1821 and had previously worked in Truro and Liskeard in Cornwall (1854) and Leicester (1856). In Cambridge he was initially based at Market Street (1858) and then moved to Plot X between 1864 and 1869 (Petty 1991). These were both apparently purely business premises and in 1861 he was living with his wife Mary Maud Mayland, an actress born in Dublin *c.* 1832, and a domestic servant Maria Morley, born *c.* 1841 at Abington, at 2 Clarendon Street, Cambridge. Mayland was a member of the Photographic Society from 1862 and earned an

'honourable mention' at the International Exhibition in the same year, for views of Cambridge University (class XIV, no. 3125).

In the 1860s he was the preferred photographer for portraits of local Cambridge eminences and in 1866 he was invited to Sandringham by the Prince of Wales to take photographs of a group of his friends. Mayland then moved to London (1869–82), going into partnership with Thomas Richard Williams (1824–71) a successful pioneer of stereoscopic photography. This partnership continued with Williams's son until 1876. Mayland then went bankrupt in 1878 and his wife Mary died in 1879. He won a medal at the Photographic Society exhibition in 1880 before retiring due to ill health in 1882; he lived in Tunbridge Wells (1888) prior to returning to London by 1901. He died in 1907.

Standing Building 72 was later used by the figurative painter and engraver Robert Farren who was born in Cambridge in 1832 and is listed in a directory of 1878 as having an 'artist's studio' at the premises. His work was exhibited in London 1868–80, particularly at the National Gallery and at Suffolk Street, and he published two books of Cambridge views (Farren 1880; Farren 1881). Farren moved to Scarborough for health reasons in 1889, although he continued to paint College portraits into the 1890s. He returned to Cambridge by 1901, and lived there until just before his death in London in 1912. Robert's daughters Mary, Jessie, Amy and Nellie were also artists and a Miss M. Farren, an artist and porcelain painter, is listed at the premises in 1878–81. Robert's father, William Farren, was a photographer in Cambridge (1864–81) and in 1875 he appears to have planned to open a studio in St Andrew's Street; although this was eventually cancelled these plans may have involved *Standing Building 72*. A plan of the mid-1870s indicates how the plot functioned with separate frontage and rear premises (Fig. 5.44D).

Plot XII

By the early nineteenth century the garden behind Plots IX–X was a single entity that measured *c.* 42m wide by *c.* 53–65m long, covering *c.* 2100 sq. m. In 1814 this garden was described as 190ft (58m) by 130ft (39.5m) in extent and had fruit trees and a greenhouse. Abutting the rear wall of *Building 29* were three early nineteenth-century structures: brick-lined drain and *Soakaway 6* and two irregularly shaped brick-lined *PBs 15–16*. Further back was *ADP 13*, which contained the partially articulated remains of a two year old pig. In 1862 the garden was leased to Robert Sayle; at this time it covered 2 roods and 3 perches (2099 sq. m) and was largely open but contained two WCs, a green house, a summer house, a pump and had a small gateway leading onto Tibb's Row (see Fig. 5.79A).

Plot XIII

In 1802 Plot XIII included a dwelling house with a shop, two parlours, a kitchen, a washhouse, four bedrooms, a chandling office, coal sheds, a yard and a garden. The main building was 'ancient and extensive' with small rooms, and would be expensive to repair. The Headley family who had occupied the plot since *c.* 1723 continued to lease it, but by 1815 most of the family had moved to Hobson Street and Sarah Headley married the Reverend James Speare who leased the plot in turn. A graduate of Clare College, Speare was at this time rector of Elmsett, Suffolk, and he immediately sublet the plot to John Furbank, a cheesemonger, grocer, tea dealer and tallow chandler born in Fulbourn *c.* 1797. The plot underwent a major reorganization *c.* 1813–23, probably linked to the transition of 1817. As part of this *Soakaway 2* (Fig. 5.46) was backfilled with ashy material and a mixed domestic assemblage (MNI 119) of pottery and glass vessels dominated by dining-related material including a soup dish from Trinity College (Fig. 5.46E) and a bottle of Dalby's carminate (Fig. 5.46I), plus an infant's medicine containing opium and some bone from food waste.

By 1823 the chandling office was in a very bad state of repair 'as much as to require being taken down' and the roof of the main house 'wants stripping'. The plaster at the end of the house next to the garden 'wants fresh doing' and one of the garden walls required new topping. Furbank occupied the plot until 1841, but then moved

Figure 5.45 (opposite). Standing Building 72 'the studio', which was constructed c. 1867–9: (A–B) ground and first floor plans of the building; (C) the northern elevation; (D) the eastern elevation; (E) photograph of building during demolition, facing southeast; (F) photograph of first floor during demolition, facing south.

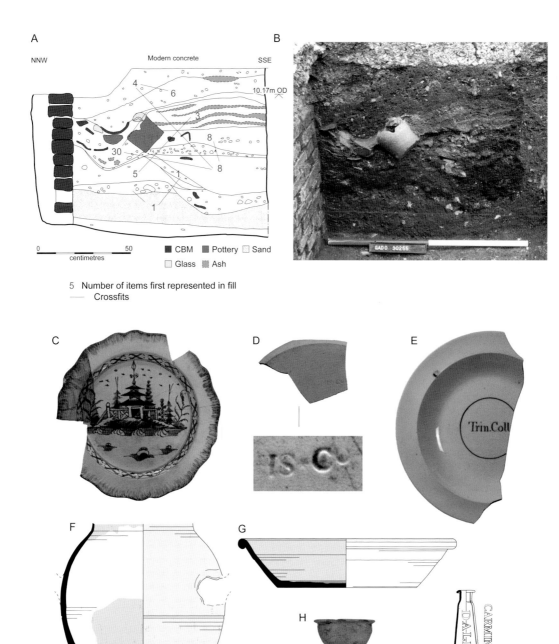

Figure 5.46. *Mid-eighteenth-century brick-lined Soakaway 2, which was backfilled c. 1813–23: (A) section; (B) photograph, facing east; (C) pearlware Rococo shell-edged plate (c. 1784–1812) with blue hand-painted pagoda scene ([30346]); (D) large plain oval creamware serving dish with impressed makers mark HS*Co ([30346]); (E) good quality creamware soup dish with hand-painted mark Trin.Coll on inside of base within circle. The base is heavily scratched indicating intensive use ([30291]); (F) Late Glazed Red Earthenware rounded jar or probably jug with single vertical strap handle, glazed internally and externally; (G) Late Glazed Red Earthenware flared bowl with clubbed rim, glazed internally ([30289], [30346], [30540]); (H) English tin-glazed earthenware ointment jar, heavily worn but complete apart from a small chip on the rim ([30346]); (I) pale green cone or steeple shaped pharmaceutical bottle that tapers towards a short cylindrical neck and has an applied flared lip. Made in a two-piece mould with side seams and pontil scar. Body embossed vertically DALBY'S CARMINATE ([30290]).*

268

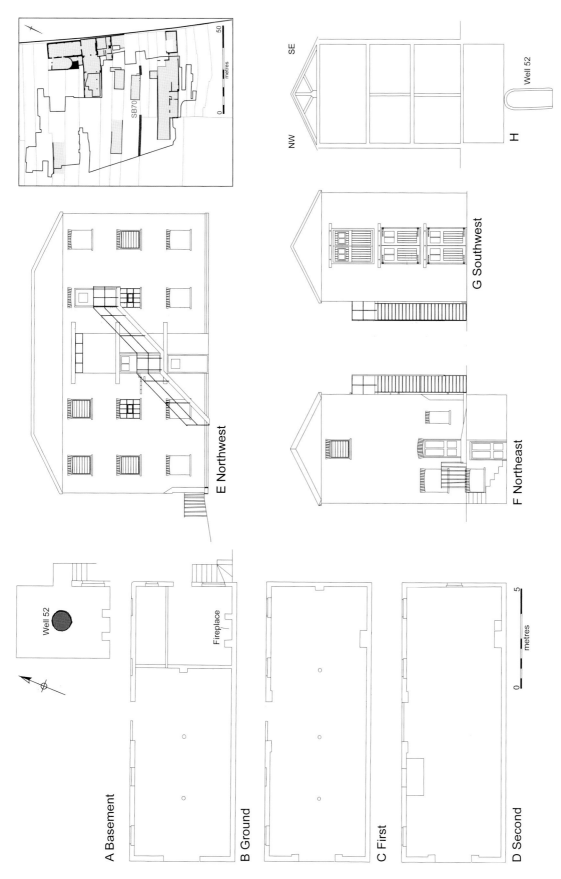

Figure 5.47. *Standing Building 70 'the Warehouse', constructed in 1845: (A–D) plans of the basement to second floors; (E–G) northwest, northeast and southwest elevations; (H) cross-section of the building.*

Figure 5.48. *Standing Building 70 'the Warehouse', constructed in 1845: (A) north side of the building from a 3D model, facing southwest; (B–D) Photographs of the building, facing southeast, northwest and east.*

away, dying in 1854. In 1843 the plot was leased to Edward Jay, a grocer, tea dealer, hop and seed merchant born *c.* 1808 at Waltham, Hertfordshire, who had previously been based at Plot XIX since *c.* 1833. In 1845, soon after the Jay's arrival, the chandling house was replaced by a 'new warehouse' and the Emmanuel College bursar's account mention Jay's 'New Warehouse', for which the College paid £200. This three-storey brick-built structure, *Standing Building 70* (Figs. 5.47–5.50), was constructed from grey Cambridge

bricks laid in Flying Flemish or Monk bond and measured 14m long by 5.5m wide, with a small basement at the east end.

Although the majority of the warehouse would have been used for storage there were two smaller basement and ground rooms. A set of steps descended to a basement at the eastern end of the building. This had a window on its east side and a large fireplace on the south wall. Sealed under the floor of the basement room was brick-lined *Well 52* (see Case Study 11). The ground floor

Case study 11: *Well 52* incorporating specialist information from Richard Darrah and Ian Tyers

Well 52 (Fig. 5.49) was constructed in 1845, presumably as the earliest element associated with warehouse *Standing Building 70* (Figs. 5.47A and 5.47H). It was sealed beneath the brick floor of the cellar of this building and was only revealed when the floor was removed by machine. In common with many nineteenth-century wells, it lacked the timber baseplate typical of earlier centuries.

The well's unmortared brick-lined shaft measured 1.2m in diameter and 2.5m deep with a domed top (Fig. 5.49A). From this protruded a lead pipe (Fig. 5.49B), which led to *Well 52* being nicknamed 'the Dalek'. This pipe led not to the cellar but instead appears to have provided water to the ground floor kitchen space, where there was presumably a non-return valve at its top end and a cast iron or wooden pump. This was the only well at the site whose lead pipe was not eventually retrieved, presumably because it was not worth the effort of lifting the brick floor to do so. The pipe was so heavy that it had to be lifted by machine, at which point it was realized that its base was perforated and that there was a rectangular Scots pine timber block at the end to seal the pipe and keep its lower end above the silt in the bottom of the well (Fig. 5.49B). The timber block was band sawn from exceptionally slow growing Scots pine (average under 0.4mm/year) with a 273-year sequence of rings that could not be matched to any softwood reference data and was presumably imported from the Baltic or North America. There is no documentary evidence as to who created *Well 52*; however, the 1851 census records that resident in Cambridge were James Gunn aged 53 a well borer and Thomas Swan aged 30 a well digger. It is unclear how long *Well 52* continued in use but it seems likely that it functioned well into the twentieth century, despite the arrival of mains water in the late 1800s.

A

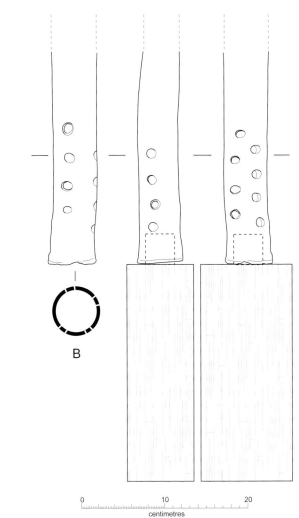

B

Figure 5.49. *Brick-lined Well 52, which was constructed in 1845: (A) photograph of the well, facing southeast, showing the brick dome; (B) the perforated circular lead pipe with rectangular Scots Pine block acting as a plug ([34630]).*

271

was divided into two, with the eastern third separated from the rest by a brick wall. The line of this wall met the north wall part way across one of the blocked ground floor windows, suggesting that it is not an original feature. Mortice holes cut in the underside of a beam just north of the doorway in the east wall show that at one stage there was a stud wall dividing off the northern third of the space. Taken together, this suggests that there was originally a separate room in the southeast corner of the building entered by a door in the east wall and lit by a window in the same wall. There is a large fireplace on the south wall similar to that below in the basement. A plan of 1845 indicates that at least one, and probably both of these rooms were utsed as kitchens, explaining the provision of a water supply and two large fireplaces. The location of kitchens in a warehouse seems an unusual arrangement, especially as the same plan indicates other kitchens in another building on the plot. One possibility is that this was not a domestic kitchen, but rather that it was used for various types of processing of foodstuffs such as blending tea, grinding and roasting coffee, cleaning fruit and weighing and packaging a range of goods.

The remainder of the ground floor of *Standing Building 70* would have been accessed via a central set of double-width doors on the north side, through which goods would have entered the warehouse from wagons which would have been able to park outside. There were also four segmented-headed windows arranged symmetrically in pairs on either side of the doors. At the northeast the corner was rounded and there was a small window on the eastern wall. There was no evidence for internal stairs, and the first and second floors must have been accessed externally. The arrangements for these staircases on the north face were similar to the ground floor, with central double-width loading doors and four symmetrical windows, although the second floor also had a window on the eastern side and later alterations mean it is unknown what arrangements were present on the western side. The first and second floors were both single open spaces. Overall, *Standing Building 70* provided c. 30 sq. m of kitchen space and c. 190 sq. m of warehouse storage space.

To the east side of the first floor door there were six brick-sized wooden blocks set rather irregularly into the fabric of the wall (Fig. 5.50). One of these was blank but five carried sets of initials and the date 1845 and all are clearly integral with the construction of the building. The lowest block, which occurred on a row by its own, had the initials of Edward Jay himself (EJ). Two courses above this was a row of four blocks. Reading from left to right the initials are those his 10-year old son Edward Jay junior (EJ with J II below), his wife Jane Maria Jay (JMJ), his assistant James Baker (JB) and his eight-year old daughter Maria Jane Anne (MJAJ). On the next row up the uppermost block does not appear to have ever been carved, but could have been painted. On the inside of the same floor near a window a brick was observed that had been carved with the initials of Edward Jay and the date 1845. The wooden blocks would not have been easily visible from ground level and it appears that the Jays, anxious to leave their mark on the building even though it was constructed at the College's expense, deliberately placed the blocks out of the casual observer's line of sight. It is interesting that Jay's assistant James Baker was commemorated, but the household servants were not. Missing from the list are two of Edward Jay's sons, Henry/Harry (aged four) and Frank (aged three), who appear to have been regarded as too young.

A number of other features were built at the same time as *Standing Building 70*, including *Drains 8–9* that used faceted 'horseshoe'-shaped pipes and ran around the northern side of the warehouse, plus a rectangular slightly sunken brick-lined toilet structure *Water Closet 1* just behind it. Slightly further back was set domed brick-lined *Well 53*, which supplied a pump located against the boundary wall. The construction deposits of this well contained part of a Willow pattern plate produced for Thomas Wicks, the cook at Emmanuel College 1807–51 who lived nearby at Plot XV. This well would have supplied water for use in the yard, while that under the warehouse/kitchen (*Well 52*) would have supplied *Standing Building 70*. Earlier stone-lined *Well 45* continued to supply the frontage building with water. Slightly later, in 1848, there was some

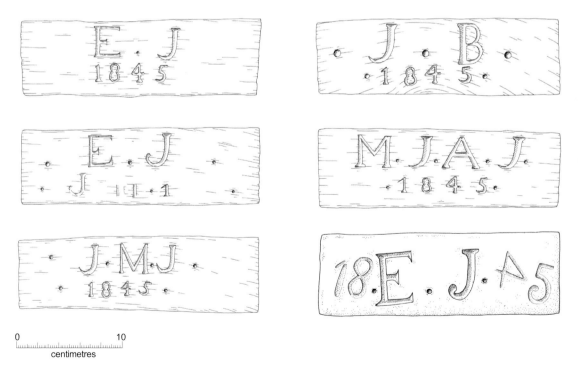

Figure 5.50. *Wooden blocks and a brick carved with the initials of the occupants of the plot from Standing Building 70 'the Warehouse', constructed in 1845.*

272

major rebuilding of the garden walls around the plot tail. Edward's wife Jane died in 1850 and in 1851 he was living with his two sons Edward junior and Frank, two visitors and his assistant James Baker.

In 1855 Edward Jay died in Great Yarmouth and was succeeded by his son Edward Jay junior, in partnership with his father's former assistant James Baker. By this time grocers stocked a much more extensive range of processed foods, including tinned goods after 1813 and cornflour after 1841. They also began to stock fresh foodstuffs, such as cheese and bacon, which had not previously been part of their repertoire. By 1863 Jay junior moved to 2 Brunswick Place and by 1866 the business also had premises nearby at 21 Corn Exchange Street and 7½ St Andrew's Hill. In 1866–7 Jay fell into arrears and Baker took sole control of the business. Jay then left Cambridge. He initially worked as a commercial traveller in Newmarket (1868 and 1874), Wood Ditton (1871) and Exining (1877), before settling in Peterborough and becoming a corn and seed merchant again (1881–1912). In 1874 the plot still reflected the constructional activities of the 1840s, but between then and 1885 a number of buildings were constructed on the southern side of the plot tail, one of which had deep cellars and contained a well (*Well M1*). James Baker died in 1887 and was succeeded by his widow Anne; after her death in 1895 the business was taken over by Harold Blinkhorn Flack and Harper Tom Judge, who only used the plot for business purposes and lived in Chesterton.

At some point *c.* 1862–1900 *Well 45*, which was located in the passage to the south of the frontage building, went out of use. This was because the plot was connected to the mains supply of the Cambridge University and Town Waterworks, which was established in 1852 with its waterworks opening in 1855 and 1500 premises being connected by 1860. Sewerage was provided at about the same time and in 1880 there is a record that there 'has some time since been laid down' a pipe leading from Plot XIV to the south 'making communication between the water closet and drain', with the drain located in the passageway. Associated with the backfilling of *Well 45* was a small spread of 11 stoneware jars and one stoneware bottle beneath *Foundation 1* (MNI 12). In the late 1880s a small pit, *Pit 61* (MNI 31), was dug in the plot tail to dispose of 27 glass bottles, mainly a set of 17 near identical beer bottles. Although very different, these two groups, one composed solely of utilitarian stoneware vessels and the other solely of utility bottles, both relate to the relatively small-scale *ad hoc* disposal of broken or otherwize worthless material related to the continuing grocery business. Rubble-built *Foundation 2* was constructed *c.* 1883–90 to provide a footing for some form of garden feature. The foundation contained a complete torpedo-shaped soda water bottle of Charles Barker & Sons (see Fig. 5.95); given the nature of the foundation this bottle must have been carefully and deliberately placed to have remained intact.

Plot XIV

Plot XIV consisted of a frontage building with a relatively extensive 'L'-shaped garden behind. It was occupied by Sarah Dobson, who was born in 1796 and came from a farming family in the nearby village of Stow cum Quy. Sarah ran a school at the premises from at least 1841, and possibly as early as *c.* 1820, until *c.* 1865–66. As well as Sarah, the household typically consisted of three to four other teachers, mainly close female relatives of Sarah, a number of pupils, mainly from Cambridge and nearby villages but including individuals from as far afield as Australia, and two servants. Part of the rear garden of Plot XV to the south was transferred to Plot XIV *c.* 1808–25 and new brick-lined *Drain 10* was added, leading into the existing cistern and two square brick-lined garden structures with iron bars over the top, whose function is uncertain, were constructed. An outside WC block, *Standing Building 99*, which had two stalls and the doors facing to the west, was also built on the footprint of a demolished building previously associated with Plot XV, possibly reflecting the increased sanitation requirements created by the school. In the garden two rectangular *PBs 17–18* plus some

circular or irregular *PHs 1–6* were dug, as well as two postholes which presumably supported trees or shrubs. These features represent a series of independent events that occurred in the garden over a period of years or even decades *c.* 1820–40.

Several of these garden features contained significant assemblages of material; these are particularly interesting as they are the only groups of material from the site where the head of the household that created them was female, and indeed in 1841 the household was entirely female in its composition. As aspects of this assemblage have been published in detail elsewhere (Cessford 2018a; see also Cessford 2009), an overview is presented here.

The largest assemblage came from a 'percolation fill' situated at the base of *PH 3* (Fig. 5.51A) that was deposited *c.* 1822–34 (MNI 129). This group dominated by dining-related material and indicates that the adults in the Dobson household used a range of relatively high-quality blue transfer-printed dining and tea drinking 'services', suggesting that Sarah subscribed to developing ideas of domesticity and gentility (Fitts 1999). The Sicilian pattern was the most common (Fig. 5.52A–D) and the literary associations of this design suggest that Sarah Dobson may have supported both the traditional moral values such as honour and integrity and the political message concerning the oppression of women in patriarchal society that the pattern could have conveyed. The children used cups decorated with images and text from the song 'Whene'er I take my walks abroad' by Isaac Watts (Fig. 5.52E–F), a leading early eighteenth-century non-conformist hymn-writer, theologian and logician whose straightforward and relatively gentle Christian ideas and lilting metre were popular in the nineteenth century. Matching cups and saucers were apparently discarded when one was broken (Fig. 5.53C–D) reinforcing the notion of 'services', while the presence of three complete blacking bottles suggests a greater than normal interest in cleanliness and appearance.

The substantial animal bone assemblage that was recovered indicates a preference for the moderately expensive topside or silverside cuts of beef, shoulders of mutton and legs of pork. Pork was one of the most expensive meats at the time and is much commoner in this group than in others of this date (17.5 per cent of the meat from the main domesticates versus 0–9.7 per cent in other assemblages). As pigs were still being raised in the plot, the pork was potentially not all obtained commercially. There were also parts of at least 22 birds, the largest number from any assemblage, with 12 chicken carcasses as well as other domestic poultry, waterfowl, pigeon and game birds including red grouse, grey partridge and pheasant. Only three clay tobacco pies were present; however, the ratio of pipes to ceramic vessels (1:18) is not significantly lower than other assemblages of *c.* 1800–50 (1:14).

It therefore appears that despite smoking being a gendered activity associated with men, and supposedly only undertaken by women of loose morals or low status, it took place in the Dobson household. There was also evidence for the consumption of alcohol, notably two wine glasses from a matching 'service' and some utility bottles, two of which are French or Belgian imports and are likely to have contained wine. At the time male working class drinking culture centred upon public houses, which respectable women did not frequent. The smoking and alcohol drinking in the Dobson household suggest that private female consumption was taking place within the home, despite the fact that both activities would have been disapproved of in more public contexts.

Other garden features including *PB 17* and *PH 1*, plus a nearby posthole, contained a child's cup with a text from 'Innocent Play' (Fig. 5.54G), another song by Isaac Watts, as well as 17 slate pencils (Fig. 5.54E–F). The pencils are 32–75mm long and have been heavily used and repeatedly sharpened. There were no identifiable writing slates, despite the presence of the pencils, and other items frequently associated archaeologically with nineteenth-century childhood such as dolls, tea sets, metal toys, marble stoppers (Wilkie 2000) were absent. This may indicate that the school was a relatively austere establishment; alternatively, it could just be that disposal was limited

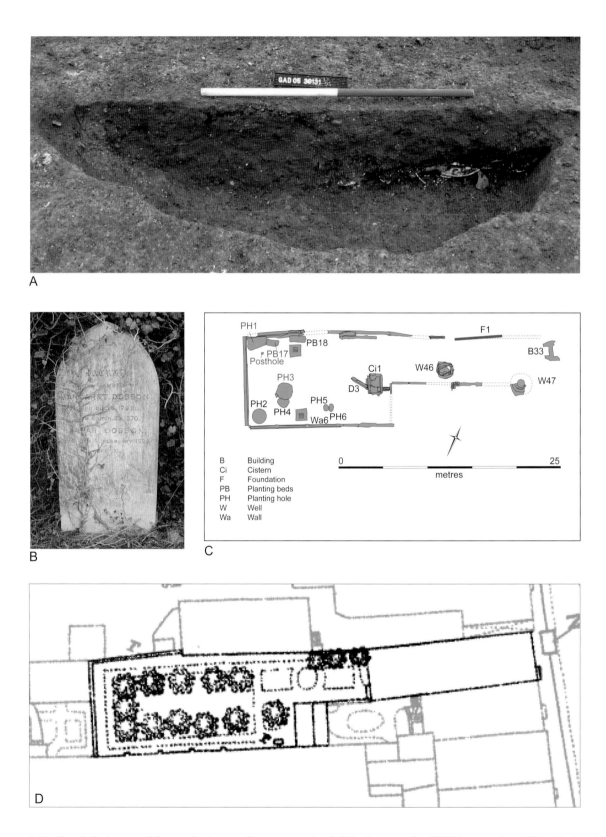

Figure 5.51. *Sarah Dobson and her mid-nineteenth-century school: (A) photograph of PH 3 created c. 1822–40 showing percolation fill (lower right), facing north; (B) headstone of Sarah Dobson, her sister Margaret and nieces Sophia and Katie at the Mill Road cemetery, facing west; (C) plan of archaeological features; (D) the property as depicted in the 1st edition Ordnance Survey map surveyed in 1885.*

Figure 5.52. *Ceramics from percolation fill of PH 3, created c. 1822–40 ([30102]): (A–D) blue transfer-printed whiteware Sicilian pattern service; (A) 14in-serving dish, with Sicilian pattern mark in cartouche on rear with impressed 14, and impressed IMPROVED STONE CHINA with a mixture or real and fake Chinese characters; (B) cup; (C) plate; (D) a serving plate; (E–F) whiteware cups with pink transfer-printed decoration and the Isaac Watts text "For I have food while others starve or beg from door to door".*

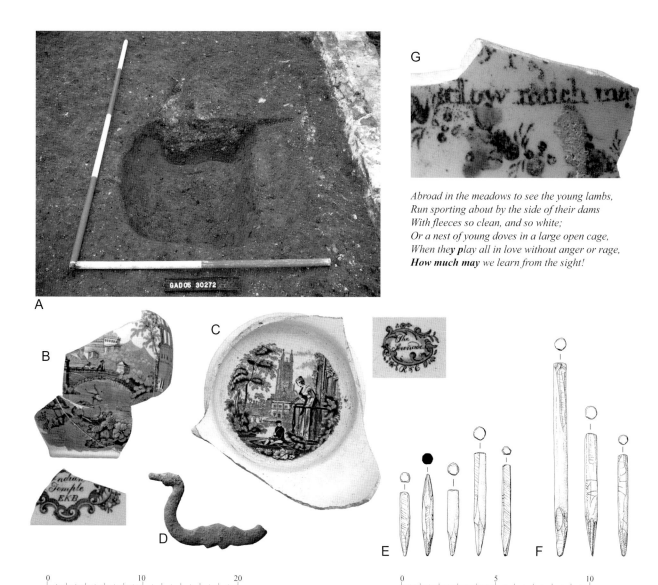

Abroad in the meadows to see the young lambs,
Run sporting about by the side of their dams
With fleeces so clean, and so white;
Or a nest of young doves in a large open cage,
*When they **p**lay all in love without anger or rage,*
***How much may** we learn from the sight!*

Figure 5.53 *(opposite). Further ceramics recovered from the percolation fill of PH 3, created c. 1822–40 ([30102]): (A) whiteware bowl with blue transfer-printed rose and thistle decoration and transfer-printed SPODE mark on the base; (B) octagonal Chinese Export porcelain plate with floral decoration; (C) matching set of bone china cup and saucer with blue transfer-printed decoration marked FELSPAR PORCELAIN/1803/Blue/M; (D) matching set of whiteware cup and saucer with blue transfer-printed Two Temples pattern; (E) whiteware cup with blue transfer-printed decoration marked Flora /16/ OPAQUE CHINA; (F) mocha-style whiteware cup with red, green and brown bands; (G) whiteware chamber pot with blue transfer-printed decoration of a romantic scene of Gothic ruins and pattern mark VERONA in cartouche; (H–J) three Utilitarian English stoneware blacking bottles, one marked BLACKING BOTTLE/6/J D.*

Figure 5.54 *(above). Various garden features of c. 1820– 40, including: (A) photograph of PB 17, facing west; (B) whiteware bowl with blue transfer-printed decoration scene with the pattern name Indian Temple and the makers mark EKB, of Elkin, Knight and Bridgwood of Lane End (1827–40) from PB 17 ([30246]); (C) whiteware chamber pot with blue transfer-printed decoration with the pattern name The/Serenade and the makers mark R&C of Reed and Clementson of Hanley (1832–9), from PB 17 ([30246]); (D) eighteenth-century copper alloy Georgian style furniture drop handle, from a posthole next to PH 1 ([30003]); (E) slate pencils from a posthole next to PH 1 ([30003]); (F) slate pencils from PH 1 ([30434]); (G) child's whiteware cup with part of the text of Isaac Watts Innocent Play, from PH 1 ([30003]).*

277

to material owned by Sarah Dobson and the personal possessions of the children were not discarded.

By 1865–6 Sarah Dobson had moved to smaller premises a short distance away at 7 St Andrew's Hill, which only had a small yard or garden. Sarah died in 1886 and was interred alongside her sister Margaret who had died in 1870; her nieces Sophia and Katie were later interred in the same burial plot in 1910 and 1913. In 1885 the plot was depicted as having an 'L'-shaped formal garden with trees, paths, regularly arranged beds and a pump, and it appears that this was largely how the garden had been when the plot was occupied by the school. It would be tempting to interpret the school garden as a pleasant, almost bucolic, location for the staff and students. This is, however, counter-pointed by the raising of pigs to eat and the presence of the WC block, apparently located so as to be concealed from the main frontage building but visible from most of the garden. This tension is paralleled in the material culture, for while ideas of gentility meant that cups and saucers were discarded when the corresponding element in the service

was damaged, there was also a strong element of frugality, again exemplified by the raising of pigs but also by the slate pencils which were repeatedly sharpened so that they could be used as intensively as possible before disposal.

Plot XIV was subsequently occupied by a solicitor, John Saunders Christmas (1867–92). After this, Plot XIV ceased to be used for residential purposes and was divided between several businesses, including a solicitors, an auctioneer, a surveyor and a tobacconist, although the garden area remained largely unchanged and was not developed.

Plot XV

In the first quarter of the nineteenth century *Building 35* was demolished and the rear 5m of Plot XV was transferred to Plot XIV. *Soakaway 3* was then backfilled and a domed brick top was added to pre-existing *Well 47*. These changes, particularly the backfilling of *Soakaway 3* (Case Study 12), appear to relate to the occupancy of Thomas Wicks, the cook of Emmanuel College 1807–51, who

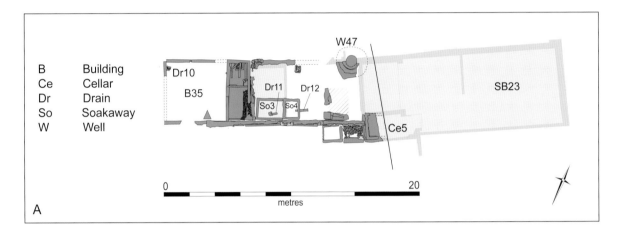

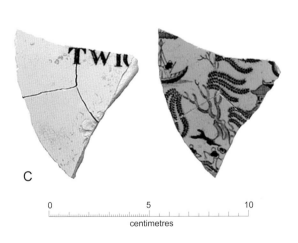

Figure 5.55. *The early–mid-nineteenth-century College cook Thomas Wicks: (A) plan of nineteenth-century features in Plot XV; (B) Celtic cross of Thomas Wicks, College cook and his wives Mary and Rose in the Mill Road cemetery, facing west; (C) sherd from a whiteware blue transfer-printed willow pattern plate marked T WIC[KS] on the reverse from construction deposits of Well 53, probably constructed in 1845 in Plot XIII ([30125]).*

Case study 12: The backfilling of *Soakaway 3*
incorporating specialist information from
Andrew Hall, Vicki Herring, Lorrain Higbee,
Mark Samuel and Simon Timberlake

The backfilling of *Soakaway 3* dates to *c*. 1808–25 and
the assemblage of over 300 items (MNI) consisting
of pottery and glass vessels, clay tobacco pipes
and bone is a mixture of domestic and business
material, dominated by items related to dining.
Some of this material predates the end of Thomas
Wicks' apprenticeship *c*. 1795 and occasionally
even his birth in 1774. Examples of this include
four Chinese export porcelain vessels (*c*. 1730–50
and 1750–60), two Staffordshire white salt-glazed
stoneware vessels (*c*. 1750–65), two glass utility
bottles (*c*. 1750–80), a bottle seal of 1770 and a
piece of English soft paste porcelain (*c*. 1760–70).
This pattern suggests that some of the material
comprised in some sense either familial or business
'heirlooms'.

The pottery has an EVE of 88.01 (EVE per MNI 0.49) with 2055
sherds weighing 40,071g (MSW 19.5g). The vessels are mainly
related to dining and tea drinking, with substantial amounts
also linked to personal hygiene and gardening. Dining vessels
included plates (MNI 29), side plates (MNI seven), bowls (MNI
eight), jugs (MNI four), deep plates/dishes (MNI three), serving
bowls/dishes (MNI three), lids (MNI four), a footed salt (MNI
one) and a sauceboat (MNI one). There is a mixture of relatively
plain creamware, highly decorated pearlware and other wares.
The creamware can be divided into three groups based on the
quality of the fabric and the lightness of the colour. Some of the
best quality material bears Wedgwood marks (MNI 12), some
material of slightly lesser quantity was produced by Turner's
(MNI nine) and the bulk of the material is lower quality and
unmarked (MNI 52). Josiah Wedgwood (1730–95) began to
experiment with creamware in 1754, set up his own pottery
works in 1759 and presented a service to Queen Charlotte in
1762. John Turner (1738–87) began working on his own in the
late 1750s and was a pioneering and successful potter; he was
succeeded by his sons William and John.

There were two slightly older Chinese export porcelain
plates of *c*. 1750–60, one of which was repaired at some stage. A
number of 'services' were identifiable. One was in a pearlware
fabric with even shell-edged decoration with even scallops and
impressed curved lines of *c*. 1802–32 (MNI eight) (Fig. 5.56A–D).
This consisted of side plates (MNI three), an even smaller plate
(MNI one), deep plates or dishes (MNI two) a lid for a large
serving vessel (MNI one) and a sauceboat (MNI one) with
T.Wic… hand-painted in gilt providing a link to Thomas Wicks
(Fig. 5.56C). There were also creamware vessels with a thick
brown hand-painted band (MNI seven), mainly plates (MNI
six) and a lid for a small serving vessel (MNI one) (Fig. 5.56E–F).
Although these were clearly a 'service' the vessels were variable;
one was better quality and marked as a Wedgwood product and
on another the band was underglaze rather than overglaze. One
of the lids with moulded and hand-painted decoration may have
been designed to resemble a beehive, suggesting that it could

come from a honey pot, while another lid is from a butter dish.
One distinctive pearlware bowl has brown transfer-printed
decoration of conch shells and other marine elements; this might
have been specifically linked to seafood (Fig. 5.56G).

Tea drinking included saucers (MNI ten), tea cups (MNI
eight), tea bowls (MNI five), tea cups/bowls (MNI eight), slops
bowls (MNI four), coffee cans (MNI two) and a teapot (MNI
one). The vessels consist principally of plain creamware, plus
pearlware and some other wares decorated with Oriental scenes.
There was some evidence of sets of material; three saucers and
three tea cups in a creamware fabric are all decorated with a
thin brown band and there are three pearlware tea bowls or
cups with identical Oriental scenes. There were also parts of a
Chinese export porcelain tea bowl and saucer with famille rose
decoration of *c*. 1730–50 that must have been of some age when
deposited. One very different piece was an almost complete
strap handled black basalt teapot with a faux bamboo reeded
body (Fig. 5.56J); this was all present but there was no trace of
its lid, suggesting that a previously broken or lost lid may be
why it was discarded.

Vessels related to personal hygiene are principally
chamber pots (MNI 16) plus a stool pan (MNI one). These were
mainly creamware (MNI ten) and were largely plain although
one has a fluted body and the stool pan is also creamware.
There were also four blackware or iron glazed chamber pots
(Fig. 5.56L) and a blackware bowl (Fig. 5.56K). There were also
two Nottinghamshire/Derbyshire-type stoneware chamber pots
(Fig. 5.56N) and one of refined white earthenware, with blue
and white transfer-printed decoration. Most features contained
one to four chamber pots, the two exceptions being *Soakaway 3*
and *Cellar 4*, which is related to an inn, which had 11 chamber
pots plus one stool pan. These two groups are too large for
purely domestic requirements and must represent business-
related groups; this group must relate to the Wicks family's
collegiate interests. In inventories chamber pots are frequently
listed alongside tablewares rather than in the bedroom and it
is clear that semi-public urination was sometimes practised
in male contexts (D'Agostono 2000). The chamber pots, both
as a whole and the individual larger feature groups, come in
a wide variety of fabrics. In general the eighteenth- and early
nineteenth-century examples are relatively plain, the exception
being the Westerwald and Scratch Blue examples. While it was
the gyps and bedmakers that would have dealt directly with
chamber pots, it is possible that the wealthier servants, such as
the cooks, bought and supplied the chamber pots which were
effectively hired to out to fellows and students, although there
is no documentary evidence for this.

Other hygiene-related vessels included three large
plain creamware water jugs and one basin used for washing.
Horticulture vessels included 18 flowerpots, one saucer and one
Mocha decorated flowerpot for inside use. Medicinal vessels
consist of five tin-glazed earthenware drug/ointment jars (Fig.
5.56O–R), two of which are complete and unbroken. They all
have different fabrics and glazes suggesting a collection built
up over time. Other drinking includes two Mocha decorated
straight-sided vessel and a creamware tankard with red transfer-
printed decoration (Fig. 5.56M).

Glass vessels include utility bottles (MNI 49), phials (MNI
11) and drinking glasses (MNI nine). The utility bottles are of
free blown black glass and include one complete example (Fig.
5.57A), two are of squat cylindrical design of *c*. 1760–80, while
the remaining 47 are of cylindrical design of *c*. 1770–1810.
Although a range of uses are possible, it is likely that most of
these bottles contained wine. There was also a seal stamped E G

Figure 5.56. *Ceramics recovered from the backfilling of Soakaway 3 in c. 1800–25 ([32901]): (A–D) pearlware fabric shell-edged service with even scallop and curved lines of c. 1802–32 including a side plate, a very small plate, a lid for a large serving vessel and a sauceboat with T.Wi[cks] hand-painted in gilt; (E–F) creamware fabric service with a thick brown hand-painted band, including a plate and a lid for a small serving vessel; (G) pearlware bowl with brown transfer-printed decoration of conch shells and other marine elements plus blue band; (H) pearlware jug with hand-painted brown and gilt bands; (I) mocha-style pearlware coffee can decorated with orange and brown bands; (J) black basalt teapot; (K) blackware or iron-glazed bowl; (L) blackware or iron-glazed chamber pot; (M) creamware tankard with red transfer-printed decoration; (N) Nottinghamshire/Derbyshire-type stoneware chamber pot, with machine turned dimple and band decoration; (O–R) tin-glazed earthenware drug/ointment jars.*

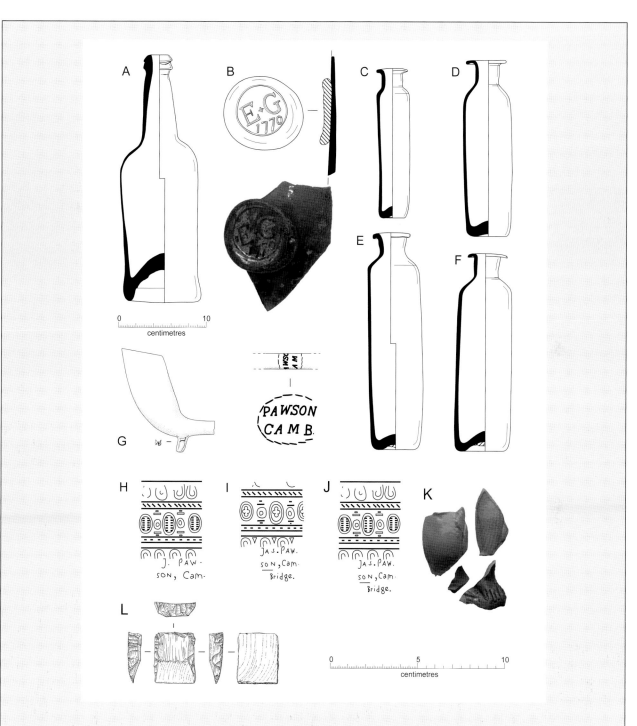

Figure 5.57. *Various materials recovered from the backfilling of Soakaway 3 in c. 1800–25 ([32901]): (A) free blown cylindrical green glass utility bottle with brown patina, high rounded base kick with disc pontil scar, short tapered but slightly bulging neck with single applied collar below rolled lip, of c. 1780–1810; (B) rounded seal from green glass utility bottle with patina, stamped E•G /1770; (C–F) colourless free blow uneven cylindrical phials, late eighteenth century; (G) type 23 clay tobacco pipe bowl of c. 1760–1800 with initial IP on spur (H–J) stem fragments with Wyer-style decoration marked J.·PAW ·/ SON, Cam· and JAS.PAW./SON, Cam·/Bridge; (K) fragments from a green and yellow painted Staffordshire-type figurine; (L) unused wedge shaped gunflint in the form of a modified blade, probably from Brandon in Suffolk and produced c. 1770–1880.*

1770 (Fig. 5.57B). The names of the occupiers of this plot in the late eighteenth century are unknown and there is no particularly plausible candidate for who EG was. Although a number of other bottle seals were recovered from the site, this is the only set of individual's initials from the site and relates to someone living in Cambridge. The earliest dated surviving English bottle seal is dated 1650 and other examples linked to Cambridge are dated 1678–1752 so this is a relatively late example. There are 10 free blown, colourless, cylindrical medicinal phials with flared lips, four of which are whole (Fig. 5.57C–F). Another phial is mould blown and has a W embossed on the side. The nine late eighteenth-century colourless drinking glasses are all incomplete and consist of a sweetmeat glass (MNI one), goblets (MNI three), wine glasses (MNI two), a jelly glass (MNI one) and tumblers (MNI two).

Soakaway 3 produced the largest clay tobacco pipe assemblage from the site (MNI 17), the next highest total being 12. One bowl is dated *c*. 1700–40, another *c*. 1730–80 and three of *c*. 1760–1800. One of the bowls of *c*. 1760–1800 has the initial IP on the spur (Fig. 5.57G) and can be linked to James Pawson. There are also nine marked stems that can be linked to the Pawson family (1786–1823); four are marked J·PAW·/SON, Cam·, Bridge or JAS.PAW./SON, Cam·/Bridge. with Wyer style decoration (Fig.5.57H–J) while five are marked PAWSON CAMB within a circle. The large number of pipes suggests a possible College connection, although the supply of pipes and tobacco to fellows and students fell within the remit of the butler rather than the cook.

Overall, 125 of the 508 bones were identified; these include a large amount of domestic waste (58 per cent), some butchery waste (32 per cent) and a small number from non-food species (dog, cat, rat and toad, all MNI one). Sheep bones are slightly more common (17 per cent NISP) than cattle bones (14 per cent). There are at least six beef joints (*c*. 65.2kg), seven mutton joints (*c*. 20.1kg), only one pork joint (*c*. 4.6kg) and shoulders of lamb appear to be particularly favoured (three joints *c*. 7.8kg) (Table 5.1). Small quantities of veal, hare and rabbit were also consumed. Pigeon (13 per cent NISP) and chicken (9 per cent) are the most commonly eaten birds. Other birds include goose, domestic and wild duck (*i.e.* teal/garganey), turkey (represented by two right tarsometatarsi and a carpometacarpus), grey partridge, grey heron (represented by a single tibiotarsus), herring gull and a small species of wader. All of the pigeon and goose bones are from juvenile birds; young pigeons are usually available between spring and autumn, whilst green geese are usually available from May to June.

The shooting season for grey partridge runs from October to February, while grey heron is resident in Britain all year round and so could have been caught in any season. It would therefore seem that the domestic waste from this feature could have been deposited at any time of year and might even include the remains of a Christmas meal, as by the eighteenth century the trend for eating turkey at this time of the year was beginning to take off amongst the wealthy in society. It is unclear whether all the bird species were eaten, although in medieval England 'few species were not eaten' by all social classes including heron and seabirds and historical sources refer to gulls as 'sea pie' (Serjeantson 2006, 133), although the bones from this feature represent the only herring gull from the site. At the time that the cellar was backfilled the plot was occupied by six people. Since annual meat consumption was typically *c*. 20kg in the nineteenth century, this would equate to around 300 days for the household. As with the chamber pots it therefore appears that this is not domestic household material.

An unused gunflint (Fig. 5.57L) in the form of a modified blade, probably from Brandon in Suffolk, produced *c*. 1770–1880 (Hanerkamp & Harris 2005; Kent 1983) may be a casual loss; alternatively, it may have been discarded as obsolete as the caplock mechanism, which used a percussion cap struck by the hammer to set off the main charge, rather than using a piece of flint to strike a steel frizzen, was patented by the Rev. Alexander in 1807. A cylinder made from a mammal long bone with axial and transverse perforations at one end and highly decorated with series of lathe turned incised lines may be a musical toy known as a 'swanny-whistle' or 'water-nightingale' (Margeson 1993, 213) but is perhaps more likely a bobbin (MacGregor 1985, 183–5). There was also part of a copper alloy purse frame and fragments of a figurine (Fig. 5.57K).

Table 5.1. *Minimum number of butchery units and meat weights from Soakaway 3.*

Species/meat	Joint	Total no. bones	MNBU	Estimated meat weight (kg)	Total estimated meat weight (kg) by meat type
Cattle/beef	Thick flank	3	3	27.9	
	Neck & clod	1	1	13.5	
	Shin	1	1	4.1	65.2
	Chuck & blade	1	1	19.7	
Cattle/veal	Chuck & blade	1	1	4.0	4.0
Sheep/mutton	Leg	6	3	9.9	
	Shoulder	8	2	8.6	
	Scrag	1	1	0.3	20.1
	?Loin	3	1	1.3	
Sheep/lamb	Shoulder	3	3	7.8	7.8
Pig (immature)/pork	Leg	1	1	4.6	4.6
Hare		8	1		
Rabbit		5	1		
Chicken		11	3		
Goose		3	1		
Duck		4	1		
Pigeon		16	3		
Turkey		3	2		
Grey partridge		1	1		
Small wader		1	1		
Grey heron		1	1		
Herring gull		5	1		
Total		87	34	101.7	

After the backfilling of *Soakaway 3* it continued to fulfil a drainage role. A roughly square pit 1.05m by 1.05m in extent and 0.65m deep was dug into its rubble infill. Into the base of this pit hundreds of fragments of thick window glass were dumped, followed by hundreds of whole and fragmentary bricks plus some roof tile and some stone mouldings, including a fragmentary shaft of *c.* 1090–1190 that derives from a monastic building that was identified petrologically as New Red Sandstone. There was also a Ketton Stone fragment from a parapet coping of *c.* 1340–1530 and a large fragment of a Niedermendig lava quernstone. There was very little domestic debris; what there was consisted of a small amount of eighteenth-century Nottinghamshire/Derbyshire-type stoneware and an intrusive mid/late nineteenth-century clay tobacco pipe bowl.

probably moved to the plot *c.* 1808 and was certainly living there by 1829 (Fig. 5.55). The assemblage deposited in *Soakaway 3* is of particular interest because it appears to represent an amalgam of domestic and collegiate material. Furthermore, after 1810 Thomas Wicks was relate to the Burbage family of butlers at Emmanuel College who lived next door in Plot XVI; this suggests that familial relationships and the proximity of the two households mean that the assemblage relates to the roles of both cook and butler.

Drains 11–12 were later inserted into *Soakaways 3–4* and they thus continued to fulfil a drainage function. Thomas Wicks was interred at the Mill Road cemetery and commemorated on a Celtic cross, which mentioned his wife Mary who had died in 1808 and his second wife Rose who died in 1872. After the death of Thomas Wicks Plot XV was occupied by his widow Rose Wicks (1851–2) and was then owned by their son Claxton/Clayton Wicks until at least 1864. After this the plot was used as mixed domestic and commercial premises; in 1885 there was a building on the frontage with some external stairs to the rear and a garden area with paths.

Plot XVI

This plot was probably occupied by the Burbage family from the late eighteenth century onwards. Charles Burbage, the butler of Emmanuel College between 1828 and 1847 lived there from 1841 to 1847, followed by his mother Anne (1847–8) and his nephew James Burbage (1848–9), who was also the College butler. It was then occupied by a series of businesses and in the 1870s the plot tail was transferred to Plot XVII. Associated with this transition, *Cellar 5* was backfilled (MNI 20) and a new brick-lined well – *Well 56*, which had a domed top and a Scots pine annulus base – was constructed. The remaining plot was only *c.* 19.5m long and by 1885 it consisted of the frontage building plus a small yard area surrounded by four small ancillary buildings.

Plot XVII

There was relatively little evidence for archaeological activity in Plot XVII in the first half of the nineteenth century, but during the late nineteenth century it went through two major phases of expansion. In the 1870s the plot was extended to *c.* 61m from the frontage and the majority of Plot XVI, plus an area behind it, was also acquired. At this time the plot was occupied by various members of the Flack family, although it is unclear whether they or the Barrett family (see below) owned the plot. The Flack family ran a number of businesses from the premises, including a Turkish Baths. Although the main structures associated with this business left little trace, some evidence did survive in the form of *Buildings 26* and *50*.

For the first half of the nineteenth century Plot XVII was owned by Misses Mary Ann and Sophia Bones (1829) and in the mid-nineteenth century it was occupied by baker Samuel Bullock (1841) and then two surgeons, George Johnson (1851–61) and Thomas Lucas (1866–71). The core of *Standing Building 25* is eighteenth-century in date, but it was remodelled and extended in the nineteenth century; the windows at the front, for example, are nineteenth-century in date. The south face was covered or constructed during the early nineteenth century using grey bricks in English bond, as was the rear, this time in Flemish bond. This build encloses the southwards extension of the eighteenth-century rear wing. The cellar has two rooms, the smaller to the front. It appears that at least parts of the north wall of the cellar are eighteenth-century in origin, the remainder nineteenth-century; this indicates an expansion at some stage, presumably contemporary with the remodelling.

The Flack family included Walter Flack a plumber, painter and glazier (1874–8), his wife Martha A. Flack a plumber, painter, glazier and lodging house keeper (1881) and their children Charles Walter Flack who ran a music and pianoforte warehouse (1874–80) and Alice M. Flack a teacher of music (1881). Their most significant business was a bathhouse founded in 1874 and known as the Turkish and Other Baths (1874–81) and the University Baths (1881–98). This was managed first by Henry/Harry Morgan who was living at No. 27 (1881–91) and then by H. Lucas (1895).

A plan of 1882 shows that there were two rectangular structures that were the 'Bath Rooms'. The southernmost of these equates to the existing *Building 26*, which had some drains and a soakaway inserted into it. Further back *Building 50* was also constructed. This measured 8.9m long by 5.2m wide and contained a cellar with a boiler at its western end and a brick-lined soakaway at its eastern end; these were connected by an iron water pipe (Fig. 5.58). There was also a chimney and a number of deep brick-lined 'bunkers'. *Building 50* comprised a secondary structure located just behind one of the 'Bath Rooms' and it may have been linked to them, although given the range of other business interests of the Flacks it might equally well have fulfilled a range of other roles.

In the area that had previously formed the rear of Plot XVI all existing buildings were demolished, and the area became a large open garden with a greenhouse. The existing *Well 43* continued in use, but the water was diverted southwards in a lead pipe. This pipe was later robbed in the late nineteenth century. The robber cut contained metapodia from at least nine sheep, representing waste generated from light tanning activity. At the rear of the garden was situated a rectangular vertically sided flat-bottomed timber-lined structure (*Cellar 12*). The Turkish Baths continued to operate until *c.* 1898–1901 and from 1895 onwards parts of the frontage were occupied by a range of other business such as a hairdresser, accountant, house/estate agent and an architect/surveyor. The bunkers and soakaway of *Building 50* were backfilled with rubble *c.* 1882–5; this infill also included some leather shoes, clay pipes produced by Anne Cleaver (active 1858, died 1864) and an object made from pipeclay. There was also a considerable quantity of plain light blue wall plaster, possibly derived from a phase of refurbishment in the Turkish Baths.

The plot then went through another major reorganization *c.* 1882–5 under the aegis of the Barrett family who acquired Plot XVII *c.* 1864–81. The Barrett family were china, earthenware and glass dealers at various premises in Cambridge between *c.* 1786–1975 (Fig. 5.59). The business was initially based at Market Hill (1813–1937/38), with warehouse(s) at Jesus Lane that were offered for sale as building material in 1831 as they were replaced by others at St Andrew's Hill. By 1830 Barrett's were the largest of the seven ceramic dealers trading in Cambridge and in 1881 the business was known as Barrett & Son with the owners living at 60 Bateman Street and 9 Parker Street.

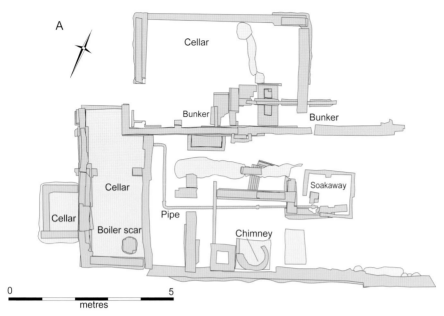

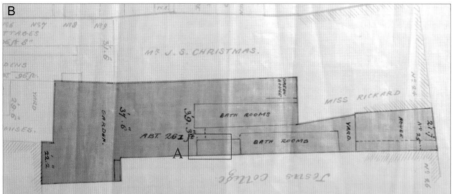

Figure 5.58. *Mid/ late nineteenth-century Building 50: (A) plan of mid/late nineteenth-century archaeological features; (B) plan of property in 1882; (C) photograph of the cellar, facing south (plan B courtesy of the Master and Fellows of Emmanuel College Cambridge).*

Figure 5.59. *Images of the Barrett family ceramics and glass business: (A–B) interior views of Barrett & Son Ltd. premises at Plot XVII, c. 1920; (C–D) exterior and interior views of Barrett & Son Ltd. glass, china and hardware shop at No.30 Market Hill, c. 1930 (all photographs courtesy of the Cambridgeshire Collection, Cambridge Central Library).*

By 1884 the rear of Plot XVII was being directly utilized by the Barrett family, who had managed to create an irregular but contiguous plot stretching *c.* 106m from St Andrew's Street to St Andrew's Hill and covering *c.* 1405 sq. m. *Cellar 12*, at the rear of the garden area that was originally part of Plot XVI but was now part of Plot XVII, was backfilled *c.* 1882–5 and contained over 300 items (MNI) (Figs. 5.60–5.62). The backfilling appears to contain two discernible elements; the majority pertains to the disposal of contemporary material relating to the Barrett family business but there is also some older material. The older material consists primarily of glass bottles of *c.* 1780–1810, including two bearing the seal of Emmanuel College (Fig. 5.60C–D). Many of the bottles are heavily encrusted with mortar, suggesting that broken bottles had been reused either as part of a foundation or projecting from the top of a wall. The dating and association with Emmanuel College indicates that they derive from features linked to the period when Plot XVI was occupied by Matthew and then Charles Burbage, the butlers at Emmanuel College.

Also possibly linked to the College is a near-complete Martaban-type storage jar (Fig. 5.62D), which was originally used to transport water, oil or some other material from Southeast Asia

to Europe. This jar may then have become a curio or collectable, and to judge from the lime-scale present in its interior, eventually served as a water container in the garden. The later Barrett family business material indicates a range of the wares that they sold to the public, such as a pattern with purple transfer-printed cereals (Fig. 5.61A). The business also stocked children's plates (Fig. 5.61G), some jugs with a classically inspired Trajan pattern (Fig. 5.61K) and high-quality red bodied stoneware (Fig. 5.62B), also classically inspired. There is evidence that the Barrett's supplied crockery to Charles Barber the cook at Sidney Sussex (Fig. 5.61D), Gonville & Caius College (Fig. 5.61E), Desiree Bruvet the cook at St John's College (Fig. 5.61F) and an unidentified Cambridge wine and spirit merchant (Fig. 5.61J).

The area was then built over by a series of large structures, *Standing Buildings 94–96* (Fig. 5.63), which comprise a set of purpose-built storage and retail spaces for the Barrett family ceramic retailing business. *Standing Building 96* was a single-storey structure measuring 13m long and 5m wide, which although substantially rebuilt was based upon and incorporated elements of earlier *Buildings 26* and *50*. The next structure to be built was *Standing Building 95*, which was keyed in to the rear wall of *Standing Building 96* and 'sandwiched'

285

dirt on the wall of *Standing Building 95* caused by earlier exposure. *Standing Building 95* was a two-storey structure measuring 15m long by 5.02m wide at ground floor level and 4.15m wide on the first floor. This disparity is accounted for on the north side, where the first floor front wall was stepped back 0.83m (13ft 7½in). The

resulting step was mostly taken up with a long skylight providing light to the ground floor and there were also skylights in the roof. A late nineteenth-century cross-section of *Standing Building 95* (Fig. 5.63B) describes it as 'Messers Barrett & Son New Premises, St Andrew's St Cambridge' and the narrower first floor with its hidden skylight and a parapet raised on the south side to hide the pitched roof from view are clearly shown. Both features were still in place at the time of demolition. Located under *Standing Building 95*, the cellar with a boiler scar at the western end of *Building 50* (Fig. 5.58C) continued in use after *c*. 1882–5 and although sealed at some point in the twentieth century was never backfilled.

Located to the north of *Standing Buildings 95–6* was a single-storey brick structure *Standing Building 94*, which measured over 42m long and 6.7m wide. Its northern and western walls were reused eighteenth-century boundary walls, while its south wall was largely shared with *Standing Buildings 95–6*, thus demonstrating that it post-dated them. Apart from the roof only a small part of it appeared purpose-built and effectively *Standing Building 94* was an expediently and cheaply constructed way to create an enclosed and roofed space that involved the minimum possible new construction by placing a cleverly designed roof between several existing walls. These were partly garden/yard boundaries and partly the walls of adjacent structures, thereby creating a building the full width of the available plot. The nineteenth-century cross-section of *Standing Building 95* (Fig. 5.63B) depicts a more complicated building in this location, indicating that the final form of *Standing Building 94* was simplified. A 1920s photograph of the interior shows that the rear of *Standing Buildings 94* and *96* were open together to form the shop floor. To the west of *Standing Building 95* were some later and much less substantial concrete footings, *Building 51* (MNI 187); these footings incorporated a large quantity of pottery as hardcore dating to *c*. 1882–1900 and presumably relating to the Barrett family business. Overall, the impression is that *Standing Buildings 94–96* and *Building 51* represent a largely successful attempt to maximize storage and retail space at the lowest possible cost.

Plot XVIII

Sometime in the early nineteenth century a particularly deep brick-lined well, *Well 57*, plus an associated structure, *Building 52*, was constructed. Pre-existing *Cellar 7* was substantially modified *c*. 1820–30; it was reduced in size and had an arch and chute inserted into one end (Fig. 5.64). Associated with this remodelling event was some refuse (MNI 78) including two cats and a kitten plus a char dish (Fig. 5.64F). The char dish plus a potted game container (Fig. 5.64E) emphasize how increasingly meat consumption might have no faunal correlate in the archaeological record. At around the same time *Cesspit 17* was backfilled with rubble, plus parts of a single large stoneware jar or bottle. By 1830 buildings extended along the northern side of the plot almost all the way to the back. The remaining part of *Cellar 7* was backfilled *c*. 1830–50 and domestic refuse associated with its infilling (MNI 49) included a plate belonging to an unidentified individual with the initials PL, a red stoneware teapot, a wine glass (Fig. 5.64G) and a clay tobacco

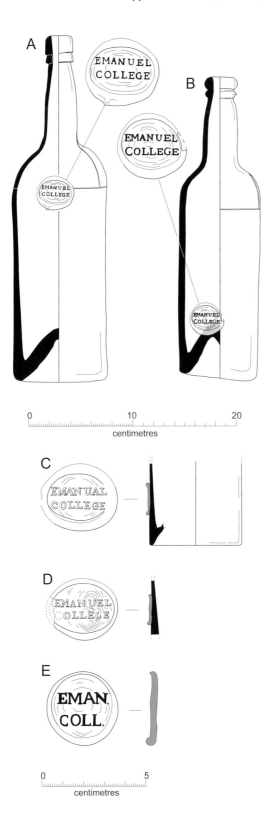

Figure 5.60. *Emmanuel College bottles: (A–B) complete bottles from the Douglas Finlay Museum of College Life of Emmanuel with seals that read EMANUEL COLLEGE; (C–D) oval seals which read EMANUEL/ COLLEGE and EMANUAL/COLLEGE from the c. 1882–5 backfilling of Cellar 12, one has an incomplete base kick probably with glass tipped pontil scar ([40023]); (E) a black glass seal which reads EMAN./COLL found at Emmanuel College, probably early nineteenth century in date.*

Figure 5.61. *Ceramics recovered from the backfilling of Cellar 12, c. 1882–5: (A) whiteware plate with mulberry or purple transfer-printed cereals pattern ([40023]); (B) whiteware Asiatic Pheasant pattern serving dish ([40023]); (C) whiteware bowl with brown transfer-printed floral pattern named BOUQUET ([40023]); (D) ornately decorated whiteware sauceboat marked C BARBER ([40023]); (E) whiteware plate with a black transfer-printed scene of Gonville & Caius College Court ([40023]); (F) whiteware plate with mulberry or purple transfer-printed crest of St John's College, the reverse is marked D.BRU[VET] ([40042]); (G) child's whiteware plate with an alphabet border and an unidentified black transfer-printed design ([40042]); (H) bone china saucer with gilt tea leaf ([40023]); (I) Nottinghamshire/Derbyshire-type stoneware bowl ([40023]); (J) large Utilitarian English stoneware bottle with a domed top labelled …Mark…/…[CA]MBRIDGE.. from an unidentified local alcohol retailer ([40042]); (K) whiteware jug with black transfer-printed Trajan pattern hunting scene ([40023]); (L–M) Utilitarian English Stoneware ink bottles manufactured by Bourne & Son of Denby ([40023]).*

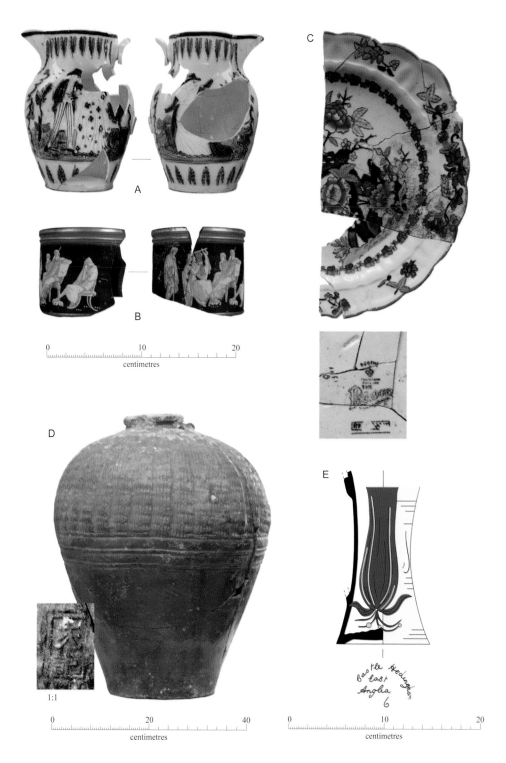

Figure 5.62. *Photographs and drawing of nineteenth–twentieth-century ceramics, including: (A) a pearlware jug with moulded and hand-painted decoration in the Pratt style of 'The Sailor's Return and Farewell' from the backfilling of Cellar 4, c. 1830–45; (B) a red bodied stoneware with gilt bands and a white and pale classical scene on a black background, which may be a Wedgwood product, from the backfilling of Cellar 12, c. 1882–5; (C) a Booth's silicon china Pomadour pattern dessert plate with red, blue and green transfer-printed floral decoration from the backfilling of Cellar 13, c. 1913–21; (D) a Martaban-type storage jar with a céladon coloured glaze, stamped with the Chinese boar symbol from the backfilling of Cellar 12, c. 1882–5; (E) 'Art' earthenware inscribed Castle Hedingham/East/Anglia/6 from the backfilling of Cellar 13 in c. 1913–21.*

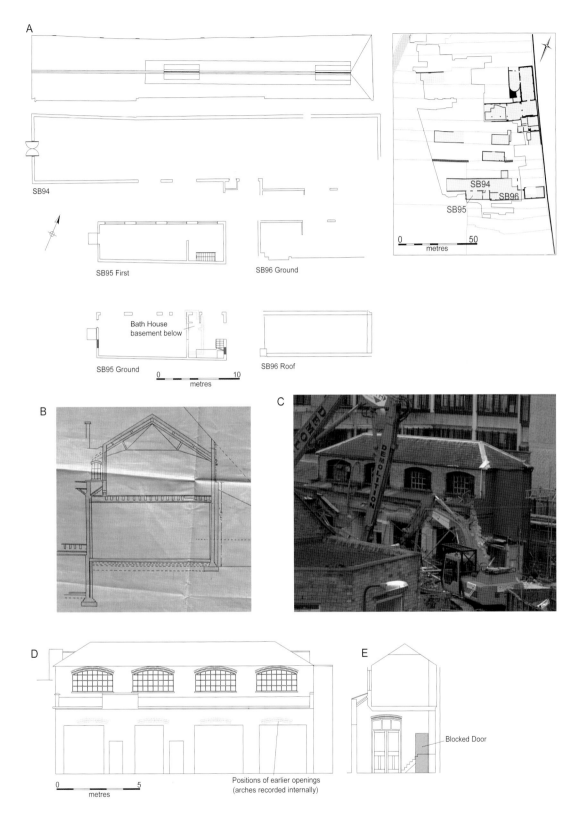

Figure 5.63. *Standing Buildings 94–6, constructed c. 1882–5: (A) plans of Standing Buildings 94–6; (B) 1880s cross-section through Standing Building 95; (C) photograph of Standing Building 95 as revealed during demolition, facing southeast; (D) north elevation of Standing Building 94; (E) cross-section through Standing Building 95 (B courtesy of the Master and Fellows of Emmanuel College Cambridge).*

289

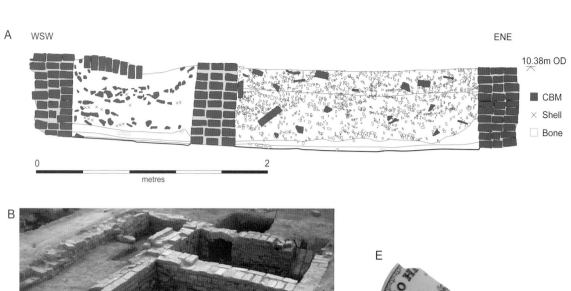

A

WSW

ENE

10.38m OD

CBM

× Shell

Bone

0   2

metres

B

E

C

F

D

Q AD05   31403

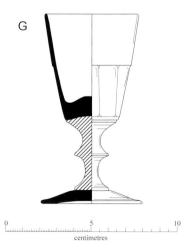

G

0   5   10

centimetres

pipe produced by Robert Nutter, known to have been active c. 1841. After this a brick floor was constructed over the cellar's remains and the building above continued in use. By the late nineteenth century, however, part of the floor had subsided into the backfilled cellar and the building was modified once again.

This plot was occupied by a butcher in 1841 and then by a series of bakers from c. 1851 onwards. By 1855 the plot has heavily built over. Many of the new structures were built in the 1840s or 1850s as they included a specialized bake house oven with 'covered flues' but this had left no trace. A small pit, *Pit 62*, was dug c. 1873–1900 to dispose of some domestic refuse (MNI 15) including a potted game container (Fig. 5.64E). Developments in the 1880s at Plot XVII meant that Plot XVIII was partially enclosed by substantial walls and by 1885 the garden had been built over.

Plot XIX

In the 1830s the plot tail of the northern part of Plot XIX was redeveloped into a series of 11 small buildings, collectively known as St Andrew's Court. This comprised an expansion of the five cottages that had existed here since 1771 and represents the creation of a small area of 'slumland' (Mayne & Murray 2001). These buildings had shallow footings and only fragments of these survived as *Building 53*, demonstrating that the individual structures were c. 5.5m wide by 4.5m deep. They consisted of a single ground floor room plus one or two upstairs bedrooms and each structure had its own separate WC and small open area. The development generally had c. 35–40 occupants at any time and was inhabited by relatively poor working class families, including lower status College servants such as bedmakers.

Plot XX

The Birdbolt Inn at Plot XX continued to develop as a coaching inn for much of the nineteenth century. By 1881 it had become a temperance hotel, but this ceased trading in 1898; bringing to an end a 420-year tradition as an inn. The plot was then briefly occupied by a tailors and robemakers and several other businesses. The only archaeological feature was a particularly deep brick-lined well, *Well 58*, which was presumably linked to the large quantities of water that the inn required, particularly for the numbers of horses that the stables on the site suggest.

Figure 5.64 *(opposite). Plot XVIII: (A–D) mid–late eighteenth-century brick-lined Cellar 7, backfilled in two stages c. 1820–30 and c. 1830–50: (A) section of the cellar; (B) photograph of cellar, facing southwest; (C) photograph of arch and chute in western wall, facing west; (D) photograph of collapsed floor, facing west; (E) a whiteware lid with green transfer-printed decoration, which reads POTTED GAME, SO H… BREAKFAST LUNCHEON & .., RW from Pit 62 c. 1873–1900 ([31207]); (F) small shallow tin-glazed earthenware char dish with polychrome decoration in a fish design, probably made in Liverpool which specialized in these pots by this date (Archer 1997, 320), from Cellar 7 ([31430]) c. 1820–30; (G) a colourless drinking glass with brown patina, consisting of a conical bowl with panel moulding on the lower half (13 panels) and a plain upper half to lip. Very short stem with bladed knop and solid conical foot, late eighteenth–early nineteenth-century from Cellar 7 ([31588]) c. 1830–50.*

Plot XXII

Throughout the medieval and post-medieval periods Plot XXII had remained a largely open area. This began to change in the late seventeenth and eighteenth centuries (see above), but it was in the nineteenth century that this situation altered fundamentally and Plot XXII became one of the most archaeologically 'active' areas in the street block. This was primarily because its lack of earlier development meant that when pressures on space increased during the nineteenth century it presented a significant opportunity, paralleled only by the large garden area that was developed by Robert Sayle (below). The Purchas family continued to own at least part of Plot XXII until 1829, although their fortunes were in decline, and by 1830 the plot was rather more densely built-upon than in the late eighteenth century but not fundamentally altered. The only archaeological feature of c. 1800–30 was brick-lined *Well 55*. The plot then came into the hands of two local spinsters, Misses Mary Ann and Sophia Bones, who died at some point between 1841 and 1851. In c. 1830–45 and probably c. 1844–5 the area was transformed, and although the Cock Inn continued to exist it shrank and lay outside the investigated area. It is unclear whether this change took place under the aegis of the Bones sisters, although it is perhaps more likely that it took place under their successors who may have been the Barrett family.

The first stage in the construction of Corn Exchange Court was the demolition of the existing above ground structures and the backfilling of various features including *Cellar 4* (Figs. 5.37, 5.65–5.69, 7.2R and 7.3). This feature contained one of the largest and most diverse nineteenth-century assemblages from the site (MNI 290, or 343 if shellfish are included), which is linked to an inn as well as several Colleges. As this material has been published in detail elsewhere (Cessford 2014a), only an overview will be presented here. The backfilling of *Cellar 4* involved the dumping of c. 3.1 cubic m of material. The primary constituent of the infill was building debris, consisting of crushed mortar and hundreds of brick and tile fragments, some of which were of the same fabric as the walls of the cellar while others appear to derive from the demolition of different structures elsewhere on the plot. There was also a considerable quantity of ash, charcoal and cinder. The material culture that was recovered was dominated by pottery (MNI 205), plus glass vessels (MNI 13), bone (46 MNBU, plus 5 others) and edible shellfish (MNI 193), plus some clay tobacco pipes (MNI 10), a small amount of window glass, some heavily corroded and unidentifiable iron fragments plus the iron portion of the heel of a shoe, part of a ceramic figurine, two bone knife handles, a whetstone, a small bone button and four copper alloy objects.

Despite the plot's known association with the Cock Inn relatively few items were recovered that appear to be inn-related. The most obvious was a half pint capacity stoneware tankard-shaped jug with a pinched spout and an ale measure mark consisting of a crown over the initials WR. This was in compliance with the act for ascertaining the measures for retailing ale and beer of 1700, which covered vessels of up to a quart capacity used in inns and other commercial establishments and was in force until 1876 (Bimson 1970). There were also several tankards (MNI eight), principally of creamware (MNI 5), and English stoneware probably from London (MNI three) as well as two nearly complete Staffordshire-type slipware two-handled cups. Also present were two complete stoneware bottles, probably from Frechen, whose stoneware industry declined in importance in the seventeenth century but continued into the 1850s. These are relatively unusual finds in Cambridge, with only one other eighteenth–nineteenth-century vessel from Grand Arcade that is substantially complete. 11 chamber pots plus a stool pan were also recovered. These are probably also linked to the inn, as the large number of these vessels indicates a level of requirement higher than that of a domestic household. The overall assemblage, however, lacks many of the distinctive characteristics normally found in inn/tavern related assemblages such as a high

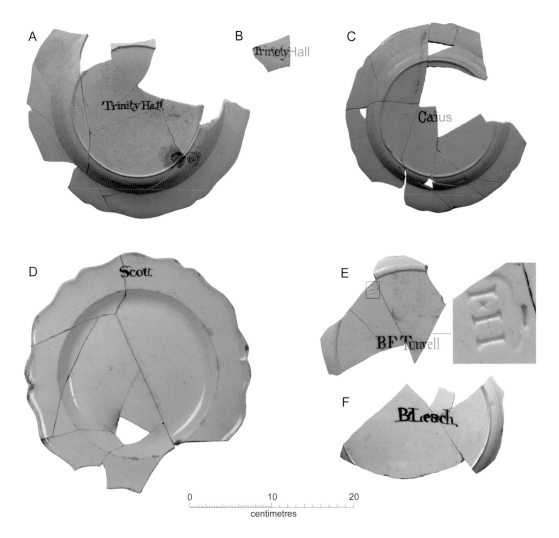

0   10   20
centimetres

Figure 5.65. *College-associated material from the backfilling of Cellar 4, c. 1830–45, including: (A) creamware dish or deep plate with Royal pattern rim with Trinity Hall on underside of base in underglaze blue writing and impressed maker's mark A ([30102], [30108]); (B) creamware vessel of unknown form marked TRINETY H… on underside of base in underglaze blue writing ([30102]); (C) creamware plate with Royal pattern rim marked CAI… for Gonville & Caius College on underside of base in underglaze blue writing ([30102], [30108]); (D) pearlware plate marked B F Tunw[ell] on underside of base in underglaze blue writing, with impressed maker's mark IH ([30101], [30108]); (E) creamware plate with a Queen's shape edge marked Scott in underglaze hand-painted blue on the upper side of the rim ([30102], [30108]); (F) creamware plate marked B Leach on underside of base in underglaze blue writing ([30102]).*

proportion of drinking vessels and high quantities of wine glasses, specialized glassware and clay tobacco pipes (Bragdon 1988; see also Cessford *et al.* 2017; Fryer & Shelley 1997; Pearce 2000; Rockman & Rothschild 1984). This is presumably because the Cock Inn continued in business and therefore retained most of its associated material culture, apart from a few unwanted items.

The ceramics (EVE 74.97, EVE per MNI 0.37) are dominated in terms of fabric by pearlware (MNI 75) and creamware (MNI 57) and functionally by dining (MNI 66) and tea drinking (MNI 61). Both the creamware and the pearlware exhibit a wide range of variation in fabric and rim form, indicating that the material was not purchased as a single group but represents a collection accumulated over time. Nearly 40 per cent of the material related to dining. This group mainly dates to *c.* 1770 or later although a single creamware plate with a richer darker yellow fabric and two Chinese export porcelain

vessels date to *c.* 1760. A number of the plates and other dining vessels were marked with the hand-painted or transfer-printed names of Colleges or College cooks. The earliest of these, dated *c.* 1770–85, were a creamware dish or deep plate with Royal pattern rim marked Trinity Hall, plus an impressed maker's mark A, (Fig. 5.65A) and a further vessel of unknown form that was probably a plate was marked TRINETY H… (Fig. 5.65B). There was also a plate with Royal pattern rim marked CAI… (Fig. 5.65C) for Gonville & Caius College.

A pearlware plate with underglaze blue lettering B F Tunw… on the base and with the impressed mark IH (Fig. 5.65E) can be linked to Bates Francis Tunwell, an apprentice cook at Emmanuel College in 1782 under his father Thomas and then himself the College cook 1794–1806. A fragment of another plate also bears the impressed mark IH; these were manufactured by John Harrison of Stoke who is listed in directories of 1781–3 (Pomfret 2008). A creamware plate with a Queens shape edge-marked Scott (Fig. 5.65D) probably relates to a cook called William Scott (*c.* 1779–94). This plate is notable as the name is painted on the upper side of the rim rather than on the underside of the base as in the other cases, making it much more visible. There was also another creamware plate marked B•Leach (Fig. 5.65F), a name more commonly represented on vessels in some other nearby features. This belonged to Barnard/Barnett Leach III and

IV, two generations of a family who were cooks at Trinity College (1770–1812) (see Fig. 7.3).

The most common name was R Hopkins, found on eight plates, a dish and a bowl belonging to Richard Hopkins, a cook at both Gonville & Caius College and Trinity Hall (*c.* 1805–12) (Fig. 5.66). The plates all have a similar moulding and blue hand-painted shell-edged Rococo decoration, but on some the name

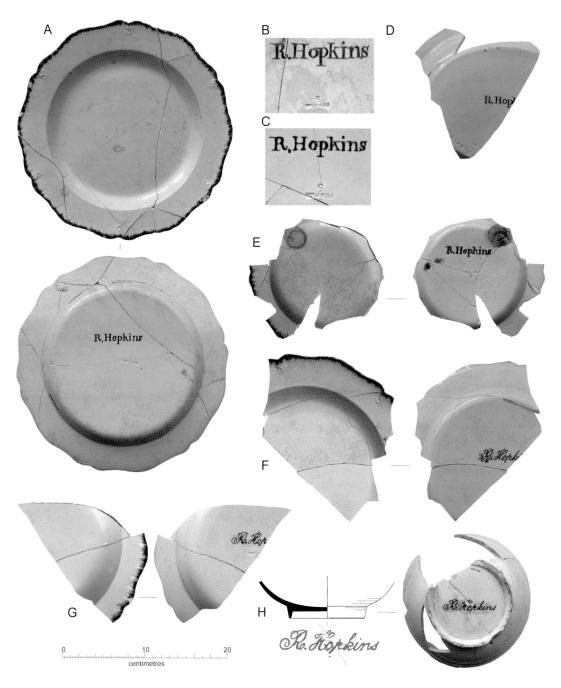

Figure 5.66. *Vessels of Richard Hopkins from the backfilling of Cellar 4, c. 1830–45, including: (A–E) creamware plates with shell-edged rims marked R Hopkins on underside of base in underglaze blue writing, with impressed maker's marks TURNER and TURNER 5 ([30102], [30108]); (F–G) creamware plates marked R Hopkins on underside of base in transfer-printed blue writing, with impressed maker's marks TURNER and TURNER 5 ([30100], [30102], [30108]); (H) plain creamware bowl with R Hopkins on underside of base in transfer-printed blue writing ([30102], [30108]).*

is hand-painted while on the others it is transfer-printed. This style of moulding and decoration has been found associated with other College cooks including Thomas Wicks (Emmanuel College, 1807–51), William Spencer (Christ's College, 1795–1833) and John Barnes (College unknown, 1814–19). The hand-painted examples are probably earlier and consist of an oval dish, three plates and a single smaller plate. All these vessels have the impressed mark TURNER and one is marked TURNER 5, manufactured by Turners of Longton who were among the best and most successful potters in the late eighteenth and early nineteenth centuries (Hillier 1965).

There are five plates with the transfer-printed name R HOPKINS, three of which are impressed TURNER 5 and one is impressed TURNER. The number 5 clearly does not relate to diameter and probably relates to rim form. The transfer printing is generally quite poor quality; this technique was invented shortly after 1750 but remained rare for a considerable period. The investment required to create the transfer print indicates that Hopkins must have commissioned a large number of vessels from Turner's. R Hopkins is Richard Hopkins, who was a cook for Gonville & Caius College by 1805 and when he died in 1810 he was the cook for both Trinity Hall and Gonville & Caius. His widow Sarah succeeded him by 1812, but resigned in 1818. There is another creamware plate with impressed mark TURNER, two plates whose fabric suggests that they were made by Turner's and a piece of creamware with the impressed mark CB (Charles Bourne of Fenton *c.* 1807–30).

While the dining vessels are mainly undecorated, the tea drinking vessels (Fig. 5.67) are dominated by pearlware vessels (MNI 42), with a mixture of hand-painted and transfer-printed blue and white decoration principally of oriental scenes. Some English soft paste porcelain vessels (MNI 5l) and Chinese export porcelain (MNI three) vessels are similarly decorated. There are individually matching saucers and teacups or bowls, but no larger services and the impression is of a collection accumulated over a considerable period. Two pearlware tea bowls that were over 90 per cent complete with multiple refitting sherds were decorated with black transfer-printed Oriental scenes (Fig. 5.67L–M). These pieces cannot be earlier than 1828, as it was only then that potters discovered that black designs could be applied in underglaze without distortion by

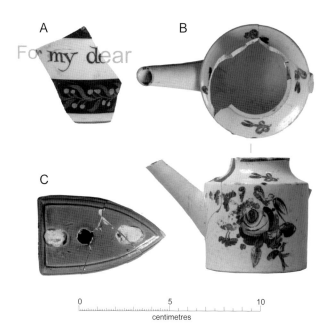

Figure 5.68. *'Personal' material from the backfilling of Cellar 4,* c. *1830–45, including: (A) creamware cup with hand-painted text '…r my de…' ([30102]); (B) creamware miniature watering can with hand-painted red and green floral decoration ([30102]); (C) green iron-shaped Staffordshire-type figurine base ([30102], [30108]).*

Figure 5.67 *(opposite). Tea and coffee drinking related vessels from the backfilling of Cellar 4,* c. *1830–45: (A) black basalt teapot lid ([30101]); (B) pearlware teapot with blue hand-painted floral decoration ([30099]); (C) mocha pattern pearlware cup with blue and brown bands ([30101], [30102]); (D) pearlware coffee can with hand-painted blue, yellow, brown and pale orange/brown stars and lines in Pratt ware style ([30102]); (E) English soft paste porcelain slops bowl with hand-painted blue scene ([30060], [30100], [30101]); (F) pearlware blue transfer-printed saucer with oriental scene ([30102]); (G) pearlware blue transfer-printed saucer with oriental scene ([30102]); (H) pearlware blue transfer-printed teacup with oriental scene ([30102]); (I) pearlware blue transfer-printed teacup or bowl with willow pattern scene ([30102]); (J) pearlware blue transfer-printed teacup or bowl with willow pattern scene ([30101], [30102]); (K) pearlware tea cup or bowl with hand-painted scenic decoration ([30101]); (L) pearlware tea bowl with black transfer-printed oriental scene ([30102]); (M) pearlware tea bowl with black transfer-printed oriental scene ([30102], [30108]).*

mixing the powdered enamel colours with Barbadoes tar (*Pisseleon Indicum*) (Majewski & O'Brien 1987, 142). This is the latest dateable material in the assemblage.

There were also a several distinctively 'personal' items, including a pearlware jug (Fig. 5.62A) with moulded and hand-painted Pratt style decoration of 'The Sailor's Return and Farewell' a common design *c.* 1790–1800 (Lewis & Lewis 2006, 2, 15, 156). This shows two scenes, first of the departing sailor and his lass waving goodbye with his ship in the background and later the returning sailor consoling his girl who has wed another in his absence. There was also a creamware cup with hand-painted text …r my de.. which probably read 'A present for my dear boy/girl' (Fig. 5.68A), a creamware miniature watering can with hand-painted red and green floral decoration (Fig. 5.68B) and a green iron-shaped Staffordshire-type figurine base (Fig. 5.68C). There were parts of two small vessels in a biscuit fabric, which has been fired once to a temperature just below vitrification and has had no glaze added. One of these is a small flat oval dish shaped like a large meat dish while the other is a circular straight sided vessel with a foot ring, with the symbol * on the side of the vessel. The function of these items is unclear, but they could potentially be miniature children's toys. There are 11 Late Glazed Red Earthenware vessels from Ely, the largest group from the site, which fulfilled a range of functions including jugs, jars and chamber pots.

Vessel glass was relatively rare and is composed of late eighteenth–early nineteenth-century pharmaceutical phials (MNI 10), which are relatively complete despite their fragility, plus utility bottles (MNI three), one of which of *c.* 1780–1810 is whole. There were fragments of at least 10 clay tobacco pipes, five were of bowls of *c.* 1730–80 and there was a stem marked PAWSON CAMB, manufactured by either James Pawson (active 1786, died 1813) or his widow Anne Pawson (active 1813, died 1823). The copper alloy objects included an eighteenth-century Rococo style furniture drop handle, two simple rings and a plate with pierced decoration. A broken square-sectioned rectangular whetstone tapers slightly towards one end and is worn round (chamfered at the edges) along its length, made of Permian sandstone.

Overall, 252 of the 1217 bones from the cellar were identified. They represent a mixture of butchery (55 per cent) and domestic waste (31 per cent). Sheep bones are relatively common (27 per cent NISP), followed by cattle (24 per cent) and pig (17 per cent). Of note amongst the butchery waste are the relatively large numbers of cattle phalanges (70 per cent of the total cattle bone assemblage) and sheep mandibles (29 per cent of the total sheep bone assemblage). The domestic refuse includes at least 43 meat joints and one portion of crabmeat. There are nine beef joints (c. 82.95kg), 12 mutton joints (c. 52.2kg), four pork joints (c. 15kg) and two lamb joints (c. 5.2kg), as well as seven chickens, six ducks, a goose, a pigeon and a teal/garganey. Very few fish bones were present, just one each from pike and salmon or trout. Edible shellfish included mussels (MNI 90), oysters (MNI 78) and cockles (MNI 25), although these only represent c. 0.6kg of meat. There were also some bones that do not relate to food waste. Cat bones (11 per cent NISP) represent a minimum of one adult and two juveniles and are scattered between three separate fills, with no signs of butchery or gnawing. There were at least two corvids that are probably crow/rook; these species act as scavengers and are generally not eaten (Albarella & Thomas 2002, 33; Dobney et al. 1996, 52; Serjeantson 2000, 184).

In addition to the infilling of *Cellar 4*, two smaller features were also backfilled at around the same time. Firstly, timber-lined *Pit 63* (MNI 97) contained vessels associated with Gonville & Caius College and the cook Barnard/Barnett Leach plus an ointment pot for Singleton's golden eye ointment. Secondly, *Pit 64* (MNI 31) contained a vessel linked to the cook Richard Hopkins. An adult dog with an estimated shoulder height of c. 0.56m was also buried on the edge of the plot in *ADP 14*; in the fill were parts of a small bowl also linked to Hopkins. These three groups of backfilling material, in *Cellar 4* and *Pits 63–64*, although of very different quantities are relatively similar, particularly in terms of the ceramic vessels. The dating of these deposits is uncertain, although *Cellar 4* must date to 1828 or later and the smaller groups are of similar origin. The assemblages are very similar in terms of vessel fabric, form *etc.* although no cross-fits were identified between features. There are also more specific links, such as the presence of vessels linked to Gonville & Caius College in two of the features. If all three assemblages were deposited at the same time this would represent c. 280 ceramic vessels. The presence of similar material in *ADP 14* and the surrounding garden soil, only a small proportion of which was investigated, indicates that much more material was not recovered. These assemblages therefore represent a palimpsest of material that built up over time (Fig. 5.69).

Identifiable elements include:

1) Mid-eighteenth-century vessels, including Chinese export porcelain of c. 1730–60, curated for almost a century.

2) Early College ceramics, plates with the names of Trinity Hall and Gonville & Caius College. This material dates to c. 1770–85 and is likely to have passed into the possession of Richard Hopkins, a later cook at both colleges.

3) Plates and a bowl of Barrett/Barnard Leach senior and junior of Trinity College 1770–1812. The Leach and Hopkins families had been linked by marriage in 1787, when Richard Hopkins was a witness, so it is likely that some Leach crockery was passed to the Hopkins c. 1812–14.

4) A plate of a cook named Scott, of St John's College.

5) A plate of Bates Francis Tunwell, Emmanuel College cook 1794–1806.

6) Plates and a bowl of Richard Hopkins, cook for both Gonville & Caius College and Trinity Hall 1805–10, probably used by his widow until 1818.

7) Items likely to be personal possessions rather than business related.

8) Material associated with the Cock Inn.

9) Material derived from a midden or similar context.

The majority of the items unfortunately lack the distinctive elements necessary to assign them to a particular group. It is notable that the majority of the vessels were of some age when deposited, but their completeness and sherd size strongly indicate against any form of middening *etc.* for most of the material. It seems likely that the backfilling material in the cellar and other features represents the disposal in the early 1840s of material belonging to a College cook that was considered out of date and no longer wanted. This collection built up over time, passing from cook to cook and many elements were c. 50 years old. Although the bulk of the assemblage related to the activities of College cooks, some was inn-related and we know that the two trades were closely linked in Cambridge. There was also more personal and domestic material; this is unsurprising as College cooks business and domestic premises were usually the same. One scenario is that the material was used by Richard Hopkins (1805–10) and later Sarah Hopkins (1810–18). The Hopkins family had premises on Slaughter House lane by 1801 and between 1816–31 Sarah was a partner in a brewers and brawn manufacturers on the same lane. In 1843 Sarah Hopkins, who was living nearby at Pembroke Place, died aged 74. At the time she was a wealthy woman, owning two breweries, two maltings, 14 inns and public houses, several cottages, accommodations and land. Her death took place just before the probable construction of Corn Exchange Court in c. 1844–45 and suggests that a significant proportion of the backfilling material represents the clearance of material that Sarah had accumulated.

Following the backfilling of these earlier features, the buildings of Corn Exchange Court, *Buildings 55*, were constructed (Fig. 5.70). These structures all had relatively shallow and ephemeral brick-built footings that did not survive well. Corn Exchange Court consisted of nine 'cottages'. Numbers 1–3 were located some distance away, closer to St Andrew's Hill, while 4–9 formed a row that fell partially within the excavated area with part of 5 and all of 6–9 being present. This rear portion of Corn Exchange Court measured 96ft (29.3m) long by 29ft 8in–31ft 6in (9.0–9.6m) wide. This would make each plot c. 15ft 4in (4.9m) wide and as they were 3.85m deep, each covered c. 18.9 sq. m. Each tenement appears to have consisted of a single ground floor room with one or two bedrooms upstairs.

To the south of the buildings was a path with a small yard at the end, while on the opposite side of the path were gardens containing three two-celled WC structures. Two of these were identified archaeologically and they measured c. 3.0m long by 0.9m wide (*Water Closets 2–3*). Pre-existing *Well 55* lay under the garden wall and fed a pump located outside Corn Exchange Court. As a result, replacement brick-lined *Well 54* was constructed. Although Corn Exchange Court might be thought of as a densely packed slum-type development, the provision of small gardens plus three two-celled WC blocks – effectively one WC per cottage – and a new well, suggests that they were relatively well catered for in terms of amenities. Numbers 5–9 Corn Exchange Court generally had around 15 occupants in total, and occasionally more than one household occupied a single premises. The occupations of the inhabitants included baker, butcher, carter, coachman, domestic servant, dressmaker, flyman, groom, nurse, omnibus driver, schoolmistress, solicitor's clerk and tailor.

Just to the south of Corn Exchange Court was a small area accessed by the same passageway. A semi-cellared structure located in this area, *Building 49* (Fig. 5.71), was backfilled c. 1879–82 when this part of the plot was owned by the Barrett family. Incorporated into its backfilling (MNI 249) were large quantities of ceramics (Figs.

Figure 5.69. *The origins of the collegiate ceramics in Cellar 4 and the temporality of the assemblage.*

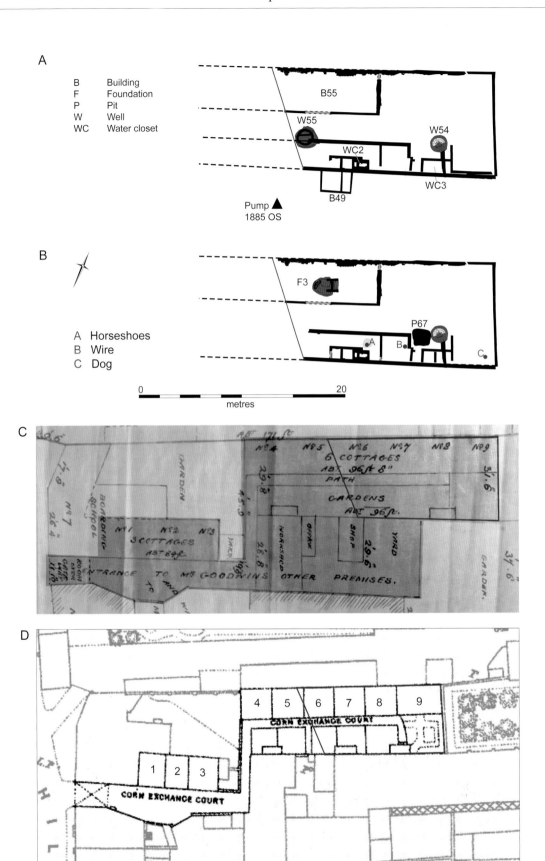

A

B Building
F Foundation
P Pit
W Well
WC Water closet

B55

W55

W54

WC2

WC3

B49

Pump ▲
1885 OS

B

A Horseshoes
B Wire
C Dog

F3

P67

A

B

C

0   20

metres

C

No 4   No 5   No 6   No 7   No 8   No 9
6 COTTAGES
ABT 96 ft 8"
PATH
GARDENS
ABT 96 ft
GARDEN
No 7
No 1   No 2   No 3
3 COTTAGES
ABT 84 ft
WORKSHOP   SHOP   SHOP   YARD
ENTRANCE TO Mrs GOODWINS OTHER PREMISES.
BOARDING SCHOOL
GARDEN

D

4   5   6   7   8   9
CORN EXCHANGE COURT
1   2   3
CORN EXCHANGE COURT
HILL

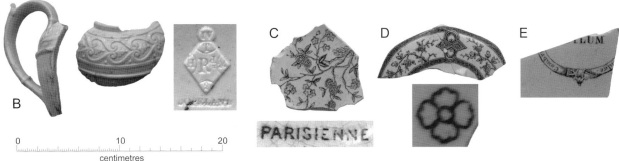

Figure 5.71 (above). Early–mid-nineteenth-century
Building 49 plus material recovered from its
backfilling in c. 1879–82 ([40000]): (A) the building
as exposed during the excavation, facing southeast;
(B) white feldspathic stoneware teapot with an
1867 diamond registration mark of William Taylor
Copeland & Sons; (C–D) whiteware vessels with black
transfer-printed floral PARISIENNE pattern and four
petalled flower maker's mark; (E) whiteware plate with
pink transfer-printed mark CAMBRIDGE in a garter
and …ILUM.

Figure 5.70 (opposite). Plans of Corn Exchange Court,
which was created c. 1844–5: (A) archaeology of initial
residential phase c. 1844/45–87; (B) archaeology of
secondary business phase c. 1887–1900; (C) plan of 1882;
(D) 1st edition Ordnance Survey map surveyed in 1885
(plan C courtesy of the Master and Fellows of Emmanuel
College Cambridge)

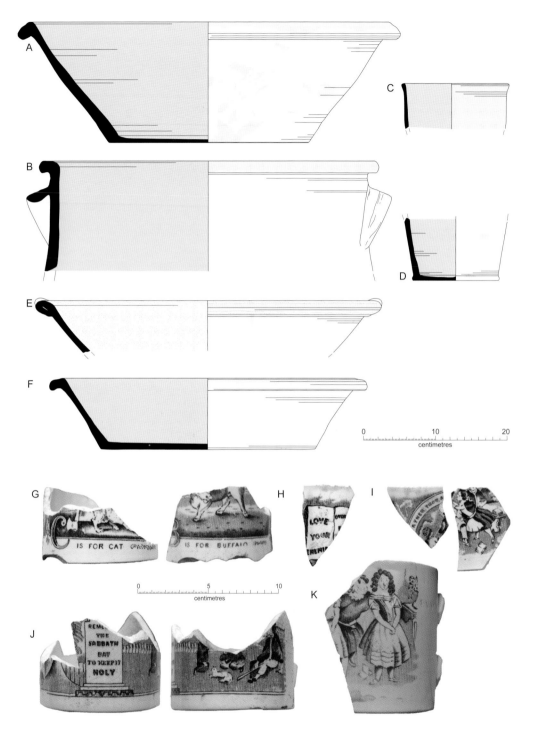

Figure 5.72. *Ceramics from backfilling of Building 49 c. 1879–82 ([40000]): (A–F) Sunderland-type earthenware; (A) bowl with clubbed rim, which is glazed internally and externally with black glaze; (B) jar with two horizontal side loop handles and clubbed rim and internal black glaze; (C) jar glazed internally and externally with black glaze; (D) jar with internal black glaze; (E) flared bowl with rolled rim and internal brown glaze plus white glaze on the rim exterior; (F) flared bowl with clubbed rim and internal brown glaze; (G–K) children's whiteware cups; (G) mulberry/purple transfer-printed alphabet cup; (H) mulberry/purple transfer-printed cup with biblical text from Matthew 5:44; (I) mulberry/ purple transfer-printed cup with a scene of children playing with biblical texts from Jeremiah 3:4 and Psalm 119:105; (J) black transfer-printed cup with the fourth commandment (Exodus 20:8) REME[MBER] THE SABBATH DAY TO KEEP IT HOLY; (K) pink transfer-printed cup.*

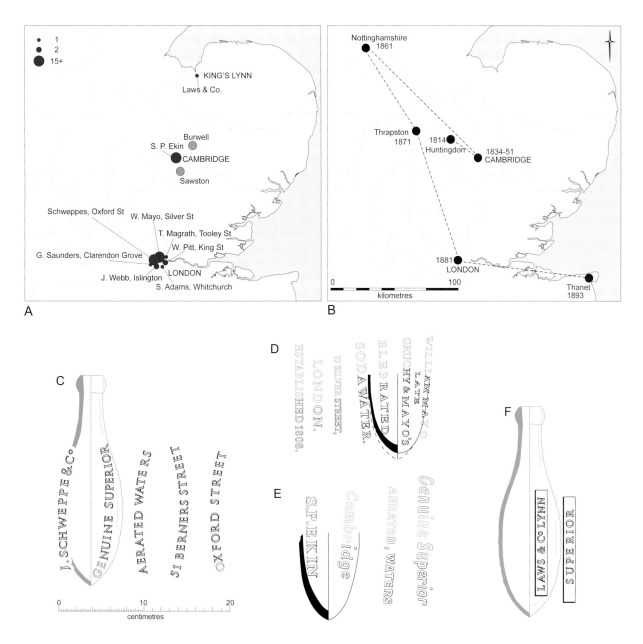

Figure 5.73. *Torpedo-shaped utility bottles recovered from the construction fill of 'H'-shaped brick Foundation 3, c. 1884–90, showing: (A) identified bottle sources; (B) the known career of Samuel Ekin 1814–93; (C) bottle embossed J. SCHWEPPE & Co/GENUINE SUPERIOR/AERATED WATERS/51 BERNERS STREET/OXFORD STREET, length 8in ([40115]); (D) bottle embossed [WILLI]AM MAYO/LATE/[DE GRUC]HY & MAYO'S/[CELEB]RATED/ [SOD]A WATER/[17 SILVER STREET]/[CITY]/[LONDON]/[ESTABLISHED 1808] ([40115]); (E) bottle embossed S.P.EKIN/Genu[ine] Superior/[AERATE]D WATERS/[Cambr]idge ([40115]); (F) bottle embossed LAWS & C° LYNN/ SUPERIOR in slightly recessed boxes ([40143]).*

5.71–5.72 and 7.2S) and many of the vessels appear unused. Most telling in terms of linking this group to the ceramic retailing activities of the Barrett family are five identical and apparently unused white feldspathic stoneware teapots of a design registered in 1867 by William Taylor Copeland & Sons (Fig. 5.71B). Also present were an eclectic group of seven 'moralizing' children's cups (Fig. 5.72G–K). In 1882 this area contained a workshop, office, shop and yard, but by 1885 the yard had been transferred to Plot XVII.

By 1887 the rear portion of Corn Exchange Court had ceased to be used as residential premises and had become a horse stables and workshop. In the 1890s this area was used by Thomas Newton, who had a carpenter's, glazier's and painter's workshop and William Chapman, who ran a builder's, carpenter's, joiner's and undertaker's workshop. *Well 55*, which served the plot to the south, was filled in but *Well 54* continued in use. The row of cottages remained standing, but their internal divisions were removed and an 'H'-shaped brick

301

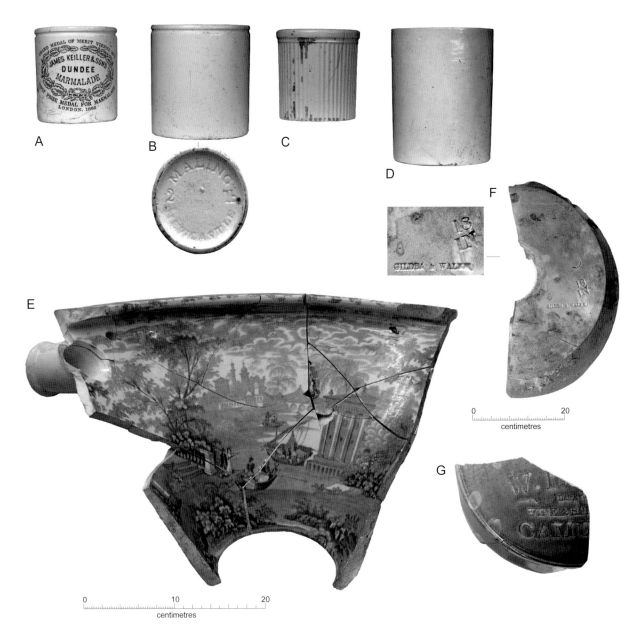

Figure 5.74. *Ceramics from plank-lined Pit 67, backfilled c. 1881–1900 ([40149]): (A) wide-mouthed Keiller marmalade whiteware jar with black transfer-printed decoration of oak wreath and text JAMES KEILLER & SONS DUNDEE MARMALADE/GRAND MEDAL OF MERIT VIENNA 1873/ONLY PRIZE MEDAL FOR MARMALADE/ LONDON, 1862, plus batch letter O possibly indicating production c. 1888; (B) plain wide-mouthed whiteware jar with text MALLING/NEWCASTLE/2lb on base; (C) wide-mouthed whiteware jar with vertical ribs; (D) plain wide-mouthed whiteware jar; (E) whiteware WC bowl decorated on the inside with a blue transfer-printed landscape scene; (F) plain whiteware washbasin stamped GILDEA & WALKER/18IN, manufactured by Gildea and Walker at Burslem Stoke-on-Trent (1881–85); (G) Utilitarian English stoneware bottle with a domed top stamped W H [APTHORPE] /LATE…./ WINE & SPI[RIT MERCHANT]/CAMB[RIDGE].*

foundation with an associated rubble base, *Foundation 3*, was created to support a piece of machinery. The rubble base (MNI 156) included 151 Hamilton soda water bottles, with 20 from the Schweppes company (Fig. 5.73C) and 16 of William Mayo (Fig. 5.73D), both based in London. Five other London businesses are represented by seven bottles in total. There were also 17 bottles of Samuel Perby Ekin (Fig.

5.73E), born in Huntingdon *c.* 1814 who had moved to Cambridge by 1834 and in 1846 was a soda water manufacturer at 10 King's Parade.

In 1850 Samuel Ekin was working at Corn Exchange Street and in 1851 he was living with his wife Mary Ann, born in London *c.* 1814, plus a servant at 47 Eden Street. Samuel Ekin's business does not appear to have survived long into the 1850s in Cambridge, and he soon changed career which meant that the bottles were several decades old when reused as rubble. One other bottle came from King's Lynn (Fig. 5.73F). The large number of Hamilton bottles indicates that this is a commercial assemblage, as the quantity is too large for domestic usage. The deposit dates to *c*. 1880–1900; at this time the Hamilton bottle was being superseded by the Codd bottle, which was invented by Hiram Codd of Camberwell in 1872 and patented in 1875 and became the dominant form in the 1880s (Talbot 1974). The assemblage therefore represents obsolete material and includes material relating to Samuel Ekin, whom we know was based at Corn Exchange Street in 1850, plus a considerable quantity from London businesses, while the single King's Lynn example is perhaps best interpreted as a stray item indicative of riverine contacts. The only local Cambridge bottles relate to a business that had not existed for *c*. 30 years, while the others come from some distance suggesting that the bottles may represent those that could not be returned to redeem the deposit.

A number of pits were dug in the garden area of Corn Exchange Court; *Pit 65* (*c*. 1880–1900, MNI 95) contained at least 37 horseshoes, a padlock, 31 pharmaceutical bottles, a cup with part of a name reading J.C… and a large stoneware bottle marked …E/[Mer]rchant/….ET of an unidentified wine and spirit merchant presumably based in Newmarket. Another small pit, *Pit 66* (*c*.1880–1900), was almost entirely filled with over 400 fragments of iron wire. A larger plank-lined vertically sided flat-bottomed square pit, *Pit 67* (*c*. 1881–1900 and probably *c*. 1892–1900, MNI 95), contained around a dozen metal paint cans. There were also 24 wide-mouthed ceramic jars, including eight Keiller Marmalade jars (Fig. 5.74A), many of which had residues indicating that they were reused as paint containers.

Also present were substantial proportions of two large WC bowls decorated on the inside with a blue transfer-printed landscape scene (Fig. 5.74E) and a large plain washbasin manufactured by Gildea & Walker (Fig. 5.74F). Other items included a large vertically sided Utilitarian English stoneware bottle with a domed top that would have held around four gallons (Fig. 5.74G) and can be linked to William Henry Apthorpe junior, a brewer and wine and spirit merchant in Cambridge born *c*. 1835 who was in business *c*. 1871–95. A substantial proportion of the material from this pit is linked to painting, in the form of ceramic wide mouth jars and tins used to contain red, blue and green paint. This suggests that the material is linked to Thomas Newton, a glazier and painter who was present in 1895. The presence of the two toilets and a wash basin suggests that one of the two three two-celled WC blocks of Corn Exchange Court may have been demolished as the area became progressively less domestic and more commercial in nature.

Twentieth century

After the many highlights of the nineteenth century, the twentieth century represents something of an anti-climax. Although the archaeology of this period is a fast-growing area of interest, there remains a strong focus upon a limited number of specialized fields, such as military remains; the 'mundane and ordinary things' of the twentieth century have not yet been fully accepted into the archaeological mainstream (Schofield 2009, 391), although exceptions are beginning to appear (Boothroyd 2009; Casella & Croucher 2010; Cessford 2012; Cessford 2013b, 100–8). During the twentieth century the nature of the archaeological remains at the Grand Arcade street block changed markedly. In comparison to the nineteenth century,

relatively few 'feature groups' were present; of those that were encountered, two were associated with the Robert Sayle department store (see below).

In contrast to the paucity of archaeological remains, the number of standing buildings – including those that were constructed during the eighteenth–nineteenth centuries, all of which underwent numerous modifications in the twentieth century – multiplied exponentially (Fig. 5.75); it is these structures that dominate our understanding of the street block during this period. Although fully recorded, the bulk of the twentieth-century buildings are of similar form and construction; as the majority are of limited interest, only the most representative examples will be discussed. Similarly, while ample twentieth-century documentary, cartographic and photographic evidence survives, the surfeit of material means that such evidence will only be presented where pertinent to the archaeological remains. Running counter to this pattern, however, the fact that most census returns are not available under the 100-year rule means that after 1911 this detailed and highly valuable data cannot be employed.

Over the course of the twentieth century the Grand Arcade street block became increasingly commercial in nature. No longer were any plots exclusively residential in focus and – excluding live-in staff at Robert Sayle (see further below) – by the end of the century the only inhabitants were students who resided on the upper floors of some of the College-owned properties. The following account presents the twentieth-century remains in a relatively broad-brush manner. The principal exception to this approach is Plot XIII, which will be dealt with in greater detail as it serves as a useful exemplar. No case studies are included for this period.

Plot X

Plot X continued to function as a chemists and went through some modifications in 1934, when it ceased to be an independent business and became instead a subsidiary branch of another local chemists. The frontage of nineteenth-century *Standing Building 18/19* (see Fig. 5.41B–C) was also modified in 1934. On the southern side of the ground floor is a rather grand six-panelled brick doorway, markedly different in colour to the upper floors, with a fanlight and ornate wrought iron grille above. Above this a large stone plaque is set into the brick (see Fig. 5.41F). The design shows a pestle and mortar with an owl, the symbol of the Roman goddess of medicine Minerva, sitting on one edge holding a scroll in one claw with the dates 1851 and 1934 to either side. The scroll beneath has a nearly illegible Latin motto which appears to read SCIENDO ET [C]ANDO. This translates as 'knowledge and candle' and is apparently based up the quote by Thomas Jefferson (1813): 'He who receives an idea from me, receives instruction himself without lessening mine; as he who lights his taper at mine, receives light without darkening me'. This is often paraphrased as 'Knowledge is like a candle: even as it lights a new candle, the strength of the original flame is not diminished'. In this inscription it has been shortened even further. Since the 1860s these premises had been occupied by H. Church & Son chemists (above), but in 1933 Henry's widow Ellen Rose Church died, providing the impetus for the family to give up the business.

Figure 5.75. *All twentieth-century archaeological remains encountered at the Grand Arcade site.*

It was taken over by G. Peck & Son Ltd., pharmaceutical chemists and opticians, a long-lived business established in 1851 and initially based at 30 Trumpington Street (Ellis 2002). This business continued until 1977 and the premises are still a pharmacy.

Behind *Standing Building 20*, small semi-sunken *Building 47* was backfilled *c*. 1920–40, possibly as part of the 1934 modifications. The backfilling contained a small quantity of pottery, a spoon, a knife and a bone typewriter brush marked + REMINGTON + on the bristle face and USED FOR TYPE ONLY on the rear (Fig. 5.76). This brush was designed to be used to clean a Remington typewriter. Remington began manufacturing typewriters in 1873 and although the business was sold in 1886 to the Standard Typewriter

Manufacturing Company, Inc. the brand name continued and in 1902 the company became the Remington Typewriter Company. In 1927 the company became Remington Rand, suggesting that the brush is earlier than this date.

Plot XIII

Plot XIII continued to be used as a grocers for much of the twentieth century, going through numerous marked changes affecting both the frontage and the yard. Although the grocery business continued, the premises was progressively downgraded to being a subsidiary branch of another local business and then part of a national chain. Partly as a result of this, as the century progressed the usage of the

0 5
centimetres

Figure 5.76. *A typewriter brush, which was probably made from a cattle long bone, marked + REMINGTON + and USED FOR TYPE ONLY, recovered from the backfilling of Building 47 of c. 1920–40 ([33866]).*

plot became more fragmented and elements were let separately to other businesses. This meant that Emmanuel College gained additional rents from those occupying the upper floors of the frontage buildings and some of the rear of the premises; in addition, it gained money through sharing drainage facilities, the presence of a telegraph pole and some garages.

In 1900 the College refused permission for the premises over the shop to be used for business purposes, stating that they must remain domestic. This was apparently ignored and from *c.* 1901 onwards various businesses occupied part of the frontage. *Standing Building 21* was rebuilt or 'restored' (Stokes 1915, 38) *c.* 1908–15, and probably in 1912–13 based upon changes in occupancy, in a version of the Queen Anne style (Fig. 5.77) with a basement and three floors, the uppermost being an attic in the roof-space. The rebuilding work relates to the fact that the building no longer provided a residence for the proprietors, as the grocers Flack & Judge who occupied the premises until 1947 lived elsewhere, so the upper floors were occupied and let separately. Prominently placed on the frontage is a stone sign that reads EMMANUEL/THE CHALICE, depicting the College coat of arms, of a lion rampant holding in his dexter paw a chaplet of laurel in chief a scroll sable, above a chalice. Plot XIII had been the Chalice Inn for around 60 years *c.* 1578–1637, but by the early twentieth century the plot had not been referred to by this name for over 250 years. This suggests that the sign is a self-consciously antiquarian statement, which may have inspired by the history of the Barnwell Gate suburb that was being researched by the Reverend H.P. Stokes (1915); one of the occupants of Plot XIII in 1910–12 was the Revered Fredrick George Walker, MA (*c.* 1858–1936), secretary to Cambridge Antiquarian Society.

Walker was the curate of Godmanchester (1902–6) and Comberton (1906–13), who began digging at Godmanchester independently and then began to excavate and survey other sites for the Cambridge Antiquarian Society (Thompson 1990, 38–40). He became assistant secretary of the society (1907), secretary (1908) and then editor and was a prolific author who also increased membership of the society and started public lectures attended by audiences of several hundred. In 1913 he left to become organizing secretary and editor of the Egypt Exploration Society, remaining an honorary member of the society. A post-medieval iron key with a cusped bow, piped stem and flat 'S'-shaped web 'found in yard, at the back of Flack

& Judge, St Andrews Street' was donated to the Cambridge Museum of Archaeology in 1907 by Walker. The interior of *Standing Building 21* had been so heavily modified that it retained few traces which can be linked to its early twentieth-century occupants. One exception to this was a large deed or legal cupboard set into the fireplace of the rear room on the first floor (Fig. 5.77E). This presumably relates to the use of this room by either Algernon and Jasper Lyon of Lyon & Sons, solicitors from 1913 onwards, or by A. Leverington, registrar of births and deaths, from 1929 onwards.

In 1908 the National Telephone Company Ltd. obtained permission to erect a telegraph pole and necessary supports in the rear of the plot; the surviving bottom 0.84m of this 0.3m diameter pole was discovered during the excavation. An associated plan indicates that the largest of the buildings on the southern side of the plot tail had been demolished by this time, but the rest of the area was much as it had been in 1885. The telegraph pole rental provided a modest, but undoubtedly useful, additional income to the College.

Between 1908 and 1926 the rear part of the plot tail was completely reorganized; *WC 1* and *Well 53* were demolished, marking the full victory of mains water and sewerage systems. The lead pipe from *Well 53* was removed, undoubtedly for its scrap metal value as it must have weighed *c.* 50kg, and the hole carefully backfilled. The buildings behind these features on the southern side of the plot were demolished and a large structure – *Building 54*, which measured 20m long by 3.8m wide – was constructed along the northern side, over what had previously been a garden. Included in the construction deposits of the building was a near-complete Bath Brick from Somerset, used for scouring or polishing. In 1915 a yard area and *Building 54*, which was described as a workshop, covering the rearmost 41.75 sq. m were leased separately to various businesses, particularly a coachbuilders.

In 1919 there were repairs to a 'shed' in the yard and between 1925 and 1929 warehouse *Standing Building 70* was redecorated. In 1921 an agreement concerning the drains was renewed and the tenants of Plot XIV had to pay a quarterly charge to the College. In 1932 a report described the plot as in an 'exceptionally favourable position …visible for some distance down Emmanuel Street … on the shady and best shopping side of St Andrew's Street … with valuable adjunct of rear access for vehicles'. *Standing Building 70* is described as a large brick and slated three-storey building 46ft (*c.* 14.0m) long by 17ft9in (*c.* 5.4m) wide, with a chain hoist for goods and all floors used for stores; 'the Warehouse is a really good building for storage purposes having a floor area on three storeys of nearly 2000 sq. ft [*c.* 186 sq. m]'.

In 1933 there were plans to erect up to five garages in the plot tail on an area of 'old stores and an ash pit', and Flack & Judge were asked to ensure that they kept the yard clear. There was no archaeological trace of the ash pit; this is however unsurprising as local byelaws indicate that such structures were raised rather than sunken. Six garages (*Standing Building 78*) with substantial concrete foundations were constructed. One of these was included in Flack & Judge's lease, but between 1934 and 1962 the other five were let separately by the College to various local businesses. Associated with the construction of the garages, the shaft of *Well 53* was relocated and a hole cut into it so that it could act as a sump for oil and other noxious liquids. These garages were a modest additional source of income for the College and mark the transition from horses to motor vehicles common *c.* 1920–40. Two single-storey lean-to stores buildings, *Standing Building 80*, were also constructed at the same time to the north.

The construction of *Standing Buildings 78* and *80* necessitated major modifications to the warehouse *Standing Building 70*, as vehicles could no longer access the loading doors on its northern side. On the northern side of the building the western halves of the ground and first floor double-width loading doors were partly blocked and narrowed, creating standard-sized doors, and the ground floor and some of the second floor windows were bricked up. The second

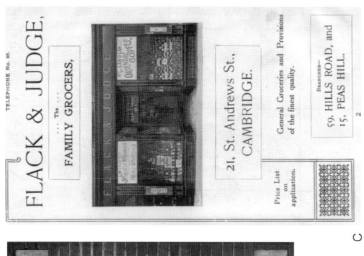

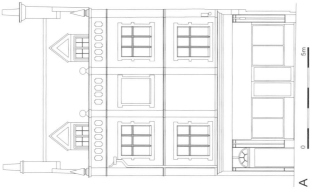

Figure 5.77.
Buildings in Plot XIII: (A) frontage of Plot XIII, (B) stone frontage sign that reads EMMANUEL/ THE CHALICE, as well as depicting the College coat of arms of a lion rampant holding in his dexter paw a chaplet of laurel in chief a scroll sable above a chalice; (C) early twentieth-century advert for Flack & Judge; (D) 1930s view of the rear entrance to plot and part of St Andrew's Hill, with signs for Foister & Jagg and Flack & Judge at Plot XIII and Barrett & Son and No. 3/4 St Andrew's Hill; (E) deed or legal cupboard set into the fireplace of the rear room on the first floor (images C–D courtesy of the Cambridgeshire Collection, Cambridge Central Library).

306

floor door was entirely bricked-up, apart from a four-pane shallow window. A new door was inserted in the position of one of the second floor windows and an external staircase added, providing the only means of access between the floors. On the eastern wall the ground and basement floor windows were bricked up.

On the western wall three double width centrally set loading doorways were inserted, replacing those on the northern wall (albeit in a less convenient location which meant that items would generally have to be moved further within *Standing Building 70*). Internally, on the ground floor the layout was altered slightly and the wall separating the eastern third was extended so that it met the north wall part way across one of the blocked ground floor windows. An axial support beam runs the length of the room, supported on two circular iron posts. As a brick pilaster has been built into the dividing wall to support the axial beam it is likely that the beam and iron pillars were also added at this time. This might indicate that the first floor required greater strength. The only associated documentation indicates that in 1933 an old and disused chimney was removed and in 1931–6 repairs to the roof were undertaken. This implies that the kitchen element of *Standing Building 70* had gone out of use by this date.

In 1936 new iron gates over 6ft (*c.* 1.8m) high were installed at the rear of the plot, perhaps as a result of the construction of the garages. In 1947 the main business became a branch of a flourishing and expanding local grocery firm Matthew & Son Ltd. (Wilson 2010, 145–6). As the premises now became a branch store this represented a relative downgrading of what had previously been the main premises of a business, and was the opposite of the earlier situation as Flack & Judge had branch stores at 59 Hills Road and 15 Peas Hill. At this time the Flack & Judge premises consisted of the ground floor and basement of the frontage building, various outbuildings immediately behind the frontage building, the warehouse, two storage buildings to the north of the warehouse and a garage.

By 1964 a considerable amount of work was needed to the property and in 1965 the status of the business was again downgraded, becoming part of Bristol Vintners Ltd., a large national chain of wine and spirit merchants. This had an immediate impact, as the warehouse *Standing Building 70* was sublet to the Robert Sayle department store, with vehicle and foot access from the rear and foot access from the front. This marks a major change and indicates that the wine and spirits merchants required much less storage space than the grocers. In 1977 the Robert Sayle department store also leased *Standing Building 79*, an elevated structure above the garages *Standing Building 78* that extended over the access way to the south supported on brick columns at the southern end as a 'first floor store'; the lease included an iron staircase for access. This structure continued in use until 2004, ultimately as the Robert Sayle department store counting house, and was accessed primarily from within buildings in Plot X to the north.

Meanwhile the frontage building continued in its role as a wine and spirit merchant in various guises, eventually becoming part of the major national chain Victoria Wine Co. (Briggs 1985). In the early 1970s the plot lost 39m at the rear because of the Lion Yard development. This effectively removed the workshop and yard that had been leased separately since 1915, plus one of the 1930s garages. The remaining structures were unchanged and the very rear of the plot tail was used as a parking area. In the later part of the twentieth century *Standing Building 21* went through a series of internal modifications; associated with its use as an off-licence, the basement was opened out to create a single storage space and the ground floor was largely opened out to create a single retail space. In contrast to the opening out of the business premises, the upper floors were sub-divided to transform what had been offices into bedrooms, toilets, kitchens and bathrooms so that it could be used as student accommodation.

In 2004 the last occupiers of Plot XIII were an off-licence on the ground and basement levels with the upper floors being used as student accommodation by Emmanuel College. In 2005 the standing buildings, apart from *Standing Building 21*, were demolished and the underground remains removed. Some eight centuries of plot history and development, over four centuries of ownership by Emmanuel College and *c.* 370 years of continuity as a chandlers/grocers/wine merchants came to an end. Although *Standing Building 21* survives, incorporating the Emmanuel College/chalice sign, Plot XIII as an entity largely disappeared; although at the time of writing *Standing Building 21* is occupied, not entirely inappropriately, by Chocolat Chocolat (see Fig. 1.10).

Plot XIV

Plot XIV was atypical as its garden, which had been extended several times in earlier centuries and had been the focus of much eighteenth–nineteenth-century activity, remained in use until the 1970s. By the 1960s this represented the last surviving garden in the street block, so its subsequent loss in some respects marked the end of the large open areas that had been such a dominant element of the area during the medieval and post-medieval periods.

At some point around 1924–40 some small buildings were erected on the northern side of the garden, possibly in 1937 when there appears to have been a reorganization of the plot and part of the garden area became a yard. The only footings associated with these structures were concrete slab *Foundation 4* (MNI 166), which had a base made up primarily of broken pottery including two souvenirs of the British Empire Exhibition held at Wembley in 1924. There is no obvious source for this pottery, although it may relate to a general clearance of material that was stored in the garden area. Some trees and bushes were removed from the garden at around the same time and a copper alloy farthing minted 1895–1936 was found in the top of *PH 3*.

Standing Building 22 was gutted by fire in March 1969. It was subsequently rebuilt to a new plan behind a façade that is either the only survival or recreates the earlier frontage. In the 1960s the plot tail was still occupied by a garden area; a plan of 1965 indicates that the small pre-WWII buildings were still present while a 1968 aerial photograph shows that the garden was densely occupied with small trees or large bushes. Following the alteration to Tibb's Row in the early 1970s the structures in the plot tail were demolished and the garden was destroyed. After this the area formed a long open yard, used predominantly for parking by the Robert Sayle department store.

Plot XX

Plot XX went through substantial building episodes in *c.* 1904–6 and *c.* 1973–5, which effectively removed the archaeological potential of one of the most significant plots in the street block.

In 1904 the Birdbolt was demolished and the offices of the Norwich Union Insurance Office (founded 1797) and Liberal Club designed by G.J. Skipper of Norwich were constructed with 'deep foundations', which were subject to limited archaeological observation and finds recovery (Hughes 1907a, 425); the offices opened in 1906 (Fig. 5.78A). Pevsner described the St Andrew's Street element of this building with its ornamental white stone façade as 'typically Edwardian, very Baroque', while on Downing Street it was 'rather more William and Mary' (Pevsner 2001, 247). It has also been described as 'gay and luscious in the richness of its Edwardian Baroque, a delightful success with its recessed arch, its garlands, and its *putti* [winged cherubic boys]' (Little 1960, 131–2). These buildings were demolished in 1973 (Fig. 5.78B), apparently with no archaeological intervention despite the proximity of the University Department of Archaeology, and replaced with and the generally unloved pre-cast concrete Norwich Union House designed by Feilden and Mawson and opened in 1975. The group of *putti* was retained rather incongruously on this structure (Fig. 5.78C–D) and then later again in the Grand Arcade development (Fig. 5.78E), appearing here even more lost and out of context.

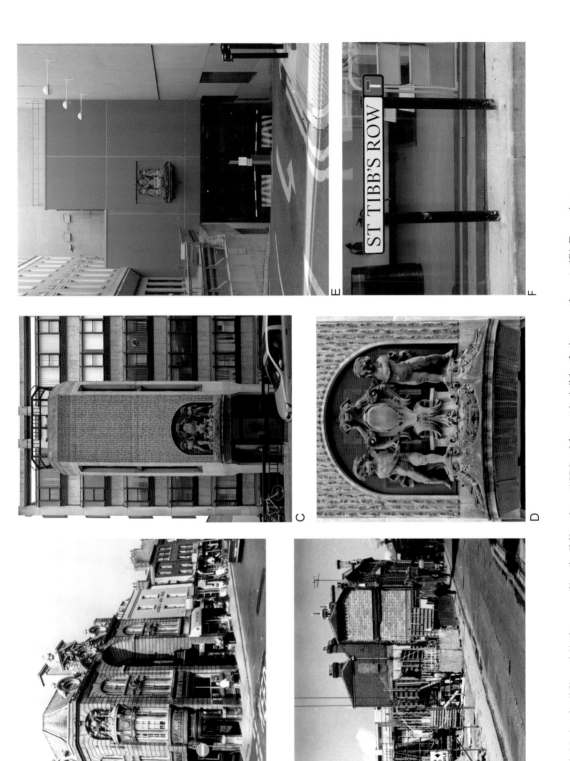

Figure 5.78. *The Norwich Union building: (A) the preceding building in c. 1970 with putti visible, facing northwest; (B) Downing Street, showing building work in progress on site of Norwich Union building c. 1973, facing northeast; (C–D) the putti on the 1970s building, facing west; (E) the putti in their current location, facing north; (F) the current St Tibb's Row road sign (located lower left in E) (images A–B courtesy of the Cambridgeshire Collection, Cambridge Central Library).*

Plot XX has played little part in the archaeological narrative of the Grand Arcade street block, despite possessing the richest documentary and cartographic records of any plot and having a uniquely favoured corner location. From the few fragments recovered in 1904, it appears that this plot may have been distinctive in the medieval period, and certainly from 1577 onwards as the Birdbolt Inn it appears to have been uniquely significant. Its loss from the archaeological record, particularly in the 1970s, is therefore all the more galling and it is important that the partiality of the archaeological story that survived until 2005–6 is not overlooked.

The Robert Sayle department store incorporating specialist information from Tony Baggs, Andrew Hall, Vicki Herring and Quita Mould

The Robert Sayle department store was first established in the 1840s and continued to develop throughout the mid-nineteenth to early twenty-first centuries. Given the scale, complexity and continuity of the department store's developmental sequence it is dealt with here as a single entity, although the account has been sub-divided into two portions – covering the nineteenth and twentieth centuries respectively – in order to aid comparison with the preceding sections. Because the department store also effectively created the context in which the archaeological investigations took place, an overview has already been presented in the introductory chapter of this volume (Chapter 1). Structurally, the following discussion has also been divided spatially into both 'frontage' and 'rear' areas, although this is a relatively arbitrary distinction. The remains relating to the department store principally consisted of standing buildings, although some below-ground features were also investigated (Fig. 5.79).

Nineteenth century

Robert Sayle (1816–83) was apprenticed at the Hitchcock, Williams & Co. drapery business in London in 1838, before setting up his own business in the southern part of Plot VIII, known as Victoria House, which he leased from Emmanuel College in 1840 (Gooch 2004; Sieveking 2004). Sayle occupied the frontage and around 100ft (c. 30m) of the plot, consisting of a ground floor shop, upper storey living quarters, a basement warehouse/stockroom, a small yard and some outbuildings. The business sold linen drapery, silk mercery, hosiery, haberdashery and straw bonnets, in competition with 18 other linen drapers and silk mercers in Cambridge plus a number of other closely related businesses. Drapers – who had always sold a variety of goods, held expensive stock requiring significant amounts of capital and dealt in textiles, which were being transformed by industrialization – were at the forefront of the development of department stores (Crossick & Jaumin 1999, 10) and the Robert Sayle department store was no exception. Department stores developed in the mid-nineteenth century and are a type of retail establishment that sold a wide range of products, without a single dominant line of merchandize, in a wide range of independent departments with their own staff and tills. They have become an important facet of modern consumerism and have been the subject of considerable academic study (Adburgham 1964; Crossick & Jaumain 1999; Hosgood 1999; Jeffreys 1954; Laermans 1993; Lancaster 1995; Miller 1981; Pasdermadijan 1954) and there has been some architectural interest in them (Calladine

2001; Wessex Archaeology 2003, 54–8), although they have been relatively neglected by archaeologists.

Although there were other department stores in Cambridge – notably Eaden Lilley of Market Street (1750–1999; Ormes 2000), which also had a strong early nineteenth-century drapery element, and Laurie & McConnal of Fitzroy Street (1883–1977) – Robert Sayle, in the phrase coined by Emile Zola in his novel *Au Bonheur des Dames* (1883), was the town's leading 'cathedral of consumption'. In 1851 Sayle expanded into the northernmost part of Plot IX, part of the large holding owned by Jesus College. In that year there were 32 people living at the premises including Robert Sayle himself, his wife and daughter plus a clerk, 19 draper's assistants, two draper's apprentices, a draper's porter and five servants. Around 1860 Sayle leased the northern part of Plot VIII. This did not form part of the main business premises as the Sayle family occupied part of this and sublet the remainder. By 1861 as well as the Sayle family, there were nine servants, 24 draper's assistants, five draper's apprentices, two draper's clerks, a mantle trimmer and a milliner. In 1865 Sayle took over the rest of Plot IX, plus Plot XII behind. The still largely open rear garden area of Plot XII covering c. 2100 sq. m (Fig. 5.79A) presented a rare and attractive opportunity for large scale expansion, based upon the contiguous landholding of Jesus College that had its origins in the medieval period.

In c. 1866–9 the Sayle family moved to Leighton House, Trumpington Road, (Fig. 6.20B) on the outskirts of Cambridge, and by November 1869 the rear of the garden next to Tibb's Row had been built up with a warehouse plus workshop over to the north and a 'strongly and substantially' built stables and carriage house with appurtenances to the south. Also in 1869 Robert Sayle opened a London office and by 1874 the business had links to both Hong Kong and Shanghai. In 1871 the head of household at the business was William Henry Lee who was a draper's clerk and manager. Also resident were his wife and two children. There were six servants, 55 drapers, a draper's clerk, a draper's assistant whose wife also resided at the premises and one lodger. In 1874 Sayle took over the northernmost part of Plot X and the adjacent portion followed by 1877. By 1881 the head of household was the housekeeper Louisa Nottage, there were six other servants and the staff consisted of a head draper, 15 drapers, 12 assistant drapers, seven commercial clerks, a commercial traveller, five dressmakers and 12 dressmaker's assistants.

After Robert Sayle's death in 1883 (see Fig. 6.20C) the business became Robert Sayle & Co. in 1884, with three owner-directors; Joseph Clark, Arthur Edward Chaplin and Hugh William Porter. At this time the business assets included goodwill (£5000), leases and buildings (£5000 related to Emmanuel College, £9500 related to Jesus College), merchandize (£27,252), furniture, fixtures and rolling stock (£3355) and six horses (£135) (Sieveking 2004, 38). By 1885 most of the area had been developed, leaving only passageways and a central yard as open spaces. In 1889 along the frontage from north to south there was a shop, a house and shop, a covered passageway and a wholesale shop and stores (Fig. 5.79C). Behind these were a warehouse, two houses, a reading room, a brew house, a coach house and a cottage. Fronting onto Tibb's Row the pre-1869 stables and carriage house with appurtenances remained largely unchanged. The warehouse plus workshop over had been expanded, and was now occupied by the Cambridge Scientific Instrument Company. The space between the St Andrew's Street and Tibb's Row elements included carpet warehouses, a down room, a stable and a building for hay straw and harnesses arranged around a central yard, which contained the pre-1877 pump house.

At the end of the nineteenth century (Fig. 5.79D) the department store complex represented more than half a century of lease acquisition, investment and building on a major scale. Although it was dwarfed by department stores in other larger cities, such as Bon Marché (Paris), Walsh's (Sheffield) and Selfridges (London), the Robert Sayle store was of a scale unparalleled regionally in East

309

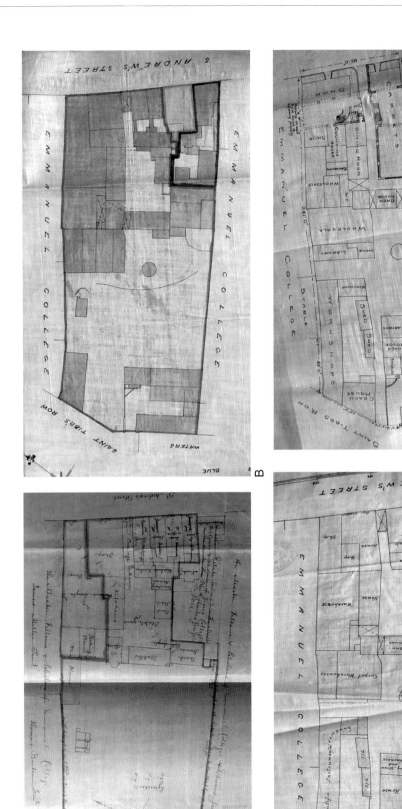

Figure 5.79. *Nineteenth-century plans of the Robert Sayle department store premises in: (A) 1862; (B) 1877; (C) 1889; (D) 1898 (all plans courtesy of the Master and Fellows of Jesus College Cambridge).*

Anglia. The overall arrangement was not, however, the inevitable conclusion of a coherent plan. There were leases acquired on properties that never became part of the department store, and failed attempts to acquire leases that were wanted. In addition, some of the structures built on the department store site were leased to others. By 1862, however, Robert Sayle had control of almost all the land that would encompass the business for the next 130 years, save some additions in the late twentieth century.

The series of detailed nineteenth-century plans allow the pattern of development to be understood. Robert Sayle began his building expansion in *c.* 1862–77, adding structures into the garden area between the frontage buildings and Tibb's Row. Initially many of the pre-existing buildings were retained; however, following the initiation of the wholesale frontage rebuild around 1870, these were also gradually replaced so that by 1938 all that remained that predated Robert Sayle was a large eighteenth-century four-storey building (*Standing Building 42/65*; see above). The evidence for these buildings includes archaeological remains, standing building recording, lease plans *etc.* plus some early photographs. Amongst the nineteenth-century buildings still standing in late 2004 were the frontage range of Plot IX and the northern part of Plot X, eighteenth-century *Standing Building 42/65*, the 1870s–1890s extension behind Plot X, the 'down room' (*Standing Building 48*) and the Cambridge Scientific Instrument Building (*Standing Building 56*). There were also below-ground remains relating to *Well 49* and *Well 50/Building 43*.

Frontage area

Originally three separate buildings, the frontage range of Plot IX was the only part of the store to have been significantly structurally altered in Robert Sayle's lifetime. In *c.* 1876–80 the buildings were entirely rebuilt, to give a new front of four storeys with a basement (Figs. 1.15 and 5.82–5.83). Behind the mask of the classically influenced ornate stone façade, the underlying structure was technologically state of the art, as the wall-line of the upper floors was supported not only on large brick piers but also by a series of riveted vertical steel and iron girders; produced by the firm of Homan & Rodgers, the girders were cased in board to form pillars. The use of a riveted metal skeleton in commercial buildings in England was relatively rare, even into the latter years of the nineteenth century (Addis 1997, 106).

Homan & Rodgers produced 'Homan's fireproof floors' and offered 'constructional steel and ironwork, roofs, piers, bridges, joists and girders and concrete floors', but 'despite … many early, but modest uses of steel and concrete, the first large steel frame buildings were not built in Britain until the last few years of the century' (Addis 1997, 106). In the *Architects & Contractors Handbook and Illustrated Catalogue of Materials and Manufacturers* of 1883 the Homan & Rodgers advertizement declared that 'The use of rolled iron to a great extent supersedes wrought-iron built girders for ordinary construction, on account of less cost and the numerous sections, which meet the requirements of length and load. A method of riveting one girder upon another was patented by Mr. Homan, whereby a great amount of additional strength is obtained, in the part of the girder usually the weakest'.

Within the building the ground and first floors were open and relatively light retail spaces, while the second–third floors were domestic accommodation for female members of staff. This was because although passenger lifts had been in use in America since the 1850s there were none at the department store, which meant that the 'upper storeys were of little use for selling space, though they served well as a hostel' (Sieveking 2004, 48). The original arrangement appears to have been two or four rooms either side of a large central stack, each with one or two windows, with simpler smaller rooms the other side of a central corridor. There are also stacks at each end. A moulded cornice runs round at ceiling level between the now blocked fireplaces, interrupted in places by later inserted stud walls. Some rooms have a picture rail; otherwise there are no internal decorative features beyond a simple skirting.

The frontage of the northern part of Plot X was rebuilt as a single structure *c.*1877–89, and further extended in the following decade. The street front, as with Plot IX, is clad in stone worked in an ornate classical style including, about halfway up the centre, an escutcheon or shield with the letters RS entwined within it (Fig. 5.82C). Although similar the two fronts are distinctly different in detail, with their separate identities remaining intact from the street view. It is clear that the creation of an impressive façade was important to the development of the department store in the late nineteenth century, and at four storeys the frontage was the tallest structure on the street block. Additionally, at around 60m long, rising to nearly 70m when Plot VIII was rebuilt in the early twentieth century, it was 10 times as long as most of the other frontage buildings.

In the last decade of the nineteenth century *c.* 1889–98, a further phase of extension and redevelopment took place apparently involving the whole range, apart from Plot VIII which was leased from a different College. At the same time Plot X was extended westwards, creating a large new retail area, the area behind Plot IX was also extended, increasing the sales area behind the main front. It seems probable that it was during these works that the internal decorative scheme within was established, including the installation of the two main staircases behind. Apart from the staircases themselves the scheme is best preserved at first floor level in Plot IX, and this is where it achieves full expression. The walls are decorated with large rectangular plaster panels and there are arches through to Plot X, the area to the west and to Plot VIII, although these must be twentieth-century copies, with keystone and plaster swags in spandrels. Above each keystone was a cherub head with wings to either side. Both the arches and windows have recessed-moulded architraves. The ceiling is plaster panelled, with three main east–west beams and two lesser north–south beams between them. There is a cornice, consisting of a moulding above dentilation above egg-and-dart above a moulding, which continues around the edge and the main beams. Under each end of the east–west beams is a double corbel with acanthus motif, below which is a narrow moulded plaster panel. The panels are the front part of a casing around the steel pillars running to the floor below.

At the base of the wall a moulded skirting runs around the edge. The decoration in Plot X is slightly simpler, with a moulded cornice at the top of the wall and a large central medallion in the ceiling with six small ceiling roses with hooks. Moving through the arches into the area behind Plot IX the decorative scheme was again well-preserved. In the east wall were situated the other sides of the two arches through from the front. The arch form is the same, but the spandrels left and right of the keystones have a decoration of plaster wreaths. To the south was the head of the main staircase. Its upper balustrade has two groups of 13 balusters separated by blocks similar to the newel posts, although these have the margent motif on all four faces. At the head of the stair the balustrade sweeps down in the four and one pattern described earlier. Behind the stair the wall curves round 180°.

There is a moulded rail at the height of the upper baluster rail; above this are five large square panels with four smaller rectangular ones in between. The plaster moulding around the panels itself has a stylized floral motif. Above the stairwell is a large decorated glass dome with a chandelier suspended from its centre. The dome is divided into 12 segments by ribs, each segment with one of two alternating designs in leaded lights broadly reflecting, though not identical to, those on the staircase below. Below the dome the opening is decorated with an egg-and-dart border above an intricately moulded plaster frieze. The ceiling has two curving triangular panels and a dentiled cornice, which continues around the whole space.

The chandelier, although superficially ornate, is quite simple, consisting of six arms linked by strings of beads with central pendants. Below the centre is a small decorated bowl, at the top a series of

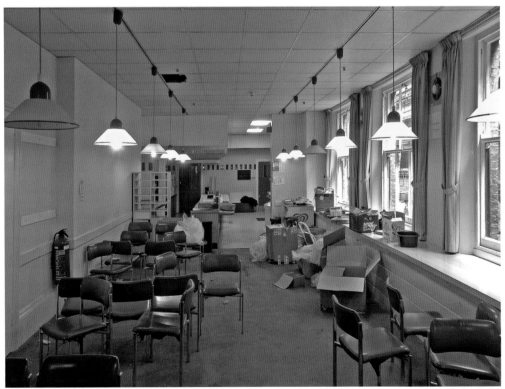

Figure 5.80. *Photographs of the aftermath of Robert Sayle – 'residues' of the former store recorded almost inadvertently during building recording in 2005: mannequins abandoned in a structure to the rear of No. 18/19 St Andrew's Street (upper) and chairs left scattered in the main staff canteen in Standing Building 42 (lower).*

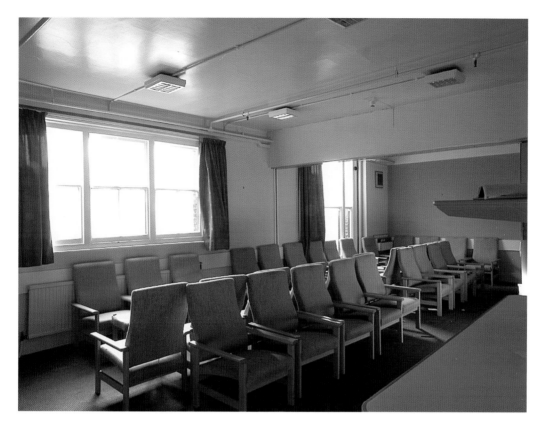

Figure 5.81. *Photographs of chairs on the first floor of Standing Building 42 left more neatly than those of the canteen (upper) and the façade of the 're-branded' John Lewis store prior to its re-opening in 2007 (lower).*

Figure 5.82. *The Robert Sayle department store frontage, which was constructed c. 1876–80 (Plot IX), c. 1877–89 (Plot X) and c. 1905–6 (Plot VIII): (A) general view of frontage, facing west; (B) double width mullion with two consoles at the top and a broad elaborate garland of flowers and fruit (Plot IX); (C) broad mullion or pilaster decorated with an ornate classically derived scheme (Plot X); (D) ornate blank cartouche over a window with fronds rising from its base (Plot IX); (E) escutcheon or shield with the letters RS intertwined (Plot X).*

Figure 5.83. *Early twentieth-century images of the Robert Sayle department store frontage: photograph of the frontage c. 1910, facing southwest (upper) and invoice head of c. 1925 (lower) (courtesy of the Cambridgeshire Collection, Cambridge Central Library).*

hanging pendants linked again to the arms by strings of beads. The west wall continues the pattern of large square and smaller rectangular panels along its length, although here the lower half to two-thirds have subsequently been removed. In the north wall are two further arches and the square-headed opening which led to the ladies' fitting rooms. The arches have moulded architraves and keystones as before but the spandrels are blank. At ground floor level only the moulded architraves and keystones are present. Photographs show that originally there were some more elaborate decorations, including plaster festoons of flowers and fruit below a large skylight.

Rear area

The two-storey structure *Standing Building 48* (Fig. 5.85), which was 21m long and 6.5m wide, was constructed *c*. 1877–85. Much of the building had a raised floor supported by dwarf walls to allow air to circulate and keep the building dry. This building functioned as the 'Down Room' and was used to process swansdown trimmings.

Standing Building 48 was built from a grey/white brick laid in Monk or Flying Flemish bond. Originally there were five segmented-headed windows on the first floor, of which only two survived. The ground floor has been more significantly altered, but there had been at least one segmented-headed window at the east end and presumably others long since removed. The western two-thirds of the building had series of dwarf walls constructed on a rough mortar surface that would have created a *c*. 0.7m-high air gap below the floor, which was presumably made of timber. There were gaps along the length of the dwarf walls and shafts along the main structural walls which would have meant that air could have circulated freely; although there is no evidence for any heating, this would nevertheless have kept the building dry. The 1889 plan identified *Standing Building 48* as a 'Down Room' (Fig. 5.79C) and it is likely that it was purpose-built for this function. By 1898 the western part of the ground floor was a coach house whilst the eastern part and the first floor remained a down room.

On the first floor there were three rooms used for the processing of swansdown trimmings. Swansdown trimming, from a range of species including ducks, geese and sheep, was used as an adornment to dresses and lingerie. It appears that birds, particularly geese, were periodically live-plucked of their breast feathers. The down was then washed and brought in from surrounding districts to the department store on Saturday mornings. Some collectors, known as 'downers', were then given down-proofed cambric, a lightweight cotton cloth used as fabric for lace and needlework, to take home and make into trimmings. This was a substantial business, involving four or five miles of cambric a month and some strips were sold to wholesale houses located as far afield as London and even China. The main feature of these rooms were a series of large metal lined bins with 16 lids along the walls that were 48ft (*c*. 14.6m) long, 2ft8in (*c*. 0.8m) wide and 2ft9in (*c*. 0.85m) high, holding *c*. 10.0 cubic m (Poole 1978; Sieveking 2004, 43–4). The Down Room in some respects represents the

Figure 5.84. *Snapshots of Robert Sayle: Plot IX glass dome with a chandelier suspended from its centre (upper); first floor Plot VIII in 1933 (middle); Plot IX central staircase (lower) (middle image courtesy of the John Lewis Partnership Archive Collection)*

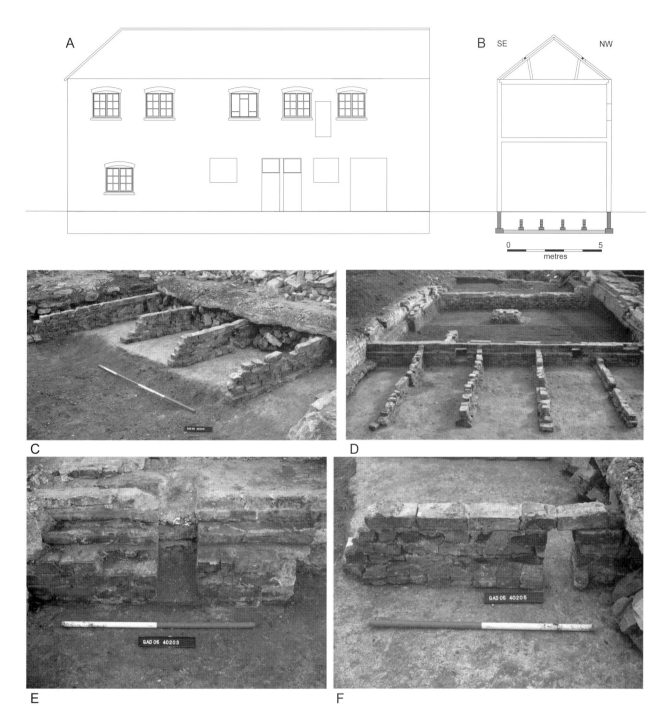

Figure 5.85. *Standing Building 48, the 'Down Room', which was constructed* c. *1877–85: (A) the northwest elevation of the building; (B) cross-section of the building; (C) photograph of the dwarf walls at the eastern end of building, facing northeast; (D) photograph of the dwarf walls at the eastern end of building, facing east; (E) detail photograph of a gap in the main wall, facing south; (F) detail photograph of a gap in a dwarf wall, facing north.*

industrialization of earlier practices, as the fact that most geese were killed when fully mature during the medieval and post-medieval periods suggests that their feathers were an important consideration.

Just to the west of *Standing Building 48* was situated *Building 44*. Constructed *c.* 1877–85, this building measured over 8.5m by 7.5m in extent and contained a series of internal walls; by 1889 it was used

as a stables. Running around *Building 42* was *Drain 7*, constructed from both salt-glazed cylindrical drains with cupped mouths and older style facetted 'horseshoe'-shaped drains produced on or near the Isle of Ely (see Fig. 5.98). Abutting the eastern side of *Building 44* and constructed at the same time was small rectangular two-roomed *Cellar 13*, which measured 6.5m by 2.2m in extent (Fig. 5.86).

317

Figure 5.86. *Cellar 13, which was constructed c. 1877–85: (A) section of the cellar; (B) photograph of the cellar after excavation, facing south; (C) photograph of the cellar during excavation, facing south; (D) photograph of the cellar during excavation, facing north.*

The original function of *Cellar 13* is not described on any of the nineteenth-century plans, but by 1938 it had changed form and become a petrol tank. The initial phase of *Cellar 13* consisted of a main cellar 4.65m long by 1.9m wide and a shallower half-height cellar area to the north 1.4m long by 1.9m wide. Bricks in a variety of fabrics were used to construct this cellar; some were local Cambridge products while others came from Burwell and the Isle of Ely. One had a stamped mark of EASTWOODS/FLETTONS, a firm based at Kempston Hardwick in Bedfordshire.

A complex of structures in the northwestern part of the area originally consisted of a warehouse plus workshop over constructed by 1869, which were entirely demolished in the 1970s. In *c.* 1877–85 the buildings were extended eastwards and part of this extension, *Standing Building 56*, did survive, although the western parts were demolished in the 1970s. In 1889 the extended warehouse plus workshop over, a series of smaller buildings and a carriage house were all arranged around a central yard. Surviving elements included a range of footings, the north wall and the roof. The north wall stood

A

B

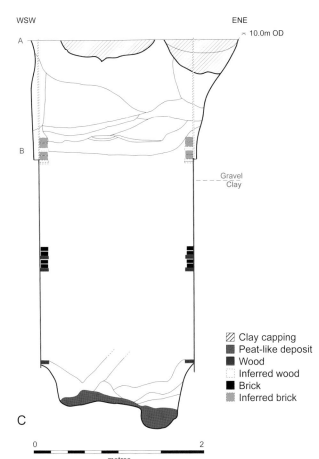

C

Clay capping
Peat-like deposit
Wood
Inferred wood
Brick
Inferred brick

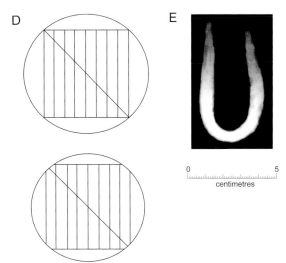

D

E

Figure 5.87. *Circular timber-lined shaft Well 49, constructed c. 1862–70: (A) the top of the shaft, facing west; (B) the upper part of the shaft, facing east; (C) section of the shaft; (D) reconstruction of the cross-section of the baulks from which the boards were sawn (based upon an original drawing by Richard Darrah); (E) simple U-shaped iron staple, possibly from the shaft lining ([37017]).*

319

A

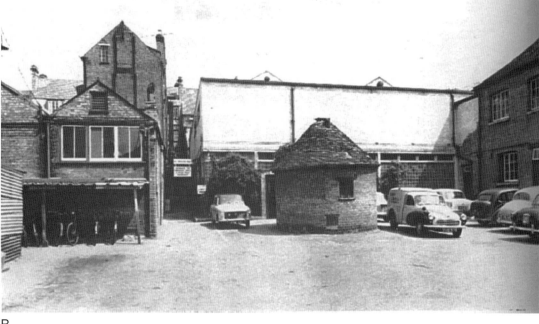

B

Figure 5.88. *The 'pump house' Building 43 and brick-lined shaft Well 50, which were constructed c. 1862–77: (A) photograph of the top of pump house and shaft showing bridge rails and later drains, facing east; (B) early 1960s photograph of the 'pump house' showing the surrounding buildings and yard area, facing east (photograph B courtesy of the John Lewis Partnership Archive Collection).*

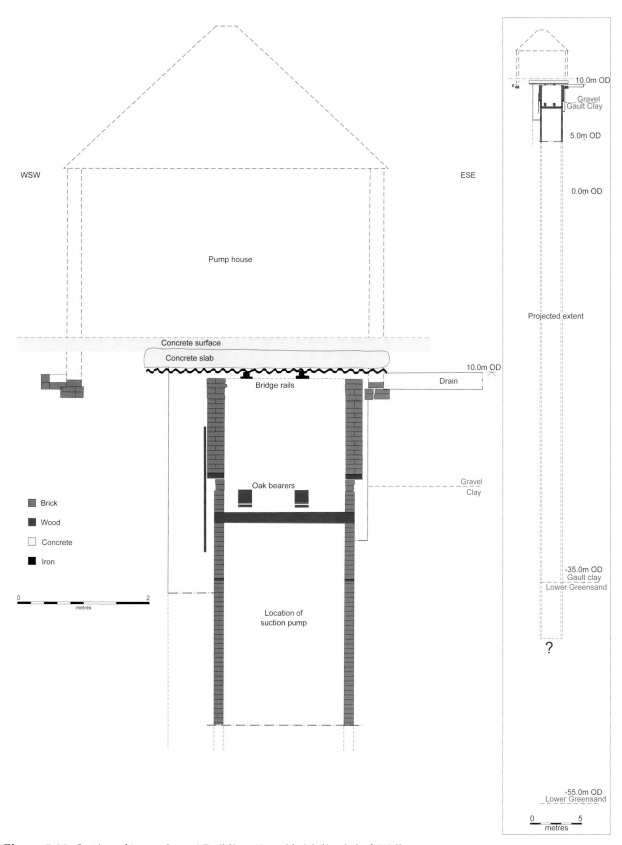

Figure 5.89. *Section of 'pump house' Building 43 and brick-lined shaft Well 50, constructed* c. *1862–77.*

to two floors, although only the upper part was visible externally. Construction was of grey/white brick laid in English bond. The first floor had five windows, three closely spaced at the west end and two more widely spaced at the east end. Although unprepossessing in its final form, *Standing Building 56* had an illustrious history. This was an early home of the Cambridge Scientific Instrument Company (CSIC), which was central to the late nineteenth-century development of science at the University (Unwin 2001), and it is likely that the additional structures of *c.* 1877–85 including *Standing Building 56* were purpose-built for the CSIC.

The company moved to St Tibb's Row in March 1882 and left for Carlyle Road in 1895. These premises consisted of a two-storey building rented from Robert Sayle for £115 per annum and the reason for the move was that 'the place formerly occupied was found to be too small for the work' (Cattermole & Wolfe 1987, 34–6). The premises were extended again in 1882 and 1883 and by 1895 the CSIC was utilizing the ground floor consisting of the front office or store room, a range of offices extending back from it and a show room and private offices at the end plus the yard to the west of the fence. The rest of the block of buildings was occupied by the Cambridge Engraving Company, who used the upper floor consisting of five rooms, yard and sheds on the east side of the recently erected fence and gateway (Cattermole & Wolfe 1987, 42). By this time the still expanding CSIC needed larger premises and moved on again (Cattermole & Wolfe 1987, 49), so their tenure here lasted only 13 years.

Although much of the area was built over in the late nineteenth century, a relatively substantial central yard remained. Located within this area was the circular shaft of *Well 49* (Fig. 5.87), which measured 2.0–2.3m in diameter and 6.65m deep. This well had an unusual timber- and brick-lining consisting of three sets of 6ft (*c.* 1.8m) high vertical boards. The boards were largely Scandinavian Scots pine, definitely felled after 1820 and probably after *c.* 1855–70, plus some reused tongue and groove silver fir Georgian floorboards. The vertical boards were connected by pairs of horizontal wooden annular rings, made from a mixture of reused boards. Placed on the horizontal annular rings were two courses of unmortared brickwork, whose principal role appears to have been to provide weight to counteract buoyancy.

The individual sets of the vertical wooden structure were built on the surface and lowered into the shaft; the boards would have expanded when wet, causing most joints to become watertight. This structure is not one that would have been designed by an experienced woodworker or builder and it seems likely that it was devized by whoever was in charge of the plot. The structure probably failed relatively rapidly, with a likely lifespan of no more than 20 years and perhaps considerably less. The scale of *Well 50*, combined with the fact that it incorporated timber probably felled after *c.* 1855 and is not shown on a plan of 1862 (Fig. 5.79A), suggests that it was constructed under the aegis of Robert Sayle, but had been abandoned and backfilled prior to 1877 (Fig. 5.79B). The shaft would have naturally filled with water to a depth of *c.* 2.7m and would have held *c.* 9.8 cubic m of liquid.

A later development in the central yard was small, low circular brick-built *Building 43* (Figs. 5.88–5.89). Measuring 4.8m in diameter with a pitched tile roof (Fig. 5.88B), this structure was constructed *c.* 1862–77 (Fig. 5.79A–B) and probably in 1868 or later. By 1889 it was known as the 'pump house'. The building contained circular brick-lined *Well 50*, whose shaft was positioned off-centre on the eastern side of the *Building 43*. The 2.3m-diameter shaft could not be fully excavated but clearly contained artesian water deriving from the Lower Greensand, which is located at a depth of *c.* 45–65/70m. Laid over the top of the shaft were two iron bridge rails (Fig. 5.88A), as used in broad gauge railway construction and presumably derived from dismantling of part of the Great Western Railway, suggesting that they were installed in 1868 or later.

The upper part of the shaft had a double thickness lining of bricks and an outer lining of upright planks. The bricks rested upon

an annular ring of reused Scots pine Georgian floorboards, below which the lining of the shaft was only one brick thick and there were two heavy 0.2m-square oak bearers with protruding large iron bolts. Within the shaft the bearers were carefully squared; however, they also projected *c.* 2.0m to one side of the shaft and were just crudely trimmed trunks from woodland trees that were over 70 years old. It is probable that a steam engine sat on the iron bridge rails, while a suction pump was located on the oak bearers. The construction of the shaft was clearly a considerable and dangerous undertaking, but by tapping into the artesian water supply so effectively, water could be obtained on an industrial scale. In many respects it is tempting to see *Well 50* as a much more expensive, well-built and successful successor to the less competently designed *Well 49*.

Twentieth century

In 1903 the department store premises were described as being 'situated … in the centre of the best trade and business part of the town, having an extensive frontage on St Andrew's Street [86 ft.] and covering 4100 sq. yd [*c.* 3400 sq. m]', although some of the premises were 'old fashioned and inconvenient'. By 1913 the business had recently spent nearly £13,000 on the 'new portion' and 'old buildings'. The site was valued at £18,088 and the buildings at £14,312. In 1919 the business became Robert Sayle & Co. Ltd. and in 1934 it was sold to Selfridges Provincial Stores (SPS); in 1940 it was sold once more to the John Lewis partnership. During the later part of the twentieth century the department store acquired or leased several 'satellite' plots and buildings, although in general this only involved minor modifications to existing buildings.

Frontage area
The bulk of the frontage had been rebuilt in the late nineteenth century, but Plot VIII was not rebuilt until *c.* 1905–6 (Fig. 5.82; see also Fig. 1.15). This was allegedly because Robert Sayle vowed never to alter the premises where he first opened a shop (Sieveking 2004, 25), an oddly sentimental decision in such a keen-minded businessman. As Plot VIII was leased from Emmanuel College rather than Jesus College, it seems likely that the later development relates to this disparity. The new structure was four storeys high plus basement, much like the existing frontage in Plots IX and X. The frontage of Plot VIII is, however, quite unlike the classically inspired stone clad frontages of the rest of the department store. The façade is constructed from yellow/white hand-made bricks laid in English bond with heavy stone 'long and short' quoins at each end of the façade. There is a single broad stone course towards the top, immediately beneath the brick parapet in front of the third floor dormer windows. The windows in the main face have arched heads at first floor level, with moulded acanthus decoration and other moulded decoration appears on the front. Inside the decorative scheme already established in the rest of the frontage buildings in the late nineteenth century was continued in the same style, although the realization was rather simpler. This was most obvious in the moulded architrave on the arches. The expression of the scheme was, however, generally smaller and simpler as the cornices are not as deep and there are no panels or mouldings on the walls.

In the westwards extension behind the front range, the underlying construction of the building was obvious in a series of beams, aligned east–west and north–south, which divided the ceiling into square bays. On these beams was a curious nod to classicism, not seen anywhere else. Around the bays was plasterwork with a Greek key pattern motif which, compared to some of the plasterwork elsewhere, was rather crudely executed. This was continued right through to the back of the complex, even including the 1970s extension. The stair from ground to first floor was also strikingly different, being made with an ornate cast iron balustrade rather than the dark wood employed elsewhere. The upper two floors are above the frontage wing only; the second floor was accessible only from a corridor in Plot VIX to the south and the third floor via a staircase from the second floor. Both were divided into small rooms, with little evidence of original features. Plot VIII was linked to the other frontage buildings at ground floor level, although it was not fully opened out until 1934–5. At a broad level the ubiquity of the decorative scheme across the entire front of the department store indicates a coherence of corporate vision, with the business being conceived of as one store rather than a series of shops joined together. Within this schema, however, Plot VIII retained a degree of individual identity due to a combination of the absence of Robert Sayle, the changing tastes of the Edwardian period and its different ownership by Emmanuel College. The ground and first floor were open shop floor areas, with the less accessible floors above used as a hostel and for other ancillary purposes.

Although visually the department store was primarily defined by its façade, its large-scale institutional nature was also apparent below ground. By the early twentieth century the entire frontage was cellared, but these were relatively small spaces of similar scale to the basements of other properties in the street block. After WWII the basements were reorganized, as they were 'desperately crowded, with a rabbit-warren of small cell-like niches in all directions off the two main rooms' (Sieveking 2004, 101). In 1971 they were extended and in 1973–4 the basement was expanded westwards in some areas under standing buildings by 'burrowing', which removed 3000 sq. ft (c. 280 sq. m) of 'mainly earth' which was sent up a conveyor belt and wheelbarrowed away (Gooch 2004, 145, 149). The basement was still rather irregular in form, but in 1985 it was decided that it could not be extended further (Gooch 2004, 154). This basement appears to have been built from largely reclaimed brick, including thousands manufactured by the Sturbridge Brick Company, based at Cheddars Lane c. 1896–1931 (Porter 1973). These basements removed almost all earlier archaeological deposits, leaving only the bases of wattle Wells 4–5 (Chapter 4; see Fig. 4.6C–D); the 1973 expansion can thus be seen as representing a hidden archaeological disaster that complemented contemporary events occurring at the Lion Yard and Norwich Union.

Rear area
Although the functions of many of individual buildings changed over time, the overall layout of the rear area survived relatively intact, although there was a significant phase of works in 1934–8 after the store was taken over by Selfridges Provincial Stores (SPS) (Sieveking 2004, 78). One of the few plans of the whole store to survive in the John Lewis archive shows these changes, and the store itself, in a fair degree of detail (see Fig. 1.15). The Selfridges' extension removed most of the few remaining pre-Robert Sayle structures, leaving only *Standing Building 42/65*. This included the buildings labelled 'store', 'cottage', 'workshop', 'coals' and 'brew house' on the 1898 plan (Fig. 5.79D). The extension created two levels of shop floor connecting back to the eastern end of *Standing Building 48*. The extent of these works clearly impacted detrimentally on neighbouring properties, as in 1938 the nearby occupants objected to the Sayles' 'extensive building operations' (Sieveking 2004, 119). Further building work occurred in 1953–4, but the next major phase of reworking came in the 1970s. When the Lion Yard redevelopment shifted Tibb's Row to its new position, the department store lost 20 per cent of the ground it occupied. This occasioned a large-scale expansion of building, so that by 1972–3 most of the open space and surviving nineteenth-century ancillary buildings had been replaced or subsumed (Gooch 2004, 146–7).

A minor, but archaeologically informative, change occurred when small rectangular two-roomed *Cellar 13* was partially backfilled and remodelled in c. 1913–21 (Figs. 5.86 and 5.90–5.92; Tables 5.8–5.9; see further Cessford 2012). The material from the backfill can be broadly grouped into three types:

1) Material relating directly to the business activities of the department store, such as fixtures and fittings, equipment and stock.
2) Material relating to the care and feeding of the staff who worked at the department store.
3) Personal possessions, belonging principally to department store staff who lived in the hostel at the premises.

Attempting to determine what material derives from what source is problematic, and is not possible in many instances. Nevertheless there are some items that can be identified with a greater or lesser degree of certainty. The only clearly business-related items are five plastic drawer fittings labelled R. SAYLE & Co. (Fig. 5.90H). Although the business had sold china and earthenware since 1864, the majority of the ceramics do not represent shop stock, especially as much of it shows signs of use such as cut marks. After the drawer labels, the most likely materials to be business-related are a number of glass bottles relating to the Wellcome Chemical Works and the Whitaker & Co. Colour Works.

The department store workforce had their meals cooked for them, with separate dining rooms for men and women and another for directors/principals plus senior and junior sitting rooms. There is a considerable body of material that appears to relate to these dining activities. The plain 'semi-porcelain whiteware' (Fig. 5.90A–B) (MNI 43 plates and one meat/serving dish) shows signs of use and is the classic type of ceramic to be provided in such a 'corporate household' (Beaudry 1999, 121–2). Of rather higher quality were the ROMA pattern vessels (Fig. 5.91A–B) (MNI one meat dish, six plates and one side plate). As this material has also been used it seems likely that this relates to the directors'/principals' dining room and the much cruder 'semi-porcelain whiteware' relates to the dining rooms for the more junior staff. 'A carver was engaged to come in every day to distribute the meat ration' (Sieveking 2004, 48–9) and it is tempting to imagine that this individual carved meat for the directors/principals using the 18in ROMA meat dish. There were also heavy tumblers (MNI 47) that in all probability relate to the dining rooms. The large food preparation vessels, particularly yellowware, also presumably derive from the kitchen. Tea drinking from a service with a design incorporating gilt bands and a tea leaf (Fig. 5.91C) (MNI 19, 15 cups and four saucers) also presumably relates to large-scale activities.

As well as the communal dining 'there were cupboards in which they [individuals living in the hostel] might keep any extras they cared to provide for themselves' (Sieveking 2004, 49). After the Sayle family moved to Leighton House on Trumpington Road c. 1866–9 (Sieveking 2004, 26) the effective but unofficial 'head of household' outside business hours appears to have been a housekeeper who looked after the hostel, and there would appear to have generally been around 70 individuals who lived in. Servants included the housekeeper who ran the hostel and several maids, who rose in number to eight or nine by the 1930s (Sieveking 2004, 79), plus a cook, a kitchen maid and a boy to carry coals, while workers consisted of a head shopman draper, who was also in some sense the head of household, plus numerous shopman drapers, draper's assistants, dressmakers, dressmaker's assistants, commercial clerks and occasional commercial travellers. Only a minority of the staff, typically less than 10 per cent, were born in Cambridge or Cambridgeshire, and even these individuals were often domestic servants rather than members of staff of the business. There were typically substantial numbers from London and Norfolk, the latter partly a reflection of Sayles' Norfolk origins. The rest were widely scattered, with no particular local concentrations, and in 1881 included individuals from 22 English counties plus Ireland. The business was male-dominated to begin with, women becoming more common later on (Sieveking 2004, 24); by the late nineteenth century over half the hostel population were female and during WWI and the 1920s this trend continued (Sieveking 2004, 59, 61) with women

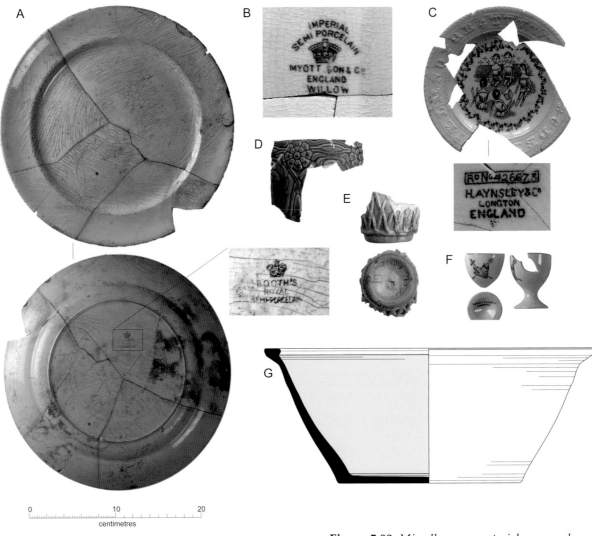

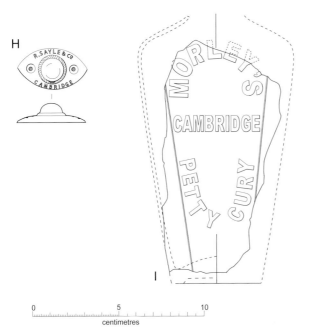

Figure 5.90. *Miscellaneous material recovered from the backfilling of a smaller part of Cellar 13 in c. 1913–21 ([40274]): (A) Booth's royal semi-porcelain plate; (B) Myott & Son imperial 'semi-porcelain whiteware' plate; (C) whiteware alphabet plate with moulded letters on the rim and a blue transfer-printed scene in the centre of a groups of dolls surrounded by the symbols of the manual sign language alphabet, manufactured by H. Aynsley and Co. of Longton; (D) poor quality green glazed small flowerpot or vase with floral pattern and a powdery white fabric; (E) poor quality green glazed small flowerpot or vase with Trellis pattern name and a powdery white fabric; (F) two egg cups with the black transfer-printed badge of Queens' College, a green stripe around the rim and a black transfer-printed retailer's mark of Barrett & Son Ltd. of Cambridge on the base; (G) Sunderland-type earthenware flared bowl with clubbed rim and internal brown glaze; (H) oval-shaped plastic fittings, probably for drawers, of R. Sayle & Co. of Cambridge; (I) spirits bottle of Morley's of Cambridge.*

Figure 5.91. *Ceramics recovered from the backfilling of a larger part of Cellar 13 in c. 1913–21: (A) whiteware meat dish with black transfer-printed geometric decoration and pattern/maker's mark "ROMA"/SPODE/COPELAND/ ENGLAND ([40306]); (B) a whiteware Roma pattern plate ([40300], [40305]); (C) gilt tea leaf pattern in the base of a bone china tea cup ([40305]); (D) Utilitarian English stoneware THE/D.B.C./[FO]OT WARMER ([40305]); (E) whiteware vessel with black transfer-printed mark L & C HARDTMUTH/VIENNA ([40300]); (F) circular biscuit ware item with three feet shaped like a gas mantle, but showing no signs of being heat-affected ([40305]).*

325

Figure 5.92. *Glass recovered from the backfilling of a larger part of Cellar 13 in c. 1913–21: (A) generic complete Codd bottle based upon several recovered; (B) Niagara patent Codd bottle with double recess with top broken of G. Gilbert of Cambridge, manufactured in London ([40305]); (C) Codd bottle with top broken of A M Pleasance & Son of Cambridge ([40305]); (D) complete Codd bottle of Potts brothers of Cambridge, manufactured in Leeds ([40300]); (E) complete Codd bottle of Woods & Son of Cambridge, manufactured in Barnsley ([40306]); (F) Codd bottle with top broken of the Sawston aerated waters company, manufactured in Barnsley ([40300]); (G) Codd bottle with top broken of the Droford mineral water works of Burwell, manufactured in London ([40306]); (H) beer bottle of the Star Brewery of Cambridge ([40300]); (I) beer bottle of Lincolne & son of Cambridge, manufactured in LONDON ([40305]); (J) lime juice bottle of Lauchlin Rose and Co. manufactured in St Helens ([40305]).*

Living above the shop and other stories

In March 2007 an extensive display was arranged of finds from the site, information about current thinking in post-excavation and video shot during the excavation process (Fig. 5.93C). In addition to this a short film was produced, in conjunction with the Robert Sayle department store, highlighting the experiences of some of those that had worked and lived in the store in the 1940s–60s. Interviews were conducted with six retired partners (to use the John Lewis terminology) with a total of 245 years' service between them by Alison Dickens (19 February–11 March 2007). Two had lived in the hostel in the

Figure 5.93. *Public engagement at Grand Arcade: (A) site tour during open day in 2005, facing south; (B) John Alexander being given site tour of the King's Ditch by Alison Dickens in 2005, facing northeast; (C) display at St Columba's Church, Cambridge, part of Cambridge University Science Week in March 2007; (D) finds on display in the Cambridge gallery of the Museum of Archaeology & Anthropology, Cambridge, which opened in 2012.*

1940s–60s and four had worked in the store only. Although initially prompted by questions, most of what follows resulted from open conversation.

Coral Gould (employee 1945–90, hostel dweller 1947–51)

I said to my mother I'd like to work there, where there's always people, I love people, so we went up and inquired, spoke to the registrar, and I was offered a job. I didn't go in at first, I travelled every day from Soham, it was in the blackout during the war, it was very frightening.

Mr Walsh who was then the Managing Director, very stern but nice man, I liked Mr Walsh. He wouldn't let me live in at that time. I was too young for being in Cambridge and with the type of …, that's what he said actually, the type of girl that was actually in the hostel at that time, he didn't want me in there, just like a real old dad he was to me. But I went in soon after that, so I must have been 15 or 16.

I had a big room, they were at one time going to be two little rooms and then changed it to have a big room for some reason, I don't know what that was.

When we were courting I was living in, and when visitors had to leave at night the watchman used to ring that bell like mad so he [her fiancé] had to run all down those stairs to get out before the gate got locked.

When you woke up and you were working, you went down for your breakfast, which spoiled you, it was there and you helped yourself. I missed that terribly when I got married.

To me it [the hostel] seemed always full, you had a job to get in. You see a lot of people wouldn't have put up with it because you had to have the night watchman on that kept a check on you. So for those that wanted to be more flighty that wouldn't have suited terribly.

[After work] I would then start getting ready to go out. I mean 'cos we'd go down again into the canteen for supper, what they called supper, I suppose it was a high tea you know, and then go up and shower or have a bath or whatever and get ready for going out. So I mean it was a damn lazy life, wasn't it?

It was never home. I loved my room to be homely, I liked the comforts that I gradually got into it for myself, but, no, it was a place of work and where I stayed at night, but it was never home. I loved it all, don't get me wrong, but it was never other than my place of work that housed me for the night. But it was a happy place, lovely to bash on somebody's door and say hello at any time.

Frances Waterson (employee 1959–69 and 1978–2006, hostel dweller 1960–4)

When I first moved in I was in a tiny room, but then somebody moved out and I got that room where I stayed for the rest of the time, at the back. The last man had just moved out when I went there.

When I was there you had loos, a bathroom [along the corridor], a kitchen at the end and then stairs going up to the attic, but originally I think they had their food in the dining room. In the attic there was washing lines and you did your ironing in there as well, if you had the windows open you got a good dry. You mustn't do it where the customers could see, oh dear me no!

The gate was locked at 12 but you weren't allowed to have anyone in your room after ten. It was very eerie, you know, if you came in late, because if you imagine you're walking up that yard, got all these vans parked up there and you're walking across

to that iron staircase and that well in the middle, you couldn't see round that little house! You'd go in, and there was a night watchman down stairs, he would occupy a rest area I think, that got taken over as all kitchen eventually, but the bottom of the stairs part of the kitchen area was where he used to sit and he was the one that was responsible for going all round the shop and checking everything was locked up and everything and locking the gate at a certain time and you would hear him coming up and down all the corridors, he'd have to shut the fire doors. Also a lot of people didn't realize that was a hostel up there and on one occasion we had a policeman came up because he saw somebody going up there and he came up because the gate was obviously open because it was during the day and the vans were coming and going, to see what was going on and he was quite surprised to find people up there!

Because of the iron staircase and the fact he [the night watchman] was sitting there below he always knew who was coming and going, there was only women there and he could tell the difference between a man and a woman, I mean, he was, yes, he was on the ball he would call out, he knew all your names, 'is that you so-and-so', and you'd have to answer because it was like a well wasn't it, so you just had to put your head over [the banister] and say 'yes it's me' sort of thing, if he called out, or he would recognize your footsteps, so you wouldn't really get away with it. There was an older lady used to live down the corridor, a section manager, and she had what we called 'eagle ears' and there was creaky floorboards and I bet if you were coming in late 'is that you!', you get the drift, you know.

And the door that was there into the shop was locked. If you went down to the basement you still couldn't get up into the shop not that part 'cos that was the kitchen area you know so obviously you couldn't get into the shop at any point at all so it was completely closed off to you, you know, even all the corridors that later on led through to the shop those as well were all locked at that time so it was just that well of stairs and that was it and the one down onto the roof so you could tell how to get out if necessary.

But it was quite good, you know, on a Sunday you'd cook your lunch and that was when if we were in we'd sort of sit at the table in the kitchen together and eat it if there was a few of us in and they used to have *Round the Horn* they would have that going, we'd put the radio on the table and listen to that while we ate our lunch.

In those days the shop was much further down, I'm talking about before they started knocking it about you know. They did eventually move some offices to the floor below and eventually they moved staff training up on that floor but that was down at the end opposite the kitchen and that didn't really affect us because when that was going on we weren't there. I can remember one year we got permission to have a Christmas in there, one of the ladies cooked us all dinner, that was quite good.

There was lots of rules and regulations as you would expect, you had to buy your milk in the dining room, she always used to have all your milk there, they didn't like it if you weren't buying your milk and looking after yourself you know what I mean and they would come and leave clean linen in your room each week, because they stopped you so much rent you see and that was what was included, bed linen, and you only had to put money in the meter in your bedroom for the fire you didn't have to put anything in the slot for the cooking so that was obviously to cover that you see, and so that just used to come out of your wages before you got them, so they looked a bit depleted. And obviously during the day you could eat in the dining room and you just needed to cook mainly at weekends upstairs. You had a cupboard with so many shelves in each and things like that. So quite interesting, quite amusing. And they used to come round and have a nose to make sure you were keeping your room clean and tidy, you know, and the cleaner used to clean the bathrooms and the kitchen and the communal areas, but you had to do your own bedrooms.

Other employees: joint interview with Pam Woollard (PW; employee for 45 years), Joyce Badcock (JB; employee for 33 years), Cynthia Yeo (CY; employee for 41 years) and Margaret Caldecoat (MC; employee for 43 years).

(PW) 1938, I was in there shopping for my birthday present, which was an armchair with dark mahogany coloured arms and a blue and brown print covering which went up in tiny squares like a stained glass window, and I had it delivered by Robert Sayles. So I must have been coming up for four then you see. Father Christmas we had upstairs, about the same time, I think it was 1938, and I remember going on the moon rocket. I put all this down when I did my 25 years. One of the top managing directors in those days, he was the one who installed it so he was thrilled to bits to think someone could actually remember it!

(PW) I went in there with my Grandmother, she always shopped in there, and a young uncle of mine started to work [in the funeral department], course the war came along and he left, he wouldn't have gone back to that after the war anyway. The funeral parlour [was] in the back yard, and in latter years it moved further out to the back yard, and display department, where I worked, had it as a model room. It wasn't very nice going in there, really, there was urns still in there left behind, and we always used to rattle the door to make sure no-one was moving in there before we went in to collect the models, it was quite a laugh really, horrible! (MC) We went in and out there didn't we, you know, if you needed anything. (PW) And there was empty coffins standing everywhere, that had been used I think! (MC) Len had his workshop and Cyril made the coffins (PW) and the French polishing, all that, they all worked there didn't they.

(PW) We used to work in there when the shop was closed, in display, and when all the lights went we had to go right over the big lovely staircase into the other part you know where our store was, and they used to cover the models in like parachute silk and when you went past them if you made a lot of movement they'd slip off! It was pitch black, and, you know, you ran out the other end as quick as you could. (JB) I do know my mother said that when they worked there they used to have to go down to the basement at night to get the covers to cover everything up and they used to make a lot of noise going down the stairs because you could hear the mice and that running. In our time we used to cover everything up at night with these old parachutes. (PW) I was a junior you see and got sent all over the staircases to pick up whatever they wanted, and I was really scared tell the truth, I wouldn't have said so at the time.

(PW) And the windows they were real old fashioned and when you walked around they were very high off the ground most of them. They were as old as the shop frontage I should think. We had lovely windows in those days, didn't we, May Balls and things like that, really went to town, and there was a gap over the top where we used to have plants (JB) and in between people used to park their prams, between the two levels of windows (PW) and leave them for us, me and Coral, to look after them, they'd say 'can we leave them here today?'. (CY) Customers were able to park outside the shop, weren't they, on more than one occasion we'd take things out to the customer's car and put it in their boot or whatever.

(PW) And it was so beautiful in parts inside, (JB) oh yes, and the staircase, (PW) and a beautiful sitting room upstairs, a lovely fire, easy chairs and a piano up there. And some of the fixturing in the department, I don't know what you'd call it, mirror glass, and we used to put all the little flowers, it was so beautiful, but I don't know what happened to some of these things, bits and pieces, we all remember differently. (JB) 'Cos they built all that bit on the back didn't they, (PW) bits kept being added on didn't they (JB) the yard got smaller and the buildings got bigger.

(PW) there was that passageway right through the two halves of the shop wasn't there, where the doors joined together, the main shop, where the furniture side of the shop was in latter years (JB) between the windows, it used to be our staff entrance (PW) so that went right from front to back (MC) that's where I used to leave my bicycle, there were bicycle racks there, if we went to the pictures in the evening that's where we used leave our bikes. (PW) They said they had a ghost used to ride through there on a bicycle, I never saw a ghost, I used to work there alone quite a lot and I never saw a ghost.

(PW) You didn't live in did you? (JB) my mother wouldn't let me, I don't know what she thought I was going to do! (MC) But those little rooms used to fascinate me. I had a friend, well she was a junior on our counter at that time, and she had a dear little room up there and I almost thought, I'd really love to have one, I mean I lived in Cambridge, my mother would have had a fit if I'd said I wanted to go and live in the hostel. (PW) There was miles of stuff up there, all different levels (JB) yes, you got to the top of the stairs and you branched one way for the ladies rooms and the other way for the mens (PW) Yes, 'cos they weren't allowed to mix were they.

(JB) You would almost know the day of the week by the people that came in, it was a regular thing, every Tuesday it would be the same people (PW) you don't have the characters now, do you, they rather expected us to know who they were.

(JB) Well people didn't leave, I mean, they just used to stay on. (PW) If you like to work in a shop with people, that was the best one to be in, unless you moved to London or somewhere, wasn't it, really, I mean there wasn't anything to touch it really, was there. (MC) My mother obviously used to go there shopping, so I only ever, don't know about you, wanted to work at Robert Sayles, 'cos we were born in Cambridge, you know? (JB) It was the nicest shop in Cambridge (PW) 'cos if you got a job at Robert Sayle, that was good, wasn't it, you had prestige.

eventually comprising over two thirds of the population, although senior positions continued to be male-dominated.

Most individuals were relatively young, with an average age of 21; only a few individuals were in their late 20s or 30s, although the housekeeper would generally be older and in her 50s or 60s. By the twentieth century all were unmarried, as married individuals had to live out, and no children were present. There was a quite rapid staff turnover, with a nucleus of long-term staff (Sieveking 2004, 52). In the early twentieth century accommodation was gender segregated and usually shared; 'living in may not have been ideal … the system was adequate' (Sieveking 2004, 48). By the 1920s individuals were trying to make their hostel rooms more comfortable. This included papering them, adding carpets and providing personal furniture (Gooch 2004, 186). By 1933/4 accommodation was mainly in single rooms with a bedstead, chest of drawers, wash stand, towel horse, chair, mirror and hanging space (Sieveking 2004, 76). Only staff who lived in could use dining rooms and meals were 'good quality and plentiful'; there were no formal tea/coffee breaks but time to get a 'glass of beer' during the day (Sieveking 2004, 48–9), which may relate to the tumblers found. Increased demand for space meant that plans to close the hostel were discussed as early as 1943, although the hostel only gradually came to an end in 1964 (Sieveking 2004, 99, 107).

Many of the ceramic vessels that were recovered may represent personal items, including a hand-painted art earthenware vase from Castle Hedingham (Fig. 5.62E) and a deaf child's sign language plate (Fig. 5.90C). No children resided at the hostel, but as this design was registered a decade or so before the plate was deposited, one possibility is that it is someone's treasured childhood memento, whose presence may reflect the increased employment opportunities WWI afforded deaf individuals. Other items that have a personal feel to them are a Pomadour pattern plate (Fig. 5.62C), two Queens' College egg cups (Fig. 5.90F) and three D.B.C foot warmers (Fig. 5.91D), while some small gas mantles (Fig. 5.91F) may relate to the personal cooking of food.

A number of the glass vessels are best interpreted as personal items. These include some Codd bottles for soda water (Fig. 5.92A–G), four whisky bottles, a Morley's bottle which also held spirits (Fig. 5.90I), beer bottles (Fig. 5.92H–I), Camp Coffee, Horlick's Malted Milk Lunch Tablets, L. Rose lime juice (Fig. 5.92J), 4711 Cologne and Ven Yusa 'Oxygen' face cream. The Holbrook & Co. Worcestershire sauce and Garton's HP sauce bottles could derive from the dining room, but are perhaps more likely to be personal in origin. Interestingly, given the lack of children living at the premises, four of the Codd bottles appear to have been deliberately broken to obtain the marbles – especially as no stray marbles were recovered – while two were unbroken. Some worn out shoes were also personal possessions, as a ladies boot and shoe department did not open until 1927 and their gender balance (MNI six female and two male) and lack of children's shoes would reflect that of the inhabitants. Other items that are personal are a toothbrush and a military button, which is presumably a memento either of a member of staff who joined up during WWI (Sieveking 2004, 55, 57) or of a sweetheart, fiancée or male relative. There are also several notable absences, the most pronounced being the total lack of flowerpots, suggesting that the plot was so heavily occupied than no opportunity for gardening remained.

Building 43 containing *Well 50* continued to provide water that was used for brewing and other purposes into the 1920s. After this the well shaft was sealed and a number of small rainwater drains were inserted under the walls of *Building 43* into the top of the shaft. After WWII *Building 43*, which became known as the 'Round House', was used as a storeroom for hardware and the large first floor water storage tank that it had supplied was removed in 1954 (Sieveking 2004, 100). In the early 1960s the business wanted to demolish *Building 43* to improve vehicular access to the yard area and although it was noted in the John Lewis Gazette in March 1962 that the structure was 'quite a conversation piece and many customers enquire about its origin. If it is ever demolished one of the ancient landmarks of old Cambridge and Robert Sayle's history will disappear', it was demolished in 1964. The shaft was then capped with concrete and a number of large drains fed into it.

The processing of down became less important during or soon after WWI and ended in 1934 (Poole 1978; Sieveking 2004, 43–4). By then some of *Standing Building 48* had been converted into a coach house and in that year it became a stores and garage. The original wooden floors were removed, the gaps between the dwarf walls were infilled with loose bricks, marked CENTRAL WHITTLESEA and manufactured by the Whittlesea Central Brick Co. Ltd. (1898–1968), and a concrete floor was poured. Just to the west of this *Building 44*, which had been a stables, was converted into a garage. A 50-gallon petrol pump was erected in the yard area in 1927, costing £50, and stabling disappeared as a result (Sieveking 2004, 67). In 1938 a petrol pump was located in the northeast corner of *Building 44*. A sunken brick-lined structure in this building relates to its use as a

garage and may be an inspection pit. *Building 44* was demolished in the early 1970s and the backfilling of the inspection pit contained paraphernalia associated with pumping petrol.

Discussion

The Robert Sayle department store was a long-lived institution, although not as long-lived as some of the other commercial entities that had previously been established in the street block; nevertheless, it operated on a much larger spatial and economic scale than any other previous or contemporary business. As a late nineteenth–early twenty-first century entity it is well-documented by cartographic, photographic, documentary evidence and even oral testimony. Yet the archaeological remains, including both standing buildings and below-ground features, do have a number of specific contributions to make to our understanding of the Robert Sayle department store.

Firstly, the remains emphasize the importance that was placed upon having an impressive façade, despite the upper storeys being of limited use as retail space (with the result that they became something of a white elephant). This circumstance led to the latter areas being used as hostel accommodation, which in turn had a strong impact upon the social history of the business. Secondly, behind the frontage the business maintained a number of specialized buildings that were constructed for particular purposes, although of these only the Down Room (*Standing Building 48*) survived in a sufficiently well-preserved state to permit its specialized role to be recognized. In addition, the presence of a timber-lined shaft (*Well 49*) and brick-built well (*Well 50*) emphasize the large-scale water requirements of the business and the lengths that were taken to meet this demand.

The assemblage(s) of *c.* 1913–21 that were recovered from *Cellar 13* shed considerable light on the staff that lived in the hostel (see also Cessford 2012). For example, there is a profound contrast between the plain and unappealing 'semi-porcelain whiteware' that was supplied for use in the dining room and the more personal items; indeed, the gaudy Pomadour plate might be seen as a direct reaction to such plainness. The contrast between the 'semi-porcelain whiteware' and the Roma pattern wares that were reserved for more senior members of staff can be linked to the signalling of status, although the 'semi-porcelain whiteware' should not be interpreted too negatively as it appears that for tea drinking all staff enjoyed the use of good-quality bone china. There are several clear expressions of individuality, perhaps most notably the deaf child's sign language plate and the Castle Hedingham art earthenware vase, as well as evidence for a whole range of drinks and other items that staff purchased for their own use.

These items could, to echo the testimony of Coral Gould – employee 1945–90, hostel dweller 1947–51 – make things 'homely' even if it was never home (see inset: 'living above the shop'). The rosy picture painted by a semi-hagiographical history of the department store, which is unsurprizingly mirrored by the oral testimony as this derives from long-term staff who must have been at least relatively happy with their lot, is unlikely to have been held by all employees (Hosgood 1999). Indeed, such a picture can be challenged slightly by the presence of four whisky bottles, whose presence hints at a somewhat darker reality. The prevalence of items associated with women, notably shoes but also various beauty products, can be linked to the increasing role of women in the workplace, whilst the deaf child's sign language plate indicates greater opportunities for the disabled.

By the time the Robert Sayle drapery business was established the street block was no longer part of a recognizable suburb. Nonetheless its establishment, expansion and success are to a considerable extent linked to the existence of large plots and especially the large contiguous area of the street block that was owned by Jesus College. Space is a vital prerequisite to a department store and it is clear that although Robert Sayle still faced profound difficulties, these were much less severe than those faced by many of its counterparts in the urban core such as Eaden Lilley (Ormes 2000). Although ancillary elements are undoubtedly significant, the most significant factor in a department store is retail space. The proportion of selling space compared to occupied or built-upon space in the department store complex, not unsurprisingly, changes with time. More meaningful, perhaps, is the way in which it changes.

Considering ground floor level only, which is all that can be meaningfully measured, by 1862 the department store occupied 4102 sq. m, of which 1926 sq. m had been built upon but only about 217 sq. m (11.3 per cent) was selling space. By 1889 the built-upon land had increased to 2279 sq. m, of which 348 sq. m (15.3 per cent) was shop floor. Into and through the twentieth century the percentage of built-upon space increases (31.6 per cent in 1898, 53.1 per cent in 1938) as more of the site is rebuilt or converted into selling space. After 1971, when the department store lost about 20 per cent of its land holding, a significant change occurred. The built area was physically smaller than before, but represented a much higher proportion of the land available (92.2 per cent); moreover, 70 per cent (2098 sq. m) of this was now retail space.

Throughout its existence the department store remained an overcrowded and obviously piecemeal shop of 'nooks and crannies' (Gooch 2004, 144). This led initially to plans to move it to an out-of-town location at either Duxford (1989) or Trumpington (1994). These plans were never implemented and ultimately the desire to retain the Robert Sayle department store in the city centre was the main factor in the wholesale redevelopment of the area in the early twenty-first century. This led to the end of the Robert Sayle name, a tripling of the floor space of the rebranded John Lewis department store and culminated in the implementation of large-scale archaeological investigations.

Material culture

At Grand Arcade, on-site refuse disposal on a significant scale ceased *c.* 1600–20. For the succeeding 150 years very little material culture was deposited. This pattern changed *c.* 1760–80, around the start of the 'classic' industrial era, but when significant refuse disposal recommenced it was a radically different phenomenon than in the preceding mid-eleventh–early seventeenth centuries and thus presents a significant set of methodological challenges. In particular, the later material derives principally from a number of short-term deliberate depositional events that can broadly be interpreted as 'feature groups'; closed assemblages of domestic artefacts that were discarded as a single deposit (Cessford 2009, 307–9; Cessford 2017a) and whose interpretation is not as straightforward as is sometimes assumed. The assemblages were recovered from a range of feature-types, including: the backfilling of redundant features such as cellars and soakaways; percolation fills in the base of planting beds/holes to aid drainage (Cotter *et al.* 1992, 161, 307–9, 450); pits dug specifically to dispose of material and, at a later date, the use of material as hardcore beneath concrete surfaces.

In the first instance, seven late eighteenth-century feature groups were recovered and studied (Table 5.2). This material has been quantified by an appropriate form of Minimum Number of Individuals/Items (MNI) count, in terms of Vessels in Studied Assemblages (VSA), and broken down in terms of function (Table 5.3), although function can be problematic to identify (Brooks 2005b). It should be also noted that large assemblages were rare and most redundant features and bases of planting beds did not contain significant amounts of material. Excluding feature groups, other contemporary features contained a variable amount of material such as pottery, clay tobacco pipe and glass vessels; some of which represents the deliberate discard of selected items. Continuing this pattern, the nineteenth-century material was also dominated by a number of large 'feature groups' (Tables 5.4–5.7). Whilst some of these can be dated quite precisely, at a more general level they can be broadly sub-divided into those of *c.* 1800–50 and those of *c.* 1850–1900;

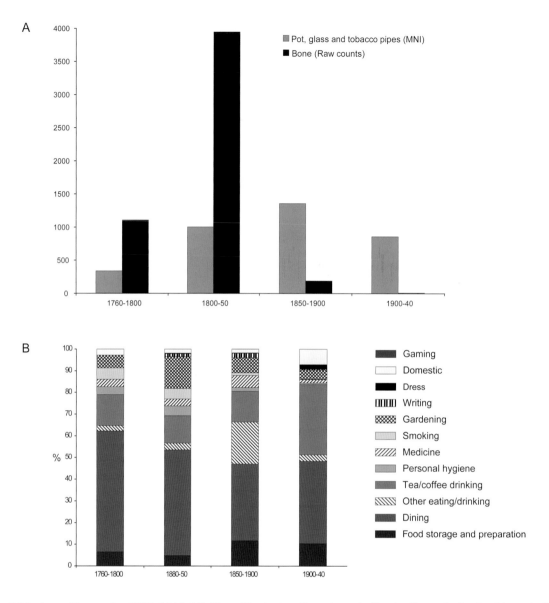

Figure 5.94. *Assemblages of c. 1760–1940: (A) The mid-nineteenth century decline in disposal of animal bone in feature groups, as demonstrated by comparing the combined number of pottery and glass vessels and clay tobacco pipes (MNIs) against the number of animal bones (raw counts, as not all assemblages studied); (B) assemblages by functional category.*

the few features that cross this boundary have been assigned to the most relevant period. Finally, during the twentieth century relatively little artefactual material was deposited. The principal exceptions comprised four 'feature groups' (Tables 5.8–5.9), two of which were related to the Robert Sayle department store. A small quantity of additional material was also recovered from plots established beside Tibb's Row (Chapter 3).

As in Chapter 4, the following reports primarily present a general overview, illustrated by a selection of the most pertinent examples, of a particular type of material. Additional information – including

methodological statements and detailed discussions as well as further tables and figures – can be found within the supplementary digital-only volume.

Coins and jettons Martin Allen
Two jettons and three coins of late sixteenth/seventeenth–twentieth-century date were recovered.

There were one definite and one probable Rose/Orb type jettons of Hans Krauwinckel II (fl. 1586–1635) and a copper alloy halfpenny of George III (1760–1820). In the top of *PH 3* created *c.* 1822–34 there was a copper alloy farthing minted 1895–1936 with the obverse and date on reverse illegible. This was deposited *c.* 1924–40, possibly during some changes to the property in 1937. Brick-lined *Soakaway*

Table 5.2. *Studied mid/late eighteenth-century assemblages; NS = not studied, + = rare, ++ = occasional, +++ = moderate, ++++ = frequent.*

Feature	General type	Plot	Date	Pottery MNI	Glass MNI	Clay Pipe MNI	Bone no.	Bone MNI	Other items	Total items	Ash	Oyster	Brick/ Tile
PBs 7–8	PF	VIII	1770–90	75	10	8	246	NS	3	87	+++	++	++
PB 10	PF	X	1760–80	27	-	1	197	24	-	52	-	-	++
PB 9	PF	XII	1760–80	11	34	6	52	NS	8	59	-	-	++++
Pit 57	Pit	XIII	1760–80	18	-	1	-	-	-	19	-	-	++
PB 11	PF	XIV	1770–90	34	5	2	286	18	3	60	-	+	+
Soakaway 4	RF	XV	1780–90	11	2	-	6	NS	-	13	-	+	++++
Cellar 6	RF	XVI	1780–90	76	12	1	320	30	4	123	-	++	++
Total				**252**	**67**	**19**	**1107**	**72**	**18**	**417**			

Table 5.3. *Major mid/late eighteenth-century assemblages quantified by function.*

Feature	General type	Plot	Date	Food storage and preparation	Dining	Other eating/ drinking	Tea/coffee drinking	Personal hygiene	Medicine	Smoking	Gardening	Domestic	Business	Total identified	Overall total	Variety (no. of functional types)
PBs 7–8	PF	VIII	1770–90	2	20	2	11	4	1	5	-	-	-	45	87	7
PB 10	PF	X	1760–80	2	16	2	4	4	1	1	3	-	15	48	52	9
PB 9	PF	XII	1760–80	2	35	1	3	-	3	6	-	8	-	58	59	7
Pit 57	Pit	XIII	1760–80	1	8	-	6	2	-	1	-	-	-	18	19	5
PB 11	PF	XIV	1770–90	4	37	-	10	1	2	2	-	1	-	57	60	7
Soakaway 4	RF	XV	1780–90	-	4	1	3	1	-	1	1	-	-	11	13	6
Cellar 6	RF	XVI	1780–90	10	60	2	9	-	4	1	15	-	-	101	123	7
Total				**21**	**180**	**8**	**46**	**12**	**11**	**17**	**19**	**9**	**15**	**342**	**417**	
Occurrence				**6**	**7**	**5**	**7**	**5**	**5**	**7**	**3**	**2**	**1**			

5 contained a George V (1910–36) copper alloy penny minted in 1916, deposited *c*. 1929–31. Neither of these coins is of any numismatic interest; however, it is worth noting that none of the late eighteenth–early twentieth-century 'feature groups' contained any coins. Both the upper part of *PH 3* and *Soakaway 5* contained little other material and whilst the coins may represent casual losses there is a strong impression that they were deliberately deposited as a form of good luck charm.

Metalwork Craig Cessford and Andrew Hall

A relatively small metalwork assemblage was recovered. The only significant artefact type comprised 11 late eighteenth–early nineteenth-century thin spatula-shaped objects that have been identified as gardening labels and were largely found in *PBs 7–8* of *c*. 1800–20 (Figs. 5.18D–G and 5.22B–C).

The quantity of eighteenth-century metalwork from the site is not great, although individual pieces are of some interest. The most interesting group are some late eighteenth–early nineteenth-century spatula-shaped objects, some of which have numbers on the head. A total of 11 were recovered, all of similar form suggesting a single source or tradition; nine came from *PBs 7–8* (Fig. 5.18D–G) and two from the garden area of Plot X (Fig. 5.22B–C). The form and context of these items indicates that they are planting labels, although they

are of different form to other known examples (Locock in Currie & Locock 1993, 182–3). The labels imply a system of record-keeping, using index numbers to track plant varieties, with an associated degree of numeracy and literacy. The only significant nineteenth-century assemblage comprised a group of 37 horseshoes in *Pit 65*.

Worked stone Simon Timberlake and Craig Cessford

In total 24 eighteenth- and nineteenth-century worked stone artefacts were recovered, consisting principally of slate pencils and whetstones. The only significant group comprised 17 slate pencils from various features of *c*. 1830–50 associated with the school in Plot XIV (Fig. 5.54E–F).

The late eighteenth–mid-nineteenth-century whetstones found at the site are clearly different to earlier examples; they are more regularly cut and shaped and are made from white orthoquartzitic sandstone that possesses acalcareous cement. This is Permian sandstone, probably from Lincolnshire or Nottinghamshire, and as this appears to be the only type of material used for whetstones at this time this marks a break with the long-established trade in Scandinavian material dating back to the eleventh–twelfth centuries.

A total of 18 slate pencils were recovered, all from nineteenth century contexts; 17 came from Plot XIV which was used as a

Table 5.4. *Studied 1800–50 assemblages by material type; NS = not studied, + = rare, ++ = occasional, +++ = moderate, ++++ = frequent.*

Feature	Plot	General type	Date	Pottery MNI	Glass MNI	Clay Pipe MNI	Bone no.	Bone MNI	Other items	Total items	Ash	Oyster	Brick/Tile	Window glass
PBs 7–8	VIII	Abandonment	1800–20	100	-	-	246	NS	9	109	-	-	-	++++
Soakaway 2	XIII	RF	1813–23	68	23	4	208	21	3	119	++++	-	+++	-
PH 3	XIV	PF	1822–34	54	23	3	1103	49	-	129	-	++	++	-
PH 1, PB 17 etc.	XIV	PF	1832–45	9	4	1	7	NS	3	17	-	+	-	-
Soakaway 3	XV	RF	1808–25	177	69	17	508	34	4	301	-	++++	+++	-
Cellar 7	XVIII	RF	1820–30	52	7	1	179	18	-	78	-	-	+++	-
Cellar 7	XVIII	RF	1830–50	35	1	12	83	NS	1	49	-	-	++	-
Cellar 4	XXII	RF	1830–45	205	13	10	1339	51	11	290	+++	++++	+++	-
Pit 63	XXII	RF	1830–45	69	10	6	179	11	1	97	++++	++	++	-
Pit 64	XXII	Pit	1830–45	28	2	1	95	NS	-	31	-	-	+++	-
Total				797	152	55	3947	184	32	1220	-	-	-	-

Table 5.5. *Studied 1800–50 assemblages by function.*

Feature	Plot	General type	Date	Food storage and preparation	Dining	Other eating/ drinking	Tea/coffee drinking	Personal hygiene	Medicine	Smoking	Gardening	Writing	Dress	Domestic	Total identified	Overall total	Variety (no. of functional types)
PBs 7–8	VIII	Abandonment	1800–20	-	-	-	-	-	-	-	109	-	-	-	109	109	1
Soakaway 2	XIII	RF	1813–23	8	58	1	9	5	4	4	16	-	-	-	105	119	8
PH 3	XIV	PF	1822–34	7	84	8	7	3	3	3	4	-	-	4	123	129	9
PH1, PB 17 etc.	XIV	PF	1832–45	1	8	1	-	5	1	2	1	16	-	1	36	42	9
Soakaway 3	XV	RF	1808–25	5	153	4	37	21	15	17	20	-	-	-	272	301	8
Cellar 7	XVIII	RF	1820–30	3	48	2	11	-	-	1	2	-	-	4	71	78	7
Cellar 7	XVIII	RF	1830–50	1	16	-	2	-	-	12	2	-	1	1	35	49	7
Cellar 4	XXII	RF	1830–45	16	115	14	61	15	12	10	10	-	2	8	247	290	10
Pit 63	XXII	RF	1830–45	7	54	3	13	2	1	6	1	-	-	2	89	97	9
Pit 64	XXII	Pit	1830–45	6	17	2	3	-	-	-	-	-	-	1	29	31	5
Total				54	553	35	143	51	36	55	166	16	3	21	1133	1245	
Occurrence				9	9	9	8	6	6	8	9	1	2	7			

school (Fig. 5.54E–F). Slate pencils were produced *c.* 1770–1900 and in 1811 a hand-operated machine was invented that allowed an individual to produce around 1200 pencils a day. The pencils, which were typically 5½in (140mm) long and were sold in boxes of a dozen or hundred, are common archaeologically on both domestic and educational sites (Davies 2005, 63–4). The examples from Grand Arcade were mostly heavily used, worn and broken and were 32–75mm (1¼–3in) long when discarded, which is slightly longer than the 17–62mm reported for the Henry's Mill site in Australia (Davies 2005, 65). No identifiable fragments of writing slates were recovered; these were larger objects that were stored more carefully and would in any case only be disposed of when broken (Davies 2005, 65).

Vessel glass Vicki Herring

Over 2300 fragments of vessel glass weighing in excess of 180kg were recovered from Grand Arcade, plus 316 pieces weighing 8.8kg from the Christ's Lane excavations. There were negligible quantities of medieval and post-medieval glass and the bulk of the assemblage dates to the mid-eighteenth to early twentieth centuries. A total of 887 vessels from selected assemblages have been subject to further examination. All the vessels are of well-understood types and their main contribution is to the understanding of the assemblages that they were

Table 5.6. *Studied 1850–1900 assemblages by material type; NS = not studied, P = present but not MNI, + = rare, ++ = occasional, +++ = moderate, ++++ = frequent.*

Feature	Plot	General type	Date	Pottery MNI	Glass MNI	Clay Pipe MNI	Bone no.	Bone MNI	Other items	Total items	Oyster	Brick/Tile	Roofing slate
Pits 68	IX	Pit	1828–80	35	2	1	-	-	1	39	-	-	-
Pit 60	X	Pit	1866–9	-	20	-	-	-	-	20	-	-	-
Well 37	XI	RF	1855–8	87	41	1	65	NS	10	139	-	++	-
Foundation 1	XIII	Hardcore	1862–1900	12	-	-	-	-	-	12	-	-	-
Pit 61	XIII	Pit	1884–90	4	27	-	-	-	-	31	-	++	-
Cellar 5	XVI	RF	1870–80	19	-	1	-	-	-	20	-	-	-
Cellar 12	XVI	RF	1882–5	178	122	5	22	NS	5	310	++	++	-
Building 51	XVII	Hardcore	1882–1900	174	10	-	-	-	3	187	-	-	-
Pit 62	XVIII	Pit	1873–1900	12	2	1	-	-	-	15	-	++++	-
Building 49	XXII	RF	1879–82	236	11	-	5	NS	2	249	-	-	-
Foundation 3	XXII	Hardcore	1884–90	1	154	P	39	NS	-	155	+	++	-
Pit 65	XXII	Pit	1880–1900	7	39	-	-	-	49	95	-	++++	-
Pit 67	XXII	Pit	1881–1900	69	20	P	2	NS	3	94	-	++++	++++
Sawpit 1	4 Tibb's Row	RF	1874–81	33	30	P	56	NS	12	75	-	++	-
Total				**867**	**478**	**9**	**189**	**NS**	**85**	**1439**			

Table 5.7. *Studied 1850–1900 assemblages by function.*

Feature	Plot	General type	Date	Food storage and preparation	Dining	Other eating/drinking	Tea/coffee drinking	Personal hygiene	Medicine	Smoking	Gardening	Writing	Dress	Domestic	Business	Gaming	Total identified	Overall total
Pits 68	IX	Pit	1828–80	5	11	-	7	-	-	1	-	1	-	2	-	-	27	39
Pit 60	X	Pit	1866–9	-	-	-	-	-	12	-	-	-	-	-	-	-	12	20
Well 37	XI	RF	1855–8	8	67	-	14	3	-	1	25	1	-	2	-	1	122	139
Foundation 1	XIII	Hardcore	1862–1900	12	-	-	-	-	-	-	-	-	-	-	-	-	12	12
Pit 61	XIII	Pit	1884–90	-	2	19	-	-	-	-	-	-	-	-	-	-	21	31
Cellar 5	XVI	RF	1870–80	-	6	-	7	-	-	1	-	-	-	-	-	-	14	20
Cellar 12	XVI	RF	1882–5	28	129	6	28	9	7	5	8	7	1	5	-	-	233	310
Building 51	XVII	Hardcore	1882–1900	20	52	1	26	1	1	-	18	1	-	1	-	-	121	187
Pit 62	XVIII	Pit	1873–1900	5	3	1	2	-	-	1	-	2	-	-	-	-	14	15
Building 49	XVII	RF	1879–82	27	55	9	55	2	-	-	9	5	-	3	-	-	165	249
Foundation 3	XXII	Hardcore	1884–90	-	-	151	-	-	-	1	-	-	-	-	-	-	152	156
Pit 65	XXII	Pit	1880–1900	1	4	1	1	-	31	-	-	1	-	3	37	-	79	95
Pit 67	XXII	Pit	1881–1900	8	14	9	3	3	4	1	3	1	-	1	24	-	71	95
Sawpit 1	4 Tibb's Row	RF	1874–81	7	26	5	4	1	3	2	9	2	1	-	11	-	71	76
Total				**121**	**369**	**202**	**147**	**19**	**58**	**13**	**72**	**21**	**2**	**17**	**72**	**1**	**1114**	**1444**
Occurrence				**10**	**11**	**9**	**10**	**6**	**6**	**8**	**6**	**9**	**2**	**7**	**3**	**1**		

Table 5.8. *Studied twentieth-century assemblages; NS = not studied, P = present but not MNI, - = rare, + = occasional, ++ = moderate, +++ = frequent.*

Feature	Plot	General type	Date	Pottery MNI	Glass MNI	Clay Pipe MNI	Bone No.	Bone MNI	Other items	Total items	Ash	Brick/Tile	Window glass
Cellar 11	Corn Exchange Street	RF	1912–21	31	4	-	-	-	2	37	-	++++	-
Cellar 13 (southern part)	Robert Sayle	RF	1913–21	121	115	P	6	NS	18	254	+++	++	+++
Cellar 13 (northern part)	Robert Sayle	RF	1913–21	379	45	-	3	NS	7	431	++++	++	-
Cellar 13 combined	Robert Sayle	RF	1913–21	500	160	P	9	NS	25	685	-	++	+++
Foundation 4	XIV	Hardcore	1924–40	157	8	-	-	-	1	166	-	-	-
Total				**688**	**172**	**P**	**18**	**NS**	**28**	**888**			

Table 5.9. *Studied 20th-century assemblages quantified by function.*

Feature	Plot	General type	Date	Food storage and preparation	Dining	Other eating/ drinking	Tea/coffee drinking	Personal hygiene	Medicine	Smoking	Gardening	Writing	Dress	Domestic	Business	Total identified	Overall total	Variety (no. of functional types)
Cellar 11	Corn Exchange Street	RF	1912–21	2	12		7	1	-	-	-	-	3	3	-	28	37	6
Cellar 13 (southern part)	Robert Sayle	RF	1913–21	26	71	15	44	1	6	1	1	1	9	13	1	189	255	12
Cellar 13 (northern part)	Robert Sayle	RF	1913–21	12	109	-	84	2	3	-	-	-	-	16	6	232	431	7
Cellar 13 combined	Robert Sayle	RF	1913–21	38	180	25	128	3	9	1	1	1	9	29	2	421	686	12
Foundation 4	XIV	Hardcore	1924–40	21	33	3	57	-	-		25	1	-	10	-	150	166	7
Total				61	225	18	192	4	9	1	26	2	12	42	7	599	889	
Occurrence				4	4	2	4	3	2	1	2	2	2	4	2			

found within and the households that created them. There were a number of bottle seals, including two of Emmanuel College (Fig. 5.60C–D), and some nineteenth–twentieth-century bottles that were embossed with the names of local firms that sold soda water and other products (Figs. 5.73E, 5.90I, 5.92, 5.95 and 6.15D).

There is some evidence that pedestal stemmed glass vessels began to be used in the seventeenth century; this is relatively late as glass vessels are found in reasonable quantities in sixteenth-century deposits elsewhere in Cambridge. The most frequent evidence for glass are fragments of free-blown thick-walled green glass wine bottles, which began to be manufactured in the 1640s and were commonplace by the 1660s (Biddle & Webster 2005, 266–7).

The eighteenth-century vessel glass is dominated by utility bottles (57 VSA; Figs. 5.23A, 5.32C and 5.33E–F), which are mainly squat cylindrical green free-blown thick-walled with pontil scars on the base and single applied collars below the lip, predominantly used as wine bottles (55 VSA). There was also a single rather earlier rounded octagonal shaped bottle of *c.* 1750–60 and an imported slim cylindrical bottle fragment. The latter may relate to an imported mineral water as does a seal (Fig. 5.23D). There were also some pharmaceutical bottles (seven VSA; Fig. 5.23B–C), these were predominantly colourless and rectangular with some with embossed lettering, and some colourless cylindrical free blown phials with pontil scars on the base and flared lips (three VSA). There were also fragments from a drinking glass (one VSA) and a bowl (one VSA).

During the nineteenth century glass vessels and drinking glasses become increasingly common. The majority of these are various types of utility bottle (442 VSA; Fig. 5.57A); there were also pharmaceutical bottles (62 VSA), phials (28 VSA; Fig. 5.57C–F), drinking glasses (20 VSA), jars and containers 20 VSA) and a few pieces of bowls, jugs and vases (six VSA). Some early–mid-nineteenth-century utility

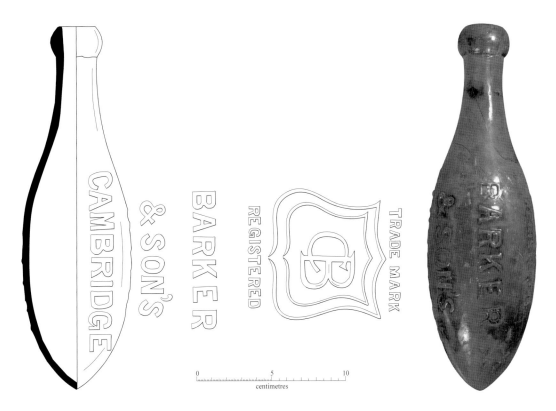

Figure 5.95. *A light green torpedo-shaped utility bottle with applied blob top and patina. It is embossed BARKER/&*
SON'S/CAMBRIDGE with the intertwined initials CB in a shield with TRADE MARK/REGISTERED around.
Recovered from Foundation 2, constructed c. 1883–90 ([40188]). See also Fig. 6.15D.

bottles bear the seal of Emmanuel College (Fig. 5.60C–D) and
there was also an eighteenth-century seal (Fig. 5.57B). Soda and
mineral water bottles are frequently embossed with the names of
local businesses, with a few examples from further afield (Figs. 5.73
and 5.95). In contrast to many types of nineteenth-century material
culture, these bottles are extremely regionally varied and require
detailed local studies (Egan 2009, 281).

The twentieth-century glass vessels are all of typical types;
some, the largest group associated with the Robert Sayle department
store, are of interest because they were manufactured in London,
Barnsley and Leeds specifically for suppliers based in Cambridge
or nearby villages (Cessford 2012) (Fig. 5.92).

Pottery Craig Cessford, Andrew Hall and David Hall
A total of 22,889 sherds of eighteenth–twentieth-century
pottery, weighing 497kg, was recovered from Grand
Arcade, plus 501 sherds weighing 8kg from Christ's
Lane. The combined eighteenth–twentieth-century
pottery is quantified here as a group, as it cross-cuts
the chapter boundaries (Table 5.10). In this context, it
is also worth noting that it appears that sherd count
is a relatively reliable method of quantifying modern
ceramics, as the results are similar to those for the
MNI of vessels in studied assemblages. In contrast,
weight over-emphasizes the significance of coarse
earthenwares and stonewares and underrepresents
refined earthenware and porcelain. The same also
holds true of specific wares. Continuing the pattern

established in Chapter 4, the sources of the various
wares are mapped over time (Fig. 5.96).

As discussed in Chapter 4, only small quantities of seventeenth-
century ceramics were recovered (Table 4.9), although this assemblage
is augmented by material recovered from the King's Ditch in 1914
(Chapter 3). At Ely there was a decline in the range of forms and
fabrics produced in the seventeenth century; there appears to have
been no production of plain pink/red ware or Broad Street Glazed
Red Earthenware Bichrome, for example, and while Babylon ware
and Broad Street Fineware may have continued to be produced in
small quantities into the early seventeenth century this soon ceased
(Cessford *et al.* 2006, 81–5). Production now focused overwhelmingly
on Glazed Red Earthenware, which was increasingly slip decorated,
reflecting the influence of the Staffordshire-type slipware industry;
this material consisted principally of large bowls, pancheons, jars
and small bowls plus smaller numbers of cisterns, chafing dishes
and pipkins.

Documentary sources indicate that there no more than two
or three master potters plus their employees were active in Ely at
any time (Cessford *et al.* 2006, table 18). There is no evidence for any
particular family traditions of potting until the arrival of John Buttey
(active 1682), whose family remained prominent until the 1780s. As
the seventeenth century progressed, however, it appears that in the
Cambridge market Ely products were increasingly challenged by
vessels from other unidentified sources.

Plain iron-glazed products, relatively similar in appearance
to Babylon ware but with a browner fabric and a lighter browner
coloured glaze, which were produced elsewhere in East Anglia,
continued to be used until at least the mid-seventeenth century.
In the latter part of the seventeenth century these are generally

337

Table 5.10. *18th–20th-century pottery from Grand Arcade.*

Fabric	No.	No. %	Weight (g)	Weight %	Vessels in studied features	Vessel %
Late Unglazed Earthenware	2641	11.5	89,676	18.1	274	10.4
Late Glazed Red Earthenware	508	2.2	28,345	5.7	65	2.5
Martaban-type jar	28	0.1	12,498	2.5	1	<0.1
Sunderland-type earthenware	446	1.9	30,854	6.2	37	1.4
Art pottery	4	<0.1	440	0.1	1	<0.1
Staffordshire-type slipware	104	0.5	1831	0.4	22	0.8
Biscuit	8	<0.1	33	<0.1	6	0.2
Powdery fabric lead glazed earthenware	127	0.6	1224	0.2	16	0.6
Total coarse earthenware	*3866*	*16.9*	*164,901*	*33.1*	*422*	*16.0*
Tin-glazed earthenware	196	0.9	3976	0.8	35	1.3
Creamware	3196	14.0	56,430	11.4	298	11.3
Pearlware	1006	4.4	13,666	2.8	159	6.0
Mocha/Industrial slipware	171	0.7	2589	0.5	52	2.0
Staffordshire-type lead glazed earthenware	464	2.0	6995	1.4	53	2.0
Iron-glazed earthenware/blackware	163	0.7	5240	1.1	11	0.4
General white earthenware	9596	41.9	132,591	26.7	1008	38.2
Refined buff earthenware/yellowware	114	0.5	4202	0.8	11	0.4
Refined blue earthenware	32	0.1	460	0.1	5	0.2
Refined red earthenware	24	0.1	784	0.2	3	0.1
Total refined earthenware	*14,962*	*65.4*	*226,933*	*45.7*	*1635*	*62.0*
Nottinghamshire/Derbyshire-type stoneware	232	1.0	10,312	2.1	30	1.1
Staffordshire white salt-glazed stoneware	319	1.4	6189	1.2	66	2.5
Staffordshire scratch blue	34	0.1	513	0.1	6	0.2
18th-century London-type stoneware	6	<0.1	553	0.1	8	0.3
Black Basalt	21	0.1	681	0.1	5	0.2
Dry red bodied stoneware	5	<0.1	277	0.1	2	0.1
Utilitarian English stoneware	713	3.1	56145	11.3	119	4.5
White bodied stoneware	28	0.1	2208	0.4	8	0.3
Frechen	45	0.2	4515	0.9	6	0.2
Westerwald	16	0.1	289	0.1	8	0.3
Total stoneware	*1419*	*6.2*	*81,682*	*16.4*	*258*	*9.8*
Chinese export porcelain	173	0.8	2208	0.4	51	1.9
English soft paste porcelain	37	0.2	704	0.1	17	0.6
Bone china/hard paste porcelain	2432	10.6	20,373	4.1	257	9.7
Total porcelain	*2642*	*11.5*	*23,283*	*4.7*	*325*	*12.3*
Overall total	**22,889**		**496,799**		**2640**	

more heavily decorated, with applied yellow coloured strips and blobs. Wares in the Midlands Yellow-ware tradition continued to be used until these were largely overtaken by similar production at Staffordshire in the late seventeenth century (Brears 1971, 31–6). There is evidence for the presence of slip decorated Staffordshire-type slipware cups and bowls, which are of rather higher quality than the Ely copies. Stoneware continued to be imported from Frechen, including one jug with an inscription, oval portrait medallions and foliage, and Westerwald stoneware appears for the first time. Tin-glazed earthenware from both the Netherlands and England also appears; although the 2005–6 excavations recovered relatively little of this the material associated with the Birdbolt Inn recovered in 1914 contained more impressive vessels that may be inn-related.

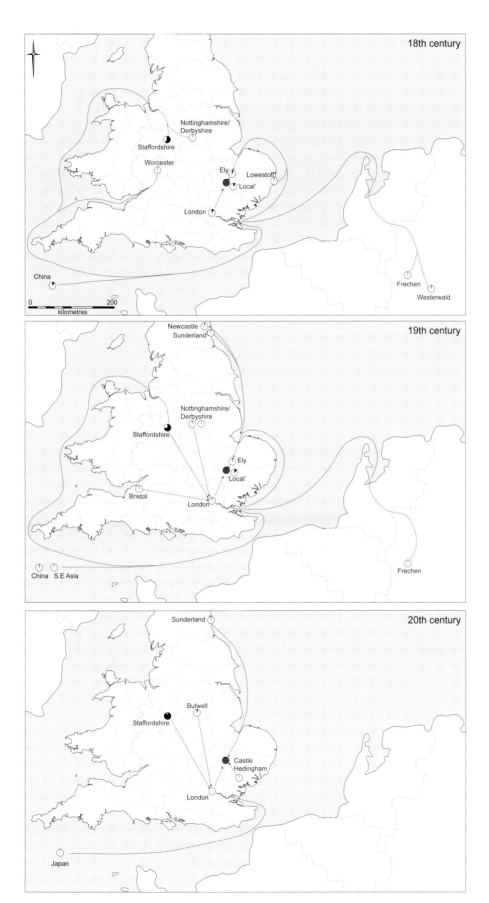

Figure 5.96. *The sources of ceramics used at Grand Arcade during the eighteenth–twentieth centuries, see Fig. 4.56 for earlier sources.*

339

In the early eighteenth century Staffordshire white salt-glazed stoneware (57 VSA; Figs. 5.18K, 5.23E–F, 5.27A–C, 5.28B–D, 5.28I and 5.33C) became relatively common *c.* 1720; it rapidly largely replaced tin-glazed earthenware (17 VSA) and Staffordshire-type slipware (nine VSA). This ware dominated functions such as dining and tea drinking until the 1760s, and was also used for vessels linked to other types of drinking and hygiene. Forms related to dining were mainly plates, with various types of moulded decoration on the rims, and bowls with smaller numbers of dishes, serving dishes, sauceboats, and pickle dishes. Tea bowls were the most common form related to tea drinking, but there were also cups, teapots and teapot lids. The tin-glazed earthenware (Figs. 5.23G, 5.27E, 5.27J, 5.33D, 5.34A, 5.46H, 5.56O–R, 5.64F and 6.11E) and Staffordshire-type slipware are both rather heterogeneous groups and represent the occasional survivals of early–mid-eighteenth-century vessels and some specialized forms. Additionally, from the mid-eighteenth century onwards smaller quantities of Chinese export porcelain (24 VSA; Figs. 5.18I, 5.27H and 5.53B) and English soft paste porcelain (six VSA; Figs. 5.27G and 5.67E) were in use, principally for tea drinking, represented mainly by tea bowls and saucers plus a single slops bowl and coffee can, and a few dining-related vessels. This pattern is similar to that for English soft paste porcelain from excavations in London (Pearce 2008). Unlike other wares the Chinese export porcelain is typologically usually several decades older than the context from which it was recovered, indicating that this material was cared for and curated.

Staffordshire white salt-glazed stoneware was eventually replaced by creamware (64 VSA; Figs. 5.18L–M, 5.27D, 5.27F, 5.28E–H, 5.33B, 5.46D–E, 5.56E–F, 5.56M, 5.65A–C, 5.65E–F, 5.66 and 5.68A–B). Creamware was first produced in the 1740s and dominated the ceramic market from the 1760s until the 1780s. The creamware vessels relate mainly to dining, with plates, side plates, bowls and dishes all relatively common, plus some serving dishes or tureen stands and a condiment vessel and a sauceboat. Tea drinking vessels include tea bowls, a teapot lid, a saucer and a jug. Other drinking is represented by tankards, hygiene by guglets (water jugs) and smoking by a spills vase. Creamware was itself largely supplanted by pearlware, although the distinction between the two wares is far from absolute and often amounts to no more than the glaze for pearlware containing a small amount of cobalt (Figs. 5.46C, 5.56A–D, 5.56G–I, 5.62A, 5.65D, 5.67B–D, 5.67F–M and 6.16B). Pearlware came into use in the mid-1770s and had achieved a dominant position by the 1780s. Although pearlware was in use (two VSA) it was not routinely discarded until later; it remained common until *c.* 1810 and both creamware and pearlware remained in limited use until *c.* 1830. The pattern of creamware from Cambridge is similar to that identified from excavations in London (Pearce 2007a). From the mid-eighteenth century some ceramics found in Cambridge begin to be marked with the names of individuals and institutions. Some tin-glazed earthenware of *c.* 1750 associated with the lessee of the Birdbolt Inn has already been mentioned (Fig. 5.34A) and the practice began to be adopted by Colleges and the cooks who worked for them in the 1760s. The practice appears to have become quite common on creamware and pearlware from the 1770s onwards; although several late eighteenth-century marked vessels were recovered they were found in nineteenth-century features.

A number of less common wares fulfilled a range of niche roles; these included decorated salt-glazed stoneware from Westerwald (seven VS; Figs. 5.18J and 5.27I) and its English equivalent Scratch Blue (six VSA; Fig. 5.32D) plus London-type stoneware (five VSA), Frechen stoneware (three VSA), Nottinghamshire/Derbyshire-type stoneware (two VSA; Figs. 5.56N and 5.61I), red bodied stoneware (two VSA; Fig. 5.62B), and Staffordshire-type lead glazed earthenware (one VSA). There were also some wares such as Black Basalt (Figs. 5.56J and 5.67A), Blackware (Fig. 5.56K–L) and Sunderland-type earthenware (Figs. 5.72A–F and 5.90G) that were presumably in use in the eighteenth century, but are not present in assemblages until the early nineteenth century.

Two more locally produced forms of pottery are Late Unglazed Earthenware (22 VSA) and Late Glazed Red Earthenware (13 VSA). Late Unglazed Earthenware (Figs. 5.18A–C, 5.42D and 5.43A–D) consists solely of flowerpots and associated saucers, these occur in a wide range of fabrics and a variety of sources are represented. Flowerpots were being produced in Cambridge by the early eighteenth century, and a kiln has been excavated at Thompson's Lane (Firman & Pullinger 1987). Flowerpots with a distinctive yellow fabric, identified as being produced in Cambridge, were found in contexts dated *c.* 1760–1825. In contrast the Ely potters do not appear to have produced flowerpots until the nineteenth century and the source of some of the flowerpot fabrics is unclear, although there are a range of relatively poorly understood vernacular potteries in Essex, Norfolk and Suffolk (Brears 1971) that could have supplied Cambridge.

The Late Glazed Red Earthenware vessels (Figs. 5.28J–K and 5.46F–G) were produced at Ely and represent the continuation of a long-established industry, although its eighteenth–nineteenth-century phase has received relatively little attention (Brears 1971, 170; Cessford *et al.* 2006, 83–5, tab. 18; Rackham 1987, 8–9). By the turn of the eighteenth century many local industries had been put out of business by the rise of Buslem and Ticknall in Staffordshire as major manufacturing centres. The Ely pottery industry survived this onslaught and continued to produce wares that were in an essentially local pre-industrial vernacular tradition (Brears 1971). Documentary sources indicate that during the eighteenth century there were between two and four master potters active in Ely at a time, with around a dozen employees. The Buttey family appears to have been particularly prominent between the late seventeenth century and the 1780s. Following marriage this became then became the Lucas family who dominated production until the 1840s. Archaeological evidence from a range of sites in Ely and Cambridge indicates that by the eighteenth century Ely potters were producing a more restricted range of fabrics and forms than in the sixteenth–seventeenth centuries. Large bowls were the most common form, plus smaller numbers of jars, dishes and chamber pots. The Ely potters also appear to have produced some rather more high quality items; although none of these have been recovered from excavations it is likely that they were in use in Cambridge so this element of their repertoire should be borne in mind.

The bulk of the nineteenth-century ceramics from the Grand Arcade site are mass-produced wares, manufactured principally in Staffordshire. Dining, tea related wares and a range of other types continued to be made of creamware (234 VSA) and pearlware (156 VSA) until *c.* 1820–30 (Sussman 1977) and eighteenth-century Chinese export porcelain continued in use (26 VSA). Although some Staffordshire-type white salt-glazed stoneware was present in assemblages up to *c.* 1850 (eight VSA) much if not all of this may be residual material. Creamware and pearlware were gradually replaced by a white-bodied clear-glazed refined earthenware, referred to simply as whiteware, introduced *c.* 1805 and common from *c.* 1820 onwards (622 VSA) although the distinction between pearlware and whiteware in particular is often relatively minor. Decoration, particularly transfer-printed decoration which had been developed as early as *c.* 1783 becomes much more common from *c.* 1830 onwards and this increases further after the cost of transfer-printed decorated and other previously expensive items fell markedly *c.* 1845–50 (Miller 1991a). A wide range of transfer-printed patterns were recovered, although only two were particularly common and most were only found in one or two features.

The Willow pattern (Coysh & Henrywood 1984, 402–3) was developed in the 1790s, the design was formalized by *c.* 1810 and by 1814 it was the cheapest transfer-printed design available (Miller 1991a, 8), while the Asiatic Pheasants pattern (Coysh & Henrywood 1984, 28) was developed in the 1830s (Fig. 5.61B). These two patterns were extremely popular, becoming ubiquitous internationally (*e.g.* Middleton 2008, 206–8). There are 22 assemblages of the correct date and composition from Grand Arcade that might reasonably be anticipated to contain these patterns; in total 89 Willow pattern vessels were found in 19 of these while Asiatic Pheasants pattern vessels were rather less common, with 26 vessels in seven assemblages. In all assemblages Willow pattern was as prevalent as or more common than Asiatic Pheasants. In addition there are a small number (MNI five) of Staffordshire-type figurines (Figs. 5.57K and 5.68C). The rather finer quality bone china (131 VSA) was introduced c. 1794 and became relatively common from c. 1820 onwards, being used principally for items linked to tea drinking, most commonly decorated with either a gold depiction of a tea leaf or alternating large and small purple sprigged plant sprays.

Utilitarian English stoneware appears c. 1800–20 (98 VSA; Figs. 5.53H–J, 5.61J, 5.61L–M, 5.74G and 5.91D), although Nottinghamshire/Derbyshire-type stoneware continued in use (28 VSA). The majority of the Utilitarian English stoneware from Grand Arcade cannot be specifically identified, but manufacturers that are represented include Maling (Newcastle), Powell (Bristol), George Skey & Co. and Bourne & Son (Staffordshire), Radnor Park and the Shipley Pottery (Derbyshire) and the Union Potteries and John Cliff & Co. (Lambeth), some of which were also found in Colchester (Cotter 2000, 254). Utilitarian English stoneware was used principally for containers; including bottles for ink (MNI 22), blacking (MNI six) and a range of other liquids (MNI 38), plus jars (MNI 30) and wide mouthed jars (MNI 18), which held various types of food including marmalade, and foot bottles (MNI seven). Rarer forms include a mug (MNI one), a jug (MNI one) and a teapot (MNI one). From c. 1870 onwards there is evidence that various local wine and spirits merchants had specially marked domed top jars or flagons produced for them, although there is no evidence where these were manufactured.

There is limited evidence for the continued use of Staffordshire-type slipware (12 VSA) in the form of cups and bowls, and tin-glazed earthenware (18 VSA), predominantly drug/ointments jars (Figs. 5.49F and 5.59O–R) plus a char dish (Fig. 5.64F). Staffordshire-type lead-glazed earthenware began to be used by the 1840s; although it is more common in the latter part of the century (35 VSA), it was used for a range of forms particularly teapots.

Coarser earthenware products continued to be produced at Ely until the 1860s, consisting principally of Late Glazed Red Earthenware (42 VSA) bowls, jars and dishes whose forms, fabric and glaze are indistinguishable from eighteenth-century products, plus some new forms principally chamber pots. There were also flowerpots in a range of Late Unglazed Earthenware fabrics (152 VSA), including some produced by the last known Ely potter Robert Sibley (Fig. 5.43A). The Ely potters also produced occasional higher quality pieces that appear to be one-off special commissions, which have been preserved in collections rather than being recovered archaeologically.

During the course of the nineteenth century the Ely Late Glazed Red Earthenware industry came under increasing competition, principally from Sunderland-type coarseware (35 VSA). This ware first occurs in Cambridge in the early nineteenth century, but was of relatively limited significance until the end of the Ely pottery industry when it briefly dominated the market in large utilitarian vessels c. 1870–80. After this Yellowware, which was used in small amounts from c. 1830 onwards and came to dominate the market nationally by c. 1880, was used (three VSA). In addition in the first half of the nineteenth century blackware or iron-glazed earthenware with a red fabric and black glaze was used for chamber pots and bowls (eight VSA), although the fabrics and glazes for the two forms are different suggesting separate sources.

A range of less common wares were also found; notable pieces include an imported Martaban-type jar (*Cellar 12*; Fig. 5.62D), a red bodied stoneware vessel decorated with a classical scene (*Cellar 12*; Fig. 5.62B) and a teapot (*Cellar 7*), two bottles from Frechen (*Cellar 4*) and a Black Basalt teapot (*Soakaway 3*) and teapot lid (*Cellar 4*).

In the early twentieth century the dominant pottery fabric continued to be whiteware (367 VSA), which fulfilled most of the dining requirements. The Robert Sayle department store-associated assemblage(s) contained a large number of plain vessels, some of which have transfer-printed marks describing them as 'semi-porcelain' (43 VSA; Fig. 5.90A–B). At this time terms such as 'semi-porcelain' were used extensively as brand names for marketing purposes as they were associated with strength and durability, but they do not necessarily mean that the vessel is made of that particular fabric (Brooks 2005a, 30). Additionally, although degree of body vitrification can be significant, those attempting to classify wares by this 'are splitting hairs by trying to distinguish among ceramic bodies that are simply points on a continuum' (Majewski & O'Brien, 1987, 120). These vessels are of a whiteware fabric of noticeably greater hardness and density than the rest of the assemblage; such wares of this date are often termed 'hotel ware' (Barker & Majewski 2006, 216–17; Myers 2016), although it is perhaps safer to restrict this term to those that bear specific institutional affiliations. As a result the term 'semi-porcelain whiteware' will be adopted to distinguish this material, with the proviso that this is a label rather than a technically accurate descriptor.

The other common ware was bone china (171 VSA), used predominantly for tea and coffee drinking. All other fabrics were much less common and were used for specific niche functions, such as Utilitarian English stoneware (27 VSA) used for food storage, foot warmers and ink bottles, and Late Unglazed Earthenware (26 VSA) used solely for flowerpots all of which were manufactured by Sankey's of Bulwell, Nottinghamshire (see Fig. 7.2Q). Sankey's products appear not to occur in Cambridge until the 1890s at the earliest, although they are known to have been supplying Ely by the 1860s. Sankey's 'garden pots' were sold at Barrett & Co. in the 1920s and by this time Sankey's were producing 500,000 flowerpots a week. Staffordshire-type lead and iron-glazed earthenware (23 VSA and three VSA) were used predominantly for teapots, while some vases were made from a lead-glazed earthenware with a distinctive poor quality powdery white fabric almost akin to Plaster-of-Paris (16 VSA). Large food preparation vessels included Sunderland-type earthenware (six VSA) and Yellowware (three VSA). Biscuit pottery, which has been fired once to a temperature just below vitrification and had no glaze added, was used to produce what may be gas mantles (two VSA) (Fig. 5.96F). There was a single piece of 'art' pottery, a hand-painted vase from Castle Hedingham (Fig. 5.62E). An art pottery studio was founded by Edward Bingham at Castle Hedingham, Essex, and was active 1864–1901 (Bartlett 1993, 53; Bradley 1968). This led to the area becoming a centre for art pottery and this piece is by a later potter.

Clay tobacco pipes Craig Cessford, incorporating specialist information from Alan Vince

In total, 1501 fragments of clay tobacco pipe weighing 6970g were recovered from Grand Arcade, representing at least 220 pipes (MNI); there were also 306 fragments weighing 1495g and representing at least 36 pipes (MNI) from Christ's Lane. In addition there were also three objects made from pipeclay: a wig curler, a mouthpiece shaped item and a hollow cone shaped item. Information on local makers derives largely from Cessford (2001c), although subsequent unpublished research has modified some of the identifications and dating of manufacturers. It appears that the earliest clay tobacco pipes – of c. 1580–1630/40 (see Chapter 4; Fig. 4.60F) – were imported from London (Fig. 5.97). Following on from this almost all the pipes were produced

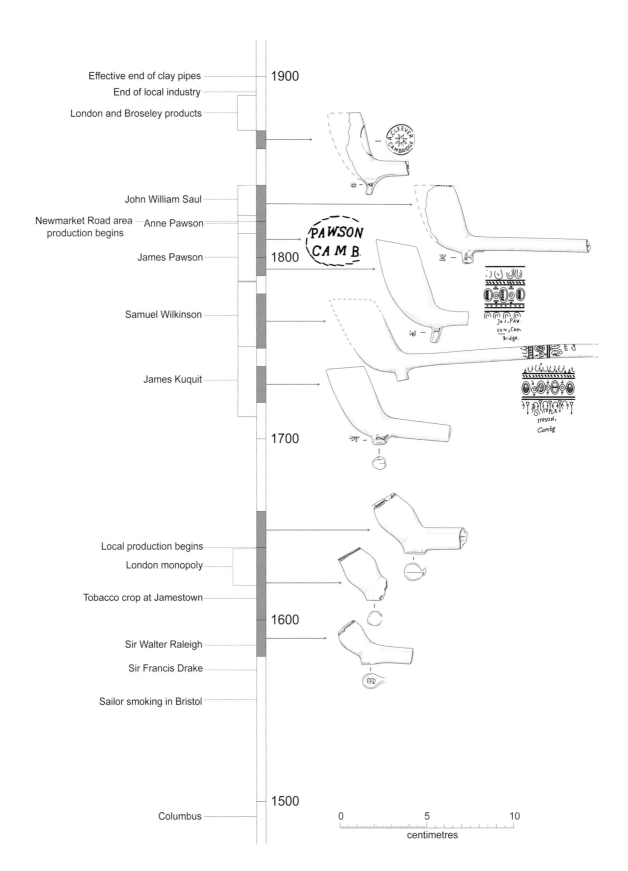

Figure 5.97. *Timeline for clay tobacco pipes in Cambridge.*

locally in Cambridge until the mid-nineteenth century, when a few London pipes are present, while from other sites it is known that pipes from Broseley also began to arrive in the town.

The use of clay tobacco pipes increased during the seventeenth century, becoming relatively common after *c.* 1660, although most of the material comes from the garden soil. The earliest documentary evidence for pipe production in Cambridge was the will of Rodger Smith, who died in 1647, and it is possible that local pipemaking did not begin until the charter granting London pipemakers a virtual monopoly ended in 1639 (Oswald 1975, 7–9). After this it appears that Cambridge pipemakers dominated the local market. Production was nonetheless small-scale with only one or two pipemakers plus their employees. Some of these pipemakers were based nearby during the late seventeenth–early eighteenth centuries, and associated material was recovered from the King's Ditch in 1914 (Chapter 3). None of the seventeenth-century Cambridge pipemakers appear to have marked or decorated their pipes; their products generally lack a high degree of finish and are almost exclusively of broad heel forms with few spurred examples. Wig curlers were rare, with just a single example from Christ's Lane (Fig. 6.11G).

A range of pipes were studied using Inductively Coupled Plasma Atomic emission Spectroscopy (ICP-AES) and in common with most British clay tobacco pipe production the Cambridge makers largely utilized Dorset/Isle of Wight Tertiary ball clay (Cessford 2011). The exception is a single pipe dated to *c.* 1600–40; this had a markedly different composition which is similar to certain East Midlands pottery such as Developed Stamford ware. It seems likely that this pipe was made using white-firing middle Jurassic clays found in Lincolnshire and Northamptonshire. The clay may have come from Northampton Field, on the east side of Northampton, which lies in an area of Jurassic clay of the Estuarine Series and in the early eighteenth century it was reputed to be the finest in the land. It was exploited from at least *c.* 1665/75 until 1771, before it became exhausted *c.* 1771–1830 (Moore 1980, 4–5) and this is the first time that it has been identified using ICP-AES. ICP-AES suggests that the single wig curler was also manufactured locally using Dorset/Isle of Wight Tertiary ball clay.

By the eighteenth century, clay tobacco pipe production was well-established in Cambridge. There appear to have been three or four makers at any point in time and there is no evidence that any pipes from elsewhere were being used in Cambridge. The pipes are of variable quality. Initially, as in the seventeenth century, broad heel forms dominate but from *c.* 1760 spurred examples become more common. Decoration is relatively rare and only a few Cambridge makers marked their pipes. Makers who did mark their pipes and whose products were recovered included James Kuquit (Fig. 5.22A), Samuel Wilkinson (Figs. 5.23H and 5.27K) and James Pawson (Fig. 5.57G–J). These makers all occupied the same premises in Sidney Street (Cessford 2001a) and in some senses their products form a local quasi-familial 'lineage' of products that continued into the nineteenth century. As well as being decorated and bearing their maker's name, Wilkinson's, and to a lesser extent Pawson's, pipes are of visibly superior quality and finish to many of the unmarked eighteenth-century pipes, which were presumably produced by other local makers. The fact that these pipemakers were wealthier and more successful than their competitors is also reflected in the fact that they have left fuller documentary records, notably in sources such as Poll Books. There is therefore a danger that the higher documentary and archaeological visibility of certain makers can lead to a self-reinforcing focus upon them to the exclusion of other makers, creating a warped view of the industry.

Clay tobacco pipe manufacturing continued in Cambridge for much of the nineteenth century. At the beginning of the century

James Pawson, succeeded by his widow Anne. Although the kiln continued in operation after Anne's death in the 1820s, its products rapidly become less archaeologically visible, and the main focus of production shifts to the rapidly expanding Barnwell suburb. From the 1870s onwards Broseley and London products begin to occur in Cambridge and the local industry went into rapid decline, ending in the early 1890s. Cambridge pipemakers were also probably producing other items made of pipeclay as a minor side-line.

Clay pipes produced in Cambridge are only occasionally marked; a few examples that can be linked to known makers including the Balls family, Anne Cleaver, James Kuquit and Thomas Moule were recovered. The most commonly marked pipes relate to Samuel Wilkinson and James and Anne Pawson. Samuel Wilkinson (active by 1762, died 1787) produced pipes with two slightly different types of Wyer style stem decoration (Walker & Wells 1979, 5–12) and his niece's husband James Pawson (active 1786, died 1813) who inherited the business also produced pipes with two slightly different types of Wyer style stem decoration, although he or possibly his wife Anne Pawson (inherited the business 1813, died 1823) eventually switched to a rather different style of stem decoration. These makers successively occupied the same premises in Sidney Street (Cessford 2001a) and supplied Cambridge and its immediate surroundings, although pipes produced by Wilkinson have been found at Ely (23km distant) and Huntingdon (27km distant) and those of Pawson at Bury St Edmund's (41km distant; Heard 2009, 5). This reflects a general pattern, as clay pipes are typically found within 25km of their place of manufacture and occasionally up to 40km (Oak-Rind 1980).

At Grand Arcade the total length of pipe stem recovered was 59.8m, giving *c.* 270mm of stem per pipe. The stem length of pipes changes through time and also varied at any given point between different makers and even different types of pipe by the same maker. Early pipes could be as little as *c.* 100mm long; this increased over time with a typical length of *c.* 360mm, although some could be as long as *c.* 910mm (Boothroyd & Higgins 2005; Jarzembowski & Jarzembowski 1981). This suggests a potential recovery rate at Grand Arcade of *c.* 75 per cent.

It was notable that many eighteenth–nineteenth-century features, such as cellars, which contained substantial numbers of pottery and glass vessels contained relatively few clay tobacco pipes. There were only a few with 10 or more clay tobacco pipes and the largest group (MNI 17) relates to collegiate usage. It should, however, be noted that even these groups are relatively small in comparison to some features from other British cities where hundreds of pipes have been recovered from individual

343

features. The infilling of such features was a relatively uncommon event, occurring only one or two times a century on any individual plot. The evidence suggests that clay tobacco pipes were frequently deposited in garden soil, a phenomenon recognized elsewhere where *c.* 120 were recovered from a single garden perhaps implying the loss of 10 per year (Higgins 1985). At the Grand Arcade site it appears that up to *c.* 1500 clay tobacco pipes were deposited in one particular garden, equating to around five per year. It appears that clay tobacco pipes were relatively much more likely to be deposited in garden soil rather than in 'feature groups'. This contrasts with contemporary ceramic and glass vessels and suggests that different depositional strategies were in action.

Clay pipes may have entered the garden soil either directly or via middens, and were disposed of relatively immediately. The larger, and potentially more hazardous, ceramic and glass vessels may have in effect been 'stockpiled' and disposed of less frequently and more 'formally'. Something of the relative patterning of deposition can be identified by comparing material types from particular features. The length of stem per pipe in the three features with the largest numbers is 132mm (*Cellar 7*), 198mm per pipe (*Soakaway 3*) and 346mm (*Cellar 4*) respectively, while the values for the two most investigated garden soils are 232mm and 248mm. The reasons for this variation are unclear, but it does seem that a substantial quantity of stem is missing from some features; perhaps because some pipes continued to be used after their stems were partially broken and this earlier breakage material was disposed of elsewhere.

18 samples of clay tobacco pipe and one wig curler from a number of sites in Cambridge were submitted for analysis of the pipeclay using Inductively Coupled Plasma Spectroscopy. The results indicated that the pipes could be divided into six groups, which correspond to a chronological sequence:

1) Group 5 (early) *c.* 1580–1620/30
2) Group 1 *c.* 1620/30–40/50
3) Group 6 *c.* 1640/50–1750/60
4) Groups 4 and 5 (late) *c.* 1750/60–1810/20
5) Group 3 *c.* 1810/20–1830
6) Group 2 *c.* 1830–70

The majority of the pipes were made of Dorset/Isle of Wight Tertiary ball clay, which is known to have been used by London pipemakers and is recorded as being traded to King's Lynn by the 1660s. The exception to this was an unmarked early seventeenth-century pipe of *c.* 1600–40, which may relate to the earliest phase of local clay pipe production in Cambridge *c.* 1620–45 and was probably made of clay from Northampton.

Table 5.11. *The Grand Arcade ceramic building materials assemblage by date. MT - Minimum number of Tiles per context, derived by dividing the number of corners present by the number of corners for a complete piece. TE - Tile Equivalent, a percentage based on the number of corners present.*

Period	No. %	Weight %	Corner %	MT %	TE %	MSW (g)
11th–12th	0.35	0.22	0.24	0.38	0.26	142.7
13th	0.09	0.02	-	-	-	45.9
14th–15th	13.02	3.50	2.85	6.83	4.10	60.2
13th–15th	27.69	1.00	0.97	1.20	1.01	8.1
16th–17th	41.63	15.49	12.51	39.19	16.07	83.4
18th–19th	15.78	77.73	81.10	50.60	76.37	1104.0
N/A	1.44	2.04	2.34	1.80	2.19	318.0

Ceramic building material Philip Mills, incorporating specialist information from Alan Vince

Overall, 9121 pieces of ceramic building material weighing 2053kg were recovered from Grand Arcade, plus 116 pieces weighing 122kg from Christ's Lane (Table 5.11). The bulk of the assemblage is seventeenth-century and later in date. For this reason, the patterns present within the overall assemblage (including material previously reported upon in Chapter 4) will be discussed here.

Slop moulded bricks are introduced in the sixteenth century, as in other parts of the country, and there is a standardization in size and increasing evidence of mass-production from the eighteenth century onwards. Brick supply is dominated by the area around Ely although there is a widening of sources from the eighteenth century, with production beginning at Cambridge itself. It appears that different plots may have obtained their bricks from different sources, although the limitations of the data make this conclusion problematic. Roof tiles are predominantly peg tiles, mainly with two rounded peg holes although there is a specifically nineteenth-century usage of peg tiles with one off set rounded peg hole and eighteenth- and nineteenth-century usage of pan tiles. Tile supply is also dominated by the Ely area, as in the rest of the region. Roof tile seems to be relatively mixed in colour until the eighteenth century when yellow came to be favoured, changing the appearance of roves in the area.

Although the vast majority of the brick and tile continued to come from Fenland sources, located on or near the Isle of Ely, during the seventeenth century there is evidence that this was a time of change and development in the local supply. It also appears that there was an increasing complexity in the types of bricks used in the later seventeenth century. Pan tiles were also introduced, although their usage appears to have been limited.

During the eighteenth century there was a major increase in the amounts of brick being used in Cambridge. Although Fenland sources located on or near the Isle of Ely still dominate, the precise sources appear to have varied and widened, and from the mid/late eighteenth century onwards there is evidence for local Cambridge-based production. Well-levigated machine-cut bricks began to be produced and specialist drain forms began to be made, both of which were employed at Grand Arcade.

The nineteenth century witnesses a continuation of trends apparent in the eighteenth century and the amounts of brick being used at Grand Arcade increases exponentially. Fenland sources, on or near the Isle of Ely, are still important but local Cambridge-based production comes to dominate. There is also evidence for the occasional use of bricks from as far afield as Bedfordshire, while other sites in Cambridge have produced evidence for bricks from the Birmingham area (Newman 2009b), presumably transported by rail. Frogged and perforated bricks begin to be commonly employed by *c.*1850 at the latest and there is evidence for several forms of specialist drain manufactured on or near the Isle of Ely (Figs. 3.25B–C and 5.98), as well as more decorative architectural elements (Fig. 3.25F).

The production of brick and tile in Ely is partially related to the pottery industry. Excavations at Potters Lane have revealed evidence for peg tile production in the thirteenth–fourteenth centuries, with production of crested ridge tiles and small thick floor tiles in the fifteenth century (Spoerry 2008, 27–9, 64). There is also evidence that glazed drain tiles were produced at Ely. The earliest documentary evidence for production dates to the second half of the fifteenth century, when there was a 'tyle kylne close' at Barton Farm (Lucas 1993, 157). Prior to this there are records that in 1339 bricks and tiles were imported to Ely from King's Lynn and Wisbech (Lucas 1993, 157), bricks were also supplied to Ely from Emneth in 1355–6 and Wiggenshall *c.*1454 (Lucas 1993, 157). In 1681 Thomas Baskerville noted that 'the great trade of this town [Ely] and the country hereabout is the making of bricks and earthenware, for which purpose they have excellent sorts of earth' (quoted in Lucas 1993, 158). The industry was also mentioned by later observers and is well-documented throughout the seventeenth–eighteenth centuries. Brick and tile production continued in Ely into the nineteenth century and the tithe map of 1843 indicates seven locations where manufacturing had occurred, although the industry appears to have declined rapidly in the 1850s–60s (Lucas 1993, 161).

The clays in the vicinity of Ely include Kimmeridge Clay, Gault Clay and alluvial clay (Gallois 1988). It has been argued that bricks made from the different clays can be identified by their different colourings, with Kimmeridge Clay products being reddish brown, alluvial clays a range of 'brindled or mottled hues' and Gault clays buff or white (Lucas 1993, 158). In fact it appears likely that all the Ely products are made from the Kimmeridge Clay (Firman 1998). In part this arises from a confusion between the term 'gault bricks', which is applied generically to all buff or white bricks even when they are not made from Gault Clay strictly speaking. The Kimmeridge Clay

is composed of a large number of beds with different compositions, which would produce a wide variety of different fabrics and colours. During the time when the Ely brick and tile industry was active the clay to produce bricks and tiles would be dug by hand, either following individual beds or in 'lifts' up to 2m high. The fabric, texture and colour of the bricks and tiles would therefore closely reflect the lithology of the individual bed or the group of beds in an individual 'lift'.

The Kimmeridge Clay around Ely was capable of producing 'brick red' bricks from darker mudstones; reddish brown bricks from medium grey mudstones and a range of yellow, buff and cream bricks from the more calcareous palest mudstones. This identification of all the clays used as deriving from Kimmeridge Clay is confirmed by the more geologically informed contemporary observers (Firman 1998). In the 1880s Thomas Roberts examined the strata in the still working or recently abandoned brick pits in and around Ely and identified the 'solid' formations as Kimmeridge Clay of Upper Jurassic Age (Roberts 1892). Thomas McKenny Hughes the Woodwardian professor of geology also stated that Ely bricks were made of Kimmeridge Clay (Hughes & Hughes 1909, 113). The Kimmeridge Clay formation was surveyed using boreholes by Gallois, who produced a detailed bed by bed description demonstrating that the more calcareous beds were favoured for brick making, and that they produced yellow or brown bricks (1988, 89). The Ely fabrics have been split into five broad groups, which can be further subdivided.

1) Ely area pottery type fabrics: these fabrics tend to have a very hard black reduced core with buff to red margins and calcareous inclusions. Forms include peg tiles and ridge tiles, some of which are crested. They are often glazed, with the ridge tiles especially having an even thick green gloss glaze, although tiles tend to have patches or stripes of thin green, yellow or brown glazes. Visual inspection suggested that these fabrics and glazes were similar to those use by potters at Ely; further analysis showed that they are varied in appearance in thin section but form a group chemically. They appear to have been made from Jurassic clays, either being highly organic, with a black core and sharp core/margin boundary, or calcareous. The thin sections indicate the presence of a mixed detrital sand, in which the finer grade grains are of Triassic origin and the coarser grade grains are of Cretaceous origin. Similar coarse sands occur in pottery produced at Colne and found at Huntingdon, classified by Spoerry as Hunts Fen Sandy ware and Colne-type ware. Chemical analysis confirms the similarity of the two Cambridge fabrics to the Colne and Huntingdon wares, but with a stronger similarity to Huntingdon. The river gravel found at Huntingdon and Colne also outcrops around Cambridge, but how similar the Cambridge gravel is to that found in these fabrics is not known, since none has been sampled. However, there is no source for Upper Jurassic clay in the immediate area of Cambridge and the closest possible source lies about five miles to the north-west. In Cambridge the occurrence of these fabrics appears to be related to the proximity of thirteenth–fourteenth-century building activity in close proximity to the site. As well as Ely itself these fabrics have been identified at

345

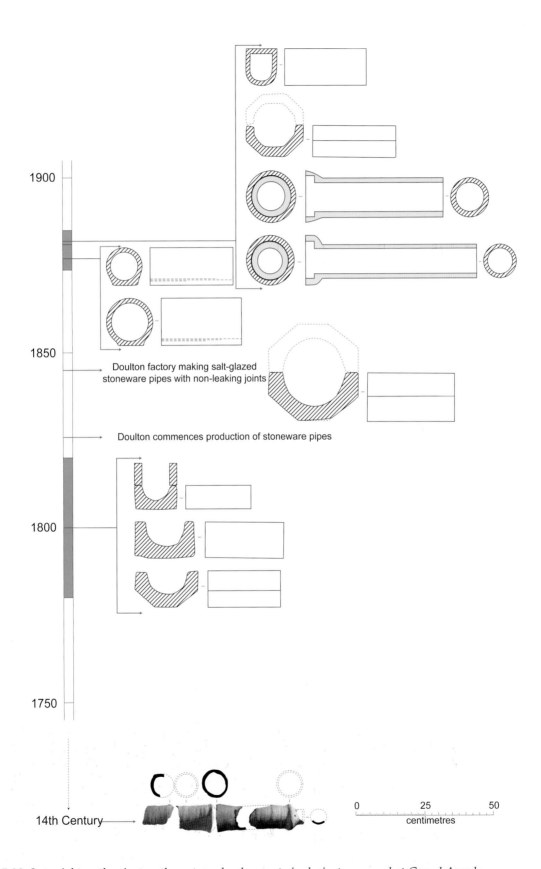

Figure 5.98. *Late eighteenth–nineteenth-century developments in drain-types used at Grand Arcade.*

King's Lynn (Mills in Cope-Faulkner 2000a) and Boston (Mills in Cope-Faulkner 2000b), as well as much further up the east coast at Newcastle (Mills in Mabbitt 2006) and Berwick (Mills in Mabbitt & Frain 2007).

2) Ely area sandy red (darker mudstone beds of Kimmeridge Clay): these are a red sandy fabric, with a range of minor variation in firings and size and sorting of inclusions. Forms include peg tiles, crested ridge tiles and bricks and they occur from the twelfth century onwards, although some variants do not appear until the thirteenth/fourteenth centuries and the fourteenth/fifteenth centuries. Production of these fabrics appears to cease by the eighteenth century. Thin section and ICP-AES examination of one of the earlier fabrics indicated that the bricks have a variable appearance in thin section and appear to be made from a mixture of silty clay of recent date and Jurassic marl. The ICP-AES analysis indicates that the bricks are all more similar to each other than to any of the other samples and that they form a distinct group, unrelated to other samples.

3) Ely area reddish brown (medium grey mudstone beds of Kimmeridge clay): a reddish brown fabric that was used rarely for bricks, but more commonly for tiles.

4) Ely area buff and white (lighter calcareous mudstone beds of Kimmeridge clay): although traditionally described as 'gault bricks' these are not made of Gault Clay.

5) Ely area mixed red and yellow (mixed darker mudstone and lighter calcareous mudstone beds of Kimmeridge clay): these fabrics do not display the pure yellow colour that perhaps should be expected with pure Gault bricks, and comprise a mixture of red and yellow lenses, in varying amounts depending on fabric, and inclusions.

Thus the Kimmeridge Clay in Cambridgeshire was capable of producing almost black bricks from inter-bedded oil shales; brick red bricks from darker mudstones; reddish brown bricks from medium grey mudstones, and a range of yellow, buff and cream bricks from the more calcareous palest mudstones.

There is a small quantity of late twelfth–thirteenth/fourteenth-century glazed relief decorated floor tiles (van Lemmen 2000) and examples of plain mosaic tile, of the same period. The plain tiles were also probably produced at Ely; the quantities involved and the distribution of the material, which is scattered across a range of plots rather than being concentrated, suggest that the material does not relate to their use at the Grand Arcade site. It appears more likely that they arrived later as refuse or rubble from elsewhere. Much smaller excavations at the Dominican friary on the opposite side of St Andrew's Street produced a much more substantial assemblage of decorated floor tile (Dickens 1999a; see also Chapter 6) and it is likely that all the material at Grand Arcade arrived after the Dissolution, either from the Dominican friary or other religious houses in Cambridge.

The earliest surviving brickwork in Cambridge is in the vault of the bone-hole of St Mary the Less dated to *c.* 1350, and there is documentary evidence for the use of brick at King's Hall (1375–6) and Gonville &

Caius College (*c.* 1390) (RCHM(E) 1959, c). The fine quality of brickwork veneer with traces of diamond or diaper patterning at Queens' College of 1448–9 is the earliest extensive use of exposed brickwork (RCHM(E) 1959, c). Bishop Alcock's work at Jesus College started 1496 and dated *c.* 1500 the diaper work near the top of the gatehouse represents the earliest 'conscious' use of white brickwork, although some is suffused with pink (Pevsner 1954, 74; RCHM(E) 1959, c). When St John's College First Court was being built in 1511–16 the brickmaker was one Recluver of Greenwich and the College paid his travelling expenses, suggesting an absence of local expertize. These bricks appear to have been purpose made and were fired using wood from Coton (RCHM(E) 1959, c). The use of brickwork by colleges became common in the sixteenth century, some of which was obtained from Ely (Lucas 1993, 158; RCHM(E) 1959, c). As well as its use by the Colleges there are sixteenth-century documentary records of brick boundary walls around domestic plots (1546, 1574–5) and named bricklayers are first attested in the 1540s (Richard Mason 1544; Charles Palmer 1546).

In the seventeenth century there is further documentary evidence for local production. In 1622 brick earth was dug for Talbot Pepys in Arbury Meadow and the bricks were piled in clamps (Wright 2002, 25). This relates to the exploitation of the loam from the extensive deposits of gravel, sand and inter-bedded loams which stretch north from Cambridge to Histon and Impington (Worssam & Taylor 1969, 111–12). The name Brickhill Lane in West Field is mentioned slightly later in 1634 (Worssam & Taylor, 1969, 111–12). When Clare College was rebuilt in 1636 brick earth was obtained for local production, whereas in 1639 the College bought bricks from Ely (RCHM(E) 1959, c). There are seventeenth-century records of non-collegiate domestic brick buildings, including a 'little brick house' (1659) and a messuage 'newly erected in brick' (1673). A considerable number of bricklayers are known from wills and apprenticeship indentures and there is the earliest named local brickmaker Richard Hallett (1636).

From the early eighteenth century large houses incorporated gauged, rubbed or moulded brick features and two-coloured brickwork (RCHM(E) 1959, ci). These were often 'hung' on existing timber framed buildings as a cheaper alternative to rebuilding in brick; the use of brick and tile was often restricted to the conspicuous frontages of the houses. The increasing use of 'white' brick potentially relates to aesthetic ideas of colour harmony as 'there is something harsh in the transition from red brick to stone, and it seems altogether unnatural; in the other, the grey stocks come so near the colour of stone that the change is less violent, and they may sort better together', although the fact that the grey are cheaper also had an effect (Ware 1756, 60–1). One local bricklayer John Brewer, who died in 1706, had a substantial number of freehold and leasehold plots in the town indicating that he was relatively wealthy. Brick and tile grounds in Chesterton parish were for sale in 1792 (Wright 2002, 25).

An early eighteenth-century kiln was excavated at Thompson's Lane (Firman & Pullinger 1987). The kiln was pear-shaped and was 5.0m by 3.65m in extent, with internal dimensions of 4.5m by 2.7m and a central pedestal. As well as a range of flowerpots it produced pinkish yellow peg tiles; the tiles are interpreted as wasters as they were 'distorted or with holes punched awry' and measured 10½in by 6½in and ½in thick (Firman & Pullinger 1987, 89). The structure appears very small for an early eighteenth-century tile kiln and it is possible that the tiles were simply used as seaters, spacers or separators for the flowerpots. The distortion and faulty holes could be due to a combination of the repeated re-firing of the tiles and the deliberate selection and use of 'seconds' in a context where faulty holes would not matter. As the flowerpots were unglazed none of the typical distinctive traces of such use as seaters, spacers or separators would be present. The only other locally investigated production site is a possible brick yard at Shippea Hill Farm on the Isle of Ely, which is not closely dated (Cra'aster et al. 1965, 147). The remains consisted of stacked bricks and tiles, the bricks were in large regularly laid stacks 10ft (3.0m) square and were 9in by 4in and 2in thick in size. The tiles were in long rows 15ft (4.6m) long and were stacked on edge lengthways; they were 11in by 6 1/6 inch in size with two holes. There was also a possible clay pit nearby.

The loam deposits north of the river were still being exploited in the nineteenth century with three kilns and associated brick grounds in 1839; these provided employment for around 10 to 15 brickmakers and up to 20 bricklayers although the area became less significant as the century progressed (Wright 2002, 25). This decline was due to the rise of the industry in the Newmarket Road area to the south of the river, which expanded throughout the nineteenth century, with several firms in existence at any point in time, some of which employed 80 to 100 men. The clay was extracted from open-topped pits up to 80ft (24m) deep and was mixed with lime-free 'silver' sand brought by cart from the east coast. The loam to the north of the river which was exploited earlier would have been easier to dig and mix than the Gault Clay to the south of the river; however, the Gault Clay could produce more heterogeneous bricks.

By the end of the eighteenth century there had developed a 'very fine-textured and regular grey-white brick of constant colour' and this is what was generally

used in the nineteenth century (RCHM(E) 1959, ci). In 1903 McKenny Hughes recorded that Cambridge bricks were made of Gault Clay, which generally burns white while Ely bricks made of Kimmeridge Clay burn red (Hughes & Hughes 1909, 113). The industry continued into the twentieth century and in the 1930s there were four companies in Cambridge, while at Ely there were 'no less than five well-established brick-works' (Page 1948, 367). The kilns in use up until the 1940s were 30ft long (9.1m), 12ft wide (3.7m) and 14ft high (4.3m), 9ft (2.7m) of which was below ground level (Porter 1973). The kilns were built from firebricks, there were two 2ft (0.6m) square flues under the floor which was built in an openwork pattern, the roof was slightly domed and pierced with 6inch diameter holes. Wood or peat were used to dry out the kiln prior to firing, while the firing itself used coal. Firing would take around 10 days, with a further 28 to 42 days for the kiln to cool.

Wood and timber Richard Darrah, incorporating specialist information from Ian Tyers and Steve Allen

The seventeenth–nineteenth-century timber primarily consisted of nine timber baseplates that had been utilized during the construction of stone or brick-lined wells (Figs. 5.4, 5.10, 5.12, 5.24C, 5.25 and 5.29) plus timber-framing of standing buildings (Fig. 5.31). There were also a range of objects (Figs. 5.5, 5.21C, 5.43K, 5.49B and 5.50), but the only individual item of note was a seventeenth-century winding block (*Well 42*; Fig. 5.10; Case Study 8).

The most striking seventeenth-century evidence for timber comes from the baseplates of three stone- and stone and brick-lined wells (*Wells 41–43*; Figs. 5.4 and 5.10). Earlier stone-lined wells did not have timber baseplates; although such baseplates would have provided additional stability for the base of the well their main function appears to relate to the construction of the features. Until the twentieth century the traditional local method of well construction was to use a cartwheel felloe *c*. 5ft (1.5m) in diameter, with the hub and spokes removed (Warboys 2003, 21–2). A circuit of unmortared stone blocks or bricks would be laid on the felloe, the soil would then be carefully removed under the wheel and the weight of material would cause the wheel to sink. This process would then be repeated as often as required. The 1620s therefore represent the earliest evidence for this local tradition, which lasted for three centuries. All these timber baseplates, and indeed the eighteenth–nineteenth-century examples, vary considerably. This is largely because they represent the *ad hoc* use of available timber, often material that had already been used once in a different context.

The eighteenth-century timber comes also comes from well baseplates. *Well 45* (Figs. 5.24C and 5.25) built in the 1720s was different from the seventeenth-century examples in that the timber appears to be boards purchased specifically for this purpose and it was constructed by nailing them together, rather than using traditional timber-framing techniques. In contrast, *Well 46* built later in 1761 is more akin to the seventeenth-century tradition of idiosyncratic use of available material and did utilize traditional timber-framing techniques (see Case Study 10; Fig. 5.29).

A number of, but not all, of the nineteenth-century wells contained wooden elements, although the most spectacular *Wells 49–50* are associated with the Robert Sayle department store. In contrast to most of the seventeenth–eighteenth-century well baseplates, the nineteenth-century baseplates and annuli part way up the shafts, such as in *Well 56*, were much less *ad hoc*, even though they were still often made from reused materials. They were generally much thinner than their predecessors, with the wood much more thoroughly reshaped into circles.

From the seventeenth century onwards timber baseplates were used in the construction of wells in the Grand Arcade street block. These were initially rather *ad hoc* structures where a broadly circular ring was constructed using traditional timber-framing techniques, apparently from whatever timber was readily available. Wood was widely imported into Cambridge during this period; a 1702 Act covering freight on the Cam lists deal boards, timber, faggots, billets (lengths of round timber), pales and staves for barrels (Chisholm 2003, 186). This pattern of *ad hoc* usage continued throughout the eighteenth century, although some baseplates were also constructed from boards – several of which were specifically purchased for the purpose – that were nailed together. By the nineteenth century only nailed boards were in use; these were much thinner than their predecessors and more thoroughly reshaped into circles. In addition to the baseplates there were also timber annuli part way up the well shafts. Wells stopped being constructed in town in the late nineteenth century due to the provision of mains water, but continued to be constructed locally in rural locations into the twentieth century where cartwheel felloes with the hub and spokes removed were employed (Warboys 2003, 21–2). There is no evidence that cartwheel felloes were ever employed in Cambridge itself, suggesting that these were either a late nineteenth–twentieth-century development or more probably that felloes that were no longer fit for their original purpose were more readily available in the countryside; an idea supported by the discovery of a wheel in a eleventh–twelfth-century pit-well at Longstanton (Patten & Evans 2005).

Leatherwork Quita Mould

The majority of the seventeenth–twentieth-century leather consisted of shoes and boots; there was also a complete moulded seventeenth-century drinking vessel (Fig. 5.6B; see also Fig. 4.37B) and an upholstery fragment (Fig. 5.21A, see also Fig. 4.37C–D). In addition, a pair of early twentieth-century boots was recovered from Christ's Lane.

Although some seventeenth-century shoes were recovered (Fig. 5.6A), the most impressive discovery was a near-complete moulded leather drinking vessel in *Cesspit 16* (see Case Study 7; Fig. 5.6B, see also Fig. 4.37B). The only eighteenth-century leather came from the

backfilling of *Well 38* in *c.* 1760–80. In addition to two wide welted shoe soles and a clump repair patch, there was a sheet fragment from a piece of upholstery or other furnishing with stamped and tooled decoration (Fig. 5.21A; see also Fig. 4.37C–D).

Several late nineteenth–early twentieth-century features contained leather items. Unlike in earlier periods these were not preserved by waterlogging but rather had not yet decayed. Overall, leather survived in eight features; recovered items included 20 shoes, all of well-known types of the period, and six other items. Three features had single shoes, three contained two shoes (including at least two pairs), one had four shoes (no pairs, plus a fifth shoe with an organic sole and textile upper) and one contained nine shoes (including only one pair). There were 17 features of this date containing large assemblages of other material where leather should potentially have survived. This suggests that in over half the large assemblages leather was not discarded, around a third of the time a single shoe or a pair of shoes was thrown away while a tenth contained larger groups, the largest of which was associated with the Robert Sayle department store.

Economic and environmental data

Mammal and bird bone Lorrain Higbee
The overall animal bone assemblage has been discussed in detail in Chapter 4; only the material directly pertaining to the seventeenth–nineteenth centuries will be presented here. This assemblage was relatively modest in size, but nevertheless produced several significant groups.

The only seventeenth-century material of note comprised a group of four carefully arranged horse skulls in *Pit 56* of *c.* 1600–30 (Fig. 5.7). In addition, *ADPs 10–12* of *c.* 1680–1720 contained the bodies of six cows that were dairy cattle and appear to have suffered from 'milk fever' (Figs. 5.13–5.14).

The eighteenth–nineteenth-century animal bone, which effectively dates to *c.* 1760–1845, will be considered as a single group. In total 1409 bones out of 5348 (26.3 per cent) were identified, including mammal (1026), bird (379), amphibian (3) and crab (1) (Table 4.15). The bone is dominated by the principal livestock species: sheep is the most common, followed by cattle and then pig, although cattle provided the bulk of the meat (Fig. 5.99A). The cattle bone is a mixture of butchery waste and prime meat joints from domestic consumption, consisting of calves fattened for meat and very old cattle. The sheep bone includes material from butchery and domestic consumption, but there was still some material from the processing of hides. Although sheep were raised primarily for their wool, supplying lambs and prime mutton was also important. Pigs were still being raised nearby, but were being culled at a younger age due to improved, faster growing breeds. No clear pattern with regards to species frequency is apparent on sites of this period (Fig. 5.99B). Hare, rabbit and fallow deer were also consumed and cats and dogs were found, mainly as complete or partially disturbed skeletons, and there were some horse bones. Chicken was the most commonly eaten bird, with evidence of a shift in importance from eggs to meat. Goose, duck, pigeon and turkey were also eaten, plus a range of wild species.

The studied eighteenth-century material primarily consists of five relatively large assemblages dating to after *c.* 1760 (*Well 38*, *PBs 10–11*, *Building 25*, *Cellar 6*). Most of the bone relates to meat joints, but some butchery waste is present and there are several groups of leatherdressers' waste. Cats and dogs were disposed of in several redundant features and it appears that pigs were still being raised in some plots. There is also the earliest evidence for the eating of turkey from *Cellar 6* dated *c.* 1780–90. Six significant

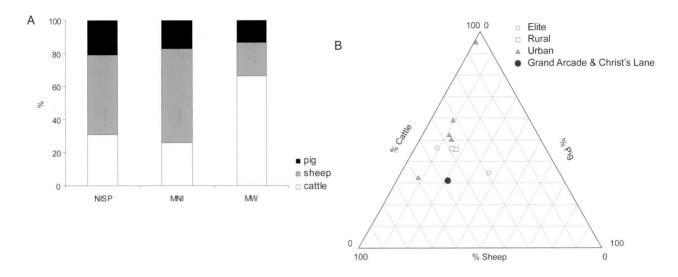

Figure 5.99. *Eighteenth–nineteenth-century livestock species: (A) the relative frequency by number of specimens identified to species (NISP), minimum number of individuals (MNI) and meat weight (MW) (Note that NISP and MNI figures exclude large industrial deposits); (B) the relative frequency (by NISP) compared to other contemporary sites. For earlier frequencies sees Figs. 4.66 and 4.67.*

assemblages of *c.* 1800–45 were studied, several of which can be contextualized through documentary evidence. They include groups associated with a grocer's household (*Soakaway 2*), a school (*PH 3*), a College cook (*Soakaway 3*) and an inn (*Cellar 4, Pit 63*). After *c.* 1850 animal bone becomes extremely rare as a component in the large assemblages of material that were still being deposited (Fig. 5.94A). This phenomenon has also been noted in London and may relate to changing attitudes of what represented 'dry and proper rubbish', plus possibly an increased use of animal bone as agricultural fertilizer (Jeffries 2006, 286). At about the same time the quantities of oyster shell in such assemblages also declined as part of the same phenomenon. There is also evidence for consumption that would not have resulted in any bone at the site, such as a jar lid for potted game (Fig. 5.64E).

Fish bone Jen Harland

Only a few fish remains relating to this period were recovered, all of which dated to the nineteenth century.

The material included Atlantic Herring, Cod and Halibut family. There was also a dish used as a container for potted Arctic char (Fig. 5.64F), a type of salmon native to Lake Windermere and Coniston Water in the Lake District. The delicate flavour of this fish's pink-tinged flesh has been popular as a potted breakfast dish in the Lake District since the sixteenth century and improved nineteenth-century transport links led to it becoming a delicacy across Britain.

Discussion

The period between the seventeenth century and the early twenty-first centuries is predominantly characterised by rapid and profound change in the Barnwell Gate suburb of Cambridge, albeit with considerable elements of continuity. For ease this discussion will, however, be sub-divided into the four chronological sections, with the Robert Sayle department store already having been considered (see above).

Seventeenth century

The seventeenth century comprised one of the most turbulent periods in English history and the archaeological sequence at Grand Arcade can be situated in regard to these events. In the early part of the century, for instance – *c.* 1600–30 – a major transformation occurred in Plots XIV–XIX: a series of brick-built structures, boundary walls and wells were created, while a group of horse skulls were also deposited. Overlapping with this, in *c.* 1616–37 the plot to the north (Plot XIII) stopped being used as an inn and was enclosed by walls. At the same time its cesspit was backfilled with a range of material that, although focused principally upon everyday and mundane eating and drinking, is also redolent of the Atlantic slave trade (Case Study 7). Broadly coeval with this, in *c.* 1625–42 the next plot to the north (Plot XI) became an inn and had its cesspit backfilled, a well created and also gained access to another well, thereby indicating that it obtained water from three separate sources.

The appearance of these brick-built structures indicates the arrival, albeit belatedly, of a form of 'great rebuilding' in the street block. The idea of a single 'Great Rebuilding' across rural England between 1570 and 1640 was first advanced by Hoskins (1953). Although broad-brush in its approach and overly narrow in its dating there is still evidence that many medieval open halls were floored over, had new chimneys and staircases inserted and glazed windows and new furnishings introduced during this period (Platt 1994; Johnson 2010, 87–112). There are suggestions that elements of this 'package' were present at Grand Arcade, although there is much more substantial evidence for structures linked to a second 'Great Rebuilding' after the Civil War; an event that emphasized regularity and the 'neat compact boxes' of Restoration England. Notably, this process started up to a century earlier at the neighbouring Christ's Lane street block (Chapter 6), suggesting that a degree of variation existed across the Barnwell Gate suburb.

It seems unlikely that households would have engaged in substantial construction works such as wells during the turmoil of the Civil War and it is therefore probable that no major features were created between 1642 and 1649. In general, archaeologically discernible impacts of the Civil War are rare in Cambridge. On the one hand, the castle's defences were strengthened at this time (Cessford 2008) and it is likely that a hoard of gold coins discovered at nearby Pembroke College was associated with the departure of royalist fellows in 1642 (Allen 1999). There is, however, no clear trace of this period in the excavated remains at Grand Arcade or Christ's Lane; at most, this period may be reflected by a temporary hiatus in constructional activity.

Nearby, the parish church of St Andrew the Great was rebuilt in the 1660s (Chapter 6) in an act that affirmed the orthodoxy of the Anglican Church after the restoration in 1660 and the Act of Uniformity in 1662. At the same time the Independents – who advocated local congregational control of religious and church matters, without any wider ecclesiastical or political geographical hierarchy – were particularly active in the St Andrew's Street and Hogg Hill area (Cam 1959, 135–6). A meeting at a house in St Andrew's Street was broken up in 1665 and the congregation escaped 'through Mr. Blackley's yard', possibly the same John Blackley who was recorded as residing at Plot XIV in 1669–70. In 1672, during the short-lived indulgence of Charles II, there was a licence to hold a congregation at a meeting house on Hog Hill (Cooper 1845, 556) and in 1675 there was a meeting 'in Robert Wilson's house in St Andrew's parish'; this latter may be The Vine at Christ's Lane as this was leased by a Robert Wilson in 1667–1702 (Chapter 6). Following the Act of Toleration of 1689 Joseph Hussey preached in 'the new meeting-house built since the liberty in 1687' on Hog Hill in 1691 (Cam 1959, 136).

In the 1680s, Plot XVI went through another transformation that resulted in a well being backfilled after only around half a century of use, along with the no doubt irksome loss of its winding block. A range of buildings and a new well were then constructed.

At around the same time or a little later a series of cattle were buried in Plot XXII. Six cows, plus three foetuses – presumably milk cattle that grazed the area and suffered from 'milk fever' caused by a lack of forage containing the right balance of minerals – were disposed of in pits situated at the rear of the property. Over the course of the seventeenth century the majority of the pottery in use was relatively unchanged, although Staffordshire-type slipware, tin-glazed earthenware and Westerwald stoneware had all become more common. Smoking with clay tobacco pipes was now widespread and glass bottles also occurred more frequently. Only a single wig curler was recovered, from Christ's Lane; such items appear, admittedly at an impressionistic level, to be relatively common discoveries as stray finds at College sites, thus indicating a potential 'town' versus 'gown' distinction.

The general lack of seventeenth-century material is part of a more widespread phenomenon, in which late medieval and early post-medieval sequences of pits and other features cease c. 1600–20 and there is no significant later activity until the late eighteenth or nineteenth centuries. From 1575 onwards the 'muck, mire, and filth' of the town was to be disposed of at a network of five 'common dunghills' established around the perimeter of the town and individuals had to regularly clear the middens from their properties (Cooper 1843, 332, 335). This system may well have had a marked impact on contemporary patterns of activity and refuse disposal, leading to a late sixteenth-century decline and early seventeenth-century cessation of on-site refuse disposal. It is notable that *Well 42*, which was backfilled in the late seventeenth century, had relatively little refuse dumped in it. This appears to mark a transition between the twelfth–sixteenth-century wells, which often contained large quantities of material within their backfills, and the eighteenth–twentieth-century wells, which did not, potentially indicating changing ideas concerning hygiene.

With the exception of the cattle skeletons, there is almost no seventeenth-century evidence pertaining to the activities that took place within the street block; similarly, there is little indication of its relative degree of 'suburban' characteristics. Loggan's 1688 map indicates that the area was less built up than most of the street blocks situated in the urban core (Fig. 5.1), and indeed neighbouring Christ's Lane (Chapter 6); there were however some street blocks located within the circuit of the King's Ditch that contained a similar proportion of buildings to open areas. Relatively few major seventeenth-century archaeological events were identified in the Grand Arcade Street block (two major construction episodes, the construction of four wells and a sequence of cattle burials) and an equally sparse assemblage of material culture was recovered. This is decidedly meagre given the population of approximately 120. The dearth may be due in large part to the fact that pit digging for various functions – the activity that had generated the bulk of the eleventh–sixteenth-century archaeological remains – had ceased but the creation of substantial brick-built features was not yet taking place on a major scale. The archaeological 'record' is largely dependent on the creation of recoverable 'context' and it is this that the seventeenth-century street block lacks rather than activity.

Eighteenth century
Archaeologically, the eighteenth century can be viewed as a period of expansion. Subdivision led to a slight increase in the overall number of plots within the street block. Rather more significantly, however, the level of 'occupation' within each individual plot also increased; marked growth occurred in the number of relatively major plot accessory buildings, for example, while many of the plot heads also expanded. These developments reflect a continuation of trends that had first begun in the 1680s with the construction of buildings in Plots IX and XVI. This pattern of expansion will have had a concomitant impact on the amount of open space that could be used for gardening/horticulture; nevertheless, such areas still accounted for a significant proportion of the street block's footprint at the end of the century. Indeed, the archaeological visibility of gardening-related activity markedly increased during this period, with the emergence of planting beds as well as garden-specific items such as flowerpots and planting labels (see further Cessford 2014b). Whilst similar materials were present in the town centre, they appear to have been much less common, presumably because of the greater restrictions on space in an urban milieu. There is no evidence for the continued grazing of cattle at Grand Arcade after the late seventeenth–early eighteenth century, however, suggesting that a shift of some kind had taken place, although pigs were still being kept in some properties.

The increasing prevalence of brick as a construction material during the eighteenth century is particularly notable. Even excluding the newly constructed frontage buildings, the many freestanding brick-built boundary walls – which averaged around 25 to 35 courses in height, and would consequently have employed 100–200 bricks per metre – would each have required thousands of bricks to construct. This represents a considerable investment, much larger than had previously been employed in relation to boundaries, to the extent that a single wall dwarfs the entire use of brick in the street block prior to the mid-seventeenth century. It therefore appears that, as

in other parts of East Anglia, Cambridge crossed the 'brick threshold' in the early–mid-eighteenth-century, when brick became the predominant material used for walling (Lucas 1997).

Documentary evidence indicates that many of the plots continued to be used for a mixture of domestic and business purposes throughout the eighteenth century. Inns remained common, with at least six examples present, and there was also a school. Other known occupations of residents included baker, barber, combmaker, grocer, tailor, tinplate worker and victualler. Archaeologically, few of these trades leave much if any trace and the only commercial activity that generated significant remains was leatherdressing. Most of the lessees appear to have been relatively wealthy and as well as businesses there is evidence for a significant presence of widows and spinsters. There were also individuals closely connected to the University, in particular those who married and were therefore barred from continuing their academic careers and often joined the clergy.

From *c.* 1760 onwards the rise of mass production, consumerism and fashion are clearly implicated in the relatively large-scale deposition of pottery and glass in discrete feature groups. The ceramics in particular predominantly represent items of globalized material culture, meaning that identical examples might well be found in any corner of the world, although a proportion remained vernacular local products that had evolved over a long period (see further Chapter 7). This was also a period of rapid change, occurring within the lifetimes of individuals such as Frances Headley (*c.* 1729–1805) who lived at Plot XIII. Over time the pottery Frances used would have changed out of all recognition, with Staffordshire white salt-glazed stoneware, creamware and pearlware all rising and receding in prominence. This marks the first time in the history of occupation at the site that such extensive changes had occurred within such a short period of time.

The newly emergent ceramics were primarily associated with dining and tea drinking, a fashionable practice that became widespread during this period. In common with most contemporary families, the Headley's even possessed a few porcelain vessels that had been imported from distant China. More mundane pots were still produced in local glazed red earthenware, although similar forms of Nottinghamshire/Derbyshire-type stoneware and Sunderland-type earthenware vessels could also be purchased that were manufactured much further afield. In addition, coarser unglazed flowerpots were available, vessels that were almost unknown a century previously, as well as lead planting labels for those with a serious interest in horticulture. The appearance of such items is somewhat paradoxical given that large areas of the plot tails were built upon during this period, thereby reducing the size of most gardens. Changes in the types of glassware that were in use were if anything even more marked than those of the ceramics, with a wide range of bottles and drinking vessels appearing, particularly wine glasses. Clay tobacco pipes also greatly increased in frequency.

During the eighteenth century almost all the plots had become shops and there was little if any connection left to the older artisanal trades and agricultural practices that had sustained the inhabitants in preceding centuries. The area was becoming significantly more urban in character. The grocery business that Frances Headly inherited would have stocked a range of luxury items imported from around the globe, such as coffee, cocoa, sugar, spices and dried fruit. Whilst long-distance trade in foodstuffs is archaeologically identifiable from the sixteenth–seventeenth centuries – in the form of wine, cod and grains-of-paradise – the eighteenth-century trade was on an altogether larger scale. The most significant of these new products would have been tea, which first appeared in Britain in the 1650s and from the 1660s was imported as a medicinal product. By the 1690s it was consumed as a beverage, albeit on a restricted scale, but by the 1750s its popularity had risen meteorically; it became the national drink and its consumption far outstripped that of coffee, which had preceded it.

By c. 1760, when the earliest feature groups were deposited at the site, vessels linked to tea drinking comprised a prominent component of the assemblages (42 VSA) compared to those associated with coffee (four VSA). Indeed, although several of the studied assemblages predate the Commutation Act of 1784, which reduced the tax on tea from 119 per cent to 12.5 per cent, there is nothing in the composition of these groups to indicate that this had an impact on the overall levels of tea consumption.

Nineteenth century

Over the course of the nineteenth century, the number of buildings present within the street block doubled and in certain plots quadrupled or more. The plot dominant frontage buildings were now almost entirely two or three storeys tall, with additional attics and basements and tiled or slated roofs. By the end of the century many of the plot accessory buildings to their rear were also of similar construction, although these structures typically lacked basements. This marks a significant change, as the majority of the early to mid-nineteenth century plot accessory buildings had comprised timber-built structures, some of which had thatched rather than tiled roofs. A further change

during the first half of the century pertained to the location of wells. For centuries previously, such features had almost exclusively been located externally within the plot tails. Now, however, the majority were located internally; either at the rear of the plot dominant buildings themselves or else in ancillary structures situated close by. Nevertheless, during the second half of the century, some – although by no means all – of these wells went out of use as piped mains water was introduced.

The expansion in building coverage meant that substantial open spaces and gardens were now a rarity in many plots, although yards still comprised a significant component of most residences. New plots were also created via a process of subdivision. Often occupying the rear of former plot tails, these new additions primarily consisted of densely packed slum-type 'court' developments comprising two rows of buildings that were accessed by a narrow lane. In the Grand Arcade street block examples of this phenomenon include St Andrew's Court (1830s, six additional plots), Corn Exchange Court (1840s, nine additional plots), Blue Lion Court (1840s, eight additional plots) Post Office Terrace (1850s, four additional plots) and St Andrew's Hill (1830s–50s, eight additional plots). The only opposing development was the emergence of the Robert Sayle department store, which led to the loss of some plots (1850s–70s, four plots). A very similar pattern of court development also occurred within the Christ's Lane street block (Chapter 6).

After the 1850s no new 'horizontal' plots were created, although it could be argued that the sub-divided usage of many of the frontage buildings – where, between 1870 and 1900, it was common for the upper storeys of the structures to be given over to different business or residential purposes than their ground floors – effectively created c. 30–40 new 'vertical' plots. To define these new entities as discrete plots would, however, be questionable, since they lack the necessary degree of individuation. A total of 64 households were recorded in the 1881 census of the Grand Arcade street block, plus five uninhabited plots. Overall, there were 351 inhabitants. The mean household size was 5.5, although a more realistic value (excluding the Robert Sayle department store) was 4.6. This may well have represented the high water mark in terms of the population of the area, which subsequently declined gradually throughout the twentieth century, and represented a c. 270 per cent increase since the late eighteenth century. It is notable that the distribution of the households recorded in 1881 was particularly varied, with a marked admixture of the identifiably 'rich' and 'poor' and a similar pattern was also identified at Christ's Lane (Chapter 6).

Despite the rapid escalation in the street block's overall population, the area nevertheless became increasingly commercial in character during the nineteenth century, although most plots retained a significant domestic component. By the end of the century, the inhabitants of a given plot and the individuals that utilized it for commercial purposes were frequently different, with the business owners typically residing elsewhere within Cambridge's newly established outlying suburbs. Such changes were part of a much broader pattern, whereby an increasingly clear demarcation developed between work and life; this was characterized by a transition from the natural rhythms of 'task time' to the commercial currency of 'clock time' (Thompson 1993). Commensurate with these developments, archaeological evidence for the emergent ideologies of personal discipline, hygiene and cleanliness (Schackel 1993) and domesticity and gentility (Fitts 1999) was identified; this is reflected by the increasing prevalence of toothbrushes, chamber pots, sets of matching ceramics and even the selection of 'dry and proper rubbish' as backfilling material (Jeffries 2006).

Perhaps the most successful business in the street block, with the notable exception of the Robert Sayle department store, was that of the Barrett family of pottery retailers (Plot XVII). College servants also became much more visible both documentarily and archaeologically; particularly relatively senior servants such as the cook Thomas Wicks (Case Study 12) and the butler Burbage, who between them left a legacy of fine Wedgwood and Turner ceramics, collegiate wine bottles and a Martaban-type jar that provide a link to the University. Much less visible are the lower level of servants, such as bedmakers, who lived in the densely packed court-type developments. There were also a significant number of students lodging in the street block (Holbrook 2006), although a lack of assemblages of the correct date from appropriate plots means that they are not discernible archaeologically.

Although the Martaban-type jar from *Cellar 12* provides the most striking evidence for long-distance trade, the most ubiquitous was that associated with tea drinking, continuing the phenomenon first noted in the eighteenth century (above). Tea drinking vessels continued at broadly the same level in the first half of the nineteenth century, but increased in frequency after *c.* 1850 (Chapter 7); indeed, from the 1820s onwards the grocers at Plot XIII were regularly described as a tea dealers. New attitudes to hygiene are demonstrated by the increasing appearance of toothbrushes and the eventual disappearance of chamber pots, plus the arrival of a Turkish Baths (Plot XVII). The character of pottery had been revolutionized by

the advent of colour transfer-printing, which dominated the market, while bone china and Utilitarian English stoneware had also risen to prominence. At the lower end of the pottery spectrum, production ended at Ely after around eight centuries, with even large heavy vessels being replaced by Sunderland-type earthenware produced much further afield. Glass vessels became ubiquitous, while almost all the brick and tile in use was supplied by local production in Cambridge.

In addition to buildings, which provide perhaps the most concrete evidence of the street block's urban character during this period, several strands of material evidence can also be adduced. The raising of pigs within certain plots continued into the nineteenth century, for example, but is last represented in a deposit of *c.* 1822–34 (*PH 3*); moreover, the practice is only evinced in one out of seven large bone assemblages of *c.* 1800–50, whereas it was evident in two out of three late eighteenth-century groups. The diminution in this activity was almost certainly associated with the gradual shrinkage of open garden areas during this period. Similarly, the discarding of gardening-related material *c.* 1800–20 in *PBs 7–8* and *c.* 1840–60 in *Well 37* probably resulted from the same process. Leatherdressing, a long-lived activity at the site, also appears to have come to an end in the nineteenth century; the last waste material associated with this industry was deposited *c.* 1840–60 in *Well 41*. Although no longer suburban, the street block nevertheless retained a number of plots that were much larger than those situated in the urban core. This situation presented a number of opportunities, most notably for the development of the Robert Sayle department store as a large-scale institution.

Archaeologically, the nineteenth century comprises the densest and most richly textured of all the periods investigated at Grand Arcade, yet beyond the broad sweeping narrative of increasing occupation it is also amongst the most fragmented. Particular highlights in broadly chronological order include the assemblages associated with the household of College cook Thomas Wicks (*c.* 1808–25, *Soakaway 3*, Plot XV; Case Study 12), Sarah Dobson's school (*c.* 1822–34, *PH 3 etc.*, Plot XIV; see also Cessford 2018a) and the Cock Inn (*c.* 1830–45, *Cellar 4 etc.*, Plot XXII; see also Cessford 2014a) plus a purpose-built grocer's warehouse and kitchen of 1845 (*Standing Building 70*, Plot XIII). Later in the century, material linked to the Newby household was encountered (*c.* 1855–8, *Well 37*, Plot X), plus a purpose-built photographic studio (*c.* 1867–9, *Standing Building 72*, Plot X) and some assemblages and purpose-built storage/retail space associated with the Barrett family of ceramics retailers (*c.* 1879–82, *Building 49*; *c.* 1882–5, *Cellar 12* and *Standing Buildings 94–6*; *c.* 1882–1900, *Building 51*, Plot XVII). This list excludes material associated with the Robert Sayle department store.

Twentieth century
Overall, the twentieth-century archaeological remains encountered at Grand Arcade were not particularly impressive. Indeed, it could be argued that they contribute little to the generic narrative of an increasingly commercial focus within the street block; the commensurate decline is in effect, the triumph of 'disposability and dispossession' (see Lucas 2002). In certain instances, however – as in the case of Plot XIII – this broader story can be resolved into closer focus. One particular change stands out above all

others during this period. Beginning in the mid–late nineteenth century, but escalating markedly during the twentieth century, the nature of households that formed the Grand Arcade street block radically altered. Prior to this, individual households had comprised locales wherein a combination of domestic, business and industrial activities took place. Over time this pattern fragmented and the different spheres became physically separated, so that those who worked and lived in a particular property were no longer the same individuals. This effectively transformed the street block and its constituent properties into 'non-places', which were not relational, historical or concerned with the establishment of a sense of identity and that were so transient that they do not hold enough significance to be regarded as 'places' (Augé 1995).

Chapter 6

Wider environs

Richard Newman

It would have been possible to publish the Grand Arcade investigations in isolation, divorced from their wider landscape; a relatively widely adopted position, since 'developers and their contractors will usually, and justly, consider their responsibilities to run no further than the boundaries of the site that needs excavation' (Perring 2002, 127). Such boundaries are, however, determined by the exigencies of the development itself, as opposed to any inherent archaeological rationale. Instead, an attempt will be made to place the Grand Arcade investigations within a range of broader contexts. Whilst many such contexts exist, practical considerations mean that three have been prioritized here. The first of these is the Barnwell Gate suburb itself, in the form of the other constituent street blocks that surrounded Grand Arcade. Second is the town's East Fields, an agricultural hinterland lying to the south and east that played an important role in the lives of many of the area's inhabitants, and third are the four additional suburbs of broadly comparable size that developed around the periphery of medieval Cambridge. The major contextual lacuna is the town centre, as a full-scale comparison with the archaeology of the urban core would be impractical (although aspects of this issue are addressed in Chapter 7).

When contextualizing the Grand Arcade investigations, it is important to recognize how relatively small-scale Cambridge has always been as an urban centre. By the late twelfth century its population was probably around 2000, whilst during the thirteenth–fifteenth centuries this is likely to have been in the region of 3000–4000. This rose to around 5000 in 1600, 6000 in 1700 and just over 10,000 by 1800. Whilst there was significant growth during the nineteenth century, rising to over 38,000 by 1900, this was dwarfed by the increase that most other British urban centres witnessed at this time. Between the thirteenth and early nineteenth centuries, when passing through the Barnwell Gate or

crossing the King's Ditch and heading out of town, it was only around 400m from the town boundary to the edge of the built-up area. Assuming a typical walking speed of around 5.0 km per hour (km/h), the suburb would have taken perhaps five minutes to traverse. Continuing onwards, the edge of the town fields was just under 2km away, or around 25 minutes' walk, whilst turning in the opposite direction the historic town itself was up to 1.6km wide, so would have taken around 20 minutes to cross.

Structurally, the following chapter employs the results of 28 investigations that have been undertaken within the wider environs of Grand Arcade (Fig. 6.1). Conducted on a piecemeal basis between 1992 and 2013, they encompass a variety of different site-types, ranging from portions of neighbouring street blocks to the nearby parish church of St Andrew the Great, as well as a number of excavations undertaken further afield in the surrounding East Fields and other Cambridge suburbs. Individually, these investigations – which were predominantly trench-based in nature and small in scale – are of limited importance. Cumulatively, however, their results are significant. Eschewing the predominantly chronological framework that has been adopted within preceding chapters, the following account uses these sites to highlight a number of broader issues in a more discursive manner.

The Barnwell Gate suburb

From around the twelfth century onwards, following its extensive reorganization, the layout of the suburb was dominated by six discrete street blocks (Fig. 6.2). As is typical in such a setting, these blocks formed long-lived topographic entities that remained consistent – in terms of their overall boundaries, although not necessarily their internal subdivisions – for a considerable period (Conzen 1960, 5). Consequently, the Barnwell Gate suburb formed a relatively stable and

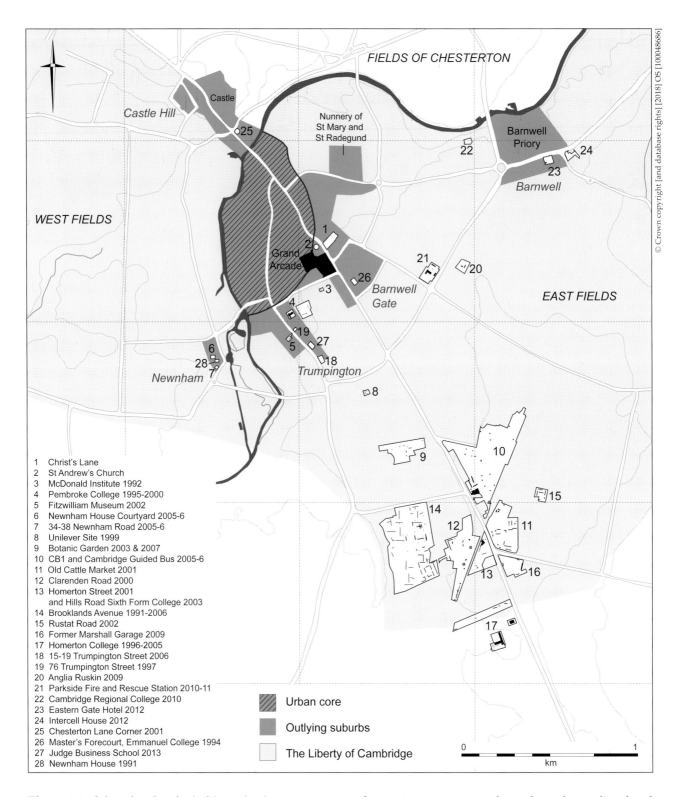

FIELDS OF CHESTERTON

Castle Hill

Castle

○25

Nunnery of
St Mary and
St Radegund

Barnwell
Priory

□22

24

23

Barnwell

WEST FIELDS

1

2○

Grand
Arcade

□26

□3

Barnwell
Gate

21

20

EAST FIELDS

4

□19 27

5

18

6

28
7

Newnham

Trumpington

□8

9

10

15

14

12

11

13

16

17

1   Christ's Lane
2   St Andrew's Church
3   McDonald Institute 1992
4   Pembroke College 1995-2000
5   Fitzwilliam Museum 2002
6   Newnham House Courtyard 2005-6
7   34-38 Newnham Road 2005-6
8   Unilever Site 1999
9   Botanic Garden 2003 & 2007
10 CB1 and Cambridge Guided Bus 2005-6
11 Old Cattle Market 2001
12 Clarenden Road 2000
13 Homerton Street 2001
     and Hills Road Sixth Form College 2003
14 Brooklands Avenue 1991-2006
15 Rustat Road 2002
16 Former Marshall Garage 2009
17 Homerton College 1996-2005
18 15-19 Trumpington Street 2006
19 76 Trumpington Street 1997
20 Anglia Ruskin 2009
21 Parkside Fire and Rescue Station 2010-11
22 Cambridge Regional College 2010
23 Eastern Gate Hotel 2012
24 Intercell House 2012
25 Chesterton Lane Corner 2001
26 Master's Forecourt, Emmanuel College 1994
27 Judge Business School 2013
28 Newnham House 1991

Urban core

Outlying suburbs

The Liberty of Cambridge

0   1
                  km

Figure 6.1. *Selected archaeological investigations undertaken within the five suburbs of Cambridge and the surrounding East Fields. Note that the extent of the suburbs includes the precincts of associated religious houses in addition to domestic occupation.*

coherent townscape zone throughout the medieval and post-medieval periods. This consistency is important, because it facilitates the construction of an 'archaeological history of neighbourhood' (*e.g.* Bowsher *et al.* 2007) or 'ethnography of place' (*e.g.* Mayne & Lawrence 1999). Whilst it is impossible to explore any of the five

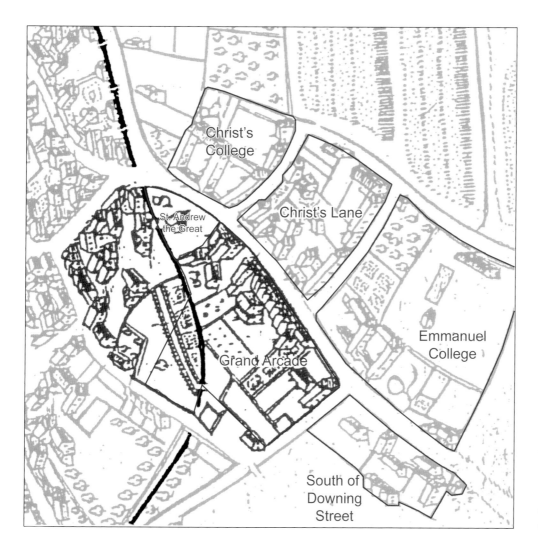

Figure 6.2. *Plan of the Barnwell Gate suburb published by John Speed in 1610, primarily based upon a map published by John Hammond in 1592, of which no complete copy now survives, showing the main constituent 'blocks'.*

additional street blocks in anything like the detail that has been achieved at Grand Arcade, a number of useful observations can nevertheless be made.

The following discussion utilises the spatial division of the suburb as an organizational framework. Beginning on the western side of St Andrew's Street, the northernmost block – that closest to the Barnwell Gate – was occupied by the parish church of St Andrew the Great. To the south of this lay the Grand Arcade street block itself and then finally beyond Downing Street lay a third block occupied by properties. To the east of the principal thoroughfare, the northernmost street block was that currently occupied by Christ's College. Next came an area that for most of its history has been occupied by domestic properties, while the southernmost block comprised that currently occupied by Emmanuel College. Although a number of archaeological investigations have been conducted across this area, their distribution has been patchy at best (Fig. 6.1). The most significant excavations have occurred within the central eastern block – the Christ's

Lane development, almost directly opposite Grand Arcade – and it is the results of this work that will dominate the following account.

St Andrew the Great

The parish church of St Andrew the Great – originally known as St Andrew without Barnwell Gate, until the foundation of St Andrew the Less in the suburb of Barnwell *c.* 1200 – was located just outside the Barnwell Gate and the King's Ditch, with the parochial area lying both inside and outside the ditch (Figs. 6.3–6.4; see also Fig. 3.27). The church would have been central to the everyday lives of the medieval inhabitants of the parish (Slater & Rosser 1998) and appears to have been established during the mid- to late eleventh century; around the same time that dispersed occupation first emerged in the area (Chapter 2). Although it is known from historical sources that the structure subsequently underwent several phases of modification/rebuilding (RCHM(E) 1959, 260–4), only isolated fragments of its medieval and post-medieval fabric now remain extant

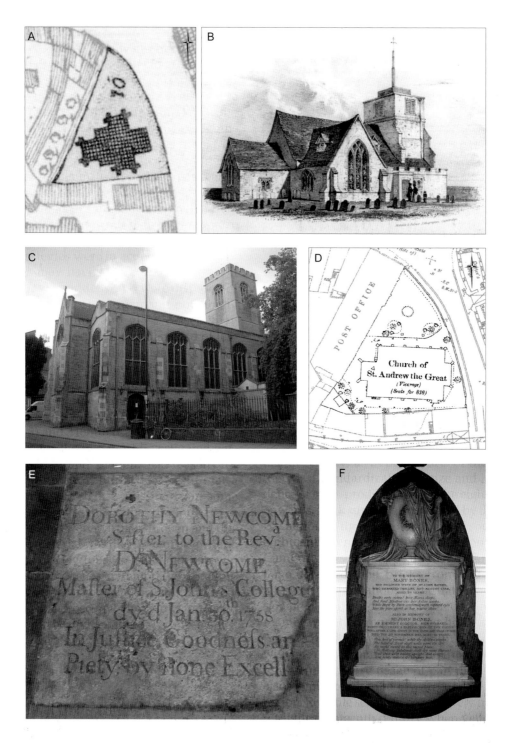

Figure 6.3. *The church of St Andrew the Great: (A) as depicted on Loggan's plan of 1688, one of the earliest reliable plans of the structure; (B) as it appeared from the southwest c. 1840, shortly prior to its demolition – in 1743 this building was described as a 'good handsome church' with a tower at the west end containing five bells, a nave, two cross aisles, two side aisles and a small chancel (Palmer 1935, 124–5); (C) a photograph of the rebuilt church as it appears today, facing southwest; (D) the post-1842 church as depicted on the 1885 1st edition Ordnance Survey map; (E) a floor slab of Dorothy Newcombe, who leased Grand Arcade Plot VIII prior to her death in 1758; (F) a white marble tablet surmounted by a draped urn on grey marble by S Manning erected by Mary Ann and Sophia Bones to John Bones who died in 1813 and his wife Martha. The Bones family was associated with various plots in the Grand Arcade street block (image B courtesy of the Cambridgeshire Collection, Cambridge Central Library).*

Figure 6.4. *The church of St Andrew the Great: (A–B) reused architectural fragments, consisting of "double capitals of two pairs of shafts, probably half-round, of the early twelfth century and carved with crude volutes" (RCHM(E) 1959, 260–61), which have been incorporated into the cellar of the rebuilt nineteenth-century church; (C) archway from the 1660s rebuilding of the church re-erected in its grounds (D) mid-seventeenth–mid-nineteenth-century iron coffin fittings recovered during the 1992 excavations at St Andrew the Great.*

following the comprehensive demolition of the original church in the mid-nineteenth century.

Archaeologically, evidence of eleventh-century burial sealed beneath a twelfth-century timber structure, possibly a chantry chapel, was identified, whilst architectural fragments suggest the presence of an early twelfth-century stone church (Fig. 6.4A–B). St Andrew the Great apparently went through a major phase of expansion in the fourteenth or early fifteenth century, but by the sixteenth century appears to have fallen on hard times. In the mid-seventeenth century it was in a ruinous state, leading to it being rebuilt in the 1660s (Figs. 6.3A–B and 6.4C). Eventually, however, in 1842 the entire structure was demolished and the present Neo-Gothic building constructed (Fig. 6.3C–D) Soon after this, in 1857, burial at the site ceased. During the twentieth century the congregation decreased as the population of the area declined, such that the church was declared redundant in 1984 before being revived as The Round Church at St Andrew the Great in 1994.

In many respects this broad sequence parallels that revealed by the Grand Arcade investigations, indicating that the sacred and profane are intimately connected. There are also more specific connections, with monuments to individuals that can be linked to excavated properties (Fig. 6.3E–F).

During small-scale excavations conducted at the site of St Andrew the Great in 1992 the earliest features to be encountered consisted of a timber-lined pit and a ditch that may represent a boundary demarcation (Fig. 6.1, no. 2; Miller 1992). Most probably eleventh-century in date, it is unclear whether these features pertained to religious or secular occupation. Soon after their creation, however, a cemetery was established that contained a number of intercutting east–west aligned inhumations, some of which were in coffins. Only a small portion of the cemetery was revealed and the skeletons were left *in situ*. Although limited in size, the majority of the associated ceramic assemblage was tenth–twelfth-century in date. This evidence, allied with the density and intercutting nature of the burials, as well as the fact that the associated cemetery soil deposits were 1.0–1.7m thick, indicates that the cemetery remained in use for a relatively substantial period of time, further supporting a probable eleventh-century foundation. Overall, therefore, it appears likely that the church had been established by 1086, when the fourth ward of Cambridge is known to have contained a church belonging to the diocese of Ely, although this cannot be proved definitively.

Given its relatively modest size, medieval Cambridge contained a large number of churches (Brooke 1985). Such a pattern was common in East Anglian towns generally, which by *c.* 1100 typically contained many more churches than areas further to the west. Notably, the escalation in church numbers occurred in the midst of a period of transition from the dispersed minster system of Anglo-Saxon England to the intensive patchwork of parishes that predominated from the twelfth century onwards. In East Anglia and the East Midlands this surge in church construction has been associated with 'individualistic parochial mentalities, bred by high population levels and fragmented land tenure' (Blair 2005, 407). Excavations conducted at a range of sites in the area have revealed that the majority of these churches were eleventh-century in origin,

with later foundations rare. Most were initially timber-built, only being converted into a more permanent single-celled, or more commonly double-celled, stone-built structures during the early twelfth century. In the present instance, it is likely that just such a twelfth-century stone-built church was the original source of two architectural elements that have been reused within the crypt of the present nineteenth-century building (RCHM(E) 1959, 260–1; Fig. 6.4A–B).

During the twelfth century a portion of the cemetery went out of use and became sealed beneath a number of postholes and thin spreads of makeup or floor layers, which together represent the remnants of a timber structure (Miller 1992). Altered/rebuilt a minimum of three times, this building continued in use into the fourteenth century. It was relatively ephemeral in form and thus most probably ancillary in nature, perhaps comprising a modest chantry chapel – at least two of which are known to have existed during the medieval period (Cam 1959, 125) – or ossuary. The church itself appears to have remained largely unaltered, although it is possible that some small-scale building work was conducted; reused architectural elements incorporated into the current structure include material of possible thirteenth-century date (RCHM(E) 1959, 260–1). Additional architectural fragments of broadly contemporary origin that were previously noted 'lying loose in the church' (Pevsner 2001, 221; RCHM(E) 1959, 263) could no longer be located when searched for. Historically, by 1200 the church was controlled from Ely and an individual named John was chaplain. In 1225–8 it was presented to Ely Cathedral by Absalom son of Algar, the rector and patron, perhaps as a restitution. Contemporary thirteenth-century church valuations indicate that it was then between the fourth and seventh wealthiest church in the town.

Subsequently, during the fourteenth or early fifteenth century, the church appears to have undergone a phase of major reconstruction. At this time the preceding timber ancillary building was truncated by a substantial west–east aligned rammed flint footing that measured 0.85m wide and over 1.3m deep (Miller 1992). The scale of this foundation indicates that it most probably pertained to the enlargement of the principal church building as opposed to a replacement ancillary structure. Nevertheless, despite its expansion, St Andrew the Great appears to have remained a relatively minor church. It was the least valuable of the seven Cambridge churches for which values were determined at the time of the Dissolution in the 1530s. Moreover, in 1598 its parish – along with those of nearby Holy Trinity and St Giles – was so 'overburdened by poor' that the other parishes in the town had to assist it (Cooper 1843, 594). Indeed, by 1650 the church was in such a ruinous state that it was proposed to unite its living with that of Holy Trinity (Cam 1959, 125). In the 1660s, however, the structure was restored via a substantial private donation; the reclaimed seventeenth-century arch that now acts as a gateway into the churchyard represents the only extant above-ground remnant of this phase (Figs. 6.3A–B and 6.4C).

In 1842 the long-standing medieval church was demolished and the present Neo-Gothic building constructed (RCHM(E) 1959, 261; Fig. 6.3C–D). Designed by Ambrose Poynter, when this new building opened in 1843 it was heavily criticized by the Cambridge Camden Society as a 'miserable and meagre ... specimen' (Anon 1843, 137); more recently, it has been described as a 'very ugly building' (Little 1960, 116). Archaeologically, disarticulated human remains and items of coffin furniture were encountered in association with its foundations (Fig. 6.4D), indicating that a number of burials were disturbed during its construction. In addition, four mid-nineteenth-century brick-built vaults were identified within the newly constructed church while a test pit to the north encountered two further vaults and two inhumations of the same period (Fig. 5.38). The provision of brick-lined burial vaults in churches was widespread from the early seventeenth century onwards, particularly in urban contexts (Gilchrist 2003, 402; Gilchrist & Morris 1996, 119), and four main types of intramural burial vault have been identified

(Litten 1991, 211–12). None of the examples at St Andrew the Great were excavated and all human remains were left *in situ*. Burial activity at the church ceased in 1857, marking the completion of a shift to the Mill Road cemetery which had been consecrated in 1848 (see Fig. 6.20A for location and Figs. 5.51, 5.55 and 6.20C for monuments there).

South of Downing Street

No archaeological investigations have taken place within the street block to the south of what is now Downing Street. Documentary and cartographic evidence indicates that the pattern of occupation was broadly similar to that at Grand Arcade, but with fields lying to the rear of the properties rather than the King's Ditch.

Christ's College

The street block currently occupied by Christ's College has seen relatively little archaeological investigation. In 1895 it was observed that along the street frontage there 'was only about 2 feet [*c*. 0.6m] of soil and made ground resting on the gravel. There were pits, extending down into the gravel to a depth of 7 feet [*c*. 2.1m] from the surface, which were full of household rubbish' (Hughes 1907b, 408). More recently, borehole observations have revealed sequences *c*. 2.0–2.5m in depth (Newman in Appleby 2010, 8; Fig. 6.5). Pottery recovered suggests that occupation of this street block began at some point during the tenth–twelfth centuries. By the mid-fifteenth century it was apparently densely occupied by seven long narrow plots described as messuages, tenements and cottages running back from the street to a watercourse, with a field beyond used as an orchard (Willis & Clark 1886 vol. II, 187–92). To the north there was also agricultural land with a dove house, pasture and a grove. The overall impression is that this street block was similar in character to the area investigated at Grand Arcade.

In 1448 God's-House, an institution for training grammar school masters, moved to the site. God's-House was a relatively small institution, comprising a proctor and four scholars, which purchased the various properties in a piecemeal fashion over time. It is likely that its impact on the suburb was relatively minor, although a chapel was constructed at some point. In 1505 God's-House was enlarged and

Figure 6.5. *Christ's College gatehouse with Lady Margret Beaufort's coat of arms, statue and Lancastrian symbols, plus boreholes being undertaken within Bath Court in 2010.*

re-founded as Christ's College, which became one of the leading Puritan Colleges in the University. This had a much more substantial and immediate impact and by 1511 the Chapel, Hall and Kitchen, Library, Gatehouse and probably the Master's Lodge had all been constructed. Unlike earlier Colleges, Christ's had an impressive frontage on a significant street, rather than being largely concealed. This was initially of clunch with lacing-courses of red brick and the current Ketton stone ashlar was added in the eighteenth century. The one significant surviving sixteenth century element is the gatehouse (Fig. 6.5); this bears the coat of arms of Lady Margaret Beaufort (1443–1509), a key figure in the Wars of the Roses and an influential matriarch of the House of Tudor, as well as a statue of her and some Lancastrian symbols. This structure represents an important stage in Colleges becoming more public institutions with significant facades and it would have had a major impact upon the streetscape of the suburb.

The Christ's Lane development
After Grand Arcade, much the largest and most significant investigation to date within the Barnwell Gate suburb were undertaken between November 2005 and August 2006 (Figs. 6.6–6.7). At this time, 10 trenches – covering 178 sq. m – were excavated at the Christ's Lane site, which is situated between the grounds of Christ's College and Emmanuel College, on the opposite side of St Andrew's Street to Grand Arcade. The restricted scale of this project, and the trench-based as opposed to open-area methodology that it employed, are much more representative of the type of excavations that are typically conducted in Cambridge. Indeed, given the many difficulties that arise from working in a densely occupied urban environment, this represents the most common type of investigation undertaken in British towns.

Undertaken on behalf of Land Securities Properties Ltd, the Christ's Lane watching brief (ten Harkel 2005) and excavation (Newman 2007) took place within the footprint of the former Bradwell's Court shopping centre. Conducted concurrently with the final stages of the excavations at Grand Arcade, the Christ's Lane investigations employed identical methodologies and recording strategies to those used at the larger site, thus ensuring close comparability between the two (although it should be noted that, due to the extent of mid-twentieth-century demolition, no standing building recording was conducted at the smaller site). Despite the work being limited in scale, several important results were obtained. These cast light upon the similarities – and, in some important instances, differences – in the patterns of

occupation that occurred within differing portions of the suburb.

Bounding the particular street block within which the Christ's Lane development took place are St Andrew's Street, previously known as Hadstock Way and later Preacher's Street, Christ's Lane, previously known as Hangman's Lane, Christ's Pieces, previously known as Barton Croft, and Emmanuel Street, previously known as Praise Be To God Street. Such a multiplicity of street frontages marks a significant divergence from the pattern that prevailed at Grand Arcade. Historically, however, the Christ's Lane street block has predominantly been utilized for a highly comparable range of domestic and commercial activities, although it is now also partially occupied by College-related buildings. Overall, a relatively intensive stratigraphic sequence was encountered (Fig. 6.8), which was dominated by the remains of a large number of well-preserved structures.

Much like at Grand Arcade, the most recent investigations were not the first to have been conducted within the Christ's Lane street block. Aside from a small number of antiquarian observations, which produced only very limited results (Hughes 1898, 377; Hughes 1901, 202; Hughes & Hughes 1909, 408–9), two more significant investigations have taken place. Firstly, during the spring and summer of 1959 a watching brief was undertaken at the Bradwell's Court construction site by Peter Addyman and Martin Biddle. Although a large basement had been excavated prior to the commencement of their work, a number of stanchion holes and drainage trenches were monitored and numerous features of twelfth–nineteenth-century date observed (Addyman & Biddle 1965, 80–3). In all, 15 areas were investigated (Fig. 6.6, Areas I–XV). In the context of contemporary archaeology at Cambridge, this investigation can be considered a notable success. Yet it was rather scathingly dismissed by Hugh Plommer, a Classical architectural historian at the Museum of Classical Archaeology, who stated that

'At best, as old Cambridge vanishes, we can publish any pits and sherds encountered by the workmen, but not the eighteenth century 'Doctor's House' sacrificed by Emmanuel [College] to the New Prudential Bank … Indeed, the pages of the local antiquaries journal would nowhere suggest that anything of interest was either being discovered or destroyed'
(Plommer 1966, 309).

It is significant that, in direct contrast to Grand Arcade, the Christ's Lane investigations produced a series of detailed, well-preserved stratigraphic sequences. Yet because of the necessarily trench-based excavation methodology that was employed – which resulted

Figure 6.6. *Archaeological investigations undertaken within the Christ's Lane development area in 1959 and 2005–6 (upper/left) and the tripartite arrangement of medieval and post-medieval plot-groups at Christ's Lane overlain upon the 1885 1st edition Ordnance Survey map (lower/right).*

Figure 6.7. *General views of the 2005–6 Christ's Lane excavations, including: (A) Areas 11 and 12, facing northeast; (B) Area 9 showing nineteenth-century building remains, facing northeast; (C) Area 11 showing adjacent brick- and cask-lined wells, facing southwest.*

from the presence of extensive twentieth-century truncation, allied with a multi-staged demolition programme that saw the initial stages of the investigations conducted *within* the extant shopping centre

– no cohesive, site-wide chronological narrative can be established. Accordingly, rather than adopting a wide-ranging feature-based approach such as that employed in Chapter 4, or a tightly focused series

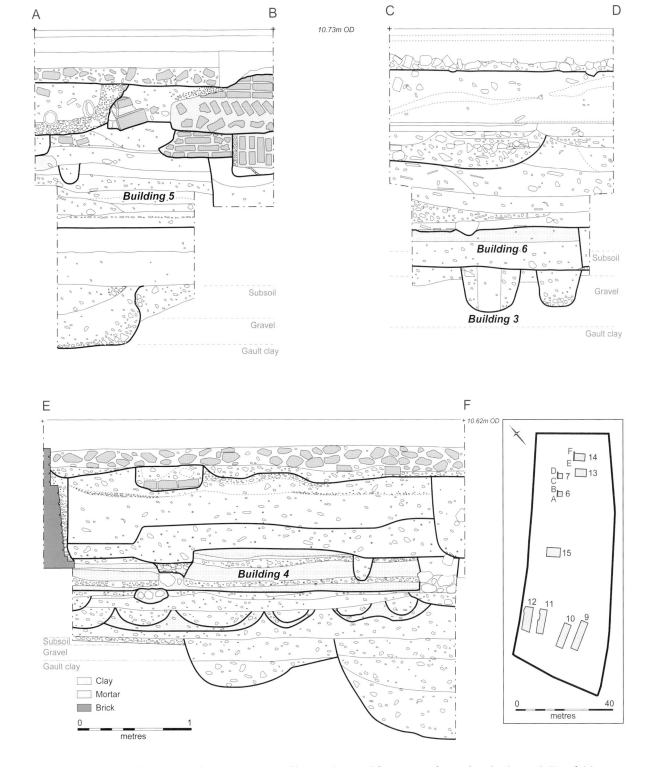

Figure 6.8. *Sections of well-stratified sequences at Christ's Lane with structural remains, in Areas 6, 7 and 14.*

of tenement narratives such as those constructed in Chapter 5, the Christ's Lane results will instead be presented in a more discursive manner. This facilitates the elucidation of the site's well-preserved structural remains, which dominated the sequence in most areas, while also highlighting its high degree of stratigraphic resolution. Both elements provide an important counterpoint to the results derived from Grand Arcade.

For reasons of clarity, the following narrative has been divided into two parts. The first covers the eleventh–seventeenth centuries, the second the eighteenth–twentieth centuries.

The Christ's Lane Street block
Unlike Grand Arcade, the Christ's Lane development area encompassed only approximately one third of the street block within which it was located. Adjoining the block's northwestern boundary – which was formed by Hangman's Lane, later renamed Christ's Lane in 1505 – the investigated area comprised one of three semi-autonomous plot groups, each of which appears to have developed independently of the others. Although the following account is entirely concerned with the most northerly plot group, which today comprises 65–68 St Andrew's Street, it is important to establish the context of this area relative to the remainder of the street block. Firstly, to the southeast of the investigated zone, the central plot group was first documented historically in the 1320s. At this time it already consisted of several tenements. By the mid-fifteenth century these tenements had been amalgamated into a single holding, known as St Nicholas Hostel, which was itself purchased by Queen's College in 1465. After passing through several different owners, by the early nineteenth century it came into the possession of Emmanuel College. Today, it forms 63–64 St Andrew's Street.

The third and southernmost plot group was also perhaps the most intensively occupied. Throughout much of its history it contained a large number of heavily sub-divided plots that fronted variously onto St Andrew's Street, Emmanuel Street and Christ's Pieces. When, in 1612, Emmanuel College acquired the eastern half of this area it was already occupied by nine messuages, two barns and a number of gardens. Eventually, between 1910 and 1914, this portion of the plot group was transformed into the North Court of the College; a notable expansion of gown over town. The western portion of the area, in contrast, appears to have remained as four separate properties throughout much of the period. These properties were gradually acquired piecemeal by Emmanuel College during the late nineteenth and early twentieth centuries, before being amalgamated into the Prudential Buildings in 1957. Of this latter structure, Pevsner caustically noted 'it is sadly lacking in a sense of occasion. It might be anywhere and would be noticed especially nowhere' (Pevsner 1970, 246). Today, this portion of the street block forms 57–62 St Andrew's Street.

Site sequence
Overall, the archaeological sequence that was encountered within the northernmost plot group was comparable to that identified at Grand Arcade. Aside from a small quantity of residual Roman and Anglo-Saxon ceramic material, comprising 13 sherds of the former and four of the latter, the earliest evidence of activity was eleventh-century in date. It was not until the beginning of the twelfth century, however, that an organized, linear arrangement of properties had definitely been established. Becoming increasingly subdivided over time, each of these properties appears to have followed its own separate developmental trajectory. Over the course of the twelfth–sixteenth centuries, for example, a series of horticultural, garden soil-type deposits accrued, the extent of which varied in relative proportion to the intensity of activity undertaken within each respective plot. Yet in no instance was this material as homogenous as the contemporary garden soil at Grand Arcade. Instead, at Christ's Lane a relatively complex stratigraphic sequence developed.

From the fourteenth century onwards, as the plots became increasingly subdivided, a number of timber-framed buildings were constructed. Unlike at Grand Arcade, such structures eventually came to dominate the sequence in the majority of areas. Moreover, no evidence of Late Medieval decline was identified. The archaeologically investigated buildings primarily comprised secondary or plot accessory structures, lying to the rear of the principal frontage. Subsequently, between the late fifteenth–eighteenth centuries, the majority of these buildings were reconstructed – and new, additional structures built – in brick. Aside from becoming increasingly subdivided, the preceding medieval layout remained largely unaltered up until the early nineteenth century; following this date, however, it was extensively remodelled. Finally, in 1959, the entire site was cleared in order to allow construction of the Bradwell's Court shopping centre, bringing to an end around 900 years of continuous domestic occupation.

Eleventh–seventeenth century, incorporating specialist information from Craig Cessford, Richard Darrah and Rosemary Horrox
Spatially, by the early/mid-twelfth century the Christ's Lane site appears to have been divided into two equally sized properties, both of which were rectangular in form and aligned perpendicular to the principal Hadstock Way frontage. Of these two, the northernmost – which longitudinally abutted a second, more minor frontage, Hangman's Lane – was itself split into two during the late twelfth or early thirteenth century. This subdivision almost certainly reflects the growing influence of the adjacent laneway. The resultant properties (Plots 1 and 2; Fig. 6.6) remained relatively consistent entities throughout the medieval

and early post-medieval periods, although over time their interiors became increasingly subdivided. To the south, the second of the two original twelfth-century properties (Plot 3; Fig. 6.6) retained its initial form until 1371, when its rear portion was transferred to Plot 2, a pattern of gradual expansion that reflects the increasing importance of the secondary frontage. This layout again remained consistent for several centuries, albeit with evidence of further internal subdivision.

These three basic 'plot-groups' thus provide a useful tripartite division that can be employed to provide a spatial framework for the following discussion. It is important to note, however, that this does not fully encompass the complex pattern of the properties' increasing subdivision. Between the early twelfth century, when the properties were first laid out, and 1534–35, when the entire group was brought into the possession of Jesus College as a single estate, documentary evidence suggests that the number of properties increased five-fold; from two to ten. Yet the trench-based nature of the investigation, which permitted only the piecemeal, fragmentary exposure of the archaeological remains, prohibits a detailed understanding of such a complex developmental history. Furthermore, the surviving documentary sources, whilst invaluable, are also fragmentary. Therefore, the broad tripartite spatial structure imparted by Plots 1–3 provides the most cohesive method with which to present the following results.

In the first instance, relatively little can be discerned of the earliest period of settlement-related activity at the site. Only one pit can be definitively dated to the eleventh century, for instance, on the basis that it exclusively contained St Neots-type ware whose fabric and form indicate a pre-twelfth-century origin. This feature was located in Area 15 (Plot 1). Yet although this period almost certainly predated the establishment of the main properties, the presence of only a single feature – in contrast to the more extensive remains that were encountered in a comparable suburban location at Grand Arcade – appears, on the surface, somewhat counterintuitive. The reasons for this dearth are probably twofold. Firstly, the limited area of exposure at Christ's Lane significantly reduces the potential to identify an ephemeral pattern of activity underlying the much more intensive twelfth-century and later occupation horizon (at the former site, for example, it appears likely that in excess of 80 per cent of the eleventh-century features had been removed by later truncation; see Chapter 2). Secondly, the limited sample size also reduces the potential to distinguish diagnostically eleventh-century ceramic material from the more generic tenth–twelfth-century assemblage.

Although it is likely that many more early features were present within the excavated area than have been positively identified, this cannot be proven with certainty. Consequently, whilst it seems probable that a pattern of mid–late eleventh-century dispersed occupation predominated at the Christ's Lane site, broadly replicating that identified at Grand Arcade (Chapter 2), such a supposition cannot be definitively corroborated. It is, however, notable that the ratio of tenth–twelfth-century to thirteenth–fifteenth-century ceramics was somewhat higher at Christ's Lane than at Grand Arcade (1:3.7 at the former versus 1:5.4 at the latter); in addition,

the density per square metre of Saxo-Norman wares was also five times higher at the former site. These factors suggest the presence of a relatively intensive early sequence. Nevertheless, the possibility remains – however tentative – that settlement activity within the Christ's Lane street block commenced slightly later, as a late eleventh/early twelfth-century first-cycle or greenfield development, than the earliest dispersed occupation at Grand Arcade.

By the early/mid twelfth century, an organized layout of rectilinear properties had been established at Christ's Lane. Across the site a range of twelfth-century domestic features were encountered, attesting to the presence of relatively intensive occupation. Whilst this development could once again have been coeval with the broadly contemporary planned layout at Grand Arcade, and thus perhaps have formed part of a much wider, over-arching programme of twelfth-century suburban expansion, there is no evidence to confirm such a direct association. Indeed, it is at least equally plausible that the two were largely unrelated, except in the broadest sense; based upon the relatively imprecise dating material available, the respective developments could well have occurred years, if not decades, apart.

Topographically, it appears likely that the boundaries of the newly established Christ's Lane street block were initially defined by ditches. Just such a feature was identified in 1959 (Area XIV), for example, running parallel to and along the perimeter of modern-day Christ's Lane. Broad and shallow in form, the ditch measured in excess of 10ft (3.0m) wide and 2ft 6in (0.75m) deep (Addyman & Biddle 1965, 80–1). Twelfth-century St Neots-type ware was recovered from its fill. The boundaries of the properties themselves were defined either by shallow gullies or relatively ephemeral fences at this time, although – resulting in part from the dispersed distribution of the archaeological trenches, which were primarily targeted at those areas with little or no twentieth-century truncation – only a small number of such features were identified during the excavation. The relatively intensive sequence of twelfth–seventeenth-century activity will now be examined on a plot-by-plot basis.

Plot 1: Three trenches were excavated within this plot in 2005–6: Area 11, which measured 10.0m by 3.0m in extent, Area 12, which measured 9.9m by 3.7m in extent and Area 15, which measured 5.2m by 3.0m in extent (Fig. 6.6). Excavations undertaken within a further five stanchion holes were also observed in 1959 (Fig. 6.6, Areas VIII, IX, X, XII and XIV). Historically, Plot 1 was first recorded in an undated, but probably early thirteenth-century, document. Between then and the early sixteenth century it passed through a variety of owners, both private individuals and religious institutions, and was subdivided a minimum of three times. Amongst the most notable of its lessees were a merchant (mid-thirteenth century), a tailor (1368), a University beadle (1372) and the Benedictine nunnery of St Mary and St Radegund, Cambridge. The last of these possessed the plot twice, firstly for a brief period during the thirteenth century and second from 1417–1534. In 1421, the main portion of the plot was leased by the nunnery as an 'empty piece of ground' that measured 208ft 6in (63.5m) long by 28ft 6in (8.7m) wide on the frontage and 35ft 3in (10.7m) at the rear but only 7ft 3in (2.2m) wide in the centre. In 1535 it became part of The Vine Estate owned by Jesus College.

Aside from a single reference to a 'shop with solar over' (1358), there are few documentary indications of the activities that were undertaken within the plot during this period. Archaeological evidence, however, strongly suggests a mixture of residential and commercial activity; a pattern that is very similar to that identified at Grand Arcade. In the first instance, evidence of twelfth-century activity was identified in all three areas. The sequence commenced with creation of a series of pits. In Areas 12 and 15, the pattern of these features was relatively intensive, indicating that these spaces probably lay immediately to the rear of the rear of the principal zone of occupation. Consisting primarily of quarry pits, a smaller number of cess- and refuse-filled pits were also present. Within one of the latter the presence of multiple cattle horn cores suggests that small-scale horn-working took place, whilst a thirteenth-century cesspit in Area 12 also produced a moderately sized insect fauna. Here, numerous synanthropic species were identified, indicating that settlement waste in various forms – both wet and dry, as well as animal- and human-related – had been dumped into the feature (see also Chapter 4).

To the southeast, in Area 11, a less intensive sequence predominated. Fewer pits were created and the area was soon sealed beneath a well-stratified garden soil layer. This latter material continued to accumulate until the early fifteenth century, when two successive phases of gravel pathway were established. Although the first of these was relatively ephemeral, the second was much more substantial. Oriented perpendicular to the principal Hadstock Way frontage, it measured 0.9m wide and was situated within a well-defined 0.4m deep cut. It seems likely that these pathways reiterated a long-standing access route that had already been in use for many years; the presence of such a route may well explain the relatively low level of earlier activity. Flanking the path, a number of pits and postholes were present.

Nearby, in Area 12, the degree of activity being undertaken escalated markedly during the fifteenth and early sixteenth centuries. Within what was most probably an open yard area, an intensive array of intercutting features was created. The sequence was dominated by a minimum of six clay-lined ovens along with numerous associated burnt clay- and banded clay-filled pits. Given the limited size of the investigated area, it is likely that many more such features also lay outside the bounds of the trench. The best preserved oven measured over 1.7m long by 0.7m wide and 0.25m deep. In form, it consisted of an irregular sub-oval 'pit' with a chamber at the one end from which a narrow flue extended. It was well maintained and had been relined at least twice. In each instance, the ovens were stratigraphically succeeded by a pit containing a large quantity of burnt clay, material which most probably represents the remnants of the preceding oven's superstructure. Also present were two enigmatic, vertically sided features that contained multiple compacted clay 'working surfaces'.

The close association of such a large number of specialized features indicates that a particular process was being undertaken. This was most probably craft-based or industrial in nature. Unfortunately, as it was common for a number of generic feature-types – including clay-lined ovens and pits – to be utilized for a wide range of industrial purposes at this date (Schofield & Vince 2003, 122), the precise nature of this process remains unclear. Moreover, aside from domestic refuse, which included five aiglets and a relatively substantial ceramic assemblage, no material residues were present that could further elucidate the issue. Elsewhere within the plot at this date, a series of pits continued to be inserted in Area 15. Nearby, in Area XII, a wattle-lined well measuring over 4ft (1.2m) in diameter and 6ft 6in (2.0m) in depth was observed in 1959. The backfill of this feature contained pottery that has recently been re-examined and assigned to the thirteenth/fourteenth century (Addyman & Biddle 1965, 81, 113, fig. 17). A second pit in this area contained a near-complete fourteenth-century Brill jug.

During the sixteenth century a substantial well was constructed beside the pathway in Area 11. Somewhat unusually, its lining was composed of a minimum of three casks stacked one on top of the other (Fig. 6.9). Of these three, the uppermost cask had been robbed when the feature went out of use whilst the lowest lay below the limit of excavation. The central cask, however, was relatively well preserved and was examined in detail by Richard Darrah. This analysis revealed that it was comprised of 27 narrow oak staves; a particularly large number for the period (Morris 2000, 2242, table 40). It also had a bunghole and a croze groove, suggesting that it had originally been constructed as a wet cask suitable for containing liquids with a capacity of 470 litres. The oak itself was fast grown, indicating that it was most probably English as opposed to imported in origin, but could not be dated using dendrochronology. Holding the cask together were two sets of four wooden hoops. Composed of half-round wood, the hoops were lashed together using strips of bark that had been sliced from the sides of small roundwood stems. Immediately prior its reuse

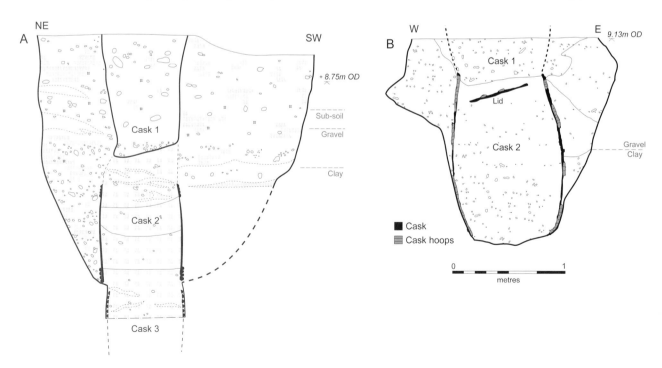

Figure 6.9. *Cask-lined well sections: (A) sixteenth-century three-tier cask-lined well in Area 11; (B) broadly contemporary late sixteenth-century cask-lined Well 38 from Grand Arcade.*

as a well lining, the cask had also had a large number of 15mm diameter holes augured into its staves.

Although comparable three-tier cask-lined wells are known nationally (*e.g.* Morris 2000, 2238), they are rare locally. In this particular instance, it appears likely that such a substantial well – which represented a relatively significant investment in terms of both labour and materials – was constructed in order to provide water to multiple properties. This stands in direct contrast to Grand Arcade, where each individual property appears to have maintained its own separate water supply. Yet by the sixteenth century Plot 1 had been subdivided numerous times, with each portion being rendered much smaller than the comparable plots at Grand Arcade. Consequently, the degree of available open space within each sub-plot is likely to have been commensurately restricted; a fact that may also explain the very low number of wells that were encountered at the Christ's Lane site overall.

Despite the scale of investment in the cask-lined well, it nevertheless appears to have been relatively short-lived. By the end of the sixteenth or beginning of the seventeenth century it had gone out of use and been replaced by a large timber-built accessory structure, *Building 1*, which once again appears to have flanked an active access route. Employing a series of earth-fast posts, *Building 1* represents a marked escalation of the degree of building coverage in the plot. Moreover, a similar pattern was also replicated in Area 12, where a contemporary late sixteenth/early seventeenth-century brick-built cellar was constructed (*Building 2*). Substantial in size, and containing a built-in soakaway, *Building 2* most probably represents the rearward expansion of a plot dominant building that fronted onto Hadstock Way. Indeed, by the end of this period only Area 15 remained an open space. Here, a gravel-lined ditch was established that may have functioned as a drainage channel.

Plot 2: Four trenches were excavated within this plot in 2005–6: Areas 6 and 7, each of which measured 2.1m by 2.1m in extent, Area 13, which measured 3.2m by 2.2m in extent and Area 14, which measured 3.7m by 2.4m in extent (Fig. 6.6). In addition, a watching brief was undertaken contemporaneously in Area 17 (Fig. 6.6). Finally, in 1959 three further stanchion holes were also observed (Fig. 6.2, Areas III, XI, XIII). Historically, no documents survive for this plot; it is known only from abuttals. As a result, its developmental history is the least clear of the three. Nevertheless, a limited number of lessees are known. These include a fumor (1272) and a tailor (1322). In 1371, the rear portion of Plot 3 – which primarily consisted of a barn with adjoining garden – was transferred to this plot, thereby almost quadrupling its size. Between then and the early sixteenth century, when it was amalgamated into a much larger holding, it is likely that Plot 2 became increasingly subdivided (although no definite historical record of this survives).

Three of the four excavated areas – Areas 6, 7 and 14 – although limited in size, contained well-stratified archaeological sequences (Fig. 6.8). The fourth, Area 13, had been very heavily truncated by the construction of a nineteenth-century cellared building. In the three former locations, twelfth-century activity was well-represented. Area 6 contained a ditch or large pit of this date; its form could not be determined with certainty as it extended outside the area of investigation. In Area 7, however, a long-lived boundary sequence was present that followed the same east-northeast to west-southwest alignment as the feature in Area 6. This sequence comprised two successive phases of postholes and gullies. Towards the end of the twelfth century, a number of much more substantial postholes indicate that an earth-fast timber building was constructed – *Building 3* – which replaced the boundary but again respected the same alignment. This structure was itself relatively short-lived, as during the thirteenth century a well-stratified garden soil deposit began to form in both areas.

A similar sequence was also identified in Area 14. Here, a series of twelfth- and thirteenth-century gravel quarry pits were succeeded by a garden soil horizon. Then, during the second half of the fourteenth century, a long-lived structural sequence commenced. Although only partially exposed, the structure in question – *Building 4* – was particularly well-preserved. Given its date, allied with its location within the northeastern portion of the plot, this building probably represents the barn that is known to have been transferred to Plot 2 from Plot 3 in 1371. Six successive phases of development were identified. In its earliest phase, the barn's southwestern wall was post-in-trench built (Fig. 6.10A). Although there is evidence to suggest that it was relatively well-maintained, as at least one post was replaced during its lifetime, the phase was nevertheless relatively short-lived. This is likely to have been a direct consequence of its form of construction, since the typical lifespan of medieval buildings employing earth-fast techniques was only around 20 to 40 years (Bowsher *et al.* 2007, 317–18; Horsman *et al.* 1988). Such structures therefore required frequent episodes of maintenance/rebuilding, with the result that their positions frequently shifted incrementally over time.

In the early fifteenth century the original posts were removed and a levelling deposit introduced across the area. *Building 4* was then rebuilt on a slightly different alignment. Once again, a post-in-trench construction technique was employed (Fig. 6.10B). The replacement barn was similarly well-maintained, with several posts being replaced during the period of its usage. In the mid–late fifteenth century, however, it was demolished and rebuilt once more. On this occasion a much more regular, flat-bottomed trench was utilized for its construction (Fig. 6.10C). No evidence of any associated posts was identified, indicating that an earth-fast timber sill beam was probably used. This phase of the building remained in use until the early sixteenth century, when it was extensively robbed; at this time, any and all traces of earlier floor deposits were removed and a further levelling deposit introduced. A new and much more robust timber-framed structure was then constructed. Employing a well-constructed mortared clunch sill wall, this fourth phase of the building comprised its most substantial incarnation to date (Fig. 6.10D).

At least one internal subdivision was now present, whilst compacted clay floor surfaces were also established. Externally, a northwest–southeast aligned gravel pathway was laid. Yet despite its more robust construction, this fourth iteration of the barn was also relatively short-lived. Around the middle of the sixteenth century the timbers were removed, a further levelling deposit was introduced and a new stone-built sill wall established. Directly overlying its predecessor, this fifth phase of *Building 4* utilized numerous clay-bonded fragments of reused architectural stone (Fig. 6.10E). In addition to clunch ashlar, the reused material included several Oolitic Limestone blocks whose mouldings could be dated to *c.* 1180–1250. The barn's internally subdivided floorplan was retained and new compacted clay floor surfaces were introduced; the external gravel pathway was also reinstated. Associated with this phase of the structure were a heavily worn pinner's bone, which had been manufactured from the distal half of a cattle metatarsal and demonstrated at least four working platforms, plus several simple copper alloy pins. Such evidence implies a potential link with small-scale pin manufacturing or similar, textile-related activity.

The sixth and final phase of *Building 4* commenced during the late sixteenth century. At this time, the preceding timber-built structure was removed; a replacement footing was then created via the introduction of mortared CBM fragments into the resultant void (Fig. 6.10F). Whilst not itself an above-ground sill wall *per se*, as its predecessors had been, this footing may well have acted as the foundation for an overlying brick-built structure. Nevertheless, given the relatively high cost of bricks at this date – allied with the secondary, ancillary nature of the building in question – it is probable that the barn remained primarily timber-built in form. The long-lived structural sequence came to an end during the early seventeenth century when *Building 4* was demolished for the last time and the

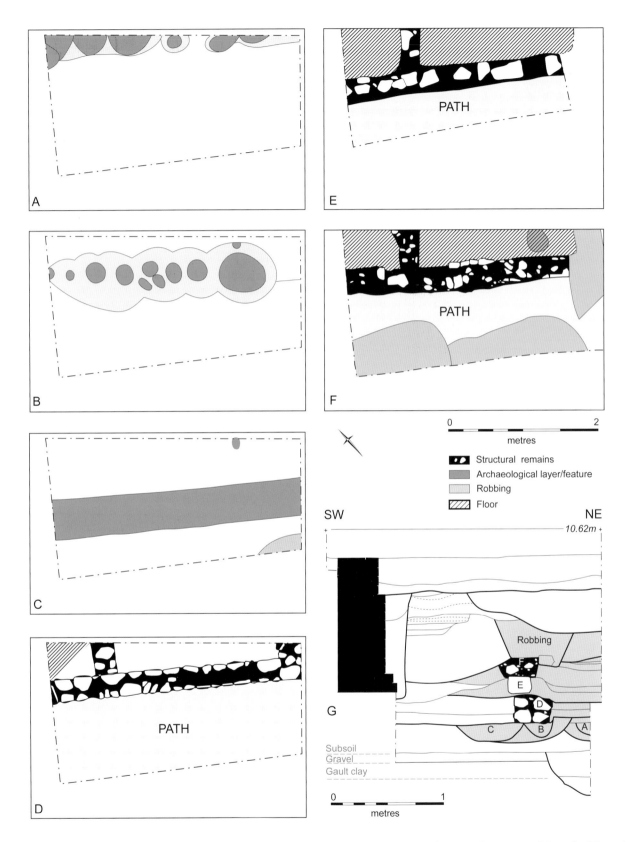

Figure 6.10. *Long-lived structural sequence of barn Building 4, Area 14: (A) mid-fourteenth century; (B) early fifteenth century; (C) mid–late fifteenth century; (D) early sixteenth century; (E) mid-sixteenth century; (F) late sixteenth century; G) section showing the well-stratified sequence of overlying structural remains.*

majority of its constituent materials were robbed. Faunal material associated with the demolition horizon included mutton joints derived from at least five sheep, possibly the remnants of a large meal. Two pits were also inserted into the flanking gravel pathway during the early seventeenth century, one of which contained two near complete ceramic vessels (Fig. 6.11H–I). Soon after their deposition, the path was reinstated.

Elsewhere within Plot 2, timber-framed buildings were also constructed in Areas 6 and 7 during the early sixteenth century, closely replicating the contemporary pattern of escalating building coverage previously identified in Plot 1. In Area 6, the form of the structure in question – *Building 5* – remains unclear, although an internal earth-fast sill beam was present within the area of investigation. It continued in use until the early seventeenth century,

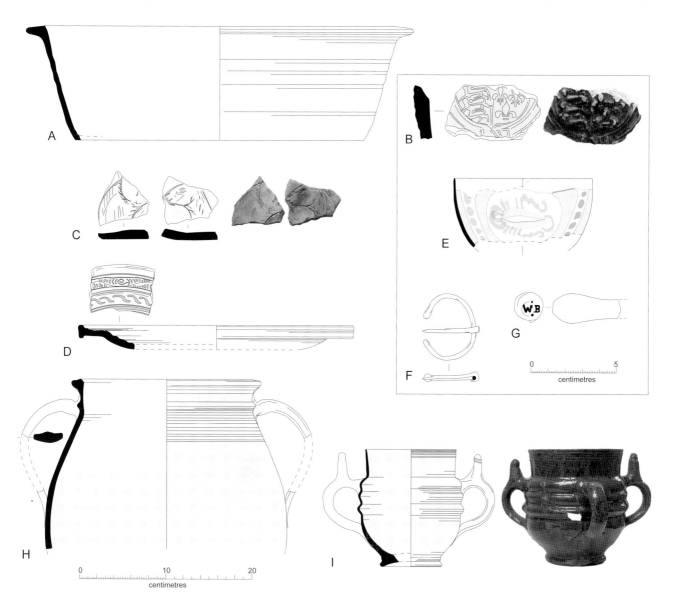

Figure 6.11. *Ceramics and other items from Christ's Lane: (A) a sixteenth-century coarse greyware flared bowl with flanged rim (F.320); (B) a sherd of sixteenth-century Glazed Red Earthenware Bichrome bearing the lower part of the royal coat of arms (F.917); (C) parts of the base of a large late sixteenth–mid-seventeenth-century Midlands Yellow-ware tradition vessel (or vessels) decorated with incised horses heads (F.819, F.821); (D) the flanged rim of a late sixteenth–mid-seventeenth-century Midlands Yellow-ware tradition large bowl with incised decoration (F.818); (E) English or Dutch tin-glazed earthenware bowl copying early seventeenth-century Ming dynasty Kraak Chinese Export porcelain (F.146); (F) copper alloy penannular buckle with pin, typologically thirteenth–fifteenth-century (F.503); (G) late seventeenth–eighteenth-century pipeclay wig curler, marked with the initials WB surmounted by a round dot inside a circle on one end (F.154); (H–I) near complete early seventeenth-century Glazed Red Earthenware large two handled jar and a three-handled cup, possibly products of the local industry based upon the Isle of Ely (F.600).*

373

when the presence of an extensive ash and charcoal deposit indicates that it may have been destroyed by fire. Subsequently, it was rebuilt in brick. In Area 7, meanwhile, a contemporary structure – *Building 6* – was established that was partially sunken in nature. Extending up to a metre below the contemporary ground surface, its walls employed earth-fast sill beams that were founded upon compacted gravel beampads. Over the course of the sixteenth century these timbers were replaced and the building re-established a minimum of three times. Nevertheless, by the end of the century it had gone out of use and the area was transformed into an open yard.

Within both *Building 5* and *Building 6* a number of ceramic vessels had been vertically inset into the structures' clay floors. Two fragmentary Glazed Red Earthenware vessels and one Babylon ware jar were encountered. Given the small size of the investigated areas, it is likely that many more such vessels were originally present. Although their function is unclear, it was most probably craft-based as opposed to domestic in nature; a similar practice is paralleled at other broadly contemporary sites (*e.g.* Cotter 2000, 219–21). Also present within *Building 6* was a sherd of Broad Street bichrome that bore the lower part of the royal coat of arms of 1406–1603; three golden leopards passant gardant and three fleurs-de-lis surrounded by a garter (Fig. 6.11B). Similar armorial decoration, although not the royal coat of arms, has previously been identified on local Ely products (Cessford *et al.* 2006, fig. 50.11). In addition, within *Building 5* three sixteenth-century sherds bearing elaborate sgraffito-type decoration were recovered. Two bore the heads of animals, the third a heavily decorated rim (Fig. 6.11C–D). None appear to be of local origin.

In its reconstructed, brick-built form, *Building 5* was relatively elaborate in form. Mortar scars testify to the presence of at least two successive tiled floor surfaces, both of which had been robbed. This may indicate an escalation in the status of the plot's occupants. By the end of the seventeenth century, however, *Building 5* had been demolished and a larger structure with a brick-built cellar established.

Plot 3: Two trenches were excavated within this plot in 2005–6; Area 9, which measured 12.0m by 3.0m in extent and Area 10, which measured 10.0m by 3.0m in extent (Fig. 6.6). Contemporary Test Pits 1, 4 and 5, as well as nearby Area 16, were all located within the footprint of a modern basement and did not encounter any archaeological remains. Excavations undertaken within a further seven stanchion holes were observed in 1959, however, all of which revealed well-stratified sequences (Fig. 6.6; Areas I, II, IV, V, VI, VII, XV). Historically, by 1352 this plot is known to have consisted of two messuages, 12 shops and a solar, plus associated agricultural land in the surrounding open fields. Up until 1371 it appears to have extended all the way back to Barton Croft, at the rear of the street block. Following this date, however, the rear portion of Plot 3 was transferred to Plot 2 (see above). The remainder of Plot 3, which probably consisted of a number of derivative sub-plots, was purchased by Jesus College in 1509; by 1534–5 it had been incorporated into the College's larger, site-wide holding The Vine Estate.

In Area 9, twelfth-century activity was well-represented. In the first instance, a gully was established that was oriented perpendicular to the principal Hadstock Way frontage; this represents the initial element in a long-lived boundary sequence. To either side of the gully were situated numerous pits and postholes. Amongst these was a twelfth-century cesspit that contained residual traces of a central rectangular timber lining. This feature went out of use and was backfilled during the thirteenth century, when a considerable quantity of animal bone was deposited. Cattle (45 per cent NISP) and sheep (38 per cent NISP) bones predominated but goat, pig, horse, chicken and frog were also represented. In addition, a concentration of horn cores from cattle (23 per cent, MNI five), sheep (5 per cent, MNI one) and goat (five per cent, MNI one) indicates that small-scale horn- and bone-working occurred (Tables 4.18–4.19; Chapter 4). All the complete cattle horn cores were from small-horned types and the

majority (63 per cent) were derived from female cattle. Mandibles (26 per cent) and metapodia (17 per cent) were also fairly common, while the remaining 24 per cent of the assemblage consisted of meat joints. Also present in this feature was a horse metatarsal that had been modified to form a skate or sledge runner as well as a relatively substantial assemblage of charred cereal grains.

By the fifteenth century a garden soil deposit had accrued across the area and this was in turn overlain by a series of compacted gravel paths that followed the same alignment as the earlier property boundary. To the south of the pathway were located a large number of intercutting pits. Then, towards the end of the fifteenth century, a small timber-framed building – *Building 7* – was constructed. Represented archaeologically by a series of floor and make-up layers, as well as a clay pad for an internal sill beam, this structure partially encroached upon the preceding access route.

A much more intensive sequence was encountered in Area 10. Here, three buildings were present – two of which underwent several phases of development. Activity initially commenced during the twelfth century when three distinct spatial 'zones' were established. The first, situated in closest proximity to the Hadstock Way frontage, consisted of a series of pits and postholes; one of which contained the partially complete skeleton of a new-born piglet. The second comprised a dense cluster of intercutting pits, whilst the third comprised a well-compacted gravel yard surface. Within the latter zone, a series of postholes were present that potentially prefigured a long-lived southwest–northeast oriented plot boundary. Then, during the thirteenth century, a timber building was established within the frontage zone. This structure, *Building 8*, employed a combination of earth-fast post and post-in-trench construction techniques. It remained in use until the early fourteenth century, when a temporary structural hiatus is indicated by the formation of a shallow garden soil deposit.

By the late fourteenth century the building sequence had recommenced. Overlying the remains of *Building 8* a new structure, *Building 9*, was constructed. Much more substantial than its predecessor, the outer walls of *Building 9* rested upon earth-fast sill beams that were packed around with clay. Internally, the scars of sill beams that were embedded within the building's compacted clay floors indicate the presence of several partition walls, whilst to the northeast the former yard area was re-established. Into this latter zone, a series of pits were inserted. From within the floors themselves over 90 oyster shells were recovered; the largest such assemblage of any date at the site. Closely mirroring the 20- to 40-year cyclical pattern previously identified within Plots 1 and 2, during the early–mid-fifteenth century *Building 9* was levelled and rebuilt in near identical form. Beneath the northeast corner of the newly erected structure a substantial pit was dug, which was infilled with domestic debris and capped with a dense layer of limestone blocks. This may have been a response to a localized subsidence event.

Broadly coeval with the reconstruction of *Building 9*, a second structure – *Building 10* – was also built to the northeast, in the area

Figure 6.12 *(opposite). The developmental sequence of Buildings 8–10 at Christ's Lane Area 10, showing: (A) Building 8, thirteenth century; (B) Building 9, late fourteenth century; (C) Buildings 9 and 10, early–mid-fifteenth century; (D) Buildings 9 and 10, late fifteenth–mid-sixteenth century (note the extensive ash and charcoal deposit associated with the oven in Building 10); (E) Buildings 9 and 10, late sixteenth century; (F) Buildings 9 and 10, early seventeenth century; (G) section of Buildings 9 and 10; (H) view of sequence, facing north.*

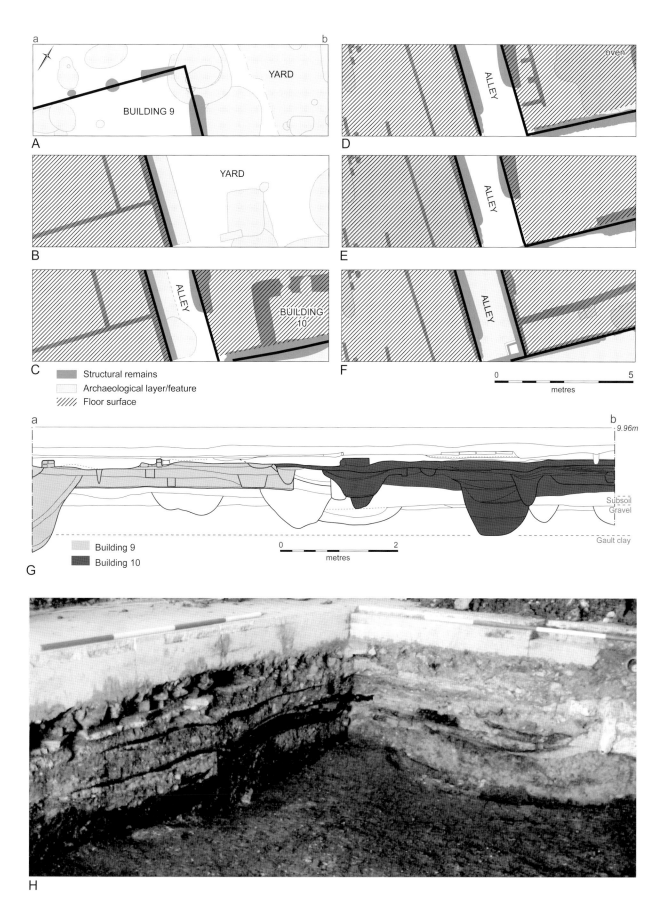

A

B

C

YARD

BUILDING 9

YARD

ALLEY

BUILDING 10

D

E

F

ALLEY

ALLEY

ALLEY

oven

Structural remains
Archaeological layer/feature
Floor surface

0   5
metres

G

a   b
9.96m

Subsoil
Gravel
Gault clay

Building 9
Building 10

0   2
metres

H

of the former yard. Separated from its neighbour by a narrow alley, *Building 10* employed a mixture of post-in-trench and mortared-clunch sill wall construction techniques. It appears to have been entered via a doorway that opened directly from the alleyway. A number of internal partitions were present, along with a series of compacted clay floor surfaces. Although no evidence pertaining to the usage of either building was recovered, it is likely that both fulfilled a combination of commercial and domestic roles. Subsequently, during the late fifteenth or early sixteenth century, these structures were again rebuilt. While this may have comprised a contemporaneous event, undertaken in a single phase by the same plot-holder, it is equally plausible that the two buildings followed entirely separate trajectories. Indeed, it is significant that *Building 9* was reconstructed in brick at this time while *Building 10* remained timber-framed. The bricks in question were not produced locally but imported from the Low Countries, reflecting a trade that had first commenced during the fourteenth century (Salzman 1952, 140). The financial investment made in *Building 9* was therefore substantially greater than that made in its near neighbour, suggesting that the former probably comprised part of the rear portion of a plot dominant frontage structure whilst the latter remained a secondary, plot accessory building.

Within the newly reconstructed *Building 10* a large brick-built oven was established. Although only partially present within the excavated area, this feature was evidently very well-constructed. Most probably circular or teardrop-shaped in form, it was repaired/rebuilt on several occasions. Moreover, extensive finely laminated deposits of trampled ash and charcoal accrued around it, radiating out several metres from the oven itself. Environmental samples recovered from these deposits reveal that the oven's principal fuel comprised great fen-sedge (evidence of which was found alongside smaller quantities of charred cereal grains, as well as numerous wild plant seeds); great fen-sedge was commonly employed within bread ovens at this date. While wood was typically utilized to get the oven up to temperature, sedge was subsequently employed to maintain the heat between batches, thus allowing multiple, successive firings to take place. Indeed, so common was this practice that 'sedge was the only fuel purchased for the bakehouse of both St John's and Corpus Christi Colleges throughout the seventeenth century' (Rowell 1986, 143). Such evidence, especially when combined with the substantial size and well-constructed nature of the oven, indicates that *Building 10* most probably functioned as a commercial bakery during this period.

Towards the end of the sixteenth century, *Building 10* was levelled and rebuilt once more. *Building 9* remained unchanged at this time, however, testifying to the more durable nature of its brick construction. Associated with *Building 10*'s reconstruction were two discrete groups of faunal remains. The first consisted of 27 metacarpals that were derived from a minimum of 14 sheep, the second of 16 metapodia derived from a minimum of seven sheep. No traces of an oven or associated rake-out deposits were present within this third iteration of the structure, although it is possible that any such activity had transferred to a room that lay outside the area of investigation. Eventually, during the early seventeenth century, *Building 10* was itself rebuilt in brick. Its overall layout, including the location of its probable entrance, appears to have been retained and the central alleyway remained in use throughout.

Returning to Area 9, timber-framed *Building 7* went out of use around the middle of the sixteenth century; it was succeeded by a fence line that closely respected the alignment of the earlier access route. Within a few decades, this fence was in turn replaced by a gravel pathway. The latter continued to be repaired/maintained until the late seventeenth century, when a structure represented by two substantial (albeit heavily truncated) brick-built cellars – *Building 11* – was constructed. Unfortunately, few additional details of this building's form could be determined. Elsewhere within Plot 3, a substantial deposit of burnt debris and brick, measuring 0.2m thick, was encountered in Area II in 1959. This material was dated to *c.* 1650–1700 and interpreted as 'the site of a burnt out house'

(Addyman & Biddle 1965, 82). However, as this stanchion hole was located immediately to the northeast of Area 10 (Fig. 6.6), it appears likely that it was associated instead with the sixteenth-century bread oven located within *Building 10*. Also present in Area II was a brick- and flint-lined cesspit that had been backfilled during the seventeenth century.

The Vine Estate: In 1534–5 Plots 1, 2 and 3 were amalgamated into a single property holding by Jesus College, Cambridge. This estate was known as *Le Vynde*, or 'The Vine'. Despite their amalgamation, however, the three earlier plots appear to have retained their distinct, semi-autonomous identities throughout the post-medieval period; the archaeological remains discussed above reveal little or no discernible evidence of alteration within the patterns of contemporary structural and/or occupational activity. Consequently, although the estate was now leased by the College to a succession of principal tenants – individuals who, nominally at least, controlled all of the various properties at the site – in practice, very little appears to have changed for the sub-tenants who occupied the majority of the estate's constituent plots. Indeed, collegiate ownership may have served to partially shield the estate from the contemporary pattern of apparent reduction and diminution that prevailed within the Grand Arcade street block (Chapter 4). No such decline was identified at Christ's Lane; the density of sixteenth–seventeenth-century ceramics was almost 14 times greater, for example, while the number of buildings continued to increase.

A wealth of historical material survives in relation to The Vine Estate, far more than for the preceding medieval plots. In part this is a reflection of the date at which it was established, since the sixteenth and particularly seventeenth centuries witnessed an increase in both the production and retention of legal documentation. In the case of The Vine Estate itself a further, compounding factor comprised the institutional nature of the estate's owner. This is because Jesus College not only maintained a relatively comprehensive archive, but – as the College remains extant, and indeed thriving, to this day – its archive has also been preserved largely intact. Thus the names and occupations of the principal tenants are known in some detail, whilst additional information pertaining to the number, and sometimes also the size, of the various plots has also survived. When it was first created, *c.* 1535, the estate appears to have been composed of around 10 separate plots. By 1667 this number had risen to 11, suggesting a degree of relative stability. In contrast, the degree of building coverage appears to have escalated much more rapidly over the course of the same period.

In addition to the extensive array of structural remains that were identified archaeologically, the presence of a large number of buildings can also be discerned within the surviving cartographic sources. In particular, two seventeenth-century plans, one of 1635 and one of 1688 (Fig. 6.13), provide detailed and highly informative depictions of the site. The first of these comprises a terrier that was drawn up in association with the lease of The Vine Estate to John Jellett. This detailed plan reveals that the Preacher's Street, and to a lesser extent Christ's Lane, frontages were relatively heavily built up by the early seventeenth century (although it should be noted that the absence of secondary, accessory buildings to the rear of the plot dominant structures does not accord with the archaeological evidence, thereby calling into question the accuracy of the interior depiction). A second, much more accurate, plan was published by David Loggan in 1688. This represents the first rectified, two-dimensional map of Cambridge to have been produced. Previous investigations conducted all across the town have generally demonstrated it to be highly reliable. At the Christ's Lane site itself, Loggan depicted an extensive array of both dominant and accessory buildings. These structures occupied more than a third of the available area; a far higher proportion than at contemporary Grand Arcade. Significantly, archaeologically identified *Buildings 2, 5, 9, 10* and *11* can all be putatively correlated with structures shown on Loggan's plan, further corroborating the accuracy of his depiction.

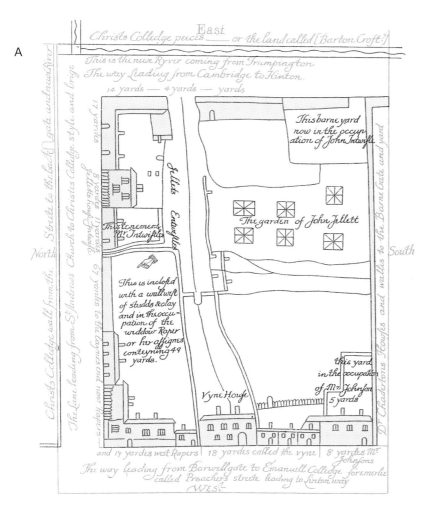

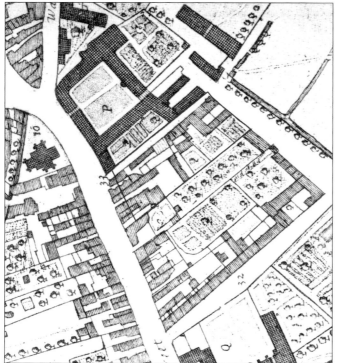

Figure 6.13. *Seventeenth-century plans of The Vine Estate, including: (A) terrier associated with the lease of John Jellett in 1635; (B) detail of David Loggan's map of 1688 (plan A courtesy of the master and fellows of Emmanuel College Cambridge).*

Eighteenth–twentieth-century, incorporating
specialist information from Craig Cessford and
Quita Mould

In many ways, the eighteenth century comprised a period of marked continuity from the preceding pattern of post-medieval occupation at the site. The three earlier plot-groups survived largely unaltered, for example, whilst the overall number of properties continued to expand incrementally; rising from 11 at the beginning of the eighteenth century to 14 at its close. But this pattern of stable continuity came to an abrupt halt during the early nineteenth century. At this time the degree of building coverage expanded markedly – thereby obfuscating, if not almost entirely eradicating, the earlier tripartite spatial layout – and the relative balance between commercial and domestic activity also shifted, with the proportion of residential occupation beginning to decline. Consequently, it is the latter period that comprises the principal focus of the following discussion.

It is important to note in this context that, although recorded in a closely comparable manner to the contemporary remains at Grand Arcade, the piecemeal exposure of the nineteenth-century archaeology at Christ's Lane – allied with the absence of any above-ground structural remains – significantly reduces the coherency of the resultant sequence. No buildings were exposed in their entirety, and few large feature groups were encountered (primarily as a result of the excavated trenches almost exclusively encountering structural remains). Because of this general dearth of complete and/or well-stratified material, the remains are of more limited potential than those recovered from Grand Arcade. The fractured nature of the trench-based investigations also inhibited the construction of comparable tenement narratives for this site.

For much of the eighteenth century the Vine Estate was leased to the Baines family. Relatively few archaeological remains of this date were identified, however, although the cellars of two earlier buildings were remodelled during this period. The first of these – *Building 5*, in Area 6 – was modified at least once before being backfilled and subsequently sealed beneath a flat-laid brick floor surface during the early nineteenth century. The second – *Building 11*, in Area 9 – was also extensively remodelled in the eighteenth century; a thick deposit of trampled coal dust indicates that it was employed as coal cellar during this period. It remained in use until the end of the nineteenth century. Finally, in Area 11, post-built *Building 1* went out of use during the early eighteenth century. A well was then inserted through its remains. Although several blocks of reused medieval moulded stone were recovered from the well's construction cut, the well-shaft itself lay beyond the limit of excavation. It remained in use until the late nineteenth century.

In direct contrast to the low quantity of eighteenth-century remains at the site, a large number of nineteenth-century buildings were encountered. Their ubiquity is testament to the rapid escalation in building coverage that occurred during the first half of the nineteenth century. A wealth of accompanying documentary and

cartographic evidence also survives from this period, allowing the pattern of redevelopment to be analysed in great detail. In particular, the 1st Edition Ordnance Survey map – which was surveyed in 1885 – provides a depiction of the site hitherto unprecedented in terms of both its accuracy and resolution. This map has therefore been used in conjunction with the 1881 census data to provide a vivid 'snapshot' of the range and variety of occupation at the site during the late nineteenth century. It is important to note, however, that the vast majority of these buildings had already been constructed by *c.* 1850. Consequently, the 1851 census data will also be employed within the following account.

Overall, seven buildings of nineteenth-century date were investigated archaeologically. In addition, two post-medieval structures – *Buildings 2* and *11* – also continued in use into this period. The investigated structures encompassed a wide range of building types. These included relatively prestigious villas with extensive gardens (such as *Building 14*), substantial frontage structures (such as *Buildings 13* and *17*), small, slum-like tenements arranged in courts (such as *Buildings 12* and *18*) and ancillary structures (such as *Buildings 15* and *16*). Although the scale and intensity of the early nineteenth-century reorganization effectively obliterated the earlier tripartite layout represented by Plots 1–3, it nevertheless represented an organic development of the preceding pattern. For this reason, a threefold spatial division remains a legitimate framework with which to present the following results.

In the first instance, the area formerly occupied by Plot 1 was subdivided into three distinct groups during the early nineteenth century; these comprised 69 St Andrew's Street, 70 St Andrew's Street and a group of properties that were situated along Christ's Lane. Number 69 St Andrew's Street was a reasonably substantial frontage property that faced onto St Andrew's Street, behind which lay a narrow yard that was lined on its southern and eastern by 13 small tenements. This yard, which was known as Field's Court, represented a formalization of the long-lived access route that was first identified in Area 11 during the early fifteenth century. Field's Court was first recorded documentarily in 1837. In 1851, it was occupied by 12 households with 50 occupants.

Archaeologically, Areas 11 and 15 lay within the central open yard of Field's Court. Two wells were located in this area. The first was that previously described above, which had been constructed during the eighteenth century; the second appears to have been constructed contemporaneously with the establishment of Field's Court itself in the early nineteenth century. The latter well was brick-lined and had been capped by a seven-coursed stone-built dome that employed several reused moulded limestone blocks. Two of these blocks were late twelfth- or thirteenth-century in date and comprised a pier element and a vault or arcade rib respectively, whilst two were fourteenth-century in date and were derived from a respond capital (Fig. 6.14). Both wells remained in use until the late nineteenth century, when they were partially robbed, probably to facilitate the removal of valuable lead pipes. This indicates that mains water had then been provided to the properties. In addition to the wells, the southern boundary of Area 11 also comprised the wall of *Building 12*, which equated to 1–3 Field's Court. *Building 12* had been constructed as a single, cellared structure that was then internally subdivided. Although little of the cellar was investigated, as it lay outside the area of excavation, a pair of suede leather ladies boots with 14 pairs of lace holes and 1¼ inch Louis heels were recovered from its backfill. Stylistically, these boots date to 1885–1920, but are most likely to have been manufactured just before the First World War.

To the north of Field's Court, 70 St Andrew's Street comprised a relatively substantial frontage property with a yard to its rear that contained a high pan-tiled building, a dung hill, cow lodges and a cow yard. In 1851 this property was occupied by George Thompson, a grocer and farmer aged 44 from Yorkshire, along with his wife, two children and two servants. To the rear of 70 St Andrew's Street were seven properties that fronted onto Christ's Lane. These buildings,

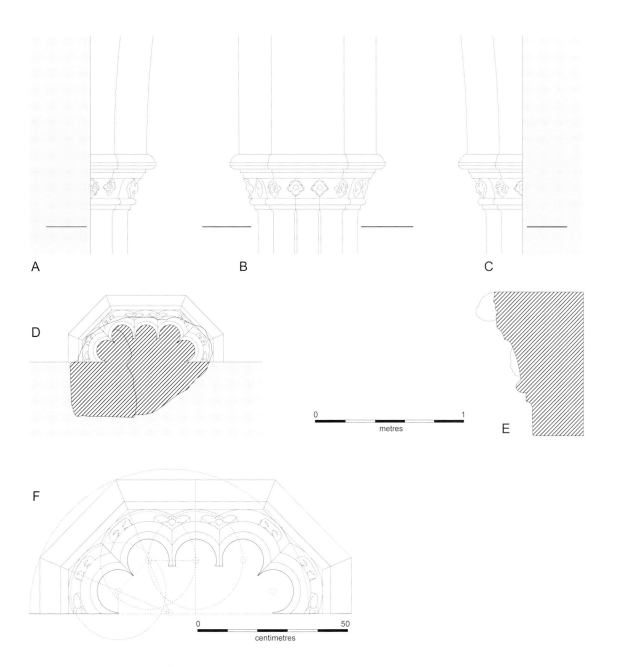

Figure 6.14. *Weldon Stone respond capital of* c. *1320–50, reused in Well F.312 in the 1830s showing: (A) transverse sectional elevation, showing fleurons (left); (B) front elevation; (C) transverse sectional elevation, showing fleurons (right); (D) reversed plan of respond showing surviving extent of fragments; (E) moulding of capital (partially restored); (F) conjectured geometrical basis of respond capital (reversed) (based upon illustrations by Mark Samuel).*

1–7 Christ's Lane, were leased to Christ's College in 1822; the College leased them again in 1837 and finally purchased them in 1862. The contract for this purchase stipulated that the properties were not to be rebuilt; instead, the land was to be used only for the enlargement and improvement of Christ's College. Yet this redevelopment never occurred and the properties therefore became increasingly dilapidated. In 1851, for example, only three out of the seven were occupied, a pattern which continued into later decades.

Area 12 was situated within the rear portion of 70 St Andrew's Street and also encompassed part of 1 Christ's Lane. The latter property was represented archaeologically by *Building 2*,

a brick-built cellar that had originally been constructed during the late sixteenth/early seventeenth century (see Part I, above). This went out of use, was partially robbed and then subsequently backfilled *c.* 1896. Incorporated into its backfilling was a relatively substantial assemblage that included a minimum of 58 glass vessels. The composition of this assemblage, which included a minimum of 11 Worcestershire sauce bottles, suggests that it was not domestic in origin. Instead, it is most likely to have been associated with the Thompson family business that operated from the adjacent property at 70 St Andrew's Street. Following on from grocer George Thompson, who had occupied these premises in the 1850s, the

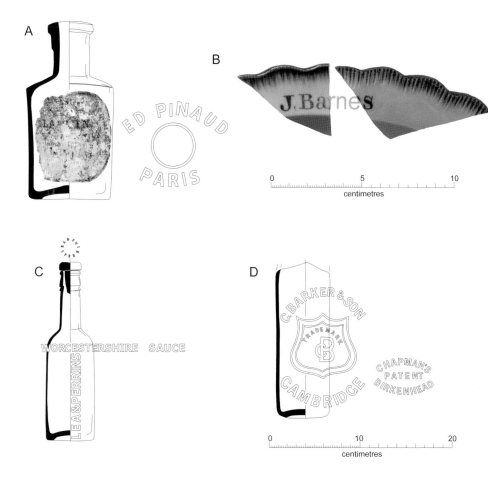

Figure 6.15. *Elements of the late nineteenth-century assemblage deposited into the cellar of Building 2 (F.473), including: (A) Ed Pinaud perfume bottle with an illegible paper label associated with its subsequent reuse; (B) sherd from early nineteenth-century pearlware plate of J Barnes, plus additional sherd from another feature (C) Lea & Perrins Worcestershire sauce bottle; (D) partially complete soda water bottle.*

business was taken over by Mrs Sarah Thompson, a grocer, glass and china dealer, between 1869 and 1879. Her son, Alfred Thompson – who was variously described as a grocer, farmer and milkman – then occupied the premises between 1881 and 1896.

Several interesting elements were present within the assemblage deposited in *Building 2* (Fig. 6.15). Whilst utility bottles made up the majority of the group, the deposit also contained a wide range of different products including vessels for soda water, food, medicine and beer. Eight of the utility bottles were rectangular in shape and may have contained pharmaceutical products, while eight additional pharmaceutical bottles and two unidentifiable vessels were also present. One of the more interesting vessels comprised a complete colourless perfume bottle that was embossed with the name of the firm of ED PINAUD, PARIS (Fig. 6.15A). This company was founded *c.* 1830 and was granted a royal patent as sole official supplier to Queen Victoria in 1845. Of the 11 Worcestershire sauce bottles in the assemblage, all were embossed LEA & PERRINS (Fig. 6.15C). This sauce was first produced commercially in 1837 and had become highly popular by the latter part of the nineteenth century (Keogh 1997).

Four of the soda water bottles in the group were associated with the Cambridge firm of C Barker & Son. Charles Barker first began production in 1875; by 1883, his firm became Barker & Son. It continued in production in this form until well into the twentieth century. Three different bottle designs were represented in the Barker group: one was torpedo-shaped, a design patented by William Hamilton in 1814 (Talbot 1974); two were Codd bottles, a design patented by Hiram Codd in 1875 (Talbot 1974); the third, to a design by Chapman & Son of Birkenhead, was only partially complete (Fig. 6.15D). Two further soda water manufacturers were also represented in the assemblage, in each instance by Hamilton bottles bearing

their embossed logos. Overall, the Barker & Son bottles provide a *terminus post quem* for the group of 1882, whilst the presence of numerous torpedo-shaped bottles suggests a depositional date in the 1880s or 1890s.

In contrast to the glass vessels, which were frequently either complete or else substantially represented, the ceramic material within the cellar backfill was highly fragmentary. Elements of over 20 vessels were present, but most were only represented by individual sherds. The single vessel of which there was a substantial surviving portion was a Keillor marmalade jar of 1873 or later. In addition, a single sherd from a pearlware plate was also present. Along its wavy edge with blue painted feather edge decoration this fragment bore part of a name; J.Ba[r]… (Fig. 6.15B). Although several possibilities exist, this vessel was most probably associated with John Barnes; a cook from Cambridge who had been apprenticed to Stephen Gurkins, the cook of Jesus College, in 1786 and later to William Spencer in 1795. By 1814 he was living at the Black Bull Yard, Cambridge, and his three sons were baptized in All Saints church between 1814 and 1819. Finally, a copper alloy button was also present in the assemblage; this was marked with the name of the nineteenth-century manufacturer EXCELSIOR around its rim.

The cellar of *Building 2* is most likely to have been infilled in 1896. This is because 1–7 Christ's Lane were demolished and replaced by five new shops and offices at this time; new structures that were erected 'in lieu of the dilapidated buildings standing thereon'. Moreover, this event also appears to have heralded the end of the Thompson family's residence at the site, as by 1898 70 St Andrew's Street was occupied by antique dealer Owen Roe. Also occurring as part of the 1896 redevelopment, a substantial brick-lined cellar, which survived in use until 1959, was constructed at the rear of 70 St Andrew's Street. This cellar – *Building 13* – was entered via

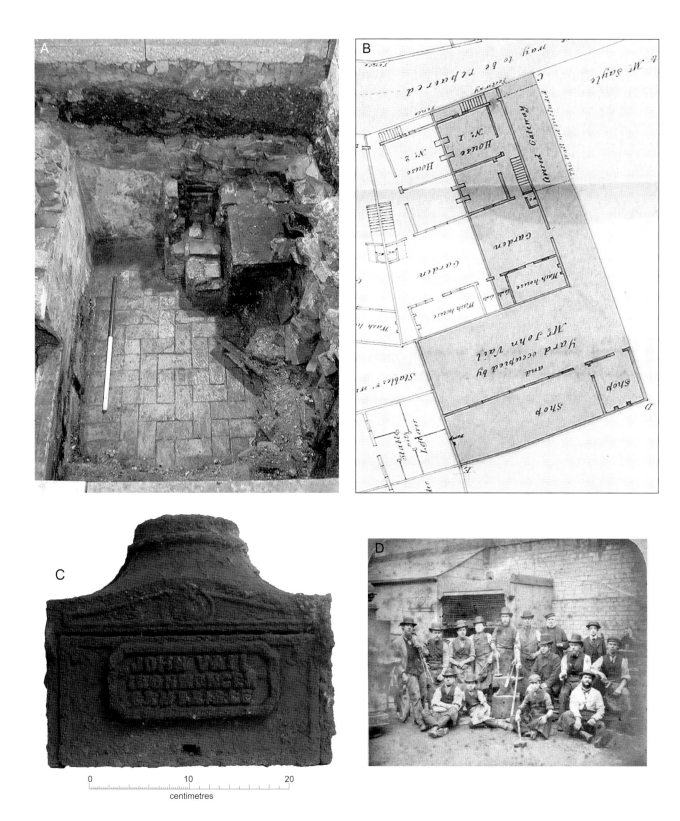

Figure 6.16. *The cellar of Building 14: (A) the excavated portion of the cellar in Area 13, including the in situ closed cast iron range, facing northeast; (B) plan of Vail premises at 1 Post Office Terrace; (C) the boiler flue, which had been partially disassembled and placed on top of the range prior to the cellar's infilling; (D) group photograph of the staff of John Vail's ironmongery business in the late nineteenth century (plan B reproduced by kind permission of the Master and Fellows of Christ's College, image D courtesy of the Cambridgeshire Collection, Cambridge Central Library).*

a flight of stairs in its northwest corner. Internally, it had a row of supporting columns as well as two light wells that faced out onto the yard of the property.

The area formerly occupied by Plot 2, which formed the easternmost third of the site, was leased in 1837 by Christ's College. It was subsequently redeveloped in order to provide housing for College servants. Indeed, with the exception of the College porter – who resided in the Porter's Lodge – the majority of Christ's College's principal servants lived here during the second half of the nineteenth century, including the cook, butler, under porter, gardener, laundress and scullions (Wroth 2004). A distinct 'hierarchy of servitude' prevailed (Brooks & Connah 2007), with the cook living in the largest property and paying the highest rent. Overall, eight properties were established by Christ's College – 7–13 Christ's Lane and 4 Drummer Street – as well as three stables and a coach house. Archaeologically, Areas 7 and 13 encountered portions of the dwelling associated with 12 Christ's Lane (*Building 14*), while Area 6 encountered an outdoor toilet block associated with 10 Christ's Lane (*Building 15*) and Area 14 encountered part of the stable block (*Building 16*). Of these three structures, the former was the most substantially investigated; both the toilet block and the stable were only partially exposed.

In Area 7 a portion of the front yard of *Building 14* was encountered, along with the foundation of the structure's northwestern wall. More significantly, however, in Area 13 part of the structure's substantial brick-built cellar was uncovered (Fig. 6.16A), as well as an external boundary wall and a portion of the rear yard area. The cellar – an original feature of *Building 14*, which was initially constructed during the late 1830s or early 1840s – housed the property's kitchen. This area was substantially remodelled during the latter part of the nineteenth century, when a light-well was inserted that faced into the open yard and a cast iron kitchen range was installed. The latter was a closed range, of a type first patented in 1802; these were much cleaner and more efficient than the open style of ranges that had preceded them (Eveleigh 1983, 23–8). The range remained *in situ* when the cellar was eventually backfilled in 1959, although it was partly dismantled prior to the building's demolition. The boiler flue, which had been placed on top of the oven, reveals that it was manufactured by John Vail, a Cambridge ironmonger (Fig. 6.16C).

Several members of the Vail family migrated from Saffron Walden, Essex, to Cambridge in the mid-nineteenth century. They were predominantly whitesmiths; that is, individuals who worked with 'white' or light-coloured metals such as tin and pewter. John Vail senior arrived in Cambridge in the 1850s. In 1858 he was listed as a whitesmith and bell hanger residing at 1 Post Office Terrace, almost directly opposite the Christ's Lane site. At the time of his death, in January 1876, he was succeeded by his son John Vail junior, a blacksmith, who continued to operate the business at Post Office Terrace until his own death in 1912. It was here, therefore, that the closed range was produced (Fig. 6.16B, 6.16D). *Building 14* itself, into which the range was installed in the later nineteenth century, was closely associated with the Nichols family of Christ's College butlers. For over 70 years, from 1841 until 1914, this property was occupied successively by Sarah Clark (née Nichols), Sarah Nichols, Sarah Ann Nichols and Harriet Addis Nichols – along with various sisters, aunts, nieces, and their female servants – at a rent of £20 per annum for most of the period. By 1871, the Nichols' household also included a dedicated cook. The late nineteenth-century transformation of the Nichols' kitchen, and in particular the transition from an open- to a closed-type range, would have had quite a substantial impact upon the range of cooking techniques that could be employed.

Figure 6.17. *Two late nineteenth-century views of Bradwell's Yard, facing northeast (images courtesy of the Cambridgeshire Collection, Cambridge Central Library).*

In the southeastern portion of the site, the area formerly occupied by Plot 3 was subdivided into five separate elements during the nineteenth century; these comprised 65–68 St Andrew's Street, plus a group of smaller properties that were arrayed along the northeastern side of Bradwell's Yard. Numbers 65–68 St Andrew's Street were all moderately sized properties that were accessed via the principal frontage. Bradwell's Yard itself lay to the rear of 67 St Andrew's Street and was accessed via a narrow alleyway (Fig. 6.17). Occupation was first documented here in 1831. By 1886, 65 and 66 St Andrew's Street had been amalgamated into a single property; the garden to the rear of 67 St Andrew's Street was also divided at this time between the newly amalgamated property and 68 St Andrew's Street. Overall, the pattern of occupation in this area was highly comparable to that which prevailed contemporaneously in the vicinity of Field's Court. Relatively substantial frontage properties, whose households typically included at least one servant, nestled cheek-by-jowl with small, slum-like tenements. Although the number of the latter fluctuated over time, in 1851 11 properties housing 19 occupants were present in Bradwell's Yard.

Archaeologically, Area 9 was situated within the rear portion of 67 St Andrew's Street (*Building 11*) and part of the garden that lay behind it, while Area 10 was situated within the rear portion of 68 St Andrew's Street (*Building 17*) and the front portion of 1 Bradwell's Yard (*Building 18*). In the first instance, the existing cellar of *Building 11* was substantially remodelled during the early nineteenth century. The rebuilt structure was then itself modified and extended on at least two occasions, prior to its eventual infilling in 1959; amongst the debris associated with this latter event was a traceried window mullion fragment of *c.* 1300–50. The Bradwell family had a long association with 67 St Andrew's Street. This probably extended back to at least 1804, when David and Thomas, the sons of David and Mary Anne Bradwell, were baptized at nearby St Andrew the Great. In 1831 the name Bradwell's Yard first appeared in parish records, indicating that the family's association with the property was now well-established. During this period, 67 St Andrew's Street and its associated yard also formed the premises for the family's construction business. In 1851, the property was occupied by builder Thomas Bradwell, aged 46, who lived there with his wife, three children and two servants. The firm appears to have ceased trading following David Bradwell senior's death in 1859; Thomas Bradwell himself probably left Cambridge shortly thereafter. Nevertheless, the Bradwells' 50-year association with the property yielded a long-lived legacy; having developed the yard that bore their name, this later influenced the naming of Bradwell's Court shopping centre.

In Area 10, post-medieval brick-built *Buildings 9* and *10* were both demolished during the early nineteenth century. Replacement structures *Buildings 17* and *18* had relatively ephemeral brick-built footings that were much less substantial than those of their predecessors, although in each instance remnants of internal tiled floor surfaces remained extant. Of the two, *Building 17* was the largest. It formed part of 68 St Andrew's Street, a moderately sized frontage property that in 1851 was occupied by Henry Lee, a boot maker aged 32 from Castle Hedingham who lived there with his wife, three children, one servant and one lodger. Significantly, this building was subject to an architectural survey shortly before its demolition in 1959. This determined that the frontage portion of the structure was early seventeenth-century in date; it was composed of two storeys, plus an attic, and had plastered, timber-framed walls (RCHM(E) 1959, 332). A short eastern return had been extended during the later seventeenth century, while the whole structure was extensively remodelled and extended in the early nineteenth century. These results accord very closely with the archaeological data that was recovered, which primarily pertained to the rear portion of the eastern return (*Building 9*).

In 1959, the topographic layout that had been established during the first half of the nineteenth century – itself an organic development of the medieval pattern, whose roots can be traced back to the early twelfth century – was eradicated. All of the standing buildings at the site were demolished, their cellars crudely and carelessly backfilled with rubble. Then, above their remains, the Bradwell's Court shopping centre was constructed. As a result, the topography of the area was substantially altered. Christ's Lane was closed, replaced by a central access route with shop units arrayed to either side, and around 900 years of unbroken occupation came to an end. In 2005, however, the shopping centre was itself demolished. Christ's Lane was re-established and the topography has reverted to a close approximation of its former medieval layout; three long narrow plots now extend back from the principal frontage, with six smaller plots facing onto Christ's Lane. A residential element has also returned.

Material culture, incorporating specialist information from Craig Cessford and David Hall

Although very similar in both range and composition to the artefactual and environmental assemblages recovered from Grand Arcade, the Christ's Lane material was much more modest in size, comprising a total of 8327 items, weighing 288kg. To avoid repetition, the two sets of material have been considered in combination on a period-by-period basis in Chapters 4 and 5; additional details can also be found within the supplementary digital-only volume. Consequently, this information will not be reiterated here. It is, however, important to briefly discuss how the two sets of data compare, as this may shed light on any potential differences in the patterns of activity that predominated within the two street blocks. To this end, three categories of material will be examined: ceramics, faunal remains and environmental remains.

In the first instance, it is notable that the depositional context of many of the assemblages recovered from Christ's Lane was different to those at Grand Arcade. Two factors in particular can be identified. Firstly, the investigated areas at Christ's Lane predominantly lay either within, or else immediately adjacent to, buildings. Contrastingly, at Grand Arcade the investigations were principally focused upon the open backlands situated towards the rear of the site's constituent properties. Accordingly, relatively few cut features were investigated at Christ's Lane; instead, a much higher proportion of material was recovered from layers. Such disparities in context and locale are likely to have had an impact on both the types and quantities of material that were discarded within them. Secondly, no large or substantial groups were encountered at Christ's Lane. Whilst by no means common at Grande Arcade, a number of large discrete groups were recovered from the backfill of features situated in the plot tails; areas that were little investigated at Christ's Lane. The absence of such groups, which are of particular archaeological importance, further inhibits the interpretive potential of the Christ's Lane material.

Contextual differences such as these may have had an impact on the eleventh–seventeenth-century ceramic assemblage. Overall, this consisted of 3402 sherds weighing 57.3kg. The assemblage has been broken down by fabric in Chapter 4, revealing a close similarity between both the range and relative proportion of wares that were present (Tables 4.4–4.11); the small number of individually significant sherds have also been illustrated above (Fig. 6.11). Yet despite the close comparability between the two assemblages, a distinction is apparent. This pertains to the relative preponderance and quality of the finewares that were in use at the smaller site. Being primarily dining-related, it is possible that this difference resulted from the context in which the sherds were deposited, with a greater quantity of material being present in the general vicinity of the buildings within which it had been used. But it is also notable that the distinction was most apparent during the sixteenth–seventeenth centuries, a period when occupation at Grand Arcade was either in decline or undergoing a period of stagnation (Chapters 4–5). Conversely, the Christ's Lane street block was thriving at this time, suggesting that a possible difference in consumption patterns may also be apparent.

Economic and environmental data, incorporating specialist information from Lorrain Higbee and Anne de Vareilles

The faunal assemblage recovered from Christ's Lane was again very similar to that from Grand Arcade (see Chapter 4). It included a mixture of primary and secondary butchery waste, domestic household refuse and waste material generated by craft/industrial activities. Amongst the domesticates sheep/goat were the most common in all periods, with the eleventh–twelfth-century assemblage comprising sheep/goat 47.1 per cent NISP, cattle 43.1 per cent NISP and pig 9.8 per cent; the thirteenth–seventeenth century assemblage of sheep/goat at 46.4 per cent NISP, cattle at 38.0 per cent NISP and pig at 15.6 per cent NISP. The somewhat lower incidence of pigs may be associated with the reduced plot-size at Christ's Lane, which would have limited the potential for raising livestock. Despite the rather modest size of the assemblage overall – 2963 fragments, weighing 37.3kg – the range of identified species was relatively broad; it closely equates to that encountered at Grand Arcade (Table 4.15). A similar range of commensal species were also present, while the fish eating habits of the two street blocks' inhabitants again appear to have been closely comparable (see Chapter 4). No variations indicative of differences in status or consumption were identified.

Finally, the environmental remains revealed perhaps the greatest disparity in the patterns of activity at the two sites. In total, nine bulk environmental samples of eleventh–sixteenth-century date were fully analysed from Christ's Lane (Table 4.27). Unlike the evidence from Grand Arcade, however – where the cereal and weed seeds in particular have been identified as predominantly rural in character and more akin to those of a *production* site as opposed to one of *consumption* (see Chapter 4) – the Christ's Lane material instead demonstrated closer affinities with sites situated in the urban core. Moreover, this disparity was not only evident during the Late Medieval period, when the degree of building coverage was relatively advanced, but from the earliest stages of occupation at the site. Although caution must be exercised, due to the low number of samples involved, a genuine pattern does appear to be present. This corroborates the 'proto-urban' nature of the archaeologically identified sequence.

Discussion

Overall, the range of medieval and post-medieval feature-types and material assemblages that were encountered during the Christ's Lane excavations were highly comparable to those recovered from Grand Arcade. This serves to underline the close physical and chronological similarities between the two sites. Nevertheless, several important differences are apparent. These primarily pertain to the density of occupation that occurred within each respective street block. Up until the mid-twelfth century, the plot layout at both sites appears to have been closely comparable. Parallel rows of long, narrow burgage-type plots predominated, each of which was aligned perpendicular to Hadstock Way. Subsequently, however, the potential for further development at Grand Arcade was inhibited by the establishment of the King's Ditch (Chapter 3). This substantial barrier restricted access to the rear portions of the block's properties. Indeed, although some limited occupation occurred along neighbouring *Landgrytheslane*, activity at the latter site appears to have remained almost entirely focused upon the principal

Hadstock Way frontage throughout the medieval period (Chapter 4).

Contrastingly, within the Christ's Lane street block two secondary frontages had developed by the early thirteenth century – along Hangman's Lane and Praise Be To God Street – while, to the rear, a backlane – Hinton Way – was also established. A much more complex spatial arrangement, commonly associated with a densely built-up proto-urban or urban environment (Palliser *et al.* 2001; Slater 1981), this evolution in layout was accompanied by a pattern of increasing plot subdivision. Over the course of the twelfth–sixteenth centuries the number of plots within the Christ's Lane development area increased fivefold, from two to 10; yet, during this same period, the number of plots at Grand Arcade remained largely unchanged. This increasingly divergent pattern of occupational usage resulted in an identifiable archaeological signature. Two elements in particular stand out: the relative density of the archaeological remains that were encountered, including both stratigraphic deposits and material assemblages, and the degree of building coverage that was established.

By either measure, a greater density of remains was encountered at Christ's Lane than at Grand Arcade. This can be demonstrated firstly by the nature of the archaeological sequences that developed at each site. Across much of Grand Arcade, for instance, only two stratigraphic horizons were present: the first was sealed by the extensive garden soil deposit that covered the majority of the site, while the second truncated it. Only close up to the principal frontage did a more complex sequence occur, although here the deposits had been extensively truncated by later cellars. Yet at Christ's Lane, where the presence of multiple frontages resulted in the development of many smaller, more intensively utilized plots, the sequence was rather different. All across this latter site a relatively well-stratified sequence was present that averaged around 2.5m in depth (Fig. 6.8). This indicates both the more intensive utilization of this particular space and the greater pace of deposition that occurred within it. Indeed, the resultant deposits are in many ways more akin to those encountered within Cambridge's urban core than its outlying suburban fringe.

This similarity can be demonstrated by comparing the Christ's Lane sequence to that identified at Corfield Court, a site situated in the core of the medieval town (Fig. 6.18). Although it is clear that a much greater degree of horizontal build-up occurred in the latter location, the principal difference between the two is not the nature of the deposits that were encountered, nor even the pattern of their deposition, but rather their *intensity*. Consisting of upcast material generated by

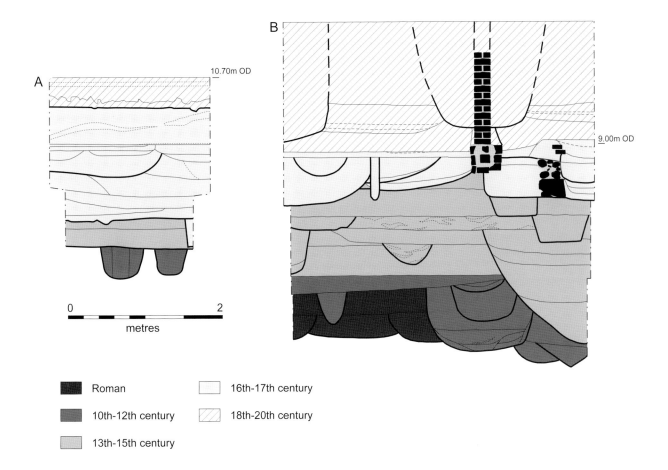

Roman

10th-12th century

13th-15th century

16th-17th century

18th-20th century

Figure 6.18. *The relative depths of the stratigraphic sequences at: (A) Christ's Lane; (B) Corfield Court.*

pit digging alongside layers, surfaces and structural remains, these deposits were primarily generated as the by-product of everyday domestic activities. Their extent thus reflects the intensity with which such activities were undertaken. A very similar pattern can also be observed in relation to the quantity of material culture that was deposited. One example of this – among many – is that the ceramic assemblages recovered from Grand Arcade, Christ's Lane and Corfield Court demonstrate a marked disparity in terms of their density per square metre (Table 6.1).

In the first instance, the density of thirteenth–fifteenth-century pottery was over four times greater at Christ's Lane than at Grand Arcade. This is a substantial difference, although it may have resulted in part from the differing excavation methodologies that were employed at each site. By its very nature, a trench-based investigation such as that conducted at Christ's Lane – where the majority of deposits were 100 per cent excavated in order to reveal the underlying strata – is likely to produce a larger finds assemblage than a more dispersed open-area excavation. Nevertheless, the material from Corfield Court, which was

recovered under near-identical trench-based conditions, was in turn over five times denser than that derived from Christ's Lane. This evidence suggests that while differences in excavation methodology may have exacerbated the scale of this distinction, they did not create it. Instead, the disparity is likely to have arisen from a combination of factors, amongst the most significant of which was the limited availability of space in many proto-urban and urban locales. This is because within small, intensively utilized plots the potential for dispersed above-ground refuse disposal

Table 6.1. *Density of sherds per sq. m at three Cambridge sites; the first is urban, the second 'proto-urban' and the third suburban. The figures in italics denote the relative percentage of the assemblage that pertains to each period. Note that for consistency, only the principal area of excavation at Grand Arcade has been included in this calculation.*

Site	10th–12th century	13th–15th century	16th–17th century
Corfield Court	53.7 (*35%*)	64.0 (*41.8%*)	35.5 (*23.2%*)
Christ's Lane	2.4 (*12.6%*)	7.7 (*40.5%*)	8.9 (*46.9%*)
Grand Arcade	0.5 (*17.2%*)	1.8 (*62.1%*)	0.6 (*20.7%*)

Table 6.2. *Buildings constructed at Christ's Lane during the twelfth–seventeenth centuries.*

Building	Plot	Area	Date	Construction technique	Nature
1	1	11	16th–17th century?	Earth-fast post	Accessory?
2	1	12	16th? –19th century	Brick-built	Dominant
3	2	7	12th century?	Earth-fast post	Accessory?
4	2	14	14th?–17th century	A = post-in-trench B = post-in-trench C = earth-fast sill beam? D = stone-built sill wall E = stone-built sill wall F = brick-built?	Accessory (barn?)
5	2	6	16th–19th century	A = earth-fast sill beam B= brick-built	Dominant
6	2	7	16th century	A = timber-built, partially sunken B = timber-built, partially sunken C = mortared-tile sill wall	Accessory?
7	3	9	15th–16th century	Timber-framed (technique unclear)	Accessory
8	3	10	13th century	Mixture of earth-fast post and post-in-trench	Accessory?
9	3	10	14th–18th? century	A = earth-fast sill beam B = earth-fast sill beam C = brick-built	Dominant
10	3	10	15th–18th? century	A = mixture of post-in-trench and stone-built sill wall B = stone-built sill wall C = stone-built sill wall D = brick-built	Accessory
11	3	9	17th–19th century	Brick-built	Dominant

– in the form of middening, for example – was highly restricted, thereby resulting in the much more rapid accumulation of 'made-ground' deposits.

The intention here is not to examine in detail the taxonomies of medieval occupation – a large, complex and multi-faceted topic – but rather to demonstrate that although closely adjacent, the Grand Arcade and Christ's Lane street blocks lay at differing points along what was a broad and relatively diverse spectrum. This fact is also underscored by a third strand of evidence. Building remains comprised the most significant facet of the Christ's Lane sequence. Overall, elements relating to 11 medieval and post-medieval buildings were investigated (Table 6.2). Dating from the twelfth century onwards, the majority of these structures were rebuilt on numerous occasions and some remained in use for several centuries (albeit in modified/updated form). Due to the trench-based nature of the excavation, however, no building was revealed in its entirety and many were only partially represented. This greatly inhibits their interpretation, as most typologies of medieval buildings are plan-based in nature (*e.g.* Grenville 1997, 165–71; Pantin 1963; Schofield 1997; see also Quiney 2003; Rees Jones 2008). Nonetheless, as at Grand Arcade the identified structures can be

subdivided into two groups: primary, *plot dominant* buildings and secondary, *plot accessory* buildings. The former typically functioned as the principal dwelling within a property, whilst the latter were associated with a range of ancillary activities such as cooking, storage or craft/industrial processes (see Conzen 1960, 31–2; Conzen 1968, 128).

In common with the differing intensities of stratigraphic deposits and material assemblages outlined above, the principal difference between the buildings within the Christ's Lane and Grand Arcade street blocks appears to have lain in their number rather than their form or method of construction. Although the physical extent of the structural remains at Grand Arcade was limited, especially when compared to the profusion of buildings that were encountered at Christ's Lane, this similarity is at least partially attested in the documentary record. During the fourteenth century, for instance, buildings at both sites were described as 'shop[s] with solar over'; probably the most common form of urban housing in the Late Medieval period (Schofield 1997, 142). This is not to suggest that both areas would have appeared architecturally uniform to a medieval visitor, however. A degree of structural variation almost certainly existed; a pattern that will only have increased over time, as each plot followed an increasingly divergent developmental trajectory. Yet it is the degree of building coverage that presents the most striking contrast. At Christ's Lane, buildings were encountered in almost every investigated area, thereby demonstrating that – by the sixteenth century, at least – they were distributed relatively evenly across the site. This contrasts markedly with Grand Arcade, where (with the exception of specialized structures such as latrines) buildings were predominantly restricted to a relatively narrow zone lying to the rear of the principal frontage.

Once again, this distinction most probably reflects the increasingly divergent spatial organization of the two street blocks. The fivefold increase in plot numbers that occurred at Christ's Lane is very likely to have had a concomitant impact on the number of structures that were present, while the presence of multiple frontages also stimulated more intensive utilization of the rear portion of the site. Indeed, despite their limited, piece-meal exposure, the buildings at Christ's Lane represent the largest and best-preserved group of medieval structures to have been excavated anywhere in Cambridge to date. Of particular significance is their chronology, as this reveals the sequence of techniques that were employed in their construction (Table 6.2). The earliest buildings, which were most probably twelfth-century in date, were composed of simple earth-fast posts. Then, during the thirteenth century, new structures were erected that employed both post-in-trench and earth-fast sill beam techniques. These were superseded during the fifteenth century when stone-built sill walls were first introduced. Finally, from the late fifteenth/early sixteenth century onwards, many structures were constructed (or, in several instances, rebuilt) in brick.

Such a pattern is by no means unique to Cambridge; similar developmental sequences have been identified in many British towns and cities (Grenville 1997; Schofield & Vince 2003, 104–9; see also Pearson 2005; Pearson 2009; Rees Jones 2008). In particular, it has been noted that the use of earth-fast timber sill beams became widespread towards the close of the twelfth century, following developments in the technology of carpentry (Schofield & Vince 2003, 109; Walker 1999). Yet in this instance, the pattern was by no means strictly unilinear; the most modern, up-to-date construction technique was not always the one that was selected. More than one method was sometimes used contemporaneously within a single structure, for example, whilst supposedly 'outdated' techniques were also sometimes employed well outside their nominal position in the sequence. It thus appears that, rather than solely being determined by the date at which the work was undertaken, the construction technique

used often represented the most suitable type, selected from a known repertoire, to solve the specific problem encountered. Cost may also have played an important role in the decision-making process. Finally, the fact that brick was used in this street block around a century earlier than at Grand Arcade may relate to issues of status and display in this proto-urban setting (see Johnson 2010, 87–112).

A further point of interest concerns the occupations of the street blocks' inhabitants. Throughout the medieval and early post-medieval periods – indeed, right up until the construction of the Bradwell's Court shopping centre in 1959 – a relatively consistent balance between commercial, agricultural and residential activities appears to have been maintained (although the relative importance of each element varied over time). Yet whilst residential occupation leaves a clearly discernible archaeological signature, commercial and agricultural activities are often harder to identify. In part this discrepancy is attributable to the ephemeral traces which many of these latter activities would have generated; a situation that is further exacerbated by the often intermingled commercial and domestic nature of many of the constituent properties. This admixture renders it difficult to distinguish between specialized craft working, such as that sufficient to have formed an individual's livelihood, and the more general 'background noise' of everyday practical activity (Schofield & Vince 2003, 122). Thus the small number of specialized bone-waste deposits that were encountered, which primarily consisted of discrete collections of sheep metacarpals and metapodia, may be indicative of craft-based processes such as tanning or tawing but could equally pertain to more general, 'workaday' bone-working activity.

Yet two instances of probable occupation-based craft/industrial activity can be identified via the close association of function-specific features – such as ovens, tanks or troughs – whose interrelationship indicates that a multi-staged *process*, as opposed to a single repeated *action*, was being undertaken. The first of these relates to *Building 10* (Plot 3), which appears to have functioned as a commercial bakery during the sixteenth century, and the second to the fifteenth–sixteenth-century group of clay-lined ovens and associated pits/troughs that were identified in Area 12 (Plot 1). Although more limited than the corresponding evidence from Grand Arcade, the presence of such features – especially when taken in conjunction with the small number of specialized waste deposits – does imply that a broadly comparable range of artisanal, craft-based activities was being undertaken.

Similar issues of archaeological identification also arise in relation to the street block's known agricultural associations. On the one hand, documents reveal that The Vine Estate retained a holding of at least 40 acres within the adjacent East Fields until their eventual inclosure in 1801–07. This holding consisted of a series of dispersed lands, or strips, that were widely distributed across multiple fields (Table 6.3, Fig. 6.19). The association of these lands with the estate almost certainly dates back well into the medieval period, when such holdings comprised a valuable economic resource (see further below). Moreover, it is likely that many other properties in the suburb originally maintained similar agricultural associations. In this particular instance, however, the relationship appears to have become 'ossified' following the estate's purchase by Jesus College; an event that henceforth perpetuated an increasingly redundant tenurial arrangement. This evidence provides a compelling argument for a close association between the inhabitants of the Christ's Lane street block and the suburb's surrounding agricultural hinterland. Yet, archaeologically, neither the site's faunal nor environmental assemblages provided evidence of a strong agricultural association; such a direct linkage would not therefore have been apparent based upon the excavated material alone.

Partial investigations inevitably produce only partial results. For this reason, the relatively limited trench-based excavation conducted at Christ's Lane cannot be compared directly with the more comprehensive open-area investigation undertaken at Grand Arcade. Nevertheless, the 'proto-urban' nature of the medieval sequence at Christ's Lane – as indicated by the intensity of its stratigraphic, structural and material culture assemblages – is identifiably distinct from the arguably more 'typical' suburban pattern encountered at Grand Arcade. This highlights the degree of variation in settlement-related activity that existed contemporaneously within a relatively discrete area. It also demonstrates that a generic model based solely upon the Grand Arcade template cannot simply be extended to cover the entire Barnwell Gate suburb; within each street block – and within each of those street blocks' constituent plots – a number of additional, localized factors must also be considered. Despite this caveat, however, many similarities can be identified between the two areas during the medieval and post-medieval periods.

The eighteenth century saw a broad continuation of the preceding the eleventh–seventeenth-century pattern of activity. Diverging from the predominantly static sequence at Grand Arcade, the intensity of occupation at Christ's Lane steadily increased throughout this period. Subsequently, however, during the early nineteenth century, *divergence* increasingly gave way to *convergence*; so much so that, by the mid-nineteenth

Table 6.3. *Lands associated with The Vine Estate, as recorded in a terrier of 1769.*

Field	Furlong	Selions	Acres	Total acres
Middle Field		3	1.5	**1.5**
Bradmore Field	?23	4	1.75	**4.75**
		2	1	
		2	1	
		2	1	
Trumpington Field	7th	3	1.75	**1.75**
Cambridge Field	13th	3	1.75	**5.25**
		4	1.75	
	17th	4	1.75	
Little Neeton (Ford Field)	1st	2	1.75	**16.75**
	2nd	2	1	
	3rd	3	1.75	
		2	1	
		2	1	
	4th	3	1.75	
		3	1.75	
	5th	6	1.75	
	6th	4	2.5	
	7th	4	2.5	
Great Soulden (Swinecroft)	1st	1	0.25	**8**
		2	0.75	
	2nd	1	0.5	
		7	4	
	3rd	2	1	
		1	0.5	
		2	1	
Little Soulden		4	1	**1**
Total	?16	78	39	39

century, very few differences remained apparent between the two sites. On the one hand, this increasing similarity can be demonstrated by examining the plot layout within the two street blocks. Over the course of the eighteenth century, for example, the number of sub-plots within The Vine Estate had risen only gradually, from 11 to 14. Yet by the mid-nineteenth century this number had almost tripled, to 39. The rapid redevelopment of the area – which saw the establishment of both large villas and small, slum-like courts, all crowded together in close proximity – mirrors that which occurred around the same date at Grand Arcade (Chapter 5). Moreover, the dominant focus of activity also shifted at this time to include an increasingly prominent commercial component.

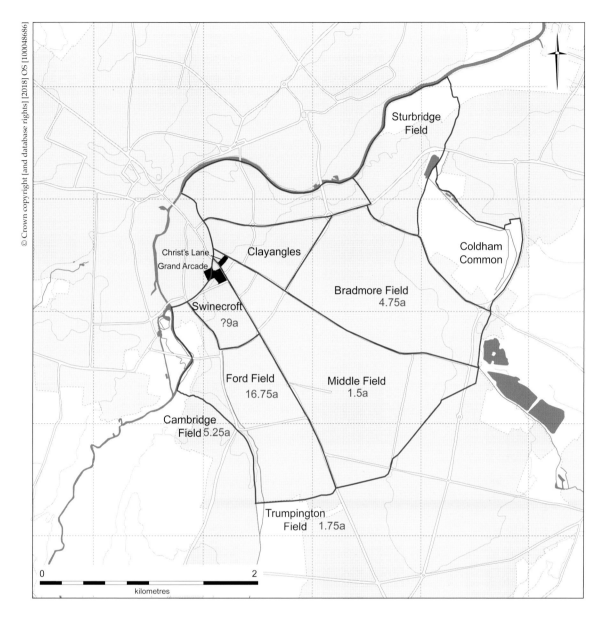

Figure 6.19. *The locations of the agricultural holdings associated with The Vine Estate within Cambridge's East Fields, as recorded in a terrier of 1769 but representing the vestiges of the medieval arrangement.*

Why this shift from divergence to convergence? What occurred during the early nineteenth century to precipitate such a change, and why did its impact extend so widely, encompassing both the Christ's Lane and Grand Arcade street blocks and beyond? Although by no means mono-causal, one of the principal factors that contributed to this transition was the inclosure of the surrounding open fields. The passing of the Cambridge Inclosure Act of 1801 and the Barnwell Inclosure Act of 1807 led to a high degree of commercial speculation, as large swathes of former agricultural land were bought up by investors with a view to large-scale development. The net result of

this process was an exponential increase in the pace of Cambridge's suburban expansion (see Bryan 1999; Bryan & Wise 2005). As is clearly shown in Figure 6.20, the suburbs' footprint increased more than tenfold over the course of the nineteenth century.

The most rapid period of growth occurred in the first few decades following inclosure. Between 1801 and 1841, for instance, the population of the outlying suburb of Barnwell increased almost 4000 per cent, rising from 252 to 9486 (Cam 1959, 110). Topographically, therefore, the Christ's Lane and Grand Arcade sites were no longer situated on the periphery of the town; within a few short years, they

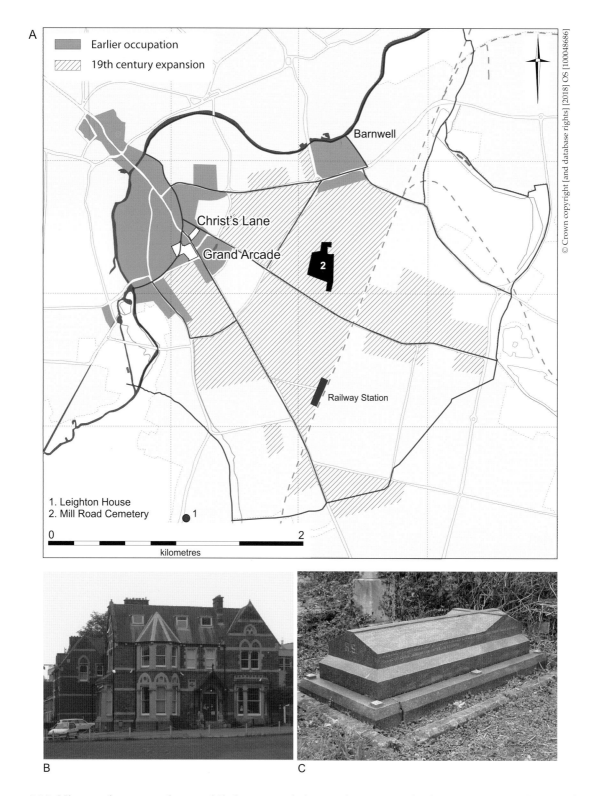

Figure 6.20. *Nineteenth-century changes: (A) the extent of nineteenth-century suburban expansion to the east of Cambridge, red lines denote the subdivisions within the former East Fields prior to their inclosure; (B) Photograph of Leighton House where the Sayle family moved c. 1866–9, facing east; (C) coped tomb with peaked (roof-shaped) top of Robert Sayle at the Mill Road cemetery, facing southwest. When Robert Sayle died in 1883 the funeral ceremony took place at the church of St Andrew the Great. The cortège formed outside his Leighton House and travelled passed the department store to the Mill Road cemetery.*

had effectively been incorporated into an expanded urban core. Further contributing to this change was the eradication of the last vestiges of the King's Ditch during the eighteenth century (Chapter 3). When the rapid escalation in suburban growth commenced, no formal demarcation of the earlier town boundary remained. The redevelopment of the Christ's Lane and Grand Arcade street blocks can thus be viewed in part as their conversion from moderately occupied, suburban spaces into intensively occupied, urban locales. Concomitant with this transformation was the increasing prevalence of commercial activity, which accompanied an attendant reduction in the degree of residential occupation. Whilst this pattern was most clearly visible at Grand Arcade, with the establishment of the Robert Sayle department store (Chapter 5), it also found expression at Christ's Lane in the assemblage of bottles associated with the Thompson family's grocery business. In 1959, the Christ's Lane site was entirely given over to commercial use following the establishment of the Bradwell's Court shopping centre.

A second major impetus for the increasing expansion of Cambridge's suburban fringe was the arrival of the Eastern Counties Railway in 1845. The new station, with its long classical façade and porte-cochère, was located to the southeast of the town as the University was vehemently opposed to a station located in the town centre (Gray 1976; Fig. 6.20). The construction of the railway greatly sped up the rate of development in nearby areas and also had other impacts; as a result of import by rail, goods such as clay tobacco pipes from Shropshire and London and bricks from Bedfordshire and Birmingham first appeared in the archaeological record. Finally, from 1860 onwards College fellows were permitted to marry and live outside their respective institutions. Although this initially occurred on a limited scale, with permission only being granted on an individual basis, by c. 1880 the escalating number of fellows seeking accommodation in the town began to have a significant impact upon the housing market.

Although marked, the sweeping changes that occurred within the Barnwell Gate suburb during the nineteenth century were by no means absolute. Despite the rapid escalation of suburban occupation, which all but eradicated the earlier East Fields, agriculture continued to play a role in the day-to-day life of the Christ's Lane inhabitants, principally in the form of dairying. A further element of continuity comprised the influence of the adjacent Colleges. Although the site had been entirely within collegiate ownership since the early sixteenth century, when The Vine Estate was first established, it was not until the nineteenth century that such an association can be identified archaeologically. As the street block became increasingly encroached

on by both Emmanuel College (who established their North Court within the southern portion of the street block in the early twentieth century) and Christ's College (whose staff occupied several plots within the Christ's Lane site itself), College-related material culture was deposited for the first time.

Overall, the piecemeal exposure of the nineteenth-century remains at Christ's Lane – allied with their extensive laceration by mid twentieth-century development, which had resulted in the survival of only scattered islands of *in situ* stratigraphy – means that they are of somewhat limited potential; they cannot add substantively to a broader understanding of life in the nineteenth-century street block. Nevertheless, as one of the few sites in the town aside from Grand Arcade where material of this date has been studied in detail, the results are of inherent value. In particular, they contribute to a broader discussion of the archaeology of modernity (see Chapter 7).

Emmanuel College

The street block occupied by Emmanuel College has witnessed several small-scale archaeological investigations, none of which have been informative about the origins of occupation. By the early thirteenth century a series of 'diverse dwellings in which many people dwelt' had apparently been established (Zutshi & Ombres 1990, 315), although 'diverse dwellings' is a standard phrase that does not necessarily equate to a large number of buildings. These structures were subsequently demolished to make way for a house of Dominican or 'black' friars of the Order of Preachers. The presence of the friary was first recorded documentarily in 1238, 17 years after the first arrival of the Order in England. Its construction had a significant impact on the local topography, which only increased as piecemeal acquisitions made by the friars over the succeeding decades led to the expansion of the precinct to around 10 acres in area (Ellis & Salzman 1948c, 272).

In 1993, archaeological excavations revealed a substantial late fourteenth-century building that was probably used as a guesthouse, with evidence for decorated glazed floor tiles and window glass (Fig. 6.21). For nearly half a century after the friary was dissolved in 1538 the site was probably occupied by a mixture of domestic properties, demolition sites and a builder's yard. Since 1584 its former site has been occupied by Emmanuel College, which was founded by a Puritan to train Protestant preachers. From the late eighteenth century onwards the Classical façade of Emmanuel College has been one of the dominant elements of the streetscape and there is strong evidence for connections between the College and the Grand Arcade street block, in terms of both property

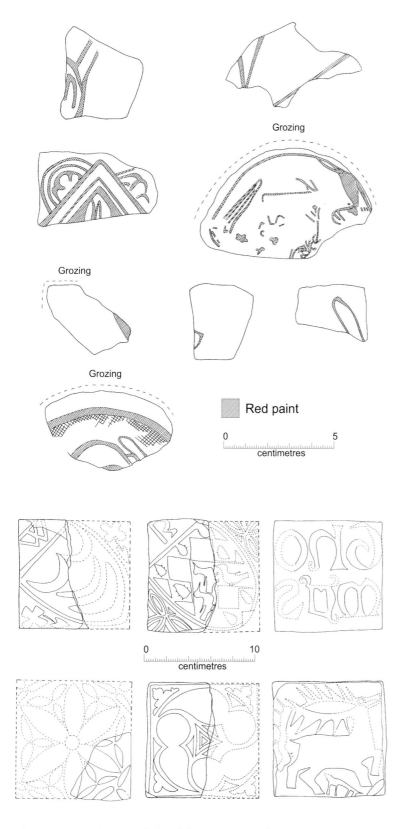

Grozing

Grozing

Grozing

Grozing

Red paint

0 _____ 5
centimetres

0 _____ 10
centimetres

Figure 6.21. *Selection of glazed floor tiles manufactured at Bawsey, near King's Lynn, and decorated window glass from late-fourteenth century building at the Dominican Friary, which preceded Emmanuel College.*

ownership and the residence of College servants. It is also probable that much of the moulded stone used to line features excavated at Grand Arcade derives from the Dominican friary, although it is impossible to prove this with certainty.

Unlike monks who lived by strict rules of self-sufficient cloistered asceticism, friars such as those of the Order of Preachers – also known as Dominicans after their founder, St Dominic de Guzman, or as Black Friars after the colour of their habits – undertook vows of poverty, chastity and obedience 'in service to society'. For this reason, the majority of their houses were situated in suburban rather than rural locations. The friars also committed to provinces that extended over relatively wide geographical areas as opposed to being tied to discrete, isolated communities. The province of England, for example, was divided into four Vicaries, of which the Cambridge house was the head of one (Ellis & Salzman 1948c, 270). Finally, the Dominicans were particularly noted for their teaching and scholastic activities; within the order, the house of Cambridge Black Friars was famed as a centre of learning second only to its sister house in Oxford (Zutshi & Ombres 1990, 314).

Archaeologically, the most significant investigation to have occurred at the former friary site took place within the Master's Forecourt of Emmanuel College in 1993 (Fig. 6.1, no. 26). As the results of this work have already been published elsewhere (Dickens 1999a), only a brief outline will be presented here. Within the excavated area the only evidence of pre-monastic activity comprised a well-worked horticultural deposit. Following the establishment of the friary, however, a large rectangular pit or tank was created that measured a minimum of 2.3m in depth. Close by a second, very similar pit was also present along with an associated ditch. Botanical and molluscan remains recovered from all three features reveal that they were perennially water-filled, indicating that they were potentially employed in a water-management capacity. They may thus have formed part of a larger complex of industrially related features. Nevertheless, during the late fourteenth century all three were deliberately backfilled in order to permit the construction of a substantial masonry building. This was represented archaeologically by the remnants of a large clunch-faced buttress, the majority of its walls having been robbed in the mid-sixteenth century when the building was demolished. Also associated with this latter event was a relatively large assemblage of discarded demolition debris that included fragments of mortar, peg tile and masonry plus over 100 glazed floor tiles – which were manufactured at Bawsey, near King's Lynn – and 25 shards of window glass (Fig. 6.21).

It is likely that this large, impressive building originally functioned as a guesthouse. Moreover, given the date of its construction it may well have been associated with the Parliament that was held in Cambridge in 1388; the only occasion such a conclave ever sat in the town (Ellis & Salzman

Reading names and signs at No. 21
Craig Cessford

In Chapter 1 there was an inset concerned with 'Doorways and windows to the past' that focussed on 21 St Andrew's Street and served to introduce some of the main themes of the volume. This inset partially returns to that property, but focuses on some other issues. When the current frontage was built in *c.* 1912–13 one of the most striking visual elements was the large stone sign that reads EMMA-NUEL/THE CHALICE, depicting the College coat of arms above a chalice (Fig. 6.22F). The sign is relatively unusual and probably owes its presence to the proximity of Emmanuel College, on the opposite side of St Andrew's Street (Fig. 6.22A–B). The

Classical façade of the west range of front court of Emmanuel College constructed 1769–75 has a central Ionic tetrastyle portico with the College coat of arms prominently displayed in a roundel on the pediment. The sign on No. 21 effectively brands the property as belonging to the College and would have been read as such by the occupants of the property, their customers, members of the College and passersby. That the unusually prominent sign was placed on a building so close to the College suggests that in some respects it was members of the College who were the most important audience.

There were few other explicit links to Emmanuel College at No. 21; indeed the only other time EMANUAL or EMANUEL COLLEGE occurs it is at a different property not owned by the College

A

B

C   D   E   F

Figure 6.22. *Emmanuel College and Grand Arcade: (A) late eighteenth-century frontage portico, facing northeast; (B) detail of College coat of arms on portico; (C) one of two College bottle seals found at No. 25 St Andrew's Street; (D) incised brick from warehouse constructed in 1845 at No. 21 St Andrew's Street; (E) sherd of pottery associated with College cook Thomas Wicks found at No. 21 St Andrew's Street; (F) early twentieth-century coat of arms on frontage of No. 21 St Andrew's Street.*

but occupied by its butler (Fig. 2.22C). The lining of Well 45 constructed in the 1720s incorporated stone blocks from two domestic windows of *c.* 1570–1640 that had probably previously graced the frontage building of the property. One of these windows itself incorporated reused stone from a window of *c.* 1200–70; the most likely source for this is the Dominican Friary founded *c.* 1221–38, which later became the site of Emmanuel College. While these probable connections can be identified through careful specialist analysis, the reused stone in the well lining was invisible – being on the rear face to 'key' the structure into the natural clay – and even when this window was putatively in the frontage of No. 21 the fact that it came from an earlier window would have similarly been concealed.

In 1845 the property went through a major re-organization. This included the construction of Well 53, the construction fill of which contained a sherd from a Willow pattern style plate marked on the rear with the name of the cook at Emmanuel College, Thomas Wicks (1807–51) (Fig. 6.22E). It is unlikely that this piece travelled directly between the College and No. 21; instead it probably moved initially to No. 23 where Wicks lived and then moved to No. 21 because of business contacts between Wicks and Edward Jay who ran the grocery business at No. 21. The sherd therefore represents indirect collegiate connections and also lacks any visible collegiate branding, despite this being common of College ceramic tablewares by this time (Cessford 2016).

Also constructed at No. 21 in 1845 was a large and impressive warehouse Standing Building 70. The warehouse lay deep within the property and was not visible from outside; although its construction was paid for by the College there was no visible collegiate branding on it. Instead there were a series of timber blocks and a brick marked with initials of members of the household that

occupied the property (Fig. 6.22D). These blocks were relatively discreet and difficult to spot from ground level. Whilst in academic terms this could be conceptualized as a form of 'resistance', it is perhaps better to think of it as a desire to leave a tangible mark from a position of relative power-lessness. This provides a form of household census of 1845 for the property, with evidence for women and children who are effectively invisible in much of the archaeological record – or perhaps more accurately the archaeological discourse – despite the fact that when combined these two groups must always have formed the majority of the population in the investigated properties. Yet even this 'census' is incomplete and biased; it omits the household servants who the censuses of 1841 and 1851 indicate would have lived at the property and the family's younger children Henry/Harry aged four and Frank aged three.

Even where there are texts that can be read literally or signs that can be easily understood, interpretation is problematic. Archaeologists have employed the literary metaphor of reading the past or reading material culture, although this is less fashionable than it once was. The interpretation of the Grand Arcade investigations involves multiple types of evidence – buildings, features, artefacts, environmental remains, documents and plans to list just the more obvious – and whilst it is possible to produce multiple complex narratives from the rich resources much probably still lies concealed (just as the moulded stone from earlier windows reused in a well, the name Wicks on the underside of a College plate and the blocks with the initials of some of the jay household were all in some senses deliberately hidden). Only a few texts or signs such as that on the frontage of No. 21 were deliberately meant to be read by the public at large. Hopefully much that was once concealed can now been read in this volume, but it is apparent that much remains hidden.

1948c, 272). As this was an important event, attended by many prestigious visitors, it could well have engendered an associated programme of construction/conversion; indeed, the sum of 20 marks was later awarded to the friars in compensation for the 'damage and inconvenience' they had incurred. The guesthouse was eventually demolished following the dissolution of the friary in 1538, most probably when the former monastic site was converted for residential use in 1544–5. A number of buildings are known to have been demolished at this time and their constituent materials sold off; at least two consignments of reclaimed masonry were purchased by Great St Mary's church, for example, for a combined sum of 88s (Ellis & Salzman 1948c, 276). In addition, smaller quantities of material – including moulded stone and timber – probably made

the shorter journey to Grand Arcade where they were reused in structures such as wells (although, given the plethora of ecclesiastical buildings that were demolished at this time throughout Cambridge and the surrounding area, the precise provenance of such fragments is difficult to determine).

Similar patterns of dispersion, involving the reuse of ecclesiastically derived material in disparate secular contexts, are frequently encountered on post-Dissolution sites (Morris 2003; Thomas 2006). Not all material-types were reclaimed equally, however. At the Dominican Friary, for instance, the majority of decorated floor tiles appear to have been discarded on site rather than retained. Contrastingly, lead – one of the most valuable commodities available for recovery (Doonan 1999; Dungworth 1999) – rarely enters the archaeological record; a situation that is well-represented at the friary by the discovery of numerous discarded quarries (irregularly shaped pieces of window glass) yet none of the associated cames (lead strips). Following the demolition of the guesthouse and the dispersal of its constituent components a timber-framed building was constructed in its place. Although large, this structure appears to have been relatively short-lived; within 30 years it had probably been demolished. A brick-built culvert was then established, perhaps in association with the foundation of Emmanuel College in 1584. Finally, the remaining sequence was dominated by made-ground deposits and planting-pits related to the subsequent collegiate use of the area as an orchard and formal garden.

With the establishment of the College almost all remnants of the preceding monastery were eradicated. This was a deliberate policy, for 'when Sir Walter Mildmay founded Emmanuel College … he was at pains that his 'spearhead of puritanism' should preserve as few traces as possible of the former priory' (Ellis & Salzman 1948c, 276). Despite the lack of physical continuity between the two institutions, however, the monastery and the College demonstrated several marked similarities; both had an exclusive membership, for example, and both employed a similar architectural vocabulary that was determined in part by the need to accommodate a sizeable, entirely male population. Thus, to the inhabitants of the surrounding suburb, their overall impact is likely to have been very similar. This is of particular importance because a second College, God's House, had also been established in the Barnwell Gate suburb in 1446 (Willis & Clark 1886 vol. II, 187–92). Situated further to the north, on the opposite side of Hadstock Way to Grand Arcade, this institution was re-founded as Christ's College in 1505. Furthermore, both Emmanuel College and Christ's College have continued to flourish up until the present day. Rather atypically, therefore, the degree of institutional presence in the suburb can be said to have *increased* rather than *decreased* following the dissolution of the friary.

Discussion

Although none of the other street blocks in the Barnwell Gate suburb are susceptible to the form of nuanced analysis made possible by the large-scale Grand Arcade investigations, they do serve to contextualize it as part of a broader community demonstrating that, *contra* the terminology of Pantin (1937, 171), no street block was an 'island', isolated unto itself. The consideration of the church of St Andrew the Great serves to foreground the religious aspects of the inhabitants' lives, whilst Christ's College and the Dominican Friary/Emmanuel College demonstrate the presence of radically different – but interlinked – communities within the suburb. Finally, the Christ's Lane investigations provide a small but important counterpoint to the much more extensive work undertaken at Grand Arcade. In particular, the presence of well-preserved stratigraphic sequences, as well as extensive structural remains – both elements that were largely absent from Grand Arcade – provide valuable insights into otherwise little-explored aspects of the lives of some of the Barnwell Gate suburb's inhabitants.

From the fourteenth century onwards a distinct 'University quarter' emerged in Cambridge, situated in the heart of the town between the main street and the river. During the sixteenth century a second University focus was created to the west with Christ's College

(1505), Emmanuel College (1584) and later to the north Sidney Sussex College (1596), which effectively linked the southern Colleges up with Jesus College (established in 1496 on the site of the twelfth-century Benedictine nunnery of St Mary and St Radegund). The creation of this secondary eastern arc of Colleges was in large part fortuitous and substantially driven by the fact that there was no space along the riverside area for new foundations. Nonetheless, this had a major impact on the topography of Cambridge and in the case of the Barnwell gate suburb meant that it now contained a substantial collegiate presence.

The agricultural hinterland

Surrounding the Barnwell Gate suburb to the south and east was an extensive, well-ordered agricultural hinterland. In the fourteenth century this area was known as the Barnwell Fields, although today it is more commonly referred to as the East Fields. Such areas comprised an intrinsic component of the medieval landscape. Between *c.* 850 and 1150 vast swathes of the English countryside were brought under intensive arable cultivation and many open hedgeless fields, composed of numerous individually worked strips known as *lands*, were established (see Astill & Langdon 1997; Gardiner & Rippon 2007; Hall 2014; Martin & Satchell 2008; Oosthuizen 2006). The systematic and repetitive practice of ploughing these lands generated a distinctive up-standing ridge, which often developed in the form of an elongated reverse 'S'. In the Cambridgeshire region each land typically measured a quarter of an acre in area, averaging eight yards (*c.* 7m) wide by 220 yards (*c.* 200m) long. Individual burgesses were allocated a number of such lands in the town's fields. In order to ensure that access to the most fertile zones was distributed equally, the allotted strips were not consolidated into a single contiguous block but instead dispersed across several different fields.

Although conforming to this general nationwide pattern, the medieval field-systems of Cambridge were relatively complex. They were subdivided into three main blocks; the East Fields, the West Fields (originally the Cambridge Fields) and the Chesterton Fields (Fig. 6.1). Although it has been suggested that these blocks all formed part of a single, over-arching three-field system (*e.g.* Maitland 1898), from around the eighth century onwards Chesterton comprised a royal *vill* – independent from Cambridge – that later developed its own, separate three-field system (Oosthuizen 2010). Moreover, despite both falling within the liberty of the town, the East and West Fields appear to have been relatively autonomous and were inclosed at different dates (Tate & Turner 1978, 73–5). In each of

Table 6.4. *Archaeological investigations in the East Fields of Cambridge undertaken by the CAU, 1996–2011.*

Site	No. on Fig 6.1	Date	Nature of investigation	Investigated area (sq. m)	Report
Anglia Ruskin	20	July 2009	Two trenches	60	Webb 2009
Botanic Garden	8	October 2003–August 2007	Eight trenches	62	Cessford 2003b; Dickens & Mackay 2007
Brooklands Avenue	14	December 1999–September 2006	Fifty-three trenches	3260	Armour 2002; Cooper 2004; Dickens & Patten 2003; Kenny 2000a; Timberlake 2006
Cambridge Guided Bus Route	10	September 2005	Monitoring only	1	Webb & Dickens 2005
CB1 development	10	May 2006–December 2010	Twenty trenches, plus one open area and monitoring	233	Michaels 2004; Mackay 2005; Mackay 2006; Slater 2010a; Slater 2010b
Clarendon Road	12	March 2000	Fifteen trenches	582	Kenny 2000b
Former Marshall Garage	16	February 2009	Four trenches	116	Newman 2009a
Hills Road Sixth Form College	13	July 2003	One trench	24	Mackay 2003
Homerton College	16	December 1996–November 2005	Twelve trenches plus monitoring	430	Alexander 1997a; Hatherley 2002; Webb & Dickens 2006; White 1997
Homerton Street	13	Feburary–August 2001	Two trenches	676	Mackay 2001a; Mackay 2001c
McDonald Institute	3	May 1992	Two trenches	58	Gdaniec 1992
Old Cattle Market	11	March–April 2001	Twenty-two trenches	748	Mackay 2001b
Parkside Fire and Rescue Station	21	July 2010–September 2011	One test pit plus three trenches	453	Newman 2010; Newman 2011
Rustat Road	15	December 2002	Six trenches	253	Cooper 2003
Unilever Site	8	April 1999	Four trenches	84	Dickens 1999b
Total			**154 trenches**	**7040**	

the latter instances, however, detailed fourteenth-century field-books survive. That pertaining to the West Fields has been intensively studied, revealing that this area consisted of four fields that were organized in a three-year cultivation regime (Hall & Ravensdale 1976). Although numerous sources relating to the East Fields also survive (Hesse 2007; Stokes 1915; see also Fig. 6.19), these have been less intensively studied. Future research therefore has the potential to greatly elucidate the detailed structure and management of this latter field-system.

In the valleys to the south of Cambridge there is evidence to suggest that intensively cultivated proto-open field-systems first emerged during the eighth–ninth centuries (Oosthuizen 2005; Oosthuizen 2006). Although the date at which the East and West Fields themselves were established remains unclear, the former was almost certainly in existence by the close of the tenth century; it had reached its maximum extent by the mid-fourteenth century (Hesse 2007).

Archaeologically, 15 trench-based investigations have been conducted within the East Fields to date, covering a combined area of 7040 sq. m (Table 6.4; see Fig. 6.1 for locations). Whilst the results of this work are perforce limited, due to the primarily evaluation-led nature of their methodology, they nevertheless shed light on an important component of the daily lives of many of the Barnwell Gate suburb's residents.

The earliest archaeologically recovered evidence of agricultural activity within the East Fields is tenth–twelfth-century in date. At a number of sites situated in close proximity to the medieval town – including the Museum of Archaeology and Anthropology, the Museum of Geology and 33 St Andrew's Street (Hurst 1956, 62–3; Hurst 1957, 52, 58), as well as the McDonald Institute (Gdaniec 1992; Fig. 6.1, no. 3) – Saxo-Norman fabrics including Thetford-type, St Neots-type and Stamford ware have been recovered. This material most probably originated as domestic waste generated within the urban core that was distributed onto the open fields via manuring. Notably, very few sherds of comparable date have been found at any greater distance from the town, despite the fact that a series of radiating trackways had almost certainly been established by this date. Elsewhere in the West Fields the discovery of a crouched inhumation close to the edge of the fields radiocarbon dated to the late tenth to early eleventh century indicates that the boundary was established by this time (Evans with Cessford in prep.).

By the early thirteenth century there were frequent documentary references to both the sale and leasing of arable holdings in the East Fields, thereby demonstrating the emergence of a thriving land market. These holdings typically consisted of areas of around seven to 10 acres that were divided into six or seven discrete land-groups, although a small number of larger holdings totalling in excess of 30 acres were also present. Such was the success of this system, by the mid-fourteenth century the area under intensive arable cultivation had doubled and many areas of common pasture and moorland that had formerly lain within the township boundary were now put to the plough (Hesse 2007). Several meadows were retained and set aside for hay, however, as well as common pastures for cattle plus wasteland that supplied rough grazing. The fields themselves followed a cyclical rotation of wheat followed by oats/barley and then fallow. In addition, zones of clay and gravel quarrying were also established; the latter were either situated in close proximity to routeways or else in areas of low agricultural potential.

Following this period of expansion the pattern of fourteenth–fifteenth-century land use within the East Fields appears to have remained relatively stable. More widespread archaeological evidence pertaining to this phase was encountered than for earlier centuries, including several ditches and furrows. Examples of the former include a 1.15m wide east-northeast–west-southwest aligned ditch that was investigated at the Former Marshall Garage site (Fig. 6.1, no. 16). This contained a type 15 copper alloy English jetton of c. 1319–43. Nearby, at Homerton College (Fig. 6.1, no. 17), several very similar features were also encountered, one of which contained fourteenth-century pottery. As these ditches were all situated on the perimeter of the Liberty of Cambridge, at the boundary of the cultivated area, their presence confirms the pattern of expansion recorded within the contemporary documentary sources. The majority of fields

remained open at this time, although some small-scale enclosure did occur. In 1381, for example, during the Great Uprising 'the townsmen thought that the Prior of Barnwell [one of Cambridge's largest landowners] had enclosed part of the field, thus depriving them of common pasture and of an ancient droveway' (Hilton 1973, 205). In response, a large mob led by the mayor attacked the priory.

Relating to the fields themselves, no upstanding headlands or ridges remain extant but a number of furrows have been identified. Firstly, at the Brooklands Avenue site (Fig. 6.1, no. 14) a series of such features were encountered. Regular in alignment and equidistant in disposition, these shallow furrows measured up to 3.0m in width. They were spaced c. 7.0m apart and in several instances contained a small quantity of fourteenth–fifteenth-century pottery. Contrary to the classic 'corrugated' appearance of ridge-and-furrow that predominated across much of the country – the 'Midlands pattern' – the Cambridge practice seems to have left the individual lands flat, separated only by a single furrow. Elsewhere, near-identical features were also encountered at the McDonald Institute (Fig. 6.1, no. 3) and Unilever sites (Fig. 6.1, no. 8). Such furrows were not ubiquitous, however. At Brooklands Avenue a portion of the site – known historically as Potmore Common, or 'frog moor' (Gelling 1984, 55) – appears to have been too damp to have been utilized for arable cultivation; no furrows were present in this area.

Archaeological evidence of gravel and clay extraction has also been encountered within the East Fields. At the CB1 site, for instance (Fig. 6.1, no. 10), numerous quarry pits measuring an average of 3.0m in diameter were investigated. These features contained pottery of fourteenth–sixteenth-century date. In addition, a much larger quarry, which measured around 50m across and up to 1.0m deep, was also investigated. The size of this latter feature indicates that extraction was being undertaken on a quasi-industrial scale; this interpretation is supported by contemporary documentary evidence, which indicates that the site lay within a furlong that contained an extensive 'pit dole' (Stokes 1915, 55). Nearby, at the Old Cattle Market site (Fig. 6.1, no. 11), a series of quarry pits

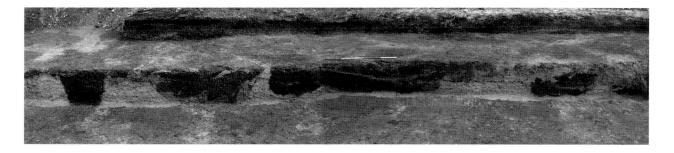

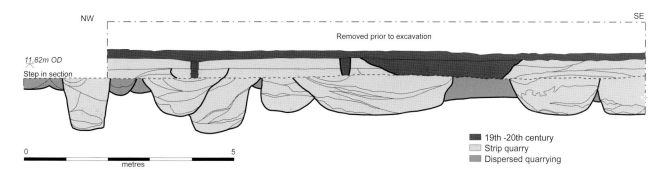

NW

SE

Removed prior to excavation

11.82m OD

Step in section

0

5

metres

19th -20th century
Strip quarry
Dispersed quarrying

Figure 6.23. *Intensive quarrying activity at the Parkside Fire and Rescue Station site; a series of dispersed late medieval pits were succeeded by a much more regimented arrangement of strip quarries during the mid-seventeenth century.*

again averaging *c.* 3.0m in diameter were encountered. Overall, both the archaeological and documentary evidence suggests that the intensity of quarrying activity within the East Fields increased during the Late Medieval period, probably as a consequence of the diminishing accessibility of natural resources in the town itself (as witnessed at Grand Arcade).

In the mid-seventeenth century the pattern of extraction-related activity intensified still further. The *ad hoc* excavation of irregular, amorphous pits gave way to a much more systematic pattern of linear 'strip-quarries'; in effect, an early form of open-cast mining. This transition was well-represented at the Parkside Fire and Rescue Station (Fig. 6.1, no. 21), where a series of seventeenth-century strip-type quarries superseded – and almost entirely eradicated – a more dispersed pattern of late medieval features (Fig. 6.23). Notably, highly comparable strip-quarries of near-identical date have also been identified elsewhere within Cambridge's hinterland, including both the West Fields (Evans & Newman 2011) and the Fields of Chesterton (Newman 2015). It thus appears that a broadly concentric 'ring' of intensive quarrying activity was established at this time, with most of the principal extraction sites located in close proximity to arterial routeways. This phase was relatively short-lived, however. By the early eighteenth century few quarry pits were being excavated in the open fields; instead, extraction appears to have escalated to a more industrial scale, utilizing larger quarries situated at a greater distance from the town. The fields themselves remained open until the passage of a series of Inclosure Acts between 1801 and 1830 (Tate & Turner 1978, 73–5).

One suburb among many

Because it forms the location of the largest excavations yet to have occurred in Cambridge, the focus of this book is almost entirely centred upon the Barnwell Gate suburb; yet it is important to note that this comprised only one of five suburbs of broadly comparable size that developed around the periphery of the medieval town (see Figs. 6.1 and 6.24). In order to situate the detailed results presented elsewhere in this volume more securely within their wider landscape context, therefore, a brief summary of these latter areas will also be presented. Although subject to much less intensive investigation than the principal area of study, between 1995 and 2013 a number of evaluations and excavations have taken place within the town's other suburbs and several significant results have been obtained. The most pertinent of these will be outlined below.

Topographically, the northernmost of Cambridge's five suburbs was centred on Castle Hill. Formerly the site of a small fortified Roman town (Alexander & Pullinger 2000; Evans & ten Harkel 2010), this area remained the principal locus of occupation at Cambridge until the early eleventh century. Although it was subsequently to retain a significant military and bureaucratic presence – in the form of Cambridge castle – the majority of domestic occupation subsequently migrated to the south of the river, where a successful inland port rapidly developed. By *c.* 1300 only 14 per cent of the town's population remained resident in the former core. To the south of Cambridge

a second suburb developed outside the Trumpington Gate. Closely mirroring the pattern of the Barnwell Gate suburb, occupation in this latter area coalesced along one of the town's principal approach roads. At the beginning of the fourteenth century five per cent of Cambridge's population resided in this suburb. A third suburb developed to the west of the river Cam, around the former hamlet of Newnham. This remained the smallest of the five suburbs; *c.* 1300, its population accounted for only four per cent of the total. Finally – and rather unusually – the fourth suburb was located a mile to the east of the town (Fig. 6.1). Here, dislocated from the urban core by a swathe of open fields, occupation was established outside the gates of Barnwell Priory (which had been re-founded in this location *c.* 1112). Despite being almost certainly the last of the five suburbs to be established, by the close of the thirteenth century Barnwell was also the largest, accommodating 18 per cent of the town's population.

Whilst there were unquestionably many similarities between each of the five suburbs, there were also a number of differences. The latter are important because they shed light on the broader pattern of suburban occupation at Cambridge as a whole. In particular, three main issues can be identified. The first relates to the economic composition of each suburb: what was the status of its occupants, for example, and what type of dwellings did they reside in? The second issue pertains to the number and type of institutions, both religious and secular, that were established in each suburb, as these will also have also had a substantial impact on the character of the area. Finally, were any additional factors present – such as an atypical location, for example, or a particular specialized and/or industrial focus – that might have served to further distinguish one area from another? Although at present the limited nature of the results precludes detailed analysis of these issues, some basic conclusions can nevertheless be drawn.

In the mid–late eleventh century, when dispersed occupation was only just emerging in the Barnwell Gate suburb (Chapter 2), the settlement on Castle Hill had already been in existence for many centuries. A small Roman town first developed on this natural promontory during the first century AD. Fortified *c.* 350, its walls

Figure 6.24 *(opposite). Lyne's map of Cambridge of 1574, with the locations of the town's various suburbs highlighted (note that Barnwell lay some distance to the east of the town; its layout was not recorded cartographically until the nineteenth century). The numbers in red denote the approximate percentage of the population that resided within each respective area c. 1300; these figures are based on an amalgamation of several medieval sources.*

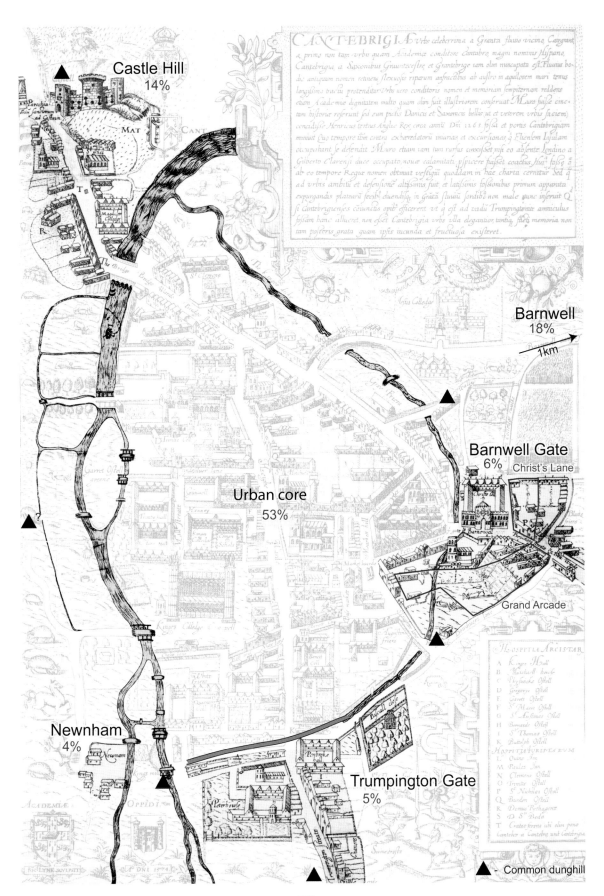

Castle Hill
14%

Barnwell
18%
1km

Barnwell Gate
6%
Christ's Lane

Urban core
53%

Grand Arcade

Newnham
4%

Trumpington Gate
5%

▲ - Common dunghill

are likely to have remained at least partially extant into the eleventh century (Alexander & Pullinger 1999, 8). Post-Roman occupation was re-established at the site by the eighth century (Cessford with Dickens 2005a), although the settlement appears to have remained relatively modest in size until the mid-tenth century (Hines 1999, 136). Following this date, as the town rapidly expanded the principal locus of occupation transferred to the south of the river, such that by 1219 the Castle Hill area was being explicitly referred to as a suburb (Maitland 1898, 176). During the medieval period one of the defining characteristics of the area was the eponymous motte-and-bailey castle. First erected in 1068, 27 houses were demolished to make way for its enlargement in 1086 (Cam 1959, 4). Although rebuilt in stone during the twelfth century, the castle's military and strategic role gradually declined until it was extensively refortified *c.* 1286–96 (Cam 1959, 116–17). Despite being officially located outside the borough – it lay instead within the royal *vill* of Chesterton – the castle nevertheless dominated the suburb physically. By 1606, however, its only upstanding remnant comprised the gatehouse, which was then employed as the town gaol. The site itself remained an important administrative centre throughout the medieval and post-medieval periods (Cam 1959, 117).

At the foot of the castle a house of Augustinian canons regular was founded *c.* 1092 (Ellis & Salzman 1948a, 234); the rapid expansion of this monastery precipitated its move to a much larger site at Barnwell, half a mile to the east of the town, 20 years after its establishment. The former monastic church, St Giles, is one of two in the suburb – along with nearby St Peter's – that are of eleventh-century origin; though both have since been comprehensively rebuilt and retain few original features. Archaeologically, the Castle Hill area was subject to a number of investigations between 1956 and 1988 (Alexander & Pullinger 1999). This work was primarily focused upon the remains of the former Roman town, however; a selective approach that, allied with the extensive truncation of the uppermost portion of the sequence across much of the area, resulted in a relative paucity of medieval material being recovered. More recently, several small-scale investigations have been conducted, much the most significant of which was undertaken at Chesterton Lane Corner (Fig. 6.1, no. 25). Here, an eighth-century execution cemetery was encountered (Cessford *et al.* 2007) that was succeeded *c.* 850 by a probable ecclesiastical structure (Cessford with Dickens 2005a, 81–3). During the medieval period a house was established at the site, beneath the floor of which a box containing a hoard of 1805 silver pennies and nine gold coins – worth £10 3s 9d – was deposited in the mid-fourteenth century (Allen 2005; Allen in Cessford with Dickens 2005a; see also Fig. 7.12).

In contrast to the relative paucity of archaeological remains that have been encountered, a number of sixteenth-century domestic buildings remain extant in the Castle Hill suburb. Primarily concentrated along Magdalene Street and Northampton Street, these structures represent the most comparable surviving examples of the type of buildings that once lined the principal thoroughfare of the Barnwell Gate suburb. Timber-framed in construction and two to three storeys in height, these structures had plastered walls, projecting upper floors and peg-tiled roofs. Internally, their ground floors typically comprised one large room that principally functioned as a workshop and/or retail space, the rear wall of which contained a fireplace. To one side of this room was an entrance passage, while on the first floor was a hall. Where a second storey was present this contained a solar, which was open to the roof (RCHM(E) 1959, xciii–xciv). Similar buildings are widely represented in towns all across Britain, where they comprised the most common form of urban housing during the late medieval and early post-medieval periods (Schofield 1997, 132–42).

To the south of Cambridge lay Trumpington; the most closely comparable suburb in terms of its size, form and location to that of Barnwell Gate. A roadside development first emerged at Trumpington during the eleventh–twelfth centuries. Over time, this was increasingly occupied by a number of wealthy households. In particular, the area came to be dominated by two prosperous families whose patrimonies were alienated to religious institutions in the thirteenth century. Firstly, on the western side of Trumpington Street the Le Rus family possessed a large masonry townhouse along with a proprietary chapel (a privately owned but publicly accessible church); this estate was alienated to the Friars of the Sack in 1258 (Ellis & Salzman 1948e, 290–1; Haigh 1988, 13; Stokes 1908, 14–43). Secondly, on the eastern side of the street a similar estate was owned by the St Edmund family; their townhouse and chapel were alienated to the Gilbertine Order in 1290 (Ellis & Salzman 1948b, 254–6; Haigh 1988, 14–15; Stokes 1908, 44–63). The suburb's parish church – originally known as St Peter without Trumpington Gates, now St Mary the Less – retains *in situ* twelfth-century elements in its west tower (RCHM(E) 1959, 280–3). In addition, a small hermitage dedicated to St Anne and a hospital dedicated to St Anthony and St Eloy were also established in this suburb during the fourteenth century (Cam 1959, 133; Ellis & Salzman 1948f), whilst a further significant institutional component of the area comprised two Colleges. The first, Peterhouse, was established in 1284 and the second, Pembroke, in 1347 (Willis & Clark 1886 vol. I, 1–76, 121–56).

Five investigations have been conducted to date within the Trumpington suburb (Fig. 6.1, nos. 4, 5, 18, 19, 27). Although limited in scale this work has nevertheless produced a number of significant results. Perhaps most notably, evaluations have taken place within the former holdings of both the St Edmund and Le Rus families. At the former site, which is now principally occupied by the Judge Business School (Fig. 6.1, no. 27), a minimum of four twelfth–fourteenth-century inhumations were encountered (Newman 2013b). Laid out in formal rows, these interments almost certainly comprised part of a larger cemetery associated either with the proprietary chapel of St Edmund (*c.* 1100–1290) or the succeeding Gilbertine Friary (1290–1539). Antiquarian discoveries of human remains made here in the eighteenth century, when Addenbrooke's Hospital was first established at the site (Stokes 1908, 62), are also likely to have derived from the same source. Contrasting with this sepulchral sequence, on the opposing side of Trumpington Street – during an evaluation conducted at the Fitzwilliam Museum (Fig. 6.1, no. 5) – a long-lived domestic sequence was encountered (Whittaker 2001b).

Activity had commenced at this site by the early twelfth century, when a number of pits and postholes were created. Then, during the thirteenth century, a timber-framed building was established. Represented archaeologically by the presence of a series of compacted mortar floor surfaces and an associated beamslot, this was most probably an ancillary structure as it was located *c.* 28m to the rear of the principal frontage. Its precise form and size are unclear due to the extent of later truncation. Given its date it may have been associated with the Le Rus family, who occupied this estate until 1258, or alternatively the succeeding monastery of the Friars of the Sack, who occupied the site until 1308 (Hall & Lovatt 1989, 31). In the early fourteenth century the timber-built structure was demolished and a replacement masonry building constructed. This was substantial in scale, measuring in excess of 10.7m by 5.7m in extent. Consonant with its size its clunch-built foundations were equally robust, varying between 1.0m and 1.3m in width, and indicating that the building was probably at least two storeys in height. From within one of the foundations a silver short cross penny of Edward I was recovered (class 9b2, *c.* 1300, of uncertain mint); the degree of wear indicates that it was probably lost/deposited during the first half of the fourteenth century.

Masonry buildings were relatively rare in medieval Cambridge (Cam 1959, 122), a dearth that is primarily attributable to the paucity of locally available building stone. The most commonly employed material, clunch, was quarried from various sources in the Cambridgeshire region (Purcell 1967, 24–8). Due to its poor weather resistance, however, its use was principally restricted to foundations and internal decorative elements. This implies that the above-ground portion of the present building may have been constructed from a different material, such as limestone, that was later robbed. Although the structure's entire footprint was not revealed, it contained a minimum of three rooms on the ground floor; the centremost of which measured at least 5.0m by 4.5m in extent. Externally, a number of glazed ridge tiles were recovered from fifteenth-century demolition deposits, indicating that its roof was originally quite ornate. Altogether, therefore, this was clearly a building of some status. The date of its construction, in the first half of the fourteenth century, suggests that it is unlikely to have been monastic in origin. Instead it was probably associated with the site's subsequent owner, Peterhouse, who purchased the estate in 1308. At the time of their acquisition a substantial masonry townhouse was present, along with additional buildings, courtyards and a large area of accompanying croftland to the rear (Hall & Lovatt 1989, 45). The College subsequently converted the main portion of the site into a number of rental properties, while the croftlands were cultivated as kitchen gardens and an orchard. Consequently, it is possible that the excavated structure represents an enlargement/modification of the pre-existing townhouse, although it is perhaps more likely that it was associated with the establishment of new residential plots at the site.

Similar evidence of probable high-status occupation was also identified during an investigation conducted at nearby Pembroke College (Fig. 6.1, no. 4). Here, a clunch-lined cesspit of pre-collegiate origin was investigated. Infilled c. 1585–1620, this feature contained a wide range of organic and non-organic material within its anaerobic backfill. Alongside substantial faunal, ceramic and botanical assemblages, the recovered items included eight timber artefacts, an ivory needle case and two jettons (Hall 2002). Furthermore, the ceramic material was notable for the presence of several continental imports, from the Netherlands and/or Germany, as well as two costrels – flat, pear-shaped drinking vessels with loops to facilitate attachment to a belt – which are not paralleled in other local groups. Historically, it appears likely that the cesspit was associated with Bradley Hall; a wealthy 'urban manorial' household that was later purchased by Pembroke College. Contemporary with the cesspit, a group of seven late fifteenth- or early sixteenth-century ceramic vessels were also incorporated into the north wall of the College's Old Library. These vessels, which have been interpreted as 'acoustic vases' (Hughes 1915b, 75–6), included a near-complete plain greyware strap-handled jug and a two-handled Cistercian ware cup.

Additional features, much more comparable to those encountered within the Barnwell Gate suburb, have also been identified in Trumpington. During a watching brief conducted within the basements and gardens of 15–19 Trumpington Street, for instance (Fig. 6.1 no. 18), a range of sixteenth–seventeenth-century features were investigated. Along with a cask-lined well a number of large pits were present that appear to have been utilized in an unidentified industrial process. Also associated with this group was a moderately sized faunal assemblage indicative of specialized craft-working activity; this included selective deposits of sheep metacarpals and cattle horn cores. In addition, eight disarticulated human bones were recovered, remains that had probably been disturbed from the cemetery associated with the adjacent hospital of St Anthony and St Eloy. Overall, therefore, despite Trumpington's marked topographical similarity to the Barnwell Gate suburb, a number of social and economic differences can be discerned. Prime amongst these are the presence of high-status masonry structures, a building-type that otherwise appears to have been primarily restricted to the most prosperous areas within the urban core (Cam 1959, 122–3; Willis & Clark 1886 vol. II, 394). There were also a variety of material-types, including coins and imported pottery, which were not encountered at either Grand Arcade or Christ's Lane. Nevertheless, alongside these wealthy high-status households it appears that a highly comparable range of artisanal, craft-based activities were also being undertaken.

A short distance to the west of Trumpington, on the far side of the River Cam, the suburb of Newnham was situated on a small island 'surrounded by fen and osier-beds [willow plantations] intersected by small streams' (Ellis & Salzman 1948e, 282; Fig. 6.1). Here, a small hamlet was recorded in Domesday Book. Its most notable feature was a watermill sited to take advantage of the adjacent river channel. Subsequently, during the twelfth century, the scale of occupation expanded until the settlement was officially recognized as a suburb, although it remained the smallest such area in Cambridge, perhaps due to the physical constraints of its flood-prone, island-based locale. In 1256 a confraternity of Carmelite friars, first established in Chesterton c. 1249, founded a monastery at Newnham. Its precinct – which included a church, a cloister, a dormitory and 'other sufficiently good buildings' (Ellis & Salzman 1948d, 282) – extended up to three acres in area. Nevertheless, around 1292 the Carmelites abandoned the site for a new location in the centre of Cambridge.

To date, three small-scale investigations have been conducted in Newnham (Fig. 6.1, nos. 6, 7, 28). The most significant took place at 34–38 Newnham Road (Hutton & Timberlake 2006; Timberlake & Webb 2006). Here, a substantial fourteenth-century gravel quarry was encountered; it was of undetermined dimensions and measured up to 2.5m deep. Once the gravel had been extracted the pit was flooded and converted into a fishpond. Associated with this latter phase was a sophisticated water management system that utilized fourteenth-century ceramic water pipes. These were produced from Medieval Ely ware. Similar pipes, in the same fabric, have been found at several sites in Ely (Briscoe & Dunning 1967; Spoerry 2008, 64) while comparable products were also manufactured at other centres in East Anglia; notably, however, no equivalent pipes have yet been encountered at any other Cambridge site. The pond itself was initially well-maintained before silting up naturally and being partially infilled. It was much more substantial than any of the water-filled pits that were encountered at Grand Arcade, thereby underlining the specialized nature of its function.

Topographically, the most atypical of Cambridge's five suburbs was that of Barnwell, whereas the Castle Hill, Trumpington and Barnwell Gate suburbs all directly adjoined the town, and the settlement at Newnham lay only a short distance away, around a kilometre of open-fields separated Barnwell from Cambridge (Fig. 6.1). Yet despite its dislocation – a situation that was unusual, although by no means unparalleled, in a national context – Barnwell rapidly developed into the town's most populous medieval suburb. This success can be attributed in no small part to Barnwell Priory, Cambridge's largest and wealthiest monastery, which relocated to Barnwell from Castle Hill c. 1112 (Ellis & Salzman 1948a, 234). Previously the site of an abandoned hermitage (Clark 1907, 40–1), by the early thirteenth century a sizeable settlement had developed outside the priory's gates. In 1279 the Hundred Roll recorded 95 messuages in the suburbium of Barnwell (Illingworth & Caley 1818, 393–401); many more than in most contemporary Cambridgeshire villages. Nevertheless, until recently the area had been the subject of only a limited number of antiquarian observations. Since 2012, however, a sustained program of redevelopment has taken place, engendering a significant program of archaeological excavation. As of 2014, this work is still ongoing. Once complete, the combined area of investigation – incorporating multiple closely adjacent sites – will be highly comparable to that of Grand Arcade.

Of the excavations that have been completed in the suburb to date, two (Fig. 6.1, nos. 22, 24; Atkins 2012) lay outside the principal area of settlement. The third, however – at the Eastern Gate Hotel site (Newman 2013a; Fig. 6.1, no. 23) – encountered an intensive and long-lived occupational sequence (this is also paralleled at several subsequent sites undertaken after this section was written; Atkins 2015a; Atkins 2015b). As the results of this excavation will be published in detail elsewhere, only an outline summary is presented here. Overall, the site is of particular significance because

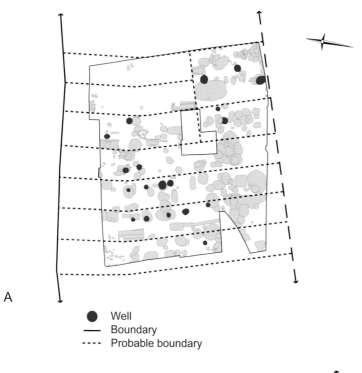

A

● Well
— Boundary
---- Probable boundary

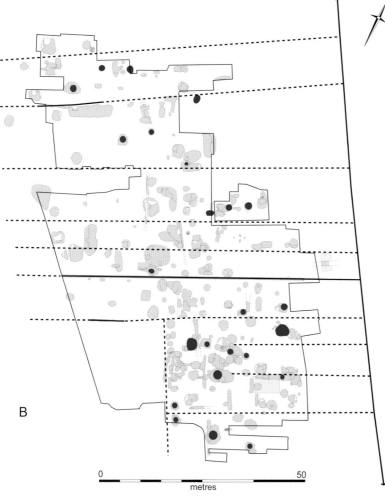

B

0   50
metres

Figure 6.25. *The density and layout of thirteenth–sixteenth-century features at Eastern Gate Hotel (A) compared to those at Grand Arcade (B), illustrating the marked morphological similarities between the long narrow properties at each site, which also holds true for the range and type of features present.*

Table 6.5. *Quantities and densities per ha of selected materials and feature-types from excavations conducted in the Barnwell and Barnwell Gate suburbs (* = estimated from percentage by count assigned to this phase). Note the close similarity between Eastern Gate Hotel and Grand Arcade; the densities at Christ's Lane, in contrast, are 'proto-urban' in character.*

Site	Investigated area (ha)	11th–12th-century pottery (count)	13th–15th-century pottery (count)	16th–17th-century pottery (count)	11th–15th-century animal bone (kg)	11th–15th-century wells (count)	11th–15th-century buildings (count)
Eastern Gate Hotel	0.19	43 (226)	3195 (16,816)	701 (3690)	94 (495)	19 (100)	7 (37)
Grand Arcade	0.70	3558 (5082)	12775 (18,221)	4539 (6484)	479.2* (685)	37 (53)	16 (23)
Christ's Lane	0.018	435 (24,438)	1374 (77,191)	1593 (89,494)	33.5 (1882)	-	6 (337)

it represents the largest suburban investigation aside from Grand Arcade to have been undertaken at Cambridge to date (Fig. 6.25). Moreover, a highly comparable range of feature-types and material assemblages were encountered. Yet, significantly, its developmental sequence was rather different to that identified in the Barnwell Gate suburb. In the early twelfth century, for instance, the area surrounding the newly founded priory remained an unoccupied agricultural hinterland, whereas by this date settlement was already well-established at Grand Arcade and Christ's Lane. Occupation first commenced at Eastern Gate Hotel *c.* 1200, when five long-lived plots were established. Linear in form and with a distinctive bend or twist at their head, each of these plots represents the occupation of a former strip within the preceding open fields. By the early fourteenth century, when a sixth plot was established that was principally industrial in focus, the level of activity at the site appears to have reached its zenith. By the late fifteenth century, however, the suburb seems to have entered a period of decline, a situation that was exacerbated by the dissolution of Barnwell Priory in 1538. Although occupation continued throughout the post-medieval period, the settlement's population was greatly reduced.

Further contrasting with the four preceding suburbs, where occupation largely appears to have developed in a piecemeal, organic fashion – albeit with localized episodes of imposed plot reorganization, as at Grand Arcade in the early twelfth century (Chapter 2) – Barnwell is likely to represent instead a deliberate, planned foundation. Converting agricultural land into domestic plots comprised one of the most effective methods of generating additional revenue in the twelfth and early thirteenth centuries. Consequently, 'plantations' of this type were relatively common (Beresford 1988; Butler 1976) and many wealthy monasteries are known to have established an associated settlement (Aston 2000, 149–52; Beresford 1988, 128–35; Slater 1987). That the settlement at Barnwell was planned does not necessarily equate to it having had an organized or regimented layout. The close morphological similarity of the plots identified at Eastern Gate Hotel, for example – which were much more regular than their contemporaries at Grand Arcade (Fig. 6.24) – may well owe more to the standardized widths of the lands they replaced rather than the existence of a regimented schema imposed by a single organizing agency.

Archaeologically, the results of the Eastern Gate Hotel excavation indicate that a highly comparable range of feature-types, material and environmental assemblages were present in Barnwell to those identified at Grand Arcade. On the one hand, this degree of similarity can be demonstrated via a comparison of the density per hectare of selected elements that were encountered (Table 6.5). From this it is apparent that certain assemblages, such as those of ceramic and faunal material, are closely proportionate; a pattern that is also replicated to a large extent in their relative composition (Newman 2013a). Both are notably different from the more urban pattern represented at Christ's Lane. In addition, the distributions

of the features from which these assemblages were recovered also demonstrate several marked similarities. Linear arrangements of wells can be identified in many instances, for example, as well as discrete clusters of pits (Fig. 6.25). Furthermore, the forms of many of the constituent features – such as the range of wattle-lined, cask-lined and stone-lined wells – are also highly consistent. As well as domestic occupation, evidence of craft/industrial activity was also represented at Eastern Gate Hotel via the presence of numerous clay-lined ovens and clay- and stone-lined tanks as well as highly selective faunal deposits. Overall, therefore, it is clear that the ongoing work at Barnwell has the potential to make a substantive contribution to the broader understanding of suburban archaeology at Cambridge, while detailed analysis of the similarities and differences between the Barnwell and Barnwell Gate suburbs may also provide insights into the wider topic of suburbanism as a whole.

In addition to the five suburbs outlined above, a further area of less well-defined extramural occupation was also present at Cambridge. This was located immediately to the east of the town, in the vicinity of Jesus Lane. Here, the Benedictine nunnery of St Mary and St Radegund had been founded in 1138 (Evans *et al.* 1997; Fig. 6.1). Adjacent to this monastery a small number of medieval properties were established, although it remains unclear whether these plots were directly associated with the nearby institution. The area does not appear to have developed a sufficiently distinct identity to warrant being individuated as a discrete suburb, instead remaining part of a somewhat nebulous 'urban fringe'. It has yet to be investigated archaeologically. Finally, a number of additional satellite villages also developed around the periphery of medieval Cambridge. Three of these villages, in particular – all of which lay a short distance outside the boundary of the liberty of the town – have been the subject of relatively extensive archaeological investigations.

Firstly, to the northeast of Cambridge lay the royal *vill* of Chesterton, where from the eighth century onwards a polyfocal settlement developed alongside the River Cam. This was re-established as a planned, nucleated development in the late eleventh/early twelfth century (Cessford with Dickens 2004). A very similar process of nucleation is known to have occurred at many villages located within the 'Central Province' of England during the eleventh–early thirteenth centuries (Roberts & Wrathmell 2000); Cambridgeshire was situated on the southern periphery of this zone (Jones & Page 2006; Taylor 1977; Taylor 2002). Chesterton's layout was transformed once again *c.* 1200, when the preceding enclosures were replaced by long, narrow rectangular plots, many of which occupied former lands within what had previously been open fields (Newman 2015). It then developed into a highly successful village. The second *vill*, Cherry Hinton, lay to the southeast of Cambridge. Occupation first emerged here during the eighth century. Then, between the late ninth and late eleventh/early twelfth centuries, a large manorial or *thegnly* centre developed (Cessford with Dickens 2005b). This was replaced in turn by a nucleated settlement in the twelfth century (Cessford & Slater 2014). Yet despite being situated a comparable distance from Cambridge to Chesterton, Cherry Hinton did not develop to an equivalent degree. Instead, by the early fifteenth century this rural settlement was in decline and had significantly contracted in size. Finally, to the northwest of Cambridge lay the hamlet of Howes. This was by far the smallest of Cambridge's satellite settlements. Although predominantly agrarian in focus, faunal evidence indicates that some of its occupants may also have had a close association with hunting (Cessford 2015b). Howes was eventually deserted in the early post-medieval period.

Discussion

By extending the field of study beyond the arbitrarily defined boundaries of the Grand Arcade development, this chapter has attempted to counteract the prevailing tendency of commercial urban excavations to exclusively focus upon a single, discrete locale. It is true that in terms of both its scale and the inclusive, 'rooftops-down' methodology that it employed, the work undertaken at Grand Arcade is unprecedented at a regional level. Yet despite the various investigations discussed in this chapter being in no way comparable in either scope or extent, they nevertheless provide a useful perspective on the more detailed work undertaken at the larger site.

Firstly, the Christ's Lane investigations illustrate that several differences existed between neighbouring street blocks within the Barnwell Gate suburb. Freed of the inhibiting influence of the King's Ditch, for example, the plots at Christ's Lane proliferated much more rapidly than those at Grand Arcade; concomitant with this growth, the degree of building coverage also increased significantly. Despite this, however – and, notably, in direct contrast to the Trumpington Gate suburb – no high-status masonry structures were identified. Instead, it appears that the Barnwell Gate's

occupants were predominantly artisanal in character, with the area also retaining a strong agrarian association. Moreover, although the impact of the nearby Dominican friary was no doubt significant (and should not be underestimated), it did not exert the same degree of influence as the much larger and wealthier Augustinian priory that dominated the outlying suburb of Barnwell. Neither was there a significant military/bureaucratic presence comparable to that of the castle which dominated Castle Hill. Finally, the Barnwell Gate suburb was not topographically isolated – like those at Newnham and Barnwell – but instead developed on the town's immediate periphery, along one of its busiest approach roads. This also provided its residents with valuable commercial opportunities.

Altogether, therefore, it appears that, whilst there were undeniably strong similarities between Cambridge's five suburbs, to some extent the Barnwell Gate area also retained its own, unique identity; a significant component of this was its close association with the surrounding East Fields, as well as the adjacent beast market. This brief overview of the archaeology of Grand Arcade's wider environs does have a notable limitation, however. Being predominantly empirical in nature, it does not address any of the broader theoretical issues that arise from such an extensive subject. Questions of taxonomy, for instance, (such as 'what defines a suburb?') as well as more esoteric issues (such as the impact of long-term processes of change, or the relative importance of local versus global trade) remain unexamined. In order to rectify this omission, these and other topics will be explored via a series of thematic essays that together comprise this volume's concluding chapter.

Chapter 7

Coda

Craig Cessford

Global urban archaeology has a long tradition at the University of Cambridge and is currently thriving, with work on the early Mesopotamian, Egyptian, Harrapan and Roman and other civilizations. It is undeniable that most of this work focuses on periods and areas that can be thought of as remote or exotic. Whilst the praxis of studying complex deeply stratified urban sites has much in common, regardless of period or geographical area, there are undoubtedly profound differences when dealing with development-led (as opposed to research-driven) work located in 'living' urban places, rather than sites abandoned in the past. Whilst many investigations of ancient urbanism are highly methodologically and theoretically developed, the focus on the deep past means that archaeology has had relatively little impact on wider urban studies. Groups such as urban geographers and historians overwhelming focus on modern post 1850 cities, leading to a profound 'recentism' (Smith 2009, 114). Arguably the best opportunities to challenge such 'temporal parochialism', from an archaeological perspective are in 'living' urban places with deep and continuous occupational sequences such as Cambridge. Such sites also potentially offer one of the most viable routes for archaeology to affect modern urban issues (Smith 2010).

The McDonald Institute for Archaeological Research was established in 1990, the same year as *Planning Policy Guidance 16: Archaeology and Planning* (PPG16) was introduced in Britain setting out the 'Secretary of State's policy on archaeological remains on land, and how they should be preserved or recorded both in an urban setting and in the countryside'. Without PPG16 it is unlikely that the trench-based evaluation covering 48 sq. m undertaken in the eastern courtyard of the Downing Site in advance of the construction of the Courtyard Building in May 1992 would have taken place (Fig. 7.1A–B; see Chapter 6). On one level the results of this evaluation were underwhelming, with relatively sparse medieval and later artefactual assemblages and a stratigraphic sequence commencing with traces of a deeply truncated and disturbed brown earth soil underlying a medieval ridge-and-furrow agricultural system with shallow *c.* 2.5–3.0m wide furrows. These furrows were associated with both tenth–twelfth- and thirteenth–fourteenth-century ceramics and there was evidence of soil build-up from the fifteenth century onwards. The University Botanic Garden created on the site after 1762 was distinguished only by a few nondescript planting holes, while the only traces associated with the occupation of the site by the University since 1851 at the Downing Site were heating ducts and services associated with the 'Dixon' hut of the Department of Pharmacology erected *c.* 1965. Walter Ernest Dixon (1871–1931) the Reader in Pharmacology, after whom the 'Dixon' hut was named, has been described as 'the man who never was', in the sense of someone who made a seminal contribution but is nonetheless largely forgotten (Cuthbert 2001). The archaeological evaluation in advance of the construction of the McDonald Institute Courtyard Building is in some regards 'the site that never was', as it would not have taken place if the Institute had been founded a few years earlier and after it took place it was effectively forgotten. The evaluation was effectively resurrected in 2005–6, when a very different archaeological investigation took place at the nearby Grand Arcade development. With the benefit of hindsight, perhaps the most interesting thing about the 1992 investigations is how a site located less than a hundred metres from a thriving and densely occupied urban site for many centuries displayed so little evidence for this. The stability of the boundary between the occupied street block and the adjacent fields is remarkable and attests to a concomitant stability of collective urban control over behaviour.

In 2002 Anthony Gormley, who studied Archaeology, Anthropology and History of Art at Trinity

College (1968–71), created the 650kg cast iron sculpture 'Earthbound: Plant' which was initially displayed in Italy. In 2009, between the Grand Arcade excavations and their publication, an unofficial largely playful archaeological watching brief was undertaken when this 185cm tall sculpture of a human body was buried upside down in the eastern courtyard of the Downing Site, just outside the McDonald Institute with only the soles of its feet visible (Fig. 7.1C–D). Gormley stated that '*Sculpture is a form of physical thinking. It is a very conscious decision to remove the body from visual perception and replace it within the body of the earth. It's reverse archaeology if you like, so I am particularly pleased that it has ended up here by the McDonald Institute as I studied just opposite in the Department of Archaeology as an undergraduate. I am very happy to be, disembodiedly, a continuing presence here*'. The generic metaphors are so obvious and numerous that they need not be laboured, however some specific resonances are worth mentioning. The fact that Gormley was a student at Cambridge in 1968–71, the sculpture was created in 2002 and subsequently used elsewhere and only 'deposited' seven years later in 2009 represents a form of temporality or biography with archaeological parallels. Gormley's collegiate connections and the inverted nature of the sculpture also find specific resonances. The sculpture represents a form of secret or hidden knowledge; most passersby appear not to notice it at all, whilst those who do often interpret it as simply a pair of footprints, unaware of the inverted body. Finally although firmly buried the sculpture is technically only on long term loan from the Royal Academy of Arts in London, just as in the long-term all buried material in urban contexts is inherently impermanent.

Despite the small scale of the 1992 Downing Site investigations, an attempt was made to undertake some more academic research. Building on the then relatively nascent field of micromorphological soil studies, samples were taken (Fig. 7.1B), contributing to a substantial corpus of development-led work within Cambridge (Fig. 7.2A–D). By the time the Grand Arcade excavations were undertaken in 2005–6 this corpus was so substantial that the relatively poorly preserved soil sequences were deemed to be not worth sampling, although the tradition of scientific micro-scale analysis was continued with regard to stone mouldings (Fig. 7.2E–K) and ceramics (Fig. 7.2L–S).

In some respects the Grand Arcade excavations were a victim of their own success, the scale of the investigations and the richness of the discoveries posing profound challenges. Although the challenges during fieldwork were daunting, those relating to publication are in some respects more intractable. As a result most of the preceding volume has had to focus on relatively

simple reportage, and makes no apologies for that. Embedded within that, both implicitly or explicitly, are broader themes of long-term and global significance. Throughout the majority of this volume a linear, chronological structure has been adopted. This contrasts with the initial grey literature where a more spatial plot-based approach was adopted (Cessford 2007; Dickens & Baggs 2009) and it would have been possible to produce a more spatially orientated publication. Whilst the chronological approach eventually adopted possesses a number of strengths, it also has weaknesses, both general and specific. In recognition of specific issues, both the King's Ditch and the Robert Sayle department store were effectively placed outside it, while more general issues are addressed below (see Temporality and biography). By discussing the sequence on a period-by-period basis, patterns of on-going change and development can be clearly elucidated. This is particularly important when analysing a long-lived and intensively occupied site such as Grand Arcade. Secondly, by grouping various categories of material together on a temporal basis, interconnections can potentially be made between relatively diverse datasets, thereby allowing a detailed and highly nuanced analysis to be undertaken. Yet such a structure also has a significant weakness. Certain issues fall largely outside a period-specific purview, as they are predominately thematic as opposed to temporal in nature. Examples include general topics (such as the nature of suburbanism, for example) as well as particular issues (such as the inhabitants' age and gender). The impact of long-term processes, which span multiple periods, can also be significantly obfuscated. This chapter is intended to redress that imbalance. Here, a number of themes that have arisen within the preceding text – either as recurrent elements, analogous in many ways to the strains of an overarching melody, or oblique references, mentioned only in passing – will be examined in greater detail.

Overall, the archaeological sequence encountered at both Grand Arcade and Christ's Lane was relatively

Figure 7.1 *(opposite). The Downing Site courtyard: (A) trench-based evaluation in advance of the construction of the Courtyard Building of the McDonald Institute for Archaeological Research in 1992, facing northwest; (B) Charles French, now Professor in Geoarchaeology of the Department of Archaeology & Anthropology, taking micromorphological samples in 1992, facing northeast; (C) Anthony Gormley sculpture 'Earthbound: Plant' being lowered into position in 2009, with the Courtyard Building of the McDonald Institute for Archaeological Research visible in the background, facing southeast; (D) view of the 'Earthbound: Plant' sculpture in 2016.*

A

B

C

D

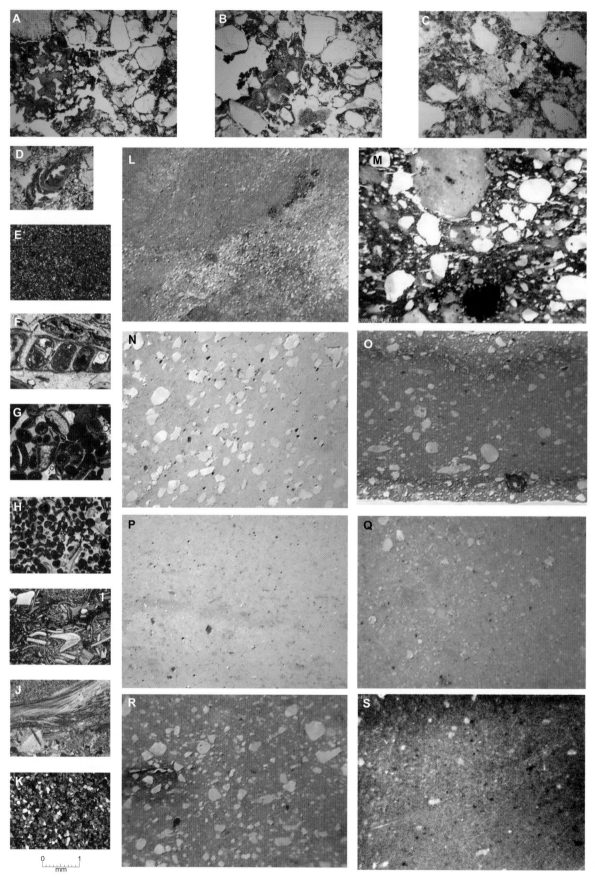

straightforward. Anthropogenic activity commenced with the clearance of the preceding woodland environment during the Neolithic period, although the earliest identifiable feature was Middle Iron Age in date. It was during the mid-eleventh century, however, that the area first emerged as a distinct *place* rather than merely an arbitrary *space*; a transformation that was brought about by the establishment of long-lived domestic occupation. Indeed, from the eleventh century to the present a largely unbroken sequence has prevailed (a situation that continues to this day, despite the substantial redevelopments of 2005–6). The excavation methodology at both sites was designed to reflect this longevity.

Features of all periods, up to and including the twentieth century, were investigated equally and all material assemblages were treated in a similar manner. A comparable approach was also adopted during the standing building investigation, with all

Figure 7.2 *(opposite). Microscopic scale analysis: (A–D) micromorphology images of soils in and around Cambridge, all plane polarized light; (A) iron-phosphate concretion and dusty/organic sandy loam in a sample from St John's College Chapel Court and Master's Garden; (B) mixed fabrics of organic or Ah sandy loam and sandy/silty B horizon material in a sample from St John's College Chapel Court and Master's Garden; (C) dirty sandy loam fabric of a disturbed brown earth in a sample from Bene't Court; (D) crescentic pure to dusty clay infills in dusty fabric material in a sample from St John's College Chapel Court and Master's Garden; (E–K) Photomicrographs of moulded stone; (E) Clunch (also known as Burwell stone and Totternhoe stone), from the lining of Well 42; (F) Barnack stone (Oolitic Limestone) from the footing of Wall 6; (G) Weldon stone from Christ's Lane Well F.312; (H) Ancaster freestone from the footing of Wall 6; (I) Derbyshire Fossil Limestone from the footing of Wall 10; (J) Alwalton Marble from the lining of Well 36; (K) 'Mansfield Red' red sandstone from the lining of Cesspit 17; (L–S) Photomicrographs of ceramic fabrics; (L) Brick fabric LZ 15.2 from footings of Wall 12; (M) Tile fabric TZ 21 from fill of the King's Ditch F.5198; (N) Brick fabric LZ 142.2 from basement wall of the main Robert Sayle building; (O) Flowerpot produced in or around Ely and marked with initials of William Newby from fill of Well 37; (P) Yellow fabric flowerpot produced in Cambridge from 'abandonment' of Planting Bed 8; (Q) Flowerpot produced by Sankey's of Bulwell from Foundation 4; (R) Glazed Red Earthenware produced in or around Ely from the fill of Cellar 4; (S) Sunderland-type coarseware from backfill of Building 49 (images A–D courtesy of Charles French, E–K courtesy of Kevin Hayward and L–S courtesy of Alan Vince).*

structures being recorded to an equivalent degree. Such methodologies, especially when taken alongside the incorporation of oral history into the project, extend into the realm of the archaeology of the 'contemporary past' (Buchli & Lucas 2001; for more recent debates, see Harrison 2011; Harrison & Schofield 2010). This effectively represents the culmination of a trend in British urban archaeology over the last half century, whereby later and later periods have come to be regarded as constituting meaningful archaeology.

The progressive assimilation of more and more recent periods contrasts starkly with what might be regarded, paradoxically, as the more 'traditional' archaeology of the contemporary past. The latter can be viewed as an – often self-consciously – avant-garde movement, which effectively leap-frogged several centuries by studying modern, late twentieth-century material culture at a time when the nineteenth and early twentieth centuries were being largely ignored. This in turn created a fault line separating the field from the archaeological mainstream, in a manner similar to that which once pertained to Industrial Archaeology. With the bridging of this gap, many of the inherent contradictions and problems associated with both the traditional archaeological study of the past, as something separate from the present, and the archaeology of the contemporary past effectively disappear. This means that the Grand Arcade and Christ's Lane investigations, when viewed from a static 2005–6 'present', can be seen as 'archaeological intervention[s] in the past, present and future tense' (Rathje 2011).

Whilst in many regards this theoretical stance has a minor impact on the results presented in this volume – since it can, by and large, be viewed as a traditional developer-funded excavation report – at a deeper level it poses fundamental questions about the disciplinary nature of archaeology itself. These questions cannot of course be answered, or even substantively addressed, here. Rather, this chapter represents an opportunity to examine eight key themes that arise from the recent excavations in light of this broader methodological standpoint. The themes selected for analysis are by no means exhaustive; the substantive nature of the results means that a wide variety of topics are available for examination. Those chosen for discussion here are simply regarded as the most pertinent to the wider topics with which this volume has been engaged. The themes consist of temporality and biography, the nature of suburban archaeology, the impact of almost exclusively investigating property tails, the nature of change over a millennium or so, age and gender, the archaeology of modernity, the local and the global, town versus gown and odd deposits and average practice.

Temporality and biography

Whilst it is often argued that sequence is all in urban archaeology, this is at best a partial truth. Equally if not more important is contemporaneity, identifying which features were in active existence at the same time. Whilst stratification and archaeological tools such as the Harris matrix can identify sequence they cannot absolutely identify contemporaneity, only constrain possibilities (Lucas 2015, 2–7). Most features in urban archaeology can be broadly categorized as short-lived or long-lived, at least in terms of their active existence. For example the active phase of a quarry pit might be the course of a few hours or a single day whilst it is dug, whereas a well might be in use as a source of water for decades or centuries. Both types of feature then have after-lives as receptacles for material, although intriguingly their temporal span is often reversed with long-lived features like wells typically being rapidly and deliberately backfilled in an urban context while short-lived features like quarry pits are often backfilled over prolonged periods of months if not years. For long-lived features in particular, sequence and contemporaneity become complex entities, with a range of possible temporal relationships that are not usually properly addressed (although it could be argued that there are up to 13 distinct possibilities: Lucas 2015, 5–6). It is effectively impossible to do justice to this level of temporal complexity in the presentation of a large-scale long-term urban site such as Grand Arcade, but it is important to remember that the broad linear temporal narrative that is presented is a simplification of a profoundly more nuanced reality.

Even this level of temporal complexity underplays the reality of the archaeological record. Artefacts are manufactured, used and deposited, or in biographical terms are 'born', go through various stages of 'life' and then 'die' (Kopytoff 1986), leading to the archaeological concept of the 'object biography' (Joy 2009). Artefacts therefore have a more complex temporality than just that of the archaeological context where they 'die'. This concept of 'object biography' can also be extended to groups of material, creating 'assemblage biographies'. Recent examples of such 'assemblage biographies' include material as diverse as pottery in Bronze Age pits (Blanco-González 2014), hoards of Iron Age torcs (Joy 2016) and nineteenth-century groups (Cessford 2014a; Cessford 2014c), all of which demonstrate that synergistically the whole can be greater than the sum of its parts. Such assemblage biographies have typically been applied to small portable items of material culture, yet it is also clear that, particularly in an urban context, structural elements such as stone blocks and timbers can also possess biographies of previous use,

creating a form of 'feature biography'. Material based archaeological biographies – be they object, assemblage or feature – are necessarily partial as they relate to what was recovered. Urban sites should, however, be conceptualized as locales that people and objects move through on various timescales and then generally leave via conduits of divestment (Gregson *et al.* 2007) or dispersal (Lucas 2014). Temporality does not exist in isolation; often it has spatial and social correlates, with movement in one also relating to movement in the others. These other aspects are equally complex. To take just one example, a well initially constructed in an open yard area might decades later be located within a built up zone or even within a building. Whilst such a well has not moved in Cartesian space its nature is nonetheless profoundly different. In another example, some assemblages of material deposited at the same time contain creamware where the earliest vessels were produced by Wedgwood in the 1760s and 1770s, while later vessels were produced by other manufacturers in the 1780s. The earlier vessels represent the height of fashion; creamware was refined by Wedgwood in *c.* 1762 and was famously supplied to Queen Charlotte in 1765. By 1778, however, it was 'no longer the choice thing it used to be, since every shop, house, and cottage is full of it' (Finer & Savage 1965, 220–1), and following the introduction of pearlware in 1779 it became much commoner and less socially exclusive. Although often almost undistinguishable physically, different creamware vessels in a single depositional group may have been radically different socio-economic entities when purchased.

Suburban archaeology

Urban archaeology has begun to address the concept of 'urbanity' or 'urban living', focussing upon materiality, practices and social processes to consider urban centres as dynamic social spaces affected by diverse everyday routines (Christophersen 2015). If 'urbanity' in this sense exists then it is concomitant that 'rurality' must have and perhaps also 'sub urbanity'. The Barnwell Gate suburb existed as a recognizable entity for around seven centuries, between the creation of the King's Ditch during the early/mid-twelfth century and the infilling of this feature in the late eighteenth century. Its identity as a discrete, self-contained area was finally obscured by the wholesale expansion of Cambridge into the surrounding East Fields during the early/mid-nineteenth century. The substantial excavations conducted at Grand Arcade mean that this site in particular can make an important contribution to our broader understanding of British suburbs. Studies of medieval towns have often concentrated on their

Peripheral biographies

The archaeological record investigated at Grand Arcade was in a sense the cumulative palimpsest of the actions of many thousands of individuals. It would be possible to construct fictionalized biographies for any of these linked specific aspects of the archaeology, but there are also numerous instances where named individuals can be linked to objects, features or buildings. The temptation would be to pick someone who had a substantial and unambiguous material impact, such as Sarah Dobson, Samuel Ekin, Richard Hopkins, Edward Jay, William Mayland or William Newby. Whilst the biographies or microhistories of these and other individuals are already present in the volume (although admittedly all could be substantially expanded) it is perhaps more apposite here to consider individuals whose archaeological presence can be viewed as more peripheral, as for every individual whose archaeological presence is relatively strong there are likely to have been many more whose presence is weaker.

Barnett Leach III (1737–92) and his son Barnett Leach IV (1764–1814) were cooks at Trinity College (1770–1812/14) and ceramics that they ordered from Staffordshire were found in several features at Grand Arcade (Fig. 7.3). Barnett Leach I, the grandfather of Barnett Leach III, and his wife Margaret moved to St Andrew's Street in 1675, whilst subsequent generations of the family who lived in Cambridge included Richard Hopkins Leach (1794–1851), the son of Barnett Leach IV, a jobbing artist best known locally as a painter of inn signs and his son Frederick Leach (1837–1904), Cambridge's finest master 'artworkman' who worked with William Morris and locally undertook work in several Colleges and churches.

There is no evidence that either Barnett Leach III or IV lived in the Grand Arcade street block; instead their pottery passed through several stages after the death of Barnett Leach IV before it was deposited. Other ceramics associated with Barnett Leach III and IV have been recovered at the Spode factory in Stoke-on-Trent, where they were manufactured, during investigations linked to the construction of a library bookstore at Trinity College, near where the ceramics were used, and in Barnwell *c.* 1.5km away from the College. These discoveries create a sense of temporal and spatial flow and biography linked to the ceramics ordered by Barnett Leach III and IV over four decades, albeit an insubstantial one given that they must have purchased thousands of marked plates. Barnett Leach III also has a rather different material biography, as his descendants still possess a portrait of him on a box lid surrounded by quill work (Fig. 7.3) and a pair of silver buckles that he owned, which have passed through several generations of the family as heirlooms.

Pottery linked to Barnett Leach III or IV was also found in an assemblage at Grand Arcade, which was linked primarily to the Newby family and deposited *c.* 1840–60. As the Newby family only moved to Cambridge *c.* 1820 there is no possibility of any direct interaction between them and Barnett Leach III or IV. The material in this later assemblage attests primarily to the adults William and Elizabeth Newby; despite them having three daughters and a son there is no material that can be unambiguously linked to their children. The temptation is therefore to see the deposition of this assemblage and the 'death' of the artefacts in terms of the literal death of William Newby (*c.* 1798–1852) or the metaphorical death of the household when Elizabeth Newby (*c.* 1812–76) moved away (*c.* 1852–8). It is, however, possible to conceptualize the 'death' of the artefacts as merely an early stage in the life of the Newby children. Their son William John Newby (1836–1933) left England in 1860 to serve as a lieutenant and later captain with a group of British volunteers in the *Risorgimento* or Italian war of unification. He subsequently returned briefly to Britain, presumably spending at least some time in Cambridge with his mother, before departing for New Zealand in 1865. In New Zealand he fought in the Second Taranaki War against the native Māori population (1864–7), took part unsuccessfully in the gold rush to the Thames goldfields, was a farmer in the Tapu district and then moved to Auckland in 1907 where he lived until his death, by which time he had 10 surviving children, 33 grandchildren and 14 great-grandchildren, some of whom are still alive today.

In terms of materiality there is no evidence that William John Newby retained any items from his childhood in Cambridge. When he left for New Zealand in 1865 he took with him a hat box, a pair of skates and a box of cricket gear, with his bats and wicket keeping pads. Later his 'greatest treasures' are described as being a photograph of Garibaldi, the badges of the Italian campaign, a letter from the officers and men he served with

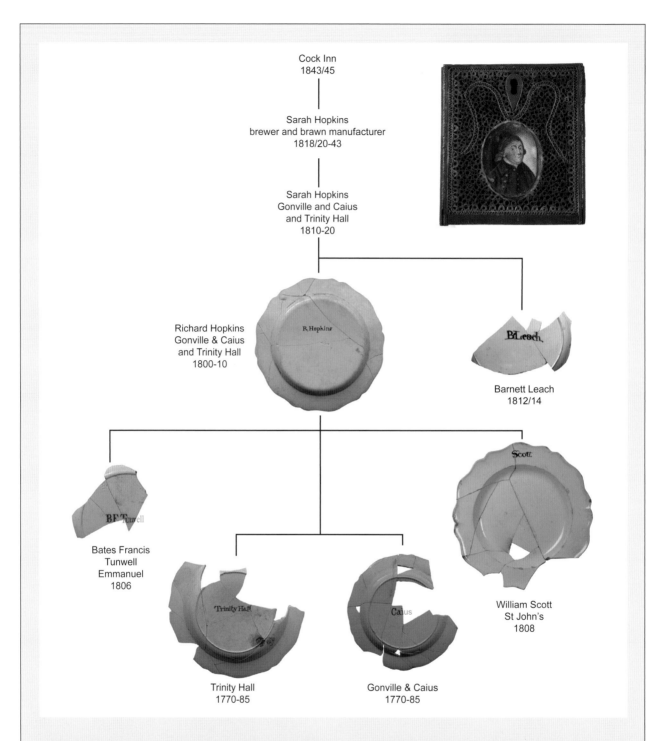

Figure 7.3. *Representation of the biography of collegiate ceramics deposited at the Cock Inn c. 1843–5 and portrait of Barnett Leach III on a box lid surrounded by quill work (photograph of box lid courtesy of Ric Leach).*

and an 'interesting relic', the 'sword he carried in the Italian campaign'. He also received telegrams on his 100th birthday from the King and Queen, as well as Mussolini, and was presented with a pipe plus tobacco and an engraved pewter pot or silver cup (the sources vary) by the Auckland Working Mens Club. The cricket gear that William John Newby took to New Zealand is, in a sense, a form of a link to Cambridge, as he must have learnt the game as a boy and played a single match of cricket for Cambridge Town Club in 1858–9. His other links to Cambridge were less tangible, including 'vivid memories of sporting affairs at Cambridge University and [he] has looked forward each year to the Oxford-Cambridge boat race. Photographs of winning Cambridge crews adorn his walls, and news of a victory by his University has always been a source of great delight to him'. Additionally William could 'remember the houses in the streets of that time [i.e. his childhood] and in many cases the names of residents and shopkeepers'.

Barnett Leach III and IV and William John Newby are at most peripheral players in the archaeological Grand Arcade narrative(s). In terms of a fully fledged global historical archaeology individuals will be linked to multiple locations during their lifetime. Whilst their documented and archaeological connections to some sites may be strong, it would be a methodological weakness to focus exclusively on these and ignore the multi-sited nature of past individual realities. The obvious risk with pursuing such weak linkages is the issue of when connections become so diffuse that they are effectively meaningless. New Zealand has featured in anecdotes and metaphors used in other Cambridge Archaeological unit publications concerned with the Iron Age and Romano-British fenland sites (Evans 2003, 250: Evans, 2013, 479–81). The archaeological connection between Grand Arcade and New Zealand is more direct – temporally at least – that these other examples, but it remains to be seen if it is truly more meaningful, given that it exists only because of documentary sources and is not inherent in anything that was excavated.

defences and intramural areas, viewing the extramural suburban spaces as both literally and metaphorically peripheral and liminal. This has often involved a stereotypically negative view of such areas, one that is principally derived from documentary sources. This view is perhaps best exemplified by Geoffrey Chaucer's *Canon's Yeoman's Tale* (c. 1380–1400), where the suburbs were described as a place for:

> Lurking in corners and in alleys blind
> Wherein these thieves and robbers, every kind
> Have all their privy fearful residence
> As those who dare not show men their presence

Yet this is not the impression gained from the archaeological investigations conducted within the Barnwell Gate suburb, although admittedly an element of criminality is archaeologically apparent.

It has been stated that 'in the suburban context above all, concrete knowledge of our medieval towns can frequently be sought only with the spade' (Keene 1976, 82). Furthermore, 'detailed studies of suburbs combining archaeological evidence with the documentary evidence' have long been advocated (e.g. Barley 1976b, 83; also Crossley 1990, 82–4; Keene 1976; Phythian-Adams 1977; Schofield & Vince 2003, 66–8), with sites located on principal suburban streets identified as a particular priority (Perring 1986). Although there have been general considerations of the suburbs of individual towns such as Northampton (Foard 1995), as well as numerous archaeological investigations undertaken within medieval suburbs – including those of

Dublin (O'Donovan 2003), Lincoln (Steane 2006; Vince in Jones *et al.* 2003, 218–47), Northampton (Shaw 1997), Norwich (Atkin 2002; Shelley 2005), Oxford (Bateman *et al.* 2004; Durham 1978; Palmer 1980; Roberts 1997), Trim (Stephens 2009), Uxbridge (Knight & Jeffries 2004), Warwick (Cracknell 1990), Winchester (Collis & Barton 1978; Rees *et al.* 2008; Serjeantson & Rees 2009) and Worcester (Dalwood *et al.* 1994) – to date there has been little synthesis of this data. In particular, few such investigations have explicitly considered the suburban nature of these sites or compared them to the towns with which they were associated. Most publications have been essentially descriptive, often treating the excavations as if they were generic urban sites.

The Barnwell Gate suburb, like all of Cambridge's medieval suburbs, fell under the town's municipal administration and jurisdiction. The reason for this is that the suburbs lay within the wider extent of the town fields, which also lay within the municipal jurisdiction and were established during the ninth–tenth centuries – well before the suburbs themselves existed. This situation appears to have been universally accepted and remained effectively unchallenged; as a result, the documents are almost entirely mute concerning the suburbs. Some indications of their status during the medieval period can however be gleaned. Firstly, from 1313 onwards legal documents relating to Cambridge frequently referred to the 'town and suburbs' together, indicating that the same rules and regulations applied to both areas, with no evidence of an administrative distinction. Secondly, from 1270 onwards a group composed of 10 burgesses was created in order to keep

413

the peace between the University and town. Three of the members of this group were recruited from the suburbs, thereby underlining the relative importance of these areas within the town's overall composition.

By the early post-medieval period, a small number of documentary sources indicate that the urban core received differential treatment from the suburbs. In 1543–4 the paving of town streets extended only part way along St Andrew's Street, thereby creating a very obvious transition (Cooper 1843, 409), whilst in 1575 it was stated that middens in the suburbs did not have to be cleared as frequently as those located in the town centre (Cooper 1843, 332). Nevertheless, economically and socially the suburbs appear to have remained an integral component of the town. Indeed, it is unclear to what extent, if any, the Barnwell Gate suburb itself possessed an individual identity that rendered it distinct from the remainder of Cambridge (although the parish church is likely to have been the centre of a relatively discrete community). The physical extent of the town's suburbs was not explicitly defined until 1561, when it was stated that they extended 'one English mile around the town in every direction' (Cooper 1843, 168). In national terms, this is relatively modest. At tenth-century Winchester, for example, the suburbs extended up to 6.2 miles from the urban core. It is however clear that the suburbanized zone extended well beyond the outer settlement fringe.

Across England generally, many suburbs appear to have reached their maximum extent during the twelfth century (Keene 1976). This initial phase of expansion was then succeeded by one of consolidation, a pattern that on the whole continued until the fourteenth century (although the character of many suburbs altered in the thirteenth century with the arrival of the mendicant orders and the proliferation of hospitals). Subsequently, the fourteenth–fifteenth centuries represented a period of widespread change and contraction, following which the succeeding patterns of development were often highly variable. Although a useful guide, such broad patterns are archaeologically problematic. This is because, on the one hand, the identifiable correlates of growth and decline may be relatively subtle, whilst on the other the majority of suburban excavations are restricted in scale. By excavating only a single property – or even less, a portion of a property – the overall pattern may not be revealed. Moreover, many individual plots are known to have progressed through a series of 'burgage cycles', wherein a pattern of gradual intensification was succeeded by a clearance event followed by a subsequent redevelopment cycle (Conzen 1960, 27). A broadly comparable notion also underpins the rather less well-defined archaeological theory of a

'development cycle' (*e.g.* Ayers 2000, 28). Yet it must not be presumed that individual property cycles can be directly correlated to wider patterns that prevailed within larger units such as street blocks, suburbs or towns. Too many variables existed at a localized, plot-specific level.

A variety of evidence pertaining to the archaeology of English suburbs has already been presented in this volume (Chapters 4–6). The key facets of this data as they relate to Grand Arcade are summarized here in tabular form (Table 7.1). Utilizing this material, it is possible to examine the potential differences that may have arisen between suburban sites and those that existed contemporaneously in both urban and rural contexts. Such a discussion is of course inherently problematic. Although it is a relatively simple matter to identify and label both the Grand Arcade and Christ's Lane excavations as 'suburban' on purely topographical grounds, it is less straightforward to determine what this means archaeologically. Can a suburb, defined here as a distinct entity with clearly demarcated boundaries, be distinguished from a more nebulous development situated around an urban fringe, for example? Furthermore, it also appears that many of the differences which existed between comparable urban and rural sites were relatively subtle in nature (Giles & Dyer 2005). Nevertheless, a comparison of the excavations undertaken within the Barnwell Gate suburb with contemporary sites excavated in both central Cambridge and nearby satellite villages does shed some light on the issue. Suburban sites, which occupy a form of middle ground between town and country, have the potential to act as a fulcrum in such debates; in particular, they challenge simplistic rural versus urban binary oppositions by stressing that medieval settlements ranged across a much more complex continuum.

Whilst it would be possible to use deductive reasoning to construct a model for likely differences between urban and suburban sites, an inductive approach has been adopted here. This is because the available evidence is predominately empirical in nature. Archaeological differences between urban and suburban sites have previously been identified at a number of British sites. Firstly, in Heigham, Norwich, the medieval pottery was dominated by steep-sided bowls rather than the cooking pots that are more common in the urban core, possibly relating to the importance of dairying (Atkin 2002, 233). There was also less imported continental pottery and the overall layout and features were more 'akin to a farmyard', with a yard and indications of animal traffic (Atkin 2002, 233). At the Hamel, Oxford, meanwhile, there was evidence for the temporary penning of sheep, with the presence of two sheep in a ditch and the identification

Table 7.1. *Potential indicators of rural, suburban and/or urban characteristics within the archaeological evidence recovered from Grand Arcade.*

Type of evidence	Date	Character
Arrangement of frontage buildings	12th onwards	Unknown
Stratigraphic depth	12th onwards	Suburban
Rarity of ditches	12th onwards	Urban/ suburban
Plot width	12th onwards	Urban
Relatively dispersed arrangement of features	12th–18th	Rural/ suburban
Absence of wells over 3m deep	12th–18th	Rural/ suburban
Individual property wells	12th–19th	Suburban
Individual property cesspits	12th–19th	Rural/ suburban
Rows of pits	12th	Rural/ suburban
Moderate density of refuse	12th–16th	Suburban
Relative absence of metalworking	12th–16th	Non-suburban
Scythe and hay rake	12th	Rural/ suburban
Low rate of burning on brick and tile	12th–15th	Rural/ suburban
Storage of large piles of timber on plot	12th–16th	Rural/ suburban
'Cut-it-yourself' wood	12th–14th	Rural/ suburban
Near equal frequencies of cattle and sheep	12th–16th	Local factors
Absence of live sheep	12th–15th	Urban/ suburban
Poached venison	12th–14th	Rural/ suburban
Field vole	12th	Rural/ suburban
'Producer' type botanical remains	12th–16th	Rural/ suburban

Type of evidence	Date	Character
Proportion of synanthropic insects	12th–16th	Unknown
Proportion of tree and cereal pollen	12th–16th	Unknown
Water-filled features	13th–15th	Rural/ suburban
Cooking pots commoner than deep sided bowls	13th–15th	Urban/ suburban
Light tanning, bone and horn working	13th–18th	Suburban
Gravel quarrying continuing	14th–16th	Rural/ suburban
Clay quarrying	14th–15th	Rural/ suburban
Disposal of complete or near complete jugs	14th–15th	Urban/ suburban
Disposal of complete or near complete bowls	14th–15th	Rural/ suburban
Disposal of horses and cows	14th–18th	Rural/ suburban
Structures for malting/drying corn	15th–16th	Rural/ suburban
Boundary of paved and unpaved streets	16th	Suburban
Less frequent midden clearance	16th	Rural/ suburban
White-tailed eagle	16th	Rural/ suburban
High rate of burning on brick and tile	16th–17th	Urban/ suburban
Presence of dairy cattle	17th–18th	Rural/ suburban
Keeping of pigs	18th–19th	Rural/ suburban
Large open areas available for 'urban' development	19th	Suburban

of Sheep keds (*Melophagus ovinus*), blood-feeding parasites that live on the sheep (Palmer 1980, 204–5, 208–9). There was also evidence for different arrangements of buildings than in the town core, especially on the frontage, which are indicative of less pressure on space (Palmer 1980, 225).

More locally, the overall form of the Barnwell Gate suburb itself was constrained by the adjacent road network, the King's Ditch and the surrounding common fields. The resultant ribbon development represents perhaps the most common form of medieval British suburb. One of the major themes in studies of suburbs is how their contraction and expansion reflects the overall fortunes of the town with which they are associated (Keene 1976). The early twelfth-century planned layout of the Barnwell Gate suburb certainly indicates that this was a period of significant growth for Cambridge; however, after this there is relatively little evidence for either contraction or expansion. This somewhat unusual situation can partially be explained by the inherent difficulties of expanding out into the common fields, while the presence of the nearby Dominican Friary may also have inhibited further commercial development (*e.g.* Keene 1976, 81).

The size of the suburb was typical for its time, as by the later twelfth century built-up areas often extended several hundred yards beyond town boundaries, although some much longer examples are known.

Furthermore, many suburbs are known to have reached their greatest extent in the twelfth century (Keene 1976, 78–9) and it is perhaps the lack of evidence of subsequent decline that is more significant. The presence of the University introduced a strong local element of economic stability, insulating Cambridge from factors that might otherwise have led to decline. The four-teenth–fifteenth-century expansion of the University between the High Street and the river must have displaced the inhabitants of this area to other parts of the town, counteracting any falls in population. Although there is evidence for fluctuations in the prosperity of individual properties, these are quite specific and do not appear to reflect general suburb-wide trends. This suggests that patterns identified from smaller excavations – which were restricted in scale to a single plot, or only part of a plot – may be misleading. Eventually, major expansion did occur, initially within the existing street blocks in the eighteenth century and then into the wider East Fields during the nineteenth century.

There is no evidence for standardized property widths within the Grand Arcade and Christ's Lane street blocks. The range of widths present, of c. 4–9m, is broadly comparable to urban properties in central Cambridge, but much less than in the rural or possibly suburban context of West Fen Road, Ely (Fig. 7.4). Some street blocks in the town centre were apparently laid out with a standardized property width of 28ft (c. 8.5m) and possibly a length of 65ft (c. 19.8m), thereby covering c. 170 sq. m. But the triangular nature of the Grand Arcade street block led to a wide variation in property lengths and areas. The smallest properties, at c. 200 sq. m, were broadly comparable to those in the town centre, but the longest properties, at over 1000 sq. m, were markedly larger. Indeed, the latter are comparable in size to some local rural properties, notably those at West Fen Road, Ely, where the ditched enclosures were typically 45–60m wide and 1000–4000 sq. m in area (Mortimer *et al.* 2005, 116), although morphologically many of the Grand Arcade properties comprised narrow rectangles rather than squares.

Such large properties were rare in the town core, although some did exist where the reclamation of low-lying wet areas meant that unusually long properties were created. Overall, the size of a property appears to have had a marked impact on the nature of the activities that could take place within it. The range of property sizes at Grand Arcade would suggest that a simple urban versus suburban dichotomy may be inappropriate, and that small versus large properties are also a factor. This distinction also appears to have engendered differences between street blocks within the same suburb; the more constrained plots at Christ's Lane, for example, appear to have been rather more

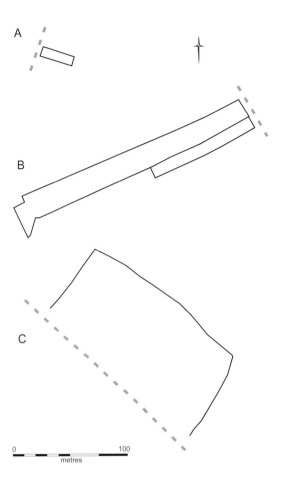

Figure 7.4. *Morphological differences between suburban, urban and rural plot-types: (A) a constricted urban plot, from the Old Divinity School site in Cambridge's central core; (B) the longest and shortest narrow rectangular suburban plots from the Grand Arcade site; (C) a spacious sub-rectangular rural plot from West Fen Road, Ely.*

'urban' in character than those at Grand Arcade. This difference was further exacerbated by the fact that while the Grand Arcade street block possessed only a single significant street frontage, Christ's Lane had at least three, thereby making it more akin to street blocks situated in the urban core.

The lack of complete building exposures from the suburb means that it is impossible to determine whether its constituent structures were identifiably 'urban' in form; especially given that medieval urban housing was not simply an adaptation of rural housing, as originally proposed by Pantin (1963), but instead consisted of distinctive, varied and innovative arrangements (Grenville 2008; Pearson 2005; Pearson 2009). Yet some feature-types that were present appear to have been simply too large to have been accommodated in an urban environment. The most obvious example of this phenomenon are ditches. Such features are commonly encountered locally on rural sites such as Cottenham (Mortimer 2000) and West Fen Road, Ely (Mortimer *et al.* 2005, 116–20), where they appear to have been used to define almost all property boundaries.

In Cambridge itself, however, ditches only appear to have been employed to define the perimeter of street blocks. Had they been used to define the divisions between properties then they would have occupied at least 20 per cent of the available space, an unacceptably high proportion. Instead, such boundaries appear to have been defined by more ephemeral fence lines and hedges, the latter indicated by pollen evidence for privet. In this respect, therefore, Grand Arcade appears to have been relatively urban in nature. There are, however, some large features – most notably the 11m long and nearly 3m wide mid-fourteenth-century *WFF 2* – which simply would not have fitted into most town centre properties (although it is questionable whether this can be categorized as a truly 'rural' element, since its rectangular shape was probably determined by the long narrow property within which it lay).

It also appears that, irrespective of size, roughly the same number of quarry pits was excavated per century in each investigated property at Grand Arcade, presumably because they represent a property-specific requirement for gravel. This means that, while the individual quarry pits themselves were similar, their relative density varied quite markedly on a plot-by-plot basis. Furthermore, although the available gravel in shorter properties was exhausted relatively rapidly, often by around the fourteenth century, in larger properties the resource proved more sustainable. In certain properties, for example, quarrying activity continued into the sixteenth century, even though by this date many neighbouring tenants had become reliant on pits situated in the common fields. Indeed, in the largest properties it appears that quarrying eventually ceased, not because the gravel was exhausted, but because the increasing depth of garden soil made it impractical to obtain. Finally, there is very little evidence for the linear arrangements of pits that comprise such a common feature of densely occupied medieval urban sites (Schofield & Vince 2003, 80–2), and those rows that did exist appear to have largely predated the intensive occupation of the area.

A further significant factor is that almost all of the properties at Grand Arcade appear to have maintained their own individual well right up until the introduction of piped mains water during the latter part of the nineteenth century. Yet there is archaeological evidence to suggest that this was not case in the town centre, and a lease of 1333 in St Benet's parish refers to a half-share in a well being leased. This pattern may again reflect the differing pressures on space in different areas. In addition, communal wells had to supply larger quantities of water, which typically led to them being deeper. Just such a well, which was a minimum of three casks deep, was encountered during the Christ's Lane development, further reinforcing the impression that the latter street block was more densely occupied than that of Grand Arcade. Rural wells, in contrast, frequently appear to have been rather different in form, with wide upper cones and only a partially lined shaft (Mortimer *et al.* 2005, 129). Wells of this form would have been impractical on narrow urban properties. It also appears that the *ad hoc* reuse of various types of timber rather than wheel felloes as well baseplates may be an urban phenomenon, implying that broken or surplus wheels were more common in the countryside. In the context of this discussion, it is also worth remembering that the area to the north and west of the King's Ditch, although technically situated inside the town, contained no wells and that it constituted a much larger open space – right up until the 1970s – than any part of the suburb itself.

Another distinctive suburban feature-type was the animal disposal pits. Although dogs and cats were routinely disposed of in town centre properties, horses and cattle were not. In part this is a reflection of the size of pit required to dispose of such large animals, but it also relates to the fact that cattle would not have been frequently taken into the centre of town; while horses would have been common, stabling facilities were predominately concentrated around the outskirts. The late seventeenth–early eighteenth-century cattle in Plot XXII were probably part of a 'flying herd', where animals from the countryside were brought as close to the town as possible to supply milk to its population; a distinctively suburban phenomenon that was part of a strand interlinking a rural-urban agricultural continuum.

In terms of material culture, there are no discernible differences between sites situated in central Cambridge and nearby rural sites of the medieval period; a pattern that is also prevalent nationally (Egan 2005b; Mellor 2005). Late medieval probate inventories indicate that there were distinctions between urban and rural material culture, but the elements that show the most marked differences – such as silver spoons, cushions and furnishings (Goldberg 2008) – are largely absent from archaeological deposits. The relative importance of some of the more archaeologically common items, such as kitchen utensils, also varies, but this is a relatively subtle distinction given the nature of the archaeological evidence. There are, however, some possibly significant patterns at Grand Arcade. A few items, such as the twelfth-century scythe and hay rake, are potentially farming tools. Such items are rarer in towns, although they do occur and could be used for various purposes in an urban context (Egan 2005b 199–200). Alternatively, they may indicate that the inhabitants of the property were involved in cultivating the nearby fields. Also from a twelfth-century context was a single fragment of field vole maxilla, reflecting the suburban location of the site.

The occasional presence of 'cut-it-yourself' wood and poached venison may suggest that slightly laxer controls and greater opportunities for certain forms of petty larceny prevailed in the suburb as opposed to the town centre. There are also several instances of the reuse of quite large fragments and even groups of timber, which probably indicate the *ad hoc* reuse of readily available material. Space to store such timber until required would not have been so readily available at many town centre properties, nor at many of the smaller properties at Grand Arcade and Christ's Lane, where again no large fragments were encountered. In addition, the majority of medieval pits within the suburb contained a lower density of refuse, both ceramic and faunal, than is typically encountered at town centre sites in Cambridge. Potentially contributing to this disparity was the tendency of many of the property tails of the suburban plots to be given over to horticultural use, with the attendant likelihood of extensive middening activity. Moreover, the close proximity of the common dunghill, the town fields and the King's Ditch meant that it was much easier to dispose of material away from the property itself than was the case in the constricted confines of a built-up urban environment.

Further conforming to this pattern, the twelfth–sixteenth-century botanical remains from Grand Arcade share some affinities with those of a rural 'producer' site, as there is evidence to suggest that certain processing activities took place in the immediate vicinity. Similarly, the predominance of sheep rather than cattle in the eleventh–twelfth-century faunal assemblage also appears to represent a relatively rural pattern; although, as the assemblage is largely post-Conquest in origin, it may equally reflect the rising importance of sheep within the local economy. A similar sheep-dominant pattern also predominated during the fourteenth–fifteenth centuries, when it may again have been attributable to localized economic factors as opposed to reflecting a more pervasive urban versus rural distinction. Indeed, determining the character of the settlement purely on the basis of its faunal remains is problematic. On the one hand, there is evidence for the keeping of pigs on some properties until the early nineteenth century, whereas this practice appears to have ceased much earlier in the town centre. Yet, on the

other hand, certain indicators of urban consumption patterns are also present. It has been suggested for example that in the medieval period town dwellers ate more beef produced more evidence for specialized butchery practices and may also have seen a rise in veal consumption during the fifteenth century (Albarella 2005). Evidence of all three of these traits was present to a greater or lesser extent.

Similar difficulties arise in relation to the site's insect assemblage. The twelfth–sixteenth-century material included a range of synanthropic species; insects that either lived exclusively in, or else favoured, habitats made or altered by man. This could be taken as evidence that the site was relatively urban in nature. Yet these species relate not to urbanism *per se*, but to the prevalence of settlement waste. Moreover, the same species have also been found on rural sites where settlement waste was deposited. Whilst it is possible that urban sites possessed a more diverse range of synanthropic species, and that certain species such as 'darkling' beetles only occurred on long-lived settlements (Kenward 1997), the distinction is a relatively subtle one and issues of formation processes and taphonomy complicate the issue. Similarly, aspects of the twelfth–sixteenth-century pollen assemblage – such as the relatively low percentages of tree and cereal pollen – could also suggest that the site was predominantly urban in nature, although once again the evidence is not clear-cut.

Nationally, it appears that particular trades were often concentrated in suburban locales (Keene 1976, 81). The most common of these were blacksmiths. In the case of the Barnwell Gate suburb, however, the negligible quantities of slag and associated material that were recovered do not support an intensive metalworking presence (although there are occasional documentary indications). Instead, much more plentiful evidence of contemporary metalworking activity has been found in the town centre (Cessford 2015a, 108). The repeated evidence for bone- and horn-working, which continued for several centuries in the Barnwell Gate suburb, is distinctive and is also paralleled in the Trumpington Street suburb. Although small groups of light tanning and bone-working waste have been found at sites located in the urban core (Higbee in Newman 2008c), bone- and horn-working do appear to have comprised predominantly suburban industries. In part this situation may not have arisen due to the nature of the industries *per se*, but rather to the proximity of the beast market from which the requisite raw materials were obtained (see inset, Chapter 3).

Towards the end of the period of study, the mid-nineteenth to mid-twentieth century rise of the Robert Sayle department store was in large part facilitated by the fact that it occupied a large, contiguous plot holding which had originally been established by Jesus College. Whilst comparable holdings, containing a similar number of contiguous properties, were present in the centre of Cambridge, the relative differences in plot size means that they were substantially smaller in area. It is therefore unsurprising that the most successful department store in Cambridge developed in a suburban location; however spatially constrained the Robert Sayle department store site eventually became, it was far more extensive than the town centre sites of its competitors.

At a broader level, a clear distinction can be made between towns like Cambridge – where the suburbs fell directly under municipal jurisdiction – and others, such as London, where suburbs including Southwark and Westminster remained largely autonomous. Consequently, these latter suburbs established their own distinctive identities, which differed from both the urban core and other suburban areas. During the medieval period, for example, Southwark was initially dominated by large residences for ecclesiastical and secular magnates (Blatherwick & Bluer 2009; Phillpotts *et al.* 2006), while in the post-medieval period it was dominated by industries such as pottery production (Tyler *et al.* 2008). Furthermore, activities that were prohibited in the urban core, such as playhouses with their distinctive structural remains and artefact assemblages (Bowsher & Miller 2009), thrived in a less regulated atmosphere. Another proscribed activity within the City of London was bowling (Rosser 1988, 54–5) and it is notable that archaeologically recovered examples of bowling balls do appear to favour suburbs such as Southwark (*e.g.* Egan in Grainger 2000, 35). By way of contrast, the recovery of a bowling ball from the King's Ditch does not appear to have been linked to its liminal position between the urban and the suburban; instead, it most probably reflects the activities taking place nearby within the large open area situated on the townward side of the ditch.

The suburb of Westminster had a very different relationship to the capital than Southwark, acting as it did as a major ecclesiastical and royal power centre, and this difference is reflected in its archaeology (Thomas *et al.* 2006). Meanwhile, other suburbs such as Spitalfields served as focal points for immigrant communities, although such individuals appear to have left little distinctive archaeological trace (Jeffries 2003). In this way, London serves as an example of how different suburbs could fulfil different roles. A similar pattern may also have predominated at Cambridge, although the limited scale of investigation to date within the town's remaining suburbs hinders detailed comparison (Chapter 6). Nevertheless, the Castle Hill

suburb, which was dominated by the eponymous castle, appears to have fulfilled a markedly different role to that of Barnwell Gate, whilst the Trumpington Gate suburb displayed both similarities (such as similar craft-based activity) and differences (including the presence of prestigious medieval masonry buildings).

Overall, no clear answer emerges to the question of how distinctively 'suburban' the Barnwell Gate suburb – and, more particularly, the Grand Arcade street block – was, or where it should be placed along any hypothetical urban to rural continuum. If it were not for the presence of the King's Ditch, plus associated topographic evidence, the archaeological remains alone would not necessarily have led to the identification of the area as a clearly defined suburb rather than a component of a more nebulous urban fringe. Yet although no clear suburban archaeological signature was identified – indeed, such a signature may in fact be an illusory concept given the variety of roles that different suburbs fulfilled – a range of factors relevant to this issue have been successfully identified (see Table 7.1). This suggests that continued examination of the issue with regard to future archaeological excavations could eventually produce useful results.

One topic that may be worthy of further investigation is the question of whether innovations commenced first in the urban core before radiating outwards, reaching the suburbs a few years or decades later. There is circumstantial evidence to suggest that such a pattern prevailed at the Barnwell Gate suburb, but due to the constituent sites' relatively poor stratigraphic resolution the archaeological dating lacks the precision necessary to resolve this issue.

A second topic of interest comprises the differing morphological characteristics of plots situated in different milieus. This is because the variations in size and form between urban (rectangular and small), suburban (rectangular and medium to large) and rural (square and large) properties appears to have had a profound impact upon the types of archeologically identified features present. Precisely what this signifies is less clear, and it could be argued that it amounts to nothing more than the ephemera of the archaeological record. But if constructed spaces, such as properties, shape daily practice and – through the bodily repetition of practices and routines, plus the construction of memories in which bodily practices were embedded – lead to social memory becoming 'embodied' (Hodder 2006; Hodder and Cessford 2004), then it is possible that dwelling in different types of properties would have conveyed profoundly different impacts. For example, the relatively ample space and lack of constraints afforded by a long suburban property might have produced different attitudes to social mores. Similarly, social relations with one's neighbours might have been profoundly impacted by whether or not they shared a communal water source or latrine. Finally, attitudes to dirt, rubbish and cleanliness may have been impacted by the disposal strategies employed.

Property tail archaeology

Archaeology in still occupied or 'living' towns is bedevilled by the fact that, at most sites, it is impossible to investigate entire properties. Instead, investigations often divide into those focused upon the buildings of the property head and those, such as Grand Arcade and to a lesser extent Christ's Lane, which are largely confined to the open areas of the property tail. Until the advent of the earliest surviving standing buildings in the eighteenth century our knowledge of the frontage buildings of the Grand Arcade street block is minimal, due to a combination of nineteenth–twentieth-century basements and the retention of some standing buildings. Whilst it is true that some aspects of the earlier frontage buildings can be inferred through elements found in the property tail, such as the discard of brick and tile or the quarrying of gravel and clay, this picture remains effectively generic. Even more specific discoveries – such as the laths in the early/mid-fifteenth century clay quarry *Pit 36*, the timber-framing from a structure demolished in the early seventeenth century in *Cesspit 16* or the stone windows of *c.* 1570–1600 reused in early/mid-eighteenth-century *Well 45* – provide only glimpses. Property tail investigations do of course have their strengths. Most notably, they often produce much larger quantities of material culture than those focused on property heads. Nonetheless, they are still restricted to only fragments of properties.

Although properties should ideally be considered as complete, holistic entities, at a practical level the frequent lack of property head investigations means that our understanding of them must often rest upon their tails. Whilst this could devolve into a simplistic or derivative check-list of features and attributes – such as wells to supply water, pits for gravel *etc.* – it is important to note that the use of the property tail 'must have been a constant source of discussion: whether to grow more vegetables, keep more pigs, build a new latrine, or, above all, devote more space to the craft which provided much of the livelihood' (Carver 1987, 70). Thus the archaeological features represent the outcomes of just such decision-making processes.

At Grand Arcade, one example of this process is represented by the decision to create cask-lined *Well 38* in the late sixteenth century, which was of better quality than preceding wattle-lined *Well 28* and moved the water supply closer to the frontage, away from what was apparently a damp and insalubrious area. In addition, the change also created a larger open area in the property tail. As a further knock-on effect, cask-lined *Cesspit 14*, which was now located inconveniently and unhealthily close to the new well, was replaced by stone-lined *Cesspit 15*. Of higher quality than its predecessor, this latter feature – whilst situated in equally close proximity to the well – may have been considered less likely to contaminate its water supply. Both the earlier well and the cesspit appear to have been in serviceable condition prior to their abandonment, indicating that these changes were not prompted by necessity. Thus, although the actual decision-making process remains opaque, the archaeological evidence does indicate its complexity. Moreover, there is also evidence that the property-dominant building was either completely or substantially rebuilt during the late sixteenth century. It is therefore possible that the property tail changes pertained to decisions that also involved, and may indeed have been primarily focused on, the property head.

Evidence from the London *Assize of Nuisance* demonstrates that issues such as the location of cesspits and their impact on adjacent plots could lead to legal conflicts (Chew & Kellaway 1973). Thus, in many cases, property tail discussions were not solely restricted to a single household, but involved at least some level of negotiation with neighbouring tenants. At Grand Arcade, one feature-type that might have engendered such negotiations are boundaries, including both gullies and fence lines.

A more specific example comprises the sixteenth-century wheel ruts that skirted around an area of clay quarry pits, thereby indicating that a cart being used in one property entered another to avoid getting stuck. Another example might be the illicit late seventeenth- or early eighteenth-century burial of cattle in *ADPs 10–12*, which may have been to some extent 'negotiated' with the property's neighbours. Some changes must also represent negotiations between the occupants and the owners of a property, mediated via the lessees who acted as intermediaries. The clearest example of the latter comprises the transference of parts of the plot tail between adjacent plots, such as the transfer of part of Plot XV to Plot XVI that allowed the construction of *Building 20* in the mid-fifteenth century. Such negotiations are well documented in College archives from the eighteenth century onwards, although – as the inscribed brick and wooden blocks in the 1845 warehouse (*Standing Building 70*) demonstrate – the documents do not necessarily convey the entire story.

420

A millennium of change

As a discipline, urban archaeology is often at its strongest when considering either the *longue durée* (long-term historical structures) or the *histoire événe-mentielle* (history of events) of the *courte durée* (short span) (see Braudel 1958; Braudel & Coll 1987). In contrast, it often pays less attention to Braudel's middle level of time, the *conjuncture* (circumstances); that is, the relatively rapid change of social and cultural history over centuries. The archaeology of the Barnwell Gate suburb covers *c*. 950 years from the mid-eleventh to the early twenty-first century. Consequently, it is possible to track the use of certain types of feature or material culture for almost a millennium. In broad terms, of course, these narratives remain relatively generic. Although site-specific, they bear close similarities to those of other sites in Cambridge, as well as to those of more distant towns at both a regional and national level. Nevertheless, they are worthy of consideration as evidence of Braudel's *conjuncture*, and several examples will therefore be considered.

Archaeology ultimately relies on the past creation of identifiable contexts and features, along with the deposition of material culture within them. Over the course of *c*. 950 years of occupation, the feature-types in use at Grand Arcade changed markedly, with no single type remaining consistent throughout. In particular, a transition occurred from a period dominated by pits of various types, along with other unlined features (mid-eleventh–mid-sixteenth century), to one where the remains were predominately stone or brick-lined (seventeenth century onwards). The dominant pattern of refuse disposal also changed markedly. Initially, most cut features contained relatively little material (mid-eleventh–mid-fifteenth centuries), although there are a few isolated exceptions. Subsequently, however, the volume of material being deposited increased substantially (mid-fifteenth–mid-sixteenth centuries). There then followed a period with very little evidence for on-site refuse disposal (mid-sixteenth–mid-eighteenth centuries), which was succeeded by a pattern of intermittent large-scale disposal in 'feature groups' (mid-eighteenth–early twentieth century) before a final return to off-site disposal practices. These changes are broadly paralleled at other British urban and suburban sites and are, of themselves, by no means unusual; they do however indicate the effective impossibility of treating all phases of the site's occupation as part of a single, seamless narrative.

Long term comparisons of different material types are problematic; the only one that is at all feasible, but which still has major limitations, is between pottery and animal bone (Fig. 7.5). This clearly shows the trend of increasing ceramic deposition, and concomitantly ownership/usage over time; with the sixteenth–seventeenth-century dip almost certainly reflecting a decline in the creation of discrete features at this time. Although it is impossible to quantify accurately, if allowance is made for the quantities of material deposited in the 'garden soil' of which only a small percentage was investigated then the quantity of sixteenth–seventeenth century-ceramics would almost certainly lie intermediately between those for the thirteenth–fifteenth centuries and the eighteenth–twentieth centuries. The pattern for animal bone is less clear, in part because the material is not inherently dateable in the way pottery is. Whilst the rise between the eleventh–twelfth century and thirteenth–fifteenth century appears genuine, albeit inflated by an unknown degree due to the presence of residual material; the sixteenth–seventeenth-century peak is almost certainly the result of the presence of a significant proportion of residual material. In contrast the nature of the eighteenth–twentieth century features renders residuality less of an issue and the decline in animal bone appears to genuinely reflect a decline in on-site deposition even if meat consumption levels probably rose.

One material type that remained consistently present throughout the occupational sequence was pottery (Fig. 7.6). This therefore provides a useful medium with which to explore potential patterns of mid- to long-term change. When the Grand Arcade street block was first occupied, *c*. 1050, the ceramics in use predominantly consisted of Thetford-type ware jugs, jars, bowls and lamps plus St Neots-type ware jars and bowls. Both of these were already well-established fabrics, which had been in use locally for over a century. Also present were a small number of higher-quality glazed Stamford ware jugs. It is difficult to assess how significant such pottery was to the inhabitants of the site, although the disposal of eight and four relatively complete vessels in *Cesspit 1* and *Pit 2* respectively may indicate that an average household did not possess a great quantity of ceramics. The situation was subsequently to remain stable for several generations. A few new wares began to appear in low numbers *c*. 1150–1200, but it was not until the early thirteenth century that the pottery in use changed significantly. The old wares lingered to a degree – with St Neots-type ware effectively replaced by pink shelly ware and Lyveden/Stanion ware and Stamford ware by Developed Stamford ware – but the assemblage rapidly became dominated by a range of grey coarsewares from unidentified sources, alongside relatively local Ely ware.

Ely ware products included cooking pots, thick-sided bowls, rather squat jars and jugs plus a few

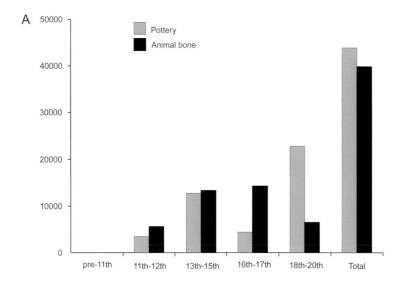

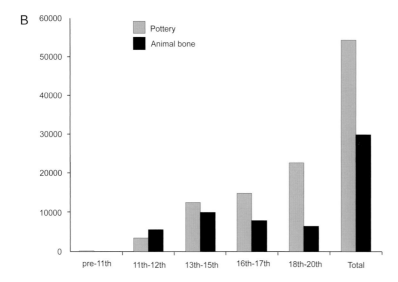

Figure 7.5. *Comparison between quantities of ceramics (sherd count) and animal bone (NISP) at Grand Arcade over time: (A) raw values; (B) modified values adjusted to take account of broadly quantifiable factors, including residuality of animal bone and less intensive excavation of 'garden soil'.*

cisterns, curfews, strainers, lamps and candlesticks, all of which bore relatively little decoration. There were also a few higher-quality glazed and decorated jugs imported from more distant sources, such as Hertfordshire, Boarstall/Brill and Scarborough. Unidentified coarsewares and Ely ware vessels continued to dominate into the fourteenth century, when they were joined in quantity by Essex Redwares and Grimston ware, while Surrey Borders fineware and material from Potterspury and Toynton were also represented in small quantities. Although the forms in use remained relatively consistent, the Essex Redwares were of notably better quality than many of the earlier wares. Also present were more distinctive products including face jugs, Hedingham ware jugs with 'barley twist handles' and Cambridge-type Sgraffito, which bore designs incised through a white slip. The succeeding fifteenth-century wares were similar to their

fourteenth-century forebears. Essex Redwares became increasingly common, while foreign imports appeared for the first time – in the form of a small quantity of stoneware from Siegburg – and a few novel new forms, such as watering pots, were introduced.

Over the course of the mid-eleventh–late fifteenth centuries, the pattern of pottery usage at the site presents a picture of gradual increase and incremental change. As there were long periods of stability, it is likely that for any given generation of inhabitants few noticeable changes occurred. This contrasts quite sharply with the first half of the sixteenth century, however, when the material in question underwent a 'post-medieval ceramic revolution' that was characterized by radical changes in form, fabric and glaze. Coarseware fabrics changed markedly, for example, and while their main forms such as jars, jugs and bowls remained consistent others such as cisterns and skillets

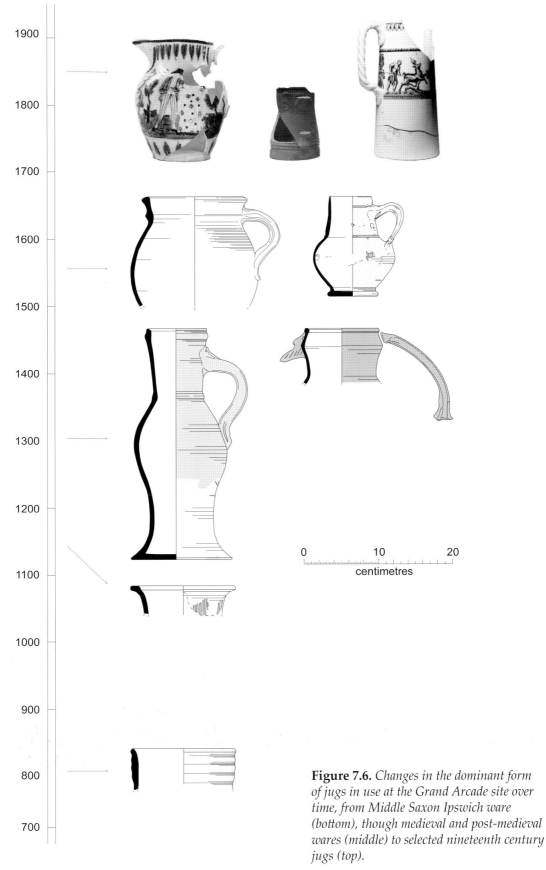

Figure 7.6. *Changes in the dominant form of jugs in use at the Grand Arcade site over time, from Middle Saxon Ipswich ware (bottom), though medieval and post-medieval wares (middle) to selected nineteenth century jugs (top).*

423

became more common. Much of the locally produced earthenware now had a rich clear glaze and is known as Glazed Red Earthenware; there were again a range of old and new forms including bowls, jugs, cisterns, pancheons, skillets, basting dishes, candlesticks, lids and pipkins, some of which indicate major changes in diet (including a shift from stewing to roasting). More novel was the locally produced Babylon-type ware, a red earthenware with a black iron-based glaze that was very different in appearance from preceding medieval wares. This was used primarily for a range of new forms linked to drinking such as tygs, cups and small jugs.

Another new fabric was Broad Street Fineware, also produced at Ely, which was used to manufacture finer, thinner-walled vessels than had previously been available. A mixture of new and old forms – such as cups, jars, jugs, strainers, platters, chafing dishes, bowls and candlestick – were produced. In addition, the quantities of imported German stoneware also increased considerably during this period. Nevertheless, at a local level this 'ceramic revolution' comprised a predominately secondary and derivative phenomenon. The new fabrics, glazes and forms mirrored those that had been developed elsewhere at an earlier date. Babylon-type ware, for example, is a local variant of the Cistercian ware tradition, which developed in in Yorkshire and Derbyshire during the late fifteenth century, while Broad Street Fineware demonstrates strong influences from the late fifteenth-century Surrey white-ware industries. Yet this secondary influence in no way lessens the impact such changes had on the local populace.

In the seventeenth century the range of local products declined, and while in many respects the ceramics remained similar to those that had predominated during the sixteenth century, some changes occurred. Staffordshire-type slipware bowls and cups began to be introduced, for example, the forms and decoration of which strongly influenced the local products. Stoneware from Westerwald and tin-glazed earthenware from both the Netherlands and England also appeared, both of which were visually very different from earlier wares. Then, from the mid-eighteenth century onwards, the ceramics entered a second period of rapid and substantial change. Firstly, Staffordshire white salt-glazed stoneware was introduced. This fabric became relatively common after *c*. 1720, rapidly replacing tin-glazed earthenware and Staffordshire-type slipware as the dominant domestic ware. It was typically used in conjunction with more decorative Chinese export porcelain and English soft paste porcelain vessels. Secondly, many novel new forms appeared, often in association with broader innovations. Thus, the range

of dining-related vessels changed markedly, and even older forms – such as plates – became rather different in character. New forms included serving dishes, sauceboats and pickle dishes.

There were also a significant number of vessels related to tea drinking. This latter product, which can be viewed as the 'essence of commodification' (Jamieson 2001), was particularly associated with tea bowls, tea cups and saucers, plus slops bowls and teapots. By *c*. 1760, when significant 'feature groups' first began to be deposited, tea had become Britain's national drink. Perhaps the best way of assessing the significance of tea drinking archaeologically is to examine the ratio of tea/coffee drinking items to dining items. Initially, *c*. 1760–1800, this ratio was somewhat disproportionate, at 1:3.9. Although this remained consistent *c*. 1800–50, the significance of tea subsequently rose *c*. 1850–1900 (ratio falls to 1:2.5); a pattern that culminated *c*. 1910–40 (when the ratio fell to 1:1.2). In addition to tea drinking, vessels related to hygiene – such as chamber pots – also became increasingly common during the eighteenth century. Although recognizable metal chamber pots had existed since the fourteenth century, and earthenware examples are mentioned documentarily from the early fifteenth century, mass production of earthenware chamber pots only began in the mid-seventeenth century. They became common archaeologically after *c*. 1640, but a lack of contemporary material culture within the Grand Arcade street block resulted in their invisibility prior to *c*. 1760.

Within a single lifetime, Staffordshire white salt-glazed stoneware was replaced by creamware. This latter fabric came to dominate the market from the 1760s until the 1780s. Creamware was rather plainer than its predecessor, with much simpler moulded decoration; its forms were generally similar, although some new types did appear such as small condiment vessels and large plain water jugs or guglets as well as spills vases linked to smoking. Creamware was itself soon largely supplanted by pearlware, which came into use in the mid-1770s and had achieved a dominant position by the 1780s. Although little pearlware was discarded at Grand Arcade during the eighteenth century, it does appear to have been in common use. The dominant forms were similar to those of creamware, but pearlware bore a much higher degree of decoration. Finally, there were also a number of less common wares that fulfilled niche roles.

In contrast to these new wares, post-medieval Glazed Red Earthenware continued to be produced at Ely throughout this period. These later vessels were largely indistinguishable from their earlier predecessors, although the range of forms was now much more limited. Production was principally restricted to bowls, jars and dishes plus at least one apparent innovation to the local repertoire, the chamber pot. Also innovatory – and perhaps even revolutionary, regardless of how mundane they now appear – were the flowerpots that this industry produced in unglazed earthenware. Flowerpots also stand out because, at a time of increasing national and international importation, a certain percentage of these vessels were manufactured in Cambridge itself (potentially the first time that pottery was produced in the town).

Overall, the evidence suggests that the quantities of ceramics in use increased substantially during the eighteenth century and that the range of fabrics and forms similarly expanded. Moreover, it appears that particular wares went in and out of fashion very rapidly, often within a single lifetime, in a way that was previously unparalleled. Creamware and pearlware continued in use until c. 1820–30, when they were superseded by whiteware; a fabric first introduced c. 1805 and common from c. 1820 onwards. Decoration, particularly transfer-printed decoration, became much more common from c. 1830, further increasing c. 1845–50. From around the same time bone china also became common. Patterns of individual vessel use also changed. From c. 1830 onwards, for example, there is much greater evidence for the presence of matching sets, used for both dining and tea drinking. Utilitarian English stoneware first appeared c. 1800–20, rapidly replacing all earlier forms of stoneware. This fabric was principally used for a range of new types of containers, including bottles for ink, blacking and a range of other liquids, as well as jars for food. Although these items could be reused, and frequently were, they were to a large extent disposable in a way that no earlier ceramics had been.

During the 1860s the production of pottery in Ely ceased, ending a c. 750-year tradition. The industry's niche role in the local market was largely filled by Sunderland-type coarseware, which had already been in use for some time, and later by yellowware. Subsequently, the twentieth century witnessed relatively few changes, although a small number of new forms, such as foot warmers, did appear. Even the market in flowerpots stopped being dominated by local suppliers, who were instead replaced by Sankey's of Bulwell in Nottinghamshire. The only 'local' ware that remained was art pottery from Castle Hedingham.

This 'broad-brush' treatment of the site's mid-eleventh–early twentieth-century pottery reveals an intriguingly cyclical pattern. Initially, between the mid-eleventh–late fifteenth centuries, the pace of change was slow; indeed, at the level of individual generations it well have been almost imperceptible. Following the early sixteenth-century 'ceramic revolution', however,

its rapidity increased markedly. There then followed a period of almost continuous change, spanning the mid-eighteenth–early nineteenth century, when both fabrics and forms underwent rapid development. Finally, there was a return to a period of relative stability. In addition, the examination also reveals the shifting balance between local and more distant production sources. While there was an undeniable trend extending from wares that supplied a local market to those operating on a national and then an international scale, this by no means represents a unilinear narrative of 'progress'. It is important not to dismiss the continued importance of the Ely pottery industry and the rise of local, Cambridge-produced flowerpots.

Similar narratives can also be constructed for other material types, although the lower quantities involved – as well as certain preservation issues – mean that in many instances a less coherent picture is produced. One potential example of such a narrative is that of worked bone and antler. These latter materials were utilized, albeit on a relatively small-scale, throughout the period of the site's occupation. In the eleventh–twelfth centuries bone was primarily used for double-ended implements as well as for flutes, toggles, buzz bones, a point and a scoop. Then, in the thirteenth–fifteenth centuries, the most common items were parchment prickers, while other items included a comb, a pen, a point, a tuning peg and a skate.

In the sixteenth–seventeenth centuries the commonest items were implement handles, while buttons and a comb were also found. In the eighteenth–nineteenth centuries common items include implement handles and brush handles, largely for toothbrushes and linked to ideas of hygiene. There were also dominoes, a 'swanny-whistle' and a range of unidentified material. In the twentieth century bone declined in significance with the rise of plastic, although there was a brush associated with a Remington typewriter, a powerful symbol of modernity. Although this list under-represents the types in use at any one time, due to the relative scarcity of deposited material, it does demonstrate how the forms of items tend to change completely over a period of a few centuries but without the raw material becoming any more significant or noticeably more frequently employed.

A further contrast is provided by glass vessels. In common with other sites investigated in Cambridge, there is no evidence for the use of such vessels prior to the fourteenth century and only extremely limited evidence for their presence for several centuries afterward. Glass may have become slightly more common in the sixteenth century, although on nothing like the scale attested at other sites in Cambridge, but is only used on any scale after the invention of green glass

Table 7.2. *Feature-types through time at Grand Arcade.*

Date	Wells	Gravel quarry pits	Clay quarry pits	Pits of unknown function	Gullies	Cesspits	Water filled features	Specialized pits	Ovens	Animal disposal pits	Planting beds/ holes	Cellars	Soakaways	Drains	WC's
11th–12th	19	163	1	59	18	13	-	-	-	-	-	-	-	-	-
13th–14th	25	113	2	169	12	-	10	5	5	2.5	-	-	-	-	-
15th–16th	16	28	4	159	-	3	8	3.5	3	5.5	6	-	-	-	-
17th	5	-	-	1	1	2	-	-	-	4	-	-	-	-	-
18th	8	-	-	-	-	1	-	-	-	-	5	7	4	1.5	-
19th	18	-	-	-	-	1	-	-	-	2	15	11	4	12	5
20th	4	-	-	-	-	-	-	-	-	-	1	6	1	10	3

wine bottles in the mid-seventeenth century. Such utility bottles become more common in the eighteenth century and remain the dominant form, although they are joined by phials and a few other vessels. During the nineteenth century glass vessels become increasingly common and there is a much wider range of forms. The use of drinking glasses become relatively widespread and there is a wide range of containers for drinks, medicines and foods. There are also products whose entire story occupies only part of the period of the occupation of the Grand Arcade street block, such as clay tobacco pipes. These have a much shorter narrative that covers their appearance, rise, decline and disappearance (see Fig. 5.97).

Change can also be tracked through features, as the nature of these altered markedly over the centuries both in terms of the types represented (Table 7.2; Fig. 7.7A) and the physical form that they took. Many feature types were present for only a part of the occupational sequence. In some cases, for example, such as quarry pits, they disappear from the archaeological record while in other instances, such as drains, they did not occur until long after the commencement of occupation. Although these results are unsurprising, and would be replicated within almost all British urban sequences, it is worth bearing them in mind rather than taking them for granted as part of an unconscious narrative of progress from the primitive past to the familiar present. Other types of feature, such as those associated with the water supply (Figs. 7.7B and 7.8–7.9), occur throughout the entire occupation of the site.

The earliest wells were located towards the rear of the property head or the front of the property tail and were wattle-lined. This was the dominant form in the eleventh–fifteenth centuries (Fig. 7.7B). Whilst the wattle-lined wells did vary slightly in form, and in aspects such as the species of wood employed and its felling season, there is relatively little to distinguish them. There were a few cask- and stone-lined wells, although these were very much in the minority. Wattle-lined wells fell out of favour around the middle of the fifteenth century (Fig. 7.7B), when the alternatives became cheaper and more readily available, and cask- and stone-lined wells that had previously been in the minority came to dominate. These tended to be rather deeper than the earlier wattle-lined wells and would have held more water.

Cask-lined wells only enjoyed a brief popularity and by the seventeenth century stone-lined wells and others incorporating both stone and brick in their linings were ubiquitous (Fig. 7.7B), reflecting the wider availability of such materials following the Dissolution. These stone-lined wells were rather different from earlier examples, as they employed timber baseplates. By the late eighteenth century stone, which was by then less readily available, had fallen out of use and well-shafts were constructed entirely from bricks, although they still retained their timber baseplates (Fig. 7.7B). One notable feature is that despite the presence of local brick production, the wells in Cambridge never employed specialist 'wedge-shaped' bricks (Noël Hume 1971, 146). This and the forms of the timber baseplates suggest a local and rather *ad hoc* vernacular 'industry' of well construction. Brick-lined wells continued into the nineteenth century. By this period, they commonly had sealed domed tops with a lead pipe through them and had shifted location closer to the frontage. Moreover, they were now typically located in either the property dominant building or an immediately adjacent property accessory building, rather than in a yard area as all earlier wells appear to have been. The nineteenth-century wells were also significantly deeper than their predecessors, and would thus have held considerably more water.

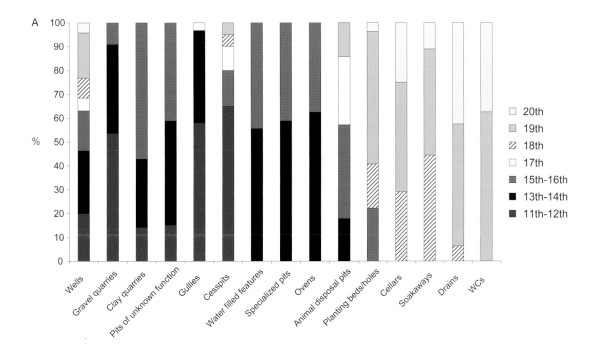

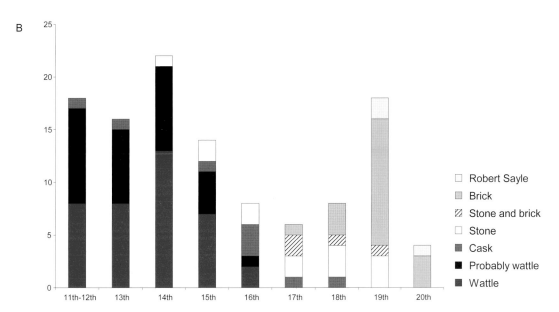

Figure 7.7. *Feature types through time at the Grand Arcade site: (A) the relative frequency of selected feature-types, showing how few feature types span the entire sequence; (B) the relative frequency of different types of well, this includes all the active wells not just those constructed in that century. The eleventh–twelfth century value is exaggerated as it covers a c. 150-year period rather than the 100 years the other columns do. The apparent fourteenth–seventeenth-century decline is somewhat illusory as the wells typically became deeper and could have supplied more water, while the seventeenth–twentieth-century rise reflects and if anything under-represents a genuine increase in water supply.*

A minority of nineteenth-century wells were much deeper still and penetrated to the Lower Greensand at a depth of c. 45–65/70m (Fig. 7.8E), thereby accessing water under artesian pressure. Beyond these examples, the well associated with the Robert Sayle department store had a much larger shaft and utilized a suction pump and steam engine to obtain artesian water on an industrial scale. This well was constructed c. 1868–77 and in many respects represents the 'last hurrah' of wells supplying water. Until this time,

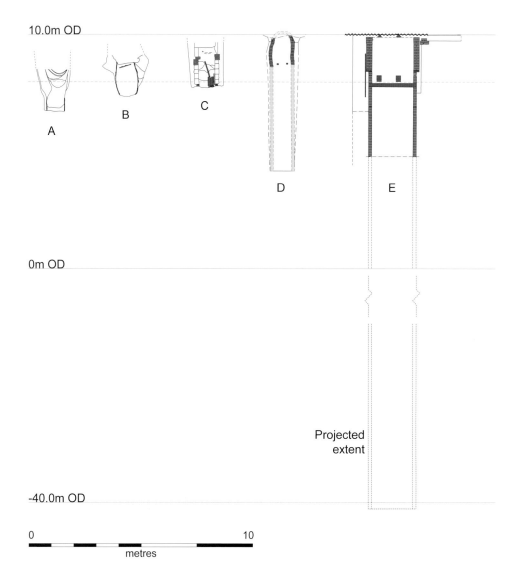

Figure 7.8. *Different types of well through time at the Grand Arcade site: (A) a wattle-lined well, typical of the eleventh–fifteenth centuries; (B) a cask-lined well, typical of the fifteenth–seventeenth centuries; (C) a stone-lined well, typical of the sixteenth–eighteenth centuries; (D) a brick-lined well, typical of the nineteenth century; (E) a brick-lined well at Robert Sayle, of late nineteenth-century date.*

wells appear to have represented effectively the sole source of water for most occupants of the Barnwell gate suburb, as other systems – such as the Franciscan Conduit, established in 1327 and taken over by Trinity College in 1546, or Hobson's Conduit (Fig. 7.9C–E), which supplied a fountain at Market Hill from 1614 onwards – were too distant to have had an impact.

In 1853, however, the Cambridge University and Town Waterworks Act was passed. A waterworks first opened in 1855 and by 1860 1500 premises in the town were being supplied. As a result of this, the wells in a number of properties went out of use during the second half of the nineteenth century, to be replaced by a mains supply (Fig. 7.9E). This narrative of well-types is, with minor variations, broadly paralleled at many other European towns such as Århus (Skov 2009, 153–7), although wells do generally appear to have considerably rarer at some densely occupied urban centres such as London (Bowsher *et al.* 2007; Burch *et al.* 2010).

This street block narrative can be further refined, to focus upon the wells associated with individual properties (Table 7.3; Fig. 7.10). Similar narratives could also be constructed for other feature types, although these are somewhat compromized by the poorer survival of less deep examples. An interesting instance of

Figure 7.9. *The changing nature of the water supply at the Grand Arcade site over time: (A) eleventh–twelfth century; (B) thirteenth–fifteenth century; (C) sixteenth–seventeenth century; (D) eighteenth century; (E) nineteenth century.*

Table 7.3. *Water supply to Plot XIII over time.*

Date	Feature	Type	Distance from frontage (m)	Capacity (cubic m)
Early 12th	Well 13	Wattle-lined well	29	0.6
Early 14th	Well 29	Wattle-lined well	18.5	1.3
Mid-15th	Well 39	Cask-lined well	35.5	0.5
Mid-16th	Outside area	Unknown well	70+	Unknown
Mid-18th	Well 45	Stone-lined well	15	1.1
1840s	Well 45	Stone-lined well	15	1.1
	Well 52	Brick-lined well	25.5	1.0
	Well 53	Brick-lined well	44	3.5
	Total			**5.6**
Late 19th	Mains supply	Mains	0	Effectively unlimited
	Well 52	Brick-lined well	25.5	1.0
	Well 53	Brick-lined well	44	3.5
	Well M1	Brick-lined well	88	Unknown
	Total			**Effectively unlimited**

constructed in the middle and rear of plots, although many such buildings known from cartographic evidence left no archaeological evidence. Furthermore, some WCs were also located within frontage buildings. The insect and botanical evidence indicates the presence of human faeces in many contexts, whilst eighteenth–nineteenth-century chamber pots, stool pans and WC bowls provide artefactual evidence for human waste disposal. The sequence of material used to construct features for the disposal of human waste broadly parallels that for wells. The two types of feature are also broadly similar, in that although there may have been some slight improvements between the twelfth–nineteenth centuries the fundamental nature

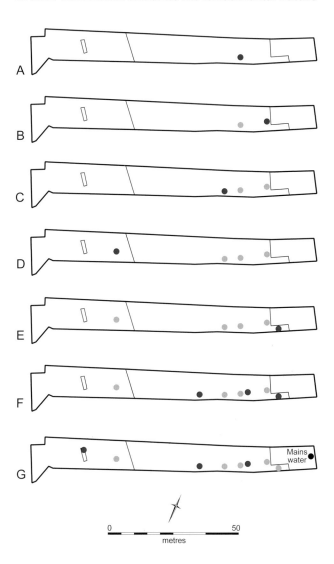

Figure 7.10. *The changing nature of the water supply to Plot XIII from the twelfth to nineteenth centuries: (A) early 12th century; (B) early 14th century; (C) mid-15th century; (D) mid-16th century; (E) mid-18th century; (F) 1840s; (G) late 19th century.*

this concerns features utilized for the disposal of human waste, which is a requirement almost as basic as water. A typical medieval household would have disposed of around 0.36 tons of faeces and 415 gallons of urine per year (Brothwell 1982). Consequently, wattle-lined cesspits comprised a relatively common feature of the twelfth century, with the majority located in timber latrine buildings. These presumably continued to be the main form of cesspit throughout the medieval period, but – due to a combination of factors – were largely invisible archaeologically. In the fifteenth century cask-lined cesspits appeared, although these may well have existed earlier. Then, in the sixteenth century, stone-lined examples also appeared. The latter were relatively uncommon and, given their high likelihood of identification and survival, this rarity is probably genuine.

In the eighteenth century, brick-lined cesspits first appeared. These were accompanied by the introduction of brick-lined soakaways, which were used to dispose of various types of liquid waste including urine. In the mid-nineteenth century small brick WC buildings were

of how practices were carried out remained constant, with the only significant change occurring during the second half of the nineteenth century.

These narratives of nearly a millennium of *conjuncture* comprise a significant strength of European urban archaeology, although they are often obscured by an excessively period-specific focus. Whilst somewhat generic, a similar narrative derived from a different Cambridge suburb or, in particular, a site located in the urban core, would be rather different. Moreover, a narrative derived from a different urban centre would provide perhaps the most telling differences of all.

Age, gender and more esoteric agencies

Throughout this volume, the archaeology of the Barnwell Gate suburb has been approached in a predominately age- and gender-neutral manner. It could therefore be argued that this unconsciously allows adult men to dominate the narrative by default; despite the fact that the majority of households in the suburb were almost certainly composed of a mixture of men, women and children. Here, some attempt will be made to redress this imbalance. The problems and complexities surrounding this issue will also be discussed.

In the first instance, there is relatively little clear-cut archaeological evidence relating to the presence of children prior to the eighteenth century. This situation is by no means unusual, as the difficulties inherent in identifying both medieval children (Lewis 2009; Orme 2008) and their toys (Crawford 2009) are well-attested. At Grand Arcade, the only unambiguous evidence was the presence of five children's shoes that were recovered from the mid-fifteenth-century backfilling of *Well 22* and *Pit 49*, and fourteenth–sixteenth-century recuts of the King's Ditch F.5192 and F.1073 respectively. In addition, a fifteenth–sixteenth-century copper alloy thimble decorated with a border of stamped roundels containing *fleur de lys* was so small that it was almost certainly intended for a child. In fact, even within the various large groups of mid-eighteenth–mid-twentieth-century material at the site, unambiguous evidence for children remained rare. The majority of such assemblages contain no material that can be definitely associated with children, despite the fact that documentary evidence clearly demonstrates their presence within the households that produced the self-same assemblages.

In all cases, the assemblages that did produce items which can be closely associated with children were relatively atypical, as they were not associated with the nuclear family units and associated businesses that generated most of the assemblages. The main

example are the garden features of *c*. 1822–45 associated with the school run by Sarah Dobson at Plot XIV, which produced material including children's cups and slate pencils (see also Cessford 2018a). At around the same time, in 1845, a warehouse was constructed in Plot XIII and letters were carved into wooden blocks incorporated in the structure with the initials of the Jay family who occupied the plot including the children Edward Jay junior aged ten and Maria Jane Anne Jay aged eight, but not their younger siblings aged four and three (Cessford 2013a, fig. 12). Children's cups and plates were also found in the backfilling of *Building 49 c*. 1879–82 in Plot XXII and *Cellar 12* of Plot XVII *c*. 1882–5, both apparently representing stock from the Barrett and Son ceramic retailing business with the Barrett family members and their children living elsewhere so there was no 'domestic' element. The backfilling of *Cellar 13* in *c*. 1913–21, associated with the residential hostel of the Robert Sayle department store, included a child's deaf sign language plate; however, as children did not live in this hostel it appears that this was a treasured childhood heirloom.

Cellar 13 also produced six glass Codd bottles for mineral water. Two of these were complete and still possessed their marbles but four were broken, apparently to obtain the marbles as these were not present. This suggests that some individuals at the Robert Sayle department store hostel were supplying Codd bottle marbles to children who lived elsewhere, possibly their relatives. The neck and top of a bottle from the backfilling of *Sawpit 1 at* 4 Tibb's Row in *c*. 1874–81 appears to have been broken to retrieve the marble, although as the occupant Thomas Reeve had no children the marble must have been intended for a child who resided elsewhere. In contrast, the bottle from *Pit 65* backfilled *c*. 1880–1900 in Plot XXII still had its marble, presumably because by this date this plot was no longer used as residential premises but as stables and workshops where no children appear to have been present.

The archaeological evidence for women is even sparser until the nineteenth century, despite the fact that documentary evidence from the fourteenth century onwards clearly indicates the importance of women in leasing plots. Although most of the nineteenth-century households that produced significant assemblages were – officially at least, in terms of census and other records – patriarchal, all the adults at the school ran by Sarah Dobson at Plot XIV were female. This female dominance does appear to be discernible in the assemblages associated with this household, as there was a greater emphasis upon the developing ideas of domesticity and gentility (Fitts 1999) than in other assemblages, and possible evidence for an interest in political statements on the oppression of women in patriarchal society. There is also evidence for a strong emphasis on frugality and cleanliness, as well as evidence that the smoking of tobacco and drinking of wine were being undertaken in private, despite the fact that both activities were disapproved of in more public contexts when women undertook them. The only other assemblage dominated by women is the backfilling of *Cellar 13*, associated with the residential hostel of the Robert Sayle department store in *c*. 1913–21. By this date the majority of staff were women. This preponderance is most apparent in the leather shoes, which are largely female, and a number of other items can be identified as having strong female associations such as a Ven Yusa face cream jar and a spinning wheel cotton reel or bobbin (see further Cessford 2012).

This, admittedly rather minimalist, discussion of women and children has shown that clear-cut archaeological evidence for their presence is relatively meagre, although some significant nineteenth–twentieth-century insights are possible. Despite this, such an examination serves as an important reminder of their presence. The consideration of age and gender raises the wider topic of agency. In general terms agency is the capacity of a person or other non-human actor to act in any given environment, whist in archaeology it has been defined as 'the way in which societies structures inhabit and empower agents, those agents' aims, ideals and desires and the material conditions of social life' (Dobres & Robb 2000, 8). Agency can be viewed as being co-produced by humans and non-humans in networks; in urban studies the concept has been extended to include animals, technological systems and resources and even whether settlements can possess a form of urban agency and be agents and proprietors of change (Brantz 2017; Lewis 2017).

Horses, cattle, pigs, dogs, cats and chickens all 'inhabited' the Grand Arcade street block. Whilst these animals have been treated primarily as resources for the benefit of humans, be that benefit nutritional or other, it could be argued that we need to consider the 'intercorporeal, sensuous and affective engagements through which humans and non-human animals are mutually constituted' (Overton & Hamilakis 2013, 111; but see also Lindstrøm 2015). Perhaps the most obvious example of this are the six late seventeenth century-cows, at least five of which were female and three of which had associated *in utero* foetuses, that appear to have been members of a 'flying herd', where animals were brought in from elsewhere whilst pregnant to give birth and then often culled or sold at the end of their lactation and cyclically replaced. These animals appear to have suffered from 'milk

fever' caused by a lack of forage containing the right balance of minerals and died. This creates a negative impression of human and non-human animal relationships, one that, whilst fundamentally driven by human nutritional benefits, relates to animal cruelty. The relationship between humans and cats and dogs is not primarily linked to nutritional benefit, however the disposal of their remains up to the mid-nineteenth century provides little evidence that they were treated as pets in the current sense (Thomas 2005). There is also evidence for bird species such as corvids, red kite and sea eagles that effectively reversed the traditional relationship, treating human urban settlements as a source of nutritional benefit by scavenging on domestic refuse. These relationships do however need to be problematized. For example, was a sixteenth-century tawny owl simply treating buildings in this part of the town as a suitable perching site at night, feeding upon rodents, birds, earthworms and beetles? Alternatively was the owl a form of human nutritional/medical benefit, consumed in the form of broth as a remedy for whooping cough? Such ambiguities, and the ability to construct almost diametrically opposed narratives from the same evidence, mean that whilst it is important to problematize the role of other species in the street block, specific interpretations are more difficult.

Whilst the concept of agency could be applied much more widely, for example to consider whether institutions such as the Colleges that owned properties possessed agency as opposed to the members of those institutions, there are practical limits to pursuing this. One particularly intriguing concept is whether plots/properties within an urban street block possess agency. To take just one example, it is apparent that the long-term development of 21 St Andrew's Street was profoundly affected by the fact that it was the only plot/property with a frontage on St Andrew's Street and rear access. Whilst individual and group human agency can clearly be identified in many particular archaeological events, longer term patterns cold be conceptualized as a form of plot/property agency.

The archaeology of modernity

As recently as the 2002 *Cities in the World 1500–2000* conference, the lack of British urban archaeology of the post-1800 period was lamented (Lawrence 2006; Symonds 2006). If the Grand Arcade excavations had taken place even a decade earlier, it is likely that the archaeological narrative would have been cut short; certainly excluding the Later Modern period (1800 onwards) and the contemporary past (1900 or 1950 onwards). Yet its timing means that Grand Arcade represents one of the first large-scale British urban archaeological excavations to take the eighteenth–twentieth centuries fully into account. Whilst treating urban deposits of this period archaeologically is hopefully now relatively uncontroversial, and does not require special justification, it does raise a series of particular issues.

It is also worth noting that archaeological studies of British towns after 1800 have tended to focus on either the imperial capital, London (Egan 1999; Jeffries *et al.* 2009), or those towns that were heavily affected by industrialization and that exported material around the globe, such as Sheffield (Symonds 2006) or Birmingham (Rátkai 2008). Cambridge is rather different, as it never underwent significant industrialization in the conventional sense, although it could be argued that in some senses it is a 'factory town' whose industry was education; as such it could be viewed as an intellectual centre of the British Empire.

The four 'haunts' of post-1500 global historical archaeology are colonialism, Eurocentrism, capitalism and modernity (Orser 1996), although it could be argued that all four are in fact simply interconnected elements of the 'incomplete project' of modernity (Habermas 1983). Archaeology as a discipline is itself part of this 'incomplete project' and, along with anthropology, has its roots in the study of the 'other' and the 'exotic' in terms of space (non-European/non-Western societies) and time (past societies). Anthropology has long moved away from this position, with the idea of an anthropology of 'proximity' not 'distance' where the anthropologist is both participatory in a society that they live in as an individual yet sufficiently distanced to comprehend it as a system (Augé 1998; Lewis 1998). By studying eighteenth–twentieth-century remains in 'living' cities, developer-funded urban archaeology has a particular strength in embedding the study of the past in the present – and even in some senses the future – as it is part of a development process that has physical as well as intellectual outcomes. In many respects, the roots of the early twenty-first-century developments at Grand Arcade and Christ's Lane can be traced back through the nineteenth–twentieth centuries, especially with regard to the history of the Robert Sayle department store, and in a more attenuated form they go back much further.

It is fruitless to try and attempt to define the origins of so complex a phenomenon as modernity, especially as it is difficult to differentiate root and proximate causes. Although controversial, it has been suggested that in some senses the origins of capitalism may go back to the thirteenth century (Macfarlane 1978) or even the ninth–tenth centuries (Hodges 1989). Whatever the case, it is clear that the fifteenth–sixteenth centuries were a key formative period in the creation of modernity. Much global historical archaeology, especially from North America, pays only lip service to this period. Yet in a British developer-funded context, disparate periods such as the fifteenth–sixteenth and nineteenth–twentieth centuries frequently occur side by side.

At Grand Arcade, for example, the late sixteenth-century cask from Ottoman Greece that may be linked to the Levant Company, and the early seventeenth-century West African grains-of-paradise that are effectively part of the Second Atlantic system of the slave trade (but are also part of a much older system of contacts between Europe and West Africa going back to the thirteenth century), both indicate some of the roots of the global modern world. Other aspects that are often thought of as distinctively nineteenth-century, and certainly developed greatly at this time, also have earlier origins. One example of this is domesticity, which is often discussed in terms of the nineteenth century (Fitts 1999) but whose roots may lie in seventeenth-century Holland (Rybzcynski 1987) or even with well-off artisans and merchants in fourteenth-century British towns (Riddy 2008). Concepts such as domesticity are of course historically contingent, so they would undoubtedly be markedly different in the Grand Arcade street block in the fourteenth as opposed to nineteenth centuries. Nonetheless, it is important to recognize the validity of both.

In excess of 95 per cent of the eighteenth–twentieth-century material came from 34 discrete assemblages that can broadly be interpreted as 'feature groups'; that is, closed assemblages of domestic artefacts that were rapidly discarded as a single deposit linked to particular households, which can in some cases be identified with known individuals (Cessford 2009, 307–9). Such feature groups are prime examples of the *courte durée* (short span) and, whilst they cannot be interpreted simplistically (Cessford 2009; Cessford 2017a), they offer significant potential for constructing new narratives about such material that are simply not possible using other archaeological sources. This is true of almost every feature group, but particularly apposite examples include the consideration of relations within the small school run by Sarah Dobson, Thomas Wicks' role as a cook at Emmanuel College or life for those who lived and worked at the Robert Sayle department store.

Another related way in which the archaeological record makes a valuable contribution is in identifying artefacts of 'resistance' (see Frazer 1999). Examples of this include the sign language plate from the Robert Sayle department store, but perhaps the best example is the contrast between the semi-concealed carved blocks bearing the initials of the tenants on the warehouse at Plot XIII and the more official frontage sign which names the College (Figs. 5.50 and 5.77B). Such resistance reveals aspects of the relations between the tenants and their landlord, the plot owner, which are often at variance to the surviving documentary records.

The various feature groups represent types of event that ranged in importance from quite minor changes to 'household clearance' events that are depicted in nineteenth-century fiction as profoundly brutal and disturbing (Trotter 2008). Objects that had been 'household gods' (Cohen 2006), with personal meaning and a past, became simply commodities with an exchange value in the present. In the case of the material in the archaeological record, it was transformed into simple 'stuff'; waste matter with no future, apart from deposition and eventual archaeological recovery (Trotter 2008). Most of the assemblages were related to less traumatic events, although almost all had some degree of emotional involvement.

All these assemblages are to a greater or lesser degree 'idiosyncratic' and they present a series of material culture 'snapshots'. One of the issues this raises is that the validity of amalgamating the results into an overall single phase assemblage becomes highly questionable, as it is unlikely to produce meaningful results (see Miller 1991b). It is also important to remember that these groups reflect only part of much wider disposal practices. Some material went into middens and 'garden soil', while more still was removed for disposal off-site.

The 'feature groups' at Grand Arcade can be subdivided into several types. The first comprises the *ad hoc* reuse of features that had been abandoned; the second, those dug expressly for the purpose of disposing of refuse; and the third, material that was used as hardcore during construction, as well as percolation fills employed to improve drainage. It would be possible to utilize these assemblages to try and examine broader issues of wealth. This is because the cost of ceramics, for example, was based primarily upon decoration, with transfer prints being the most expensive (Miller 1980; Miller 1991a) and their relative ratios can be quantified from the archaeological remains. But the constitution and organization of households was probably more important in determining the nature of the ceramics in use than wealth, and as ceramics were relatively inexpensive they are not particularly useful as economic indicators. Instead, documentary sources and building sequences are more significant (Tarlow 2007, 178–83).

Probate inventories illustrate the economic and physical insignificance of ceramics in terms of both value and quantity in the majority of households. It is also clear that there are major temporal changes and that function played a major role in influencing decoration.

Perhaps a more informative approach, therefore, is to consider the functional aspects of the assemblages (Tables 5.3, 5.5, 5.7 and 5.9); although such ascriptions are themselves problematic (Brooks 2005a, 63–5; Brooks 2005b). At a broad level, this approach indicates the prevalence of dining, with material associated with tea/coffee drinking and food storage and preparation being present in nearly as many features but much lower in number. Next come the categories of other eating/drinking and gardening, examples of which are not present in as many features but are more common where they do occur. Material associated with smoking, personal hygiene, medicine and domestic occupation is relatively common, occurring in large numbers, while other functions are much less significant.

It must be remembered, however, that refuse disposal was not a simple process (Cessford 2009, 307–9; Cessford 2017a). The material deposited within the various feature groups had been carefully selected. Still fashionable or valuable material was often saved for further use, either on the same site or elsewhere, for example (Johnson 1996, 182–3). Furthermore, some types of material may have been much more susceptible to the vagaries of fashion, so that dining or tea/coffee drinking vessels may have been disposed of as out of date, whereas flowerpots might be retained as their form was much more stable. Nevertheless, the functional approach does provide useful information. The disposal of flowerpots, for example, indicates a prior interest in gardening while their disposal suggests a cessation of this interest. This can clearly be seen at Plot VIII, where the late eighteenth-century interest in gardening apparently ended in the early nineteenth century or at Plot XIV where the same pattern can be identified a century later.

At Plot XI this pattern becomes much more personal. Here, William Newby's gardening activities were not shared by his successor, Elizabeth Price. What, however, of the many feature groups that lacked gardening-related material? Does this reflect a genuine lack of interest in gardening, or is it simply that the interest continued and so the flowerpots were saved to continue in use. The latter scenario is almost certainly the case with regard to the relative absence of flowerpots and other gardening-related material in the basal percolation fills of planting beds in the late eighteenth–mid-nineteenth centuries, as the features themselves attest to a continuing interest in gardening. The early twentieth-century cellars at the Robert Sayle department store contained very little gardening-related material, presumably because the surrounding area was hard-surfaced. The same arguments can also be extended to a range of other functions such as smoking, albeit with different caveats.

Grouping items together by function does to an extent involve the rather spurious notion that all items are of equal significance. Thus, while there is little issue with equating chamber pots with stool pans as items of personal hygiene, this is not true if toothbrushes are added to the equation. Some items are clearly more significant, or at least have greater interpretive potential. An example of this might be the detailed study of a few 'literary' plates, dishes and mugs from a site at High Wycombe (Lucas 2003), which arguably have more to say about the inhabitants of the site than the overall functional analysis of the assemblage of hundreds of items (Lucas & Regan 2003). Whilst an accusation of 'cherry picking' could be levelled, it is clear that greater attention should perhaps be applied to the more distinctive or idiosyncratic elements of the assemblages. Instances of this could include the children's cups with text and illustrations from the works of Isaac Watts associated with the school at Plot XIV, which are unparalleled in the other groups (see also Cessford 2013a; Cessford 2018a).

The strongest approach is, however, to try and meld the evidence of these individual items with the larger assemblages from which they were derived. Thus the Isaac Watts cups are best understood in light of the Sicilian pattern vessels, and even the blacking bottles, which were recovered from the same feature, while the slate pencils from nearby features also add context. Another example might be how the flowerpots marked by both their maker Robert Sibley and their owner William Newby have greater resonance when combined with other evidence for gardening derived from the same feature, and also with the fact that although Newby owned ceramics by Copeland & Garrett, Davenport and Wedgwood it was a flowerpot that he marked. While there must be a comparative element to such an approach, it is best expressed in the contextualized and intimate discussions of individual feature groups that are scattered throughout the relevant property narratives (Chapter 5) rather than by a bland and homogenized attempt to construct an overall story.

Many aspects of modernity can be viewed as parts of an unproblematic 'familiar past' (see Tarlow & West 1999) and have been largely ignored by archaeologists. One such aspect in a rural context is field drainage (Tarlow 2007, 59–62). Similarly, urban drainage has also been largely been ignored archaeologically. Locally, there is evidence that the technology for sophisticated water management existed by the fourteenth century, but there is no evidence that it was applied in an urban context until the early nineteenth century. At this point, a range of drain forms began to be produced on and around the Isle of Ely. A broad 'evolutionary' progression occurred, extending from horseshoe-shaped to facetted horseshoe, enclosed D to cylindrical with spouted base and, finally, salt-lazed cylindrical with cupped mouth (Fig. 5.98). There is, however, evidence for different types being used at the same time and for 'archaic' types being used long after other, newer forms had been introduced.

In 1827 John Doulton began manufacturing ceramic pipes. Following the publication of the 'General Report on the Sanitary Condition of the Labouring Population' by Edwin Chadwick in 1842, which drew attention to the death and disease caused by poor sanitation, Doulton opened a new factory in 1845 to make salt-glazed stoneware drain pipes with a special non-leaking joint (Brown in Killock & Meddens 2003, 48–9). In the Grand Arcade street block, it was not until the 1870s that there is evidence for the use of salt-glazed cylindrical pipes with cupped mouths and even then unglazed facetted horseshoe and cylindrical with flattened base pipes continued in use for several decades. This suggests that globalizing narratives which focus on well-known individuals in major centres need to be nuanced by local comparisons. Other examples of such modern phenomena could include the abandonment of wells as mains water became available, although this was a prolonged process lasting several decades during which some wells were never abandoned.

Modernity is also of course expressed archaeologically through buildings. While the Robert Sayle department store provides the most imposing example in the Grand Arcade street block, and a similar theme is also expressed by the surviving frontage buildings, it is also eloquently conveyed by some of the buildings that covered the majority of the property tails during the nineteenth century. At this time there was a proliferation of purpose-built structures whose forms, despite later modifications, contained significant traces of their specific functions. These include a grocer's warehouse and kitchen (*Standing Building 70*, Plot XIII), a photographic studio (*Standing Building 72*, Plot X) and ceramic retailing storage and retail space (*Standing Buildings 94–96*, Plot XVII). More prosaically, there were also the slum-like court developments (*Buildings 53*, Plot XIX and *Buildings 55*, Plot XXII) and a WC block associated with a school (*Standing Building 99*, Plot XIV). These structures, and others like them that eventually covered most of the plot tails, created a densely occupied townscape redolent of modernity.

The twentieth century is of course not the end of the story. The archaeological investigations of 2005–6 comprised part of the £101 million Grand Arcade development, a process which lasted over three years and thus, in itself, forms a slice of the temporal sequence. The retention of many of the buildings of the

St Andrew's Street frontage, and more incongruously of the *putti* (Fig. 5.78D), means that the Grand Arcade development did not represent a complete abrogation of the past. It did, however, mark perhaps the most drastic change since the twelfth century, as well as the final extinction of the King's Ditch as even a residual topographic feature.

Yet it could be argued that the commercial and retail forces that put in train the development are the same as those represented in the archaeological record, particularly with regard to the Robert Sayle department store, and are therefore part of Braudel's *conjuncture* (circumstances) of the change of social and cultural history over centuries. While the John Lewis store, which occupies nearly 60 per cent of the retail floor space of Grand Arcade, largely represents continuity between pre- and post-development phases, it is notable that few of the other retail outlets mirror this pattern. At the time of writing (2015), the remaining businesses at Grand Arcade are dominated by clothing and footwear (28 retailers), accessories (13 retailers), home and entertainment (six retailers), food (five retailers), hair and beauty (four retailers), children (three retailers and travel (one retailer). None of these 60 retailers are businesses that occupied the development footprint prior to 2005, and several types of retailer that used to be represented in the area such as dry cleaners are now entirely absent.

Even in the relatively short time since the Grand Arcade development took place, further changes have occurred. In 2011, for example, the 1930s Post Office vacated its premises, emphasizing that, when dealing with the modern world, any archaeological investigation is not a full stop, but at most a comma.

The local and the global

It is a truism that archaeologists of the Late Modern period must 'think globally, dig locally' (Orser 1986, 183). Whilst many potential approaches to this issue could be adopted, one appropriate method on long-lived urban and suburban sites is to consider the balance between locally produced, 'vernacular' material and items that were traded over a longer distance. Such relationships are demonstrated to a degree by examining the provenance of the various ceramics that were in use over time (Figs. 4.56 and 5.96), although it must be noted that a rather different picture emerges when other material types are considered (Figs. 7.11–7.12). It is also possible to compare the origins of various tenants who were linked to the Grand Arcade street block via documentary evidence.

To a varying degree, throughout its long history the Grand Arcade street block had always comprised part of a 'world system' (see Wallerstein 1984); a fact that is rendered apparent archaeologically via the use of timber from Scandinavia and the Baltic region throughout the majority of its occupation. Moreover, by the late sixteenth–early seventeenth century this 'world' appears to have expanded, as revealed by the deposition of a cask from Ottoman Greece as well as West African grains-of-paradise, thereby reflecting the impact of the wider European Age of Discovery.

During the eleventh–twelfth centuries, the archaeological evidence for long distance contacts within the Grand Arcade street block includes the presence of Niedermendig Mülstein lava querns as well as whetstones from Eidsbrog in Norway (Fig. 7.11). Although fragments of a twelfth-century Scandinavian chest were also recovered, this item did not necessarily arrive at the site much in advance of its deposition during the fourteenth century. Similar querns and whetstones continued to be imported to the site throughout the medieval period, where, by the fourteenth century, they had been joined by fish from the North Sea, bricks from the Low Countries and timber from the Baltic (Fig. 7.11). In addition, pottery from, Siegburg, Germany, is also known to have reached Cambridge by this date (Newman & Evans 2011), although none of the sherds from the Grand Arcade could definitely be assigned to a pre fifteenth-century context.

Usefully, a rather different perspective can also be obtained regarding Cambridge's fourteenth-century 'economic world'. This is provided by the contents of a hoard of 1805 silver pennies and nine gold coins that was assembled *c.* 1351–2 and deposited beneath the floor of a building located within the town's Castle Hill suburb (Allen 2005). The hoard contained coins that were minted all over England as well as Ireland, Scotland and a large swathe of the European mainland (Fig. 7.12). As such, they demonstrate the extent of the international mercantile network with which the town was connected. This evidence can be contrasted with the relatively limited range of contemporary commodities that were identified archaeologically within the Barnwell Gate suburb. A small number of later silver coins have also been recovered from elsewhere in Cambridge, including those of Eric VII of Denmark (1412–39) and Leonardo Loredan of Venice (1501–21).

Within the Grand Arcade street block itself, many of the earlier imports continued into the sixteenth century. Both Niedermendig querns and Eastern Baltic timber remained present, for example. A range of pottery was also being imported from a variety of different sources, including the Netherlands, Langerwehe, Raeren, Frechen and – from the seventeenth century onwards – Westerwald. Jettons from Nuremberg became relatively common in the

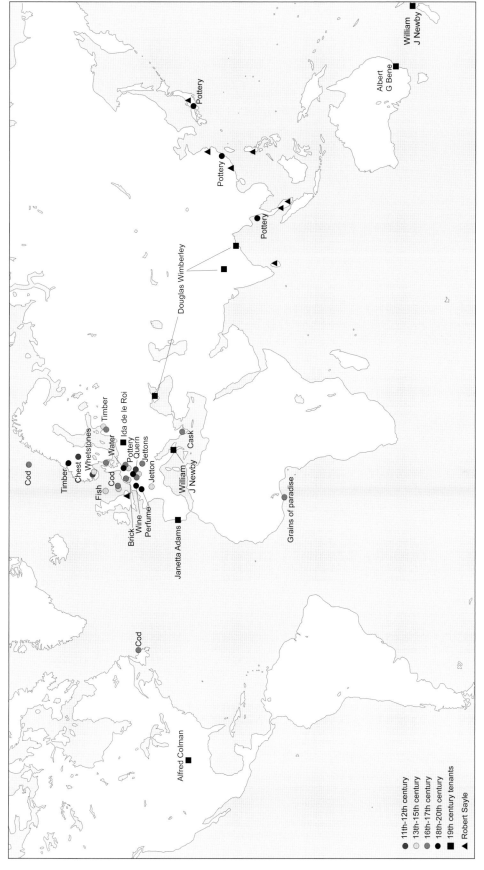

Figure 7.11. *International linkages with the Barnwell Gate suburb over time, including both imported materials and the origins of various nineteenth-century tenants.*

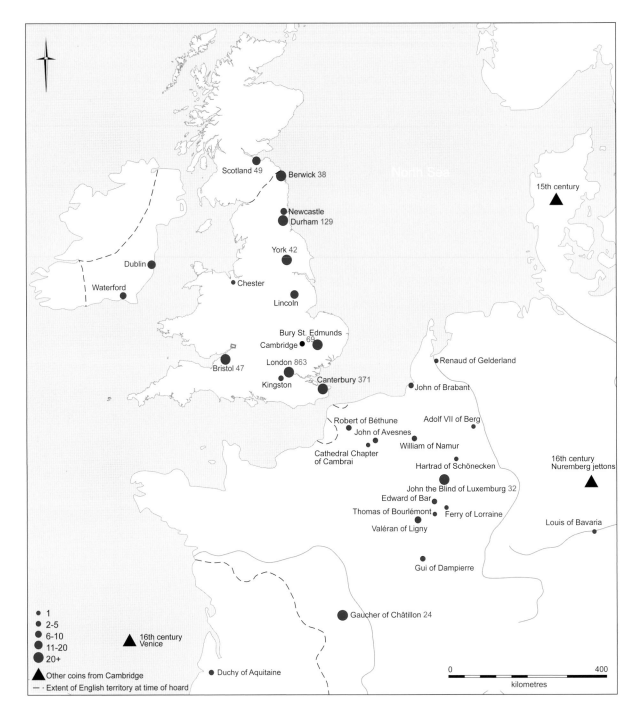

Figure 7.12. *The 'economic world' of the Chesterton Lane Corner coin hoard. This shows the derivations of the various coins that were included in the hoard, which was assembled c. 1351–2.*

late sixteenth–early seventeenth century. At around the same time, *c.* 1563–90, a cask was reused that has its origins in the Central and Western region of mainland Greece; its presence may thus have been related to the contemporary upswing in commercial relations with the Ottoman Empire and the formation of the Levant Company in 1581. Slightly later, *c.* 1616–37,

there were grains-of-paradise imported from coastal West Africa as part of the Second Atlantic system of the burgeoning slave trade.

In the eighteenth century pottery continued to be imported from both Frechen and Westerwald, while from the same general area there were also bottles of mineral water from Pyrmont and wine from France or Belgium. Porcelain was imported from China and the forms of the ceramic vessels themselves indirectly attest to the importation of tea from China, coffee from the Far East and their vital adjunct – to a British palate, at least – cane sugar from the Caribbean. But perhaps the most notable, if also ultimately the most tenuous, international link to the area can be found within the adjacent church of St Andrew the Great (Fig. 7.13). It consists of a memorial tablet to Captain James Cook (1728–79), who died at Kealakekua Bay, Hawaii.

Although Captain Cook's body was initially retained by the Hawaiian chiefs and elders, and some of the flesh potentially cut from his bones and roasted, his partial remains were eventually returned to the British for formal burial at sea (Collingridge 2003, 413). Although Cook himself had no personal connection to Cambridge during his lifetime, his son Hugh – the first of his children to die after infancy – perished while he was a student at Christ's College. Hugh was buried in the middle aisle of St Andrew the Great in 1793, subsequently to be followed by his brother James in 1794 and his mother Elizabeth in 1835. The family memorial thus became associated with the parish church of a small Cambridge suburb, thereby emphasizing the extent to which the world-view of this area had shifted from the local to the global. Captain Cook explored New Zealand in 1769, mapping the country and botanical exploration just under a century before William John Newby would arrive there (see inset above).

During the nineteenth century, Frechen pottery was still being imported to the site. Also present was Scandinavian timber from the area around Trondheim, as well as perfume from Paris, medicines containing opium from India and a Martaban-type jar from Southeast Asia. It was also during the nineteenth century that the first documentary evidence for international linkages among the inhabitants of the street block can be established. In 1851, census data reveals that individuals were present who had been born in America, Portugal and India. Perhaps the most telling of these is one Janetta Adams, a British citizen and army officer's daughter who was born in Portugal c. 1821. It appears likely that Janetta's father served with the British forces who ruled Portugal in the name of the absent king after the Peninsular War (1807–14) until a revolution of 1820, when they were driven out and the king returned as constitutional monarch.

In 1861, in contrast, the only resident born outside the British Isles was Albert Bene of Sydney, Australia. Ultimately, Albert became a clergyman in Staffordshire and Kew. In 1861, however, Albert was a pupil at the school run by Sarah Dobson in Plot XIII. In contrast to Albert, Sarah herself never appears to have travelled more than 20km from her birthplace, although there

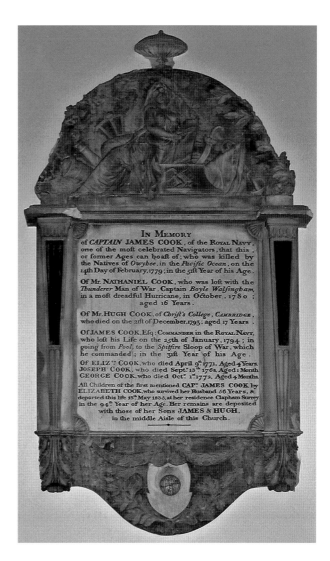

Figure 7.13. *The Cook family monument in the church of St Andrew the Great. This is headed by Captain James Cook, even though he died in Hawaii and never actually visited Cambridge.*

was some emigration to Australia from her home village during her lifetime. Whilst deposited rather earlier than Albert's time as a pupil, the Dobson household used 'Sicilian-pattern' pottery; a design that is also known to have been used contemporaneously in Australia. It is therefore possible that Albert used near indistinguishable ceramics 17,000km apart that were the 'same under a different sky' (Connah 2007, 191; see also Brooks & Connah 2007, 140). Although physically identical, this nevertheless raises the issue of whether the meaning(s) that the Sicilian-pattern conveyed remained the same in Cambridge as they had been Australia.

The 1871 census recorded no foreign-born residents, while that of 1881 recorded only one, who had been born in Prussia. Moreover, whilst the presence of

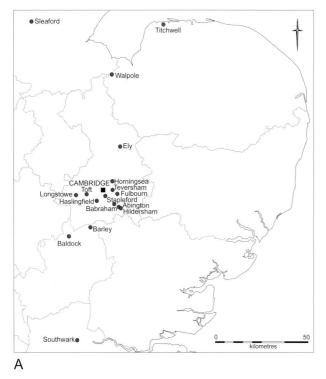

A

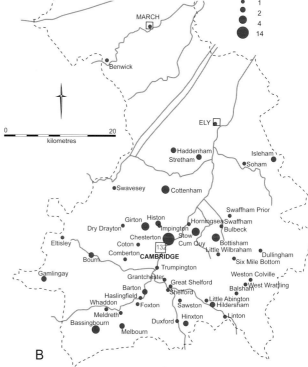

B

foreign inhabitants does indicate potential linkages to a broader global world, it is important to consider the fact that in 1881 the vast majority of the street block's inhabitants had been born in either Cambridge (39.3 per cent) or Cambridgeshire (26.2 per cent), with the rest deriving mainly from East Anglia (14.3 per cent) or elsewhere in England (18.5 per cent), and that only the remainder (1.7 per cent) originated from Scotland, Ireland or further afield (Fig. 7.14B–C). This highlights the degree to which, even at this late date, the street block remained predominately local in character. Yet in contrast to this residential pattern, by 1874 the Robert Sayle department store had established offices in Hong Kong and Shanghai and was involved in import and export trade that also encompassed Singapore, Ceylon, Penang, Manila and Japan. This far-flung business activity lasted until *c.* 1907 (Sieveking 2004, 32–3).

Over the centuries that the Grand Arcade street block was occupied, there is evidence to suggest that its connections gradually expanded in extent. This transition reflects broader trends that were often occurring at a national and indeed international scale. Nevertheless, despite its importance, this fact must not be allowed to obscure the significant role that local factors continued to play throughout all periods in its history. It is also notable that many of the linkages which have

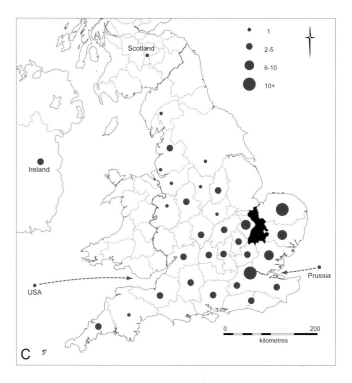

C

Figure 7.14. *Origins of people resident in the Grand Arcade and Christ's Lane street blocks: (A) individuals recorded in the thirteenth–fourteenth centuries, based on named attributions and toponymic surnames; (B) individuals from Cambridgeshire listed in the 1881 census; (C) individuals from the British Isles and beyond listed in the 1881 census.*

440

been outlined above were revealed via the isolated survival of fragile organic materials. Utilizing such evidence, connections have been made that would not necessarily have been established by the analysis of more traditional archaeological materials, such as pottery, alone.

Town versus gown

Any discussion of the archaeology of Cambridge must always bear in mind the 'town versus gown' issue; that is, the often asymmetrical relationship between the townspeople and, first, Cambridge's numerous religious institutions plus, later, the University. The biased nature of the surviving documentary records, which derive principally from the 'perpetual institutions' that make up the University, means that most aspects of the relationship have previously been considered from a College-dominated perspective (*e.g.* Lee 2003; Lee 2005). In contrast, the limited and generally small-scale opportunities for investigations on College and other University sites mean that the archaeological evidence is typically biased in the opposite direction, in favour of the town. Although often viewed primarily as adversarial (Parker 1983), the relationship between 'town' and 'gown' is in fact much more nuanced (Shephard 2000). Whilst this relationship is Cambridge-specific, the issue of the archaeological recognition of distinct social groups within towns is of much broader significance. Several aspects of the town versus gown relationship are revealed by the archaeology of the Grand Arcade street block. The reuse of moulded stone is one obvious example. The majority of this material was derived from the town's various religious institutions, particularly following the mid-sixteenth century Dissolution, when many such foundations were converted for collegiate use.

Perhaps the most striking signifiers of this relationship comprise the late eighteenth–twentieth-century ceramics that were marked during the manufacturing process with the names of Colleges and their cooks (Cessford 2016; Cessford 2017c; Cessford 2018c). These cooks were semi-independent contractors, who often maintained a number of varied business interests. They thus acted as middlemen whose activities spanned the two spheres, thereby challenging a simple 'town versus gown' distinction. The existence of such a group in Cambridge was of long standing; since at least the fourteenth century there have always been groups that enjoyed a 'privileged' position as 'scholars servants' and fell under the jurisdiction of the University and in the late sixteenth century they probably accounted for *c.* 12 per cent of the town's households (Shepard 2004, 7–8,

n. 10). In 1802 there were 145 'principal servants' of the Colleges, plus a 'considerable number more' in 'less honourable' positions (Pickles 2007). Although non-carceral, Cambridge Colleges are in a sense 'total institutions' with an isolated, enclosed social system whose primary purpose is to control most aspects of its participants' lives (Goffman 1961; also Macfarlane 2009, 106, 135). As most servants and a significant number of students lived outside the College boundaries they were extremely permeable entities. College-related crockery has, unsurprisingly, been found at a number of College sites, including St Johns College and Trinity College, despite the limited scale of many College-based investigations to date. Similar finds have also been made at a number of non-collegiate sites that were associated with College cooks, such as Thomas Wicks in Plot XV. Other discoveries relate to probable commercial links, such as the Jay family of grocers in Plot XIII (who may well have supplied Wicks with provisions). Similarly, fragments of College ceramics were also found in deposits associated with the Barrett family of china, earthenware and glass merchants in Plot XVII, suggesting that this business played a role in supplying ceramics to both cooks and Colleges.

Although the ceramics themselves often comprised the personal property of the cook rather than the College, many had a subsequent 'afterlife' following the end of that individual's employment. Continuing to be used and to circulate, such ceramics were sometimes employed in quite different environments from that for which they were originally intended (Cessford 2018b). One example of this is the varied assemblage of College-related material that was recovered from the Cock Inn in Plot XXII. In other instances, where no legitimate explanation apparently exists for their presence, some items were perhaps acquired illicitly by those who had no right to them. Whilst many of these latter ceramics were eventually dumped into convenient nearby features, others were taken off-site to the 'common dunghills' on the outskirts of the town; a situation that might explain how a disparate group of College material ended up being incorporated into the backfilling of the Civil War ditch of Cambridge Castle (Hall in Cessford 2008, 146, fig. 6).

Presumably, a small proportion was also subsequently conveyed out of the town on to the common fields. This process is less archaeologically visible, although at the North West Cambridge site – located within the city's encircling green belt – a pit containing utilitarian whitewares with a predominance of table and service wares, including numerous College-related vessels, was encountered (Cessford in Evans with Cessford in prep.; Cessford 2016). Finally, a few vessels – no doubt a vanishingly small percentage of the

Figure 7.15. *Nineteenth-century collegiate ceramics that have survived intact until the present day that parallel fragments discovered at Grand Arcade: (A) a plate of the cook of Gonville & Caius College showing the College court, this service was introduced c. 1820–38, was still being purchased until the 1960s and was employed on feast days until at least the 1990s. An example from Grand Arcade was deposited c. 1882–5 (see Fig. 5.61E); (B) a polychrome plate of Thomas Wicks, the cook at Emmanuel College; no examples of this or any other collegiate polychrome service have been recovered archaeologically but two other services associated with Wicks were recovered at Grand Arcade (see also Figs. 5.55C, 5.56A–D) (photographs courtesy of Peter Stoivin).*

original number – never broke and are still owned by Cambridge Colleges and private collectors (Fig. 7.15).

Significantly, these marked ceramics act as a form of archaeological 'tracer dye'. Highly distinctive and readily identifiable, they constitute a small percentage of the complex urban 'flow' of material culture, thus allowing the spatial and temporal passage of this material to be tracked. Densely occupied urban and suburban sites are amongst the most challenging to

investigate archaeologically, as they pose numerous methodological and intellectual challenges. One particularly important issue pertains to the relationship that prevailed between individual artefacts and the contexts in which they were deposited, in regards to the extent that the latter were related – or, potentially, unrelated – to the original usage of the item. Ceramics marked with the names of Cambridge Colleges and their cooks provide one mechanism for approaching the multi-dimensional complexity of such deposits, as well as elucidating to an extent the nature of the relationship(s) between 'town' and 'gown'.

Odd deposits and average practice

Concepts of 'placed', 'structured' or 'special' deposits originally developed in the context of prehistoric Britain have increasingly come to be applied to later periods, such as the Anglo-Saxon period (Hamerow 2006; Morris & Jervis 2011), at the same time that the concepts have come under sustained critique (Chadwick 2012; Garrow 2012). The large-scale of the investigations at Grand Arcade and the significant temporal span provides a useful context to consider 'odd' deposits and 'average' practice (Garrow 2012). Average depositional practice at Grand Arcade clearly involved a wide range of variation and there are many deposits that if analogously replicated in a prehistoric context would often be interpreted as 'structured' or 'ritual'. In most instances at Grand Arcade such an interpretation appears highly unlikely, even if many deposits are clearly structured in the broadest sense of the term. Even from a ritual-phobic perspective, however, a core of 'odd' or inexplicable deposits remains.

Prominent amongst these 'odd' deposits are the iron scythe head in twelfth-century *Pit 6* (Fig. 4.9), the two *in situ* ladders in mid-sixteenth-century *WFFs 14* and *15* (Figs. 4.46 and 4.48), and the four carefully arranged horse skulls in seventeenth-century *Pit 56* under *Wall 4* (Fig. 5.7). How to interpret these is unclear, but perhaps the main conclusion to recognize is simply the rarity of such apparently inexplicable deposits. In terms of material composition, feature type, location etc. particular sets of material do occur in specific contexts, an obvious and highly distinctive example being nearly complete ceramic jugs in the base of thirteenth–fifteenth-century wells (Figs. 4.14–4.16 and 4.24). There is also clear structuring in terms of the large assemblages found in certain types of late eighteenth–early twentieth-century features. At the broadest level the concept of structured deposition is applicable to medieval and later material, although its application needs to be relatively nuanced and holistic to represent a substantive improvement upon empirical common sense (Cessford 2017a).

Conclusion

The Cambridge Archaeological Unit has been undertaking fieldwork in Cambridgeshire for 25 years. Over the course of this period many important sites have been excavated, several of which have been published within the unit's *New Archaeologies of the Cambridge*

Region monograph series. Yet the present book marks the first occasion that Cambridge itself has played a significant role in any such study. The reasons for this are two-fold. Firstly, there is the issue of *temporality*; arguably, Cambridge only became the central place in the region from the tenth century onwards, whereas most previous studies have been prehistoric and Roman in focus. Secondly, there is the issue of *location*; the present work marks much the largest investigation yet to have been undertaken in close proximity to the town.

Another important facet of this observation is that it highlights the concept of 'place'. At its heart this volume is unashamedly empiricist and, in common with most archaeological fieldwork, has been structured around the concept that excavations occur in a particular place and consist of antecedent and successive phases. This default position of Cartesian nihilism, whilst undeniable, is not necessarily 'true' at a deeper level. During the prehistoric to Anglo-Saxon periods, for example, there is no compelling evidence to suggest that the investigated area comprised a meaningful *place*; it appears, in contrast, to have been little more than a generic *space* within a broader landscape that was utilized but not inhabited. It can only be defined as an identifiable place, or perhaps conglomerate of places, following the establishment of dispersed occupation in the mid-eleventh century. Nevertheless, with the advent of a large-scale imposed layout during the early twelfth century it could be argued that the site's previous identity was lost and a new and different place created.

Similarly, despite some limited evidence of continuity, the early/mid-twelfth-century creation of the King's Ditch potentially altered the area to such a degree that it was to all intents and purposes re-established once again. These extensive twelfth-century changes led to the creation of the Grand Arcade and Christ's Lane street blocks – or, more poetically, 'islands' (Pantin 1937, 171) – establishing the form in which they were to survive, largely unaltered, until the late eighteenth–early nineteenth century. Following this date, however, the final infilling of the King's Ditch – and, even more significantly, the rapid expansion of the town out beyond its former suburbs into what had previously been open fields – altered the character of the area irrevocably. The street blocks were transformed from elements of a well-defined suburb into adjuncts of the expanded urban core, although such extensive changes also went hand in hand with a few pronounced continuities.

Indeed, even between the mid-twelfth to the late eighteenth century, a period of relative archaeological stability, a number of significant changes had occurred at a broader, town-wide level. At the start of this period, for example, Cambridge was only a minor county town, whilst by its close it was the home of a world-renowned University. Therefore, even had the suburb itself remained entirely consistent in character throughout (which it did not), it would nevertheless have been transformed in relation to the town of which it comprised a part. During the medieval period both street blocks were composed of a series of essentially self-contained properties, where people lived, carried out craft activities and grew or raised much of their own food. By the late eighteenth century, however, these property 'islands' no longer existed in the same manner, as people's lives had become much more spatially divided; a process that effectively culminated during the nineteenth–twentieth centuries.

The exigencies and imperatives of the modern capitalist world meant that, in the early twenty-first century, around 900 years of largely organic development came to an end. Yet some of the minor by-products of those same forces ensured that major archaeological investigations took place, which attempted to make this transition an ultimately creative as opposed to destructive process (see Lucas 2001). This is especially true as a *longue durée* view of the archaeological record would suggest that many of these same forces were already in existence by the twelfth century, and that the Grand Arcade development should thus be regarded as merely one facet of a much larger narrative. Given the pressures and constrictions on space that predominate in a modern, thriving city, it is highly unlikely that so large a contiguous site as Grand Arcade will ever be excavated in Cambridge again. As such, the material presented in this volume must represent something of a high watermark. Nevertheless, additional small-scale investigations located within the town core, the King's Ditch, the suburbs and the town fields will doubtless continue, providing scope for the further refinement and elaboration of the ideas presented here.

Rather belatedly, perhaps, the archaeology of Cambridge is viewed not only as *Prehistory at Cambridge and Beyond* (Clarke 1989), but as a more holistic subject, where all periods are treated equally and College crockery or Keiller marmalade jars comprise a legitimate subject for investigation. It has long been recognized that 'working within the pressures of a living town' raises particular problems and requires long-term commitment to avoid the fragmentation so common in post-1990 British archaeology, which in turn leads to 'intellectually and financially ineffective … technician's archaeology' (Biddle 1983, 128–9). It is ironic that whilst PPG 16 and developer-funded archaeology have undeniably produced some negative results in many British towns – and have been decried by two leading archaeologists whose early work arguably represented the most successful precursor to the current work of the Cambridge Archaeological Unit (Addyman 2005; Biddle 2005) – for Cambridge itself, their advent has represented a major advance.

Unfortunately, the constraints inherent in British developer-funding meant that no organized 'ethno-archaeological' recording of the area was undertaken in the period 1997–2005, when businesses such as Robert Sayle remained functioning entities at the site. Instead, work only commenced during the redevelopment's initial 'aftermath', when their constituent buildings had already been abandoned. The standing building recording, in particular, took place within what was effectively a ghost town. Yet although many fixtures and fittings had been removed prior to the start of fieldwork, much remained. This situation led to certain notable disjunctions, such as that engendered by encountering a room filled with abandoned shop-floor mannequins (Fig. 5.80). It also meant that selected elements, such as tables and chairs (Figs. 5.80–5.81), found continued, secondary employment by the project's archaeologists; indeed, almost all of the paper archive is still held within reclaimed ring-binders. Of course, a further aftermath comprises the completed, re-branded John Lewis store (Fig. 5.81), which has expunged most – though by no means all – traces of its predecessor. But as the pace of Cambridge's physical and economic development continues to increase, it is clear that further opportunities for archaeological excavation will arise. In this respect, therefore, the present investigations can also potentially be regarded as a prelude.

Bibliography

Adburgham, A., 1964. *Shops and Shopkeeping 1800–1914: where and in what manner the well-dressed Englishwoman bought her clothes*. London: George Allen & Unwin.

Addis, W., 1997. Concrete and steel in twentieth century construction: from experimentation to mainstream usage, in *Structure and Style: conserving 20th century buildings*, ed. M. Stratton, M. London: Taylor & Francis, 103–42.

Addyman, P.V., 1997. York Archaeological Trust: 25 years a growing. *Archaeology York* 22, 5–12.

Addyman, P.V., 2005. Peter Addyman. *Current Archaeology* 200, 436–8.

Addyman, P.V. & Biddle, M., 1965. Medieval Cambridge: recent finds and excavations. *Proceedings of the Cambridge Antiquarian Society* 63, 74–137.

Albarella, U., 1997. Size, power, wool and veal: zooarchaeological evidence for late medieval innovations, *Environment and Subsistence in Medieval Europe*, eds. G. de Bow & F. Verhaeghe. Bruges: Institute for the Archaeology Heritage of Flanders, 19–30.

Albarella, U., 2005. Meat production and consumption in town and country, in *Town and country in the Middle Ages: contrasts, contacts and interconnections 1100–1500*, eds. K. Giles & C. Dyer. (Society for Medieval Archaeology Monograph 22.) Leeds: Maney, 131–48.

Albarella, U., 2006. Pig husbandry and pork consumption in medieval England, in *Food in Medieval England: diet and Nutrition*, eds. C.M. Woolgar, D. Serjeantson & T. Waldron. Oxford: Oxford University Press, 72–87.

Albarella, U. & Davis, S., 1996. Mammal and bird bones from Launceston Castle: decline in status and the rise of agriculture. *Circaea* 12(1), 1–156.

Albarella, U., Beech, M. & Mulville, J., 1997. *Saxon, Medieval and Post-Medieval Mammal and Bird Bones Excavated 1989–91 from Castle Mall, Norwich, Norfolk*. (Ancient Monuments Laboratory Report 72/97.) London: Ancient Monuments Laboratory.

Albarella, U. & Thomas, R., 2002. They dined on Crane: bird consumption, wild fowling and status in medieval England, *Actazoologica Cracoviensia* 45, 23–38.

Alexander, J.A., 1970. Red Lion Car Park, Cambridge. *Archaeological Excavations 1969*, 63.

Alexander, J.A., 1972. Red Lion Car Park, Cambridge. *Archaeological Excavations 1971*, 68.

Alexander, J.A. undated. *The Lion Yard Excavation Archive*. Unpublished archive. Cambridge: Cambridgeshire County Records Office.

Alexander, J.A. & Pullinger, J., 1999. Roman Cambridge: excavations on Castle Hill 1956–1988. *Proceedings of the Cambridge Antiquarian Society* 87.

Alexander, J.S., 1995. Building stone from the East Midlands quarries: sources, transportation and usage. *Medieval Archaeology* 39, 106–35.

Alexander, M., 1997a. *An archaeological evaluation at Homerton College, Cambridge*. (CAU Report 198.) Cambridge: Cambridge Archaeological Unit.

Alexander, M., 1997b. *Excavations for the New Library Extension, Trinity Hall College, Cambridge*. (CAU Report 222.) Cambridge: Cambridge Archaeological Unit.

Alexander, M., 2003. A medieval and post-medieval street frontage: investigations at Forehill, Ely. *Proceedings of the Cambridge Antiquarian Society* 92, 135–82.

Allen, M., 1999. The Pembroke College, Cambridge hoard of Tudor and Stuart gold coins. *British Numismatic Journal* 69, 222–6.

Allen, M., 2005. The fourteenth-century hoard from Chesterton Lane Corner, Cambridge. *British Numismatic Journal* 75, 63–90.

Alsleben, A., 2009. Changes in food consumption during the period of urbanisation in northern Central Europe, in *Archaeology of Medieval Towns in the Baltic and North Sea Area*, eds. N. Engberg, A.N. Jørgensen, J. Kieffer-Olsen, P.K. Madsen, & C. Radtke. (National Museum Studies in Archaeology and History 17.) Copenhagen: Aarhus University Press, 65–72.

Anon., 1843. New churches. *The Ecclesiologist* 2, 136–8.

Appleby, G. 2010. *New Library Building, Christ's College, Cambridge: an archaeological desktop assessment*. (CAU Report 975.) Cambridge: Cambridge Archaeological Unit.

Armour, N., 2002. *Archaeological evaluation at the former government offices site, Brooklands Avenue, Cambridge*. (CAU Report 467.) Cambridge: Cambridge Archaeological Unit.

Arndt, B. & Wiethold, J., 2001. Pflaume, Pfeffer und Paradieskorn. *Archäologie in Niedersachsen* 4, 35–9.

Ashley, S., 2002. *Medieval Armorial Horse Furniture in Norfolk*. (East Anglian Archaeology 101.) Dereham: Archaeology

& Environment Division, Norfolk Museums & Archaeology Service.

Astill, G., 2000. Archaeology and the late-medieval urban decline, in *Towns in Decline, AD 100–1600*, ed. T.R. Slater. Aldershot: Ashgate, 214–34.

Astill, G. & Langdon, J., 1997. *Medieval Farming and Technology: the impact of agricultural change in northwest Europe*. Leiden: Brill.

Aston, M., 1992. *Interpreting the Landscape: landscape archaeology and local history*. London: Batsford.

Aston, M., 2000. *Monasteries in the Landscape*. Stroud: Tempus.

Atkin, M., 2002. Excavations in the suburb of Heigham, *Excavations in Norwich 1971–1978 part III*, M. Atkin & D.H. Evans. (East Anglian Archaeology 100.) Norwich: Norwich Survey, 199–234.

Atkins, P.J., 1977. London's intra-urban milk supply, circa 1790–1914. *Journal of the Institute of British Geographers* 2, 383–99.

Atkins, P.J., 1980. The retail milk trade in London, *c.*1790–1914. *Economic History Review* 33(4), 522–37.

Atkins, R., 2012. Between river, priory and town: excavations at the former Cambridge Regional College site, Brunswick, Cambridge. *Proceedings of the Cambridge Antiquarian Society* 101, 7–22.

Atkins, R. 2015a. *Early Iron Age and medieval to modern settlement remains at Harvest Way, Barnwell, Cambridge: PXA and UPD*. (OAEast Report 1632.) Bar Hill: Oxford Archaeology East.

Atkins, R., 2015b, *Medieval to modern remains at Newmarket Road, Barnwell, Cambridge - PXA and UPD*. (OAEast Report 1669a.) Bar Hill: Oxford Archaeology East.

Atkinson, T.D., 1899. On a bridge over the King's Ditch. *Proceedings of the Cambridge Antiquarian Society* 9 (1), 33–5.

Atkinson, T.D., 1907. On a survey of the King's Ditch at Cambridge made in 1629. *Proceedings of the Cambridge Antiquarian Society* 11 (2), 251–4.

Augé, M., (translated J. Howe). 1995. *Non-Places: introduction to an anthropology of supermodernity*. London: Verso.

Augé, M., (translated A. Jacobs). 1998. *A Sense for the Other: the timeliness and relevance of anthropology*. Stanford: Stanford University Press.

Ayers, B., 1987. *Excavations at St Martin-at-Palace Plain, Norwich, 1981*. (East Anglian Archaeology 37.) Dereham: Norfolk Archaeological Unit, Norfolk Museums Service.

Ayers, B., 2000. Anglo-Saxon, medieval and post-medieval (urban), in *Research and Archaeology: a framework for the eastern counties. 2. Research agenda and strategy*, eds. N. Brown, & J. Glazebrook. (East Anglian Archaeology Occasional Paper 8) Norwich: Scole Archaeological Committee for East Anglia, 27–32.

Ayers, B. & Murphy, P., 1983. A waterfront excavation at Whitefriars Street Car Park, Norwich, 1979, in *Waterfront excavation and Thetford ware production, Norwich*, ed. P. Wade Martin. (East Anglian Archaeology 17.) Gressenhall: Norfolk Archaeological Unit, Norfolk Museums Service, 1–60.

Baart, J.M., 1994. Dutch redwares. *Medieval Ceramics* 18, 19–27.

Baggs, T. & Bryan, P., 2002. *Cambridge 1574–1904. A portfolio of twelve maps illustrating the changing plan of Cambridge from the sixteenth to the twentieth century*. Cambridge: Cambridgeshire Records Society.

Baggs, T. & Dickens, A., 2005. *22–25 St. Andrew's Street, Cambridge. Historic Building Survey: the listed buildings*. (CAU Report 698.) Cambridge: Cambridge Archaeological Unit.

Bagshawe, T.W., 1956. Rake and scythe-handle making in Bedfordshire and Suffolk. *Gwerin* 1, 34–46.

Baillie, M.G.L. & Pilcher, J.R., 1973. A simple crossdating program for tree-ring research. *Tree Ring Bulletin 33*, 7–14.

Baker, N. & Holt, R., 2004. *Urban Growth and the Medieval Church: Gloucester and Worcester*. Aldershot: Ashgate.

Ballantyne, R., 2004. Islands in wilderness: the changing medieval use of the East Anglian peat fens, England: *Environmental Archaeology* 9(2), 189–98.

Barker, D. & Majewski, T., 2006. Ceramic studies in Historical Archaeology, in *The Cambridge Companion to Historical Archaeology*, eds. D. Hicks & M. Beaudry Cambridge: Cambridge University Press, 205–31.

Barley, M.W., 1961. Excavation of the Borough Ditch, Slaughterhouse Lane, Newark, 1961. *Transactions of the Thoroton Society of Nottinghamshire* 65, 10–18.

Barley, M.W., 1976a. (ed.) *The Plans and Topography of Medieval Towns in England and Wales,* Council for British Archaeology Research Report 14. York.

Barley, M.W., 1976b. Town defences in England and Wales after 1066, in *The Plans and Topography of Medieval Towns in England and Wales,* ed. M.W. Barley. (Council for British Archaeology Research Report 14.) Council for British Archaeology: York, 57–71.

Barrett, J.H., Locker, A.M. & Roberts, C.M., 2004a. 'Dark Age Economics' revisited: the English fish bone evidence AD 600–1600. *Antiquity* 78 (301), 618–36.

Barrett, J.H., Locker, A.M. & Roberts, C.M., 2004b. The origins of intensive marine fishing in medieval Europe: the English evidence. *Proceedings of the Royal Society of London B* 271 (1556), 2417–21.

Barrett, J.H., Orton, D., Johnstone, C., Harland, J., van Neer, W., Ervynck, A., Roberts, C., Locker, A., Amundsen, C., Enghoff, I.B., Hamilton-Dyer, S., Heinrich, D., Hufthammer, A.K., Jones, A.K.G., Jonsson, L., Makowiecki, D., Pope, P., O'Connell, T.C., de Roo, T. & Richards, M., 2011. Interpreting the expansion of sea fishing in medieval Europe using stable isotope analysis of archaeological cod bones. *Journal of Archaeological Science* 38(7), 1516–24.

Bartlett, J.A., 1993. *British Ceramic Art 1870–1940*. Atlgen: Schiffer.

Bassett, S.R., 1982. *Saffron Walden: excavation and research 1972–80*. (Council for British Archaeology Research Report 45.) York: Council for British Archaeology.

Bateman, C., Enright, D. & Hancocks, A., 2004. The development of Oxford's northern suburb: evidence from 1–12 Magdalene Street (SP 5016 0646). *South Midlands Archaeology* 34, 58–65.

Beaudry, M., 1999. House and household: the archaeology of domestic life in Early America, in *Old World and New*, eds. G. Egan & R.L. Michael. Oxford: Oxbow Books, 117–26.

Bellamy, B., 1983. Medieval pottery kilns at Stanion. *Northamptonshire Archaeology* 18, 153–61.

Bellamy, P.S., 2006. Bridport's 13th-century defences: archaeological observations to the rear of 41 and 43 East Street, Bridport. *Proceedings of the Dorset Natural History and Archaeology Society* 127, 59–66.

Beresford, M. 1988. *New Towns of the Middle Ages: town plantation in England, Wales and Gascony.* Gloucester: Alan Sutton.

Biddle, M., 1976. Towns, in *The Archaeology of Anglo-Saxon England*, ed. D.M. Wilson. London: Methuen, 99–150.

Biddle, M., 1983. The study of Winchester: archaeology and history in a British town. *Proceedings of the British Academy* 69, 93–135.

Biddle, M., 2005. Martin Biddle. *Current Archaeology* 200, 442–3.

Biddle, M., 2008. Recollections of a student archaeologist, *Pembroke College Cambridge Gazette* 82, 51–5.

Biddle, M. & Webster, J., 2005. Green glass bottles, in *Nonsuch Palace: the material culture of a noble restoration household*, M. Biddle. Oxford: Oxbow, 266–92.

Bimson, M., 1970. The significance of ale-measure marks. *Post-Medieval Archaeology* 4. 165–6.

Blacker, J.F., 1922. *The A B C of English Salt-glaze Stoneware from Dwight to Doulton.* London: Stanley Paul.

Blair, J., 2005. *The Church in Anglo-Saxon Society.* Oxford: Oxford University Press.

Blanco-González, A., 2014. Tracking the social lives of things: biographical insights into Bronze Age pottery in Spain. *Antiquity* 88(340), 441–55.

Blatherwick, S. & Bluer, R., 2009. *Great Houses, Moats and Mills on the South Bank of the Thames: medieval and Tudor Southwark and Rotherhithe.* (MoLAS Monograph 47.) London: MoLAS.

Boessneck, J., von den Driesch, A., Meyer-Lempennau, U. & Weschler-von Ohlen, E., 1971. *Das Tierknochenfunde aus dem Oppidum von Manching. Die Ausgrabungen in Manching 6.* Wiesbaden: Franz Steiner Verlag.

Bond, J.M. & O'Connor, T.P., 1999. *Bones from Medieval Deposits at 16–22 Coppergate and Other Sites in York.* (Archaeology of York 15/5). York: Council for British Archaeology.

Boothroyd, N., 2009. *'A small liberty of scattered farm-houses and collieries': excavations at Cotehouse Farm and Lawn Farm, Berryhill, Stoke-on-Trent, Staffordshire, 2003–2007.* (Stoke-on-Trent Archaeological Service Monograph 3.) Stoke-on-Trent: Stoke-on-Trent Museums.

Boothroyd, N. & Higgins, D., 2005. An inn-clearance group, *c.* 1800, from the Royal Oak, Eccleshall, Staffordshire. *Post-Medieval Archaeology* 39, 197–203.

Bowsher, D., Dyson, T., Holder, N. & Howell, I., 2007. *The London Guildhall. An archaeological history of a neighbourhood from early medieval to modern times.* (MoLAS Monograph 36.) London: MoLAS.

Bowsher, J. & Miller, P., 2009. *The Rose and the Globe – playhouses of Shakespeare's Bankside, Southwark: excavations 1988–91.* (MoLAS Monograph 48.) London: MoLAS.

Bradley, R.J., 1968. The story of Castle Hedingham pottery (1837–1905) Part I. *The Connoisseur* (February–April 1968), 16–20.

Bragdon, K.J., 1988. Occupational differences reflected in material culture, in *Documentary Archaeology in the New World*, ed. M.E. Beaudry. Cambridge: Cambridge University Press, 83–91.

Bramwell, D., 1986. Report on the bird bone, in *Coventry: excavations on the town wall 1976–78*, J. Bateman & M. Redknap. (Coventry Museums Monograph Series 2.) Coventry: Coventry Museums, 120–1.

Brantz, D., 2017. Assembling the multitude: questions about agency in the urban environment. *Urban History* 44(1), 130–6.

Braudel, F., 1958. Histoire et sciences sociales: la longue durée. *Annales. Histoire, Sciences Sociales* 13(4), 725–53.

Braudel, F. & Coll, A., 1987. Histoire et sciences sociales: la longue durée. *Réseaux* 5, 7–37.

Brears, P.C.D., 1971. *The English Country Pottery: its history and techniques.* Newton Abbot: David & Charles.

Briggs, A., 1985. *Wine for Sale: Victoria Wine and the liquor trade 1860–1984.* London: Batsford.

Briggs, A., 1988. *Victorian Things.* London: Batsford.

Briscoe, G. & Dunning, G.C., 1967. Medieval pottery, roof-fittings and a water-pipe found at Ely. *Proceedings of the Cambridge Antiquarian Society* 40, 81–9.

Bronk Ramsey, C. & Lee, S. 2013. Recent and planned developments of the program OxCal. *Radiocarbon* 55(2–3), 720–30.

Brooke, C.N.L., 1985. The Medieval churches of Cambridge, in *History, Society and the Churches: essays in honour of Owen* Chadwick, eds. D. Beales & G. Best. Cambridge: Cambridge University Press, 49–76.

Brooks, A., 2005a. *An Archaeological Guide to British Ceramics in Australia, 1788–1901.* Sydney: Australasian Society for Historical Archaeology.

Brooks, A., 2005b. Observing formalities - the use of functional artefact categories in Australian historical archaeology. *Australasian Historical Archaeology* 23, 7–14.

Brooks, A. & Connah, G., 2007. A hierarchy of servitude: ceramics at Lake Innes Estate, New South Wales. *Antiquity* 81 (311), 133–47.

Brooks, C.M., 1983. Aspects of the sugar-refining industry from the 16th to the 19th century. *Post-Medieval Archaeology* 17, 1–14.

Brothwell, D., 1982. Linking urban man with his built environment, *Environmental Archaeology in the Urban Context*, eds. R.A. Hall & H.K. Kenward. (Council for British Archaeology Research Report 43.) York: Council for British Archaeology, 126–9.

Browne, D.M., 1974. An archaeological gazetteer of the city of Cambridge, 1973. *Proceedings of the Cambridge Antiquarian Society* 65, 1–38.

Bruce-Mitford, R.S.L., 1939. The archaeology of the site of the Bodleian Extension, Broad Street, Oxford. *Oxoniensia* 4, 89–146.

Bryan, P., 1999. *Cambridge: the shaping of the city.* Cambridge: Privately published.

Bryan, P. & Wise, N., 2002. A reconstruction of the medieval Cambridge market place. *Proceedings of the Cambridge Antiquarian Society* 91, 73–87.

Bryan, P. & Wise, N., 2005. Cambridge New Town – a Victorian microcosm. *Proceedings of the Cambridge Antiquarian Society* 94, 199–216.

Bryant, J.G. & Steane, J.M., 1969. Excavations at the deserted medieval settlement at Lyveden [Northamptonshire]: a second interim report. *Journal of the Northampton Museum and Art Gallery* 5, 1–50.

Buchli, V. & Lucas, G., (eds.) 2001. *Archaeologies of the Contemporary Past*. London: Routledge.

Buck C.E., Christen J.A. & James G.N., 1999. BCal: an on-line Bayesian radiocarbon calibration tool. *Internet Archaeology* 7. Available at: http://intarch.ac.uk/journal/issue7/buck/ Accessed 7 July 2011.

Buckley, R., 1987. *Leicester Town Defences: excavations 1958–74.* (Leicestershire Museum Publications 85). Leicester: Leicestershire Museums, Art Galleries & Records Service.

Burch, M. & Treveil, P. with Keene, D.J., 2010. *The Development of Early Medieval and Later Poultry and Cheapside: Excavations at 1 Poultry and vicinity, City of London.* (MoLAS Monograph 38.) London: MoLAS.

Bushnell, G.H.S. & Hurst, J.G., 1952. Some further examples of sgraffito ware from Cambridge. *Proceedings of the Cambridge Antiquarian. Society* 46, 21–6.

Butler, L., 1976. The evolution of towns: planned towns after 1066, in *The Plans and Topography of Medieval Towns in England and Wales*, ed. M.W. Barley. (Council for British Archaeology Research Report 14.) York: Council for British Archaeology, 32–47.

Butler, R., 2001. The City defences at Aldersgate. *Transactions of the London and Middlesex Archaeological Society* 52, 41–111.

Caius, J., 1568. *Historia Cantabrigiensis Acadimae.* London.

Calladine, T., 2001. 'A paragon of lucidity and taste': the Peter Jones department store. *Transactions of the Ancient Monuments Society* 45, 7–28.

Cam, H.M., 1934. The origin of the Borough of Cambridge: a consideration of Professor Carl Stephenson's theories. *Proceedings of the Cambridge Antiquarian Society* 35, 33–53.

Cam, H.M., 1959. The City of Cambridge, in *A History of the County of Cambridge and the Isle of Ely Vol. 3: the City and University of Cambridge*, ed. J.P.C. Roach. London: Oxford University Press, 1–149.

Campbell, B.M.S. & Overton, M., 1992. Norfolk livestock farming 1250–1740: a comparative study of manorial accounts and probate inventories. *Journal of Historical Geography* 18(4), 377–96.

Campbell, B.M.S. & Overton, M., 1993. A new perspective on medieval and early modern agriculture: six centuries of Norfolk farming, c.1250–c.1850. *Past & Present* 141, 38–105.

Carter, A., 1972. Nottingham Town Wall Park Row excavations. *Transactions of the Thoroton Society of Nottinghamshire* 75, 33–40.

Carter, A., 1977. Wooden objects, in *Excavations in King's Lynn 1963–1970*, H. Clarke & A. Carter. (Society for Medieval Archaeology Monograph 7.) London: Society for Medieval Archaeology, 366–74.

Carter, S., 2001. A reassessment of the origins of the St Andrews 'garden soil'. *Tayside and Fife Archaeological Journal* 7, 87–92.

Carver, M.O.H., 1987. *Underneath English Towns: interpreting urban archaeology.* London: Batsford.

Carver, M.O.H., 2010. *The Birth of a Borough: an archaeological study of Anglo-Saxon Stafford.* Woodbridge: Boydell.

Casella, E.C.C. & Croucher, S.K., 2010. *The Alderley Sandhills Project: an archaeology of community life in (post) industrial England.* Manchester: Manchester University Press.

Cattermole, M.J.G. & Wolfe, A.F., 1987. *Horace Darwin's Shop: A History of the Cambridge Scientific Company 1878 to 1968.* Bristol: Adam Hilger.

Cessford, C., 2001a. Pipemaking at No. 11 Sidney Street, Cambridge. *Society for Clay Pipe Research Newsletter* 57, 13–22.

Cessford, C., 2001b. Clay tobacco pipe kiln muffle from Cambridge. *Society for Clay Pipe Research Newsletter* 58, 17–25.

Cessford, C., 2001c. The clay tobacco pipe industry in Cambridgeshire and Huntingdonshire. *Cambridgeshire Local History Society Review* 10, 3–19.

Cessford, C., 2003a. *Cambridge and County Folk Museum: an archaeological excavation.* (CAU Report 574.) Cambridge: Cambridge Archaeological Unit.

Cessford, C., 2003b. *Cambridge University Botanic Garden, Cambridge: an archaeological evaluation.* (CAU Report 575.) Cambridge: Cambridge Archaeological Unit.

Cessford, C., 2005. *Hostel Yard, Corpus Christi College, Cambridge: an archaeological excavation.* (CAU Report 673.) Cambridge: Cambridge Archaeological Unit.

Cessford, C., 2006. Tobias Anthony of Cambridge. *Society for Clay Pipe Research Newsletter* 69, 14–15.

Cessford, C., 2007. *Grand Arcade Cambridge: an archaeological excavation.* (CAU Report 800.) Cambridge: Cambridge Archaeological Unit.

Cessford, C., 2008. Excavation of the Civil War bastion ditch of Cambridge Castle. *Proceedings of the Cambridge Antiquarian Society* 96, 137–48.

Cessford, C., 2009. Post-1550 urban archaeology in a developer-funded context: an example from Grand Arcade, Cambridge, in *Crossing Paths or Sharing Tracks? Future directions in the archaeological study of post-1550 Britain and Ireland*, eds. A. Horning & M. Palmer, M. Woodbridge: Boydell & Brewer, 301–21.

Cessford, C., 2011. The use of 'local' clay for making pipes in 17th century Cambridge [based upon work by the late A. Vince]. *Society for Clay Pipe Research Newsletter* 79, 25–6.

Cessford, C., 2012. Life in a 'cathedral of consumption': corporate and personal material culture recovered from a cellar at the Robert Sayle department store in Cambridge, England, c. 1913–21. *International Journal of Historical Archaeology* 16(4), 784–808.

Cessford, C., 2013a. Different times, different materials and different purposes: writing on objects at the Grand Arcade site in Cambridge, in *Writing as Material Practice: substance, surface and medium*, eds. K.E. Piquette & R.D. Whitehouse. London: Ubiquity Press, 289–317.

Cessford, C., 2013b. Huntingdon Street, St Neots: from medieval suburb to early 20th century household. *Proceedings of the Cambridge Antiquarian Society* 102, 93–110.

Cessford, C., 2014a. Assemblage biography and the life course: an archaeologically materialized temporality

448

of Richard and Sarah Hopkins. *International Journal of Historical Archaeology* 18(4), 555–90.

Cessford, C., 2014b. The archaeology of garden-related material culture: a case study from Grand Arcade, Cambridge, 1760–1940. *Garden History* 42(2), 257–65.

Cessford, C., 2014c. An assemblage of collegiate ceramics: mid-nineteenth century dining at Trinity Hall, Cambridge. *Archaeological Journal* 171(1), 340–80.

Cessford, C., 2015a. The St John's Hospital cemetery and environs, Cambridge: contextualizing the medieval dead. *Archaeological Journal* 172(1), 52–120.

Cessford, C., 2015b. Howes: a hunting-related medieval hamlet near Cambridge? *Medieval Archaeology* 59, 319–22.

Cessford, C., 2016. Cambridge College ceramics *c.* 1760–1900: a brief overview. *Proceedings of the Cambridge Antiquarian Society* 105, 109–25.

Cessford, C., 2017a. Throwing away everything but the kitchen sink? Large assemblages, depositional practice and post-medieval households in Cambridge, *Post-Medieval Archaeology* 51(1), 164–93.

Cessford, C., 2017b. Riparian Cambridge, archaeological excavations near the River Cam at WYNG Gardens, Thompson's Lane, and elsewhere. *Proceedings of the Cambridge Antiquarian Society* 106, 61–88.

Cessford, C., 2017c. Cambridge colleges and their crockery from the mid-18th century to the present day. *English Ceramic Circle Transactions* 28, 105–18.

Cessford, C., 2018a. Educating Victorian children: a material culture perspective from Cambridge, in *The Oxford Handbook of the Archaeology of Childhood*, eds. S. Crawford, D.M. Hadley & G. Shephard. Oxford: Oxford University Press, 228–50.

Cessford, C., 2018b. Moving in mysterious ways: the use and discard of Cambridge college ceramics. *Antiquity* 92, 1076–93.

Cessford, C., 2018c. Corporate branding and collegiate coats of arms as logos: marked ceramics and the University of Cambridge, *International Journal of Historical Archaeology* 22, 883–904.

Cessford, C., Alexander, M. & Dickens, A., 2006. *Between Broad Street and the Great Ouse: waterfront archaeology in Ely* (East Anglian Archaeology 114.) Cambridge: CAU.

Cessford, C. with Dickens, A., 2004. The origins and early development of Chesterton. *Proceedings of the Cambridge Antiquarian Society* 93, 125–42.

Cessford, C. with Dickens, A., 2005a. Cambridge Castle Hill: excavations of Saxon, medieval and post-medieval deposits, Saxon execution site and a medieval coin hoard. *Proceedings of the Cambridge Antiquarian Society* 94, 73–101.

Cessford, C. with Dickens, A., 2005b. The manor of *Hintona*: the origins and development of Church End, Cherry Hinton. *Proceedings of the Cambridge Antiquarian Society* 94, 51–72.

Cessford, C. with Dickens, A., Dodwell, N. & Reynolds, A., 2007. Middle Anglo-Saxon justice: the Chesterton Lane Corner execution cemetery and related sequence, Cambridge. *Archaeological Journal* 164(1), 197–226.

Cessford, C., Hall, A., Herring, V. & Newman, R., 2017. To Clapham's I go: material from a mid–late 18th century

Cambridge coffee house, *Post-Medieval Archaeology* 51(2), 372–426

Cessford, C. & Mortimer, R., 2004. *Land Adjacent to 63 Church End, Church End, Cherry Hinton: an archaeological excavation.* (CAU Report 607.) Cambridge: Cambridge Archaeological Unit.

Cessford, C. & Slater, A., 2014. Beyond the Manor of Hintona; further thoughts on the origins and development of Church End, Cherry Hinton. *Proceedings of the Cambridge Antiquarian Society* 103, 39–59.

Chadwick, A.M., 2012. Routine magic, mundane ritual: towards a unified notion of depositional practice. *Oxford Journal of Archaeology* 31(3), 283–315.

Challis, C.E., 1978. *The Tudor Coinage.* Manchester: Manchester University Press.

Chapman, A., 1998. Excavation of the town defences at Green Street, Northampton, 1995–96. *Northamptonshire Archaeology* 28, 25–60.

Chapman, P., Blinkhorn, P. & Chapman, A., 2008. A medieval potters' tenement at Corby Road, Stanion, Northamptonshire. *Northamptonshire Archaeology* 38, 215–70.

Chesterton, G.K., 1938. *The Coloured Lands.* New York: Sheed & Ward.

Chew, H.M. & Kellaway, W., (eds.) 1973. *London Assize of Nuisance 1301–1431: a calendar* (London Records Society 10.) London: London Records Society.

Chisholm, M., 2003. Conservators of the River Cam: 1702–2002. *Proceedings of the Cambridge Antiquarian Society* 92, 183–200.

Christophersen, A., 2015. Performing towns. Steps towards an understanding of medieval urban communities as social practice. *Archaeological Dialogues* 22(2), 109–32.

Clark, J.W., 1907. *Ecclesie de Bernewelle Liber Memorandum.* Cambridge: Cambridge University Press.

Clark, J.W. & Gray, A. 1921. *Old Plans of Cambridge.* Cambridge: Bowes & Bowes.

Clarke, G., 1989. *Prehistory at Cambridge and Beyond.* Cambridge: Cambridge University Press.

Clarke, R., 2006. *Prehistoric Activity, Medieval Occupation and Post-medieval Industry to the rear of Walden House, Huntingdon, Cambridgeshire. Post Excavation Assessment and Updated Project Design.* (Cambridgeshire County Council Archaeological Field Unit Report 858.) Bar Hill: Cambridgeshire County Council Archaeological Field Unit.

Clarke R., 2009. *Late Saxon to Post-Medieval Occupation to the Rear of Gazeley House and Lawrence Court (Huntingdon Town Centre), Huntingdon, Cambridgeshire. Post Excavation Assessment and Updated Project Design.* (Oxford Archaeology East Report 1056) Bar Hill: Oxford Archaeology East.

Clarke, S, & Bray, J., 2003. The Norman town defences of Abergavenny. *Medieval Archaeology* 47, 186–9.

Cohen, D., 2006. *Household Gods: the British and their possessions.* New Haven (Conn): Yale University Press.

Collard, M., 1988. Excavations at Desborough Castle, High Wycombe, 1987. *Records of Buckinghamshire* 30, 15–41.

Collingridge, V., 2003. *Captain Cook: the life, death and legacy of history's greatest explorer.* London: Ebury.

Collis, J., 2011. The urban revolution: Martin Biddle's excavations in Winchester, 1961–1971, in *Great Excavations.*

Shaping the Archaeological Profession, ed. J. Schofield. Oxford: Oxbow, 74–86.

Collis, J. & Barton, K.J., 1978. *Winchester Excavations Vol. 2, 1949–60. Excavations in the suburbs and the western part of the town.* Winchester: City of Winchester.

Connah, G., 2007. *The Same Under a Different Sky?: a country estate in nineteenth-century New South Wales.* (British Archaeological Reports, International Series 1625.) Oxford: John & Erica Hedges.

Conzen, M.R.G., 1960. *Alnwick, Northumberland: a study in town plan analysis* (Institute of British Geographers Publication 27.) London: George Philip.

Conzen, M.R.G., 1968. The use of town plan analysis in the study of urban history, in *The Study of Urban History: the proceedings of an international round-table conference of the Urban History Group at Gilbert Murray Hall, University of Leicester on 23-26 September 1966,* ed. H.J. Dyos. London: Edward Arnold, 113–30.

Cooper, A., 2003. *Archaeological evaluation on land at the Cambridge Water Company, Rustat Road, Cambridge: phase 1- the north area.* (CAU Report 525.) Cambridge: Cambridge Archaeological Unit.

Cooper, A., 2004. *Former government offices, Brooklands Avenue, Cambridge; archaeological evaluation on the proposed residential redevelopment site, part 2.* (CAU Report 608.) Cambridge: Cambridge Archaeological Unit.

Cooper, C.H., 1842. *Annals of Cambridge Vol. 1. From the earliest times to 1547.* Cambridge: Warwick.

Cooper, C.H., 1843. *Annals of Cambridge Vol. 2. 1547 to 1602.* Cambridge: Warwick.

Cooper, C.H., 1845. *Annals of Cambridge Vol. 3. 1603 to 1688.* Cambridge: Warwick.

Cope-Falkner, P., 2000a. *Archaeological Investigations at Raynham House, King's Lynn, Norfolk (5530KLY).* (Archaeological Project Services Report 35/00.) Heckington: Archaeological Project Services

Cope-Falkner, P., 2000b. *Archaeological Evaluation of land adjacent to Petticoat Lane and Mitre Lane, Boston, Lincolnshire (BSBA00).* (Archaeological Project Services Report 25/00.) Heckington: Archaeological Project Services.

Cotter, J., 2000. *Post-Roman Pottery from Excavations in Colchester 1971–85.* (Colchester Archaeological Reports 7.) Colchester: Colchester Archaeological Trust.

Cotter, J.L., Roberts, D.G. & Parrington, M., 1992. *The Buried Past, an Archaeological History of Philadelphia.* Philadelphia (Pa): University of Pennsylvania Press.

Cowgill, J., Neergaard, M. de & Griffiths, N., 2000. *Knives and Scabbards.* (Medieval Finds from Excavations in London 1.) Woodbridge: Boydell Press.

Coysh, A.W. & Henrywood, R.K., 1984. *The Dictionary of Blue and White Printed Pottery 1780–1880. Vol. 1.* Woodbridge: Antique Collectors Club.

Cra'aster, M.D., Hutchinson, P. & Tebbutt, C.F., 1965. Archaeological notes. *Proceedings of the Cambridge Antiquarian Society* 58, 141–7.

Cracknell, S., 1990. Bridge End, Warwick: archaeological excavation of a medieval street frontage. *Birmingham and Warwickshire Archaeological Society Transactions* 95, 17–72.

Crawford, S., 2009. The archaeology of play things: theorising a toy stage in the 'biography' of objects. *Childhood in the Past* 2, 55–70.

Creighton, O.H., 2005. *Castles and Landscapes: power, community and fortification in medieval England.* London: Equinox.

Creighton, O.H. & Higham, R., 2005. *Medieval Town Walls: an archaeological and social history of urban defence.* Stroud: Tempus.

Creighton, O.H. & Wright, D., 2016. *The Anarchy: war and status in 12th-century landscapes of conflict.* Liverpool: Liverpool University Press.

Crone, B.A., 2005. A tale of three tuns: a 12th-century French barrel from the High Street, Perth. *Tayside and Fife Archaeological Journal* 11, 70–3.

Crossick, G. & Jaumain, S., (eds.) 1999. *Cathedrals of Consumption: the European department store, 1850–1939.* Aldershot: Ashgate.

Crossley, D., 1990. *Post-Medieval Archaeology in Britain.* London: Leicester University Press.

Crummy, N., 1988. *The Post-Roman Small Finds from Excavations in Colchester 1971–85.* (Colchester Archaeological Reports 5.) Colchester: Colchester Archaeological Trust.

Crummy, P., 1979. The system of measurement used in town planning from the ninth to the thirteenth centuries. *Anglo-Saxon Studies in Archaeology and History* 1, 149–64.

Cumberpatch, C., 2003. The transformation of tradition: the origins of the post-medieval ceramic tradition in Yorkshire. *Assemblage* 7. Available at: http://www.shef.ac.uk/assem/issue7/cumberpatch. Html [accessed 7 July 2011].

Curnow, P.E. & Thompson, M.W., 1969. Excavations at Richard's Castle, Herefordshire, 1962–64. *Journal of the British Archaeological Association* 32, 105–27.

Currie, C.K. & Locock, M., 1993. Excavations at Castle Bromwich Hall gardens 1989–91. *Post-Medieval Archaeology* 27, 111–99.

Cuthbert, A.W., 2001. The man who never was – Walter Ernest Dixon FRS. *British Journal of Pharmacology* 133(7), 945–50.

D'Agostono, M.E., 2000. Privy business: chamber pots and sexpots in Colonial life. *Archaeology* 53(4), 33–7.

Dalwood, C.H., Buteux, V.A. & Darlington, J., 1994. Excavations at Farrier Street and other sites north of the city wall, Worcester 1988–92. *Transactions of the Worcestershire Archaeological Society* 14, 75–114.

Daniel, G., 1939. A note on finds of archaeological interest recently made in the College. *The Eagle* 51, 144–7.

Daniell, J. & Leeds, E.T., 1939. The City Wall and Ditch in the Clarendon Quadrangle. *Oxoniensia* 4, 153–61.

Daniels, R., 1986. The medieval defences of Hartlepool, Cleveland: the .results of excavation and survey. *Durham Archaeological Journal* 2, 1986, 63–72.

Daubney, A., 2010. Credit crunch and Venetian coins. *Current Archaeology* 243, 38–42.

Davey, W. & Walker, H., 2008. *The Harlow Pottery Industries* (Medieval Pottery Research Group Occasional Report 3.) London: Medieval Pottery Research Group.

Davies, P., 2005. Writing slates and schooling. *Australasian Historical Archaeology* 23, 63–9.

Davies, S.M., 1983. Excavations at Christchurch, Dorset, 1981 to 1983. *Proceedings of the Dorset Natural History and Archaeology Society* 105, 21–56.

Davis, S.J.M., 1992. *A rapid method for recording information about mammal bones from archaeological sites.* (Ancient Monuments Laboratory Report 19/92.) London: Ancient Monuments Laboratory.

Davis, S.J.M., 2002. British agriculture: texts for the zoo-archaeologist. *Environmental Archaeology* 7(1), 47–60.

de Clercq, W., Caluwé, D., Cooremans, B., de Buyser, F., de Groote, K., Deforce, K., Ervynck, A., Lentacker, A., Mortier, S., Pype, P., Vandenberghe, S., van Neer, W. & Wouters, H., 2007. Living in times of war: waste of c. 1600 from two garderobe chutes in the castle of Middelburg-in-Flanders (Belgium). *Post-Medieval Archaeology* 41, 1–63.

Denham, V., 1985. The pottery, in *Middle Saxon Palaces at Northampton,* eds. J.H. Williams, M. Shaw & V. Denham. (Northampton Development Corporation Monograph Series 4.) Northampton: Northampton Development Corporation, 46–64.

Dickens, A., 1992. *A Watching Brief at Emmanuel College Kitchens. Cambridge.* (CAU Report 55.) Cambridge: Cambridge Archaeological Unit.

Dickens, A., 1993. *An Archaeological Assessment at The Master's Forecourt, Emmanuel College, Cambridge.* (CAU Report 81.) Cambridge: Cambridge Archaeological Unit.

Dickens, A., 1994. *Archaeological Excavations in the Master's Forecourt, Emmanuel College, Cambridge 1993.* (CAU Report 110.) Cambridge: Cambridge Archaeological Unit.

Dickens, A., 1997. *The Lion Yard Cambridge: An Archaeological Desktop Study.* (CAU Report 212.) Cambridge: Cambridge Archaeological Unit.

Dickens, A., 1999a. A new building at the Dominican Priory, Emmanuel College, Cambridge, and associated fourteenth-century Bawsey floor tiles. *Proceedings of the Cambridge Antiquarian Society* 87, 71–80.

Dickens, A., 1999b. *Archaeological investigations at the new Unilever Cambridge Centre, Union Road, Cambridge.* (CAU Report 316.) Cambridge: Cambridge Archaeological Unit.

Dickens, A., 1999c. *The Grand Arcade Cambridge: an archaeological test pit evaluation.* (CAU Report 346.) Cambridge: Cambridge Archaeological Unit.

Dickens, A., 2001a. *The Lion Yard Cambridge: Archaeological Observations made on Structural Engineer's Test Pits.* (CAU Report 431.) Cambridge: Cambridge Archaeological Unit.

Dickens, A., 2001b. *A Statement of Archaeological Strategy at the Grand Arcade, Cambridge (TL 451 583).* Unpublished CAU document. Cambridge: Cambridge Archaeological Unit.

Dickens, A., 2003. *The Lion Yard Cambridge: an archaeological desktop study.* (CAU Report 565.) Cambridge: Cambridge Archaeological Unit.

Dickens, A., 2004. *A Written Scheme of Investigation for Archaeological Mitigation at the Grand Arcade, Cambridge (TL 451 583).* Unpublished CAU document. Cambridge: Cambridge Archaeological Unit.

Dickens, A., 2007. *Updated Project Design for Analysis and Publication of Archaeological Excavations at the Grand Arcade, Cambridge.* Unpublished CAU document. Cambridge: Cambridge Archaeological Unit.

Dickens, A. & Baggs, T., 2009. *Grand Arcade, Cambridge. Building Survey 2004–2006.* (CAU Report 801.) Cambridge: Cambridge Archaeological Unit.

Dickens, A. & Cessford C., 2003. *The Grand Arcade, Cambridge: test pit evaluation in the Lion Yard Car Park.* (CAU Report 516.) Cambridge: Cambridge Archaeological Unit.

Dickens, A. & Mackay, D., 2007. *Botanic Garden, Cambridge: an archaeological evaluation on the site of the proposed Sainsbury Laboratory.* (CAU Report 785.) Cambridge: Cambridge Archaeological Unit.

Dickens, A. & Patten, R., 2003. *The former government offices site, Brooklands Avenue, Cambridge: residential site: an archaeological evaluation, part 1.* (CAU Report 524.) Cambridge: Cambridge Archaeological Unit.

Dobney, K., Jacques, D. & Irving, B., 1996. *Of Butchery and Breeds: report on the vertebrate remains from various sites in the City of Lincoln.* (Lincoln Archaeological Studies 5.) Lincoln: City of Lincoln Archaeology Unit.

Dobres, M.A. & Robb, J., 2000. Agency in archaeology: paradigm or platitude?, in *Agency in Archaeology*, eds. M.A. Dobres & J. Robb. London: Routledge, 3–17.

Dobson, R.B., 1977. Urban decline in late medieval England. *Transactions of the Royal Historical Society* 27, 1–22.

Dodwell, N., Lucy, S. & Tipper, J., 2004. Anglo-Saxons on the Cambridge backs: the Criminology site settlement and King's Garden Hostel cemetery. *Proceedings of the Cambridge Antiquarian Society* 93, 95–124.

Doonan, R., 1999. *Metallurgical debris from Eynsham Abbey, Oxfordshire.* (Ancient Monuments Laboratory Report 70/1999.) Portsmouth: Ancient Monuments Laboratory.

Drewett, P., 1999. *Field Archaeology: an introduction.* London: UCL Press.

Dungworth, D., 1999. *Assessment of iron working slags and lead waste from Dunwich Greyfriars, Suffolk.* (Ancient Monuments Laboratory Report 49/1999.) Portsmouth: Ancient Monuments Laboratory.

Dunn, A., 2004. *The Peasants' Revolt: England's failed revolution of 1381.* Stroud: Tempus.

Dunning, G.C., 1950. Notes on the Trinity College jug. *Proceedings of the Cambridge Antiquarian Society* 44, 49–50.

Durham B., 1978. Archaeological investigations in St Aldates, Oxford. *Oxoniensia* 42, 83–203.

Dyer, A., 1991. *Decline and Growth in English Towns, 1400–1640.* Basingstoke: Macmillan Education.

Dyer, A., 2000. Appendix: ranking lists of English medieval towns, *The Cambridge Urban History of Britain Vol. 1, 600–1540,* ed. D.M. Palliser. Cambridge: Cambridge University Press, 747–70.

Dyer, C., 2003. The archaeology of medieval small towns. *Medieval Archaeology* 47, 85–114.

Dyer, C., 2006. Seasonal patterns in food consumption in the Later Middle Ages, in *Food in Medieval England: Diet and Nutrition,* eds. C.M. Woolgar, D. Serjeantson & T. Waldron. Oxford: Oxford University Press, 201–14.

Eddy, M.E. & Petchey, M.R., 1983. *Historic Towns in Essex: an archaeological survey of Saxon and medieval towns, with guidance for their future planning.* Chelmsford: Essex County Council.

Edwards, B.J.N., 2002. A group of pre-Conquest metalwork from Asby Winderwath Common. *Transactions of the Cumberland and Westmorland Antiquarian and Archaeological Society* 2, 111–43.

Edwards, D. & Hall, D.N., 1997. Medieval pottery from Cambridge. *Proceedings of the Cambridge Antiquarian Society* 86, 153–68.

Egan, G., 1999. London - axis of the Commonwealth?, in *Old World and New*, eds. G. Egan & R.L Michael. Oxford: Oxbow Books, 61–71.

Egan, G., 2005a. *Material Culture in London in an Age of Transition: Tudor and Stuart period finds c. 1450–1700 from excavations at riverside sites in Southwark* (MoLAS Monograph 19.) London: MoLAS.

Egan, G., 2005b. Urban and rural finds: material culture of country and town *c. 1050–1500*, in *Town and Country in the Middle Ages: contrasts, contacts and interconnections 1100–1500*, eds. K. Giles & C. Dyer. (Society for Medieval Archaeology Monograph 22.) Leeds: Maney, 197–210.

Egan, G., 2009. Material concerns: The state of post-medieval finds studies, in *Crossing Paths or Sharing Tracks? Future directions in the archaeological study of post-1550 Britain and Ireland*, eds. A. Horning & M. Palmer. Woodbridge: Boydell & Brewer, 273–86.

Egan, G. & Pritchard, F., 2002. *Dress Accessories c.1150–1450.* (Medieval Finds from Excavations in London 3.) London: HMSO.

Ellis, D.M.B. & Salzman, L.F., 1948a. Houses of Augustinian canons: Priory of Barnwell, in *A History of the County of Cambridge and the Isle of Ely: Vol. 2*, ed. L.F. Salzman. Oxford: Oxford University Press, 234–49.

Ellis, D.M.B. & Salzman, L.F., 1948b. Priory of St Edmund, Cambridge, in *A History of the County of Cambridge and the Isle of Ely: Vol. 2*, ed. L.F. Salzman. Oxford: Oxford University Press, 254–6.

Ellis, D.M.B. & Salzman, L.F., 1948c. Friaries: Dominicans, Cambridge, in *A History of the County of Cambridge and the Isle of Ely: Vol. 2*, ed. L.F. Salzman. Oxford: Oxford University Press, 269–76.

Ellis, D.M.B. & Salzman, L.F., 1948d. Friaries: Carmelites, Cambridge, in *A History of the County of Cambridge and the Isle of Ely: Vol. 2*, ed. L.F. Salzman. Oxford: Oxford University Press, 282–6.

Ellis, D.M.B. & Salzman, L.F., 1948e. Priory: Friars of the Sack, Cambridge, in *A History of the County of Cambridge and the Isle of Ely: Vol. 2*, ed. L.F. Salzman. Oxford: Oxford University Press, 290–1.

Ellis, D.M.B. & Salzman, L.F., 1948f. The Hospital of St Anthony and St Eloy, Cambridge, in *A History of the County of Cambridge and the Isle of Ely: Vol. 2*, ed. L.F. Salzman. Oxford: Oxford University Press, 307.

Ellis, P., 1985. Excavations at Friarn Street and West Quay, Bridgwater, 1983/4. *Proceedings of the Somerset Archaeology and Natural History Society* 129, 69–80.

Ellis, S., 2002. A century and a half of pharmacy in Trumpington Street, Cambridge. *Pharmaceutical History* 32(4), 61–4.

Engle, B.S., 1929. The use of Mercury's caduceus as a medical emblem, *Classical Journal* 25(3), 204–8.

English Heritage, 2001., *Archaeometallurgy.* Centre for Archaeology Guidelines 2001/01.

Ennis, T., 2007. The 'magnum fossatum' at Saffron Walden: excavations at Elm Grove, off Goul Lane 2001. *Essex Archaeology and History* 36, 204–7.

Epstein, M., 1908. *The Early History of the Levant Company.* Dutton: New York.

Evans, C., 2003. *Power and Island Communities: Excavations at the Wardy Hill Ringwork, Coveney, Ely.* (East Anglian Archaeology 103.) Cambridge: CAU.

Evans, C. with Appleby, G. Lucy, S. & Regan, R. 2013. *Process and History: Roman fen-edge communities at Colne Fen, Earith.* (CAU Landscape Archives – The Archaeology of the Lower Ouse Valley 2.) Cambridge: CAU.

Evans, C. & Cessford, C., in prep. *North West Cambridge.*

Evans, C., Dickens, A. & Richmond, D.A.H., 1997. Cloistered communities: archaeological and architectural investigations in Jesus College, Cambridge, 1988–97. *Proceedings of the Cambridge Antiquarian Society* 86, 91–144.

Evans, C. & Newman, R., 2011. 'An Imperial Philosophical Machine': the archaeology of the Cambridge Observatory and early modern science. *Antiquity* 85(330), 1369–84.

Evans, C. & ten Harkel, L., 2010. Roman Cambridge's early settlements and *Via Devana*: Excavations at Castle Street. *Proceedings of the Cambridge Antiquarian Society* 99, 35–60.

Evans, N. & Mould, Q., 2005. Footwear, in *Before the Mast. Life and death aboard the Mary Rose*, eds. J. Gardiner with M.J. Allen. (Archaeology of the Mary Rose 4.) Portsmouth: Mary Rose Trust, 59–94.

Eveleigh, D.E., 1983. *Firegrates and Kitchen Ranges.* Oxford: Shire Publications.

Everson, P., 1988. What's in a name? 'Goltho, Goltho and Bullington'. *Lincolnshire Historical Archaeology* 23, 93–9.

Every, R. & Richards, M., 2005. Knives and knife sheaths, in *Before the Mast. Life and Death Aboard the Mary Rose*, eds. J. Gardiner with M.J. Allen. (Archaeology of the Mary Rose 4.) Portsmouth: Mary Rose Trust, 144–53.

Farley, M., 1982. A medieval pottery industry at Boarstall, Buckinghamshire. *Records of Buckinghamshire* 24, 107–17.

Farmer, P.G. & Farmer, N.C., 1979. *An Introduction to Scarborough ware and a Re-assessment of Knight Jugs.* Hove: Privately published.

Farmer, P.G. & Farmer, N.C., 1982. The dating of the Scarborough ware pottery industry. *Medieval Ceramics* 6, 66–86.

Farren, R., 1880. *Twenty Etchings of Cambridge, for the Re-issue of Cooper's Enlargement of Le Keux's Memorials of Cambridge.* Cambridge: privately published.

Farren, R., 1881. *Cambridge and its Neighbourhood, Drawn & Etched by R. Farren.* Cambridge: Macmillan.

Ferraby, R., 2011a. *Archaeological Survey at Sidney Sussex College, Cambridge: magnetometer and topographic survey June 2011.* Unpublished report for Sidney Sussex College. Cambridge: Sidney Sussex College archives.

Ferraby, R., 2011b. *Archaeological Survey at Sidney Sussex College, Cambridge: ground penetrating radar survey June*

2011. Unpublished report for Sidney Sussex College. Cambridge: Sidney Sussex College archives.

Finer, A. & Savage, G., 1965. *The Selected Letters of Josiah Wedgwood.* London: Cory, Adams & Mackay.

Firman, P. & Pullinger, J., 1987. Excavation at Riverside, Thompson's Lane, Cambridge. *Proceedings of the Cambridge Antiquarian Society* 76, 83–95.

Firman, R., 1998. Gault: a geologist's cautionary tale of words as a barrier to understanding. *British Brick Society Information* 74, 4–13.

Fitter, R.S.R. & Manuel, R., 1986. *Field Guide to the Freshwater Life of Britain and North-West Europe.* London: Collins.

Fitts, R.K., 1999. The archaeology of middle-class domesticity and gentility in Victorian Brooklyn, *Historical Archaeology* 33(1), 39–62.

Foard, G., 1995. The early topography of Northampton and its suburbs. *Northamptonshire Archaeology* 26, 109–22.

Fort, T., 2003. *The Book of Eels: on the trail of the thin-heads.* London: Harper Collins.

Fox, C., 1923. *The archaeology of the Cambridge region.* Cambridge: Cambridge University Press.

Fox, R., Barton, K.J. & Hoad, M.J., 1986. Excavations at Oyster Street, Portsmouth, Hampshire, 1968–71. *Post-Medieval Archaeology,* 20, 31–255.

Framework Archaeology, 2008., *From Hunter Gatherers to Huntsmen: a history of the Stansted landscape* (Framework Archaeology Monograph 2.) Salisbury: Framework Archaeology.

Frazer, B., 1999. Reconceptualizing resistance in the historical archaeology of the British Isles: an editorial, *International Journal of Historical Archaeology* 3(1), 1–10.

Friedlander, W.J., 1992. *The Golden Wand of Medicine: a history of the caduceus symbol in medicine.* New York: Greenwood Press.

Fryer, K. & Shelley, A., 1998. Excavation of a pit at 16 Tunsgate, Guildford, Surrey, 1991. *Post-Medieval Archaeology* 31, 139–230.

Fulford, M. & Holbrook, N., (eds.), 2015. *The Towns of Roman Britain: The contribution of commercial archaeology since 1990* (Britannia Monograph Series 27.) London: Society for the Promotion of Roman Studies.

Fuller, T., 1840. *The History of the University of Cambridge since the Conquest to the year 1634.* London: John W. Parker.

Gailey, A., 1970. Irish corn drying kilns. *Ulster Folk Life* 15/16, 52–71.

Gaimster, D., 1994. The archaeology of post-medieval society, *c.* 1450–1750: material culture studies in Britain since the War, in *Building on the Past,* ed. B. Vyner. London, Royal Archaeological Institute, 281–311.

Gaimster D. & Nenk, B., 1997. English households in transition *c.*1450–1550: the ceramic evidence, in *The Age of Transition: the archaeology of English culture 1400–1600,* eds. D. Gaimster & P. Stamper. Oxford, Oxbow Books, 171–95.

Gallois, R.W., 1988. *Geology of the Country around Ely. British Geological Survey sheet memoir 173.* London: HMSO.

Gardiner, J. with Allen, M.J., (eds.) 2005. *Before the Mast: life and death aboard the Mary Rose* (The Archaeology of the Mary Rose 4.) Portsmouth: The Mary Rose Trust.

Gardiner, M.F. & Rippon, S., 2007. *Medieval Landscapes.* Macclesfield: Windgather Press.

Garrison, F.H., 1920. The use of the caduceus in the insignia of the army medical officer. *Bulletin of the Medical Library Association* 9(2), 13–16.

Garrow, D., 2012. Odd deposits and average practice. A critical history of the concept of structured deposition. *Archaeological Dialogues* 19(2), 85–115.

Gdaniec, K., 1992. *Archaeological Investigations at the McDonald Institute, 1992.* (CAU Report 58.) Cambridge: Cambridge Archaeological Unit.

Geertz, C., 1973. Thick description: towards an interpretive theory of culture, in *The Interpretation of Cultures,* ed. C. Geertz. New York (NY): Basic Books, 3–30.

Gelling, M., 1984. *Place-names in the Landscape.* London: Dent.

Gidney, L., 1991. *Leicester, The Shires, 1988 Excavations: the animal bones from the medieval deposits at Little Lane.* (Ancient Monuments Laboratory Report 57/91.) London: Ancient Monuments Laboratory.

Gidney, L., 1992. *Leicester, The Shires, 1988 Excavations: the animal bones from the post-medieval deposits at Little Lane.* (Ancient Monuments Laboratory Report 24/92.) London: Ancient Monuments Laboratory.

Gidney, L., 2000. Economic trends, craft specialisation and social status: bone assemblages from Leicester, in *Animal Bones, Human Societies,* ed. P. Rowley-Conwy. Oxford: Oxbow Books, 170–8.

Gilchrist, R., 2003. Dust to dust: revealing the Reformation dead, in *The Archaeology of Reformation, 1480–1580,* eds. D. Gaimster & R. Gilchrist. (Society for Post-Medieval Archaeology Monograph 1.) Leeds: Maney, 399–414.

Gilchrist, R., 2008. Magic for the dead? The archaeology of magic in later medieval burials. *Medieval Archaeology* 52, 119–59.

Gilchrist, R., 2012. *Medieval Life. Archaeology and the life course.* Woodbridge: Boydell & Brewer.

Gilchrist, R. & Morris, R., 1996. Continuity, reaction and revival: church archaeology in England *c.* 1600–1880, in *Church Archaeology: research directions for the future,* eds. J. Blair & C. Pyrah. (Council for British Archaeology Research Report 104.) York: Council for British Archaeology, 112–26.

Gilchrist, R. & Sloane, B., 2005. *Requiem. The Medieval Monastic Cemetery in Britain.* London: MoLAS.

Giles, K. & Dyer, C., 2005. *Town and Country in the Middle Ages: contrasts, contacts and interconnections 1100–1500.* (Society for Medieval Archaeology Monograph 22.) London: Society for Medieval Archaeology

Giorgi, J., 1997. Diet in Late Medieval and Early Modern London: the archaeobotanical evidence, in *The Age of Transition: the archaeology of English culture 1400–1600,* eds. D. Gaimster & P. Stamper. Oxford, Oxbow Books, 197–213.

Giorgi, J., 1999. Archaeobotanical evidence from London on aspects of post-medieval urban economies, in *Old World and New,* eds. G. Egan & R.L. Michael. Oxford: Oxbow Books, 342–8.

Goffman, E., 1961. *Asylums: essays on the social situation of mental patients and other inmates.* Garden City: Doubleday & Co.

Goldberg, P.J.P., 2008. The fashioning of bourgeois domesticity in later medieval England: a material culture

453

perspective, in *Medieval Domesticity: home, housing and household in medieval England,* eds. M. Kowaleski & P.J.P. Goldberg. Cambridge: Cambridge University Press, 124–44.

Gooch, J., 2004. A history of Robert Sayle. Part 2 1969–2004, in Sayle, R. (ed.) *A History of Robert Sayle. Revised Edition 2004.* Cambridge: Robert Sayle, 131–90.

Goodall, I.H., 2011. *Ironwork in Medieval Britain: an archaeological study.* (Society for Medieval Archaeology Monograph 31.) London: Society for Medieval Archaeology.

Goodburn D., 2008. Possible dugout trawled from sea near Covehithe. *Saxon; Newsletter of the Sutton Hoo Society* 48, 1–3.

Gooder, E., Woodfield, C. & Chaplin, R.E., 1964. The walls of Coventry. *Birmingham and Warwickshire Archaeological Society Transactions* 81, 88–138.

Goose, N., 1980. Household size and structure in early-Stuart Cambridge. *Social History* 5(3), 347–85.

Graham-Campbell, J., 1968. The School of Pythagoras (Merton Hall). *The Eagle* 62, 243–53.

Grainger, I., 2000. Excavations at Battle Bridge Lane in 1995: medieval and early post-medieval development along Tooley Street, Southwark. *Surrey Archaeological Collections* 87, 1–47.

Grant, A., 1988. Animal resources, in *The Countryside of Medieval England,* eds. G. Astill & A. Grant. Oxford: Blackwell, 149–261.

Gray, A., 1898. *The Priory of Saint Radegund Cambridge* (Cambridge Antiquarian Society Octavo Series 31.) Cambridge: Cambridge Antiquarian Society.

Gray, A., 1908. *The Dual Origin of the Town of Cambridge* (Cambridge Antiquarian Society Quarto Publications New Series 1.) Cambridge: Cambridge Antiquarian Society.

Gray, A., 1976. Cambridge's quest for a central station. *Journal of the Railway & Canal History Society* 22, 22–4.

Gray, J.M., 1922. *Biographical Notes on the Mayors of Cambridge.* Cambridge: Privately published.

Green, F.J., 1979. Phosphatic Mineralization of Seeds from Archaeological Sites. *Journal of Archaeological Science* 6(3), 279–84.

Green, F.J., 1982. Problems of interpreting differentially preserved plant remains from excavations of medieval urban sites, in *Environmental Archaeology in the Urban Context,* eds. A.R. Hall & H.K. Kenward. (Council for British Archaeology Research Report 43.) Oxford: Council for British Archaeology, 40–6.

Green, F.J., 1984. The archaeological and documentary evidence for plants from the medieval period in England, in *Plants and Ancient Man: studies in palaeoethnobotany,* eds. W. van Zeist & W.A. Casparie. Rotterdam: Balkema, 99–114.

Gregson, N., Metcalfe, A. & Crewe, L., 2007. Moving things along: the conduits and practices of divestment in consumption, *Transactions of the Institute of British Geographers* 32(2), 187–200.

Greig, J., 1996. Archaeobotanical and historical records compared - a new look at taphonomy of edible and other useful plants from the 11th to the 18th centuries AD. *Circaea* 12(2), 211–47.

Grenville, J., 1997. *Medieval Housing.* London: Leicester University Press.

Grenville, J., 2008. Urban and rural houses and households in the late Middle Ages: a case study from Yorkshire, in *Medieval Domesticity: home, housing and household in medieval England,* eds. M. Kowaleski & P.J.P. Goldberg. Cambridge: Cambridge University Press, 92–123.

Grey, P.C., 1972. The changing face of St Andrew's Street, Cambridge. *Cambridgeshire Local History Society Review* 27, 19–22.

Grover, M.D., 2004. Household succession as a catalyst of landscape change. *Historical Archaeology* 38(4), 25–43.

Habermas, J., 1983. Modernity: an incomplete project, in *The Anti-Aesthetic: essays on postmodern culture,* ed. H. Foster. Seattle (Wash): Bay Press, 3–15.

Haigh, D., 1984. Excavation of the town ditch at Swavesey, 1984. *Proceedings of the Cambridge Antiquarian Society* 73, 45–53.

Haigh, D., 1988. *The Religious Houses of Cambridge.* Cambridge: Cambridgeshire County Council.

Hall, A., 2002. A late 16th-century pit group from Pembroke College, Cambridge. *Proceedings of the Cambridge Antiquarian Society* 91, 89–101.

Hall, A. & Brudenell, M., 2003. *King's Parade: an archaeological watching brief.* (CAU Report 568.) Cambridge: Cambridge Archaeological Unit.

Hall, C.P. & Lovatt, R., 1989. The site and foundations of Peterhouse. *Proceedings of the Cambridge Antiquarian Society* 78, 5–46.

Hall, C.P. & Ravensdale, J.R., 1976. *The West Fields of Cambridge.* (Cambridge Antiquarian Records Society III.) Cambridge: Cambridge Antiquarian Records Society.

Hall, D.N., 1975. A group of post-medieval pottery from the Manor House, Strixton, Northampton. *Bedfordshire Archaeological Journal* 10, 65–70.

Hall, D.N., 2001. The pottery from Forehill, Ely, Cambridgeshire. *Medieval Ceramics* 25, 2–21.

Hall, D.N., 2014. *The Open Fields of England.* Oxford: Oxford University Press.

Hall, R.A. & Hunter-Mann, K., 2002. *Medieval Urbanism in Coppergate: refining a townscape* (Archaeology of York 10/6.) York: Council for British Archaeology.

Hamerow, H., 2006. Special deposits in Anglo-Saxon settlements. *Medieval Archaeology* 50, 1–30.

Hammond, P.J., 2009. Ebenezer Church: clay tobacco pipe manufacturer of Pentonville, London. *Transactions of the London and Middlesex Archaeological Society* 60, 225–48.

Hanerkamp, N. & Harris, N., 2005. Unfired Brandon gunflints from the Presidio Santa Maria de Galve, Pensacola, Florida. *Historical Archaeology* 39(4), 95–111.

Hansen, M., 1986. *The Hydrophilidae (Coleoptera) of Fennoscandia and Denmark Fauna* (Fauna Entomologyca Scandinavica 18.). Leiden: Brill.

Harrington, P., 2004. *English Civil War Archaeology.* Batsford: London.

Harris, J., 2007. More Malmsey, your grace? The export of Greek wine to England in the Later Middle Ages, in *Eat, Drink and be Merry (Luke 12:19)- Food and Wine in Byzantium: papers of the 37th annual spring symposium of byzantine studies, in honour of professor A.A.M. Bryer,* eds. L. Brubaker & K. Linardou. Aldershot: Ashgate, 249–53.

Harrison, R., 2011. Surface assemblages. Towards an archaeology in and of the present. *Archaeological Dialogues* 18(2), 141–61.

Harrison, R. & Schofield, J., 2010. *After Modernity: archaeological approaches to the contemporary past.* Oxford: Oxford University Press.

Harvey, P.D.A., 1969. Banbury, in *Atlas of Historic Towns I,* ed. M.D. Lobel. Oxford: Lovell Johns, 1–8.

Haslam, J., 1978. The excavation of the defences of Devizes, Wilts, 1974. *Wiltshire Archaeological Magazine* 72–3, 59–65.

Haslam, J., 1984. The development and topography of Saxon Cambridge. *Proceedings of the Cambridge Antiquarian Society* 72, 13–29.

Hatcher, J., 1993. *The History of the British Coal Industry Vol. 1: before 1700, towards the age of coal.* Oxford: Clarendon Press.

Hatherley, C., 2002. *An archaeological evaluation at Homerton College, Cambridge.* (CAU Report 495.) Cambridge: Cambridge Archaeological Unit.

Healey, R.H., 1969. Bourne Ware. *Lincolnshire Historical Archaeology* 4, 108–9.

Healey, R.H., 1975. *Medieval and Sub-Medieval Pottery in Lincolnshire.* Unpublished M.Phil. thesis, University of Nottingham.

Heard, K., 2009. Clay tobacco pipes from an excavation on the site of the former Cattle Market, Bury St Edmunds (BSE 252). *Society for Clay Pipe Research Newsletter* 75, 2–15.

Hebditch, M., 1968. Excavations on the medieval defences, Portwall Lane, Bristol, 1965. *Transactions of the Bristol and Gloucestershire Archaeological Society* 87, 131–43.

Heighway, C., (ed.) 1972. *The Erosion of History: archaeology and planning in towns. A study of historic towns affected by modern development in England, Wales and Scotland.* York: Council for British Archaeology.

Hesse, M., 2007. The East Fields of Cambridge. *Proceedings of the Cambridge Antiquarian Society* 96, 143–60.

Hey, G. & Lacey, M., 2001. *Evaluation of Archaeological Decision-making Processes and Sampling Strategies.* Oxford: Kent County Council/Oxford Archaeological Unit.

Hicks, D., 2004. From 'questions that count' to 'stories that matter' in Historical Archaeology, *Antiquity* 78 (302), 934–9.

Hicks, D., 2007. *'The Garden of the World': a historical archaeology of eastern Caribbean sugar plantations, AD 1600–2001.* (British Archaeological Reports, International Series 1632.) Oxford: Archaeopress.

Higgins, D.A., 1985. Clay tobacco pipes from 27 George Street, Hemel, Hempstead, in *The Archaeology of the Clay Tobacco Pipe, IX: more pipes from the Midlands and southern England,* ed. P. Davey. (British Archaeological Reports, British Series 146 Vol. 2) Oxford: British Archaeological Reports, 337–62.

Hillier, B., 1965. *Master Potters of the Industrial Revolution: the Turners of Lane End.* London: Cory, Adams & McKay.

Hilton, R.H., 1973. *Bond Men Made Free: medieval peasant movements and the English rising of 1381.* London: Maurice Temple Smith.

Hines, J., 1999. The Anglo-Saxon archaeology of the Cambridge region and the Middle Anglian kingdom. *Anglo-Saxon Studies in Archaeology and History* 10, 135–89.

Hinton, D.A., 1990. Harness pedants and swivels, in *Object and Economy in Medieval Winchester (Artefacts from Medieval Winchester Part II),* ed. M. Biddle. (Winchester Studies 7ii.) Oxford: Oxford University Press, 1047–53.

Hodder, I., 2006. The spectacle of daily performance at Çatalhöyük, in *Archaeology of performance. Theaters of power, community, and politics,* eds. T. Inomata & L.S. Coben. Altamira: Lanham, 81–102.

Hodder, I. & Cessford, C., 2004. Daily practice and social memory at Çatalhöyük. *American Antiquity* 69(1), 17–40.

Hodges, R., 1989. *The Anglo-Saxon Achievement: archaeology and the beginnings of English society.* London: Duckworth.

Holbrook, M., 2006. *Where do you Keep? Lodging the Cambridge undergraduate.* Great Malvern: Capella Archive.

Holt, R., 2000. Society and population 600–1300, in *The Cambridge Urban History of Britain Vol. 1, 600–1540,* ed. D.M. Palliser. Cambridge: Cambridge University Press, 79–104.

Hooper, B., 1989. A horse-skull house-charm from Manuden. *Essex Journal* 24, 45–6.

Horniker, A.L., 1942. William Harborne and the beginning of Anglo-Turkish diplomatic and commercial relations. *Journal of Modern History* 14(3), 289–316.

Horsman, V., Milne, C. & Milne, G., 1988. *Aspects of Saxo-Norman London. 1: building and street development near Billingsgate and Cheapside.* (London Middlesex Archaeological Society Special Paper 11.) London: London and Middlesex Archaeological Society.

Hosgood, C.P., 1999. Mercantile monasteries: shops, shop assistants and shop life in Late-Victorian and Edwardian Britain. *Journal of British Studies* 38(3), 322–52.

Hoskins, W.G., 1953. The rebuilding of rural England, 1570–1640. *Past & Present* 4, 44–59.

Huelsbeck, D.R., 1991. Faunal remains and consumer behavior: what is being measured?, *Historical Archaeology* 25(2), 62–76.

Hughes. T. McK., 1894a. On the recent discovery of two ancient ditches and objects of medieval date between Hobson Street and Sidney Street, Cambridge. *Proceedings of the Cambridge Antiquarian Society* 8(1), 32–55.

Hughes. T. McK., 1894b. On some ancient ditches and medieval remains found in the course of recent excavations near the Pitt Press, Cambridge. *Proceedings of the Cambridge Antiquarian Society* 8(3), 255–83.

Hughes. T. McK., 1898. Further observations on the ditches round ancient Cambridge, with special reference to the adjoining ground. *Proceedings of the Cambridge Antiquarian Society* 9(3), 370–84.

Hughes, T. McK., 1901. On the natural forms which have suggested some of the commonest implements of stone, bone and wood, *Archaeological Journal* 58(1), 199–213.

Hughes, T. McK., 1907a. On the section seen and the objects found during excavations on the site of the Old Bird Bolt Hotel. *Proceedings of the Cambridge Antiquarian Society* 11(3), 424–45.

Hughes, T. McK., 1907b. On the superficial deposits under Cambridge, and their influence upon the distribution of the colleges. *Proceedings of the Cambridge Antiquarian Society* 11(3), 393–423.

Hughes, T. McK., 1915a. On some objects found in the King's Ditch under the Masonic Hall. *Proceedings of the Cambridge Antiquarian Society* 19, 16–27.

Hughes, T. McK., 1915b. Acoustic vases in ancient buildings. *Proceedings of the Cambridge Antiquarian Society* 19, 63–90.

Hughes, T. McK. & Hughes, M.C., 1909. *Cambridgeshire.* Cambridge: Cambridge University Press.

Hunt, J., 2004. Sculpture, dates and patrons: dating the Herefordshire School of Sculpture. *Antiquaries Journal* 84, 185–222.

Hurcombe, R. & Lemieux, L., 2005. Basketry, in *Before the Mast. Life and Death Aboard the Mary Rose,* eds. J. Gardiner with M.J. Allen. (Archaeology of the Mary Rose 4.) Portsmouth: Mary Rose Trust, 400–8.

Hurst, J.G., 1956. Saxo-Norman pottery in East Anglia: part I St Neots Ware. *Proceedings of the Cambridge Antiquarian Society* 49, 43–70.

Hurst, J.G., 1957. Saxo-Norman pottery in East Anglia: part II Thetford Ware. *Proceedings of the Cambridge Antiquarian Society* 50, 29–60.

Hurst, J.G., 1958. Saxo-Norman pottery in East Anglia: part III Stamford Ware. *Proceedings of the Cambridge Antiquarian Society* 51, 37–65.

Hurst, J.G., 1970. Medieval Britain in 1969. II. Post-Conquest. *Medieval Archaeology* 14, 166–208

Hurst, J.G., 1976. The pottery, in *The Archaeology of Anglo-Saxon England,* ed. D.M. Wilson. Cambridge: Cambridge University Press, 283–348.

Hutton, J. & Timberlake, S., 2006. *34–38 Newnham Road, Cambridge: a report on the January 2006 archaeological evaluation.* (CAU Report 728.) Cambridge: Cambridge Archaeological Unit.

Illingworth, W. & Caley, J., 1812–18. *Rotuli hundredorum temp. Hen. III. & Edw. I. in Turr' Lond' et in curia receptae scaccarij Westm.* London: Record Commissioners.

Isserlin, R.M.J. & Connell, P., 1997. A previously unknown medieval earthwork in Maldon; excavation behind the Moot Hall, 39 High Street, Maldon 1991. *Essex Archaeology and History* 28, 133–41.

ITC (Independent Transport Commission)., 2004. *Suburban Future.* London: ITC.

Ivens, R.J., 1981. Medieval pottery kilns at Brill, Buckinghamshire: preliminary report on excavations in 1978. *Records of Buckinghamshire* 23, 102–6.

Ivens, R.J., 1982. Medieval pottery from the 1987 excavations at Tempse Farm, Brill. *Records of Buckinghamshire* 24, 144–70.

Jamieson, R.W., 2001. The essence of commodification: caffeine dependencies in the early modern world, *Journal of Social History* 35(2), 269–94.

Jaques, D. & Dobney, K., 1996. *Vertebrate Remains from Excavations at Tower 10, City Walls, York: technical report.* (Environmental Archaeology Unit York Report 96/28.) York: Environmental Archaeology Unit.

Jarzembowski, E. & Jarzembowski, B., 1981. Complete restoration pipes from London (*c.* 1660–1680), in *The Archaeology of the Clay Tobacco Pipe VI*, ed. P. Davey.

(British Archaeological Reports, British Series 97.) Oxford: British Archaeological Reports, 79–85.

Jefferys, J.B., 1954. *Retail Trading in Britain 1850–1950: a study of trends in retailing with special reference to the development of co-operative, multiple shop and department store methods of retailing.* Cambridge: Cambridge University Press.

Jeffries, N., 2003. Historically visible but archaeologically invisible? The Huguenots in 17th-century Spitalfields. *Medieval Ceramics* 25, 54–64.

Jeffries, N., 2006. The Metropolis Local Management Act and the archaeology of sanitary reform in the London Borough of Lambeth 1856–86. *Post-Medieval Archaeology* 40, 272–90.

Jeffries, N., Owens, A., Hicks, D., Featherby, R. & Wehner, K., 2009. Rematerialising metropolitan histories? People, places and things in modern London, in *Crossing Paths or Sharing Tracks? Future directions in the archaeological study of post-1550 Britain and Ireland*, eds. A. Horning & M. Palmer. Woodbridge: Boydell & Brewer, 323–50.

Jervis, B., 2017. Assessing urban fortunes in six late medieval ports: an archaeological application of assemblage theory. *Urban History* 44(1), 2–26.

Jessop, L., 1986. *Coleoptera: Scarabaeidae.* (Handbooks for the Identification of British Insects 5/11.) London: Royal Entomological Society of London.

Johnson, M., 1996. *An Archaeology of Capitalism.* Oxford: Blackwell.

Johnson, M., 2010. *English Houses, 1300–1800: Vernacular Architecture, Social Lives.* London: Longman.

Jones, C., Eyre-Morgan, G., Palmer, S. & Palmer, N., 1997. Excavations in the outer enclosure of Boteler's Castle, Oversley, Alcester, 1992–93. *Birmingham and Warwickshire Archaeological Society Transactions* 101, 1–98

Jones, G., 1984. Interpretation of archaeological plant remains: ethnographic models from Greece, in *Plants and Ancient Man: studies in palaeoethnobotany*, eds. W. van Zeist & W.A. Casparie. Rotterdam: Balkema, 43–61.

Jones, G., Straker, V. & Davis, A., 1991. Early medieval plant use and ecology in London, in *Aspects of Saxo-Norman London: II. Finds and environmental evidence*, ed. A.G. Vince. (Transactions of the London and Middlesex Archaeological Society Special Paper 12.) London: London and Middlesex Archaeological Society, 347–85.

Jones, M.J., Stocker, D. & Vince, A., 2003. *The City by the Pool. Assessing the archaeology of the city of Lincoln.* (Lincoln Archaeological Studies 10.) Oxford: Oxbow Books.

Jones, R.T & Page, M., 2006. *Medieval Villages in an English Landscape: beginnings and ends.* Macclesfield: Windgather Press.

Jope, E.M., 1950. A late medieval pottery kiln at Potterspury, Northants. *Archaeological Newsletter* 2, 156–7.

Jope, E.M., 1954. Medieval pottery kilns at Brill, Buckinghamshire. Preliminary report on excavations in 1953. *Records of Buckinghamshire* 16, 39–42.

Jope, E.M., 1956. The tinning of iron spurs: a continuous practice from the tenth to the seventeenth centuries. *Oxoniensia* 21, 35–42.

Jope, E.M. & Ivens, R.J., 1981. Some early products of the Brill pottery, Buckinghamshire. *Records of Buckinghamshire* 23, 32–8.

Joy, J., 2009. Reinvigorating object biography: reproducing the drama of object lives. *World Archaeology* 41(4), 540–56.

Joy, J., 2016. Hoards as collections: re-examining the Snettisham Iron Age hoards from the perspective of collecting practice. *World Archaeology* 48(2), 239–53

Jütte, D., 2014. Entering a city: on a lost early modern practice. *Urban History* 41(2), 204–27.

Kaner, S., 2000. *The Grand Arcade Cambridge: a brief for archaeological excavation.* Unpublished Cambridgeshire County Archaeological Office document. Cambridge: Cambridgeshire County Archaeological Office.

Keene, D.J., 1976. Suburban growth, in *The Plans and Topography of Medieval Towns in England and Wales*, ed. M.W. Barley. (Council for British Archaeology Research Report 14.) York: Council for British Archaeology, 71–82.

Keene, D.J., 1982. Rubbish in medieval towns, in *Environmental Archaeology in the Urban Context*, eds. A.R. Hall & H.K. Kenward. (Council for British Archaeology Research Report 43.) York: Council for British Archaeology, 26–30.

Keene, D.J., 1996. Landlords, the property market and urban development in England, in *Power, Profit and Urban Land. Landownership in medieval and early modern northern European towns*, eds. F.-E. Eliassen & G.A. Ersland. Aldershot: Scolar Press, 93–119.

Kellet, J.H., 1969. Glasgow, in *Atlas of Historic Towns 1*, ed. M.D. Lobel. Oxford: Lovell Johns, 1–13.

Kenny, D.A., 2000a. *An archaeological evaluation at the former government offices site, Brooklands Avenue, Cambridge.* (CAU Report 347.) Cambridge: Cambridge Archaeological Unit.

Kenny, D.A., 2000b. *Archaeological evaluation at the former Charrington Oil Depot, 22–24 Clarendon Road, Cambridge.* (CAU Report 360.) Cambridge: Cambridge Archaeological Unit.

Kent, B.C., 1983. More on gunflints, *Historical Archaeology* 17(2), 27–40.

Kenward H.K., 1997. Synanthropic insects and the size, remoteness and longevity of archaeological occupation sites: applying concepts from biogeography to past 'islands' of human occupation, *Quaternary Proceedings* 5, 135–52.

Kenward, H.K. & Hall, A.R., 1997. Enhancing bio-archaeological interpretation using indicator groups: stable manure as a paradigm. *Journal of Archaeological Science* 24(7), 663–73.

Kenyon, J.R., 1990. *Medieval Fortifications.* London: Leicester University Press.

Keogh, B., 1997. *The Secret Sauce: a history of Lea and Perrins.* Privately published.

Kerridge, E., 1967. *The Agricultural Revolution.* London: Allen & Unwin.

Killock, D. & Meddens, F., 2005. Pottery as plunder: a 17th-century maritime site in Limehouse, London. *Post-Medieval Archaeology* 39, 1–91.

Kilmurry, K., 1980. *The Pottery Industry of Stamford Type, Lincs. c. AD 850–1250.* (British Archaeological Reports, British Series 84.) Oxford: British Archaeological Reports.

Klingelhofer, E., 1978. Barrack Street excavations, Warwick, 1972. *Birmingham and Warwickshire Archaeological Society Transactions* 88, 87–104.

Knight, H. & Jeffries, N., 2004. *Medieval and later urban development at High Street, Uxbridge: excavations at the Chimes Shopping Centre, London Borough of Hillingdon.* (MoLAS Archaeological Studies Series 12.) London: MoLAS.

Knight, M. & Murrell, K., 2010. *Must Farm, Whittlesey 2010 Palaeochannel Investigations. Interim statement.* (CAU Report 989.) Cambridge: Cambridge Archaeological Unit.

Koch, K., 1992. *Die Kafer Mitteleuropas.* (Ökologie Band 3.) Krefeld: Goecke & Evers.

Kopytoff, I., 1986. The cultural biography of things: commoditization as process, in *The Social Life of Things: commodities in cultural perspective*, ed. A. Appadurai. Cambridge: Cambridge University Press, 64–91.

Kowaleski, M., 2000. The expansion of the south-western fisheries in late medieval England. *Economic History Review* 53(3), 429–54.

Kruse, K.M. & Sugrue, T.J., (eds.). 2006. *The New Suburban History.* Chicago: University of Chicago Press.

Laermans, R., 1993. Learning to consume: early department stores and the shaping of the modern consumer culture. *Theory, Culture & Society* 10(4), 79–102.

Lancaster, B., 1995. *The Department Store: a social history.* London: Leicester University Press.

Langdon, J., 1986. *Horses, Oxen and Technological Innovations.* Cambridge: Cambridge University Press.

Lawrence, S., 2006. Overburden: the importance of the archaeology of the Modern period in Britain, in *Cities in the World, 1500–2000*, eds. A. Green & R. Leach. Leeds: Maney, 307–19.

Le Cheminant, R., 1981. Clay tobacco pipes from London and the south east, in *The Archaeology of the Clay Tobacco Pipe VI: pipes and kilns in the London region*, ed. P. Davey. (British Archaeological Reports, British Series 97.) Oxford: British Archaeological Reports, 127–72.

Leach, P., (ed.) 1984. *The Archaeology of Taunton: excavations and fieldwork to 1980* (Western Archaeological Trust Excavation Monograph 8.) Bristol: Western Archaeological Trust.

Leah, M., 1994. *The Late Saxon and Medieval Pottery Industry of Grimston, Norfolk: excavations 1962–92.* (East Anglian Archaeology 64.) Dereham: Field Archaeology Division, Norfolk Museums Service.

Leahy, K., 2013. A deposit of early medieval iron objects from Scraptoft, Leicestershire. *Medieval Archaeology* 57, 223–37.

Lee, S.J., 2003. Feeding the colleges: Cambridge's food and fuel supplies, 1450–1560. *Economic History Review* 56(2), 243–64.

Lee, S.J., 2005. *Cambridge and its Economic Region, 1450–1560.* Hatfield: University of Hertfordshire Press.

Lethbridge, T.C., 1949. Byzantine influence in Late Saxon England. *Proceedings of the Cambridge Antiquarian Society* 43, 2–6.

Lewis, C., 1989. Paired mottes in East Chelborough, Dorset, in *From Cornwall to Caithness: some aspects of British field archaeology. Papers presented to Norman V Quinnell*, eds.

M. Bowden D. Mackay & P. Topping. (British Archaeological Reports, British Series 209.) Oxford: British Archaeological Reports, 159–71.

Lewis, C., 2009. Children's play in the later medieval English countryside. *Childhood in the Past* 2, 86–108.

Lewis, H.S., 1998. The misrepresentation of anthropology and its consequences. *American Anthropologist* 100(3), 716–31.

Lewis, J.N.C. & Lewis, G., 2006. *Pratt Ware: English and Scottish relief decorated and underglaze coloured earthenware, 1780–1840*. 2nd edition. Woodbridge: Antique Collectors' Club.

Lewis, R., 2017. Comments on urban agency: relational space and intentionality. *Urban History* 44(1), 137–44.

Lilley, K.D., 2015. Urban planning after the Black Death: townscape transformation in later medieval England (1350–1530), *Urban History* 42(1), 22–42.

Lindroth, C.H., 1974. *Coleoptera: Carabidae* (Handbooks for the Identification of British Insects 4/2.) London: Royal Entomological Society of London.

Lindstrøm, T.C., 2015. Agency 'in itself'. A discussion of inanimate, animal and human agency. *Archaeological Dialogues* 22(2), 207–38.

Lintonbon, J., 2006. 'Designer Shopping': the development of the department store in nineteenth century Sheffield, in *Materializing Sheffield: Place, Culture and Identity*, ed. S. Macdonald. Available at: http://www.hrionline.ac.uk/matshef/lintonbon/MSlintonbon.htm. Accessed: 7 July 2011.

Litten, J., 1991. *The English Way of Death: the common funeral since 1450*. London: Robert Hale.

Little, B., 1960. *Cambridge Discovered*. Cambridge: W. Heffer & Sons.

Lobel, M.D., 1975. *The Atlas of Historic Towns, Vol. 2: Bristol; Cambridge; Coventry; Norwich*. Aldershot: Scholar Press.

Loewe, J.A., 2009. Cambridge's collegiate crisis: King Henry VIII and the suppression of Colleges, 1546. *Reformation Renaissance Review* 11(2), 139–64.

Lucas, G., 1998. A medieval fishery on Whittlesea Mere, Cambridgeshire. *Medieval Archaeology* 42, 19–44.

Lucas, G., 2001. Destruction and the rhetoric of excavation. *Norwegian Archaeological Review* 34(1), 35–46.

Lucas, G., 2002. Disposability and dispossession in the twentieth century. *Journal of Material Culture* 7(1), 5–22.

Lucas, G., 2003. Reading pottery: literature and transfer-printed pottery in the early nineteenth century. *International Journal of Historical Archaeology* 7(2), 127–43.

Lucas, G., 2014. Conduits of dispersal. Dematerializing an early twentieth-century village in Iceland, in *Ruin Memories Materiality: aesthetics and the archaeology of the recent past*, eds. B. Olsen & Þ. Pétursdóttir. Abingdon: Routledge, 305–18.

Lucas, G., 2015. Archaeology and contemporaneity. *Archaeological Dialogues* 22(1), 1–15.

Lucas, G. & Regan, R., 2003. The changing vernacular: archaeological excavations at Temple End, High Wycombe, Buckinghamshire. *Post-Medieval Archaeology* 37, 165–206.

Lucas R., 1993. Ely bricks and roof-tiles and their distribution in Norfolk and elsewhere in the sixteenth to eighteenth centuries. *Proceedings of the Cambridge Antiquarian Society* 82, 157–62.

Lucas, R., 1997. When did Norfolk cross 'the brick threshold'? *Vernacular Architecture* 28(1), 68–80.

Luff, R., 1993. *Animal Bones from Excavations in Colchester, 1971–85*. (Colchester Archaeological Reports 12.) Colchester: Colchester Archaeological Trust.

Mabbit, J., 2006. *MCH02, One Trinity*. (Tyne & Wear Museums Report). Newcastle: Tyne & Wear Museums.

Mabbit, J. & Frain T., 2007. *Excavations at the Former Tweedale Press, Walkergate, Berwick upon Tweed*. (Tyne & Wear Museums Report). Newcastle: Tyne & Wear Museums.

Macfarlane, A., 1978. *The Origins of English Individualism: the family, property and social transition*. Blackwell: Oxford.

Macfarlane, A., 2009. *Reflections on Cambridge*. New Delhi: Social Science Press,

MacGregor, A., 1985. *Bone, Antler, Ivory and Horn. The technology of skeletal materials since the Roman period*. London: Croom Helm.

Mack, R.P., 1966. Stephen and the Anarchy, 1135–1154. *British Numismatic Journal* 35, 38–112.

Mackay, D., 2001a. *Land around Homerton Street, Cambridge: an archaeological evaluation*. (CAU Report 423.) Cambridge: Cambridge Archaeological Unit.

Mackay, D., 2001b. *The Old Cattle Market, Cambridge: an archaeological evaluation*. (CAU Report 437.) Cambridge: Cambridge Archaeological Unit.

Mackay, D., 2001c. *An archaeological investigation at Homerton Street, Cambridge*. (CAU Report 448.) Cambridge: Cambridge Archaeological Unit.

Mackay, D., 2003. *Hill's Road Sixth Form College: an archaeological evaluation*. (CAU Report 566.) Cambridge: Cambridge Archaeological Unit.

Mackay, D., 2005. *Cambridge Business and Cultural Centre: an archaeological watching brief and radar survey*. (CAU Report 685.) Cambridge: Cambridge Archaeological Unit.

Mackay, D., 2006. *Archaeological test pitting and watching brief at the CB1 Development, Cambridge: an archaeological evaluation*. (CAU Report 736.) Cambridge: Cambridge Archaeological Unit.

Macphail, R.I., Galinié, H. & Verhaeghe, F., 2003. The fate of Dark Earth, *Antiquity* 77 (296), 349–58.

Maitland, F.W., 1898. *Township and Borough*. Cambridge: Cambridge University Press.

Maitland, F.W. & Bateson, M., 1901. *The Charters of the Borough of Cambridge*. Cambridge: Cambridge Antiquarian Society.

Majewski, T. & O'Brien, M.J., 1987. The use and misuse of nineteenth-century English and American ceramics in archaeological analysis. *Advances in Archaeological Method and Theory* 11, 97–208.

Malcolm, G., 1999. Excavations at Island site, Finsbury Pavement, London EC2. *Transactions of the London and Middlesex Archaeological Society* 48, 33–58.

Malim, T., 1990. *The King's Ditch, 1989*. (Cambridgeshire County Council Archaeological Field Unit Report 4.) Fulbourn: Cambridgeshire County Council Archaeological Field Unit.

Maloney, J. & Harding, C., 1979. Dukes Place and Houndsditch: the medieval defences. *London Archaeology* 3, 347–54.

Maltby, J.M., 1979. *Faunal Studies on Urban Sites: the animal bones from Exeter 1971–1975.* (Exeter Archaeology Report 2.) Sheffield: Department of Prehistory and Archaeology, University of Sheffield.

Mandich, M.J., 2015. Re-defining the Roman 'suburbum' from Republic to Empire: a theoretical approach, in *TRAC 2014. Proceedings of the Twenty-Fourth Theoretical Roman Archaeology Conference*, eds. T. Brindle, M. Allen, E. Durham & A. Smith. Oxford: Oxbow Books, 81–99.

Margeson, S., 1993. *Norwich Households: the medieval and post-medieval finds from Norwich Survey excavations 1971–1978* (East Anglian Archaeology 58.) Norwich: The Norwich Survey/Norfolk Museums Service.

Martin, E.A. & Satchell, M., 2008. *'Where most Inclosures be' East Anglian Fields: history, morphology and management* (East Anglian Archaeology 124.) Ipswich: Archaeological Service, Suffolk County Council.

Martin, E., Plouviez, J. & Ross, H., 1984. Archaeology in Suffolk 1983. *Proceedings of the Suffolk Institute of Archaeology & History* 35, 321–8.

Masefield, R., Branch, N., Coultrey, P., Goodburn, D. & Tyers, I., 2003. A later Bronze Age well complex at Swalecliffe, Kent. *Antiquaries Journal* 83(1), 47–121.

Mather, J., 2009. *Pashas: Traders and Travellers in the Islamic World.* London: Yale University Press.

Matthew, D., 2002. *King Stephen.* Stroud: Tempus.

Mayne, A. & Lawrence, S., 1999. Ethnographies of Place: a new urban research agenda. *Urban History Yearbook* 26, 325–48.

Mayne, A. & Murray, T., (eds.) 2001. *The Archaeology of Urban Landscapes: explorations in slumland.* Cambridge: Cambridge University Press.

McCarthy, M.R. & Brooks, C.M., 1988. *Medieval Pottery in Britain, AD 900–160.* London: Leicester University Press.

McCobb, L.M.E., Briggs, D.E.G., Evershed, R.P., Hall, A.R. & Hall R.A., 2001. Preservation of fossil seeds from a tenth-century AD cess pit at Coppergate, York. *Journal of Archaeological Science* 28(9), 929–40.

Meeson, R.A. & Welch, C.M., 1993. Earrthfast posts: the persistence of alternative building techniques. *Vernacular Architecture* 24(1), 1–17.

Mellor, M., 2005. Making and using pottery in town and country, in *Town and Country in the Middle Ages: contrasts, contacts and interconnections 1100–1500*, eds. K. Giles & C. Dyer. (Society for Medieval Archaeology Monograph 22.) Leeds: Maney, 149–64.

Merrifield, R., 1987. *The Archaeology of Ritual and Magic.* London: Batsford.

Michaels, T., 2004. *Triangle Site, Station Road, Cambridge: an archaeological evaluation.* (Foundations Archaeology Report.) Swindon: Foundations Archaeology.

Middleton, A., 2008. *Te Puna. A New Zealand Mission Station: Historical Archaeology in New Zealand.* New York (NY): Springer-Verlag.

Miles, T.J., 1998. Flint: excavations at the castle and on the town defences 1971–1974. *Archaeologia Cambrensis* 145, 67–151.

Miller, G.L., 1980. Classification and economic scaling of 19th-century ceramics. *Historical Archaeology* 14(1), 1–40.

Miller, G.L., 1991a. A revised set of cc index values for classification and economic scaling of English ceramics from 1787 to 1880. *Historical Archaeology* 25(1), 1–25.

Miller, G.L., 1991b. Thoughts towards a user's guide to ceramic assemblages, part I: lumping sites into mega-assemblages by those that cannot tell time. *Council for Northeast Historical Archaeology Newsletter* 18, 2–5.

Miller, J., 1992. *Archaeological Investigations at St Andrew's the Great, Cambridge.* (CAU Report 70.) Cambridge: Cambridge Archaeological Unit.

Miller, M.B., 1981. *The Bon Marché: bourgeois culture and the department store.* Princeton (NJ): Princeton University Press

Milne, G., 1992. *Timber Building Techniques in London c. 900–1400: an archaeological study of waterfront installations and related material.* (London and Middlesex Archaeological Society Special Paper 15.) London: London and Middlesex Archaeological Society.

Milne, G. & Cohen, N., 2002. *Excavations at Medieval Cripplegate: archaeology after the Blitz, 1946–68.* Swindon: English Heritage.

Minns, E.H., 1934. A Cambridge vintner's accounts *c.* 1511. *Proceedings of the Cambridge Antiquarian Society* 34, 50–8.

Mitchiner, M., 1988. *Jetons, Medalets and Tokens. Vol. 1. The Medieval Period and Nuremberg.* London: BA Seaby.

Mitchiner, M., 1998. *Jetons, Medalets and Tokens. Vol. 3. British Isles circa 1558 to 1830.* London: BA Seaby.

Moffett, L.C., 1991. The archaeobotanical evidence for free-threshing tetraploid wheat in Britain, in *Palaeoethnobotany and Archaeology*, ed. E. Hajnalova. (Acta Interdisciplinaria Archaeologica VII.) Nitra: Archeologický ústav Slovenskej akadémie vied, 233–44.

Moffett, L.C., 1994. Charred cereals from some ovens/kilns in late Saxon Stafford and the botanical evidence for the pre-*burh* economy, in *Environment and Economy in Anglo-Saxon England*, ed. J. Rackham. (Council for British Archaeology Research Report 89.) York: Council for British Archaeology, 55–64.

Moffett, L.C. & Smith, D.N., 1997. Insects and plants from a Late Medieval tenement in Stone, Staffordshire. *Circaea* 12(2), 157–75.

Monckton, A., 1999. The plant remains, in *Roman and Medieval Occupation in Causeway Lane, Leicester*, by A. Connor & R. Buckley. (Leicester Archaeological Monograph 5.) Leicester: University of Leicester Archaeological Services, 346–61.

Monk, M.A., 1981. Post-Roman drying kilns and the problem of function: a preliminary statement, in *Irish Antiquity*, ed. D. Ó Corráin. Dublin: Four Courts Press, 216–30.

Monk, M.A., 1986. Evidence from macroscopic plant remains for crop husbandry in prehistoric and early historic Ireland. *Journal of Irish Archaeology* 3, 31–6.

Moore, W.J. & Corbett, M.E., 1975. Distribution of dental caries in ancient British populations: III, the 17th century. *Caries Research* 9(2), 163–75.

Moore, W.R.G., 1980. *Northamptonshire Clay Tobacco-Pipes and Pipemakers.* Northampton: Northampton Museums & Art Gallery.

Morris, C.A., 2000. *Wood and Woodworking in Anglo-Scandinavian and Medieval York* (Archaeology of York 17/13.) York: Council for British Archaeology.

Morris, C.A., 2007. Wooden gaming pieces, in *Finds from the Eell at St Paul-in-the-Bail, Lincoln*, ed. M. Archibald. (Lincoln Archaeological Studies 9.) Oxford: Oxbow, 59–65.

Morris, J. & Jervis, B., 2011. What's so special? A re-interpretation of Anglo-Saxon 'special deposits'. *Medieval Archaeology* 55, 66–81.

Morris, R.K., 2003. Monastic architecture: destruction and reconstruction, in *The Archaeology of Reformation, 1480–1580*, eds. D. Gaimster & R. Gilchrist. (Society for Post-Medieval Archaeology Monograph 1.) Leeds: Maney, 235–51.

Mortimer, J., 1712. *The whole Art of Husbandry, in the way of Managing and Improving of Land*. 3rd edition. London: Mortlock & Robinson.

Mortimer, R., 2000. Village development and ceramic sequence: the Middle to Late Saxon village at Lordship Lane, Cottenham, Cambridgeshire. *Proceedings of the Cambridge Antiquarian Society* 89, 5–33.

Mortimer, R., 2006. *Mill Common, Huntingdon, Cambridgeshire: trench evaluation and community archaeology project*. (Cambridgeshire County Council Archaeological Field Unit Report 823.) Bar Hill: Cambridgeshire County Council Archaeological Field Unit.

Mortimer, R., Regan, R. & Lucy, S., 2005. *The Saxon and Medieval Settlement at West Fen Road, Ely: the Ashwell site* (East Anglian Archaeology 110.) Cambridge: CAU.

Murphy, P., 1997. Environment and economy [urban medieval and post-medieval], in *Research and Archaeology: A framework for the Eastern Counties, 1. Resource assessment*, ed. J. Glazebrook. (East Anglian Archaeology Occasional Paper 3.) Norwich: Scole Archaeological Committee, 63–4.

Murphy, P., 1998. Plant macrofossils, in *Excavations at St Martin-at-Palace-Plain, Norwich, 1981*, by B. Ayers. (East Anglian Archaeology 37.) Dereham: Norfolk Archaeological Unit, 118–33.

Murphy, P. & Scaife, R.G., 1991. The environmental archaeology of gardens, in *Garden Archaeology: papers presented to a conference at Knuston Hall, Northamptonshire, April 1988*, ed. A.E. Brown. (Council for British Archaeology Research Report 78.) York: Council for British Archaeology, 83–99.

Murray, H.K., Murray, J.C. & Lindsay, W.J., 2009. Medieval timber-lined wells in Elgin. *Proceedings of the Society of Antiquaries of Scotland* 139, 213–28.

Myers, A., 2016. The significance of hotel-ware ceramics in the twentieth century. *Historical Archaeology* 50(2), 110–26.

Mynard, D.C., 1970. Medieval pottery of Potterspury type. *Bulletin of the Northamptonshire Federated Archaeology Society* 4, 49–55.

Myrdal, J., 1984. The hayrake. *Ethnologia Scandinavica* 1984, 237–45.

Naton, A. & Cockin, G., 2008. Excavations at the Classics Centre, 65–67 St Giles, Oxford. *Oxoniensia* 73, 161–94.

Newman, R., 2007. *The Christ's Lane development at Bradwell's Court, Cambridge: an archaeological excavation*. (CAU Report 775.) Cambridge: Cambridge Archaeological Unit.

Newman, R., 2008a. *Thompson's Lane, Cambridge: an archaeological investigation*. (CAU Report 809.) Cambridge: Cambridge Archaeological Unit.

Newman, R., 2008b. *The Kavli Institute for Cosmology, Cambridge: an archaeological excavation*. (CAU Report 820.) Cambridge: Cambridge Archaeological Unit.

Newman, R., 2008c. *St John's Triangle, Cambridge: an archaeological excavation and watching brief*. (CAU Report 851.) Cambridge: Cambridge Archaeological Unit.

Newman, R., 2009a. *The Former Marshall Garage, Cambridge: an archaeological evaluation*. (CAU Report 877.) Cambridge: Cambridge Archaeological Unit.

Newman, R., 2009b. *The Old Schools, University of Cambridge: an archaeological excavation*. (CAU Report 903.) Cambridge: Cambridge Archaeological Unit.

Newman, R., 2010. *Parkside Fire and Rescue Station, Cambridge: an archaeological test pit investigation*. (CAU Report 955.) Cambridge: Cambridge Archaeological Unit.

Newman, R., 2011. *Parkside Fire and Rescue Station, Cambridge: an archaeological evaluation*. (CAU Report 1049.) Cambridge: Cambridge Archaeological Unit.

Newman, R., 2013a. *The Eastern Gate Hotel site, Cambridge: an archaeological excavation*. (CAU Report 1176.) Cambridge: Cambridge Archaeological Unit.

Newman, R., 2013b. *Judge Business School, Cambridge: an archaeological evaluation*. (CAU Report 1187.) Cambridge: Cambridge Archaeological Unit.

Newman. R., 2015. Planned redevelopments in medieval and early post-Medieval Chesterton. *Proceedings of the Cambridge Antiquarian Society* 104, 89–105.

Newman, R. & Evans, C., 2011. Archaeological investigations at the Old Schools, University of Cambridge. *Proceedings of the Cambridge Antiquarian Society* 100, 185–96.

Newton, A.A.S., 2010. A medieval clunch-working site at Fordham Road, Isleham, Cambridgeshire. *Proceedings of the Cambridge Antiquarian Society* 99, 103–12.

Nilsson, A.N. & Holmen, M., 1995. *The Aquatic Adephaga (Coleoptera) of Fennoscandia and Denmark II. Dytiscidae*, (Fauna Entomologyca Scandinavica 35.) Leiden: Brill.

Noël Hume, I., 1971. *A Guide to Artifacts of Colonial America*. New York (NY): Alfred A. Knopf.

Oak-Rind, H., 1980. Distribution of clay tobacco pipes around their place of manufacture, in *The Archaeology of the Clay Tobacco Pipe III: Britain, the north and west*, ed. P. Davey. (British Archaeological Reports, British Series 78.) Oxford: British Archaeological Reports, 349–61.

O'Connor, T.P., 1982. *Animal bones from Flaxengate, Lincoln c. 870–1500*. (Archaeology of Lincoln 18/1.) London: Council for British Archaeology.

O'Connor, T.P., 1984. *Selected Groups of Bones from Skeldergate and Walmgate* (Archaeology of York 15/1.) London: Council for British Archaeology.

O'Connor, T.P., 1993. Process and terminology in mammal carcass reduction. *International Journal of Osteoarchaeology* 3(2), 63–7.

O'Connor, T.P., 1995. Size increase in post-medieval English sheep: the osteological evidence. *Archaeofauna* 4, 81–91.

O'Donovan, E., 2003. The growth and decline of a medieval suburb? Evidence from excavations at Thomas Street, in *Medieval Dublin IV. Proceedings of the Friends of Medieval*

Dublin Symposium 2002, ed. S. Duffy. Dublin: Four Courts Press, 127–71.

Oosthuizen, S., 2000. The Cambridgeshire Lodes, in *An Atlas of Cambridgeshire and Huntingdonshire History*, eds. T. Kirby & S. Oosthuizen. Cambridge: Centre for Regional Studies Anglia Polytechnic University.

Oosthuizen, S., 2005. New light on the origins of open-field farming?. *Medieval Archaeology* 49, 165–93.

Oosthuizen, S., 2006. *Landscapes Decoded: the origins and development of Cambridgeshire's medieval fields*. Hatfield: University of Hertfordshire.

Oosthuizen, S., 2010. The distribution of two- and three-field systems on south Cambridgeshire before about 1350. *Medieval Settlement Research* 25, 21–31.

Orme, N., 2008. Medieval childhood: challenge, change and achievement. *Childhood in the Past* 1, 106–19.

Ormes, I., 2000. *Eaden Lilley: 250 years of retailing*. Saffron Walden: W. Eaden Lilley.

Orser, C.E., 1986. *A Historical Archaeology of the Modern World*. London: Plenum.

Osborne, M., 1990. *Cromwellian Fortifications in Cambridgeshire*. Huntingdon: Cromwell Museum.

Osborne, P.J., 1983. An insect fauna from a modern cesspit and its comparison with probable cesspit assemblages from archaeological sites. *Journal of Archaeological Science* 10(5), 453–63.

Oswald, A., 1975. *Clay Pipes for the Archaeologist* (British Archaeological Reports, British Series 14.) Oxford: British Archaeological Reports.

Ottaway, P. & Rogers, N., 2002. *Craft, Industry and Everyday Life: finds from medieval York*. (Archaeology of York 17/15.) York: Council for British Archaeology.

Otway-Ruthven, J., 1938. Translation of the text of Cambridgeshire Domesday, in *A History of the County of Cambridge and the Isle of Ely Vol. 1.*, ed. L.F Salzman. Oxford: Oxford University Press, 358–99.

Overton, N.J. & Hamilakis, Y., 2013. A manifesto for a social zooarchaeology. Swans and other beings in the Mesolithic. *Archaeological Dialogues* 20(2), 111–36.

Page, F.M., 1948. Industries, in *A History of the County of Cambridge and the Isle of Ely: Vol. 2*, ed. L.F. Salzman. London: Oxford University Press, 357–76.

Palliser, D.M., Slater, T.R. & Dennison, P.E., 2001. The topography of towns, 600–1300, in *The Cambridge Urban History of Britain Vol. 1*, ed. D.M. Palliser. Cambridge: Cambridge University Press, 153–86.

Palmer, N.J., 1980. A Beaker burial and medieval tenements in The Hamel, Oxford. *Oxoniensia* 45, 124–225.

Palmer, W.M., 1935. *William Cole of Milton*. Cambridge: Galloway & Porter.

Pantin, W.A., 1937. The recently demolished houses in Broad Street, Oxford. *Oxoniensia* 3, 171–200.

Pantin, W.A., 1963. Medieval English town-house plans. *Medieval Archaeology* 7, 202–39.

Parker, R., 1983. *Town and Gown: the 700 years' war in Cambridge*. Cambridge: Patrick Stephens.

Partridge, C., 1973. *Report on Petty Cury for the Cambridge Archaeological Committee*. Unpublished document. Cambridge: Cambridgeshire County Archaeology Office.

Pasdermadjian, H., 1954. *The Department Store, its Origins, Evolution, and Economics*. London: Newman Books.

Patten, R. & Evans, C., 2005. *Striplands Farm West, Longstanton, Cambridgeshire: an archaeological excavation*. (CAU Report 703.) Cambridge: Cambridge Archaeological Unit.

Payne, S., 1973. Kill-off patterns in sheep and goats: the mandibles from Asvan Kale. *Anatolian Studies* 23, 281–303.

Pearce, J.I., 1992. *Post-Medieval Pottery in London, 1500–1700, Vol. 1, Border Wares*. London: HMSO.

Pearce, J.I., 1999. The pottery industry of the Surrey-Hampshire borders in the 16th and 17th centuries, in *Old World and New*, eds. G. Egan & R.L. Michael. Oxford: Oxbow Books, 246–63.

Pearce, J.I., 2000. A late 18th-century inn clearance assemblage from Uxbridge, Middlesex. *Post-Medieval Archaeology* 34, 144–86.

Pearce, J.I., 2007a. Consumption of creamware: London archaeological evidence, in *Creamware and Pearlware Re-examined*, eds. T. Walford & R. Massey. London: English Ceramic Circle, 231–3.

Pearce, J.I., 2007b. *Pots and Potters in Tudor Hampshire*. London: Guildford Museum & MoLAS.

Pearce, J.I., 2008. English porcelain of the 18th century in archaeologically excavated assemblages from London. *English Ceramic Circle Transactions* 20(2), 273–314.

Pearce, J.I. & Vince, A., 1988. *A Dated Type-series of London Medieval Pottery, Part 4: Surrey White Wares*. (Transactions of the London and Middlesex Archaeological Society Series Special Paper 10.) London: London and Middlesex Archaeological Society.

Pearce, J.I., Vince, A.G., White, R. & Cunningham, C., 1982. A dated type series of London medieval pottery 1: Mill Green ware. *Transactions of the London and Middlesex Archaeological Society* 33, 266–98.

Pearson, S., 2005. Rural and urban houses 1100–1500: urban adaptation reconsidered, in *Town and Country in the Middle Ages: contrasts, contacts and interconnections 1100–1500*, eds. K. Giles & C. Dyer. (Society for Medieval Archaeology Monograph 22.) Leeds: Maney, 43–63.

Pearson, S., 2009. Medieval houses in English towns: form and location. *Vernacular Architecture* 40, 1–22.

Perring, D., 1986. Pianificazione strategica nell'archeologia urbana. *Archeologia Uomo Territorio* 5, 119–38.

Perring, D., 2002. *Town and Country in England: frameworks for archaeological research* (Council for British Archaeology Research Report 134.) York: Council for British Archaeology.

Petty, M., 1991. William Mayland, *Cambridge Weekly News* 4 April 1991.

Pevsner, N., 1954. *The Buildings of England: Cambridgeshire*. 1st edition. Harmondsworth: Penguin.

Pevsner, N., 1970. *Cambridgeshire; the buildings of England No. 10*. 2nd edition. Harmondsworth: Penguin.

Pevsner, N., 2001. *Cambridgeshire; the buildings of England No. 10*. Revised 2nd edition. Harmondsworth: Penguin.

Phillpotts, C., Samuel, M. & Seeley, D., 2006. *Winchester Palace: excavations at the Southwark residence of the bishops of Winchester*. (MoLAS Monograph 31.) London: MoLAS.

Phythian-Adams, C., 1977. Jolly cities: goodly towns. The current search for England's urban roots. *Urban History Yearbook* 1977, 30–9.

Pickles, J.D., 2007. Servants of the Cambridge colleges in 1802. *Cambridgeshire Family History Society Journal* 16(4), 12–13

Pinder, L.C.V., Marker, A.F.H., Mann, R.H.K., Bass, J.A.B. & Copp, G.H., 1997. The River Great Ouse, a highly eutrophic, slow-flowing, regulated, lowland river in Eastern England. *Regulated Rivers: Research & Management* 13(3), 203–19.

Piper P.J. & O'Connor, T.P., 2001. Urban small vertebrate taphonomy: a case study from Anglo-Scandinavian York. *International Journal of Osteoarchaeology* 11(5), 336–44.

Pitt. K. with Taylor, J., 2009. *Finsbury's Moated manor. Medieval land use and later development in the Finsbury Square area, Islington.* (MoLAS Archaeological Studies 20.) London: MoLAS.

Platt, C., 1994. *The Great Rebuildings of Tudor and Stuart England: Revolutions in Architectural Taste.* London: Routledge.

Plommer, H., 1966. 'Omnia Fatis' The Proposals for replanning Cambridge. *Cambridge Review* 88, 304–9.

Pluskowski, A., 2007. Communicating through skin and bone: approaching animal bodies in medieval western European seigneurial culture, in *Breaking and Shaping Beastly Bodies: animals as material culture in the middle ages,* ed. A. Pluskowski. Oxford: Oxbow Books, 32–51.

Pomfret, R., 2008. Attribution of the 'IH' mark. *Transferware Collectors Club Bulletin* 9(3), 4–5.

Poole, L.N., 1978. Feathers, feathers everywhere. *Gazette* 16 March 1978, 149–50.

Pooley, C.G., 1979. Residential mobility in the Victorian city. *Transactions of the Institute of British Geographers* 4(2), 258–77.

Poore, D., Score, D. & Dodd, A., 2006. Excavations at No. 4A Merton St., Merton College, Oxford: the evolution of a medieval stone house and tenement and an early college property. *Oxoniensia* 71, 211–342.

Porter, E., 1969. *Cambridgeshire Customs and Folklore.* London: Routledge & Kegan Paul.

Porter, E., 1973. Cambridge brickmakers. *Cambridge Society for Industrial Archaeology Newsletter* 5, 2–3.

Potter, K.R., (ed.) 1976. *Gesta Stephani.* Oxford: Oxford University Press.

Poulton, R., 1998. Excavation between Castle Street and Bear Lane, Farnham. *Surrey Archaeological Collections* 85, 133–43.

Poulton, R. & Riall, N., 1998. The town ditch and the origins and early development of Farnham. *Surrey Archaeological Collections* 85, 147–51.

Priddy, D., 1982. Excavation in Essex, 1981. *Essex Archaeology and History* 14, 133–45.

Purcell, D., 1967. *Cambridge Stone.* London: Faber.

Quiney, A., 2003. *Town Houses of Medieval Britain.* London: Yale University Press.

Quinnell, H. & Blockley, M.R., 1994. *Excavations at Rhuddlan, Clwyd: 1969–73 Mesolithic to medieval* (Council for British Archaeology Research Report 95.) York: Council for British Archaeology.

Rackham, B., 1948. *Medieval English Pottery:* Faber & Faber.

Rackham, B., 1987. *Catalogue of the Glaisher Collection of Pottery and Porcelain in the Fitzwilliam Museum Cambridge.* Woodbridge: Antique Collectors' Club.

Rackham, O., 1980. *Ancient Woodland, its History, Vegetation and Uses in England.* London: Edward Arnold.

Rahtz, P. & Meeson, R., 1992. *An Anglo-Saxon Watermill at Tamworth* (Council for British Archaeology Research Report 83.) York: Council for British Archaeology.

Rathje, W., 2011. Archaeological intervention in the past, present and future tense. *Archaeological Dialogues* 18(2), 176–180.

Rátkai, S., (ed.) 2008. *The Bull Ring Uncovered: excavations at Edgbaston Street, Moor Street, Park Street and The Row, Birmingham City Centre, 1997–2001.* Oxford: Oxbow Books.

Rawlinson, H.G., 1922. The embassy of William Harborne to Constantinople, 1583–8. *Transactions of the Royal Historical Society* 5, 1–27.

RCHM(E)., 1959. *An Inventory of the Historical Monuments in the City of Cambridge.* London: HMSO.

Reaney, P.H., 1943. *The Place-Names of Cambridgeshire and the Isle of Ely* (English Place-Name Society 19.) Cambridge: Cambridge University Press.

Reece, R., 1984. Sequence is all: or archaeology in an historical period, *Scottish Archaeological Review* 3(2), 113–15.

Rees, H., Crummy, N., Ottaway, P.J. & Dunn, G., 2008. *Artefact and Society in Roman and Medieval Winchester: small finds from the suburbs and defences, 1971–1986.* Winchester: Winchester Museums Service.

Rees Jones, S., 2008. Building Domesticity in the city: English urban housing before the Black Death, in *Medieval domesticity: home, housing and household in medieval England,* eds. M. Kowaleski & P.J.P. Goldberg. Cambridge: Cambridge University Press, 66–91.

Regan, R., 1997. *Archaeological Excavations at Angel Court, Trinity College, Cambridge.* (CAU Report 199.) Cambridge: Cambridge Archaeological Unit.

Regan, R., 1998. *Salvage recording at Portugal Place/New Park Street.* Unpublished CAU document. Cambridge: Cambridge Archaeological Unit.

Reimer, P.J., Bard, E., Bayliss, A., Beck, J.W., Blackwell, P.G., Bronk Ramsey, C., Grootes, P.M., Guilderson, T.P., Haflidason, H., Hajdas, I., HattŽ, C., Heaton, T.J., Hoffmann, D.L., Hogg, A.G., Hughen, K.A., Kaiser, K.F., Kromer, B., Manning, S.W., Niu, M., Reimer, R.W., Richards, D.A., Scott, E.M., Southon, J.R., Staff, R.A., Turney, C.S.M. & van der Plicht, J., 2013. IntCal13 and Marine13 radiocarbon age calibration curves 0–50,000 Years cal BP. *Radiocarbon* 55(4), 1869–87.

Relph, E., 1976. *Place and Placelessness.* London: Pion.

Rex, P., 2006. *The English Resistance: the underground war against the Normans.* Stroud: Tempus.

Riall, N., 1998. Excavation at Borelli Yard, Farnham: the town ditch. *Surrey Archaeological Collections* 85, 120–32.

Richards, M. & Maddocks, J., 2005. Personal hygiene and sanitary arrangements, in *Before the Mast. Life and Death Aboard the Mary Rose,* eds. J. Gardiner with M.J. Allen. (Archaeology of the Mary Rose 4.) Portsmouth: Mary Rose Trust, 153–62.

Riddy, F., 2008. 'Burgeis' domesticity in late-medieval England, in *Medieval Domesticity: home, housing and household in medieval England,* eds. M. Kowaleski & P.J.P. Goldberg. Cambridge: Cambridge University Press, 14–36.

Rigby, S.H., 1979. Urban decline in the later middle ages: some problems in interpreting the statistical data. *Urban History Yearbook* 6, 46–59.

Rigold, S., 1975. Structural aspects of medieval timber bridges. *Medieval Archaeology* 19, 48–91.

Roberts, B.K. & Wrathmell, S., 2000. *An Atlas of Rural Settlement in England.* London: English Heritage.

Roberts, M.R., 1997. A tenement of Roger of Cumnor and other archaeological investigations in medieval North Oseney, Oxford. *Oxoniensia* 61, 181–224.

Roberts, T., 1892. *The Jurassic Rocks of the Neighbourhood of Cambridge: being the Sedgwick Prize essay for 1886.* Cambridge: Cambridge University Press.

Rockman, D. de Z. & Rothschild, N.A., 1984. City tavern, country tavern: an analysis of four colonial sites. *Historical Archaeology* 18(2), 112–21.

Rogerson, A. & Dallas, C., 1984. *Excavations in Thetford 1948–59 and 1973–80.* (East Anglian Archaeology 22.) Dereham: Archaeology & Environment Division, Norfolk Museums & Archaeology Service.

Rogers, E., 2002. A wooden eating spoon found at Harleston. *Norfolk Archaeology* 44(1), 129.

Rolleston, J.D., 1942. Laryngology and folk-lore. *Journal of Laryngology & Otology* 57(12), 527–32.

Rosser, A.G., 1988. London and Westminster: the suburb in the urban economy in the later middle ages, in *Towns and Townspeople in the Fifteenth Century,* ed. J.A.F. Thomson. Gloucester: Sutton, 145–61.

Rowell, T.A., 1986. Sedge (*Cladium mariscus*) in Cambridgeshire: its use and production since the 17th century. *Agricultural History Review* 34(2), 140–8.

Royal, J.G. & McManamon, J.M., 2010. At the transition from Late medieval to early modern: the archaeology of three wrecks from Turkey. *International Journal of Nautical Archaeology* 39(2), 327–44.

Rudd, G.T. & Tebbutt, C.F., 1973. 'The Church Street ditch', in Late Saxon settlements in the St Neots area by P.V. Addyman. *Proceedings of the Cambridge Antiquarian Society* 64, 68–70.

Rybzcynski, W., 1987. *Home, a short history of an idea.* New York: Penguin.

Salway, P., 1996. Sidney before the college, in *Sidney Sussex College, Cambridge: historical essays in commemoration of the quatercentenary,* eds. D. Beales, E. Dawson & H.B. Nisbet. Woodbridge: Boydell, 3–34.

Salzman, L.F., 1952. *Buildings in England down to 1540: a documentary history.* Oxford: Clarendon Press.

Sayer, D., 2009. Medieval waterways and hydraulic economics: monasteries, towns and the East Anglian fen. *World Archaeology* 41(1), 134–50.

Schackel, P.A., 1993. *Personal Discipline and Material Culture, an Archaeology of Annapolis, Maryland, 1695–1870.* Knoxville (Tenn): University of Tennessee Press.

Schofield, J., 1997. Urban housing in England, 1400–1600, in *The Age of Transition: the archaeology of English culture 1400–1600,* eds. D. Gaimster & P. Stamper. Oxford: Oxbow Books, 127–44.

Schofield, J., 2009. The modern age, in *The Archaeology of Britain. An introduction from earliest times to the twenty-first century,* eds. J. Hunter, & I. Ralston. London, Routledge, 390–409.

Schofield, J., Palliser, D. & Harding, C., 1981. *Recent Archaeological Research in English Towns* (Council for British Archaeology Occasional Paper. 12.) York: Council for British Archaeology.

Schofield, J. & Vince, A., 2003. *Medieval Towns: the archaeology of British towns in their European setting.* 2nd edition, London: Continuum.

Scott, L., 1951. Corn-drying kilns. *Antiquity* 25(100), 196–208.

Secord, A., 2007. Hotbeds and cool fruits: the unnatural cultivation of the eighteenth century cucumber, in *Medicine, Madness and Social History: essays in honour of Roy Porter,* eds. R. Bivens & J.V. Pickstone. Basingstoke: Palgrave Macmillan, 90–104.

Seetah, K., 2007. The middle Ages on the block: animals, guilds and meat in the medieval period, in *Breaking and Shaping Beastly Bodies: animals as material culture in the middle ages,* ed. A. Pluskowski. Oxford: Oxbow Books, 18–31.

Serjeantson, D., 2000. Good to eat and good to think with: classifying animals from complex sites, in *Animal Bones, Human Societies,* ed. P. Rowley-Conwy. Oxford: Oxbow Books, 179–89.

Serjeantson, D., 2006. Birds: food and a mark of status, in *Food in Medieval England: diet and nutrition,* eds. C.M. Woolgar, D. Serjeantson & T. Waldron, T. Oxford: Oxford University Press, 131–47.

Serjeantson, D. & Rees, H., (eds.) 2009. *Food, Craft and Status in Medieval Winchester: the plant and animal remains from the suburbs and city defences.* Winchester: Winchester Museums Service.

Serjeantson, D & Woolgar, C., 2006. Fish consumption in Medieval England, in *Food in Medieval England: Diet and Nutrition,* eds. C.M. Woolgar, D. Serjeantson & T. Waldron. Oxford: Oxford University Press, 102–30.

Serpell, J., 1996. *In the Company of Animals: a study of human-animal relationships.* Cambridge: Cambridge University Press.

Shaw, M., 1997. Recent work in medieval Northampton: archaeological excavations on St Giles' Street, 1990, and at St Edmund's End, 1988. *Northamptonshire Archaeology* 27, 101–41.

Shelley, A., 2005. *Dragon Hall, King Street, Norwich: excavation and survey of a late medieval merchant's trading complex.* (East Anglian Archaeology 112.) Norwich: Norfolk & Norwich Heritage Trust.

Shepard, A., 2000. Contesting communities? 'Town' and 'gown' in Cambridge, *c.* 1560–1640 in *Communities in Early Modern England: networks, place, rhetoric,* eds. A. Shepard & P. Withington. Manchester: Manchester University Press, 216–34.

Shepard, A., 2004. Litigation and locality: the Cambridge university courts, 1560–1640. *Urban History* 31(1), 5–28.

Sieveking, L.M., 2004. A history of Robert Sayle. Part 1 1840–1969, in *A History of Robert Sayle,* ed. R. Sayle. Cambridge: Robert Sayle, 7–130.

Silver, I.A., 1969. The ageing of domestic animals, in *Science in Archaeology*, eds. D. Brothwell & E.S. Higgs. 2nd edition. London: Thames & Hudson, 283–301.

Skilliter, S.A., 1977. *William Harborne and the Trade with Turkey, 1578–1582: a documentary study of the first Anglo-Ottoman relations*. London: Oxford University Press.

Skov, H., 2009. The infrastructure of Århus between 900 and 1600 AD, in *Archaeology of Medieval Towns in the Baltic and North Sea Area*, eds. N. Engberg, A.N. Jørgensen, J. Kieffer-Olsen, P.K. Madsen & C. Radtke. (National Museum Studies in Archaeology and History 17) Copenhagen: Aarhus University Press, 151–66.

Slater, A., 2010a. *Excavations at the CB1 development site, Hills Road, Cambridge*. (CAU Report 933.) Cambridge: Cambridge Archaeological Unit.

Slater, A., 2010b. *Great Eastern House, Station Road, Cambridge: archaeological evaluation and watching brief*. (CAU Report 979.) Cambridge: Cambridge Archaeological Unit.

Slater, T.R., 1981. The analysis of burgage patterns in medieval towns. *Area* 13(3), 211–16.

Slater, T.R., 1987. Ideal and reality in English episcopal medieval town planning. *Transactions of the Institute of British Geographers* 12(2), 191–203.

Slater, T.R., (ed.) 2000. *Towns in Decline, AD 100–1600*. Aldershot: Ashgate.

Slater, T.R. & Rosser, G., (eds.) 1998. *The Church in the Medieval Town*. Aldershot: Ashgate.

Smith, D.N., 1996. Thatch, turves and floor deposits: A survey of Coleoptera in materials from abandoned Hebridean blackhouses and the implications for their visibility in the archaeological record. *Journal of Archaeological Science* 23(2), 161–74.

Smith, D.N., Letts J.P. & Cox, A., 1999. Coleoptera from Late Medieval smoke blackened thatch (SBT): its archaeological implications. *Environmental Archaeology* 4(1), 9–18.

Smith, D.N., Letts, J. & Jones, M., 2005. The insects from non-cereal stalk smoked blackened thatch. *Environmental Archaeology* 10(2), 171–8.

Smith K.G.V., 1989. *An Introduction to the Immature Stages of British Flies* (Handbooks for the identification of British Insects Vol. 10 part 14.) London: Royal Entomological Society of London.

Smith, M.E., 2009. Editorial – just how comparative is comparative urban geography? A perspective from archaeology. *Urban Geography*, 30(2), 113–17.

Smith, M.E., 2010. Sprawl, squatters and sustainable cities: can archaeological data shed light on modern urban issues?. *Cambridge Archaeological Journal*, 20(2), 229–53.

Spence, C., 1994. *Archaeological Site Manual*. 3rd edition, London: MoLAS.

Spoerry, P., 2007. Town and country in the medieval fenland, in *Town and Country in the Middle Ages: contrasts, contacts and interconnections 1100–1500*, eds. K. Giles & C. Dyer. (Society for Medieval Archaeology Monograph 22.) Leeds: Maney, 85–110.

Spoerry, P., 2008. *Ely Wares* (East Anglian Archaeology 122.) Bar Hill: CAM ARC.

Spoerry, P., 2016. *The Production and Distribution of Medieval Pottery in Cambridgeshire*. (East Anglian Archaeology 159.) Bar Hill: Oxford Archaeology East.

Spoerry, P., Atkins, R., Macaulay, S. & Shepherd Popescu, E., 2008. Ramsey Abbey, Cambridgeshire: excavations at the site of a fenland monastery. *Medieval Archaeology* 40, 171–210.

Spufford, P., 1963. Continental coins in late medieval England. *British Numismatic Journal* 32, 127–39.

Spurrell, M., 1995. Containing Wallingford Castle, 1146–1153. *Oxoniensia* 60, 257–70.

Stace, C., 1997. *New Flora of the British Isles*. Cambridge: Cambridge University Press.

Stallibras, S., 1993. *Post-medieval cattle burials from St Giles by Brompton Bridge, North Yorkshire*. (Ancient Monuments Laboratory Report 94/93.) London: Ancient Monuments Laboratory.

Steane, J.M., 1967. Excavations at Lyveden. *Journal of Northampton Museum & Art Gallery* 2, 1–37.

Steane, K., 2006. *The Archaeology of The Upper City and Adjacent Suburbs*. (Lincoln Archaeology Studies 3.) Oxford: Oxbow.

Stephens, M., 2009. SubUrbia: evidence for suburban activity in the medieval town of Trim, in *Uncovering Medieval Trim. Archaeological excavations in and around Trim, Co. Meath*, eds. M. Potterton & M. Seaver. Dublin: Four Courts Press, 121–44.

Stephenson, C., 1933. *Borough and Town: a study of urban origins in England*. Cambridge (MA): Medieval Academy of America.

Stokes, H.P., 1908. *Outside the Trumpington Gates before Peterhouse was founded: a chapter in the intimate history of medieval Cambridge* (Cambridge Antiquarian Society Octavo Series 44.) Cambridge: Cambridge Antiquarian Society.

Stokes, H.P., 1915. *Outside the Barnwell Gate: another chapter in the intimate history of medieval Cambridge* (Cambridge Antiquarian Society Octavo Series 47.) Cambridge: Cambridge Antiquarian Society.

Stone, D.J., 2006. The consumption and supply of birds in late medieval England, in *Food in Medieval England: diet and nutrition*, eds. C.M. Woolgar, D. Serjeantson & T. Waldron, T. Oxford: Oxford University Press, 148–61.

Streeten, A.D.F., 1977. Excavations at Lansdowne Road, Tonbridge, 1972 and 1976. *Archaeologia Cantiana* 92, 105–18.

Sussman, L., 1977. Changes in Pearlware Dinnerware, 1780–1830. *Historical Archaeology* 11(1), 105–11.

Swann, J., 1975. Shoe Fashions to 1600. *Transactions Museum Assistants' Group for 1973* 12, 14–27.

Swann, J., 1982. *Shoes*. London: Batsford.

Sykes, N.J., 2006. From cu and sceap to beffe and motton, in *Food in Medieval England: diet and nutrition*, eds. C.M. Woolgar, D. Serjeantson & T. Waldron, T. Oxford: Oxford University Press, 56–71.

Sykes, N.J., 2007. *The Norman Conquest: A Zooarchaeological Perspective* (British Archaeological Reports, International Series 1656.) Oxford: Archaeopress.

Symonds, J., 2006. Tales from the city: brownfield archaeology - a worthwhile challenge, in *Cities in the World, 1500–2000*, eds. A. Green & R. Leach. Leeds: Maney, 235–48.

Tabor, J.L., 2010. *Land East of Days Road, Capel St Mary, Suffolk: an archaeological excavation*. (CAU Report 957.) Cambridge: Cambridge Archaeological Unit.

Tabor, R., 1992. The rake factory. *Tool & Trades History Society Newsletter* 37, 15–33.

Talbot, O., 1974. The evolution of glass bottles for carbonated drinks. *Post Medieval Archaeology* 8, 29–62.

Tarlow, S., 2007. *The Archaeology of Improvement in Britain 1750–1850.* Cambridge: Cambridge University Press.

Tarlow, S. & West, S., (eds.) 1999. *The Familiar Past? Archaeologies of later historical Britain.* London: Routledge.

Tate, W.E. & Turner, M., 1978. *A Domesday of English Enclosure Acts and Awards.* Reading: The Library.

Taylor, A., 1988. *Note on observations at the Department of Metallurgy, Pembroke Street.* Unpublished document. Cambridge: Cambridgeshire County Archaeology Office.

Taylor, A., 1999. *Cambridge: the hidden history.* Stroud: Tempus.

Taylor, C.C., 1974a. *Fieldwork in Medieval Archaeology.* London: Batsford.

Taylor, C.C., 1974b. Total Archaeology or studies in the history of the landscape, in *Landscapes and Documents*, eds. A. Rodgers & R.T. Rowley. London: Bedford Square Press, 15–26.

Taylor, C.C., 1977. Polyfocal settlement and the English village. *Medieval Archaeology* 21, 189–93.

Taylor, C.C., 2002. Nucleated settlement: a view from the frontier. *Landscape History* 24(1), 53–71.

ten Harkel, L., 2005. *Bradwell's Court, Cambridge: an archaeological watching brief.* (CAU Report 682.) Cambridge: Cambridge Archaeological Unit.

Thomas, C., Cowie, R. & Sidell, J., 2006. *The Royal Palace, Abbey and Town of Westminster on Thorney Island: archaeological excavations (1991–8) for the London Underground Limited Jubilee Line Extension* (MoLAS Monograph 22.) London: MoLAS.

Thomas, G., McDonnell, G., Merkel, J. & Marshall, P., 2016. Technology, ritual and Anglo-Saxon agriculture: the biography of a plough coulter from Lyminge, Kent. *Antiquity* 90(351), 742–58.

Thomas, J., 2006. Evidence for the Dissolution of Thorney Abbey: recent excavations and landscape analysis at Thorney, Cambridgeshire. *Medieval Archaeology* 50, 179–241.

Thomas, R., 2005. Perceptions versus reality: changing attitudes towards pets in medieval and post-medieval England, in *Just Skin and Bones? New Perspectives on Human-Animal Relations in the Historical Past*, ed. A. Pluskowski. (British Archaeological Reports, International Series 1410.) Oxford: Archaeopress, 95–104.

Thomas, R. & Locock, M., 2000. Food for the dogs? The consumption of horseflesh at Dudley Castle in the eighteenth century. *Environmental Archaeology* 5(1), 83–91.

Thompson, E.P., 1993. *Customs in Common.* London: Penguin.

Thompson, J.D.A., 1956. *Inventory of British Coin Hoards A.D. 600–1500* (Royal Numismatic Society Special Publication 1.) London: Royal Numismatic Society.

Thompson, M.W., 1990. *The Cambridge Antiquarian Society 1840–1990.* Cambridge: Cambridge Antiquarian Society.

Thomson, D.F.S. & Porter, H.C., 1963. *Erasmus and Cambridge: the Cambridge letters of Erasmus.* Toronto: University of Toronto Press.

Timberlake, S., 2006. *An archaeological evaluation of the former government offices site, Brooklands Avenue: phase 3.* (CAU Report 744.) Cambridge: Cambridge Archaeological Unit.

Timberlake, S. & Webb, D., 2006. *Further Investigations at 34–38 Newnham Road, Cambridge.* (CAU Report 732.) Cambridge: Cambridge Archaeological Unit.

Todd, M., 1975. Excavations on the medieval defences of Newark, 1972. *Transactions of the Thoroton Society of Nottinghamshire* 78, 27–53.

Tomlinson, P. & Hall, A.R., 1996. A review of the archaeological evidence for food plants from the British Isles: an example of the use of the Archaeobotanical Computer Database (ABCD). *Internet Archaeology* 1. Available at: http://intarch.ac.uk/journal/issue1/tomlinson_index. html. Accessed 7 July 2011.

Tottenham C.E., 1954. *Coleoptera Staphylinidae. Section (a) Piestinae to Euaesthetinae* (Handbooks for the Identification of British Insects Vol. 4 Part 8a.) London: Royal Entomological Society of London.

Trotter, D., 2008. Household clearances in Victorian fiction, *19 Interdiciplinary Studies in the Long Nineteenth Century* 6. Available at: http://www.19.bbk.ac.uk/issue6/papers/ trotterhouseholdclearances.pdf. Accessed 7 July 2011.

Trow-Smith, R., 1957. *A History of British Livestock Husbandry to 1700.* London: Routledge & Kegan Paul.

Trust, W.G., 1956. The hazel underwood industry, in utilisation of hazel coppice. *Forestry Commission Bulletin* 27, 8–9.

Tuan, Y., 1977. *Space and Place: the perspective of experience.* Minneapolis (Minn): University of Minnesota.

Turner, M.E., Beckett, J.V. & Afton, B., 2001. *Farm Production in England 1700–1914.* Oxford:

Turner-Rugg, A., 1995. Medieval pottery from St Albans. *Medieval Ceramics* 19, 45–65.

Tyler, K., 2001. The excavation of an Elizabethan/Stuart waterfront site on the north bank of the River Thames at Victoria Wharf, Narrow Street, Limehouse, London E14. *Post-Medieval Archaeology* 35, 53–95.

Tyler, K. Betts, I. & Stephenson, R., 2008. *London's Delftware Industry: the tin-glazed pottery industries of Southwark and Lambeth.* (MoLAS Monograph 40.) London: MoLAS.

Unwin, D.J., 2001. *'The Scientific': the story of the Cambridge Instrument Company.* Cambridge: Cambridge Industrial Archaeology Society.

Unwin, T., 1991. *Wine and the Vine: an historical geography of viticulture and the wine trade.* London: Routledge.

van de Mieroop, M., 1997. *The Ancient Mesopotamian City.* Oxford: Oxford University Press.

van der Veen, M., 1989. Charred grain assemblages from Roman-period corn driers in Britain. *Archaeological Journal* 146(1), 302–19.

van Houts, E., 1992. Nuns and goldsmiths: the foundation and early benefactors of St Radegund's Priory at Cambridge, in *Church and City, 1000–1500: essays in honour of Christopher Brooke*, eds. D. Abulafia, M. Franklin & M. Rubin. Cambridge: Cambridge University Press, 59–79.

van Lemmen, H., 2000. *Medieval Tiles.* Aylesford: Shire.

Vaughan, L., (ed.) 2015. *Suburban Urbanities. Suburbs and the Life of the High Street.* London: UCL Press.

Verslype, L. & Brulet, R., (eds.) 2004. *Terres Noires-Dark Earth actes de table-ronde, Louvain-la-Neuve 2001.* Louvain-la-Neuve: Université catholique de Louvain.

Waldron, T., 2007. *St Peter's, Barton-upon-Humber, Lincolnshire: a parish church and its community. vol. 2 the human remains.* Oxford: Oxbow Books.

Walker, H., 2012. *Hedingham Ware, a Medieval Pottery Industry in North Essex, its production and distribution.* (East Anglian Archaeology 148.) Chelmsford: Essex County Council, Historic Environment, Environment and Commerce.

Walker, I.C. & Wells, P.K., 1979. Regional varieties of clay tobacco pipe markings in eastern England, in *The Archaeology of the Clay Tobacco Pipe 1,* ed. P. Davey. (British Archaeological Reports, British Series 63.) Oxford: British Archaeological Reports, 3–66.

Walker, J., 1999. Twelfth and early-thirteenth-century aisled buildings: a comparison. *Vernacular Architecture* 30, 21–53.

Wallerstein, I., 1984. *The Politics of the World-Economy.* Cambridge: Cambridge University Press.

Walton Rogers, P., 2003. Sewing threads on leatherwork from 16–22 Coppergate and Bedern Foundry, in *Leather and Leatherworking in Anglo-Scandinavian and Medieval York,* eds. Q. Mould, I. Carlisle & E. Cameron. (Archaeology of York 17/16.) York: Council for British Archaeology, 3259–61.

Warboys, R.T.C., 2003. Oakington wells and water supply. *Cambridgeshire Local History Review* 12, 21–8.

Ware, I., 1756. *A Complete Body of Architecture, Adorned with Plans and Elevations from Original Designs.* London: Osborne, Shipton, Rodgers, Davis, Ward & Baldwin.

Waterer, J.W., 1950. *Leather and Craftsmanship.* London: Faber & Faber.

Webb, D., 2009. *Anglia, Ruskin University, Cambridge: an archaeological evaluation.* (CAU Report 906.) Cambridge: Cambridge Archaeological Unit.

Webb, D. & Dickens, A., 2005. *The Cambridge Guided Bus System: archaeological monitoring of geotechnical test pits.* (CAU Report 704.) Cambridge: Cambridge Archaeological Unit.

Webb, D. & Dickens, A., 2006. *Homerton College, Cambridge: archaeological evaluation on the site of new undergraduate accommodation.* (CAU Report 720.) Cambridge: Cambridge Archaeological Unit.

Webley, L. & Hiller, J., 2009. A fen island in the Neolithic and Bronze Age: excavations at North Fen, Sutton, Cambridgeshire. *Proceedings of the Cambridge Antiquarian Society* 98, 11–36.

Weinstein, R., 2005. Eating and drinking vessels and utensils, in *Before the Mast. Life and Death Aboard the Mary Rose,* eds. J. Gardiner with M.J. Allen. (Archaeology of the Mary Rose 4.) Portsmouth: Mary Rose Trust, 448–58.

Wessex Archaeology., 2003. *Charter Quay. The Spirit of Change. The Archaeology of Kingston's Riverside.* Salisbury: Trust for Wessex Archaeology.

West, S.E., 1971a. Excavation of the town defences at Tayfen Road, Bury St Edmunds. 1968. *Proceedings of the Suffolk Institute of Archaeology & History* 32(1), 17–24.

West, S.E., 1971b. The excavation of Dunwich town defences, 1970. *Proceedings of the Suffolk Institute of Archaeology & History* 32(1), 25–37.

White, L., 1997. *Archaeological monitoring of construction works at Homerton College, Cambridge.* (CAU Report 224.) Cambridge: Cambridge Archaeological Unit.

White, L., 1998. *Report on Phase 1 Archaeological Monitoring of Preliminary Ground Investigations, Grand Arcade Development, Cambridge.* (CAU Report 280.) Cambridge: Cambridge Archaeological Unit.

White, L. & Mortimer, R., 1998. *Downing Place: Transco Pipe Pit (DPH 98).* Unpublished CAU document. Cambridge: Cambridge Archaeological Unit.

Whitehand, J.W.R., 2001. British urban morphology: the Conzenian tradition. *Urban Morphology* 5(2), 103–9.

Whittaker, P., 2001a. *An Archaeological Watching Brief on Land behind Fitzbillies Bakery, 52–54 Trumpington Street, Cambridge.* (CAU Report 444.) Cambridge: Cambridge Archaeological Unit.

Whittaker, P., 2001b. *Medieval Buildings found during an Archaeological Watching Brief on Land beside Fitzwilliam Museum, Trumpington Street, Cambridge.* (CAU Report 502.) Cambridge: Cambridge Archaeological Unit.

Whittaker, P., 2002. *An Archaeological Evaluation at the ADC Theatre, Park Street, Cambridge.* (CAU Report 511.) Cambridge: Cambridge Archaeological Unit.

Wilcox, R.A. & Witham, E.M., 2003. Symbol of modern medicine: why one snake is more than two. *Annals of Internal Medicine* 138(8), 673–77.

Wilkie, L.A., 2000. Not merely child's play: creating a historical archaeology of children, in *Children and Material Culture,* ed. J.S. Derevenski. London: Routledge, 100–13.

Willan, S., 1955. Some aspects of English trade with the Levant in the sixteenth century. *English Historical Review* 70(276), 399–410.

Willcox, G.H., 1977. Exotic plants from Roman waterlogged sites in London. *Journal of Archaeological Science* 4(3), 269–82.

Williams, J.H., 1982. Four small excavations on Northampton's medieval defences and elsewhere. *Northamptonshire Archaeology* 17, 60–73.

Willis, R. & Clark, J.W., 1886. *The Architectural History of the University of Cambridge.* Cambridge: Cambridge University Press.

Wilson, B., 1999. Displayed or concealed? Cross cultural evidence for symbolic and ritual activity depositing Iron Age animal bones. *Oxford Journal of Archaeology* 18(3), 297–305.

Wilson, B. & Edwards, P., 1993. Butchery of horse and dog at Witney Palace, Oxfordshire, and the knackering and feeding of meat to hounds during the post-medieval period. *Post-Medieval Archaeology* 27, 43–56.

Wilson, C.A., 1973. *Food and Drink in Britain from the Stone Age to Recent Times.* London: Constable.

Wilson, J., 2010. *Cambridge Grocer: The Story of Matthew's of Trinity Street 1832–1962.* Cambridge: R.A. Wilson.

Winter, G., 1973. *A Country Camera 1844–1914.* Harmondsworth: Penguin.

Wood, A., 1935. *History of the Levant Company.* London: Oxford University Press.

Woolgar, C.M., 1999. *The Great Household in Late Medieval England*. New Haven (Conn): Yale University Press.

Worssam, B.C. & Taylor, J.H., 1969. *Geology of the Country around Cambridge. Explanation of One-inch Geological Sheet 188, New Series*. London: HMSO.

Wrathmell, S., 1989. Peasant houses, farmsteads and villages in north-east England, in *The Rural Settlements of Medieval England. Studies dedicated to Maurice Beresford and John Hurst*, eds. M. Aston, D. Austin & C. Dyer. Oxford: Basil Blackwell, 247–67.

Wright, A.P.M., 2002. Chesterton, in *A History of the County of Cambridge and the Isle of Ely Vol. 9. Chesterton, Northstowe and Papworth Hundreds (North and North-West of Cambridge)*, eds. A.P.M. Wright & C.P. Lewis. London: Oxford University Press, 5–39.

Wroth, R., 2004. The Christ's College servants in the 19th century (or how the other half lived): college porters. *Christ's College Magazine 229*, 56–9.

Yeomans, L., 2005. Spatial determinants of animal carcass processing in post-medieval London and evidence for a co-operative supply network. *Transactions of the London and Middlesex Archaeological Society 55*, 69–83.

Yeomans, L., 2007. The shifting use of animal carcasses in medieval and post-medieval London, in *Breaking and Shaping Beastly Bodies: animals as material culture in the Middle Ages*, ed. A. Pluskowski. Oxford: Oxbow Books, 98–115.

Zola, E., 1883. *Au Bonheur des Dames*. Paris: Charpentier.

Zutshi, P.N.R., 2011. When did Cambridge become a studium generale?, in, *Law as Profession and Practice in Medieval Europe: essays in honour of James A. Brundage*, eds. K. Pennington & M.H. Eichbauer. Ashgate: Farnham. 153–71.

Zutshi, P.N.R., 2012. The dispersal of scholars from Oxford and the beginnings of a University at Cambridge: a study of the sources. *English Historical Review* 127(528), 1041–62.

Zutshi, P. & Ombres, R., 1990. The Dominicans in Cambridge, 1238–1538. *Archivum Fratrum Praedicatorum* 60, 314–15.

Index

Page numbers in *italics* denote illustrations, those in **bold**, tables. Finds are listed by material type, i.e. basketry, bone, glass, etc.

A

abbreviations and acronyms 20, **20**
ADC Theatre, Park Street 47, **203–4**
agricultural hinterland *358*, 395–8, **396**, *397*
Alexander, John 5, 47, *327*
Anarchy, The 86–7
animal disposal pits *110*, 122, *133*, 151, 417
animal disposal pits (numbered)
  ADP 1 108, **191**; *ADP 2 108*, 151, **191**; *ADP 4 110*, **191**; *ADPs 5 & 6 131*, **191**; *ADP 8 131*, 151, **189**, **191**; *ADP 9 133*, 151, **191**, *192*, *193*; *ADPs 10–12* **190**, *193*, 228, 230–1, *234*, 249, 349, 420; *ADP 13* **191**, *259*, 267; *ADP 14* **191**, *259*, 296
animals and humans 432
antiquarian investigations 4–5
artificial water channels 89
assemblages **333–6**, 410–13, *412*, 433–5

B

barns *371*, *372*, *373*
Barnwell Gate 48
Barnwell Gate suburb 4–5, 357–9, *358–9*, **403**, *404*
  see also Christ's College; Christ's Lane development; Emmanuel College; South of Downing Street; St Andrew the Great
Barnwell suburb 398, *399*, 401, **403**
Barrett & Son Ltd. 283, 285–6, *285*, 301, *306*, *324*, 431
basketry objects
  basket *71*, *72*

eel grig *120*, 121
bathhouse 283, *284*
Birdbolt Inn 7, 169, 249, *253*, 291, 307
bone objects 170–1
  bird bone: *see* mammal and bird bone
  corer/scoop 219
  decorative object *145*
  dominoes *263*, 264
  flute *170*
  implements *99*
  knife handles 71, *71*, *170*, 171
  musical toy? 282
  parchment prickers/styli 170
  square-sectioned object 37, *39*
  stylus?/point *170*
  toothbrush handle 262, 264
  typewriter brush 304, *305*
bone-working 64, 68, 171, 187, *188*, 189, **189**, 418
Bones family 283, 291, *360*
Bradwell's Court 364, *365*
Bradwell's Yard *382*, 383
brick, inscribed 272, *272*, *393*, 394
brick kilns 348
bricks 81, *81*, 169–70, 213, 344–5
brickwork 169, 347–8, 352
buildings – Christ's Lane 386–7, **386**; *Buildings 1–3 371*; *Building 2 371*, 379–80; *Building 4 371*, *372*, 373; *Buildings 5–7 373–4*; *Buildings 8–10 374*, *375*, 376; *Building 11 376*, 378, 383; *Building 12 378*; *Building 13 380*, 382; *Building 14 381*, 382; *Building 17* 383
buildings (numbered)
  Building 1 36, *37–8*; *Building 2 37*, *37*; *Building 3 97*, *102*, *163*; *Building 6 98*, *164*, 167, *183*, **190**; *Buildings 7 & 8 108*, 117, *131*; *Buildings 9 & 10 108*, 169; *Building 12 108*, 151; *Building 12/14 138*, *144*; *Building 14 131*, *218*; *Building 15 138*, *217*, *218*; *Building*

16 138, 185, **191**; *Building 20 133*, *144*, *145*, *146*; *Building 22 216*, *217*, *234*, *235*, 237–8; *Building 23 217*, *218*; *Building 24 217*, *224*, *234*, 247, *252*; *Building 25* **189**, *217*, 224–5, *224–5*, 228, *234*, 247, *253*, 349; *Building 26 217*, 228, *234*, 247, *259*, 283, 285; *Building 27 234*, 238; *Building 28 234*, *235*, 238, 257, *259*; *Building 29 234*, *235*, 257, *259*, 262; *Building 30 234*, *235*; *Buildings 31–33 234*, 244; *Building 34 234*, 247; *Building 35 234*, 247, *252*, *259*, 278, *278*; *Buildings 36 & 37 234*, 247; *Building 38 234*, 249; *Building 41* 80, 81–2; *Building 43 259*, 320–1, 322, 330; *Building 44 259*, 317, 330; *Building 47 262*, 264, 304, *304*, *305*; *Building 48 259*; *Building 49 296*, 298–300, **335**; *Building 50 259*, 283, *284*, 285; *Building 51 259*, 286, **335**; *Building 52 259*, 283; *Building 53 259*, 291; *Building 54 304*, *305*; *Building 55 296*, *298*, 435
burgage plots 98
butchery 59, **59**, 72, **72**, 79, 81, 113, **113**, 152, 195–6, 282, **282**, 296, 349

C

Cambridge Engraving Company 322
Cambridge Scientific Instrument Company 309, 322
Carrier's Arms 79, 81, 82
castle 86, 87, 400
Castle Hill suburb 398, *399*, 400
cellars (numbered)
  Cellar 4 234, 249, 256, *259*, 288, 291–2, 292–5, 297, **334**, 350; *Cellar 5* **190**, *234*, 247, *259*, 278, 283, **335**; *Cellar 6 234*, 247, *253*, **333**, 349; *Cellar 7* **190**, *234*, 247, *259*, 283, 290, **334**; *Cellar 10* 80, 82; *Cellar 11 258*, **336**; *Cellar 12 259*, 283, 285, 287–8, **335**; *Cellar*

Q

R

S

St Andrew's Court 291
21 St Andrew's Street *3*, *6*, 16–20, *18*,
   393–4, *393*
57–62 St Andrew's Street 368
63–64 St Andrew's Street 368
65–68 St Andrew's Street 383
69 St Andrew's Street 378
70 St Andrew's Street 378–80
St Andrew's Street plots 31–2, *32*, *215*,
   216
stable isotope analyses 199
stables 235
standing buildings
   introduction to 28–9, *29–30*, 31–2,
      32–3, 34, 214
   plans *29*, *233–4*, *258*
standing buildings (numbered)
   Standing Building 18/19 257, *261*,
   303; *Standing Building 20* 235, 257,
   264, *265*, 267; *Standing Building
   21* 16, *18*, 305, *306*, 307; *Standing
   Building 22* 244, *250*, 307; *Standing
   Buildings 23 & 24* 234, 244, 247,
   250–1; *Standing Building 25* 234,
   247, 283; *Standing Buildings 28
   & 29* 235; *Standing Building 42*
   31, 234, 235, 237–8, *312–13*, 323;
   Standing Building 48 316, *317*, 323,
   330; *Standing Building 56* 319,
   322; *Standing Building 65* 31, 234,
   235, 237–8, 323; *Standing Building
   70* 269–70, *270*, 272, *272*, 305, 307;
   Standing Building 72 264, *265–6*,
   267; *Standing Building 78* 304, 305;
   Standing Building 79 307; *Standing
   Building 80* 305; *Standing Building
   94* 31, 286, *289*; *Standing Building
   95* 171, 285–6, *289*; *Standing Building
   96* 31, 285, *289*; *Standing Building
   99* 273; *Standing Building 105*
   234, 244; *Standing Building 106*
   247; *Standing Building 110* 234,
   244
stone objects 159, 296, 333–4
   chalk tablet 58, *63*, 159
   cresset? or heating tray *154*, 159
   gunflint *281*, 282
   mortar *147*, 159
   slate pencils 273, *277*, 333–4
   whetstones 333
stone, reused 171–2, *171–4*, 174–5,
   249, 392, 394
   architectural fragments 114, *134*
   ashlar blocks 143
   beak *255*
   blind arcading *173*
   blocks 222, 228
   capital 378, *379*
   column base *255*
   cornice *255*

gravestone *255*
   mouldings, various 249
   parapet crenellation *174*, *175*, *255*
   windows 16–17, *227*, 228, *241*, *243*,
      244, 394
stratigraphic resolution 93
suburban archaeology 410, 413–20,
   415, *416*, 419
suburbs 389, *390*, 391, 398, *399*, 400–1,
   402, 403–4, **403**
surfaces 123, *133*, 151, *217*, 222

T

tea drinking 353, 354, 424
telegraph pole *304*, 305
temporality and biography 410
tenements 107
test pits 8, *9*
textile remains 181
Thoday and Clayton 79
4 Tibb's Row 79, *80–2*, *81–3*
Tibb's Row 31, 34, 79, *80*, 83, *258*
tile kilns 348
timber framing *251*
timber supplies 175
toads 151, 193
topography of Cambridge 84
town ditches 45, 83, 89, **90**, 91, *91*
   see also King's Ditch
town versus gown 441–3, *442*
tree-ring data: *see* dendrochronology
Trumpington Gate suburb 398, *399*,
   400–1
15–19 Trumpington Street *358*, 401
Tunwell family 235, 240, 292, *292*,
   412

V

Vine Estate 376, *377*, 388, **388**, *389*

W

walls *217*, 222–3, *234*, 238, 247, 249
walls (numbered)
   Wall 1 222; *Wall 2* 222; *Wall 3* 222–3;
   Wall 4 223, 228, 249; *Wall 5* 223, 224;
   Wall 6 223, 228, *408*; *Wall 8* 238;
   Wall 10 171, 174, 175, 228, 234, 249,
   254–5, 259, *408*; *Wall 11* 249; *Wall 12*
   247, *408*; *Wall 13* 247; *Wall 14* 247
Ward, Mary 244
Warehouse 269–70, *270*, 272, 394
water channels 89
Water Closet 1 259, 272, *304*, 305
Water Closets 2 & 3 296, *298*
water closets 273, 430
water-filled features 110, *110*, 117,
   121–2, *133*, 147

water-filled features (numbered)
   WFF 2 108, 121, *122*, *131*, 175; *WFF
   3* 108, *118*, 119, 121; *WFF 4* 108,
   119, *119*, 121; *WFF 5* 108, 119, *120*,
   121, 122; *WFF 6* 17, *110*; *WFF 7* 17,
   110, 117, 121, *133*; *WFF 8* 110, 121,
   133; *WFF 9* 110, 121; *WFF 10* *110*,
   205, **205–6**; *WFF 11* *131*, 148–9, *149*;
   WFF 12 *131*, 149; *WFF 13* *131*, *146*,
   147, *179*; *WFF 14* 17, 147, *147*, 176–7;
   WFF 15 17, 147, *150*, 176; *WFF 16*
   133, *151*, **187**, **189**
water requirements 230
water supply 19, 273, 417, 426–8,
   427–30, **429**
   see also Wells
wattle structures
   fence or revetment 75, *75*
   revetment 67
   wells 17, *18*, 36–7, *37–8*, 42, 99,
      100–1, *101*, 111, *112*, 114, 177–9, **177**,
      178, 370
Watts, Isaac 273, *275*, 277
wells 37, 417, 426–8, *427–30*, **430**
   mid–late 12th C. *96–8*, 99–100, 102
   13th–14th C. 109, *109–12*, 110–11,
      113–14, **113**, *114–16*, 117
   15th–16th C. 132, *132–40*, 136, 139–
      43, *142*
   17th C. 217–18, *218*, 222, 226–8,
      226–7, 229
   18th C. 234, 235, 239, 240, *241–3*,
      244, 247–9, *248*
   19th C. 257, *259*
   Christ's Lane 370–1, *370*, 378
wells (numbered)
   Well 1 17, *18*, 36–7, *37–8*, 136; *Well
   2* 37, *37*, 42, *110*; *Well 3* 40, 42, *95*;
   Well 4 97, **177**; *Well 5* 97, 100–1, *101*,
   108, *164*, **177**, 179; *Well 6* 97, 100,
   101, 108, 114, *157*, **179**; *Well 7 & 8* 97,
   100, **177**; *Well 9* 97, 100; *Well 10* 97,
   100, 108; *Well 12* 97, *163*; *Well 13* 17,
   18, 98, 100, *110*, **177**; *Well 14* 98, 100,
   110; *Well 15* 98, 100, *110*, *163*; *Well
   18* 98–9, 110, 170, **177**; *Well 20* 108,
   187, *188*, **189**; *Well 21* 108, **177**; *Well
   22* 108, 110, 114, 131–2, *133*, 136,
   136, 143, *171*, **190–1**; *Well 23* 108,
   116, **177**; *Well 25* 108, 114, 116, 175,
   177; *Well 26* 108, 131, **177**; *Well 28*
   136, 138, 420; *Well 29* 17, *18*, *110*,
   133, *166*, **177**; *Well 30* 110, 133, **191**;
   Well 31 110, 113, *133*, **177**; *Well 32*
   110, 111, *112*, 113, **113**, 136, 167, **177**;
   Well 33 110, 114, 115, 136, 167, **177**;
   Well 34 110, 133, *166*; *Well 35* *131*,
   136, **177**; *Well 36* 124, 132, *134*, 138,
   143, 171, 175; *Well 37* 138, 143, 216,
   217, *218*, 234, 235, 262, *263*, 264, **335**;